PREFACE

A preliminary edition of Subclass KF, *Law of the United States,* developed by Werner Ellinger and John Fischer, was published in 1969. A 1999 edition cumulated all changes that had been made to the schedule since the 1969 edition was published. The 2004, 2005, and 2008 editions cumulated additions and changes made since the publication of the previous editions. This 2012 edition cumulates changes made since the 2008 edition was published.

Classification numbers or spans of numbers that appear in parentheses are formerly valid numbers that are now obsolete. Numbers or spans that appear in angle brackets are optional numbers that have never been used at the Library of Congress but are provided for other libraries that wish to use them. In most cases, a parenthesized or angle-bracketed number is accompanied by a "see" reference directing the user to the actual number that the Library of Congress currently uses, or a note explaining Library of Congress practice.

Access to the online version of the full Library of Congress Classification is available on the World Wide Web by subscription to Classification Web. Details about ordering and pricing may be obtained from the Cataloging Distribution Service at:

<http://www.loc.gov/cds/>

New or revised numbers and captions are added to the L.C. Classification schedules as a result of development proposals made by the cataloging staff of the Library of Congress and cooperating institutions. Upon approval of these proposals by the editorial meeting of the Policy and Standards Division, new classification records are created or existing records are revised in the master classification database. Lists of newly approved or revised classification numbers and captions are posted on the World Wide Web at:

<http://www.loc.gov/aba/cataloging/classification/weeklylists/>

Jolande Goldberg, law classification specialist in the Policy and Standards Division and Libby Dechman, senior subject cataloging policy specialist in the Policy and Standards Division, are responsible for coordinating the overall intellectual and editorial content of class K and its various subclasses. Kent Griffiths and Ethel Tillman, assistant editors of classification schedules, are responsible for creating new classification records, maintaining the master database, and creating index terms for the captions.

Barbara B. Tillett, Chief
Policy and Standards Division

June 2012

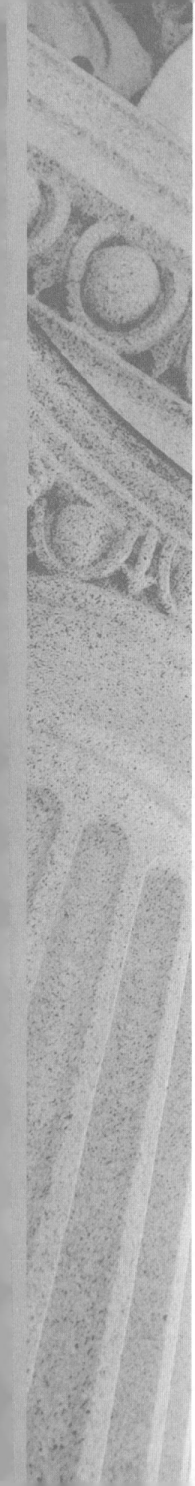

KF

Law of the United States

Library of Congress Classification 2012

Prepared by the Policy and Standards Division
Library Services

LIBRARY OF CONGRESS
LIBRARY OF CONGRESS Cataloging Distribution Service
Washington, D.C.

This edition cumulates all additions and changes to subclass KF through List 2012/04, dated April 16, 2012. Additions and changes made subsequent to that date are published in lists posted on the World Wide Web at

<http://www.loc.gov/aba/cataloging/classification/weeklylists/>

and are also available in *Classification Web*, the online Web-based edition of the Library of Congress Classification.

Library of Congress Cataloging-in-Publication Data

Library of Congress.

Library of Congress classification. KF. Law of the United States / prepared by the Policy and Standards Division, Library Services.

pages cm

"This edition cumulates all additions and changes to subclass KF through List 2012/04, dated April 16, 2012. Additions and changes made subsequent to that date are published in lists posted on the World Wide Web ... and are also available in Classification Web, the online Web-based edition of the Library of Congress Classification"--Title page verso.

Includes index.

ISBN 978-0-8444-9552-1

1. Classification, Library of Congress. 2. Classification--Books--Law. 3. Classification--Books--United States. 4. Law--United States--Classification. I. Library of Congress. Policy and Standards Division. II. Title. III. Title: Law of the United States.

Z696.U5K55 2012
025.4'634973--dc23

2012024576

Copyright ©2012 by the Library of Congress except within the U.S.A.

For sale by the Library of Congress Cataloging Distribution Service, 101 Independence Avenue, S.E., Washington, DC 20541-4912. Product catalog available on the Web at **www.loc.gov/cds**.

United States (General)

States

Cities

Territories, Confederate States of America

OUTLINE

Call Number	Subject
KF1-9827	Law of the United States (Federal)
KF1-11	Bibliography
KF12-49	Congressional documents
KF50-90	Statutes and administrative regulations
KF101-153	Law reports and related materials
KF154	Encyclopedias
KF156	Law dictionaries. Words and phrases
KF159	Legal maxims. Quotations
KF165	Uniform state law
KF170	Form books
KF(175)	Periodicals
KF178	Yearbooks
KF180-185	Judicial statistics
KF190-195	Directories
KF200	Society and bar association journals
KF202	Congresses
KF209-213	Collections
KF219-224	Criminal trials
KF226-228	Civil trials
KF240-247	Legal research. Legal bibliography
KF250-251	Legal composition and draftsmanship
KF255	Law reporting
KF261-292	Legal education
KF294	Law societies
KF297-(334.2)	The legal profession
KF336-337.5	Community legal services. Legal aid
KF338	Lawyer referral services
KF350-374	History
KF379-382	Jurisprudence and philosophy of American law
KF384	Criticism. Legal reform. General administration of justice
KF385-391	General and comprehensive works
KF394-395	Common law in the United States
KF398-400	Equity
KF410-418	Conflict of laws
KF420	Retroactive law. Intertemporal law
KF425-435	General principles and concepts
KF445-450	Concepts applying to several branches of law
KF465-553	Persons
KF465-485	General. Status. Capacity
KF501-553	Domestic relations. Family law
KF560-720	Property
KF560-562	General. Ownership
KF566-698	Real property. Land law

OUTLINE

Law of the United States (Federal)

Property - Continued

KF701-720	Personal property
KF726-745	Trusts and trustees
KF746-750	Estate planning
KF753-780	Succession upon death
KF801-1241	Contracts
KF801	General and comprehensive works
KF807-839	General principles
KF841-869.5	Government contracts
KF871-1241	Particular contracts
KF871-890	Comprehensive. Commercial law. Mercantile transactions
KF894	Contract of service. Master and servant
KF898-905	Contract for work and labor. Independent contractors
KF911-935	Sale of goods
KF939-951	Contracts involving bailments
KF956-962	Negotiable instruments
KF966-1032	Banking
KF1033	Foreign-exchange brokerage
KF1035-1040	Loan of money
KF1045	Suretyship. Guaranty
KF1046-1062	Secured transactions
KF1066-1084	Marketing of securities. Investments. Stock exchange transactions
KF1085-1087	Commodity exchanges. Produce exchanges
KF1091-1137	Carriers. Carriage of goods and passengers
KF1091	General. Liability
KF1092	Carriage by land
KF1093	Carriage by air
KF1096-1114	Carriage by sea. Maritime (Commercial) law. Admiralty
KF1121-1132	Maritime labor law
KF1135-1137	Marine insurance
KF1146-1238	Insurance
KF1241	Aleatory contracts
KF1244	Restitution. Quasi contracts. Unjust enrichment
KF1246-1327	Torts
KF1328	Compensation to victims of crime. Reparation
KF1341-1348	Agency
KF1355-1480	Associations
KF1355-1359	General

OUTLINE

Law of the United States (Federal)

Associations - Continued

	Unincorporated associations
KF1361-1381	General
KF1361-1362	Business associations. Partnership
KF1365-1381	Corporations. Juristic persons
KF1384-1480	General
KF1384-1386	Nonprofit corporations
KF1388-1390	Business corporations
KF1396-1477	Government-owned corporations and business
KF1480	organizations
KF1501-1548	Insolvency and bankruptcy. Creditors' rights
KF1570-1575	Economic policy
KF1600-2940	Regulation of industry, trade, and commerce. Occupational law
KF1600	General and comprehensive
KF1601-1668	Trade regulation. Control of trade practices
KF1601-1611	General. Unfair trade practices
KF1614-1617	Advertising
KF1619-1620	Labeling
KF1624-1625	Restraint of trade
KF1626-1629	Price fixing
KF1631-1657	Monopolies. Antitrust laws
KF1659-1659.1	Small business
KF1661	Trade associations
KF1663	State jurisdiction. Trade barriers
KF1665-1666	Weights and measures. Containers
KF1668	Standard time
KF1681-1873	Primary production. Extractive industries
KF1681-1755	Agriculture. Forestry
KF1770-1773	Fishery
KF1801-1873	Mining. Quarrying
	Including petroleum, oil, and gas
KF1874-1893	Manufacturing industries
KF1900-1944	Food procesing industries
KF1950	Construction and building industry. Contractors
KF1970-2057	Trade and commerce
KF2076-2140	Public utilities
KF2161-2849	Transportation and communication
KF2900-2940	The professions
KF2971-3193	Intellectual property
KF2971-2980	General
KF2986-3080	Copyright

OUTLINE

Law of the United States (Federal)

Intellectual property - Continued

KF3084	Author and publisher. The publishing contract
KF3086	Design protection
KF3091-3193	Patent law and trademarks
KF3195-3198	Unfair competition
KF3300-3771	Social legislation
KF3300	General
KF3301-3580	Labor law
KF3600-3686	Social insurance
KF3720-3745	Public welfare. Public assistance
KF3750	Disaster relief
KF3760-3771	Human reproduction
KF3775-3816	Public health. Sanitation
KF3821-3838	Medical legislation
KF3832	Eugenics. Sterilization
KF3835-3838	Veterinary medicine and hygiene
KF3841-3845	Prevention of cruelty to animals
KF3861-3896	Food. Drugs. Cosmetics
KF3901-3925	Alcohol. Alcoholic beverages. Prohibition
KF3941-3977	Public safety
KF3941-3942	Weapons. Firearms. Munitions
KF3945-3965	Hazardous articles and processes
KF3970	Accident control
KF3975-3977	Fire prevention and control. Explosives
KF3985-3995	Control of social activities
KF3985	General
KF3987	Amusements
KF3989	Sports. Prizefighting. Horse racing
KF3992	Lotteries
KF4101-4257	Education
KF4270-4330	Science and the arts. Research
KF4270	General
KF4280	Particular branches and subjects
KF4288-4302	The arts
KF4305	Museums and galleries
KF4310-4312	Historical buildings and monuments
KF4315-4319	Libraries and library services
KF4325	Archives. Historical documents
KF4330	Educational, scientific, and cultural exchanges
KF4501-5130	Constitutional law
KF4501-4515	Sources
KF4520	Works on legislative history of the Constitution

OUTLINE

Law of the United States (Federal)

Constitutional law - Continued

Call Number	Subject
KF4525-4528.5	Texts of the Constitution
KF4529-4530	State constitutions (Collections)
KF4541-4545	Constitutional history of the United States
KF4546-4554	General works
KF4555	Amending process
KF4558	Particular amendments
KF4565-4579	Separation of powers. Delegation of powers
KF4581-4583	Sources and relationships of law
KF4600-4629	Structure of government. Federal and state relations. Jurisdiction
KF4635	National territory. Noncontiguous territories
KF4650-4694	Foreign relations
KF4695	Public policy. Police power
KF4700-4856	Individual and state
KF4700-4720	Nationality and citizenship
KF4741-4786	Civil and political rights and liberties
KF4788	Political parties
KF4791-4856	Control of individuals
KF4791	Identification
KF4794-4794.5	Passports
KF4800-4848	Aliens
KF4850-4856	Internal security
KF4865-4869	Church and state
KF4880-5130	Organs of the government
KF4881-4921	The people. Election law
KF4930-5005	The legislative branch
KF5050-5125	The executive branch
KF5130	The Judiciary. Judicial power
KF5150	National emblem. Flag. Seal. Seat of government. National anthem
KF5152	Patriotic customs and observances
KF5153-5154	Decorations of honor. Awards
KF5155-5156	Commemorative medals
KF5300-5332	Local government
KF5336-5398	Civil service. Government officials and employees
KF5399-5399.5	Police and power of the police
KF5401-5425	Administrative organization and procedure
KF5500-5865	Public property. Public restraints on private property
KF5500-5501	General
KF5505-5510	Conservation of natural resources
KF5521-5536	Roads

OUTLINE

Law of the United States (Federal)

Public property. Public restraints on private property - Continued

KF5540-5541	Bridges
KF5551-5590	Water resources. Watersheds. Rivers. Lakes. Water courses
KF5594	Weather control. Meteorology. Weather stations
KF5599	Eminent domain
KF5601-5646	Public land law
KF5660-5662	Indian lands
KF5670-5673	Homesteads
KF5675-5677	Land grants
KF5691-5710	Regional and city planning. Zoning. Building
KF5721-5740	Housing. Slum clearance. City redevelopment
KF5750-5857	Government property
KF5750-5755	Administration. Powers and controls
KF5760-5810	Land and real property
KF5820-5857	Personal property
KF5865	Public works
KF5900-6075.5	Government measures in time of war, national emergency, or economic crisis. Emergency economic legislation
KF6200-6795	Public finance
KF6200-6200.5	General
KF6201-6219	Money. Currency. Coinage
KF6221-6227	Budget. Government expenditures
KF6231-6239	Expenditure control. Public auditing and accounting
KF6241-6245	Public debts. Loans. Bond issues
KF6251-6708	National revenue
KF6251-6256	History
KF6260	General
KF6265-6708	Particular sources of revenue
KF6265	Charges
KF6271-6645	Taxation
KF6651-6708	Tariff. Trade agreements. Customs
KF6720-6795	State and local finance
KF7201-7755	National defense. Military law
KF7201-7225	Comprehensive. General
KF7250-7680	The military establishment. Armed Forces
KF7250-7298	General
KF7305-7479	Particular branches of service
KF7485-7488.7	Auxiliary services during war or emergency
KF7590	Military discipline
KF7595-7596	Law enforcement. Criminal investigation

OUTLINE

Law of the United States (Federal)

National defense. Military law

The military establishment. Armed Forces - Continued

KF7601-7679	Military criminal law and procedure
KF7680	Criminal status of members of the Armed Forces
KF7682-7683	Other defense and intelligence agencies
KF7685	Civil defense
KF7701-7755	War veterans
KF8201-8228	Indians
KF8700-9075	Courts. Procedure
KF8700-8709	Administration of justice. Organization of the judiciary
KF8711-8807	Court organization and procedure
KF8810-9075	Civil procedure
KF9084	Negotiated settlement. Compromise
KF9085-9086	Arbitration and award. Commercial arbitration
KF9201-9461	Criminal law
KF9601-9760	Criminal procedure
KF9771-9827	Juvenile criminal law and procedure
KFA-KFW	Laws of the states
KFX	Laws of the cities
KFZ	Laws of the territories. Laws of the Confederate States of America

KF UNITED STATES (GENERAL) KF

United States (General)

Including American statutory law, and common law and equity as developed by the courts of the United States and the states of the union in general and collectively; for the law of particular states, see the states

For Anglo-American law and doctrine in general see KD1+

Bibliography

For manuals of legal bibliography and legal research and on the use of law books (How to find the law) see KF240+

1	General
2	Checklists of statutes
3	Checklists of law reports
4	Library catalogs. Union lists
6	Sales catalogs. Want lists. Duplicates
8	Indexes to periodical literature, society publications, collections
	Congressional documents
11	American State Papers
12	United States congressional serial set
	Bills
16	Prints
18	Digests
	Calendars
	Senate
20.8	General
21.A-Z	By committee, A-Z
	House
21.8	General
22.A-Z	By committee, A-Z
	Committee hearings
	Joint
24.8	Serials. By committee (Table KF20)
	Subarrange by title
25	Monographs. By committee (Table KF20)
	Subarrange by initial date of hearings
	Senate
	Standing committees
25.8	Serials. By committee (Table KF21)
	Subarrange by title
26	Monographs. By committee (Table KF21)
	Subarrange by initial date of hearings
	Special and select committees
26.3	Serials. By committee (Table KF22)
	Subarrange by title
26.5	Monographs. By committee (Table KF22)
	Subarrange by initial date of hearings

Congressional documents
Committee hearings -- Continued
House
Standing committees

26.8	Serials. By committee (Table KF23)
	Subarrange by title
27	Monographs. By committee (Table KF23)
	Subarrange by initial date of hearings
	Special and select committees
27.3	Serials. By committee (Table KF24)
	Subarrange by title
27.5	Monographs. By committee (Table KF24)
	Subarrange by initial date of hearings

Committee reports

| 29.7 | General collections |

Joint

29.8.A-Z	Serials. By committee, A-Z
	Subarrange by title
30	Monographs. By committee (Table KF25)
	Subarrange by date of original publication

Senate

30.7	General collections
	Standing committees
30.8.A-Z	Serials. By committee, A-Z
	Subarrange by title
31	Monographs. By committee (Table KF26)
	Subarrange by date of original publication
	Special and select committees
31.3.A-Z	Serials. By committee, A-Z
	Subarrange by title
31.5	Monographs. By committee (Table KF27)
	Subarrange by date of original publication

House

31.7	General collections
	Standing committees
31.8.A-Z	Serials. By committee, A-Z
	Subarrange by title
32	Monographs. By committee (Table KF28)
	Subarrange by date of original publication
	Special and select committees
32.3.A-Z	Serials. By committee, A-Z
	Subarrange by title
32.5	Monographs. By committee (Table KF29)
	Subarrange by date of original publication

Miscellaneous documents (Collections)
Class individual miscellaneous documents with the appropriate subject

KF UNITED STATES (GENERAL) KF

Congressional documents

Miscellaneous documents (Collections) -- Continued

33	Senate. By date
34	House. By date

Congressional Record

Class here editions of the Congressional Record and all predecessor publications, disregarding title and treating as one publication with continuous numbering

35	Text
36	Abridgments, summaries, digests

Debates

37	Senate
38	House

Other legislative documents

40	Index to the proceedings

History of bills and resolutions. Legislation passed or vetoed

42	Serials
42.2	Monographs. By date
43	Daily digest

Journals

Senate

45.A2-.A29	Official editions
	Arrange chronologically
45.A3-Z	Unofficial editions. By editor or publisher

House

46.A2-.A29	Official editions
	Arrange chronologically
46.A3-Z	Unofficial editions. By editor or publisher
47	Presidential messages. By date
	Class here only presidential messages regarding legislation
47.5	Recommended legislation
48	United States Code Congressional and Administrative News
49.A-Z	Other materials relating to legislative history, A-Z
49.C57	Congressional daily
49.C58	Congressional hearings calendar
49.C6	Congressional index (Commerce Clearing House)
49.C62	Congressional Information Service
49.C65	Congressional quarterly
	Including Congressional quarterly almanac and CQ ... almanac plus
49.C653	Congress and the Nation
49.L43	Legislative reference checklist
49.T56	THOMAS
49.W5	Witness index to hearings

Statutes and administrative regulations

KF UNITED STATES (GENERAL) KF

Statutes and administrative regulations -- Continued

Session laws. Statutes at large

50 Serials

51 Monographs. By initial date of session

Codification. Revision of statutes

53 Legislative documents. By date

56.A-Z Code commissions. Revision committees. By committee, A-Z

Under each:

.xA15-.xA159	*General serials*
.xA2	*Organic acts. By date*
.xA3-.xA34	*Reports (Serials)*
.xA35	*Reports (Monographs). By date*
.xA4	*Notes. By date*
.xA5	*Draft revisions. By date*
.xA8	*Other. By date*

For commissions or committees limited to a specific subject, see the subject

59 Code revision bills

Compilations of statutes

60 United States Revised Statutes

United States Code

Official editions

Including annotated official editions

61 Serials

62 Monographs. By date of edition

e.g. KF62 1964, United States code. 1964 ed., containing the general and permanent laws of the United States in force on January 3, 1965. Washington, 1965

62.5 Unofficial editions. By editor or publisher

Not further subarranged by date

63 Supplemental services

Other general compilations

Comprehensive

64 Unannotated. By date

65.A-Z Annotated. By editor, A-Z

68.A-Z Selective. By editor, A-Z

Administrative regulations

70.A2 Federal Register

70.A3 Code of Federal Regulations

Indexes

70.A34 Serials

70.A35 Monographs. By date

Proclamations and executive orders

70.A473 Codification of Presidential Proclamations and Executive Orders

70.A5 Other general compilations

KF UNITED STATES (GENERAL) KF

Statutes and administrative regulations
Administrative regulations
Proclamations and executive orders -- Continued
70.A55 Indexes
Rules of court see KF8816+
70.A8-Z Other. By editor, title, etc.
Attorneys General's opinions see KF5406.A6+
75 Digests of statutes
78 Citators to statutes and/or administrative regulations
For citators to both reports and statutes, see citators to reports
80 Indexes to statutes
85 Digests of and indexes to state legislation
90 Other bibliographic aids. Tables of popular names
Law reports and related materials
Including federal and regional reports
For regional reports including selected federal decisions, see regional reports. For reports of individual states or territories, see the law of the respective jurisdiction
For reports relating to particular subjects, and for reports of courts of limited jurisdiction other than those listed below, see relevant subject
For federal court rules see KF8816+
Federal courts
Supreme Court
101 Reports
101.1 Digests
101.2 Citators. Tables of cases overruled, etc.
101.4 Conversion tables. Blue books
101.6 General indexes
For indexes relating to a particular publication, reporter system, or digest (e. g. descriptive-word indexes), see that publication
101.7 Dockets of cases pending
101.8.A-Z Selective reports (other than by subject). By editor, A-Z
101.9 Records and briefs
Lower courts
Including Supreme Court and lower courts combined
105 General. Various courts (Table KF31)
For Federal rules decisions see KF8830
Intermediate appellate courts. Circuit courts of appeals. Courts of appeals
110 General. Collective (Table KF31)
112 Particular appellate courts. By circuit (1st, 2nd, etc.)
Subarrange each by Table KF31
113 Federal Circuit of the Court of Appeals (Table KF31)

Law reports and related materials
Federal courts
Lower courts
Intermediate appellate courts. Circuit courts of appeals.
Courts of appeals
Particular appellate courts -- Continued

114 District of Columbia Circuit of the Court of Appeals (Table KF31)
Class here works published after August 1, 1970
For works published before July 29, 1970, see KFD1245
For works published before July 29, 1970, and continuing after that date, see KFD1245

Circuit courts

115 Collective (Table KF31)

117 Particular courts. By circuit (1st, 2nd, etc.)
Subarrange each by Table KF31

District courts

120 Collective and by circuit
Subarrange each by Table KF31

122.A-Z Particular courts. By district, A-Z
Subarrange each by Table KF32

122.D57-.D576 District Court for the District of Columbia (Table KF32)
Class here works published after August 1, 1970
For works published before July 29, 1970, see KFD1252
For works published before July 29, 1970, and continuing, see KFD1252

125.A-Z Other courts, A-Z
Assign Cutter numbers according to distinguishing part of the name of the court
Commerce Court see KF2184

125.C5-.C56 Court of Claims. Claims Court (Table KF32)

125.C8-.C86 Court of Customs and Patent Appeals (Table KF32)

127 Digests and indexes of federal decisions

128.A-Z Decisions of federal courts in, or of cases before federal courts arising in, particular states. By state, A-Z
Cf. KFC47+ California
Cf. KFN5047+ New York

State courts
Reports covering all states
Including territories and the District of Columbia, or selected states, or state and federal courts. Selective reporting systems

132 American Law Reports (Table KF31)
Including ALR Federal

KF UNITED STATES (GENERAL) KF

Law reports and related materials
State courts
Reports covering all states -- Continued
133.A-Z Other, A-Z
Subarrange each by Table KF32
Regional reports
National Reporter system
For editions for a particular state, see state law
For Supreme Court reporter see KF101+
For Federal rules decisions see KF8830
135.A-Z Particular regions. By title, A-Z
135.A7-.A76 Atlantic Reporter (Table KF32)
135.N6-.N66 North Eastern Reporter (Table KF32)
135.N7-.N76 North Western Reporter (Table KF32)
135.P2-.P26 Pacific Reporter (Table KF32)
135.S6-.S66 South Eastern Reporter (Table KF32)
135.S7-.S76 South Western Reporter (Table KF32)
135.S8-.S86 Southern Reporter (Table KF32)
American Digest
139 Century edition
140 1st-3d Decennial digests
141 4th- Decennial digests
144 Classification. Subject headings. Scope notes
146.A-Z Other regional reports. By region, A-Z
146.M5-.M56 Middle Atlantic States (Table KF32)
146.N4-.N46 New England (Table KF32)
148.A-Z Digest of various state reports. By author or title, A-Z
For American Digest see KF141
150 Citators to various state reports. Tables of cases overruled, etc.
152 Other auxiliary publications
Including conversion tables, chronological tables, tables of popular names of cases
153 Decisions of federal administrative agencies (Table KF31)
For decisions of particular agencies, see the subject
Cf. form divisions following subclass KFX
154 Encyclopedias
Under each, as required: Citations. Notes
156 Law dictionaries. Words and phrases
For bilingual and multilingual dictionaries, see subclass K
For dictionaries on a particular subject, see the subject
159 Legal maxims. Quotations
Uniform state law
Class here general works only
For uniform state laws on a particular subject, see the subject
165.A2 Proceedings of the National Conference of Commissioners
Other documents

KF UNITED STATES (GENERAL) KF

Uniform state law

Other documents -- Continued

165.A3-.A39	Serials
165.A4	Monographs. By date
165.A5	Texts. By date
165.A8-Z	Treatises. Monographs
170	Form books
	Class here general works only
	For form books on a particular subject, see the subject
<175>	Periodicals
	For periodicals consisting primarily of informative material (newsletters, bulletins, etc.) relating to a particular subject, see the subject and form division, "Periodicals"
	For law reports, official bulletins or circulars, and official gazettes intended chiefly for the publication of laws and regulations, see appropriate entries in the text or form division tables
	For periodicals consisting predominantly of legal articles, regardless of subject matter and jurisdiction see K1+
178	Yearbooks
	Class here only publications issued annually, containing information, statistics, etc. about the year just past
	For other publications appearing yearly see K1+
	Judicial statistics
180	General
183	Criminal statistics
184	Juvenile crime
185.A-Z	Other. By subject, A-Z
185.B2	Bankruptcy cases
185.E58	Environment. Natural resources
	Natural resources see KF185.E58
	Directories
	General
190	National. Regional
192.A-.W	By state, A-W
193.A-Z	By county or city, A-Z
195.A-Z	By specialization, A-Z
195.A4	Administrative law
195.A47	Aeronautics. Space law
195.A57	Antitrust law
195.A8	Automobile law
195.B3	Banking law
195.B35	Bankruptcy
	Building law see KF195.C58
195.C57	Commercial law
195.C573	Communications law
195.C574	Computer law
195.C58	Construction law. Building law

KF UNITED STATES (GENERAL) KF

Directories
By specialization, A-Z -- Continued

195.C6	Corporation law
	Disability law see KF195.H36
195.D6	Domestic relations. Family law
195.E58	Entertainment law
195.E6	Environmental law
195.E75	Estate planning
195.E96	Expert evidence. Forensic science
	Forensic science see KF195.E96
195.F73	Franchise law
	Fraternities see KF289
195.H36	Handicapped. People with disabilities. Disability law
	Health law see KF195.M43
195.H67	Hospital law
195.H68	Housing law
195.I45	Immigration and naturalization law
195.I5	Insurance law
195.I52	Intellectual property law
	Cf. KF3165.A3 Patent attorneys
195.I54	International law
	Including international trade law
	International trade law see KF195.I54
	Judicial officers see KF8700.A19
	Juvenile court judges see KF9787.9
195.J8	Juvenile law
195.L3	Labor law
	Law schools see KF292.A+
	Law teachers see KF266
	Lawyer referral services see KF338.A33+
	Legal aid societies see KF336.A33+
195.L43	Legal assistants. Paralegal personnel
195.L53	Litigation. Trial practice
195.L6	Lobbyists
195.L62	Local government
	Including state government and municipal government
195.M37	Maritime law
195.M43	Medical law. Health law
195.M54	Military justice
	Municipal government see KF195.L62
195.N4	Negligence law
	Patent attorneys see KF3165.A3
195.P47	Personal injuries
195.P7	Probate law
	Procurement see KF195.P83
195.P75	Property law
195.P83	Public contracts. Procurement

KF UNITED STATES (GENERAL) KF

Directories
By specialization, A-Z -- Continued
Public defenders see KF9646.A15
195.P85 Public utility law
195.R3 Railroad law
195.R44 Religion and law
195.S43 Science and law. Technology and law
Space law see KF195.A47
State government see KF195.L62
Student bar associations see KF288
195.T38 Taxation
Technology and law see KF195.S43
195.T5 Title abstracting. Title investigation
195.T7 Transportation law (General)
Trial practice see KF195.L53
200 Society and bar association journals
Class here only journals restricted to society or bar association activities
For proceedings and annual reports of societies and bar associations, see the appropriate Cutter numbers in KF294 and KF325+
For journals devoted to legal subjects, either wholly or in part see K1+
202 Congresses
Collections
209 Monographic series
Several authors. Festschriften
210 General works
211 Minor collections. Anthologies
211.5 Digests (Summaries, condensations of periodical articles, essays, etc.)
213.A-Z Individual authors, A-Z
Under each:
.x *By date*
.xA-.xZ *By editor*
Including collected opinions, instructions to juries, and charges to grand juries
Criminal trials
For courts-martial (Army) see KF7642.A+
For courts-martial (Navy) see KF7652.A+
For courts-martial (Air Force) see KF7657.5.A+
219 Bibliography
220 General collections
Including both criminal and civil
221.A-Z Particular offenses, A-Z
221.B74 Bribery
221.C55 Communism

Criminal trials

Particular offenses, A-Z -- Continued

Call Number	Topic
221.C6	Conspiracy
221.L5	Libel and slander
221.M8	Murder. Assassination
221.P57	Piracy
221.P6	Political offenses
	Including treason, sedition, etc.
221.S49	Sex crimes
	Slander see KF221.L5

Particular trials

Call Number	Topic
223.A-Z	Early through 19th century. By defendant or by best known name, A-Z
224.A-Z	20th century. By defendant or by best known name, A-Z
224.B55	Black Panthers Trial, New York, 1970-1971
224.C47	Chicago Seven
224.H27	Harrisburg Seven
224.L64	Los Siete de la Raza Trial, San Francisco, 1970
224.N28	Nazi Saboteurs Trial, Washington, D.C., 1942
224.S49	Sleepy Lagoon Trial, Los Angeles, 1942-1943
224.W33	Watergate Trial, Washington, D.C., 1973
225.A-Z	21st century. By defendant or by best known name, A-Z

Civil trials

Call Number	Topic
226	General collections

Particular trials. By plaintiff, A-Z

Including records and briefs

Cf. "Particular cases" under subjects, and "Particular companies" under "Regulation of industry, trade and commerce"

Call Number	Topic
228.A-Z	Early through 20th century. By plaintiff, A-Z
229.A-Z	21st century. By plaintiff, A-Z

Legal research. Legal bibliography

Methods of bibliographic research and of how to find the law

Call Number	Topic
240	General
241.A-Z	By subject, A-Z
241.A35	Administrative law
241.A57	Antitrust law
241.B34	Banking law
241.B36	Bankruptcy
241.B57	Birth control
241.C64	Commercial law
241.C65	Communications
241.C66	Constitutional law
241.C67	Corporation law
241.C75	Criminal law
241.D65	Domestic relations
241.E38	Educational law and legislation

KF UNITED STATES (GENERAL) KF

Legal research. Legal bibliography
By subject, A-Z -- Continued

241.E5	Election law. Initiative and referendum
241.E85	Export controls
	Initiative see KF241.E5
241.I58	Insurance
241.L33	Labor law and legislation
	Liability see KF241.T67
241.M34	Malpractice
241.M45	Medical laws and legislation
241.P75	Products liability
	Referendum see KF241.E5
241.S66	Sports
241.T38	Taxation
241.T67	Torts
	Electronic data processing. Information retrieval
	General
242.A1	Federal law
	Including federal and state law combined
242.A12	Collective state law
	For particular states, see the state
242.A3-Z	By subject
242.A45-.A46	Agricultural law and legislation (Table KF37)
242.A65-.A66	Apportionment (Election law). Redistricting (Table KF37)
242.A85-.A86	Automobile litigation (Table KF37)
242.B3-.B32	Bankruptcy (Table KF38)
242.C65-.C66	Commercial law (Table KF37)
242.C67-.C672	Corporation law (Table KF38)
242.C68-.C69	Court administration (Table KF37)
242.C72-.C73	Criminal justice administration (Table KF37)
242.C76-.C77	Criminal law (Table KF37)
242.D65-.D66	Domestic relations (Table KF37)
242.E37-.E38	Educational law and legislation (Table KF37)
242.E58-.E59	Environmental law (Table KF37)
242.I42-.I43	Immigration law (Table KF37)
242.I46-.I47	Industrial property (Table KF37)
242.I5-.I52	Inheritance and succession (Table KF38)
242.I55-.I56	Insurance law (Table KF37)
242.J85-.J86	Juvenile courts (Table KF37)
	Litigation see KF242.P746+
242.M8-.M82	Municipal corporations (Table KF38)
242.N43-.N44	Negligence (Table KF37)
242.P3-.P32	Patent laws and legislation (Table KF38)
242.P73-.P74	Pretrial procedure (Table KF37)
242.P746-.P7462	Procedure. Litigation (Table KF38)
242.P75-.P76	Real property (Table KF37)
242.P8-.P82	Public law (Table KF38)

KF UNITED STATES (GENERAL) KF

Legal research. Legal bibliography
Electronic data processing. Information retrieval
By subject -- Continued
Redistricting see KF242.A65+

242.S43-.S432	Securities (Table KF38)
242.T38-.T382	Taxation (Table KF38)
245	Systems of citation
246	Legal abbreviations
247	Abstracting and indexing systems

Legal composition and draftsmanship
Including works on legal document preparation
For legislative drafting see KF4950

250	General works
251	Brief writing
255	Law reporting

For court reporters see KF8805
Classification of the law see KF435
Legal education

261	Bibliography
262	Periodicals

Class here periodicals consisting primarily of informative material (newsletters, bulletins, etc.)
For periodicals consisting predominantly of legal articles, regardless of subject matter and jurisdiction see K1+

263	Society publications
264	Congresses. Conferences
(265)	Yearbooks. Annual and periodical surveys
	see KF262
266	Directories
270.A-Z	Law school catalogs and bulletins. By school, A-Z

General works. Standards. Criticism

272	Treatises. Monographs
273	Addresses, essays, lectures

Continuing (Post-admission) legal education

275	General (Table KF6)
276	Judicial education (Table KF6)
276.5	In-house training (Table KF6)

Study and teaching
General works see KF272+

277.A-Z	Particular subjects, A-Z
277.A35	Aged. Older people
277.A64	Appellate procedure
277.B55	Bill drafting
277.C6	Conflict of laws
277.C65	Court administration
277.D57	Dispute resolution
277.E5	Environmental law

Legal education
Study and teaching
Particular subjects, A-Z -- Continued

Call Number	Subject
277.L33	Labor law and legislation
277.L38	Law and literature
	Class here works on the teaching of courses that focus on the interdisciplinary connection between law and literature
277.L4	Legal ethics
	Medical care see KF277.P82
277.P68	Pretrial procedure
277.P7	Procedure
277.P82	Public health. Medical care
	Teaching methods
279	General
280	Case method
	Moot courts
281.A2	General
281.A5-Z	Particular. By school
	Under each:
	.A2 — *Rules. By date*
	.A5-.Z — *Treatises. Monographs*
	Casebooks, practice books, etc. (Civil procedure) see KF8918
	Casebooks, practice books, etc. (Criminal procedure) see KF9657
282	Clinical method (Table KF6)
282.5	Computer assisted instruction (Table KF6)
283	Students' guides and textbooks
	For introductions to legal literature (legal bibliography) see KF240
	For introductory surveys of the law see KF385.A4+
	For moot court practice see KF8918
	Prelaw-school education. Admission to law school
	For study and teaching of law in elementary and secondary schools see KF4208.5.L3
	For universities and colleges see KF4245.5.L3
285.A1-.Z8	General works
285.Z9	Examination aids
	Law students
287	General
	Including sociology and psychology of law students; particular groups
287.5	Student ethics
288	Student bar associations
289	Legal fraternities
	For Law clubs see KF292.A+

Legal education -- Continued

Call Number	Description
292.A-Z	Particular law schools, A-Z
	Subarrange each by Table KF11
294.A-Z	Law societies, A-Z
	Subarrange each by Table KF33
	e. g.
	Cf. KF200 Society and bar association journals (under each society)
294.A3	American Bar Foundation (Table KF33)
294.A4	American Judicature Society (Table KF33)
294.A5	American Law Institute (Table KF33)
294.A8	Association of Trial Lawyers of America (Table KF33)
294.C6	Commercial Law League of America (Table KF33)
294.F7	Fraternal Society Law Association (Table KF33)
294.N28	National Association of Attorneys General (Table KF33)
294.N38	National Institute of Municipal Law Officers (Table KF33)
294.W35	Walter E. Meyer Research Institute of Law (Table KF33)
	The legal profession
297	General. Law as a career (Table KF8)
298	Particular aspects. The lawyer and society
299.A-Z	Particular classes of lawyers and types of careers, A-Z
299.A32	Administrative law
	Admiralty see KF299.M37
299.A35	African American lawyers
299.A55	Animal welfare lawyers. Animal rights lawyers
299.B65	Bond lawyers
299.C47	Christian lawyers
299.C54	Communications law
299.C6	Court administration
299.C7	Criminal lawyers
299.D6	Domestic relations. Family law
299.E57	Entertainment law. Performing arts
299.E6	Environmental lawyers
	Family law see KF299.D6
299.G6	Government service
	Health law see KF299.M43
299.I5	Industry. Corporate practice
299.I75	Irish American lawyers
299.J35	JD/MBA professionals
299.J4	Jewish lawyers
299.J8	Judge advocates. Military lawyers
299.L3	Labor law
299.L4	Legislators
299.M37	Maritime law. Admiralty
299.M43	Medical law. Health law
	Military lawyers see KF299.J8
299.M56	Minority lawyers

KF UNITED STATES (GENERAL) KF

The legal profession
Particular classes of lawyers and types of careers, A-Z --
Continued
Negro lawyers see KF299.A35
Patent lawyers see KF3165.A3+
Performing arts see KF299.E57
299.P8 Public interest lawyers
299.T3 Tax lawyers
299.T46 Temporary lawyers
299.W6 Women lawyers
Practice of law
For attorneys in nonjudicial government service (General)
see KF299.G6
For corporate practice as a career see KF299.I5
For corporate legal departments see KF1425
For attorneys in nonjudicial government service (City
attorneys) see KF5322
For attorneys as judicial officers see KF8795
300 General works (Table KF8)
Surveys of the legal profession
301 General
301.5.A-.W By state, A-W
Biography of lawyers
see KF334, KF354, KF362+ KF367+ KF372+
Admission to the bar
302 General (Table KF6)
Administrative bar see KF5414
303 Bar examinations
304 Loyalty oaths (Table KF6)
304.5 Residence requirements (Table KF6)
Legal ethics and legal etiquette
Cf. KF287.5 Law student ethics
Cf. KF8779 Judicial ethics
305-306 General. Attorney-attorney relationship (Table KF5
modified)
305.A2 Documents. Canons. By date of publication
307 Directories of lawyer disciplinary agencies (Table KF6)
Discipline. Unauthorized practice. Disbarment
Cf. KF9201+ Criminal law
308 General (Table KF6)
309.A-Z Particular cases. By attorney, A-Z
310.A-Z Special topics, A-Z
310.A3 Advertising (Table KF7)
310.A4 Ambulance chasing (Table KF7)
310.A43 Ancillary business activities (Table KF7)
310.C6 Contingent fees (Table KF7)
310.G7 Group arrangements (Table KF7)

The legal profession
Practice of law
Legal ethics and legal etiquette
Special topics, A-Z -- Continued

310.O34	"Of counsel" relationships (Table KF7)
310.P63	Public relations (Table KF7)
	Attorney and client
311	General. Counseling (Table KF6)
313	Malpractice. Liability (Table KF6)
314.A-Z	Other topics, A-Z
314.C45	Client security funds (Table KF7)
	Economics of law practice
315	General (Table KF6)
	For surveys see KF301+
316	Fees (Table KF6)
	For contingent fees see KF310.C6
	For fees in workers' compensation cases see KF3623.A8
316.5	Marketing of legal services (Table KF6)
317	Labor unions (Table KF6)
	Law office management
318	General (Table KF8)
319	Attorneys' and legal secretaries' handbooks, manuals, etc.
	Form books see KF170
320.A-Z	Special topics, A-Z
320.A2	Accounting
	For works in accounting in general, for the use of lawyers, see subclass HJ
320.A9	Automation
	Design see KF320.L39
320.E44	Emergency management. Disaster preparedness
320.I56	Insurance
320.L39	Layout. Design
	Legal advertising see KF450.N6
320.L4	Legal assistants. Paralegal personnel
	Legal records see KF320.R42
320.L48	Letter writing
320.N48	Newsletters. Publications
320.O35	Office equipment and supplies
	Publications see KF320.N48
320.R42	Legal records. Records management and retention
	Retention see KF320.R42
320.S4	Shorthand
	Including individual shorthand systems
	For works on specific systems for use in law reporting see KF255

The legal profession
Practice of law
Law office management
Special topics, A-Z -- Continued

Call Number	Topic
320.S73	Statistics. Statistical methods
320.T44	Telecommuting
320.T73	Translating
320.T9	Typewriting
	Including automatic typewriting
	Word processing see KF322+
	Word processing
322	General works
322.5.A-Z	By program, A-Z
322.5.M53	Microsoft Word
322.5.W66	WordPerfect
322.5.W67	WordStar 2000
	The organized bar. Bar associations
323	General (Table KF6)
	For monographs and publications on particular subjects, see the subject
	For membership directories see KF190+
	For bar association publications see KF200
	Particular types of organization
	National bar associations
	American Bar Association
	Documents
325.A2	Proceedings (Serial)
	For proceedings of particular meetings, see KF325.A8
325.A23-.A239	Programs (Serial)
	For programs of particular meetings, see KF325.A8
	Presidents' reports
325.A29-.A299	Serials
325.A3	Monographs. By date
	Organization handbooks. Constitution and bylaws
325.A39-.A399	Serials
325.A4	Monographs. By date
325.A6-.A629	Committee reports and other reports on organization
325.A8	Particular meetings. By date
	Including proceedings, programs, etc.
325.A9	Anniversary publications, etc.
325.A95	Other

KF UNITED STATES (GENERAL) KF

The legal profession
The organized bar. Bar associations
Particular types of organization
National bar associations
American Bar Association
Documents -- Continued

325.1-.29 Subordinate organizations: Sections, Conferences, etc. By name (alphabetically)
Subarrange by title
For directories of members specializing in a
particular branch of law see KF195.A+

326 General works. History
Biography
see KF354, KF363, KF368, KF373

328.A-Z Other national bar associations, A-Z
Under each (using successive Cutter numbers):
.x1-.x19 *Proceedings. Yearbooks*
.x2 *Organization handbooks.*
Constitution and bylaws. By date
.x3-.x39 *Other documents*
.x4-.x49 *General works*
State bar associations

330 General. Integrated bar (Table KF6)

332.A-Z Particular associations. By state and by association, each A-Z
Under each association (using successive Cutter numbers):
.x1-.x19 *Proceedings. Yearbooks*
Organization handbooks.
Constitution and bylaws
.x195-.x199 *Serials*
.x2 *Monographs. By date*
.x3-.x39 *Other documents. Special*
meetings. Anniversaries
.x4-.x49 *General works. Collective*
biography of members.
Memorials, etc.
Individual biography, see
KF363, KF368, KF373

KF UNITED STATES (GENERAL) KF

The legal profession
The organized bar. Bar associations
Particular types of organization -- Continued

334.A-Z Local bar associations, lawyers' clubs, etc. By city and by association, each A-Z

Under each association (using successive Cutter numbers):

Call number	Description
.x1-.x19	*Proceedings. Yearbooks*
.x2	*Organization handbooks. Constitution and bylaws. By date*
.x3-.x39	*Other documents. Special meetings. Anniversaries*
.x4-.x49	*General works*
.x5-.x59	*Collective biography of members. Memorials, etc. Individual biography, see KF363, KF368, KF373*

e. g.

334.N4A81-.N4A859 Association of the Bar of the City of New York

(334.2) Lawyers in literature, legal anecdotes, wit and humor see subclass K

Community legal services. Legal aid. Legal services to the poor

General. National organizations

Including the Legal Services Corporation

336.A2 Bibliography

336.A3 Society publications

Directories of legal aid societies

336.A33-.A39 Serials

336.A4 Monographs. By date

336.A7-.A79 Official reports and monographs

336.A8-Z General works

For collections of, and works on, substantive law see KF390.5.P6

337.A-Z Local agencies and legal aid societies. By state or place, A-Z

337.5.A-Z Legal services to particular groups, A-Z

337.5.A27 Abused wives (Table KF7)

337.5.A33 Aged. Older people (Table KF7)

337.5.A34 AIDS patients. Persons with AIDS (Table KF7)

Aliens, Illegal see KF337.5.I45

337.5.A7 Armed Forces personnel (Table KF7)

Battered wives see KF337.5.A27

337.5.G38 Gays (Table KF7)

337.5.I45 Immigrants (Table KF7)

Including illegal aliens

337.5.J88 Juveniles (Table KF7)

337.5.M46 Mental disabilities, People with (Table KF7)

Older people see KF337.5.A33

KF UNITED STATES (GENERAL) KF

Community legal services. Legal aid. Legal services to the poor

Legal services to particular groups, A-Z -- Continued

337.5.P7	Prisoners (Table KF7)
337.5.R4	Refugees (Table KF7)
	Wives, Abused see KF337.5.A27
	Lawyer referral services
	Directories of lawyer referral services
338.A33-.A39	Serials
338.A4	Monographs. By date
338.A5-Z	General works
	Public defenders see KF9646
	History
	General
350	Sources
351	Extracts. Readings
352	General works (Table KF8)
	Collective biography
353	General
354.A-.W	By state, A-W
	Cf. KF332.A+ State bar associations
355.A-Z	By county, city, etc., A-Z
	Cf. KF334.A+ Local bar associations
358	Particular aspects. Influence of foreign (e.g. Roman) law
	By period
	Colonial
361	General works (Table KF8)
	Biography
	For Supreme Court justices see KF8744+
362	Collective
	For local biography see KF353+
363.A-Z	Individual (including nominations of judges, attorneys-general, district attorneys, etc.), A-Z
	Subarrange each by Table KF39
364.A-Z	Special topics, A-Z
364.P7	Privilegium fori
364.W73	Writs of assistance
	19th century
366	General works (Table KF8)
	Biography
	For Supreme Court justices see KF8744+
367	Collective
	For local biography see KF353+
368.A-Z	Individual (including nominations of judges, attorneys-general, district attorneys, etc.), A-Z
	Subarrange each by Table KF39
369.A-Z	Special topics, A-Z

KF UNITED STATES (GENERAL) KF

History
By period
19th century
Special topics, A-Z -- Continued

369.Y3	Yazoo Fraud
	20th-21st centuries
371	General works (Table KF8)
	Biography
	For Supreme Court justices see KF8744+
372	Collective
	For local biography see KF353+
373.A-Z	Individual (including nominations of judges, attorneys-general, district attorneys, etc.), A-Z
	Subarrange each by Table KF39
374.A-Z	Special topics, A-Z

Jurisprudence and philosophy of American law. General doctrines of American legal institutions

Class here doctrines peculiar to American legal institutions
For works by American authors on philosophy of law in general, see subclass K
For works on the philosophy of particular branches of law (e.g. Constitutional law, Criminal law), see these branches

General works

379	Casebooks. Readings
380	Treatises
382	Rule of law in the United States (Table KF8)

Relationship of law to other disciplines, subjects, or phenomena
see subclass K

384	Criticism. Legal reform. General administration of justice (Table KF8)
	Cf. KF8700 Judiciary
	Cf. KF9223 Criminal justice

General and comprehensive works
For collections see KF209+

385.A4	Casebooks. Readings
385.A5-Z	Treatises
386	Compends. Courses of study
387	Minor and popular works
388	Examination aids
389	Miscellaneous individual addresses and essays
	For collected essays see KF209+
390.A-Z	Works for particular groups of users, A-Z
390.A3	Accountants
390.A4	Aged. Older people. Retired persons
390.A5	Americans abroad
390.A67	Armed Forces personnel

General and comprehensive works
Works for particular groups of users, A-Z -- Continued

Call Number	Subject
390.A69	Artisans. Craftsmen
390.A7	Artists and art collectors
390.A74	Athletes
390.A96	Authors
390.A97	Automobile collectors
390.A98	Automobile racers
390.B8	Works on doing business abroad
	Class here general works only
	For works on a particular country, see the country
	Business consultants see KF390.C65
390.B84	Businesspeople. Foreign investors
390.C5	Clergy
390.C65	Consultants, Business
	Craftsmen see KF390.A69
390.D38	Day care providers
390.D4	Detectives
390.D64	Domestics. Servants
390.E3	Educators
390.E54	Engineers
390.E57	Entertainers
390.E87	Ex-convicts
390.E9	Executives
390.F3	Farmers
	Foreign investors see KF390.B84
390.H53	Homeowners
(390.H6)	Horse breeders
	see KF390.5.H6
390.I5A-.I5Z	Immigrants. By nationality, A-Z
390.I54	Independent contractors
390.L8	Lumbermen. Lumber trade
	Medical personnel see KF390.P45
390.N8	Nurses
	Older people see KF390.A4
390.O7	Oral historians
390.P4	Pet owners
390.P45	Physicians. Medical personnel
	Cf. KF390.N8 Nurses
390.P65	Police
390.P8	Purchasing agents
390.R4	Retail trade
	Retired persons see KF390.A4
390.S2	Sales personnel
390.S35	Scout leaders
	Servants see KF390.D64
390.S6	Social workers

KF UNITED STATES (GENERAL) KF

General and comprehensive works
Works for particular groups of users, A-Z -- Continued

390.W6	Women
390.5.A-Z	Works on diverse legal aspects of a particular subject and falling within several branches of the law, A-Z
390.5.A5	Animals (Table KF7)
390.5.C35	Cats (Table KF7)
390.5.C6	Computers (Table KF7)
390.5.D6	Dogs (Table KF7)
390.5.H6	Horses (Table KF7)
390.5.H85	Human body (Table KF7)
390.5.M37	Martial arts (Table KF7)
390.5.P6	Poverty. Legal protection of the poor. Handbooks for legal services (Table KF7)
390.5.P78	Public interest law (Table KF7)
390.5.P8	Public relations (Table KF7)
390.5.S9	Swimming pools (Table KF7)
390.5.T73	Trees (Table KF7)
391.A-Z	Foreign languages treatises. By language, A-Z For translations from English, see the original
394	Common law in the United States (Table KF8 modified) For works on common law in both the United States and the United Kingdom see KD671
(394.A7)	Casebooks, readings see KF379
	Restatement of the common law
<395.A2>	Texts. By subject, A-Z Prefer subject For state annotations, see state law
395.A3	Digests of decisions. Restatement in the courts
395.A4	Citators
395.A5-Z	Treatises. Monographs (General)
	Equity
398	Casebooks
399	Treatises
400	Examination aids, etc.
	Usage and custom see KF427
	Conflict of laws
	General
410	Casebooks
411	Treatises. Monographs
412	Examination aids, etc.
413.A-Z	Particular aspects, A-Z
413.C5	Classification. Qualification
413.J87	Jurisdiction
413.P6	Points of contact
413.R4	Renvoi

KF UNITED STATES (GENERAL) KF

Conflict of laws -- Continued

416.A-Z	Between the United States and particular countries, A-Z
417	Interstate (Table KF6)
418.A-Z	Particular branches and subjects of the law, A-Z
418.B3	Bankruptcy
418.C48	Civil procedure
418.C58	Confiscations
418.C6	Contracts. Obligations. Debtor and creditor
418.C64	Corporations
	Criminal jurisdiction see KF9230
418.C78	Custody of children
418.D3	Decedents' estates
418.E4	Eminent domain
	Foreign judgments see KF8729
418.L5	Life insurance
418.L55	Limitation of actions
418.M2	Marriage. Divorce. Marital property
418.S2	Sales
418.S7	Statute of frauds
418.S82	Succession upon death
418.T6	Torts
418.T7	Trusts and trustees
420	Retroactive law. Intertemporal law
422	Retroactive judicial decisions. Prospective overruling
	General principles and concepts
	Particular aspects
425	Statutory construction and interpretation
427	Usage and custom
429	Stare decisis
	Cf. K574 Stare decisis in general jurisprudence
431	Conflicting decisions
434	Codification
435	Classification
	For classification of library collections of legal literature see Z697.L4
	Concepts applying to several branches of law
	Damages
445	Casebooks
446	Treatises. Monographs
446.Z9	Minor works
450.A-Z	Other, A-Z
450.A8	Authentication. Acknowledgments. Certification
450.D85	Duress
	Cf. KF820 Contracts
450.E7	Estoppel
	Cf. KF8992 Res judicata
450.G6	Good faith

KF UNITED STATES (GENERAL) KF

Concepts applying to several branches of law
Other, A-Z -- Continued

450.L5	Liability
450.L55	Limitation of actions
	Cf. KF8881 Civil procedure
450.N6	Notice. Legal advertising
450.P8	Public policy
450.T5	Time (Computation of time)
450.W3	Waiver

Persons

General. Status. Capacity

465	General works

Natural persons

Civil status

466	Domicile (Table KF6)
468	Name (Table KF6)
470	Absence and presumption of death (Table KF6)
471	Missing persons (Table KF6)

Capacity and disability

Cf. KF760.C3 Capacity to make wills

475	General (Table KF6)
477-478	Women (Table KF5)
478.5	Intersex people (Table KF6)
479	Minors (Table KF6)

Including liability

Persons of unsound mind. People with physical or mental disabilities

For care of the mentally ill see KF3828

480	General (Table KF6)
480.5.A-Z	Particular diseases or impairments, A-Z
480.5.A94	Autism (Table KF7)
480.5.D4	Deafness (Table KF7)
480.5.E6	Epilepsy (Table KF7)
481	Unborn children. Nasciturus (Table KF6)
481.5	Conservatorship

Cf. KF553+ Guardian and ward

Slaves

482.A2	Casebooks
482.A5-Z	Treatises. Monographs
485	Recording and registration. Registers of births, marriages, deaths. Census. Vital statistics. National Data Center. Birth and death certificates (Table KF6)

Juristic persons see KF1384+

Domestic relations. Family law

501-505	General (Table KF4)
505.5	Domestic relations courts (Table KF6)

Persons
Domestic relations. Family law -- Continued
Marriage. Husband and wife
Cf. KF9322 Conjugal violence

506-510	General (Table KF4)
511	Particular aspects
512	Certificates. Premarital examinations (Table KF6)
514	Performance of marriage. Civil and religious celebration (Table KF6)
516	Common-law marriage (Table KF6)
517	Interracial marriage. Miscegenation (Table KF6)
518	Invalid and voidable marriages. Nullity (Table KF6)
	Rights and duties of husband and wife
521	Civil status of married women (Table KF6)
	Property relationships
524	General (Table KF6)
	Particular modes of property relationships
526	Community property (Table KF6)
527	Separate property (Table KF6)
529	Marriage settlements. Prenuptial agreements (Table KF6)
	Divorce. Separation
	Including divorce settlements
531.A1	Bibliography
531.A3	Periodicals
	Class here periodicals consisting primarily of informative materials (newsletters, bulletins, etc.)
	For periodicals consisting predominantly of legal articles, regardless of subject matter and jurisdiction, see K1+
	Statutes. Regulations. Rules of practice
532	Comparative state laws
532.5	Uniform state laws. Conferences
533.5	Form books
534	Casebooks. Readings
535.A2	Collected papers and essays. Symposia
535.A7-.Z8	Treatises. Monographs
535.Z9	Compends. Outlines. Popular works
535.Z95	Works on comparative and uniform state and local law
535.7	Equitable distribution (Table KF6)
536	Relationship between civil and religious divorces (Table KF6)
537	Separate maintenance. Alimony (Table KF6)
538	Unmarried couples (Table KF6)
539	Same-sex marriage. Civil unions (Table KF6)
	Including quasi-marital relationships
	Parent and child
	Cf. KF9323 Child abuse

KF UNITED STATES (GENERAL) KF

Persons
Domestic relations. Family law
Parent and child -- Continued

540	General (Table KF6)
542	Legitimacy. Legitimation. Paternity (Table KF6)
543	Illegitimate children. Affiliation (Table KF6)
545	Adoption (Table KF6)
	Parental rights and duties. Property of minors. Custody
	Including access to children, and parental kidnapping
547	General (Table KF6)
548	Grandparents' rights (Table KF6)
549	Desertion and nonsupport (Table KF6)
550	Interstate and reciprocal enforcement (Table KF6)
	Guardian and ward
	Cf. KF3736.5 Foster home care
553	General (Table KF6)
554	Guardians ad litem (Table KF6)
	Agency see KF1341+
	Property
	General. Ownership. Actions in rem
560	Casebooks
561	Treatises
562	Particular aspects and relationships. Private property
	Including right of property
564	Alien property (Table KF6)
	Real property. Land law
566-570	General (Table KF3)
572	General special
573	Alien landownership (Table KF6)
	Land tenure
574	General (Table KF6)
	Ownership
575	General (Table KF6)
576	Community associations of property owners (Table KF6)
	Cf. KF581 Condominium associations
577	Estates and interests. Freehold. Fee simple (Table KF6)
578	Estates for life. Possessory estates (Table KF6)
579	Underground space (Table KF6)
580	Airspace (Table KF6)
581	Horizontal property. Housing condominium (Table KF6)
	Tenancy
585	General (Table KF6)
	Leaseholds. Landlord and tenant. Rent
586-590	General (Table KF3)
593.A-Z	Particular kinds of tenancy and leases, A-Z

KF UNITED STATES (GENERAL) KF

Property
Real property. Land law
Land tenure
Ownership
Tenancy
Leaseholds. Landlord and tenant. Rent
Particular kinds of tenancy and leases, A-Z --
Continued
Building leases see KF593.G7
593.C6 Commercial leases (Table KF7)
Including both real and personal property
For personal property see KF946
593.F3 Farm tenancy (Table KF7)
593.G7 Ground leases. Building leases (Table KF7)
Oil and gas leases see KF1865
593.Q5 Quitrent (Table KF7)
595 Housing courts
597 Contingent estates. Defeasible fees
598 Other interests (Table KF6)
Equitable ownership
601 Equitable conversion
Future estates and interests in land
Including works on future interests in both real and
personal property
Cf. KF708+ Personal property
General. Limitations. Rule in Shelley's case
604 Casebooks
605 Treatises
607 Power of appointment
Estate planning see KF746+
608 Reversions. Reversionary interests
Remainders
609 General
610 Contingent remainders
613 Rule against perpetuities
615 Worthier title
Concurrent ownership
Including works on concurrent ownership in both real and
personal property
Cf. KF709 Personal property
619 General (Table KF8)
620 Joint tenancy (Table KF6)
Tenancy by the entirety
621 General (Table KF6)
622 Tenancy in common (Table KF6)
623 Housing cooperatives (Table KF6)
626 Partition (Table KF6)

KF UNITED STATES (GENERAL) KF

Property
Real property. Land law
Land tenure
Ownership -- Continued

629	Estates and interests arising from marriage. Dower. Curtesy (Table KF6)
	Rights and interests incident to ownership and possession
634	General (Table KF8)
636	Fixtures. Improvements (Table KF6)
637	Rights of user. Waste (Table KF6)
639	Boundaries. Fences (Table KF6)
	Riparian rights. Water rights of individuals
	For state water rights see KF5575
641-645	General (Table KF4)
646	Western States (Table KF6)
649	Animals and fish. Game and fishing rights (Table KF6)
	Actions to recover the possession of land. Ejectment
652	General (Table KF6)
	Trespass to land see KF1272
	Rights to dispose of land
654	Restraints on alienation (Table KF6)
	Rights to use and profits of another's land
656	General (Table KF8)
	Easements
657	General (Table KF8)
658.A-Z	Particular kinds, A-Z
658.C65	Conservation easements (Table KF7)
661	Covenants running with the land
662	Restrictive covenants (Table KF6)
664	Equitable restrictions (Table KF6)
	Transfer of rights in land
	Land grants see KF5675+
	Transfer inter vivos
	General. Vendor and purchaser
	Cf. KF2042.R4 Real estate agents
665.A15	Periodicals
	Class here periodicals consisting primarily of informative materials (newsletters, bulletins, etc.)
	For periodicals consisting predominantly of legal articles, regardless of subject matter and jurisdiction, see K1+
	Statutes. Regulations. Rules of practice
665.A29	Serials
665.A3	Monographs. By date of publication
665.A4	Casebooks

KF UNITED STATES (GENERAL) KF

Property
Real property. Land law
Transfer of rights in land
Transfer inter vivos
General. Vendor and purchaser -- Continued

665.A65	Formbooks
665.A75	Collected papers and essays. Symposia
665.A8-.Z8	Treatises. Monographs
665.Z9	Popular works
665.Z95	Works on comparative and uniform state and local law
	Conveyances. Title investigation. Abstracts
666-670	General. Deeds (Table KF3)
	Particular kinds of deeds
672	Acknowledgments (Table KF6)
674	Father-son operating agreements. Family farm operating agreements (Table KF6)
675	Installment land contracts (Table KF6)
	Title investigation. Abstracts
678	General (Table KF6)
679	Registration. Torrens system (Table KF6)
680	United States land acquisition (Table KF6)
681	Settlement costs (Table KF6)
683	Description of land. Surveying (Table KF6)
	Transfer by will see KF755+
	Gifts mortis causa see KF760.G4
	Intestate succession see KF771+
	Unclaimed estates see KF780
685.A-Z	Other modes of transfer, A-Z
685.A3	Accretion (Table KF7)
685.A4	Adverse possession (Table KF7)
685.J8	Judicial process or judicial decree. Judicial sales (Table KF7)
685.T2	Tax deeds. Tax sales (Table KF7)
	Mortgages
691-695	General (Table KF3)
	Particular aspects
696	Mortgages as investments
697.A-Z	Special topics, A-Z
697.D5	Discrimination in mortgage loans (Table KF7)
697.F6	Foreclosure (Table KF7)
697.M63	Modification or restructuring of existing mortgages (Table KF7)
697.R48	Reverse mortgages (Table KF7)
697.S43	Secondary mortgage market (Table KF7)
697.S83	Subprime mortgage loans (Table KF7)
697.V37	Variable rate mortgage loans (Table KF7)

Property

Real property. Land law -- Continued

698 Equitable liens (Table KF6)

Trust indentures see KF1457

Personal property

701-705 General. Personal action (Table KF3)

706 Choses in action (Table KF6)

For negotiable instruments see KF956+

Stocks and shares (Marketing) see KF1065.2+

Stocks and shares (Corporation finance) see KF1441+

Intellectual and industrial property see KF2971+

Ownership and possession

708 Interests. Future interests (Table KF6)

For future interest in real and personal property see KF604+

709 Concurrent ownership (Table KF6)

For concurrent ownership in both real and personal property see KF619+

Fixtures see KF636

Acquisition of property

711 General

Original acquisition

712 General

713.A-Z Particular modes of acquisition, A-Z

713.A3 Accession and confusion

Adverse possession see KF685.A4

713.T7 Treasure troves. Lost articles

Transfer

715 Choses in possession

Bill of sale see KF949

Sale see KF911+

716 Gifts inter vivos (Table KF6)

Including gifts in general

Gifts causa mortis see KF760.G4

Bailment

For contracts involving bailments see KF939+

718.A2-.Z8 Treatises

718.Z9 Minor works

Transfers as security see KF1046+

720 Actions to recover personal property. Replevin (Table KF6)

Trover and conversion see KF1274

Trusts and trustees

726-730 General (Table KF3)

731 Particular aspects

Trusts

Private trusts

Trusts and trustees
Trusts
Private trusts -- Continued

733	General trusts (Table KF6)
	Particular aspects
734	Living trusts (Table KF6)
735	Testamentary trusts (Table KF6)
736.A-Z	Particular trusts, A-Z
736.L3	Land trusts (Table KF7)
736.L4	Life insurance trusts (Table KF7)
	Massachusetts trusts, business trusts see KF1381
736.P3	Pension trusts (Table KF7)
	Cf. KF3512 Labor fringe benefits
736.S6	Spendthrift trusts (Table KF7)
739-740	Charitable trusts (Table KF5)
741	Cy pres doctrine (Table KF6)
742	Resulting trusts (Table KF6)
	Trustees
	Trust companies
744	General (Table KF6)
	Escrow business see KF1027
745	Liability. Breach of trust
746-750	Estate planning (Table KF3)
	For estate tax planning see KF6576+
	Succession upon death
753	General (Table KF6)
	Testate succession. Wills
755	General (Table KF6)
	Texts of wills see CS1+
759.A-Z	Contested will cases. By testator, A-Z
760.A-Z	Special topics, A-Z
760.C3	Capacity to make a will (Table KF7)
760.C6	Contracts to make wills (Table KF7)
	Cy pres doctrine see KF741
	Estate planning see KF746+
760.F2	Family provisions. Legitime (Table KF7)
760.G4	Gifts causa mortis (Table KF7)
760.J6	Joint wills (Table KF7)
760.M2	Mass stipends (Table KF7)
	Power of appointment see KF607
760.R44	Religious wills (Table KF7)
	Worthier title see KF615
	Probate law and practice
765	General. Probate courts (Table KF6)
	For probate records see KF8755.A+
	Particular federal courts
	American Consular Courts in China see KF8768.C4

KF UNITED STATES (GENERAL) KF

Succession upon death
Probate law and practice -- Continued

769.A-Z	Special topics, A-Z
	Adoption see KF545
769.C6	Contested wills (Table KF7)
769.E65	Estate settlement costs (Table KF7)
769.J83	Judgments (Table KF7)
769.L6	Lost wills (Table KF7)
	Intestate succession
771	General (Table KF6)
772.A-Z	Special topics, A-Z
772.C6	Consanguinity (Table KF7)
	Dower and curtesy see KF629
	Administration of decedents' estates. Execution of wills.
	Personal representatives
774-778	General (Table KF3)
779.A-Z	Special topics, A-Z
779.A3	Accounting (Table KF7)
779.F6	Foreign personal representatives (Table KF7)
779.L5	Liability of estate for debts of deceased (Table KF7)
	Estate taxes, death duties see KF6576+
780	Unclaimed estates. Heirless property (Table KF6)
	Contracts
	General and comprehensive works
801.A1	Serial publications. Collections
801.A2	Congresses. Symposia. Collected papers and essays
801.A65	Form books
801.A7	Casebooks. Readings
801.A75-.Z8	Treatises. Monographs
801.Z9	Examination aids, popular works, etc.
	Including compends, outlines, and works for particular classes of users.
	General principles
	Formation of contract
807	General
807.2	Consideration
807.5	Contracts through correspondence, telephone, teletype, wire, computer, etc. (Table KF6)
808	Standard clauses. Standard forms
809	Adhesion contracts
810	Formalities. Written contract. Contract under seal. Statute of frauds
811	Option
812.A-Z	Particular frauds, A-Z
812.I5	Indemnity against liability. Hold harmless agreements
	Parties to contract
814	Assignment of contracts. Subrogration

KF UNITED STATES (GENERAL) KF

Contracts
General principles -- Continued
Void and voidable contracts

817	General
818.A-Z	Unlawful contracts, A-Z
	Restraint of trade see KF1624+
818.T6	Trading with the enemy (Table KF7)
818.U7	Usury (Table KF7)
	Cf. KF1036 Loan of money
819	Mistake
820	Duress. Undue influence
821	Fraud. Misrepresentation
	Discharge
825	General
	Performance
826	General
	Payment. Tender
827	General (Table KF8)
828	Gold clause
830	Accord and satisfaction
832	Supervening impossibility
	Limitation of actions see KF450.L55
	Limitation of actions (Procedure) see KF8881+
	Bankruptcy see KF1506+
	Breach of contract. Remedies
	Including damages, quantum meruit, assumpsit
836	General works (Table KF6)
837	Specific performance
839	Rescission and restitution
	Government contracts. Public contracts. Purchasing and procurement
841-850	General (Table KF2)
	For Court of Claims reports see KF125.C5+
850.5	Municipal contracts (Table KF6)
	War contracts. Defense contracts. Military procurement
851-855	General (Table KF4)
	Nondiscrimination clause see KF3464+
858-859	Settlement (Table KF5)
861-862	Renegotiation (Table KF5)
863-864	Cancellation. Termination (Table KF5)
865	Construction and building contracts (Table KF6)
869	Research and development contracts (Table KF6)
	Cf. KF4280.D3 Science and the arts
869.3	Subcontracting (Table KF6)
	Cf. KF3475 Labor law
869.5.A-Z	Particular federal departments, agencies, etc.
869.5.E5	Department of Energy (Table KF7)

KF UNITED STATES (GENERAL) KF

Contracts
Government contracts. Public contracts. Purchasing and procurement
Particular federal departments, agencies, etc. -- Continued

869.5.E54	Environmental Protection Agency (Table KF7)
869.5.N3	National Aeronautics and Space Administration (Table KF7)
869.5.R47	Resolution Trust Corporation (Table KF7)
869.5.T73	Federal Transit Administration (Table KF7)
869.5.T75	Department of Transportation (Table KF7)
	Particular contracts
871-890	Comprehensive. Commercial law. Mercantile transactions (Table KF1)
	Agency see KF1341+
	Contract of service. Master and servant
894	General (Table KF6)
	Merchant mariners see KF1121+
	Civil service see KF5336+
	Contract for work and labor (Contract for services). Independent contractors
898	General (Table KF6)
899-900	Mechanics' liens (Table KF5)
	Particular types
901-902	Building and construction (Table KF5)
905.A-Z	Other, A-Z
905.B87	Business practices (Table KF7)
905.C6	Computer contracts (Table KF7)
905.C67	Consulting contracts (Table KF7)
905.F34	Facility management (Table KF7)
	Government construction contracts see KF865
905.P5	Plumbing and heating (Table KF7)
	Sale of goods
911-915	General (Table KF3 modified)
915.Z93A-.Z93Z	Particular goods, A-Z
915.Z93C65	Computers
915.Z93H6	Horses
	Formation of contract
918	General (Table KF8)
919.A-Z	Special topics, A-Z
	C.I.F. and F.O.B. clauses see KF934
919.C6	Conditions and warranties. Implied warranties (Table KF7)
	Products liability see KF1296+
	Transfer of property and title
920	Auction sales (Table KF6)
	Cf. KF2038.A8 Auction houses
	Documents of title

KF UNITED STATES (GENERAL) KF

Contracts
Particular contracts
Sale of goods
Documents of title -- Continued

924	General (Table KF6)
925-926	Bills of lading (Table KF5)
	Ocean bills of lading see KF1109
	Trust receipts see KF1061
930	Warehouse receipts (Table KF6)
	Conditional transfer, conditional sale, installment sale, lease-purchase see KF1056
	Performance
933	General
934	Overseas sales. C.I.F. clause. F.O.B. clause
935	Other clauses
	Rights of unpaid seller. Lien see KF1058+
	Contracts involving bailments
	Cf. KF718.A+ Bailments
	General
939	Casebooks
940	Treatises
941	Compends. Outlines
942	Examination aids
	Particular contracts
945	Deposit of goods. Warehouses (Table KF6)
	For warehouse receipts see KF930
	For warehouse regulation see KF2050+
946	Hire of goods (Table KF6)
947	Consignment of goods (Table KF6)
	Pledge (Pawn) see KF1060
949	Bill of sale (Table KF6)
951	Innkeeper and guest (Table KF6)
	For hotel and restaurant trade see KF2042.H6
	Carriers see KF1091+
	Partnership see KF1371+
	Negotiable instruments
956-957	General (Table KF5)
	Bills of exchange
958	General (Table KF6)
959.A-Z	Special topics, A-Z
959.A3	Acceptance (Table KF7)
959.E5	Endorsement (Table KF7)
959.H6	Holder in due course (Table KF7)
959.P6	Protest (Table KF7)
	Checks
960	General (Table KF6)
961.A-Z	Special topics, A-Z

Contracts
Particular contracts
Negotiable instruments
Checks
Special topics, A-Z -- Continued

961.D8	Duplicates (Table KF7)
961.F6	Forgeries. Alterations (Table KF7)
	Cf. KF9367 Criminal law
962	Promissory notes (Table KF6)
	Securities (Marketing) see KF1065.2+
	Securities (Issuing and sale) see KF1431+
	Warehouse receipts see KF930
	Banking
966-975	General (Table KF2)
977	Management. Directors (Table KF6)
	Particular kinds of banks
981-990	Federal Reserve banks (Table KF2)
	Cf. KF6219 Federal Reserve Board
	Rediscount see KF1026
	National banks
991-1000	General (Table KF2)
1001	Comptroller of the Treasury (Table KF6)
1001.5	Foreign banks (Table KF6)
1002	Mortgage banks (Table KF6)
	Including government-sponsored enterprises
1004	Savings banks (Table KF6)
1006	Investment banks (Table KF6)
1008	Cooperative banks. Credit unions (Table KF6)
1009	Building and loan associations (Table KF6)
	Industrial banks see KF1039+
	Trust companies see KF1011
1011	Agricultural credit banks (Table KF6)
	Cf. KF1701 Farm loans
1012	Regulatory agencies
1012.F2	Farm Credit Administration (Table KF7)
	Including Farm Credit Corporation, Farm Loan Commissioner, Federal Farm Loan Board, Federal Farm Loan Bureau
	Commodity Credit Corporation see KF1692.1
	Export-Import Bank see KF1978
1015	Clearinghouses (Table KF6)
1017	Bank holding companies (Table KF6)
1018	Bank mergers (Table KF6)
1019	Branch banking (Table KF6)
1020	State banks (Table KF6)
	Deposits and accounts
1022	General (Table KF6)

KF UNITED STATES (GENERAL) KF

Contracts
Particular contracts
Banking
Deposits and accounts -- Continued

1023	Deposit insurance. Federal Deposit Insurance Company (Table KF6)
1023.5	NOW accounts (Table KF6)
1023.6	Savings accounts (Table KF6)
1024	Collecting of accounts. Collection laws (Table KF6)
	For collection agencies see KF2042.C6
1026	Discount. Discount rate. Rediscount (Table KF6)
1027	Escrow business (Table KF6)
1028	Letters of credit (Table KF6)
1029	Repurchase agreements (Table KF6)
1030.A-Z	Other, A-Z
	Bank secrets see KF1030.R3
1030.E4	Electronic funds transfer (Table KF7)
1030.F6	Foreign banking (Table KF7)
	Investment services see KF1030.S43
	Money laundering see KF1030.R3
1030.R3	Record keeping (Table KF7)
	Including bank secrets, money laundering
1030.R35	Reserves. Specie (Table KF7)
1030.S2	Safe-deposit boxes (Table KF7)
1030.S43	Securities processing. Investment services (Table KF7)
1032.A-Z	Particular banks, A-Z
1033	Foreign exchange brokerage
	Loan of money
1035	General (Table KF6)
1036	Interest. Usury (Table KF6)
	Cf. KF818.U7 Unlawful contracts
1039-1040	Consumer credit. Small loans. Industrial banks. Morris plan. Finance charges (Table KF5)
	Including credit cards
	Small business investment companies see KF1080
	Government lending. Government insurance of loans (General) see KF6241+
	Government lending. Government insurance of loans (Housing) see KF5737
1045	Suretyship. Guaranty (Table KF6)
	For suretyship insurance, bonding see KF1223+
	Secured transactions
1046-1050	General (Table KF4)
	Particular transactions
	Chattel mortgages
1053	General (Table KF6)
1054.A-Z	Particular kinds of personal property, A-Z

Contracts
Particular contracts
Secured transactions
Particular transactions -- Continued

1056	Conditional sale. Installment sale. Lease purchase (Table KF6)
	Liens
1058	General (Table KF6)
	For equitable liens on real property see KF698
1059.A-Z	Particular kinds, A-Z
	Prefer secured obligation
	Maritime liens see KF1114.B6
	Mechanics' liens see KF899+
	Railroad liens see KF2305
	Tax liens see KF6316
1060	Pledge (Table KF6)
	For pawnbrokers see KF2038.P3
	Suretyship and guaranty see KF1045
	Trust indentures see KF1457
1061	Trust receipts (Table KF6)
1062	Other
	Marketing of securities. Investments. Stock exchange transactions
	Issuing and sale of securities, Federal Securities Act, Securities and Exchange Commission see KF1431+
1066-1070	General (Table KF4)
1071	Stockbrokers (Table KF6)
1072	Investment advisors (Table KF6)
1073.A-Z	Particular transactions, A-Z
	Calls see KF1073.P88
1073.I5	Insider trading in corporate securities (Table KF7)
1073.M3	Trading on margin (Table KF7)
	Options, Stock see KF1073.P88
1073.P88	Put and call transactions (Table KF7)
1074.A-Z	Particular stock exchanges, A-Z
1074.N3	New York Stock Exchange (Table KF7)
1075	Over-the-counter markets (Table KF6)
	Investment trusts. Investment companies. Mutual funds
1078	General (Table KF6)
1078.3	Hedge funds (Table KF6)
1078.5	Private equity funds (Table KF6)
1079	Real estate investment companies (Table KF6)
	Cf. KF1535.R43 Bankruptcy
1080	Small business investment companies (Table KF6)
	Particular securities

Contracts
Particular contracts
Marketing of securities. Investments. Stock exchange transactions
Particular securities -- Continued

Call Number	Description
1083	Legal investments. Trust investments (Table KF4)
	For mortgages see KF696+
	For stocks see KF1441+
	For industrial bonds (debentures) see KF1456
	For government bonds see KF6241+; KF6775
1084.A-Z	Special topics, A-Z
1084.I5	Insurance. Securities Investor Protection Corporation (Table KF7)
	Commodity exchanges. Produce exchanges
1085	General. Futures trading (Table KF6)
1086.A-Z	Particular commodities, A-Z
1086.C6	Coffee (Table KF7)
1086.C65	Cotton (Table KF7)
1086.G7	Grain (Table KF7)
1086.W6	Wool (Table KF7)
1087.A-Z	Particular commodity exchanges, A-Z
1087.C55	Chicago Board of Trade (Table KF7)
	Carriers. Carriage of goods and passengers
1091	General. Liability (Table KF6)
1092	Carriage by land. Affreightment (Table KF6)
	For Interstate commerce act, Interstate Commerce Commission see KF2181
	For Commerce Court see KF2184
	For motor carriers see KF2246+
	For railroads see KF2271+
1093	Carriage by air (Table KF6)
	Cf. KF2421+ Regulation of commercial aviation
	Carriage by sea. Maritime (Commercial) law. Admiralty
1096-1105	General (Table KF2)
1105.2	Federal Maritime Board
	Liability
1107	General. Maritime torts. Collisions at sea (Table KF6)
	Government liability see KF1325.M2
1108	Average (Table KF6)
1109	Ocean bills of lading (Table KF6)
	Admiralty proceedings
1111.A25	Legislative documents. By date
	Court rules
1111.A4	Drafts. By date
1111.A5	Texts. By date
1111.A6-Z	Particular courts. By jurisdiction
1111.5	Form books

Contracts

Particular contracts

Carriers. Carriage of goods and passengers

Carriage by sea. Maritime (Commercial) law. Admiralty

Admiralty proceedings -- Continued

1112	Treatises. Monographs
1114.A-Z	Special topics, A-Z
1114.B2	Barratry (Table KF7)
1114.B6	Bottomry and respondentia. Ship mortgages. Maritime liens (Table KF7)
1114.B65	Federal ship mortgage insurance (Table KF7)
1114.C4	Charter parties (Table KF7)
1114.S2	Salvage. Wreck (Table KF7)

Maritime labor law. Merchant mariners

For manning requirements see KF2553

For war services see KF7488+

1121	General (Table KF6)
1123	Minimum age (Table KF6)
1124	Citizenship requirements (Table KF6)
1125	Certification. Suspension. Revocation (Table KF6)
1127	Maritime unions. Collective labor agreements (Table KF6)
1128.A-Z	Particular types of maritime labor, A-Z Subarrange each by Table KF6
1130	Labor disputes and arbitration (Table KF6)
1130.5	Maritime Labor Board (Table KF6)
1131	Wages and nonwage benefits. Hours of labor (Table KF6)

Social insurance

1132	Workers' compensation. Death on the high seas (Table KF6)

Coastwise navigation see KF2556

Inland water transportation see KF2645+

Marine insurance

1135	General (Table KF6)
1136	Warranty of seaworthiness (Table KF6)

Particular risks

1137	War risks (Table KF6)

Insurance

Including regulation of insurance business

For taxation see KF6614.I5

1146-1165	General (Table KF1)
1167	Insurance business. Agents. Broker (Table KF6)

Tort liability of insurance companies see KF1301.5.B36

Insurance fraud see KF9368

1169.A-Z	Particular plans and modes of premiums, A-Z
1169.A7	Assessment insurance (Table KF7)

Contracts
Particular contracts
Insurance
General
Particular plans and modes of premiums, A-Z --
Continued

1169.G7	Group insurance (Table KF7)
1170.A-Z	Particular clauses, A-Z
1170.E94	Excess and surplus lines (Table KF7)
	Particular branches
1170.5	Multiple-line underwriting (Table KF6)
	Personal insurance
	Life
1171-1175	General (Table KF4)
1176	Life insurance companies. Finance. Investment of funds (Table KF6)
1177.A-Z	Particular plans and modes of payment, A-Z
1177.G7	Group life (Table KF7)
1177.V3	Variable contracts. Variable annuities (Table KF7)
1177.V53	Viatical settlements (Table KF7)
1178.A-Z	Particular clauses, A-Z
1178.D5	Disability (Table KF7)
1178.I5	Incontestability. Suicide (Table KF7)
1178.N6	Non-forfeiture (Table KF7)
1180.A-Z	Particular types of benefits, A-Z
1180.B8	Business life (Table KF7)
1180.E5	Endowment (Table KF7)
1181.A-Z	Special topics, A-Z
1181.A8	Assignment (Table KF7)
1181.B6	Breach of contract (Table KF7)
1181.E5	Doctrine of election (Table KF7)
1181.R8	Rule against perpetuities (Table KF7)
1181.W2	Waivers (Table KF7)
1181.W25	War risks (Table KF7)
1182	Disability insurance (Table KF6)
	Cf. KF3641+ Social insurance
	Health. Medical care
1183	General (Table KF6)
1184.A-Z	Particular plans and modes of premium, A-Z
1184.G7	Group insurance. Blue Shield. Group Health (Table KF7)
1184.H4	Health maintenance organizations (Table KF7)
1184.P73	Preferred provider organizations (Table KF7)
1185	Hospitalization (Table KF6)
1186	Dental care (Table KF6)
1187	Accident (Table KF6)

Contracts
Particular contracts
Insurance
Particular branches
Personal insurance -- Continued

1188	Burial (Table KF6)
1189	Other
1189.5	Business insurance (Table KF6)
	Including bank insurance
	Property insurance
1190	General (Table KF6)
	Ocean marine see KF1135+
1192	Inland marine. Transportation (Table KF6)
1194	Aviation (Table KF6)
1196	Fire (Table KF6)
1198	Fire insurance business (Table KF6)
1200	Theft. Burglary. Robbery (Table KF6)
1202.A-Z	Other hazards, A-Z
1202.B8	Business interruptions (Table KF7)
1202.C58	Climate change (Table KF7)
1202.E2	Earthquakes (Table KF7)
1202.W5	Windstorms (Table KF7)
	Particular kinds of property
	Agricultural
	For Government insurance see KF1701
1203	General (Table KF6)
	Crops
1204	General (Table KF6)
1205.A-Z	Particular crops, A-Z
1207	Tornado (Table KF6)
1210	Motor vehicles (Table KF6)
1212.A-Z	Other, A-Z
1212.M2	Machinery (Table KF7)
1212.P5	Plate glass (Table KF7)
	Casualty insurance
1215	General liability (Table KF6)
	Particular risks
	Atomic damage see KF1220.N8
1218	Automobile (Table KF6)
1218.8	Uninsured motorists (Table KF6)
1219	Unsatisfied judgment funds (Table KF6)
	For financial responsibility laws see KF2219
1219.5	No-fault (Table KF6)
1220.A-Z	Other, A-Z
	Deposit, Federal Deposit Insurance Company see KF1023
1220.E83	Executives' liability (Table KF7)

KF UNITED STATES (GENERAL) KF

Contracts
Particular contracts
Insurance
Particular branches
Casualty insurance
Particular risks
Other, A-Z -- Continued

1220.G68	Government risks (Table KF7)
1220.M2	Malpractice (Table KF7)
1220.N8	Nuclear damage (Table KF7)
1220.P5	Pollution (Table KF7)
1220.P6	Products liability (Table KF7)
	Suretyship. Guaranty. Title insurance
	For contract of suretyship see KF1045
1223	General (Table KF6)
	Bonding
1225	Bonding of employees (Table KF6)
	Including government employees
1226	Bail bonds (Table KF6)
1228	Other
	Guaranty
1231	Credit insurance (Table KF6)
1232	Mortgage. Mortgage guaranty (Table KF6)
	For government mortgage insurance see KF5737
1232.5	Ship mortgage (Table KF6)
1233	Other
1234	Title insurance (Table KF6)
1236	Reinsurance (Table KF6)
1238	Fraternal insurance. Friendly societies (Table KF6)
	Group insurance see KF1169.G7
	Social insurance see KF3600+
	Aleatory contracts
1241	Gambling. Wagering. Speculation (Table KF6)
	Lotteries (Regulation) see KF3992
	Insurance see KF1146+
	Lotteries (Criminal law) see KF9440
1244	Restitution. Quasi contracts. Unjust enrichment (Table KF6)
1244.5	Remedies. Constructive trust
	Torts (Extracontractual liability)
1246-1250	General. Liability. Damages (Table KF3 modified)
	Cf. KF8944 Evidence
1249.4	Restatements
1251	Particular aspects
1253	Privilege. Respondeat superior (Table KF6)
1254	Proximate cause (Table KF6)
	Particular torts

Torts (Extracontractual liability)
Particular torts -- Continued
Torts in respect to the person

1256-1257	Personal injuries (Table KF5)
	Cf. KF1300.2+ Parties to actions in torts
	Cf. KF1315.P3 Vicarious liability
	Cf. KF1325.P3 Government liability
	Cf. KF8925.P4 Trial practice
1259	Wrongful life (Table KF6)
1260	Death by wrongful act (Table KF6)
	Violation of privacy
1262	General (Table KF6)
1263.A-Z	Special topics, A-Z
	Banking information and privacy see KF1030.R3
1263.C65	Computers and privacy. Internet and privacy (Table KF7)
	Including data protection
	Financial information and privacy see KF1030.R3
	Internet and privacy see KF1263.C65
1263.M43	Mass media and privacy (Table KF7)
1263.U5	Unauthorized publication of picture (Table KF7)
1264	Anguish and fright (Table KF6)
	Torts in respect to reputation
1266	General. Libel and slander (Table KF6)
1266.5.A-Z	Particular instances of tort liability, A-Z
1266.5.C7	Credit information (Table KF7)
	Disparagement (Unfair competition) see KF3198
1267.A-Z	Defenses, A-Z
1267.P7	Privileges. Truth (Table KF7)
1269	Torts in respect to domestic relations (Table KF6)
	Abuse of legal process
1270	Malicious prosecution (Table KF6)
1270.5	Abuse of discovery (Table KF6)
1271	Deceit. Fraud (Table KF6)
	Unfair competition see KF3195+
1272	Trespass to land (Table KF6)
	Ejectment see KF652+
1273	Nuisance (Table KF6)
1274	Torts affecting chattels. Trespass to goods. Conversion. Trover (Table KF6)
	Replevin see KF720
	Negligence
1276-1285	General (Table KF2)
	Cf. KF8925.N4 Trial practice
	Cf. KF8944 Evidence
1286	Contributory negligence. Comparative negligence. Last clear chance (Table KF6)

KF UNITED STATES (GENERAL) KF

Torts (Extracontractual liability)
Particular torts
Negligence -- Continued
Liability for condition and use of land
Including premises liability

1287	General (Table KF6)
1287.5.A-Z	Particular kinds, A-Z
1287.5.A8	Attractive nuisance (Table KF7)
1287.5.B8	Building accidents (Table KF7)
1287.5.E45	Elevator accidents. Escalator accidents (Table KF7)
1289	Malpractice. Professional liability (Table KF6)
	For malpractice and tort liability of particular professions, see the profession
1290.A-Z	Particular types of accidents, A-Z
1290.A8	Automobile accidents (Table KF7)
	For financial responsibility laws see KF2219
1290.A9	Aviation accidents (Table KF7)
	Including helicopter accidents
	For liability of common air carriers see KF2454+
	Fall accidents see KF1290.S55
1290.F4	Fire accidents (Table KF7)
	Helicopter accidents see KF1290.A9
	Marine accidents (General) see KF1107
	Marine accidents (Government liability) see KF1325.M2
1290.P5	Playground accidents. Public recreation (Table KF7)
	For liability of school districts see KF1309
	For liability of teachers see KF1310
	Railroad accidents (General. Damage to property) see KF2371+
	Railroad accidents (Personal injury) see KF2375
	School accidents see KF1309; KF1310
1290.S55	Slip and fall accidents (Table KF7)
1290.S66	Sports accidents (Table KF7)
1290.S7	Streetcar, subway, bus accidents. Liability of local transit lines (Table KF7)
	Strict liability. Liability without fault
1292	General (Table KF6)
1293	Damage caused by animals (Table KF6)
1293.5	Damage resulting from intoxication. Dramshop acts (Table KF6)
1294.A-Z	Ultrahazardous activities or occupations. By risk, A-Z
	Products liability
	Cf. KF3945+ Product safety
1296	General (Table KF6)
1297.A-Z	By product, A-Z
1297.A57	Airplanes (Table KF7)
1297.A73	Asbestos (Table KF7)

Torts (Extracontractual liability)
Strict liability. Liability without fault
Products liability
By product, A-Z -- Continued

1297.A77	Athletic equipment and supplies (Table KF7)
1297.A8	Automobiles, automotive equipment (Table KF7)
1297.B74	Breast implants (Table KF7)
1297.C4	Chemical products (Table KF7)
1297.C65	Contraceptive drug implants (Table KF7)
1297.D7	Drugs (Table KF7)
1297.F55	Firearms (Table KF7)
1297.F6	Food (Table KF7)
1297.L33	Ladders (Table KF7)
1297.L5	Liquor (Table KF7)
1297.M4	Medical instruments and apparatus (Table KF7)
1297.R33	Radioactive substances (Table KF7)
1297.T63	Tobacco (Table KF7)
	Including works on claims for injuries from smoking
1297.V32	Vaccines (Table KF7)
	Environmental damages
1298	General (Table KF6)
1299.A-Z	Particular types of damages, A-Z
1299.H39	Hazardous substances (Table KF7)
1299.W38	Water pollution (Table KF7)
1300	Enterprise liability. Industry-wide liability
	Parties to actions in torts
	Children, minors see KF479
	Corporations
	General
1301.A2	Torts in general (Table KF7)
1301.A3-Z	Particular kinds of torts or accidents
	Civil liability for racketeering. Civil RICO actions see KF9375
1301.H39	Hazardous substances, Improper disposal of (Table KF7)
1301.5.A-Z	Particular kinds of corporations, A-Z
1301.5.B36	Banks. Lender liability
1301.5.I58	Insurance
	Lender liability see KF1301.5.B36
	Municipal corporations
1302.A2	Torts in general (Table KF7)
1302.A3-Z	Particular kinds of torts or accidents, A-Z
	Subarrange each by Table KF7
	Nonprofit corporations
	General
1303.A2	Torts in general (Table KF7)

Torts (Extracontractual liability)
Parties to actions in torts
Corporations
Nonprofit corporations
General -- Continued

Call Number	Topic
1303.A3-Z	Particular kinds of torts or accidents, A-Z
	Subarrange each by Table KF7
1303.2.A-Z	Particular kinds, A-Z
1303.2.C6	Colleges and universities (Table KF7)
	Hospitals see KF3825.3
	Public officers and government employees
1306.A2	General (Table KF7)
1306.A3-Z	Particular kinds of torts or accidents
	Civil rights see KF1306.C64
1306.C64	Constitutional torts. Civil rights (Table KF7)
1306.T7	Traffic accidents (Table KF7)
1307	Police (Table KF6)
1308	Correctional personnel (Table KF6)
1309	School districts (Table KF6)
1309.5	Foreign governments and employees. Alien tort claims (Table KF6)
1310	Teachers (Table KF6)
1311	Social service agencies (Table KF6)
1312	Joint tortfeasors (Table KF6)
1313	Victims of crimes (Table KF6)
	Including claims against third parties
	Liability for torts of others. Vicarious liability
1314	Employer and independent contractor
1315	Master and servant
1315.A2	General (Table KF7)
	Fellow servant rule see KF1319.F4
1315.P3	Personal injuries (Table KF7)
	Respondeat superior see KF1253
	Employer's liability
1316	General (Table KF6)
1317.A-Z	Particular groups of employees or industries, A-Z
1317.M3	Merchant mariners (Table KF7)
1317.M5	Mines (Table KF7)
	Railroads
1317.R2	General
1317.R22A-.R22Z	Particular railroad companies, A-Z
1319.A-Z	Special topics, A-Z
1319.A7	Assumption of risk (Table KF7)
1319.F4	Fellow servant rule (Table KF7)
	Government torts
1321	General. Federal Tort Claims Act (Table KF6)
	Including constitutional torts

KF UNITED STATES (GENERAL) KF

Torts (Extracontractual liability)
Liability for torts of others. Vicarious liability
Government torts -- Continued

1322	Suability of states (Table KF6)
1325.A-Z	Particular kinds of accidents and torts arising from particular conditions, activities, etc., A-Z
1325.C58	Civil rights
1325.E58	Environmental damages
1325.L36	Land use. Zoning
	Including planning
1325.M2	Maritime torts
1325.P3	Personal injuries
1325.T7	Traffic accidents. Highway conditions
	Zoning see KF1325.L36
	Remedies. Defenses
1326	General (Table KF6)
1327.A-Z	Particular remedies, A-Z
	Compensation to victims of crimes. Reparation
1328	General (Table KF6)
1328.5.A-Z	Particular crimes, A-Z
1328.5.C45	Child sexual abuse (Table KF7)
	Assistance in emergencies. Good Samaritan laws
1329	General (Table KF6)
	Medical emergency assistance see KF2905
	Agency
1341-1345	General (Table KF3)
1346	Conflict of interests (Table KF6)
1347	Power of attorney (Table KF6)
1348.A-Z	Particular types of agency, A-Z
1348.A38	Advertising. Marketing (Table KF7)
	Auctioneers (Auction sales) see KF920
	Auctioneers (Second-hand trade) see KF2038.A8
1348.B7	Brokers. Commission merchants. Factors (Table KF7)
	Real estate agents see KF2042.R4
1348.C6	Commercial travelers. Traveling sales personnel (Table KF7)
	Forwarding agents see KF2745
	Forwarding agents (Air freight forwarders) see KF2462
	Forwarding agents (Ocean freight forwarders) see KF2654
	Marketing see KF1348.A38
	Associations
1355	General (Table KF6)
	Including business enterprises in general, regardless of form of organization
1357	Accounting law. Auditing. Financial statements (Table KF6)
	For corporation accounting see KF1446
	For practice of accountancy see KF2920

KF UNITED STATES (GENERAL) KF

Associations
General -- Continued

Call Number	Description
1357.5	Business records. Records keeping and retention (Table KF6)
	Publicly chartered corporations. Patriotic societies
1359.A1	General (Table KF7)
1359.A2-Z	Particular societies, A-Z
	Subarrange each by Table KF7
	Unincorporated associations
1361	General (Table KF7)
1362.A-Z	Particular types of associations, A-Z
	Building and loan associations see KF1009
1362.C5	Clubs (Table KF7)
	Community associations of property owners see KF576
	Condominium associations see KF581
	Credit unions see KF1008
1362.F7	Freemasons (Table KF7)
	Labor unions see KF3381+
	Business associations. Partnership
	General
1365	Casebooks
1366	Treatises
	Partnership
1371-1375	General (Table KF3)
1377	Particular aspects
1380	Limited partnership (Table KF6)
	Including limited liability companies and private companies
1380.5	Joint ventures (Table KF6)
	Strategic alliances. Corporate alliances
1380.6	General (Table KF6)
1380.7	Research and development partnership (Table KF6)
1381	Massachusetts trusts. Business trusts (Table KF6)
1382	Family partnerships (Table KF6)
	Corporations. Juristic persons
1384	Corporations in general (Table KF6)
1385	Particular aspects
1386.A-Z	Special topics, A-Z
1386.B9	Bylaws (Table KF7)
1386.D6	Domicile (Table KF7)
1386.U5	Ultra vires doctrine (Table KF7)
	Nonprofit corporations
1388	General (Table KF6)
	Management
1388.5	General (Table KF6)
1388.7	Board of directors. Officers (Table KF6)
	Particular types
	Foundations. Endowments

Associations
Corporations. Juristic persons
Nonprofit corporations
Particular types
Foundations. Endowments -- Continued

1389	General (Table KF6)
1389.5	Fund raising (Table KF6)
1390.A-Z	Other, A-Z
1390.C6	Collective settlements. Communes (Table KF7)
	Professional associations see KF2902
	Religious corporations and societies see KF4865
	Business corporations
1396-1415	General (Table KF1)
1416	Special aspects
1418	Government regulation and control. Licensing (Table KF6)
1419	Foreign corporations. Corporations doing business in other states, or engaged in interstate commerce (Table KF6)
1420	Incorporation. Corporate charters and bylaws. Promoters (Table KF6)
1422	Management (Table KF6)
1423	Board of directors. Officers (Table KF6)
1424	Remuneration, salaries, pensions, etc. (Table KF6)
	Interlocking directorates see KF1657.I57
1425	Corporate legal departments (Table KF6)
	Corporate finance. Capital. Dividends
1428	General (Table KF6)
	Issuing of securities
	For security exchanges see KF1066+
1431-1440	General (Table KF2)
	Particular types of stocks
	Common stock
1441	General (Table KF6)
1442.A-Z	Particular kinds, A-Z
1442.N6	Nonvoting (Table KF7)
1442.W5	Without par value (Table KF7)
1443	Credit rating. Credit rating agencies (Table KF6)
1444	Securities and Exchange Commission (Table KF6)
1446	Accounting. Auditing. Financial statements (Table KF6)
	Shares and shareholders' rights. Stock transfers
1448	General (Table KF6)
1448.5	Minority stockholders (Table KF6)
1449	Disclosure requirements (Table KF6)
	Stockholders' meetings
1450	General (Table KF6)
1451	Proxy rules (Table KF6)

KF UNITED STATES (GENERAL) KF

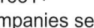

Associations
Corporations. Juristic persons
Business corporations
Shares and shareholders' rights. Stock transfers
Stockholders' meetings -- Continued

1452	Voting trusts (Table KF6)
1454	Stock transfers (Table KF6)
1456	Debentures. Bonds. Preferred stocks (Table KF6)
1457	Trust indentures (Table KF6)
	Particular types of corporations
1465	Subsidiary and parent companies. Holding companies (Table KF6)
	For particular industries (Railroads) see KF2293
	Combines, trusts, monopolies see KF1631+
	Private companies. Limited liability companies see KF1380
1466	Close corporations (Table KF6)
1470	Cooperative societies (Table KF6)
	Agricultural cooperatives see KF1715
	Housing cooperatives see KF623
	Building associations see KF1009
	Farm corporations see KF1713
	Professional corporations see KF2901
1475	Dissolution. Liquidation (Table KF6)
1477	Consolidation and merger (Table KF6)
	For monopoly and antitrust aspects see KF1654+
1478	Divestiture. Spinoffs (Table KF6)
1480	Government-owned corporations and business organizations (Table KF6)
	For particular industries (Public utilities) see KF2076+
	For particular industries (Railroads) see KF2295
	Municipal corporations see KF5304+
	Insolvency and bankruptcy. Creditors' rights
1501	General (Table KF6)
	Bankruptcy
1506-1525	General (Table KF1)
1526	Particular aspects
	Procedure
	General
	Court rules
1527.A2	Collections. By date of publication
	Supreme court rules. General orders and forms
1527.A3	Drafts. By date

Insolvency and bankruptcy. Creditors' rights
Bankruptcy
Procedure
General
Court rules
Supreme court rules. General orders and forms --
Continued

1527.A31-.A329	Text editions
	Arrange chronologically by means of successive Cutter numbers, according to date of adoption or revision of rules
	Under each:
	.xA2 *Unannotated texts. By date of publication*
	.xA3-.xZ *Annotated editions. Commentaries*
1527.A4	District court rules. By district
	Subdivide by date of publication
1527.A5-.A7	Official reports and monographs
1527.A8-Z	Treatises. Monographs
1530.A-Z	Special topics, A-Z
1530.A88	Automatic stays (Table KF7)
	Costs see KF1530.F54
1530.D4	Discharge (Table KF7)
1530.E44	Electronic filing of court documents (Table KF7)
1530.E87	Evidence (Table KF7)
1530.F54	Filing fees. Costs (Table KF7)
1530.J8	Jurisdiction (Table KF7)
1530.P3	Petitions (Table KF7)
1530.R3	Receivers in bankruptcy (Table KF7)
1530.R35	Referees (Table KF7)
1532	Priority of claims (Table KF6)
1534	Fraudulent conveyances (Table KF6)
1535.A-Z	Particular types of bankrupts, A-Z
1535.A37	Airlines. Aviation industry (Table KF7)
	Aviation industry see KF1535.A37
1535.C65	Computer industry (Table KF7)
1535.D58	Divorced people (Table KF7)
1535.E44	Electronic commerce (Table KF7)
1535.G73	Grain elevators (Table KF7)
1535.I58	Insurance companies (Table KF7)
1535.M44	Medical and health care industry (Table KF7)
1535.M85	Municipal corporations (Table KF7)
1535.P48	Petroleum industry (Table KF7)
1535.R43	Real estate investment companies (Table KF7)
1535.R45	Retail trade (Table KF7)
1536.A-Z	Other topics, A-Z
1536.E93	Exclusions. Exemptions (Table KF7)

KF UNITED STATES (GENERAL) KF

Insolvency and bankruptcy. Creditors' rights
Bankruptcy
Other topics, A-Z -- Continued
Exemptions see KF1536.E93
1536.S34 Sale of assets (Table KF7)
Debtors' relief
1539 General (Table KF6)
1540 Composition. Receivership to avoid bankruptcy (Table KF6)
1542 Real property arrangements (Table KF6)
Corporate reorganization
For taxation see KF6499.C6
1544 General (Table KF6)
1546.A-Z Particular types of corporations or lines of business, A-Z
1546.B2 Banks (Table KF7)
1546.F35 Farms (Table KF7)
1546.H35 High technology industries (Table KF7)
1546.I5 Insurance companies (Table KF7)
1546.M8 Municipal corporations (Table KF7)
1546.P83 Public utilities (Table KF7)
1546.R2 Railroads (Table KF7)
1548 Other forms of debt relief
1548.A7 Assignments for benefit of creditors (Table KF7)
1548.B8 Bulk transfers (Table KF7)
1548.M6 Moratorium (Table KF7)
Cf. KF5901+ Wartime and emergency legislation
Economic policy. Economic planning
For economic emergency legislation see KF5900+
1570 General (Table KF6)
1575 Foreign investment (Table KF6)
Cf. KF1419 Foreign corporations
Regulation of industry, trade, and commerce. Occupational law
1600 General. Comprehensive (Table KF6)
Trade regulation. Control of trade practices. Consumer protection
Cf. KF3096+ Patent law, unfair competition, trademarks, etc.
Economic emergency legislation see KF5900+
1601-1610 General. Unfair trade practices (Table KF2)
Federal Trade Commission
General
1611.A2A-.A2Z Federal Trade Commission documents. Reports
Procedure
1611.A3 Rules. By date
1611.A4 Treatises. Monographs
1611.A5-Z History and general works
Advertising

KF UNITED STATES (GENERAL) KF

Regulation of industry, trade, and commerce. Occupational law
Trade regulation. Control of trade practices. Consumer
protection
Advertising -- Continued

1614	General (Table KF6)
	Cf. Professional ethics, e. g. KF310.A3 Lawyers
	Legal advertising see KF450.N6
1616.A-Z	By industry or product, A-Z
1616.A5	Alcoholic beverages (Table KF7)
1616.B33	Bakery products (Table KF7)
1616.B34	Banking (Table KF7)
1616.D78	Drugs (Table KF7)
1616.F6	Food (Table KF7)
1616.I5	Insurance (Table KF7)
	Liquor see KF1616.A5
1616.O6	Optical industry (Table KF7)
1616.T5	Tobacco (Table KF7)
1617.A-Z	By medium, A-Z
1617.B7	Broadcasting (Table KF7)
1617.C65	Computer networks (Table KF7)
	Including the Internet
	Signboards see KF5532
	Labeling
	Including misbranding
1619	General (Table KF6)
1620.A-Z	By product, A-Z
	Alcoholic beverages
1620.A5	General (Table KF7)
1620.A53	Beer (Table KF7)
1620.A57	Whiskey (Table KF7)
1620.A58	Wine (Table KF7)
1620.A6	Household appliances (Table KF7)
	Bedding see KF1620.F83
	Cosmetics see KF3896
	Cotton fabrics see KF1620.T33
	Drugs, pharmaceutical products, narcotics see KF3885
1620.F66	Food (Table KF7)
1620.F8	Fur (Table KF7)
1620.F83	Furniture (Table KF7)
	Including bedding
	Hazardous substances see KF3945+
1620.I58	Insulating materials (Table KF7)
1620.P2	Paint. Lacquer. Varnish. Linseed oil (Table KF7)
	Poisons see KF3958+
	Textile fabrics
1620.T3	General (Table KF7)
1620.T33	Cotton (Table KF7)

Regulation of industry, trade, and commerce. Occupational law
Trade regulation. Control of trade practices. Consumer protection
Labeling
By product, A-Z
Textile fabrics -- Continued

1620.T38	Wool (Table KF7)
	Toxic substances see KF3958+
1620.T7	Trout (Table KF7)
1624-1625	Restraint of trade (Table KF5)
	Price fixing. Price discrimination. Basing-point pricing
	For price maintenance (Fair trade laws) see KF2016+
1626-1627	General (Table KF5)
1629.A-Z	By product, A-Z
1629.C6	Coal (Table KF7)
1629.N6	Nonferrous metals (Table KF7)
1629.P6	Portland cement (Table KF7)
1629.S7	Steel (Table KF7)
1629.S8	Sugar (Table KF7)
	Monopolies. Antitrust laws
	Works on antitrust aspects of a particular industry or profession are classed in KF1681+ ; those relating to an individual company, with that company
	Cf. KF1465 Holding companies
1631-1650	General (Table KF1)
1652	Particular aspects
1653	Antitrust Division of the Department of Justice (Table KF6)
1654-1655	Industrial mergers (Table KF5)
1657.A-Z	Special topics, A-Z
	For civil procedure in suits brought by the United States see KF9066.A5
1657.C6	Consent decrees (Table KF7)
1657.C7	Criminal law. Criminal prosecution (Table KF7)
1657.I57	Interlocking directorates (Table KF7)
	Labor unions see KF3402
1657.P3	Parens patriae suits (Table KF7)
	Patents see KF3116
1657.P74	Private antitrust actions (Table KF7)
1657.S72	State action doctrine (Table KF7)
1657.T53	Tie-ins. Tying arrangements (Table KF7)
	Tying arrangements see KF1657.T53
1657.T7	Triple-damage suits (Table KF7)
1659	Small business (Table KF6)
	For small business investment companies see KF1080
	For taxation see KF6491
1659.1	Small Business Administration (Table KF6)

Regulation of industry, trade, and commerce. Occupational law
Trade regulation. Control of trade practices. Consumer
protection -- Continued

1661	Trade associations (Table KF6)
	Professional associations see KF2902
1663	State jurisdiction. Trade barriers (Table KF6)
	Weights and measures. Containers
1665	General. Standards (Table KF6)
1666.A-Z	By product, A-Z
1666.B3	Beverages (Table KF7)
1666.S3	Seeds (Table KF7)
1668	Standard time (Table KF6)
	Including regulation of calendar
	For computation of time see KF450.T5
	For Sunday legislation see KF2009+
	Primary production. Extractive industries
	Agriculture. Forestry
1681-1682	General (Table KF5 modified)
	Surveys of legislation
1681.A24-.A248	Serials
1681.A249	Monographs. By date
1683	Department of Agriculture
1686	Conservation of agricultural and forest lands. Soil conservation. Field irrigation. Erosion control (Table KF6)
	For soil banks see KF1705+
	Cf. KF5615+ Land reclamation
	Control of agricultural pests, plant diseases, predatory animals. Weed control. Plant quarantine
	Cf. KF3835+ Veterinary law
1687-1688	General (Table KF5)
1689.A-Z	Particular diseases, pests, etc., A-Z
1689.W3	Weeds (Table KF7)
	Pesticides, herbicides, etc. see KF3959
	Economic assistance
1691	General. Agricultural Adjustment Act (Table KF6)
	Agricultural banks see KF1011
	Price supports. Production control
1692	General (Table KF6)
1692.1	Commodity Credit Corporation (Table KF6)
	Processing taxes see KF6630+
	By commodity
	For cattle, meat, poultry products, dairy products, see KF1730+
1693.A-Z	Field crops, A-Z
	Grain
1693.G7	General (Table KF7)

Regulation of industry, trade, and commerce. Occupational law
Primary production. Extractive industries
Agriculture. Forestry
Economic assistance
Price supports. Production control
By commodity
Field crops, A-Z
Grain -- Continued
Particular cereals

1693.G75	Rice (Table KF7)
1693.G76	Rye (Table KF7)
1693.S8	Sugar beets. Sugar cane (Table KF7)
1693.T6	Tobacco (Table KF7)
1694	Fruit and vegetables (Table KF6)
	Marketing agreements. Marketing orders
1696	General (Table KF6)
1697.A-Z	By commodity, A-Z
1697.F78	Fruit and vegetables (Table KF7)
1701	Farm loans. Farm mortgage insurance. Bankhead-Jones Farm Tenant Act (Table KF6)
	Acreage allotments. Soil banks. Marketing quotas
1705	General (Table KF6)
	By commodity
1706.A-Z	Field crops, A-Z
1706.C6	Cotton (Table KF7)
	Grain
1706.G7	General (Table KF7)
	Particular cereals
1706.G73	Corn (Table KF7)
1706.G78	Wheat (Table KF7)
1706.P6	Potatoes (Table KF7)
1707	Fruit and vegetables
	Agricultural surpluses
1709	General (Table KF6)
1710.A-Z	Particular commodities, A-Z
	For cattle, meat, poultry, poultry products, dairy products see KF1730+
1712	Disaster relief. Disaster loans. Flood and drought relief (Table KF6)
	Cf. KF3750 Disaster relief in general
1713	Farm corporations (Table KF6)
1715	Farm producers' and marketing cooperatives (Table KF6)
	Marketing. Market forecasts
	For produce exchanges see KF1085+
1718	General (Table KF6)
1719.A-Z	Particular commodities, A-Z
1719.A6	Apples (Table KF7)

Regulation of industry, trade, and commerce. Occupational law
Primary production. Extractive industries
Agriculture. Forestry
Marketing. Market forecasts
Particular commodities, A-Z -- Continued

Code	Description
1719.G7	Grain (Table KF7)
1719.P3	Perishable agricultural products (Table KF7)
	Standards and grading
	For containers, measurements see KF1665+
1721	General
	Particular commodities
1722	Seeds (Table KF6)
1724.A-Z	Field crops, A-Z
1724.C6	Cotton (Table KF7)
	Grain
1724.G7	General (Table KF7)
	Particular cereals
1724.G79	Wheat (Table KF7)
1724.T6	Tobacco (Table KF7)
	Fruit and vegetables
1725.A1	General (Table KF7)
1725.A3-Z	Particular fruits or vegetables
1725.A6	Apples (Table KF7)
	Livestock and meat
1726.A1	General (Table KF7)
1726.A3-Z	Particular kinds
1726.C2	Cattle. Beef (Table KF7)
1726.P6	Poultry (Table KF7)
	Poultry products see KF1915+
	Dairy industry see KF1921+
	Livestock industry and trade. Cattle raising
1730	General. Cattle industry (Table KF6)
	For meat packing industry see KF1911+
1730.1	Bureau of Animal Industry (Table KF6)
1730.12	Trade practices. Trade regulations (Table KF6)
1730.2	Prices. Consumer protection (Table KF6)
1730.3	Economic assistance. Price supports. Surpluses (Table KF6)
1730.4	Sanitation. Product inspection (Table KF6)
1730.8.A-Z	Special topics, A-Z
1730.8.B7	Cattle brands. Brand inspection (Table KF7)
1734	Sheep raising (Table KF18)
1738	Poultry industry (Table KF18)
	Dairy industry see KF1921+
1750	Forestry. Timber laws (Table KF6)
	National forests see KF5631+
1755	Beekeeping. Apiculture (Table KF6)

Regulation of industry, trade, and commerce. Occupational law
Primary production. Extractive industries
Agriculture. Forestry -- Continued
Game laws see KF5640+

1760	Aquaculture (Table KF6)
	Fishery
1770	General (Table KF6)
1770.1	Administration. Fish and Wildlife Service (Table KF6)
	Fishing industry
1771	General (Table KF6)
1772	Coastal and inland fishery, by area
	For particular species see KF1773.A+
	Atlantic coast
1772.2	General (Table KF6)
1772.25	New England (Table KF6)
	Pacific coast
1772.4	General. North Pacific (Table KF6)
1772.45	Alaska (Table KF6)
1772.48	Washington (Table KF6)
	Inland waters
1772.8.A2	Great Lakes (Table KF7)
1772.8.A5-Z	Particular rivers
1772.8.C65	Columbia River (Table KF7)
1772.8.M5	Mississippi (Table KF7)
1773.A-Z	Particular fish or marine fauna, A-Z
	Including conservation, control, and regulation of industry. Classification by species has priority over classification by area
1773.S23	Salmon (Table KF7)
1773.S25	Sardines (Table KF7)
1773.S33	Seals (Table KF7)
	Including fur-seal fishing
	Shellfish
1773.S4	General. Crustaceans (Table KF7)
1773.S45	Lobsters (Table KF7)
1773.S49	Oysters (Table KF7)
1773.T8	Tuna (Table KF7)
	Mining. Quarrying
1801-1820	General (Table KF1)
	For mine safety see KF3574.M5
1820.5	Administration. Bureau of Mines (Table KF6)
1823	Strip mining (Table KF6)
1826-1830	Coal (Table KF4)
1830.5	Bituminous Coal Commission (Table KF6)
	Nonferrous metals
1835	General (Table KF6)
1836.A-Z	Particular metals, A-Z

Regulation of industry, trade, and commerce. Occupational law
Primary production. Extractive industries
Mining. Quarrying
Nonferrous metals
Particular metals, A-Z -- Continued

1836.A5	Aluminum (Table KF7)
1836.C6	Copper (Table KF7)
1836.P5	Platinum (Table KF7)
1836.U6	Uranium (Table KF7)
	Petroleum. Oil and gas
1841-1850	General (Table KF2)
	Conservation. Interstate compacts
1852	General (Table KF6 modified)
	Statutes. Regulations. Rules of practice
	Comparative and uniform state and local
	legislation. Interstate compacts
1852.A415	Interstate Compact to Conserve Oil and Gas
1853	Pooling and unit operation of oil fields (Table KF6)
1856	Submerged land legislation. Tidal oil (Table KF6)
	Cf. KF4627 Constitutional law
	Trade practices. Regulation of industry
1860	General (Table KF6)
1862	Standards. Product inspection (Table KF6)
1865	Oil and gas leases (Table KF6)
1866.A-Z	Particular companies, A-Z
1867.A-Z	Particular oil fields, reserves, etc., A-Z
1870	Natural gas (Table KF6)
	Pipelines see KF2398
1873.A-Z	Other nonmetallic minerals and gases, A-Z
1873.M48	Methane (Table KF7)
	Manufacturing industries
1874	General (Table KF6)
	Chemical industries
1875	General (Table KF6)
1876.A-Z	Particular products, A-Z
1876.A5	Alcohol (Industrial) (Table KF7)
1876.D9	Dyes and dyestuffs (Table KF7)
1876.F3	Fertilizer (Table KF7)
1876.R8	Rubber, Synthetic (Table KF7)
	Synthetic rubber see KF1876.R8
1879	Drug and pharmaceutical industries (Table KF6)
	Cf. KF3885+ Drug laws
	Textile industries
1881	General (Table KF6)
	Textile fabrics
1885	General (Table KF6)
1886.A-Z	Particular products, A-Z

Regulation of industry, trade, and commerce. Occupational law
Manufacturing industries
Textile industries
Textile fabrics
Particular products, A-Z -- Continued

1886.C6	Cotton fabrics (Table KF7)
1886.H6	Hosiery (Table KF7)
1886.K5	Knitwear (Table KF7)
1886.L4	Linen (Table KF7)
1886.S4	Silks (Table KF7)

Individual types of manufacture
Major and heavy industries, A-Z

1890.A-Z	Major and heavy industries, A-Z
1890.C6	Computers (Table KF7)
1890.D45	Defense industries (Table KF7)
1890.E4	Electric machinery (Table KF7)
1890.H53	High technology (Table KF7)
1890.P5	Plumbing and heating fixtures (Table KF7)
1890.R8	Rubber (Table KF7)

For synthetic rubber see KF1876.R8

Shipbuilding

For federal ship mortgage insurance see KF1114.B65

Cf. KF2635+ Merchant fleet

1890.S4	General (Table KF7)
1890.S41	Finance. Subsidies (Table KF7)
1890.S7	Steel (Table KF7)

Consumer products. Light industries, A-Z

1893.A-Z	Consumer products. Light industries, A-Z
1893.B2	Barber and beauty supplies (Table KF7)
1893.B56	Biotechnology industries (Table KF7)
1893.B57	Book industries and trade (Table KF7)
1893.B6	Bookbinding (Table KF7)
1893.B7	Brushes (Table KF7)
1893.C5	Clocks and watches (Table KF7)
1893.C8	Curled hair (Table KF7)
1893.E44	Electronic games (Table KF7)
1893.H2	Handbags (Table KF7)
1893.J3	Jewelry (Table KF7)
1893.M2	Marking devices (Table KF7)
1893.M4	Mirrors (Table KF7)
1893.P3	Pens and pencils (Table KF7)
1893.P46	Phonorecords (Table KF7)
1893.R2	Radio and television receivers (Table KF7)
1893.R3	Resistance welders (Table KF7)
1893.S3	Seam binding (Table KF7)
1893.S5	Slide fasteners (Table KF7)
1893.S8	Sunglasses (Table KF7)

Television receivers see KF1893.R2

Regulation of industry, trade, and commerce. Occupational law
Manufacturing industries
Individual types of manufacture
Consumer products. Light industries, A-Z -- Continued

1893.T68	Toys (Table KF7)
1893.U5	Umbrellas (Table KF7)
1893.U55	Uniforms (Table KF7)
1893.V53	Video tape recorders (Table KF7)
	Food processing industries
1900	General (Table KF6)
	Agricultural products
	Cereal products
1902	Flour milling (Table KF17)
1903	Baking industry (Table KF17)
1904.A-Z	Particular cereal products, A-Z
1904.C6	Corn (Table KF7)
1907	Sugar refining (Table KF6)
	Fruit and vegetables
1908	General (Table KF17)
1909.A-Z	Particular, A-Z
1909.B3	Beans (Table KF7)
1909.C57	Citrus fruit (Table KF7)
1909.G6	Grapefruit (Table KF7)
1909.O5	Olives (Table KF7)
1909.P3	Peas (Table KF7)
1909.T6	Tomatoes (Table KF7)
1910.A-Z	Other, A-Z
1910.T6	Tobacco products (Table KF7)
	Meat industry
1911	General (Table KF17)
	Poultry products
1915	General. Dressed poultry (Table KF17)
1916	Eggs and egg products (Table KF17)
1917.A-Z	Particular poultry, A-Z
	Dairy industry. Dairy products industry
1921	General. Milk production and distribution (Table KF17)
1924.A-Z	Particular products, A-Z
1924.C5	Cheese
1924.C6	Concentrated milk
1924.E8	Evaporated milk
1924.F4	Filled milk
1924.I3	Ice cream
	Fishery products. Seafood industry
1930	General (Table KF17)
1932.A-Z	Particular products, A-Z
1932.5.A-Z	Related fishery products other than food, A-Z
	For fish meal see KF3879.F5

Regulation of industry, trade, and commerce. Occupational law
Food processing industries -- Continued
Vegetable oils and fats

1935	General (Table KF17)
1936.A-Z	Particular products, A-Z
1936.O5	Oleomargarine
	For taxation see KF6628.O5
1939	Spices. Herbs (Table KF6)
1940.A-Z	Beverages, A-Z
	Liquor, alcoholic beverages see KF3901+
1940.M5	Mineral water. Bottled water
1940.S65	Soft drinks
1944.A-Z	Related industries and products, A-Z
1944.B2	Baking powder
1950	Construction and building industry. Contractors (Table KF6)
	For building contracts see KF901+
	For building laws see KF5701+
	Trade and commerce
	For commercial law see KF871+
	For trade regulation see KF1601+
1970	General (Table KF6)
1971	Department of Commerce (Table KF6)
	International trade
	Cf. KF4678 Economic sanctions
1975-1976	General. Export and import controls and regulations (Table KF5)
	For trade agreements see KF6665+
1978	Export-Import Bank of the United States (Table KF6)
	Formerly Export-Import Bank of Washington
1979	Special Representative for Trade Negotiations. Committees for Reciprocity Information (Table KF6)
1979.A4	Rules of practice. By date
1980	Trading with the enemy (Table KF6)
1984.A-Z	Particular commodities, A-Z
1984.A9	Automobiles (Table KF7 modified)
1984.A9Z9-.A9Z99	By country, A-Z
1984.C6	Coffee (Table KF7 modified)
1984.C6Z9-.C6Z99	By country, A-Z
1984.M6	Motion pictures (Table KF7 modified)
1984.M6Z9-.M6Z99	By country, A-Z
1984.M8	Munitions (Table KF7 modified)
1984.M8Z9-.M8Z99	By country, A-Z
1984.P3	Petroleum (Table KF7 modified)
1984.P3Z9-.P3Z99	By country, A-Z
1984.T5	Tin (Table KF7 modified)
1984.T5Z9-.T5Z99	By country, A-Z

Regulation of industry, trade, and commerce. Occupational law
Trade and commerce -- Continued
Export trade. Export controls and regulations

1987	General (Table KF6)
1988	Export trading companies (Table KF6)
1989.A-Z	Particular countries, A-Z
1990.A-Z	Particular commodities, A-Z
1990.A4	Agricultural commodities. Farm produce (Table KF7, modified)
1990.A4Z9-.A4Z99	By country, A-Z
1990.C54	Coal (Table KF7, modified)
1990.C54Z9-.C54Z99	By country, A-Z
1990.C6	Cotton (Table KF7, modified)
1990.C6Z9-.C6Z99	By country, A-Z
1990.M8	Munitions (Table KF7, modified)
1990.M8Z9-.M8Z99	By country, A-Z
1990.N82	Nuclear materials (Table KF7, modified)
1990.N82Z9-.N82Z99	By country, A-Z
	Import trade. Import controls and regulations
	For tariff see KF6651+
1993	General (Table KF6)
1995.A-Z	Particular countries, A-Z
1996.A-Z	Particular commodities, A-Z
1996.A5	Alcoholic beverages (Table KF7, modified)
1996.A5Z9-.A5Z99	By country, A-Z
1996.A96	Automobiles (Table KF7, modified)
1996.A96Z9-.A96Z99	By country, A-Z
1996.C6	Cotton (Table KF7, modified)
1996.C6Z9-.C6Z99	By country, A-Z
1996.F8	Furs (Table KF7, modified)
1996.F8Z9-.F8Z99	By country, A-Z
1996.M5	Milk and cream (Table KF7, modified)
1996.M5Z9-.M5Z99	By country, A-Z
1996.P2	Paper. Newsprint (Table KF7, modified)
1996.P2Z9-.P2Z99	By country, A-Z
1996.P3	Petroleum and petroleum products (Table KF7, modified)
1996.P3Z9-.P3Z99	By country, A-Z
1996.S55	Silk (Table KF7, modified)
1996.S55Z9-.S55Z99	By country, A-Z
1996.S8	Sugar (Table KF7, modified)
1996.S8Z9-.S8Z99	By country, A-Z
1996.T6	Tobacco and tobacco products (Table KF7, modified)
1996.T6Z9-.T6Z99	By country, A-Z
1996.W6	Wool (Table KF7, modified)
1996.W6Z9-.W6Z99	By country, A-Z
	Wholesale trade

Regulation of industry, trade, and commerce. Occupational law
Trade and commerce
Wholesale trade -- Continued

1998	General (Table KF6)
1999.A-Z	By commodity, A-Z
1999.C65	Cotton (Table KF7)
1999.C66	Cotton textiles (Table KF7)
1999.F5	Flour (Table KF7)
	Fruit and vegetables, perishable agricultural products
	see KF1719.P3
	Meat see KF1911+
1999.P5	Plumbing and heating fixtures (Table KF7)
	Retail trade
2005	General (Table KF6)
	Conditions of trading
2009	Sunday legislation (Table KF6)
	Price maintenance. Competition
2015	General (Table KF6)
	Fair trade legislation
2016.A25	Legislative documents. By date
2016.A5	Decisions (Digests)
2016.A75-Z	Treatises. Monographs
2017	Works on comparative state law
	Particular products see KF2036.A+
2020	Discount houses. Cutrate trade (Table KF6)
2022	Unfair trade practices (Table KF6)
2023	Franchises (Table KF6)
	Labor relations see KF3452.R3
	Particular modes of trading
2026	Markets. Fairs (Table KF6)
2026.5	Direct selling (Table KF6)
	Including telemarketing
2027	Peddling (Table KF6)
2028	Mail-order business (Table KF6)
2030	Department stores (Table KF6)
2031	Chain stores (Table KF6)
2034	Vending machines (Table KF6)
2036.A-Z	Particular products, A-Z
2036.A8	Automobiles. Motor vehicles (Table KF7)
	Contact lenses see KF2036.E93
2036.D7	Drugs. Pharmaceutical products (Table KF7)
2036.E93	Eyeglasses. Contact lenses (Table KF7)
2036.G7	Groceries (Table KF7)
2036.H4	Hearing aids (Table KF7)
2036.M63	Mobile homes (Table KF7)
	Motor vehicles see KF2036.A8
	Radio receivers see KF2036.T4

Regulation of industry, trade, and commerce. Occupational law
Trade and commerce
Retail trade
Particular products, A-Z -- Continued

2036.T4	Television and radio receivers (Table KF7)
	Secondhand trade
2038.A1	General (Table KF6)
2038.A3-Z	Particular types
2038.A8	Auction houses (Table KF7)
	Cf. KF920 Auction sales
2038.P3	Pawnbrokers (Table KF7)
	Service trades
2041	General. Licensing (Table KF6)
2042.A-Z	Particular trades, A-Z
	Art dealers see KF2042.A76
2042.A76	Art galleries (Table KF7)
2042.A8	Automobile repair shops (Table KF7)
2042.C35	Camps (Table KF7)
2042.C6	Collection agencies (Table KF7)
	For collection laws see KF1024
	Customhouse brokers see KF6696.5
2042.D3	Day care centers. Nursery schools (Table KF7)
2042.D48	Detectives. Private investigators (Table KF7)
2042.E5	Employment agencies (Table KF7)
2042.H6	Hotels. Restaurants (Table KF7)
	Cf. KF951 Innkeeper and guest
	Insurance agents see KF1167
2042.L3	Laundries. Cleaners. Linen supply (Table KF7)
	Life care communities see KF2042.O43
2042.M6	Motels (Table KF7)
2042.O43	Old age homes. Life care communities (Table KF7)
2042.P45	Photographers (Table KF7)
2042.P49	Physical fitness centers (Table KF7)
	Private investigators see KF2042.D48
2042.R4	Real estate agents (Table KF7)
	Cf. KF5698.3 Real estate development
	Stockbrokers see KF1071
	Ticket brokers (Railroads) see KF2366
2042.T7	Trailer camps (Table KF7)
2042.T75	Travel agents (Table KF7)
2042.U5	Undertakers (Table KF7)
	Cf. KF3781 Disposal of the dead
	Warehouses
	For warehouse contracts see KF945
2050	General. Storage (Table KF6)
	Special-purpose warehouses
2054	Bonded warehouses (Table KF6)

Regulation of industry, trade, and commerce. Occupational law
Trade and commerce
Warehouses
Special-purpose warehouses -- Continued

2056	Agricultural warehouses (Table KF6)
	Including United States Warehouse Act
2057	Cold storage (Table KF6)

Public utilities
Including private and publicly owned utilities
Cf. KF5900+ War and emergency legislation
Regulated industries in general

2076-2095	General. Comprehensive (Table KF1)
2096	Federal, state, and local jurisdiction (Table KF6)
2099	Corporate structure. Holding companies (Table KF6)
2101	Valuation. Accounting (Table KF6)
2103	Ratemaking (Table KF6)
2105	Operation (Table KF6)

Particular utilities
Power supply. Energy policy

2120	General. Comprehensive (Table KF6)
	Administration. Regulatory agencies
2120.1	Federal Power Commission (1920-1977) (Table KF6)
	Energy Research and Development Administration
	(1974-1977) see KF4280.E53
2120.13	Department of Energy (1977-) (Table KF6)
2120.15	Federal, state, and local jurisdiction (Table KF6)
2120.2	Corporate structure. Holding companies. Antitrust
	measures (Table KF6)
2120.3	Finance (Table KF6)
2120.4	Valuation. Accounting (Table KF6)
2120.5	Ratemaking (Table KF6)
2120.6	Operation (Table KF6)
2120.65	Liability (Table KF6)
2120.8.A-Z	Particular companies, A-Z

Particular sources of power

2125-2125.8	Electricity (Table KF35)
2130-2130.8	Gas (Table KF35)
2133-2133.8	Water. Hydroelectric power (Table KF35)
2138-2138.9	Atomic power (Table KF35 modified)
2138.1	Atomic Energy Commission (Table KF6)
2138.15	Federal, state and local jurisdiction (Table KF6)
	Comparative state law
2138.9.A3	Collected statutes and regulations
2138.9.A8-.A89	Official reports and monographs
2138.9.A9-.Z8	Treatises. Monographs
2140.A-Z	Other sources of power, A-Z
2140.G45-.G457	Geothermal resources (Table KF36)

KF UNITED STATES (GENERAL) KF

Regulation of industry, trade, and commerce. Occupational law
Public utilities
Particular utilities
Power supply. Energy policy
Other sources of power, A-Z -- Continued

2140.S65-.S657	Solar energy (Table KF36)
2140.S95-.S957	Synthetic fuels (Table KF36)
2140.W56-.W567	Wind power (Table KF36)

Transportation and communication see KF2161+
Transportation and communication
Including state-owned and municipal services
NOTE: Under Transportation (General) are classed editions of the Interstate Commerce Act including the amendment of August, 1935, and later editions, and works thereon
For separately published editions of Part II of the Act see KF2246+
For earlier editions and related works see KF2271+
For editions of Part III (Amendment of September, 1940) see KF2531+

2161-2180	General. Comprehensive (Table KF1)
2181	Procedure. The Interstate Commerce Commission (Table KF6)
2181.5	Administration. Officials and employees (Table KF6)
2184	The Commerce Court (Table KF6)
	Express companies see KF2740+
	Freight forwarders see KF2745
2186	Finance. Federal aid to transportation (Table KF6)
2187	Ratemaking (Table KF6)
	Freight. Freight claims
2190	General (Table KF6)
2192.A-Z	By commodity, A-Z
	Road traffic. Automotive transportation
2201-2210	Motor vehicles in general (Table KF2)
2212	Safety equipment. Weight restrictions (Table KF6)
2213	Fuel consumption. Fuel efficiency (Table KF6)
2215	Registration. Title transfer (Table KF6)
2218	Drivers' licenses (Table KF6)
2219	Safety responsibility laws. Financial responsibility laws. Compulsory insurance (Table KF6)
	Cf. KF1218.8 Uninsured motorist insurance
	Cf. KF1219 Unsatisfied judgment funds
2220.A-Z	Particular vehicles, A-Z
	Ambulances see KF3826.E5
2220.B5	Bicycles (Table KF7)
2220.M58	Mopeds (Table KF7)
2220.M6	Motorcycles (Table KF7)
2220.S6	Snowmobiles. All terrain vehicles (Table KF7)

KF UNITED STATES (GENERAL) KF

Regulation of industry, trade, and commerce. Occupational law
Transportation and communication
Road traffic. Automotive transportation
Particular vehicles, A-Z -- Continued

2220.T6	Trailers (Table KF7)
2220.T7	Trucks (Table KF7)
	Traffic regulation and enforcement
2226-2230	General (Table KF4)
2231	Criminal provisions. Traffic violations. Drunk driving (Table KF6)
2232	Traffic courts (Table KF6)
2234	Highway safety. Traffic signs. Grade crossings. Railroad crossings (Table KF6)
2235	Right turn on red (Table KF6)
2236	Parking rules (Table KF6)
2239	School buses (Table KF6)
2239.5	Ride sharing. Car pools. Van pools (Table KF6)
2240	Pedestrians (Table KF6)
	Carriage of passengers and goods
	General motor carrier regulation
2246	Bibliography
2247	Periodicals
	Class here periodicals consisting primarily of informative materials (newsletters, bulletins, etc.) For periodicals consisting predominantly of legal articles, regardless of subject matter and jurisdiction, see K1+
2248	Regulations
2249	Comparative state legislation
2250	Decisions
2250.5	Looseleaf services
2251	Treatises
2252	Compends
2254	Works on comparative state law
2257	Ratemaking (Table KF6)
2258	Freight. Freight claims (Table KF6)
2260	Passenger carriers. Bus lines (Table KF6)
2263	Taxicabs (Table KF6)
2265	Carriers of goods. Truck lines (Table KF6)
2268.A-Z	Special topics, A-Z
2268.T7	Trip leasing (Table KF7)
	Railroads
	Class here editions of the Interstate Commerce Act earlier than those including the amendments of August, 1935 For later editions of the Act see KF2161+

Regulation of industry, trade, and commerce. Occupational law
Transportation and communication
Railroads -- Continued

2271-2290	General. Corporate structure. Regulation of industry (Table KF1)
	For Interstate Commerce Commission see KF2181
	For Commerce Court see KF2184
2293	Consolidation. Mergers. Holding companies
	For reorganization in insolvency proceedings see KF1546.R2
2295	Government ownership. Government tenure. Emergency seizure (Table KF6)
2298	Railroad lands. Land grants. Rights of way (Table KF6)
2300	Valuation (Table KF6)
2301	Finance (Table KF6)
2305	Security devices. Car trusts. Liens (Table KF6)
2308	Accounting. Record-keeping (Table KF6)
	Operation of railroads
	Rolling stock. Equipment
2315	General (Table KF6)
2318	Private cars (Table KF6)
2326-2330	Railroad safety. Railroad sanitation (Table KF4)
	For railroad crossings see KF2234
2332	Full-crew laws. Length of trains (Table KF4)
	Rates and ratemaking
2336-2345	General (Table KF2)
	Freight. Freight classification
2346-2347	General (Table KF5)
2349	Through routes. Long and short haul (Table KF6)
2351	Rate discrimination (Table KF6)
2353	Demurrage (Table KF6)
2355.A-Z	Particular commodities, A-Z
	Agricultural products
2355.A4	General (Table KF7)
2355.A46	Grain (Table KF7)
2355.C6	Coal (Table KF7)
2355.I7	Iron ore (Table KF7)
2355.L8	Lumber (Table KF7)
2355.P2	Paper and pulp (Table KF7)
	Passenger fares
2360	General (Table KF6)
	Special rates. Passes
2362	General (Table KF6)
2364.A-Z	Particular classes of passengers, A-Z
2366	Ticket brokers (Table KF6)
	Liability
2371	General. Damage to property (Table KF6)

KF UNITED STATES (GENERAL) KF

Regulation of industry, trade, and commerce. Occupational law
Transportation and communication
Railroads
Operation of railroads
Liability -- Continued

2372	Freight claims (Table KF6)
2375	Personal injury (Table KF6)
	Cf. KF1317.R2+ Employer's liability
2377	Abandonment of lines. Discontinuance of service (Table KF6)
2379.A-Z	Particular railroads and railroad companies, A-Z
	Including litigation, decisions, rulings, etc.
	Local transit
2391	General (Table KF6)
2393	Electric railroads. Streetcar lines. Subways (Table KF6)
2395	Accounting. Recordkeeping (Table KF6)
	Tort liability see KF1290.S7
	Particular cities
	see KFX for city
2398	Pipelines (Table KF6)
	Cf. KF1841+ Oil and gas
	Aviation
	Aviation in general
2400	General. Comprehensive (Table KF6)
2406	Air traffic rules. Air safety. Airworthiness (Table KF6)
	Airports
2415	General (Table KF6)
2418.A-Z	Particular airports, A-Z
	Commercial aviation. Airlines
2421-2440	General (Table KF1)
	Regulatory agencies. Civil Aeronautics Board, Civil Aviation Agency, etc.
	General counsel's opinions
2441.A55-.A559	Serials
2441.A56	Monographs. By date
2441.A57	Digests
2441.A575	Citators
2441.A58	Indexes
2441.A9-.Z8	Treatises. Monographs
2441.Z9	Compends. Outlines
2445	Ratemaking. Rate agreements. Passenger fare (Table KF6)
2446	Air charters (Table KF6)
2447	Cargo. Air freight. Air express (Table KF6)
2449	Airmail subsidies (Table KF6)

Regulation of industry, trade, and commerce. Occupational law
Transportation and communication
Aviation
Commercial aviation. Airlines -- Continued
Liability
For general tort liability for aviation accidents see KF1290.A9

2454	General. Damage to property (Table KF6)
2455	Personal injuries (Table KF6)
2459.A-Z	Particular airlines, A-Z
2462	Air freight forwarders (Table KF6)
2471-2480	Space law (Table KF2)
	Cf. KF4280.S7 Space exploration
	Water transportation. Navigation and shipping
2531	General. Comprehensive (Table KF6)
	Merchant mariners see KF1121+
	War legislation see KF7488+
	Ships
2536	General (Table KF6)
2538	Ships' papers. Registry (Table KF6)
	Safety regulations
2541-2550	General. Inspection (Table KF2)
2550.5	Steamboat Inspection Service (Table KF6)
	Coast Guard see KF7445+
2553	Manning requirements (Table KF6)
2556	Load line (Table KF6)
2558.A-Z	Particular types of vessels, A-Z
2558.B2	Barges (Table KF7)
2558.M6	Motor boats (Table KF7)
2558.P36	Passenger ships (Table KF7)
2558.P5	Pleasure craft (Table KF7)
2558.T2	Tank vessels (Table KF7)
2560.A-Z	Particular types of cargo, A-Z
2560.D2	Dangerous cargo (Table KF7)
2560.E85	Explosives. Munitions (Table KF7)
2560.G6	Grain (Table KF7)
2564.A-Z	Special topics, A-Z
2564.E4	Electrical engineering (Table KF7)
	Navigation and pilotage
	Including coastwise and inland navigation
2566	General (Table KF6)
2566.5	Regulatory agency. Bureau of Navigation (Table KF6)
2568	Obstructions to navigation. Public works in navigable waters (Table KF6)
	Particular waterways
	Cf. KF5580+ Waterway development
2571	Great Lakes (Table KF6)

Regulation of industry, trade, and commerce. Occupational law
Transportation and communication
Water transportation. Navigation and shipping
Ships
Navigation and pilotage
Particular waterways -- Continued
Canals

2573	General (Table KF6)
2574.A-Z	Particular canals, A-Z
	Subarrange each by Table KF6
	Rivers
2575	General (Table KF6)
2576.A-Z	Particular rivers, A-Z
2578.A-Z	Other, A-Z
	Harbors and ports
2581	General (Table KF6)
2583	Port charges. Tonnage fees (Table KF6)
2585.A-Z	Particular ports, A-Z
	Bridges see KF5540+
	Lighthouses
2588	General (Table KF6)
2588.5	Lighthouse Service (Table KF6)
2589.A-Z	Particular lighthouses, A-Z
2594	Artificial islands (Table KF6)
	Marine radio see KF2826
	Shipping laws. The merchant marine
2601-2605	General (Table KF4)
	War and emergency measures see KF7485+
	Regulation of shipping industry
2606	General. Procedure (Table KF6)
2608	Shipping Board (Table KF6)
2609	Maritime Commission (Table KF6)
2615	Ratemaking and rate agreements (Table KF6)
2625	Passenger accommodations. Steerage passengers (Table KF6)
	Merchant fleet
2635	General (Table KF6)
2636	Government ownership. Government vessels. Emergency seizure (Table KF6)
2637	Finance
	Shipbuilding subsidies see KF1890.S41
2639	Shipping subsidies (Table KF6)
2640	Ocean mail subsidies
	Domestic shipping. Inland water carriers
2645	General. Coastwise shipping (Table KF6)

Regulation of industry, trade, and commerce. Occupational law
Transportation and communication
Water transportation. Navigation and shipping
Shipping laws. The merchant marine
Domestic shipping. Inland water carriers -- Continued

2649.A-Z	Particular waterways, A-Z
	Under each (using successive Cutter numbers):
	.x General
	.x2 By commodity, A-Z
	.x3 Passengers
2654	Ocean freight forwarders (Table KF6)
	Custom house brokers see KF6696.5
	Postal service
2661-2665	General (Table KF4)
	Organization and administration. The Post Office Department
2668	General (Table KF6)
	Officers and personnel
2670	General (Table KF6)
2670.5	Salaries and pensions (Table KF6)
2670.55	Special allowances. Allowances in kind. Moving expenses (Table KF6)
2670.56	Leave regulations (Table KF6)
2670.58	Other benefits (Table KF6)
2670.6	Hours of labor. Holidays. Overtime pay (Table KF6)
2670.7	Travel regulations (Table KF6)
2670.8	Postal unions. Collective labor agreements (Table KF6)
	Bonding see KF1225+
	Particular classes of employees
	Postmasters
2675	General (Table KF6)
2675.5	Salaries and pensions (Table KF6)
2675.55	Special allowances. Allowances in kind. Moving expenses (Table KF6)
2675.56	Leave regulations (Table KF6)
2675.58	Other benefits (Table KF6)
2675.6	Hours of labor. Holidays. Overtime pay (Table KF6)
2675.7	Travel regulations (Table KF6)
2675.8	Postal unions. Collective labor agreements
	Bonding see KF1225+
	Railway postal employees
2679	General (Table KF6)
2679.5	Salaries and pensions (Table KF6)
2679.55	Special allowances. Allowances in kind. Moving expenses (Table KF6)

Regulation of industry, trade, and commerce. Occupational law
Transportation and communication
Postal service
Organization and administration. The Post Office
Department
Officers and personnel
Particular classes of employees
Railway postal employees -- Continued

2679.56	Leave regulations (Table KF6)
2679.58	Other benefits (Table KF6)
2679.6	Hours of labor. Holidays. Overtime pay (Table KF6)
2679.7	Travel regulations (Table KF6)
2679.8	Postal unions. Collective labor agreements
	Bonding see KF1225+
2684	Accounting. Auditing (Table KF6)
	Classification of mails. Rates
2688	General (Table KF6)
	Special classes
2690	Second class (Table KF6)
2692	Fourth class. Parcel post (Table KF6)
2692.5	C.O.D. shipments (Table KF6)
2693	Foreign mail (Table KF6)
	Nonmailable merchandise
2695	General (Table KF6)
2696.A-Z	Particular kinds of merchandise, A-Z
	Particular types of transportation
2700	Air mail (Table KF6)
	Surface mail
2704	By railroad (Table KF6)
2707	Ocean mail (Table KF6)
	Subsidies see KF2640
	Special mail services
2712	General. Collective (Table KF6)
	C.O.D. shipments see KF2692.5
2716	Rural free delivery (Table KF6)
2717	Star routes (Table KF6)
	Other services
2725	Postal savings (Table KF6)
2727	Postal notes (Table KF6)
	Rates. Postage. Modes of collecting
	For rates of a particular service, see the service
2730	General (Table KF6)
2733	Stamped envelopes (Table KF6)
2734	Franking privilege. Postage-free mails (Table KF6)
	Congressional franking privilege see KF4969.F7

Regulation of industry, trade, and commerce. Occupational law
Transportation and communication
Postal service -- Continued

2736.A-Z	Postal service in relation to foreign countries. By country, A-Z
	Nonpostal functions
2737	Censorship. Detention of mail (Table KF6)
2738	Control of subversive propaganda (Table KF6)
	Crimes committed through the mails see KF9460+
	Electronic mail see KF2847
	Express companies
2740	General (Table KF6)
2743.A-Z	Particular companies, A-Z
2745	Forwarding agents. Freight forwarders (Table KF6)
	For air freight forwarders see KF2462
	For ocean freight forwarders see KF2654
2750	Mass media. Press law (Table KF6)
	For student publications see KF4165
	For freedom of the press see KF4774
	For censorship of the press see KF4775
	Telecommunication
2761-2765	General. Comprehensive (Table KF4)
2765.1	Federal Communications Commission (Table KF6)
	Government ownership. Emergency legislation. By period
2765.2	1939-1945 (Table KF6)
2765.21	Board of War Communications (Table KF6)
2765.3	Mergers (Table KF6)
2765.5	Accounting (Table KF6)
2765.6	Ratemaking (Table KF6)
2765.65	Liability (Table KF6)
	Particular companies see KF2849.A+
2770	Artificial satellites in telecommunication (Table KF6)
	Telegraph. Teletype
2775	General (Table KF6)
	Government ownership. Emergency legislation. By period
2775.2	1939-1945 (Table KF6)
2775.21	Board of War Communications (Table KF6)
2775.3	Mergers (Table KF6)
2775.5	Accounting (Table KF6)
2775.6	Ratemaking (Table KF6)
2775.65	Liability (Table KF6)
	Particular companies see KF2849.A+
	Telephone
	Including radio telephone
2780	General (Table KF6)

Regulation of industry, trade, and commerce. Occupational law
Transportation and communication
Telecommunication
Telephone
General -- Continued
Government ownership. Emergency legislation. By period

2780.2	1939-1945 (Table KF6)
2780.21	Board of War Communications (Table KF6)
2780.3	Mergers (Table KF6)
2780.5	Accounting (Table KF6)
2780.6	Ratemaking (Table KF6)
2780.65	Liability (Table KF6)
	Particular companies see KF2849.A+
	Radio and television communication
	Cf. KF2750 Mass media
2801-2805	General (Table KF4)
	Federal Radio Commission see KF2765.1
2810	Radio and television stations. Frequency allocations. Licensing. Networks (Table KF6)
2812	Fairness doctrine. Equal time rule (Table KF6)
	Radio broadcasting
2814	General (Table KF6)
2815	Programming (Table KF6)
2819.A-Z	Other topics, A-Z
2819.C3	Censorship (Table KF7)
2819.C64	Contests (Table KF7)
2824	Public radio (Table KF6)
2826	Marine radio (Table KF6)
2828	Amateur radio (Table KF6)
2829	Citizens band radio (Table KF6)
	Television broadcasting
2840	General (Table KF6)
2844	Community antenna television. Cable television (Table KF6)
	Educational television see KF4209.T3
2847	Electronic mail (Table KF6)
2849.A-Z	Particular companies, A-Z
	The professions
	Including occupations
2900	General (Table KF6)
2901	Professional corporations (Table KF6)
2902	Professional associations (Table KF6)
	Class here general works only
	For particular associations, see the profession
	Liability see KF1289
	Particular professions

Regulation of industry, trade, and commerce. Occupational law
The professions
Particular professions -- Continued
The health professions
For medical legislation see KF3821+
General. Physicians

2905	General. Legal status, etc. (Table KF15)
2907.A-Z	Special topics, A-Z
2907.E3	Medical education (Table KF7)
2907.F3	Fees. Medical economics (Table KF7)
2907.G7	Group practice (Table KF7)
2907.P38	Patient referral (Table KF7)
2910.A-Z	Particular branches of medicine, A-Z
2910.A5-.A53	Anesthesiologists (Table KF16)
2910.C37-.C373	Cardiologists (Table KF16)
	Counselors see KF2910.P75+
2910.D3-.D33	Dentists and dental specialists (Table KF16)
2910.G45-.G453	Geriatricians (Table KF16)
2910.G94-.G943	Gynecologists. Obstetricians (Table KF16)
2910.I56-.I563	Internists (Table KF16)
2910.N45-.N453	Neurologists (Table KF16)
	Obstetricians see KF2910.G94+
2910.O64-.O643	Ophthalmologists (Table KF16)
2910.O78-.O783	Orthopedists (Table KF16)
2910.P42-.P423	Pediatricians (Table KF16)
2910.P64-.P643	Podiatrists (Table KF16)
2910.P75-.P753	Psychiatrists. Psychotherapists. Psychologists. Counselors (Table KF16)
	Psychologists see KF2910.P75+
	Psychotherapists see KF2910.P75+
2910.R33-.R333	Radiologists (Table KF16)
2910.S65-.S653	Sports physicians (Table KF16)
2910.U75-.U753	Urologists (Table KF16)
2913.A-Z	Other health practitioners, A-Z
2913.A28-.A283	Acupuncturists (Table KF16)
2913.C4-.C43	Chiropractors (Table KF16)
2913.C45-.C453	Christian-Science healers (Table KF16)
2913.F3-.F33	Faith healers (Table KF16)
2913.N38-.N383	Naturopaths (Table KF16)
2913.Q2-.Q23	Quacks (Table KF16)
	Auxiliary professions
2914	General (Table KF15)
2915.A-Z	Particular professions, A-Z
	Audiologists see KF2915.S63+
	Counselors see KF2910.P75+
	Dental hygienists see KF2910.D3+
2915.D53-.D533	Dietitians. Nutritionists (Table KF16)

Regulation of industry, trade, and commerce. Occupational law
The professions
Particular professions
The health professions
Auxiliary professions
Particular professions, A-Z -- Continued

Call Number	Description
2915.E4-.E43	Emergency medical personnel (Table KF16)
2915.E95-.E953	Exercise personnel (Table KF16)
2915.M5-.M53	Midwives (Table KF16)
2915.N8-.N83	Nurses (Table KF16)
	Nurses, Practical see KF2915.P73+
2915.N84-.N843	Nursing home administrators (Table KF16)
	Nutritionists see KF2915.D53+
	Occupational therapists see KF2915.T45+
2915.O6-.O63	Optometrists (Table KF16)
2915.P4-.P43	Pharmacists (Table KF16)
	Physical therapists see KF2915.T45+
2915.P45-.P453	Physicians' assistants (Table KF16)
2915.P73-.P733	Practical nurses (Table KF16)
2915.S63-.S633	Speech therapists. Audiologists (Table KF16)
2915.T45-.T453	Therapists, Physical. Occupational therapists (Table KF16)

Economic and financial advisers

Call Number	Description
2920	Accountants. Auditors (Table KF15)
	For accounting law see KF1357
2921	Financial planners (Table KF15)
	Investment advisers see KF1072
	Tax consultants see KF6320
	Lawyers see KF297+; KF8795

Engineering and construction

Call Number	Description
2925	Architects (Table KF15)
2928	Engineers (Table KF15)
2930.A-Z	Other, A-Z
2930.I54-.I543	Industrial designers (Table KF16)
2930.I58-.I583	Interior decorators (Table KF16)
2930.S67-.S673	Sprinkler irrigation contractors (Table KF16)
	Surveyors see KF2940.S87+

Performing artists

Call Number	Description
2932	General (Table KF6)
2933.A-Z	Particular types of artists, A-Z
2940.A-Z	Other professions, A-Z
2940.C45-.C453	Chemists (Table KF16)
	Clergy see KF4868.C44
2940.C66-.C663	Consultants (Table KF16)
	Journalists see KF2750
	Librarians see KF4316
	School psychologists see KF4192.5.P8

Regulation of industry, trade, and commerce. Occupational law
The professions
Particular professions
Other professions, A-Z -- Continued
Social workers see KF3721+

2940.S87-.S873	Surveyors (Table KF16)
	Teachers see KF4175+
2940.V3-.V33	Veterinarians (Table KF16)
	Intellectual property
2971-2980	General (Table KF2)
	Antitrust aspects see KF3116
2983	Litigation (Table KF6)
	Cf. KF3080 Copyright litigation
	Cf. KF3155+ Patent litigation
	Cf. KF9359 Criminal law
	Copyright
2986-2995	General (Table KF2)
2996	Special aspects
	For antitrust aspects see KF3116
3000	Common-law literary property
	Formalities. Administration. Copyright Office
3002	General (Table KF6)
3004	Registration (Table KF6)
3005	Deposit (Table KF6)
	Scope of protection
3010	Duration and renewal (Table KF6)
3012	Moral rights (Table KF6)
3015	Manufacturing clause (Table KF6)
	Particular branches
	Literary copyright
3020	General. Authorship (Table KF6)
	Protected works
3021	General (Table KF6)
3022	Public domain (Table KF6)
3024.A-Z	Particular types of works, A-Z
3024.A3	Addresses. Sermons (Table KF7)
3024.C6	Computer programs (Table KF7)
3024.E44	Electronic information resources (Table KF7)
	Including electronic publishing
3024.M32	Machine-readable bibliographic data (Table KF7)
	Scope of protection
	General see KF3020
3030.1	Mechanical reproduction. Reprinting. Dissemination (Table KF6)
3030.2	Performing rights (Table KF6)
3030.3	Broadcasting rights (Table KF6)
3030.4	Recording devices (Table KF6)

KF UNITED STATES (GENERAL) KF

Intellectual property
Copyright
Particular branches
Literary copyright
Scope of protection -- Continued

3030.5	Loudspeakers. Phonographs. Juke boxes (Table KF6)
3030.6	Filming (Table KF6)
3030.7	Translation (Table KF6)
3030.95	Other
3033	Duration (Table KF6)

Musical copyright
General. Authorship (Table KF6)

3035	General. Authorship (Table KF6)
	Protected works
3036	General (Table KF6)
3037	Public domain (Table KF6)
3039.A-Z	Particular types of works, A-Z
3045	Scope of protection
3045.1	Mechanical reproduction. Reprinting. Dissemination (Table KF6)
3045.2	Performing rights (Table KF6)
3045.3	Broadcasting rights (Table KF6)
3045.4	Recording devices (Table KF6)
3045.5	Loudspeakers. Phonographs. Juke boxes (Table KF6)
3045.6	Filming (Table KF6)
3045.7	Translation (Table KF6)
3045.95	Other
3048	Duration (Table KF6)

Works of art and photography
General. Works of art

3050	General. Authorship
	Protected works
3051	General (Table KF6)
3052	Public domain
3054.A-Z	Particular types of works, A-Z
	Scope of protection
	General see KF3050+
3060.1	Mechanical reproduction. Reprinting. Dissemination (Table KF6)
3060.2	Performing rights (Table KF6)
3060.3	Broadcasting rights (Table KF6)
3060.4	Recording devices (Table KF6)
3060.5	Loudspeakers. Phonographs. Juke boxes (Table KF6)
3060.6	Filming (Table KF6)
3060.7	Translation (Table KF6)

Intellectual property
Copyright
Particular branches
Works of art and photography
General. Works of art
Scope of protection -- Continued
3060.8 Droit de suite (Table KF6)
3060.95 Other
3063 Duration (Table KF6)
3065 Designs and models (Table KF6)
3067 Works of photography (Table KF6)
Violation of rights in one's own picture see KF1263.U5
3070 Motion pictures (Table KF6)
3072 Prints and labels (Table KF6)
3074 Maps (Table KF6)
Quasi copyright. Neighboring rights
3075 General (Table KF6)
3076 Performing artists (Table KF6)
Cf. KF3580.S7 Labor law
3080 Infringement. Litigation (Table KF6)
Cf. KF9359 Criminal law
3084 Author and publisher. The publishing contract (Table KF6)
3086 Design protection (Table KF6)
Cf. KF3065 Design copyright
Cf. KF3142 Design patents
Patent law and trademarks
3091-3095 General (Table KF4)
Patent law
3096-3115 General (Table KF1 modified)
Court decisions
For cases decided by the Court of Customs and Patent Appeals see KF125.C8+
Reports
3105.A2 Serials
3105.A5-Z Monographs
Each divided by date of publication
3105.3 Digests of reports (Case finders)
3105.5 Citators
Including citators for both cases and statutes
3105.7 Indexes
<3105.8> Individual cases. By date
see KF223+ and KF228.A+
3116 Special aspects
Including relationship to antitrust laws
Procedure. The Patent Office
General

KF UNITED STATES (GENERAL) KF

Intellectual property
Patent law and trademarks
Patent law
Procedure. The Patent Office
General -- Continued

3120.A25	Legislative documents. By date
	Rules of practice
3120.A39	Serials
3120.A4	Monographs. By date
3120.A535	Citators
3120.A59	Collections of summaries of cases. By editor or title
3120.A6	Looseleaf services
3120.A65	Form books
3120.A68	Dictionaries
3120.A7	Casebooks. Readings
3120.A8-.Z8	Treatises. Monographs
3120.Z9	Minor works
3124	Interference practice
3125.A-Z	Special topics, A-Z
3125.C5	Claim drafting. Applications (Table KF7)
3125.F3	Fees (Table KF7)
3128	War and emergency measures. Secret inventions (Table KF6)
	Scope of protection see KF3096+
	Invention
3131	General (Table KF6)
3133.A-Z	Particular products, processes, etc., A-Z
3133.A38	Art (Table KF7)
3133.B56	Biotechnology (Table KF7)
3133.B87	Business methods (Table KF7)
3133.C4	Chemicals (Table KF7)
3133.C65	Computer programs (Table KF7)
	For works discussing patent and copyright or computer programs see KF3024.C6
3133.D78	Drugs (Table KF7)
3133.E5	Electrical implements and appliances (Table KF7)
3133.P53	Plants (Table KF7)
3133.P7	Printing (Table KF7)
3133.R2	Radio (Table KF7)
	Employees' inventions
3135	General (Table KF6)
3136	Government employees (Table KF6)
3139	Government-developed inventions. Patents and government research contracts (Table KF6)
3142	Designs and models (Table KF6)
	Licenses. Compulsory licenses
3145	General (Table KF6)

KF UNITED STATES (GENERAL) KF

Intellectual property
Patent law and trademarks
Patent law
Licenses. Compulsory licenses -- Continued
3147 Foreign licensing agreements (Table KF6)
3149 Assignments (Table KF6)
Infringement. Patent litigation and procedure
Cf. KF9359 Criminal law
3155 General (Table KF6)
3157 Court of Appeals (Federal circuit) (Table KF6)
Formerly Court of Customs and Patent Appeals
3159.A-Z Particular patents. By product or claimant, A-Z
3159.E56 Electric controllers (Table KF7)
3159.F52 Fiber optics. Optical fibers (Table KF7)
3159.G56 Glass fruit jars (Table KF7)
Optical fibers see KF3159.F52
3159.R83 Rubber (Table KF7)
3159.S43 Sewing machines (Table KF7)
3159.S72 Steamboats (Table KF7)
Patent attorneys. Patent practice
3165.A3 Directories
3165.A4 Society publications
3165.A6 American Patent Law Association. Bylaws. Reports. By date
3165.A8-Z Treatises. Monographs
3165.Z9 Compends. Outlines. Popular works
Trademarks
3176-3180 General. Common-law trademarks (Table KF4)
3181 Procedure. Registration (Table KF6)
3184 Marks of origin (Table KF6)
3185 Union label (Table KF6)
3188 Classification (Table KF6)
3189.A-Z Particular trademarks, A-Z
3192 Licenses (Table KF6)
3193 Infringement. Trademark litigation and procedure (Table KF6)
Cf. KF9359 Criminal law
3194 Business names (Table KF6)
Including Internet domain names
Unfair competition
Cf. KF1601+ Unfair trade practices
3195 General (Table KF6)
Particular aspects and special topics
3197 Trade secrets. Industrial espionage. Commercial espionage (Table KF6)
3197.5 Product counterfeiting (Table KF6)
3198 Disparagement in advertising (Table KF6)

Unfair competition -- Continued
Particular industries
see the industry
Social legislation

3300	General
	Labor law
3301-3320	General (Table KF1)
3321	Special aspects
	Administration. Department of Labor. Organization and administration
3325	General (Table KF6)
3326.A-Z	Special topics, A-Z
3326.T7	Travel regulations (Table KF7)
3327.A-Z	Special divisions, A-Z
3327.B8	Bureau of Labor Statistics (Table KF7)
	Women's Division, Women's Bureau see KF3555.5
	Management-labor relations
3351-3370	General (Table KF1)
3372	National Labor Relations Board (Table KF6)
	Fair and unfair labor practices
	see KF3438, KF3455, KF3544
	Labor unions
3381-3390	General (Table KF2)
	Union security. Union shop
3391	General (Table KF6)
3394-3395	Open and closed shop. Right-to-work laws (Table KF5)
3397	Company unions. Yellow-dog contracts (Table KF6)
	Union organization
3400	General (Table KF6)
	Including Labor-Management Reporting and Disclosures Act
3402	Antitrust law aspects (Table KF6)
3404	Election of officers (Table KF6)
	Collective bargaining. Collective labor agreements
3407-3408	General (Table KF5, modified)
3408.Z94A-.Z94Z	Foreign language works. By language, A-Z
	Particular clauses and benefits
	see the subject
3409.A-Z	Particular industries and occupations, A-Z
3409.A3	Actors (Table KF7)
3409.A4	Agricultural machinery (Table KF7)
3409.A43	Airlines (Table KF7)
3409.A45	Airplane manufacture (Table KF7)
3409.A5	Aluminum industry (Table KF7)
3409.A7	Atomic workers (Table KF7)
3409.A8	Automobile industry (Table KF7)

Social legislation
Labor law
Management-labor relations
Labor unions
Collective bargaining. Collective labor agreements
Particular industries and occupations, A-Z --
Continued

3409.C2	Canning and preserving industry (Table KF7)
3409.C4	Chemical industries (Table KF7)
3409.C5	Clerks (Table KF7)
3409.C56	Clothing industry (Table KF7)
3409.C6	Coal industry (Table KF7)
3409.C65	Construction industry (Table KF7)
	Educational personnel see KF3409.S3; KF3409.T4
3409.E5	Electric industry (Table KF7)
	Government employees see KF3409.P77
3409.H66	Hospitals (Table KF7)
3409.L3	Leather industry (Table KF7)
3409.M3	Meat packing industry (Table KF7)
3409.M66	Motion picture industry (Table KF7)
3409.N3	Newspapers (Table KF7)
3409.N8	Nurses (Table KF7)
3409.P2	Paper industry (Table KF7)
3409.P3	Petroleum industry (Table KF7)
3409.P5	Plastics industry (Table KF7)
	Postal service see KF2670.8
3409.P7	Printing industry (Table KF7)
3409.P77	Public employees (Table KF7)
	For Federal civil service see KF5365
3409.P8	Public utilities (Table KF7)
3409.R2	Radio and television (Table KF7)
3409.R25	Railroads (Table KF7)
3409.R37	Retail and service establishments (Table KF7)
3409.S3	School employees (Table KF7)
	Cf. KF3409.T4 Teachers
	Service establishments see KF3409.R37
3409.S6	Soft drink industry (Table KF7)
3409.S7	Steel industry (Table KF7)
3409.T4	Teachers (Table KF7)
3409.T45	Textile industry (Table KF7)
3409.T6	Tobacco industry (Table KF7)
3409.T65	Trucking industry (Table KF7)
3409.W5	White collar workers (Table KF7)
	Collective labor disputes
3415	General (Table KF6)
3416-3425	Arbitration. Conciliation (Table KF2)
3427	Factfinding boards (Table KF6)

Social legislation
Labor law
Management-labor relations
Labor unions
Collective labor disputes
General -- Continued
Particular industries see KF3448+
Strikes. Boycotts

Call Number	Topic
3430-3431	General (Table KF5)
3432	Picketing (Table KF6)
3435	Labor injunctions (Table KF6)
	Particular industries see KF3448+
3438	Oppressive labor practices. Strike breakers. Labor spies (Table KF6)
	Wartime disputes. National War Labor Board. Defense Mediation Board
3444	1917-1919 (Table KF6)
3445	1941-1945 (Table KF6)
	By industry or occupation
3448	Railroads (Table KF6)
3448.1	Railroad Labor Board (Table KF6)
3448.5.A-Z	Particular cases. By company, A-Z
3450.A-Z	Other, A-Z
3450.C6-.C61	Coal mining (Table KF34)
3450.C65-.C651	Construction industry (Table KF34)
	Government employees see KF3450.P8+
3450.H4-.H41	Health facilities (Table KF34)
3450.I7-.I71	Iron and steel industry (Table KF34)
3450.P53-.P531	Plumbing and heating industry (Table KF34)
3450.P8-.P81	Public employees (Table KF34)
3450.S4-.S41	Shipbuilding industry (Table KF34)
3450.T43-.T431	Teachers (Table KF34)
3450.T7-.T71	Trailer industry (Table KF34)
3450.T8-.T81	Transportation (Table KF34)
3452.A-Z	Particular industries and groups of employees, A-Z
3452.A3	Agricultural laborers (Table KF7)
3452.A8	Automobile industry (Table KF7)
3452.C6	Construction workers (Table KF7)
3452.H6	Hospitals (Table KF7)
	Lawyers see KF317
3452.N65	Nonprofit organizations (Table KF7)
3452.R3	Retail trade (Table KF7)
3452.S5	Sheltered workshops (Table KF7)
3452.T45	Telecommunication (Table KF7)
3452.T73	Transportation (Table KF7)
	Labor standards
3455	General. Labor conditions (Table KF6)

Social legislation
Labor law
Labor standards -- Continued
Employment and dismissal

3457	General (Table KF6)
	For individual labor contract see KF898+
3457.3	Employment tests (Table KF6)
3457.5	Personnel records (Table KF6)
3457.6	Employment references (Table KF6)
3457.7	Employment interviewing (Table KF6)
3457.8	Rating. Employee appraisals (Table KF6)
	Preferential employment
3458	Seniority (Table KF6)
3460	Veterans (Table KF6)
3462	Other (Table KF6)
3463	Covenants not to compete (Table KF6)
	Discrimination in employment and its prevention
3464	General. Racial discrimination (Table KF6)
3464.15	Administration. Equal Employment Opportunity Commission (Table KF6)
	Particular groups or types of discrimination
	For particular industries see KF3580.A+
3465	Aged. Older people (Table KF6)
3466	Linguistic minorities (Table KF6)
3466.5	Religious discrimination (Table KF6)
3467	Sex discrimination (Table KF6)
	Including sexual harassment and pregnancy discrimination
3467.5	Sexual minorities. Sexual orientation discrimination (Table KF6)
	Including gays, lesbians, and transgender people
3468	Ex-convicts (Table KF6)
3469	People with disabilities (Table KF6)
	Including the mentally ill
3470	AIDS patients (Table KF6)
3470.5	Cancer patients (Table KF6)
	Dismissal. Resignation. Job security
3471	General (Table KF6)
3472	Dismissal pay (Table KF6)
3475	Subcontracting (Table KF6)
	Seniority see KF3458+
3478	Mandatory retirement (Table KF6)
	Wages. Minimum wage
	Including Wage and Hour Laws and Fair Labor Standards Act
3481-3490	General (Table KF2)

Social legislation
Labor law
Labor standards
Wages. Minimum wage -- Continued
War and emergency legislation. By period
Prefer KF3505, Particular industries and groups of employees

3492	1939-1945 (Table KF6)
3493	1945- (Table KF6)
	Wage discrimination. Equal pay for equal works see KF3464+
	Types of wages. Mode of remuneration
3495	Annual wage. Guaranteed wage
3496	Incentive wages. Bonus system. Profit sharing (Table KF6)
3499	Cost-of-living adjustments. Escalator clause (Table KF6)
3501	Family allowances (Table KF6)
3503	Overtime payments. Night differentials (Table KF6)
3505.A-Z	Particular industries and groups of employees, A-Z
3505.A4	Agriculture (Table KF7)
3505.A5	Airplane industry (Table KF7)
3505.A9	Automobile industry (Table KF7)
3505.B25	Banks (Table KF7)
3505.B27	Battery industry (Table KF7)
3505.B8	Butane dealers (Table KF7)
	Cleaning industry see KF3505.L2
3505.C5	Clerks (Table KF7)
3505.C6	Coal industry (Table KF7)
3505.C65	Construction industry (Table KF7)
3505.C7	Crushed stone industry (Table KF7)
3505.E3	Education (Table KF7)
3505.E5	Electric lamp industry (Table KF7)
3505.H58	Hospitals. Medical personnel (Table KF7)
3505.H6	Hotels, restaurants, taverns, etc. (Table KF7)
3505.I3	Ice industry (Table KF7)
3505.I6	Iron and steel industry (Table KF7)
3505.L2	Laundry and cleaning industry (Table KF7)
3505.L28	Lease and rental services (Table KF7)
3505.L3	Leather industry (Table KF7)
	Medical personnel see KF3505.H58
3505.R2	Railroads (Table KF7)
	Rental services see KF3505.L28
3505.R3	Retail and service establishments (Table KF7)
3505.S4	Shoe trade (Table KF7)
3505.Y68	Youth (Table KF7)
	Nonwage payments. Fringe benefits

Social legislation
Labor law
Labor standards
Nonwage payments. Fringe benefits -- Continued
3509 General (Table KF6)
Pension and retirement plans
Including individual retirement accounts (IRAs)
3510 General (Table KF6)
3512 Pension trusts (Table KF6)
Health benefits. Health insurance plans
3515 General (Table KF6)
3515.3 Health care continuation coverage (Table KF6)
Dismissal pay see KF3472
3517 Other
Including voluntary employees' beneficiary associations, cafeteria benefit plans
3519.A-Z By industry or occupation, A-Z
3519.T6 Tobacco workers (Table KF7)
Hours of labor. Night work
3525 General (Table KF6)
Overtime payments see KF3503
Women and children see KF3551+; KF3555
3528.A-Z Particular industries and groups of employees, A-Z
Government employees see KF3528.P8
3528.H5 Highway transportation (Table KF7)
Merchant mariners see KF1131
3528.P8 Public employees (Table KF7)
3528.R2 Railroads (Table KF7)
3531 Vacations. Holidays. Leaves of absence (Table KF6)
3532 Sick leave (Table KF6)
Labor discipline. Work rules
3540 General (Table KF6)
3542 Shop committees. Shop stewards. Works councils (Table KF6)
3544 Grievances. Grievance procedure (Table KF6)
3546 Labor supply. Manpower controls (Table KF6)
Protection of labor. Labor hygiene and safety
3550 General (Table KF6)
3551-3552 Child labor (Table KF5)
Including hours of child labor
3555 Woman labor (Table KF6)
Including hours of woman labor
3555.5 Administration. Women's Bureau (Table KF6)
3557 Home labor (Table KF6)
3559 Apprentices. Learners (Table KF6)
Labor hygiene and safety. Hazardous occupations. Safety regulations

Social legislation
Labor law
Protection of labor. Labor hygiene and safety
Labor hygiene and safety. Hazardous occupations.
Safety regulations -- Continued

3566-3570	General (Table KF4)
3571	Factory inspection (Table KF6)
3574.A-Z	By industry or type of labor, A-Z
3574.A7	Atomic industry (Table KF7)
3574.B84	Building cleaning industry (Table KF7)
3574.C65	Construction industry (Table KF7)
3574.E5	Electric industry (Table KF7)
3574.F6	Foundries (Table KF7)
3574.G68	Government employees and laborers (Table KF7)
3574.H39	Hazardous waste management industry (Table KF7)
	Health facilities see KF3574.H66
3574.H66	Hospitals. Health facilities (Table KF7)
3574.L32	Laboratories (Table KF7)
3574.L6	Longshoremen (Table KF7)
3574.M43	Medical instruments and apparatus industry (Table KF7)
3574.M5	Mining (Table KF7)
3574.M53	Coal mining (Table KF7)
3574.P2	Paper industry (Table KF7)
3574.P3	Petroleum industry (Table KF7)
3574.R48	Retail trade (Table KF7)
3574.S4	Shipyards. Shipbuilding and repairs (Table KF7)
3574.W6	Wood-using industries (Table KF7)
3575.A-Z	By machinery, equipment, etc., A-Z
	Prefer subdivision by industry
3580.A-Z	Labor law of particular industries or types of employment, A-Z
3580.A4	Agricultural migrant labor (Table KF7)
3580.A8	Aviation industry (Table KF7)
3580.B34	Banks (Table KF7)
3580.B84	Building cleaning industry (Table KF7)
3580.C2	Canning and preserving industry (Table KF7)
3580.C6	Construction industry (Table KF7)
3580.C7	Crushed stone industry (Table KF7)
3580.D64	Domestics. Servants (Table KF7)
3580.G6	Government employees and laborers (Table KF7)
3580.G7	Grocery workers (Table KF7)
3580.H4	Health facilities (Table KF7)
3580.I3	Ice cream industry (Table KF7)
3580.L5	Liquor industry (Table KF7)
3580.L52	Libraries (Table KF7)
3580.N48	Newspapers (Table KF7)

KF UNITED STATES (GENERAL) KF

Social legislation
Labor law
Labor law of particular industries or types of employment,
A-Z -- Continued

3580.N65	Nonprofit organizations (Table KF7)
3580.P3	Petroleum industry (Table KF7)
3580.P74	Professional corporations (Table KF7)
3580.R2	Railroads (Table KF7)
3580.R3	Retail trade and service establishments (Table KF7)
3580.R6	Road construction workers (Table KF7)
	Servants see KF3580.D64
3580.S7	Stagecraft (Table KF7)
3580.S8	Sugar industry (Table KF7)
	Teachers see KF4175+
3580.T45	Temporary employees (Table KF7)
3580.T7	Transportation (Table KF7)
	Universities and colleges see KF4225+
	Labor injunctions see KF3435
	Social insurance
3600	General (Table KF6)
3601	Organization and administration (Table KF6)
3603	Special aspects
	Particular branches
	Health insurance
	Cf. KF1183+ Private insurance
	Cf. KF3515+ Fringe benefits
3605	General (Table KF6)
3608.A-Z	Particular industries or groups, A-Z
3608.A4	Aged. Older people. Medicare (Table KF7)
	Civil service see KF5385
3608.C6	Coal miners (Table KF7)
	Medicaid see KF3608.P66
	Older people see KF3608.A4
3608.P66	Poor. Medicaid (Table KF7)
3608.R2	Railroads (Table KF7)
3609.A-Z	Particular services and benefits, A-Z
3609.R44	Renal disease program (Table KF7)
3609.R87	Rural health services
	Workers' compensation
3611-3615	General (Table KF4)
3616	Special aspects
3622	Occupational diseases (Table KF6)
3623.A-Z	Special topics, A-Z
3623.A8	Attorneys' fees (Table KF7)
3623.S8	Subrogation (Table KF7)
	Particular industries or groups of employees
3626	Federal employees (Table KF6)

Social legislation
Social insurance
Particular branches
Workers' compensation
Particular industries or groups of employees
Federal employees -- Continued
U.S. Employees Compensation Commission

3626.5.A2-.A5	Documents
3626.5.A7-Z	Treatises. Monographs
3628	Longshoremen and harbor workers (Table KF6)
3629	Railroads (Table KF6)
3632.A-Z	Other, A-Z
3632.A4	Agricultural workers (Table KF7)
3632.A7	Atomic workers (Table KF7)
3632.B6	Brewery workers (Table KF7)
3632.C6	Coal miners (Table KF7)
3632.I53	Independent contractors (Table KF7)
3632.P8	Public works (Table KF7)
3634.A-Z	Particular cases, A-Z

Social security. Retirement. Old age and disability pensions. Survivors' benefits

3641-3650	General (Table KF2)
	For works for particular groups of users see KF3659+
	Cf. KF1182 Disability insurance
3650.5	Administration. Federal Security Agency (Table KF6)
3651-3655	Contributions. Social security taxes (Table KF4)
	For withholding of both income and social security taxes see KF6436+
3658.A-Z	Special topics, A-Z
3658.C66	Cost-of-living adjustments (Table KF7)
3658.M6	Mothers' pensions (Table KF7)
3658.T5	Tips

Particular industries, occupations, or groups

3659-3660	Railroad employees (Table KF5)
3664.A-Z	Other, A-Z
3664.A4	Agricultural laborers (Table KF7)
3664.C58	Clergy (Table KF7)
3664.H6	Household employees. Servants (Table KF7)
3664.N6	Nonprofit corporations (Table KF7)
3664.P73	Prisoners (Table KF7)
3664.R2	Radio broadcasting (Table KF7)
3664.S4	Self-employed (Table KF7)

Unemployment insurance

3671-3675	General (Table KF4)
3676	Administration. U.S. Employment Service (Table KF6)

KF UNITED STATES (GENERAL) KF

Social legislation
Social insurance
Particular branches
Unemployment insurance -- Continued

3679.A-Z	Special topics, A-Z
3679.M3	Merit rating (Table KF7)
3680.A-Z	Particular industries or occupations, A-Z
3680.F3	Federal employees (Table KF7)
3680.M5	Migrant labor (Table KF7)
3680.R2	Railroads (Table KF7)
3685.A-Z	Particular industries or occupations, A-Z
3686	Particular insurance plans
	Cf. KF1169.A+ Private insurance
	Cf. KF3510+ Fringe benefits
	Public welfare. Public assistance
3720	General (Table KF6)
3720.5	Administration. Department of Health, Education and Welfare. Federal Security Agency
	Social work. Social workers
3721	General (Table KF6)
3721.5	Volunteer workers (Table KF6)
3723	Domicile requirements (Table KF6)
3724.A-Z	Special topics, A-Z
3728	Maternal and infant welfare (Table KF6)
	For private day care centers see KF2042.D3
	Particular groups
3731-3735	Children. Child welfare. Youth services (Table KF4)
	Cf. KF9323 Child abuse
3736	Administration. Children's Bureau. Regulatory agencies (Table KF6)
3736.5	Foster home care (Table KF6)
	Older people
3737	General (Table KF6)
	Meals on wheels programs see KF3745.M42
	People with disabilities. Vocational rehabilitation
3738	General (Table KF6)
3739	Blind (Table KF6)
	Education of the blind see KF4212
3740	Deaf-mute (Table KF6)
3742	Homeless persons (Table KF6)
3743	Immigrants. Aliens (Table KF6)
	Including illegal aliens
	Veterans (1939-1945) see KF7739.E3
	Veterans (1945-) see KF7749.E3
3745.A-Z	Particular relief measures, A-Z
3745.F62	Food stamp program (Table KF7)
3745.M42	Meals on wheels program (Table KF7)

Social legislation
Public welfare. Public assistance
Particular relief measures, A-Z -- Continued

3745.R4	Rent supplements (Table KF7)
3750	Disaster relief. Emergency management (Table KF6)
	Drought relief see KF1712
	Agricultural disaster relief see KF1712
	Human reproduction
	Cf. KF3830+ Human reproductive technology
3760	General (Table KF6)
3766	Birth control. Family planning. Population control (Table KF6)
	Cf. KF3832 Eugenics. Sterilization
	Cf. KF9445 Contraceptive devices (Criminal law)
3771	Abortion (Table KF6)
	Cf. KF9315 Abortion (Criminal law)
	Cf. KF9445 Contraceptive devices (Criminal law)
	Environmental law. Public health
	Including environmental pollution and sanitation
	Cf. KF1298+ Liability for environmental damages
3775	General (Table KF6 modified)
3775.Z9	Examination aids, popular works, etc.
	Including compends, outlines, and works for particular classes of users
	Public Health Service
3776.A25	Legislative documents. By date
3776.A3	Statutes. By date
3776.A5	Decisions. By date
3776.A7-.Z8	General works. Treatises. Monographs
3776.Z9A-.Z9Z	Particular divisions
3776.Z9C6	Commissioned Corps
3776.Z9F6	Division of Foreign Quarantine
3779.A-Z	Particular kinds of group hygiene, A-Z
	Labor hygiene see KF3550+
3779.M5	Military hygiene (Table KF7)
	School hygiene see KF3826.S3
3781	Disposal of the dead. Burial and cemetery laws
	For undertakers see KF2042.U5
3783	Global warming. Climatic changes (Table KF6)
	Water pollution. Drainage
	Cf. KF1299.W38 Liability for water pollution damages
3786-3790	General (Table KF4)
3790.5	Administration. Regulatory agency (Table KF6)
3792.A-Z	Particular bodies of water, A-Z
3794	Drinking water standards (Table KF6)
	Contagious, infectious, and other diseases
3800	General. Reporting (Table KF6)

Environmental law. Public health
Contagious, infectious, and other diseases -- Continued

	Particular diseases, A-Z
3803.A-Z	Particular diseases, A-Z
3803.A54	AIDS (Table KF7)
3803.A56	Alzheimer's disease (Table KF7)
3803.C3	Cancer (Table KF7)
3803.C37	Cardiovascular disease (Table KF7)
3803.L3	Leprosy (Table KF7)
3803.M84	Multiple sclerosis (Table KF7)
3803.O24	Obesity (Table KF7)
	Including obesity in children
3803.P4	Phenylketonuria (Table KF7)
3803.S55	Sickle cell anemia (Table KF7)
3803.S62	Sleep disorders (Table KF7)
3803.T8	Tuberculosis (Table KF7)
3803.V3	Venereal diseases (Table KF7)
	Particular measures
3806	Animal products inspection (Table KF6)
	Meat inspection see KF1911+
3807	Immigration inspection. Quarantine (Table KF6)
	Immunization. Vaccination
3808	General (Table KF6)
3809.A-Z	Particular diseases, A-Z
3809.P6	Poliomyelitis (Table KF7)
3811	Mosquito abatement
	Air pollution. Control of smoke, noxious gases, etc.
3812	General (Table KF6)
3812.2	Carbon (Table KF6)
	Including carbon emissions trading and carbon offsetting
3812.3	Tobacco smoking (Table KF6)
	Class here works on measures to restrict tobacco smoking
	For works on claims for injuries from smoking see KF1297.T63
3812.5.A-Z	Particular measures, A-Z
3812.5.E55	Emission density zoning (Table KF7)
3813	Noise control (Table KF6)
3816.A-Z	Other public health hazards and measures, A-Z
3816.R4	Refuse disposal (Table KF7)
	Cf. KF3946 Hazardous waste disposal
	Cf. KF5510 Recycling waste
3816.S49	Sewage disposal (Table KF7)
	Medical legislation
	For physicians and related professions see KF2905+
3821	General (Table KF6)
3823	Patients' rights (Table KF6)

KF UNITED STATES (GENERAL) KF

Medical legislation -- Continued
Health facilities and services. Hospitals
Cf. KF3828 Psychiatric hospitals and mental health facilities
Cf. KF7298 Armed Forces hospitals
Cf. KF7739.M35 Veterans' hospitals (1939-1945)
Cf. KF7749.M35 Veterans' hospitals (1945-)

3825	General (Table KF6)
3825.1	Licensing (Table KF6)
3825.3	Liability (Table KF6)
3825.5	Planning. Finance. Costs (Table KF6)
	Including certificate of need, construction, etc.
3826.A-Z	Other health services, A-Z
3826.A45	Ambulatory medical care (Table KF7)
3826.B55	Blood banks (Table KF7)
3826.C48	Child health services (Table KF7)
3826.E5	Emergency medical services. Ambulance service (Table KF7)
3826.H64	Home health services (Table KF7)
3826.L3	Laboratories, Medical (Table KF7)
3826.M38	Maternal health services (Table KF7)
3826.N8	Nursing homes (Table KF7)
3826.R34	Radiological services (Table KF7)
3826.S3	Schools. School health services (Table KF7)
	Cf. KF5702.S3 School buildings
3827.A-Z	Special topics, A-Z
3827.A58	Antitrust aspects (Table KF7)
	Assisted suicide see KF3827.E87
3827.B4	Behavior modification (Table KF7)
3827.C78	Cryonics (Table KF7)
3827.D4	Death, Definition of (Table KF7)
3827.D66	Donation of organs, tissues, etc. (Table KF7)
	Embryonic stem cells see KF3827.S74
3827.E87	Euthanasia. Right to die. Living wills. Assisted suicide (Table KF7)
3827.G4	Medical genetics (Table KF7)
3827.I5	Informed consent (Table KF7)
	Living wills see KF3827.E87
3827.M38	Medical experiments with humans (Table KF7)
3827.M4	Medical instruments and apparatus. Medical devices (Table KF7)
	Organ donation see KF3827.D66
3827.P7	Professional standards review organization (Table KF7)
3827.P78	Psychosurgery (Table KF7)
3827.R4	Medical records. Hospital records. Records management (Table KF7)
	Right to die see KF3827.E87

Medical legislation
Special topics, A-Z -- Continued

3827.S73	Medical statistics (Table KF7)
3827.S74	Stem cells (Table KF7)
	Including embryonic stem cells
	Tissue donation see KF3827.D66
	Pharmacies see KF2915.P4+
3828	The mentally ill (Table KF6)
	Including psychiatric hospitals and mental health facilities
	For civil status of insane persons see KF480+
	For criminal liability see KF9241+
3828.5	Mental health courts (Table KF6)
3829.A-Z	Disorders of character, behavior, and intelligence, A-Z
3829.A5	Alcoholism (Table KF7)
	Including works on the treatment and rehabilitation of alcoholics in the criminal justice system
	Drug addiction see KF3829.N2
3829.N2	Narcotic addiction. Drug addiction (Table KF7)
	Human reproductive technology
	Including artificial insemination and fertilization in vitro
	Cf. KF3760+ Human reproduction
3830	General (Table KF6)
3831	Human cloning (Table KF6)
3832	Eugenics. Sterilization (Table KF6)
	Veterinary medicine and hygiene. Veterinary public health
	For veterinarians, practice of veterinary medicine see KF2940.V3+
3835	General. Reporting (Table KF6)
3836.A-Z	Particular measures, A-Z
3836.Q2	Quarantine (Table KF7)
3838.A-Z	Particular animal diseases and causative agents, A-Z
	Animal protection. Animal welfare. Animal rights
	Including prevention of cruelty to animals
	For animal rights as a social issue see HV4701+
3841	General (Table KF6)
3842	Transportation (Table KF6)
3843	Animal experimentation and research (Table KF6)
	Including vivisection and dissection
3844	Slaughtering of animals (Table KF6)
3845.A-Z	Particular animals, A-Z
	Food. Drugs. Cosmetics
3861-3870	General. Comprehensive (Table KF2)
	For regulation of industry (Drugs) see KF1879
	For regulation of industry (Food processing) see KF1900+
3871	Administration. Food and Drug Administration (Table KF6)
	Food law

Food. Drugs. Cosmetics
Food law -- Continued

3875	General (Table KF6)
3878	Adulteration. Inspection (Table KF6)
3879.A-Z	Particular food and food related products, A-Z
3879.B2	Baking powder (Table KF7)
3879.C64	Color additives (Table KF7)
3879.D5	Dietary supplements (Table KF7)
3879.F5	Fish meal (Table KF7)
3879.F55	Flavoring essences (Table KF7)
3879.P7	Preservatives. Food additives (Table KF7)
3879.S9	Syrups (Table KF7)

Drug laws

3885	General. Labeling (Table KF6)

Narcotics

3890	General (Table KF6)
3890.1	Administration. Bureau of Narcotics (Table KF6)
3891.A-Z	Particular narcotics, A-Z
3891.C62	Cocaine (Table KF7)
3891.H4	Heroin (Table KF7)
3891.M2	Marijuana (Table KF7)
3891.M3	Methadone (Table KF7)
3891.O3	Opium (Table KF7)
3894.A-Z	Other, A-Z
3894.B5	Biological products (Table KF7)
	Including antibiotics, hormones, vaccines, etc.
	Cigarettes see KF3894.T63
3894.G45	Generic drugs (Table KF7)
3894.H34	Hallucinogenic drugs (Table KF7)
3894.P3	Patent medicines. Proprietary drugs (Table KF7)
3894.R33	Radiopharmaceuticals (Table KF7)
3894.T63	Tobacco. Cigarettes (Table KF7)
3895	Drug paraphernalia (Table KF6)
3896	Cosmetics (Table KF6)
	Pharmacies see KF2915.P4+

Alcohol. Alcoholic beverages. Prohibition

Cf. KF9456 Criminal law

3901-3920	General. Alcohol production (Table KF1)
3921	Administration. Bureau of Prohibition (Table KF6)
3924.A-Z	Particular products, A-Z
3924.B4	Beer. Malt liquors (Table KF7)
3924.D3	Denatured alcohol (Table KF7)
3924.M3	Medicinal spirits (Table KF7)
3924.W5	Wine (Table KF7)
3925.A-Z	Special topics, A-Z
3925.D74	Drinking age (Table KF7)
3925.L6	Local option (Table KF7)

KF UNITED STATES (GENERAL) KF

Public safety
Weapons. Firearms. Munitions

3941	General (Table KF6)
3942.A-Z	Particular, A-Z
3942.B6	Body armor (Table KF7)
3942.H3	Handguns (Table KF7)
3942.K56	Knives (Table KF7)
	Hazardous articles and processes. Product safety
	Including transportation by land
	For transportation by sea see KF2560.D2
	Cf. KF1296+ Products liability
	Cf. KF2695+ Nonmailable merchandise
3945	General (Table KF6)
3946	Hazardous waste disposal (Table KF6)
	Particular products and processes
3948	Atomic power. Radiation (Table KF6)
3950	Atomic waste disposal (Table KF6)
3953	Explosives (Table KF6)
3955	Inflammable materials. Fireworks (Table KF6)
	Poisons. Toxic substances
3958	General. Economic and industrial poisons (Table KF6)
3959	Pesticides. Herbicides (Table KF6)
3964.A-Z	Particular substances, A-Z
3964.A67	Arsenic (Table KF7)
3964.A73	Asbestos (Table KF7)
3964.B45	Benzene (Table KF7)
3964.D53	Dibromopropanol phosphate. Tris (Table KF7)
3964.L43	Lead (Table KF7)
3964.M64	Molds. Toxigenic fungi (Table KF7)
3964.P47	Petroleum (Table KF7)
3964.P64	Polychlorinated biphenyls (Table KF7)
3964.R35	Radon (Table KF7)
	Toxigenic fungi see KF3964.M64
	Tris see KF3964.D53
3964.V46	Vinyl chloride (Table KF7)
3964.W4	White phosphorus (Table KF7)
3965.A-Z	Other, A-Z
3965.A87	Automobiles. Motor vehicles (Table KF7)
	Motor vehicles see KF3965.A87
	Accident control
3970	Steam boilers (Table KF6)
	Fire prevention and control
	Cf. KF3955 Inflammable materials
3975	General (Table KF6)
3976	Fire departments. Fire fighters (Table KF6)
3977	Forest fires (Table KF6)
	Flood control see KF5588+

KF UNITED STATES (GENERAL) KF

Control of social activities

3985	General (Table KF6)
3987	Amusements (Table KF6)
3989	Sports. Prizefighting. Horse racing (Table KF6)
	Cf. KF4166 School sports
3992	Lotteries. Games of chance. Gambling (Table KF6)
	Cf. KF9440 Criminal law
3994	Video games. Computer games (Table KF6)
3995	Other

Education

Education in general. Public education

4101-4120	General and comprehensive (Table KF1)
4121	Administration. Office of Education (Table KF6)
4124	Church and education. Denominational schools (Table KF6)
4124.5	Other special aspects (not A-Z)

School government and finance

4125	General (Table KF6)
4127	School districts (Table KF6)
	Individual school districts are classed under the jurisdiction from which they derive their authority
4131	School boards (Table KF6)
4133	School superintendents (Table KF6)
4134	Charter schools (Table KF6)
4135	School lands (Table KF6)
	Including community use of school facilities
4136-4137	Finance. Federal aid to education (Table KF5)

Related activities

4141	School transportation (Table KF6)
	For school bus regulations see KF2239
4143	School lunch programs (Table KF6)

Students. Compulsory education

Cf. KF4825.S7 Admission of foreign students to the United States (Immigration law)

4150	General (Table KF6)
4151-4155	Right to education. Admission. Discrimination and segregation (Table KF4)
4156	Educational tests and measurements (Table KF6)
4156.5	Student records (Table KF6)
4157	Ability grouping (Table KF6)
4158	School attendance and truancy (Table KF6)
4159	School discipline. Tort liability of school boards and staff for disciplinary actions (Table KF6)
	Liability for school and playground accidents
	see KF1290.P5 KF1309 KF1310

Education
Education in general. Public education
Students. Compulsory education -- Continued

4162	Religious and patriotic observances in public schools (Table KF6)
	Including Bible reading, religious instruction, school prayers, flag salute, exercise of freedom of religion by students and school employees
4164	Students' societies (Table KF6)
4165	Student publications (Table KF6)
4166	School sports (Table KF6)
	Teachers
4175	General. Tenure (Table KF6)
	Education and training
4177	General (Table KF6)
	Teachers' colleges
4178	General (Table KF6)
4179.A-Z	Particular colleges, A-Z
4180	Qualifications. Certifications (Table KF6)
4183	Loyalty oaths (Table KF6)
4185	Salaries, pensions, etc. (Table KF6)
4188	Leaves of absence (Table KF6)
4190.A-Z	Special topics, A-Z
4190.S8	Student teachers (Table KF7)
4190.T43	Teachers' assistants (Table KF7)
	Nonteaching school personnel
4192	General (Table KF6)
4192.5.A-Z	Particular classes of employees, A-Z
4192.5.G8	Guidance workers (Table KF7)
4192.5.P8	School psychologists (Table KF7)
4192.5.S63	Social workers (Table KF7)
	Elementary and secondary education
4195	General (Table KF6)
4197	Pre-elementary education. Kindergartens (Table KF6)
	For nursery schools see KF2042.D3
	Cf. KF3728 Maternity and infant welfare
4199	Secondary education (Table KF6)
	Curricula. Courses of instruction
4201	General (Table KF6)
4203	Physical education (Table KF6)
4203.5	Reading (Table KF6)
4204	Language instruction (Table KF6)
	Including bilingual education
	Vocational instruction
4205	General (Table KF6)
	For vocational rehabilitation see KF3738+
4208	Technical education. Manual training (Table KF6)

Education
Elementary and secondary education
Curricula. Courses of instruction -- Continued

Code	Description
4208.5.A-Z	Other special courses, A-Z
4208.5.L3	Law (Table KF7)
4208.5.S34	Science (Table KF7)
4209.A-Z	Particular teaching methods and media, A-Z
4209.A8	Audiovisual education (Table KF7)
4209.E38	Educational technology (Table KF7)
4209.T3	Television (Table KF7)
	Special education
4209.3	General (Table KF6)
	Particular types of students
4209.5	Gifted children
	Students with physical disabilities
4210	General (Table KF6)
4212	Blind (Table KF6)
4215	Students with mental disabilities (Table KF6)
4216	Students with social disabilities (Table KF6)
4217.A-Z	Particular types, A-Z
4217.H68	Homeless children (Table KF7)
4217.I46	Children of immigrants (Table KF7)
	Including children of illegal aliens
4217.M5	Children of migrant laborers (Table KF7)
4218	Extracurricular school programs (Table KF6)
	School buildings see KF5702.S3
4219	School libraries (Table KF6)
	Including censorship
4220	Private education. Private schools (Table KF6)
	Denominational schools see KF4124
4221	Domestic education. Home schools (Table KF6)
4222	Correspondence schools. Home study schools (Table KF6)
4223	Adult education (Table KF6)
	Indian education see KF8210.E3
	Higher education. Colleges and universities
4225	General (Table KF6)
4230	Land grant colleges (Table KF6)
4232	African American universities and colleges (Table KF6)
4234	Finance. Federal aid to higher education (Table KF6)
4235	Student aid. Scholarships (Table KF6)
4240	Faculties. Legal status of academic teachers (Table KF6)
4242	Academic freedom (Table KF6)
	Students
	Including legal status, discipline
	Cf. KF4825.S7 Admission of foreign students to the United States (Immigration law)

KF UNITED STATES (GENERAL) KF

Education
Higher education. Colleges and universities
General
Students -- Continued

4243	General (Table KF6)
4244.A-Z	Particular types of students, A-Z
4244.M45	Mental disabilities, Students with (Table KF7)
4244.P58	Physical disabilities, Students with (Table KF7)
	Curricula. Courses of instruction
4245	General (Table KF6)
4245.5.A-Z	Particular fields of study, A-Z
4245.5.I5	International education. General area studies (Table KF7)
4245.5.L3	Law (Table KF7)
4248	Student personnel services (Table KF6)
4250	Cooperative education (Table KF6)
	Professional education. Professional schools
4256	General
4257	Particular types of professional education (Table KF6) Prefer profession or subject
	Science and the arts. Research
4270	General (Table KF6)
4280.A-Z	Particular branches and subjects, A-Z
4280.D3	Defense research and development (Table KF7) Cf. KF869 Research and development contracts
4280.E53	Energy research. Energy Research and Development Administration (Table KF7)
4280.I53	Industrial research (Table KF7)
4280.L35	Language and languages (Table KF7)
	Meteorology see KF5594
4280.O3	Oceanography (Table KF7)
4280.R2	Radiobiology (Table KF7)
4280.S6	Social sciences (Table KF7)
4280.S7	Space exploration. National Aeronautics and Space Administration (Table KF7)
	The arts
4288	Fine arts (Table KF6)
	Performing arts
4290	General (Table KF6) Including cultural centers
	Music
4291	General (Table KF6)
4293	Conservatories (Table KF6)
4294	Orchestras (Table KF6)
4296	Theater and theaters (Table KF6) Cf. KF3987 Amusements (Control of social activities) Cf. KF5702.T4 Building laws

KF UNITED STATES (GENERAL) KF

Science and the arts. Research
The arts
Performing arts -- Continued
Motion pictures

4298	General (Table KF6)
4300	Censorship (Table KF6)
4302	Regulation of industry. Trade practices (Table KF6)
4305	Museums and galleries (Table KF6)

Historic buildings and monuments. Architectural landmarks
Including vessels, battlefields, etc.

4310	General (Table KF6)
4311.A-Z	By place, A-Z

Under each:
.xA2-.xA49 General
.xA5-.xZ *Particular buildings, monuments, etc., A-Z*

4312.A-Z	Other, A-Z

Buildings and monuments not located in, or associated with, a particular city or town

Libraries and library services

4315	General. Library development (Table KF6)
4316	Librarians (Legal status, qualifications, certification, etc.)

Cf. KF3580.L52 Labor law
Depository libraries see KF5003

4317	Library of Congress (Table KF6)

Presidential libraries

4318.A1	General (Table KF7)
4318.A5-Z	Particular libraries, A-Z

Subarrange each by Table KF7

4319.A-Z	Other, A-Z
4319.I5	Information networks (Table KF7)

Library surveillance see KF4858.L5
School libraries see KF4219

4325	Archives. Historical documents

Record management, the National Archives see KF5752

4330	Educational, scientific, and cultural exchanges

Constitutional law
Sources

4501	Bibliography
4502	Collections

Individual sources other than the Constitution

4505	Proceedings and journals of the Continental Congress, 1774-1789
4506	Declaration of Independence, 1776
4508	Articles of Confederation
4510	Constitutional Convention, 1787-1788

State conventions

Constitutional law
Sources
Individual sources other than the Constitution
State conventions -- Continued

4511	General works
4512.A-.W	By state, A-W
4513	Other documents
4515	Contemporary writings. The Federalist
	Class here editions of the Federalist and legal (constitutional) commentaries
	For works on political theory and political commentary see JK155
4520	Works on legislative history (origin and making) of the Constitution (Table KF8)
	Class here legal works only
	For general works on political institutions of the constitutional period (1776-1829) see JK116+
	Texts of the Constitution
4525	Unannotated. By date
4526.A-Z	Foreign language editions. By language, A-Z
4527	Annotated
4528	Commentaries
4528.5	Indexes
	Amendments and proposed amendments see KF4558+
	State constitutions. State constitutional conventions
4529	Bibliography
4530	Collections
	Including digests and indexes
	Constitutional history of the United States
4541	General (Table KF8)
4545.A-Z	Special topics, A-Z
	For history of a particular subject of constitutional law, see the subject
	Admission to the Union see KF4545.S7
4545.D57	District of Columbia (Constitutional status) (Table KF7)
4545.S5	Slavery. Fugitive slave act (Table KF7)
4545.S7	Statehood (U.S. states). Admission to the Union (Table KF7)
	For individual states, see the state
4546-4550	Constitutional law in general (Table KF3)
	State constitutions see KF4530
	Particular aspects
4551	Religious aspects
4552	Other aspects
4554	U.S. Constitution and foreign constitutions compared
4555	Amending process (Table KF6)
	Amendments

Constitutional law
Amendments -- Continued
Collective. By author or editor
Particular amendments
1st-10th amendments treated collectively see KF4741+

4557	Collective. By author or editor
	Particular amendments
	1st-10th amendments treated collectively see KF4741+
4558 1st	1st amendment
	2nd amendment see KF3941+
4558 3rd	3rd amendment
4558 4th	4th amendment
4558 5th	5th amendment
4558 6th	6th amendment
4558 7th	7th amendment
4558 8th	8th amendment
4558 9th	9th amendment
4558 10th	10th amendment
4558 11th	11th amendment
4558 12th	12th amendment
	13th-15th amendments treated collectively see KF4756+
	13th amendment see KF4545.S5
4558 14th	14th amendment
	15th-27th amendments
	see the subject, e.g. 15th amendment, see KF4891+ 16th amendment, see KF6351+ etc.
	Rule of law see KF382
4565	Separation of powers. Delegation of powers (Table KF6)
4568	Conflict of interests (General). Incompatibility of offices. Ethics in government (Table KF6) Cf. KF4970 Legislature
4570	Executive privilege (Table KF6)
4575	Judicial review of legislative acts (Table KF6)
4578	Congressional nullification of Supreme Court decisions (Table KF6)
4579.A-Z	Other topics, A-Z
4579.A38	Advisory opinions (Table KF7)
4579.I4	Executive impoundment of appropriated funds (Table KF7)
	Sources and relationships of law
4581	International and municipal law. Treaties and agreements
4583	Statutory law and delegated legislation. Ordinances. Rules President's ordinance powers see KF5068
	Structure of government. Federal and state relations. Jurisdiction
4600	General (Table KF6)
4605	Comity clause (Privileges and immunities of state citizens)
4606	Commerce clause
4608	Contract clause
4612	Federal-state disputes

KF UNITED STATES (GENERAL) KF

Constitutional law
Structure of government. Federal and state relations.
Jurisdiction
Federal-state disputes -- Continued

4613	Secession. Nullification
4615	Disputes between states
4618	Interstate compacts
	Federal and state jurisdiction in particular areas
4621	Sedition (Table KF6)
	e. g. works on the Virginia and Kentucky resolutions, 1798
4625	Federal areas within states (Table KF6)
4627	Submerged land (Table KF6)
	Cf. KF1856 Petroleum legislation
4629	Welfare clause
4635	National territory. Noncontiguous territories (Table KF6)
	Foreign relations
4650-4651	General (Table KF5, modified)
	General works
4651.A59	Attorneys General's opinions
4665	Mutual security program
	Foreign assistance program
4668	General (Table KF6)
4669.A-Z	Particular countries, A-Z
4670.A-Z	Particular kinds of assistance, A-Z
4670.A35	Agricultural assistance (Table KF7, modified)
4670.A35Z9-.A35Z99	By country, A-Z
4670.F66	Food relief (Table KF7 modified)
4670.F66Z9-.F66Z99	By country, A-Z
4670.M54	Military assistance (Table KF7 modified)
4670.M54Z9-.M54Z99	By country, A-Z
4670.P2	Patent and technical information. "Know-how" assistance (Table KF7 modified)
4670.P2Z9-.P2Z99	By country, A-Z
4675	Neutrality laws (Table KF6)
4678	Economic sanctions (Table KF6)
4689	Peace Corps (Table KF6)
	Foreign service see KF5112+
4694.A-Z	Particular topics, A-Z
	Consuls, Foreign see KF4694.F67
4694.F67	Foreign consuls (Table KF7)
4695	Public policy. Police power (Table KF6)
	Individual and state
	Nationality and citizenship
4700	General (Table KF6)
	Acquisition and loss
4704	General (Table KF6)
4706-4710	Naturalization (Table KF4, modified)

KF UNITED STATES (GENERAL) KF

Constitutional law
Individual and state
Nationality and citizenship
Acquisition and loss
Naturalization -- Continued
4706.A45 Directories. By date
Loss of citizenship
4715 Expatriation (Table KF6)
4718 Criminal sentence (Table KF6)
4720.A-Z Particular groups, A-Z
4720.E3 East Indians (Table KF7)
4720.P83 Puerto Ricans (Table KF7)
4720.V3 Veterans (Table KF7)
4720.W6 Women (Table KF7)
Civil and political rights and liberties
General. The Bill of Rights
4741 Bibliography
4742 Periodicals
Class here periodicals consisting primarily of informative materials (newsletters, bulletins, etc.)
For periodicals consisting predominantly of legal articles, regardless of subject matter and jurisdiction, see K1+
4743.5 Legislative documents. By date
4744 Collections of sources. By date of publication
4744.5 Texts of Bill of Rights
Statutes
Collections. Compilations
4744.512 Serials
4744.513 Monographs. By date of publication
4744.514-.579 Particular acts
Arrange chronologically, by means of successive decimal numbers, according to date of original enactment or revision of law
Under each:
Legislative history
.A15 Compilations of documents. By date of publication
.A16 Treatises
Unannotated texts
Including official editions, with or without annotations
.A19 Serials
.A2 Monographs. By date of publication
.A5-.Z Annotated editions. Commentaries. By author of commentary or annotations

Constitutional law
Individual and state
Civil and political rights and liberties
General. The Bill of Rights -- Continued
Court decisions
Reports

Call Number	Description
4745.A2	Serials
4745.A5-Z	Monographs
4745.3	Digests of reports (Case finders)
4745.5	Citators
	Including citators for both cases and statutes
4745.7	Indexes
4746.3	Collections of summaries of cases ("Digests" of cases decided by courts or regulatory agencies). By editor or title
4746.5	Looseleaf services
4747.5	Dictionaries
4748	Casebooks. Readings
	General works
4749.A1	Collections. Monographic series
4749.A2	Collected papers and essays. Symposia
4749.A7-Z	Treatises. Monographs
4750	Compends. Outlines
4750.Z95	Works on comparative and uniform state and local law
	Particular amendments see KF4558+
	Particular groups
4753	Business (Table KF6)
4754	Labor (Table KF6)
	People with disabilities see KF480+
4754.5	Sexual minorities (Table KF6)
	Including gays, lesbians and transgender people
	Cf. KF539 Same-sex marriage
	Prisoners see KF9731
4755	Racial and ethnic minorities. Antidiscrimination in general (Table KF6)
	For discrimination in a specific field, see the field, e. g. KF3464+, Discrimination in employment
4755.5	Affirmative action (Table KF6)
	For affirmative action in particular fields, see the number for discrimination in the field, e.g. KF3464, Employment discrimination
4756-4757	African Americans (Table KF5, modified)
	Including works on the 13th to 15th amendments treated collectively, and works on discrimination against African Americans in public accommodations
	Cf. Special subjects, e.g. KF4893 (Suffrage)

KF UNITED STATES (GENERAL) KF

Constitutional law
Individual and state
Civil and political rights and liberties
Particular groups
African Americans. 13th to 15th amendments. Access
to public accommodations -- Continued

4756.A28	Compilations of legislative histories of 13th to 15th amendments
	General works
4757.A59	Attorneys General's opinions
	Indians see KF8210.C5
4757.5.A-Z	Other groups, A-Z
4757.5.A75	Asian Americans (Table KF7)
4757.5.C47	Chinese Americans (Table KF7)
4757.5.L38	Latin Americans (Table KF7)
4757.5.M4	Mexican Americans (Table KF7)
4757.5.O94	Overweight persons (Table KF7)
4758	Sex discrimination (Table KF6)
	Cf. KF697.D5 Discrimination in mortgage loans
	Particular constitutional guarantees
4764	Equal protection of the law (Table KF6)
4765	Due process of law (Table KF6)
4767	Linguistic rights. Bilingualism (Table KF6)
4769	Free choice of employment (Table KF6)
	Freedom of expression
4770	General (Table KF6)
4772	Freedom of speech (Table KF6)
4774	Freedom of the press and of information (Table KF6)
	For press law see KF2750
4775	Press censorship (Table KF6)
	School library censorship see KF4219
	Access to public records see KF5753
4778	Freedom of assembly and of association (Table KF6)
4780	Freedom of petition (Table KF6)
4783	Freedom of religion and of conscience (Table KF6)
	Cf. KF4865+ Church and state
4785	Freedom of movement (Table KF6)
	Habeas corpus see KF9011
	Right of privacy see KF1262+
	Self incrimination see KF9668
4786	Right to resistance against government (Table KF6)
4788	Political parties (Table KF6)
	Control of individuals
4791	Identification. Registration (Table KF6)
	For alien registration see KF4840
	For foreign agents registration see KF4854
4794	Passports (Table KF6)

Constitutional law
Individual and state
Control of individuals
Passports -- Continued
4794.5 Administration. Passport Office (Table KF6)
Aliens
For services for immigrants, etc. see KF3743
4800 General (Table KF6)
Immigration
4801-4820 General (Table KF1)
4821 Immigration and Naturalization Service (Table KF6)
Admission of particular groups
For ethnic groups see KF4845+
4824.A-Z Seasonal laborers. By country, A-Z
4825.A-Z Other, A-Z
4825.B87 Businesspeople (Table KF7)
4825.E53 Engineers (Table KF7)
4825.E93 Exchange visitors' program (Table KF7)
4825.M43 Medical personnel (Table KF7)
4825.S7 Students (Table KF7)
Particular controls and procedures
4827 Visas (Table KF6)
Public health inspection, quarantine see KF3807
4829 Other (Table KF6)
Including controls on employment
Particular classes of immigrants. Quota preferences
and restrictions
4836 Refugees (Table KF6)
4840 Identification and registration (Table KF6)
For foreign agents' registration see KF4854
4842 Deportation and expulsion (Table KF6)
Particular ethnic groups
4845 Chinese (Table KF6)
4846 Japanese (Table KF6)
Cf. KF7224.5 Japanese American internment,
1942-1945
4848.A-Z Other, A-Z
4848.A83 Asians (Table KF7)
4848.M48 Mexicans (Table KF7)
4848.S26 Salvadoreans (Table KF7)
Internal security. Control of subversive activities
Cf. KF9397 Criminal law
4850 General (Table KF6)
For loyalty-security program see KF5346
4851 Procedure. The Subversive Activities Control Board
(Table KF6)
4852.A-Z Cases. By respondent, A-Z

KF UNITED STATES (GENERAL) KF

Constitutional law
Individual and state
Control of individuals
Internal security. Control of subversive activities --
Continued

4854	Foreign agents. Foreign propaganda
4856.A-Z	Particular groups, A-Z
4856.C6	Communists (Table KF7)
4858.A-Z	Special topics, A-Z
4858.L5	Library surveillance (Table KF7)
	Church and state
4865	General. Religious corporations (Table KF6)
4868.A-Z	Special topics, A-Z
4868.A84	Atheism (Table KF7)
4868.C4	Church property (Table KF7)
4868.C44	Clergy (Table KF7)
4868.F35	Faith-based human services (Table KF7)
	Flag salute see KF4162
4868.R45	Religious observances on public property (Table KF7)
	School prayers see KF4162
4869.A-Z	Particular religions, denominations, sects, etc., A-Z
4869.A45	Amish (Table KF7)
4869.C2	Catholic Church (Table KF7)
4869.C4	Christian Scientists (Table KF7)
	Christian Science healers see KF2913.C45+
	Friends, Society of see KF4869.Q83
4869.J3	Jews (Table KF7)
4869.M3	Methodists (Table KF7)
4869.M6	Mormons (Table KF7)
4869.M86	Muslims (Table KF7)
4869.N45	Neopagans. Pagans (Table KF7)
	Pagans see KF4869.N45
4869.P7	Presbyterians (Table KF7)
4869.Q83	Quakers (Society of Friends) (Table KF7)
4869.S35	Scientologists (Table KF7)
	Society of Friends see KF4869.Q83
	Organs of the government
4880	General (Table KF6)
	The people
4880.5	General works (Table KF6)
4881	Initiative and referendum. Plebiscite (Table KF6)
4884	Recall (Table KF6)
	Including recall of judges and judicial decisions
	Political parties see KF4788
	Election law
4885-4886	General (Table KF5)
	Suffrage

Constitutional law
Organs of the government
The people
Election law
Suffrage -- Continued

Number	Description
4891	General
	Including voting age
	Particular groups of voters
4893	African Americans (Table KF6)
4894	Soldiers (Table KF6)
4895	Women (Table KF6)
4896.A-Z	Other, A-Z
4896.C64	College students (Table KF7)
4896.E92	Ex-convicts (Table KF7)
	Indians see KF8210.S84
4896.L56	Linguistic minorities (Table KF7)
	Including bilingual ballots
4898	Registration. Qualifications. Educational tests. Poll tax requirements (Table KF6)
4901	Absentee voting (Table KF6)
	Soldiers see KF4894
4904	Voting machines. Voting systems (Table KF6)
4905	Election districts. Apportionment. Gerrymandering (Table KF6)
4907	Primaries (General) (Table KF6)
	Election to particular offices
	President. Vice President
4910	General (Table KF6)
4911	Electoral college (Table KF6)
	Contested elections see KF5073+
	Congress
	Both houses see KF4885+
	Contested elections see KF4975+
4913	Senate (Table KF6)
4914	House of Representatives (Table KF6)
4916	Other
	e.g. Local and municipal elections, comparative state law
4920	Campaign funds and expenditures (Table KF6)
4921	Corrupt practices. Illicit political activities (Table KF6)
	Cf. KF9409 Criminal law
	The legislative branch
4930	General. Legislative power (Table KF6)
4932	Special and local legislation (Table KF6)
4933	Organization of legislative bodies. Procedure. General and comparative state law (Table KF6)
4934	Legislative branch employees (Table KF6)

KF UNITED STATES (GENERAL) KF

Constitutional law
Organs of the government
The legislative branch -- Continued
The Congress

Call Number	Topic
4935	General. Organization (Table KF6)
4937	Rules and procedure (Table KF6)
	Joint committees
4939	General
4939.5.A-Z	Particular committees, A-Z
4939.5.A8	Atomic Energy (Table KF7)
4939.5.C66	Congressional Operations (Table KF7)
4939.5.E36	Economic (Table KF7)
4939.5.L5	Library (Table KF7)
4939.5.P7	Printing (Table KF7)
4939.5.T39	Taxation (Table KF7)
	Powers and duties
4940	General. Legislative functions and limitations (Table KF6)
	Cf. KF4600+ Federal and state relations
	Particular powers
	Prefer subject
4941	Declaration of war (Table KF6)
	Cf. KF5060 War and emergency powers of the president
4942	Investigative power (Table KF6)
	Cf. KF4570 Executive privilege
4943	Sunset reviews of government programs (Table KF6)
4944	Legislative veto (Table KF6)
	Commerce power see KF4606
	The legislative process
	Cf. KF8709 Judicial impact statements
4945	General (Table KF8)
4946	Committees (Table KF6)
4948	Lobbying (Table KF6)
4950	Bill drafting (Table KF6)
	For legal composition, language of the law (General) see K103.B54
	For legal composition, language of the law (United States) see KF250+
4951	The Legislative Counsel
4952	Legislative reference services
	Veto see KF5067
4958	Impeachment power and procedure (Table KF6)
	Cf. KF5075+ Impeachment of the President
	Cf. KF8781+ Impeachment of judges
	Discipline of legislators

Constitutional law
Organs of the government
The legislative branch
The Congress
Discipline of legislators -- Continued

4960	General (Table KF8)
	Cases
4961.A2	Collections. By date
4961.A5-Z	Particular cases. By respondent, A-Z
	Legal status of legislators
4966	Parliamentary immunity (Table KF6)
4967	Salaries, pensions, etc. (Table KF6)
4969.A-Z	Other privileges, A-Z
4969.F7	Franking privilege (Table KF7)
4970	Conflict of interests. Incompatibility of offices (Table KF6)
	Cf. KF9410 Criminal law
	Contested elections
4975	General
	Cases
	Senate
4976.A2	Collections. By date
4976.A5-Z	Particular cases. By incumbent, A-Z
	House
4977.A2	Collections. By date
4977.A5-Z	Particular cases. By incumbent, A-Z
	The Senate
4980	General
4982	Rules and procedures
4984	Cloture. Filibustering
	Committees
4986	General (Table KF6)
4987.A-Z	Particular committees, A-Z
4987.A25	Aging (Table KF7)
4987.A3	Agriculture and Forestry (Table KF7)
4987.A35	Agriculture, Nutrition, and Forestry (Table KF7)
4987.A67	Appropriations (Table KF7)
4987.A7	Armed Services (Table KF7)
4987.B36	Banking, Housing and Urban Affairs (Table KF7)
4987.C6	Commerce, Science, and Transportation (Table KF7)
4987.E54	Energy and Natural Resources (Table KF7)
4987.E57	Environment and Public Works (Table KF7)
4987.E84	Ethics (Table KF7)
4987.F5	Finance (Table KF7)
4987.F6	Foreign Relations (Table KF7)
4987.G6	Government Operations (Table KF7)

KF UNITED STATES (GENERAL) KF

Constitutional law
Organs of the government
The legislative branch
The Congress
The Senate
Committees
Particular committees, A-Z -- Continued

Call Number	Description
4987.G63	Government Operations with Respect to Intelligence Activities (Table KF7)
4987.G65	Governmental Affairs (Table KF7)
4987.H4	Health, Education, Labor, and Pensions (Table KF7)
4987.H65	Homeland Security and Governmental Affairs (Table KF7)
4987.H654	Permanent Subcommittee on Investigations (Table KF7)
4987.H86	Human Resources (Table KF7)
4987.I45	Indian Affairs (Table KF7)
4987.I47	Intelligence (Table KF7)
4987.I5	Interior and Insular Affairs (Table KF7)
4987.J8	Judiciary (Table KF7)
4987.L3	Labor and Public Welfare (Table KF7)
4987.N8	Nutrition and Human Needs (Table KF7)
4987.P7	Presidential Campaign Activities (Table KF7)
4987.R85	Rules and Administration (Table KF7)
4987.S6	Small Business (Table KF7)
4987.V47	Veterans' Affairs (Table KF7)

Powers and duties

4988	General (Table KF6)
4988.5	Confirmation of Presidential nominations (Table KF6)
4989	Treaties (Table KF6)

The House of Representatives

4990	General (Table KF6)
4992	Rules and procedure (Table KF6)

Committees

4996	General (Table KF6)
4997.A-Z	Particular committees, A-Z
4997.A33	Administrative Review (Table KF7)
4997.A34	Aging (Table KF7)
4997.A35	Agriculture (Table KF7)
4997.A6	Appropriations (Table KF7)

Constitutional law
Organs of the government
The legislative branch
The Congress
The House of Representatives
Committees
Particular committees, A-Z -- Continued

4997.A7	Armed Services (Table KF7)
	The committee existed under this name during the periods 1946-1994 and 1999- . During the period 1995-1998 it was called the Committee on National Security
	For works on the committee during the period 1995-1998 see KF4997.N375
4997.B3	Banking and Currency (Table KF7)
4997.B8	Budget (Table KF7)
4997.C6	Commerce (Table KF7)
4997.E3	Education and Labor (Table KF7)
4997.E35	Education and the Workforce (Table KF7)
4997.E53	Energy and Commerce (Table KF7)
4997.F5	Financial Services (Table KF7)
4997.F6	Foreign Affairs (Table KF7)
4997.G6	Government Operations (Table KF7)
4997.G67	Government Reform (Table KF7)
4997.H66	Homeland Security (Table KF7)
4997.H68	House Administration (Table KF7)
4997.I46	Intelligence (Table KF7)
4997.I48	Internal Security (Table KF7)
	Formerly Un-American Activities Committee
4997.I5	International Relations (Table KF7)
4997.J8	Judiciary (Table KF7)
4997.M4	Merchant Marine and Fisheries (Table KF7)
4997.N37	Narcotics Abuse and Control (Table KF7)
4997.N375	National Security (Table KF7)
	The committee existed under this name during the period 1995-1998. During the periods 1946-1994 and 1999- it was called the Committee on Armed Services
	For works on the committee during the periods 1946-1994 and 1999- see KF4997.A7
4997.N38	Natural Resources (Table KF7)
4997.O94	Oversight and Government Reform (Table KF7)
4997.P6	Post Office and Civil Service (Table KF7)
4997.P8	Public Works and Transportation (Table KF7)
4997.R4	Resources (Table KF7)
4997.R8	Rules (Table KF7)
4997.S25	Science (Table KF7)

KF UNITED STATES (GENERAL) KF

Constitutional law
Organs of the government
The legislative branch
The Congress
The House of Representatives
Committees
Particular committees, A-Z -- Continued

4997.S3	Science and Astronautics (Table KF7)
4997.S34	Science and Technology (Table KF7)
4997.S6	Small Business (Table KF7)
4997.S73	Standards of Official Conduct (Table KF7)
4997.T7	Transportation and Infrastructure (Table KF7)
	Un-American Activities see KF4997.I48
4997.V47	Veterans' Affairs (Table KF7)
4997.W3	Ways and Means (Table KF7)
	Powers and duties
4998	General (Table KF6)
4999	Treaties (Table KF6)
	General Accounting Office see KF6236
5001	Government printing. Government Printing Office. The Public Printer (Table KF6)
5003	Depository libraries (Table KF6)
5005	Other offices and agencies of the legislative branch
	Library of Congress see KF4317
	The executive branch
5050	General. Executive power (Table KF6, modified)
5050.Z95	State executive. Governors
	The President
5051	General (Table KF8)
	Powers and duties
5053	General (Table KF8)
5055	Treaty-making power (Table KF6)
	Consent of Senate see KF4989
5057	Executive agreements
5060	War and emergency powers (Table KF6)
	Cf. KF4941+ Declaration of war
5063	Martial law. Military government (Table KF6)
	Military commissions see KF7661
	Legislative powers
5065	General
5067	Veto power (Table KF6)
5068	Ordinance power (Table KF6)
	Cf. KF4583 Delegated legislation
	Impoundment of appropriated funds see KF4579.I4
	Appointing and removal power
	Cf. KF4988.5 Senate confirmation
5069.A7-.Z8	General works

Constitutional law
Organs of the government
The executive branch
The President
Powers and duties
Appointing and removal power -- Continued

Call Number	Description
5069.Z9A-.Z9Z	Particular cases. By incumbent
	Contested elections
5073	General
	Particular cases
5074	Hayes-Tilden, 1876
5074.2	Bush-Gore, 2000
	Impeachment
5075	General (Table KF6)
5076.A-Z	Particular cases. By president, A-Z
	Under each:
	.A2 *Documents. By date*
	.A3-.Z *General works*
	Including proposed impeachments
	Legal status
5080	General (Table KF8)
	Election see KF4910+
5081	Term of office (Table KF8)
5082	Disability. Succession (Table KF8)
5085	The Vice President (Table KF6)
	The Cabinet
5089	General (Table KF6)
	Impeachment of cabinet officers
5090	General (Table KF6)
5091.A-Z	Particular cases. By name of cabinet official, A-Z
	Executive departments
5101-5105	General (Table KF4)
5105.5	Public meetings (Table KF6)
	Particular departments
	For the administrative law of an individual department, see the respective branches of the law and particular subjects under its jurisdiction
	Department of Justice. Attorney General
	Cf. KF5406+ Attorneys General's opinions
	Cf. KF8790 Solicitor General, United States Attorneys and Marshals
5106-5107	General (Table KF5, modified)
	For nominations to office see KF361+
5106.A15	Registers
5107.A2	Administrative reports. By date
5107.A6-.A69	Official reports and monographs
5107.A7-.Z8	Treatises. Monographs

Constitutional law
Organs of the government
The executive branch
Executive departments
Particular departments
Department of Justice. Attorney General
General -- Continued

5107.Z9	Works on state attorneys general (Collective)
5107.5	Office of Independent Counsel. Special prosecutors (Table KF6)
5108	Federal Bureau of Investigation (Table KF6)
	Department of State
5110	General
	The Foreign Service
5112	General (Table KF6)
5113	Legal status of Foreign Service personnel. Salaries, allowances, pensions, etc. (Table KF6)
5118.A-Z	Other, including proposed departments, A-Z
	Prefer subject
	Independent agencies. Special bureaus
5120	General
5121.A-Z	Particular agencies and bureaus (not classed elsewhere), A-Z
	Cf. KF5406+ Regulatory agencies
	Special Representative for Trade Negotiations see KF1979
5125	Executive advisory bodies. Presidential commissions (Table KF6)
	Special district, public authorities see KF5332
	Civil service see KF5336+
5130	The Judiciary. Judicial power (Table KF6)
	Constitutional status only
	For judicial review see KF4575
	Cf. KF8699.2+ Courts, administration of justice, and organization of the judiciary
5150	National emblem. Flag. Seal. Seat of government. National anthem (Table KF6)
5152	Patriotic customs and observances (Table KF6)
	For school flag salute see KF4162
	Patriotic societies see KF1359.A1+
	Decorations of honor. Awards
5153	Civilian (Table KF6)
5154	Military (Table KF6)
	Commemorative medals
5155	General
5156.A-Z	Particular commemorations, A-Z

Local government

5300	General (Table KF6)
	Municipal government. Municipal services
5304-5305	General. Municipal corporations (Table KF5)
5311	Municipal powers and services beyond corporate limits (Table KF6)
	Particular services see KF2076+
5313	Charters and ordinances. Local law
	Including model ordinances and drafting manuals
	Model ordinances relating to a particular subject and not limited to one state, see the subject, with form divisions for "Comparative and uniform state legislation" in Tables KF1-KF6
	Tort liability see KF1302.A2+
5315.A-Z	Special topics, A-Z
5315.A5	Annexation (Table KF7)
5315.M78	Municipal franchises (Table KF7)
5315.M8	Municipal ownership (Table KF7)
	Zoning see KF5691+
	Municipal officials. Organs of government
5316	General (Table KF6)
	Particular officers or organs
5317	City councils (Table KF6)
5319	Mayors (Table KF6)
5322	City attorneys (Table KF6)
5324	Other
5325.A-Z	Special topics, A-Z
5325.I5	Impeachment (Table KF7)
5325.R46	Residence requirements (Table KF7)
	Municipal civil service see KF5393+
5330	County government. County charters. General and comparative (Table KF6)
5332	Special districts. Public authorities (Table KF6)
	Class here general works; for individual special districts or public authorities, see the jurisdiction from which they derive their authority
	For particular kinds of districts, prefer subject, e.g. KF4127, School districts
	Civil service. Government officials and employees
	Federal civil service
	For works limited to legislative branch employees see KF4934
	For works limited to judicial branch employees see KF8770+
5336-5337	General. Qualifications for employment (Table KF5)
5338	Merit Systems Protection Board. Office of Personnel Management. Civil Service Commission (Table KF6)

KF UNITED STATES (GENERAL) KF

Civil service. Government officials and employees
Federal civil service -- Continued
Conditions and restrictions of employment. Employment discipline

5340	General (Table KF6)
5342	Nondiscrimination (Table KF6)
5344	Illicit political activities (Table KF6)
	Conflict of interests see KF4568
5346	Loyalty-security program (Table KF6)
5349	Performance rating (Table KF6)
	Types and modes of employment
5352	Veterans' preference (Table KF6)
5353	Retired military personnel (Table KF6)
5355	People with disabilities (Table KF6)
5357	Consultants (Table KF6)
5362	Re-employment and reinstatement (Table KF6)
	Employment relations
5365	Labor unions (Table KF6)
	Tenure and remuneration
5370	General (Table KF6)
5372	Classification (Table KF6)
5372.5	Administration. Personnel Classification Board. Personnel Classification Division (Table KF6)
5375	Salaries (Table KF6)
5377	Promotions (Table KF6)
5380	Retirement. Pensions (Table KF6)
5384	Leave regulations (Table KF6)
5385	Other benefits (Table KF6)
	e.g. Life insurance, health insurance
	Compensation for injuries see KF3626
	Unemployment insurance see KF3680.F3
5387	Travel regulations (Table KF6)
	Bonding see KF1225+
	Particular departments
	see the department
5390	State civil service (Table KF6)
	General and comparative
	Municipal civil service
	General and comparative
5393	General (Table KF6)
5394	Labor unions (Table KF6)
5396	Retirement pensions (Table KF6)
5398.A-Z	Particular departments or positions, A-Z
	Firemen see KF3976
5398.P6	Police (Table KF7)
	Teachers see KF4175+

KF UNITED STATES (GENERAL) KF

Police and power of the police. Federal and comparative state law

5399	General (Table KF6)
5399.5.A-Z	Special topics, A-Z
5399.5.L4	Legal advisors (Table KF7)
	Policemen (Salaries, tenure, etc.) see KF5398.P6
5399.5.P7	Private police (Table KF7)
	Tort liability see KF1307
	Administrative organization and procedure
5401-5402	General. Administrative law (Table KF5)
5406-5407	The administrative process. Regulatory agencies (Table KF5 modified)
	Attorneys General's opinions
	Reports
5406.A6-.A619	Serials
	For opinions on specific subjects, see the subject
5406.A62	Monographs. By date
5411	Legislative functions. Rulemaking power. Regulations (Table KF6)
5414	Admission of attorneys and rules of practice (Table KF6)
5415	Citizen participation (Table KF6)
	Legislative veto see KF4944
	Judicial functions. Procedure. Administrative tribunals
5416-5417	General (Table KF5)
5421	Hearing examiners (Table KF6)
5422	Administrative agency investigations. Governmental investigations (Table KF6)
5423	Abuse of administrative power. Ombudsman (Table KF6)
5425	Judicial reviews. Appeals (Table KF6)
	Tort liability of the government and of public officers see KF1321
	Public property. Public restraints on private property
5500	General (Table KF6)
5501	Department of the Interior (Table KF6)
	Conservation of natural resources
5505	General (Table KF6)
5508	Mineral resources (Table KF6)
5510	Recycling of waste (Table KF6)
	Roads
5521-5525	General. Highway law (Table KF4)
5528	Highway finance (Table KF6)
5530	Express highways. Parkways (Table KF6)
5532	Roadside protection. Rights of way (Table KF6)
	Including restrictions on signboards, advertising, etc.
	Cf. KF5710 Structures other than buildings
5534	Foot trails (Table KF6)
5535	Pedestrian areas (Table KF6)

KF UNITED STATES (GENERAL) KF

Public property. Public restraints on private property
Roads -- Continued

5536.A-Z	Particular roads, A-Z
	Bridges
5540	General (Table KF6)
5541.A-Z	Particular bridges, A-Z
	Water resources. Watersheds. Rivers. Lakes. Water courses
5551-5570	General. Conservation. Water resources development (Table KF1)
	Including water power development
	Federal Power Commission see KF2120.1
5571	Special aspects
5575	State water rights (Table KF6, modified)
	Decisions
5575.A5	Digests
5575.A55A-.A55Z	Particular cases. By plaintiff
	Riparian rights see KF641+
	Pollution see KF3786+
	River and harbor improvement
5580	General (Table KF6)
5581	Dredging (Table KF6)
5582.A-Z	Particular inland waterways and channels, A-Z
	Canals
	For navigation see KF2573+
5584	General (Table KF6)
5585.A-Z	Particular canals, A-Z
	Flood control. Levees. Dams
5588	General (Table KF6)
5589.A-Z	Particular dams, bodies of water, etc., A-Z
	Under each:
	.xA35-.xA39 *Interstate compacts*
	.xA5-.xA7 *Other documents*
	.xA8-.xZ *Treatises. Monographs*
5590.A-Z	Particular bodies of water, particular districts, A-Z
	Subarrange each by Table KF19
	e. g.
5590.D4	Delaware River Basin and Bay area (Table KF19)
5590.E8	Everglades National Park (Table KF19)
5590.P6	Potomac River Basin (Table KF19)
5590.S9	Susquehanna River Basin (Table KF19)
5590.T4	Tennessee Valley Authority (Table KF19)
5594	Weather control. Meteorology. Weather stations (Table KF6)
5599	Eminent domain (Table KF6, modified)
5599.A28	Court rules. By date
	Military requisitions see KF5901+ subdivision (1)
	Public land law
5601-5605	General (Table KF4)

Public property. Public restraints on private property
Public land law -- Continued

Number	Description
5607	Public Land Office (Table KF6)
5609	Rights-of-way across public lands (Table KF6)
	Reclamation. Irrigation. Drainage
5615	General (Table KF6)
5616-5620	Arid lands (Table KF4)
5624	Swamps. Marshes. Wetlands (Table KF6)
5627	Shore protection. Coastal zone management (Table KF6)
	National preserves
5630	Grazing districts (Table KF6)
	National forests
5631	General (Table KF6)
5631.5	Administration. Forest Service (Table KF6)
	National parks and monuments. Wilderness preservation
5635	General (Table KF6)
5638	Recreation areas (Table KF6)
	Wildlife protection
	Including game, bird, and fish protection
	Cf. KF1770+ Fishery law
5640	General. Game laws. Protection of migratory birds (Table KF6)
	Wildlife and waterfowl refuges
5643	General (Table KF6)
5644.A-Z	Particular refuges, A-Z
5645.A-Z	Particular animals and birds, A-Z
5645.H65	Wild horses. Burros (Table KF7)
5646.A-Z	Particular parks, monuments, etc., A-Z
5648	State preserves. State parks and forests (Table KF6)
	Architectural and historic monuments see KF4310+
	Indian lands
5660	General (Table KF6)
5662.A-Z	Particular lands, by tribe, reservation, etc., A-Z
5662.I53	Indian Territory (Oklahoma)
	Homesteads
5670	General (Table KF6)
5673.A-Z	Particular groups, A-Z
5673.S6	Soldiers (Table KF7)
	Land grants
5675	General (Table KF6)
5677.A-Z	Particular claims. By claimant, A-Z
	Land grant colleges see KF4230
	Railroads see KF2298
	Regional and city planning. Zoning. Building
	Federal, state, and local laws, collectively
5691-5692	General (Table KF5)
	Land use. Zoning. Land subdivision

Public property. Public restraints on private property
Regional and city planning. Zoning. Building
Land use. Zoning. Land subdivision -- Continued

Code	Description
5697-5698	General (Table KF5)
5698.3	Real estate development (Table KF6)
	Cf. KF2042.R4 Real estate agents
5698.5	Development rights transfer (Table KF6)
5698.7	Solar access zoning. Shade control (Table KF6)
	Particular land uses and zoning controls
5699	Sex-oriented businesses (Table KF6)
5700	Rural and agricultural uses (Table KF6)
	Emission density zoning see KF3812.5.E55
5700.5.A-Z	Other land uses and zoning controls, A-Z
5700.5.A58	Antennas. Telecommunication towers (Table KF7)
5700.5.G74	Group homes (Table KF7)
5700.5.H65	Home-based businesses (Table KF7)
5700.5.L36	Landslide and rockslide prevention (Table KF7)
	Telecommunication towers see KF5700.5.A58
	Building laws
5701	General (Table KF6)
5702.A-Z	Particular types of buildings, A-Z
5702.C6	Court buildings (Table KF7)
5702.I53	Industrial buildings (Table KF7)
5702.M63	Mobile homes (Table KF7)
5702.P74	Prefabricated buildings (Table KF7)
5702.S3	School buildings (Table KF7)
5702.S45	Shopping centers (Table KF7)
5702.T4	Theaters (Table KF7)
5703	Roofs (Table KF6)
5704	Electric installations (Table KF6)
5704.5	Gas installations (Table KF6)
5705	Elevators (Table KF6)
5708	Heating and ventilating. Air conditioning (Table KF6)
	Including energy conservation provisions
5709	Plumbing (Table KF6)
5709.3.A-Z	Other topics, A-Z
5709.3.A78	Artists' studios (Table KF7)
5709.3.H35	Handicapped, Provisions for. People with disabilities, Provisions for (Table KF7)
	People with disabilities, Provisions for see KF5709.3.H35
5710	Structures other than buildings (Table KF6)
	Including billboards and outdoor advertising in cities
	Cf. KF5532 Roadside protection
	Housing. Slum clearance. City redevelopment
5721-5730	General (Table KF2)
5733	Special aspects

Public property. Public restraints on private property
Housing. Slum clearance. City redevelopment -- Continued
Housing finance

5735	General (Table KF6)
5737	Government mortgage insurance (Table KF6)
5738	Housing receiverships (Table KF6)
5740	Discrimination in housing (Table KF6)
	Cf. KF662 Restrictive covenants
	Housing courts see KF595
	Government property
	Administration. Powers and controls
5750	General. The General Services Administration (Table KF6)
5752	Records management (Table KF6)
5752.5	Computerized data files (Table KF6)
	Court records see KF8733+
5753	Access to public records. Freedom of information (Table KF6)
	Cf. KF7695.S3 Security classification
5755	The National Archives (Table KF6)
	Including administration of the federal register
	Land and real property
	Including surplus real property
5760	General (Table KF6)
	Particular properties
	Government buildings
5765	General (Table KF6)
5767.A-Z	By city, A-Z
5769.A-Z	By department or agency, A-Z
	Subdivided, as needed, by city, A-Z
5769.T7	Treasury Department (Table KF7)
5775	Particular buildings (Table KF6)
	Embassies. Consulates
5780	General (Table KF6)
5781.A-Z	By place, A-Z
5800	Military installations (Table KF7)
5810	National cemeteries (Table KF7)
	Personal property
5820	General (Table KF6)
5824	Disposal (Table KF6)
5828.A-Z	Particular departments, agencies, etc. A-Z
	Surplus property
5840	General (Table KF6)
	Agricultural surplus see KF1709+
	Military surplus. War materiel. Military property
5845	General (Table KF6)
	By period

Public property. Public restraints on private property
Government property
Personal property
Surplus property
Military surplus. War materiel. Military property
By period -- Continued
World War I

5846	General (Table KF6)
5847.A-Z	By plant, article, commodity, etc., A-Z
	Subarrange each by Table KF7
	World War II
5851	General (Table KF6)
5852.A-Z	By plant, article, commodity, etc., A-Z
	Subarrange each by Table KF7
	Post-war period, 1945-
5856	General (Table KF6)
5857.A-Z	By plant, article, commodity, etc., A-Z
	Subarrange each by Table KF7
5865	Public works (Table KF6)
	Government measures in time of war, national emergency, or economic crisis. Emergency economic legislation
5900	General (Table KF6)
	By period
	In case of doubt, prefer classification with general subject
	1789-1861
5901	General (Table KF6)
5902	Military requisitions from civilians (Table KF6)
5903	Enemy property. Alien property. International trade (Table KF6)
5904	War damage compensation. Foreign claims settlements (Table KF6)
5905	Other (Table KF6)
	1861-1914
5906	General (Table KF6)
5907	Military requisitions from civilians (Table KF6)
5908	Enemy property. Alien property. International trade (Table KF6)
5909	War damage compensation. Foreign claims settlements (Table KF6)
5910	Other (Table KF6)
	1861-1865
5911	General (Table KF6)
5912	Military requisitions from civilians (Table KF6)
5913	Enemy property. Alien property. International trade (Table KF6)
5914	War damage compensation. Foreign claims settlements (Table KF6)

Government measures in time of war, national emergency, or economic crisis. Emergency economic legislation

By period

1861-1914

1861-1865 -- Continued

5915	Other (Table KF6)
5921-5945	1914-1939 (Table KF14)
5951-5975	1914-1918 (Table KF14)
5981-6005	1929-1939 (Table KF14)
	New Deal legislation
6011	General (Table KF6)
6015.A-Z	Particular subjects and measures, A-Z
	Including National Recovery Administration codes of fair competition
6015.E4	Emergency Relief Appropriation Act, 1935 (Table KF7)
6015.R3	Reconstruction Finance Corporation (Table KF7)
6020	Other
6021-6045	1939-1945 (Table KF14)
6037.5-6045	Procedure. U.S. Emergency Court of Appeals
6051-6075	1945- (Table KF14)
6075.5	Youth Conservation Corps (Table KF6)
	Peace Corps see KF4689
	Public finance
6200	General (Table KF6)
6200.5	The Treasury Department (Table KF6)
	Money. Currency. Coinage
6201-6205	General (Table KF4)
6211	Gold trading. Gold standard (Table KF6)
6213	Silver regulations (Table KF6)
6215	Coinage. Mint regulations (Table KF6)
	Federal Reserve System
6218	General (Table KF6)
6219	Federal Reserve Board (Table KF6)
	Federal Reserve banks see KF981+
	Rediscount see KF1026
	Budget. Government expenditures
	Cf. KF4579.I4 Executive impoundment of appropriated funds
6221-6225	General (Table KF4)
6227	Zero-base budgeting (Table KF6)
6231-6235	Expenditure control. Public auditing and accounting (Table KF4)
6236	General Accounting Office. Comptroller General (Table KF6)
6239	Investment of public funds (Table KF6)

KF UNITED STATES (GENERAL) KF

Public finance
Expenditure control. Public auditing and accounting --
Continued
Particular departments
see Administration or name of department under subject
6241-6245 Public debts. Loans. Bond issues (Table KF4)
National revenue
History
Wartime finance
Cf. KF6406 Wartime surtaxes
6251 General (Table KF6)
6252 Civil War (Table KF6)
6253 Spanish American War (Table KF6)
6254 World War I (Table KF6)
6255 World War II (Table KF6)
6256 Later emergencies (Table KF6)
6260 General (Table KF6)
Treasury Department see KF6200.5
Particular sources of revenue
Charges
6265 Fees
Taxation
6271-6290 General (Table KF1 modified)
6290 Tables
Tax saving. Tax planning
Tax planning relating to particular taxes, except income
tax, see these taxes, e.g. KF6571+ Estate and gift
taxes
6296-6297 General (Table KF5)
6297.5 Tax shelters (Table KF6)
6298 Tax expenditures (Table KF6)
Tax administration and procedure
Including administration and procedure relating to federal
taxes in general and to federal income tax
General works and works on particular aspects and
topics (e.g., KF6310+) relating to other taxes are
classed with these taxes
Cf. KF6750+ State taxation
Cf. KF6780+ Local taxation
6300 General
Internal Revenue Service
6301 General (Table KF6, modified)
6301.A18 Directories. Districts
Statutes. Regulations. Rules of practice
Federal legislation
Regulations. Instructions
Collections. Compilations

Public finance
National revenue
Particular sources of revenue
Taxation
Tax administration and procedure
General
Internal Revenue Service
General
Statutes. Regulations. Rules of practice
Federal legislation
Regulations. Instructions
Collections. Compilations -- Continued

Call Number	Description
6301.A329	Serials
6301.A33	Monographs. By date
	Administration
6301.3	Officers and personnel. Salaries, pensions, etc. (Table KF6)
6301.5	Travel regulations. By date
6301.9	Other administrative rules. By date
	Particular divisions, units, etc.
6302	Income tax unit (Table KF6)
6303	Collection Division (Table KF6)
	Federal and state jurisdiction see KF6736+
6306	Double taxation
	For collections of treaties see K4473.2
	For individual treaties see K4473.6
	Tax collection
6310	General (Table KF6)
6312	Taxpayers' identification (Table KF6)
6314	Tax accounting (Table KF6)
6316	Tax liens (Table KF6)
	Procedure. Practice
6320	General (Table KF6)
6321	Enforcement (Table KF6)
	Including tax penalties
6324	Remedies. Tax courts. Tax appeals (Table KF6 modified)
6324.A48	Court rules. By date
6327	Refunds (Table KF6)
6328	Confidentiality of returns (Table KF6)
6329	Exemption (Table KF6)
	Class here general and income tax; for other taxes, see the particular tax
6330	State and city property, bonds, etc. (Table KF6)
	Tax treatment of special activities
6332	Bankruptcy (Table KF6)
6333	Divorce (Table KF6)

Public finance
National revenue
Particular sources of revenue
Taxation -- Continued

6334	Criminal law. Tax evasion (Table KF6)
	Particular taxes
6335	Several, collective (Table KF6)
	e.g. Income, estate, and gift taxes
	Income tax
6351-6370	General (Table KF1 modified)
6370	Income tax tables
	Administration, Income tax unit see KF6302
	Procedure, practice see KF6320+
6374	Special aspects
	Tax planning see KF6296+
	Estate planning see KF746+
	Income. Exclusion from income
6375	General (Table KF6)
6376	Profits (Table KF6)
6377	Business expenses (Table KF6)
6379	Deferred compensation. Stock options (Table KF6)
6383	Tax-exempt securities. Government bonds (Table KF6)
	Deductions
6385	General
	Particular kinds
6386	Amortization. Depreciation allowances (Table KF6, modified)
6386.Z95	Tables
6388	Charitable or educational gifts and contributions (Table KF6)
6389	Investment credit (Table KF6)
6390	Taxes (Table KF6)
6392	Interest (Table KF6)
	Expenses
6394	General
6395.A-Z	Particular kinds, A-Z
6395.A96	Automobile expenses (Table KF7)
6395.B88	Business use of home (Table KF7)
6395.E3	Educational expenses (Table KF7)
6395.H63	Hobbies (Table KF7)
	Individual retirement accounts (IRAs) see KF6395.R35
6395.L63	Lobbying expenses (Table KF7)
6395.M3	Medical expenses (Table KF7)
6395.M68	Moving expenses (Table KF7)

Public finance
National revenue
Particular sources of revenue
Taxation
Particular taxes
Income tax
Deductions
Particular kinds
Expenses
Particular kinds, A-Z -- Continued

6395.R3	Repairs (Table KF7)
6395.R35	Retirement contributions (Table KF7)
	Including individual retirement accounts (IRAs)
6395.S73	Start-up expenses (Table KF7)
6395.T7	Travel and entertainment expenses (Table KF7)
6396	Losses (Table KF6)
6396.5	Income averaging (Table KF6)
6397	Tax credits (Table KF6)
	Cf. KF6419 Foreign investments
	Refunds see KF6327
6400	Community property of husband and wife (Table KF6)
6401	Joint returns (Table KF6)
	Surtaxes
6404	General (Table KF6)
6405	Unjust enrichment (Table KF6)
6406	Wartime surtaxes. War revenue tax. Victory tax (Table KF6)
	Excess profit tax see KF6471+
	Particular sources of income
	Salaries and wages
6410	General (Table KF6)
	Social security tax see KF3651+
6411.A-Z	Particular payments or benefits, A-Z
6411.M5	Military pay (Table KF7)
6411.S3	Scholarships, awards, etc. (Table KF7)
	Capital investment
6415	General. Securities (Table KF6)
6417	Dividends. Interest (Table KF6)

Public finance
National revenue
Particular sources of revenue
Taxation
Particular taxes
Income tax
Particular sources of income
Capital investment -- Continued
6419 Foreign investments (Table KF6)
Including works on taxation of international
business transactions in general
For foreign investors in the United States
see KF6441
For income taxation of foreign income from
business transactions see KF6445
6425 Pensions and annuities (Table KF6)
6428.A-Z Other, A-Z
6428.A4 Alimony and support (Table KF7)
6428.D36 Damages. Settlements (Table KF7)
6428.E9 Extinguishment of debts (Table KF7)
6428.I5 Industrial property (Table KF7)
Including copyright, patents, trademarks
6428.L3 Leases (Table KF7)
6428.L5 Life insurance proceeds (Table KF7)
Real estate transactions see KF6540
Settlements see KF6428.D36
Particular methods of assessment and collection
Payment at source of income
6435 General (Table KF6)
Payroll deduction. Withholding tax
6436 General (Table KF6 modified)
6436.Z95 Tables
Social security tax see KF3651+
Particular classes of taxpayers
6441 Aliens (Table KF6)
6442 Clergy (Table KF6)
6443 Trusts (Table KF6)
6445 United States citizens living abroad (Table KF6)
6449 Income of nonprofit organizations, nonprofit
corporations, foundations, endowments,
pension funds (Table KF6)
Income of business organizations
Including taxation of business organizations in
general
6450 General (Table KF6)
6452 Partnerships and joint ventures (Table KF6)

Public finance
National revenue
Particular sources of revenue
Taxation
Particular taxes
Income tax
Income of business organizations -- Continued
Juristic persons. Corporations
For nonprofit corporations see KF6449

6455	General (Table KF6)
6456-6465	Corporation income tax (Table KF2)
	Surtaxes
6471-6475	Excess profits tax (Table KF4)
6477	Undistributed profits (Table KF6)
	Allowances and deductions
6481-6482	Depletion allowances. Oil and gas income tax (Table KF5)
6484	Close corporations (Table KF6)
6485	Cooperatives (Table KF6)
6491	Small business corporations (Table KF6)
6493	Domestic international sales corporations (Table KF6)
6495.A-Z	Particular lines of corporate business, A-Z
6495.A47	Agriculture. Forestry (Table KF7)
6495.A8	Automotive transportation (Table KF7)
6495.B2	Banks (Table KF7)
6495.C57	Computer industry. Software industry (Table KF7)
6495.C6	Construction industry (Table KF7)
6495.E45	Electronic commerce (Table KF7)
	Forestry see KF6495.A47
6495.H4	Health facilities (Table KF7)
6495.H45	High technology industries (Table KF7)
6495.H67	Hospitality industry (Table KF7)
	Including hotels and restaurants
	Hotels see KF6495.H67
6495.I5	Insurance companies (Table KF7)
6495.I55	Investment companies (Table KF7)
6495.L4	Legal services corporations. Corporate practice of law (Table KF7)
6495.M5	Mining (Table KF7)
6495.M6	Motion picture industry (Table KF7)
6495.P2	Paper and pulp industry (Table KF7)
6495.P7	Professional corporations (Table KF7)
6495.P8	Public utilities (Table KF7)
6495.R2	Railroads (Table KF7)
	Restaurants see KF6495.H67

KF UNITED STATES (GENERAL) KF

Public finance
National revenue
Particular sources of revenue
Taxation
Particular taxes
Income tax
Income of business organizations
Juristic persons. Corporations
Particular lines of corporate business, A-Z --
Continued
Software industry see KF6495.C57
6495.T6 Trust companies (Table KF7)
6499.A-Z Special topics, A-Z
6499.C58 Consolidated returns (Table KF7)
6499.C6 Corporate reorganization (Table KF7)
6499.D3 Damages (Table KF7)
Including antitrust payments and recoveries
6499.D5 Dissolution. Liquidation (Table KF7)
6499.M4 Mergers (Table KF7)
6499.S34 Sale of business enterprises. Stock transfer
(Table KF7)
Stock transfer see KF6499.S34
Property taxes. Taxation of capital
6525 General (Table KF6)
6528 Tax valuations (Table KF6)
6529 Depreciation (Table KF6)
Federal taxes affecting real property
Including income tax, estate taxes, and others, and
works on both federal and state taxation
For ad valorem taxes upon real estate see
KF6760+
6535 General (Table KF6)
6540 Real estate transactions (Table KF6)
6558 Corporate franchises (Special franchises).
Corporate stock (Table KF6)
General franchises see KF6456+
Other taxes on capital and income
6566 Capital gains tax
Poll taxes see KF4898
Estate, inheritance, and gift taxes
6571-6572 General (Table KF5)
6576-6585 Estate tax. Inheritance tax (Table KF2)
6588 Life insurance proceeds (Table KF6)
6590 Marital deductions (Table KF6)
6594 Gift taxes (Table KF6)
Indirect taxes. Sales or turnover taxes
6598 Value-added tax (Table KF6)

Public finance
National revenue
Particular sources of revenue
Taxation
Particular taxes
Indirect taxes. Sales or turnover taxes -- Continued
Excise taxes. Taxes on transactions

6600	General (Table KF6)
6606	Retail sales tax (Table KF6)
6609	Use taxes (Table KF6)
	Particular commodities, services, transactions
6611	A to Alcoholic a
6611.A3	Admissions. Amusements (Table KF7)
	Aeronautics see KF6614.A9
6611.A5	Alcohol (Table KF7)
	Alcoholic beverages. Liquor taxes
6612	General (Table KF6)
6613.A-Z	Particular beverages, A-Z
6613.B3	Beer (Table KF7)
6613.B7	Brandy (Table KF7)
6613.R8	Rum (Table KF7)
6613.W4	Whiskies (Table KF7)
6613.W5	Wine (Table KF7)
6614	Alcoholic c to Motor fr
6614.A5	Ammunition (Table KF7)
	Amusements see KF6611.A3
6614.A8	Automobile licenses (Table KF7)
	Automobiles see KF6619+
6614.A9	Aviation. Air user taxes (Table KF7)
6614.B4	Bills of exchange (Table KF7)
6614.B6	Boats (Table KF7)
6614.C4	Cheese (Table KF7)
6614.C5	Cigarette paper (Table KF7)
	Cigars see KF6635
6614.C56	Clothing (Table KF7)
6614.C6	Coal (Table KF7)
6614.C68	Cotton (Table KF7)
6614.D4	Distilling apparatus (Table KF7)
6614.D7	Drugs (Table KF7)
	Entertainments see KF6611.A3
6614.E94	Excess benefits (Table KF7)
6614.F5	Firearms (Table KF7)
	Gambling see KF6636.W2
6614.I5	Insurance policies (Table KF7)
	Liquor see KF6612+
6614.L8	Luxury articles (Table KF7)
6614.M55	Mines and mineral resources (Table KF7)

Public finance
National revenue
Particular sources of revenue
Taxation
Particular taxes
Indirect taxes. Sales or turnover taxes
Excise taxes. Taxes on transactions
Particular commodities, services, transactions --
Continued
Motor fuels

6615	General (Table KF6)
	Particular fuels
6616	Gasoline (Table KF6)
6617.A-Z	Other fuels, A-Z
6617.D4	Diesel fuel (Table KF7)
	Motor vehicles
6619	General (Table KF6)
6620.A-Z	Particular types, A-Z
6622	Motor vi to Narcotic
	Narcotics
6623	General (Table KF6)
6624.A-Z	Particular, A-Z
6624.O6	Opium (Table KF7)
6625	Narcotics to Oil (Table KF7)
	Oils and fats
6627	General (Table KF6)
6628.A-Z	Particular, A-Z
6628.O5	Oleomargarine (Table KF7)
6629	Ok to Proc
6629.P3	Petroleum, Crude (Table KF7)
6629.P5	Playing cards (Table KF7)
	Processing of agricultural commodities
6630	General (Table KF6)
6631.A-Z	By commodity, A-Z
6631.H6	Hogs (Table KF7)
6631.O4	Oil (Table KF7)
6631.W4	Wheat (Table KF7)
6633	Prod to Tobab
	Real property see KF6540
6633.S65	Steam boilers (Table KF7)
6633.S7	Stock exchange transactions (Table KF7)
6633.S8	Sugar (Table KF7)
6633.T3	Telecommunication facilities. Telegraph.
	Telephone (Table KF7)
6635	Tobacco and tobacco products (Table KF6)
6636	Tobad-Z
6636.T7	Transportation (Table KF7)

KF UNITED STATES (GENERAL) KF

Public finance
National revenue
Particular sources of revenue
Taxation
Particular taxes
Indirect taxes. Sales or turnover taxes
Excise taxes. Taxes on transactions
Particular commodities, services, transactions
Tobad-Z -- Continued

6636.V4 Vinegar (Table KF7)
6636.W2 Wagering. Gambling (Table KF7)

Particular methods of assessment and collection
For assessment and collection of particular taxes, see these taxes, e.g., Income tax, Excise taxes

6645 Stamp duties

Tariff. Trade agreements. Customs
For foreign trade regulations see KF1975+

6651-6660 General (Table KF2)
6662 U.S. Tariff Commission (Table KF6)

Trade agreements. Particular tariffs
For North American Free Trade Agreement see KDZ1+

6665 General
6666 Collected agreements
6668.A-Z Particular countries, A-Z

Under each:
.x General
.x2 *Individual trade agreements*
Arrange by date. Subarrange each as follows:
.x2A3-.x2A39 *Collected papers and essays*
.x2A4-.x2A59 *Official reports and monographs*
.x2A6-.x2Z *Treatises. Monographs. Commentaries*

6668.C3-.C32 Canada
6669.A-Z Particular commodities, A-Z
6669.C34 Chemicals (Table KF30)
6669.M6 Motor vehicles (Table KF30)
6669.P48 Petroleum (Table KF30)
6669.R85 Rum (Table KF30)
6669.S83 Steel (Table KF30)
6669.W66 Wool (Table KF30)

Customs administration

6676-6695 General. Procedure. Remedies (Table KF1)
6696 Administration. Customs Service (Table KF6)
6696.5 Customhouse brokers (Table KF6)

KF UNITED STATES (GENERAL) KF

Public finance
National revenue
Particular sources of revenue
Tariff. Trade agreements. Customs
Customs administration
General. Procedure. Remedies -- Continued
6698 Customs Court. Court of Customs Appeals. Court of Customs and Patent Appeals (Table KF6, modified)
6698.A48 Court rules. By date
6698.A7 Administrative documents
6699 Enforcement. Criminal law. Smuggling (Table KF6)
Special topics
6701 Drawbacks (Table KF6)
Exemptions. Duty-free imports
6704 General (Table KF6)
Particular commodities see KF6669.A+
6705 Foreign trade zones (Table KF6)
6708.A-Z Other, A-Z
6708.A66 Appraisal of goods (Table KF7)
6708.D8 Dumping. Antidumping duties (Table KF7)
6708.O75 Origin, Rules of (Table KF7)
6708.P7 Preferences, Tariff (Table KF7)
Tariff preferences see KF6708.P7
State and local finance
6720 General (Table KF6)
6722 Budget. Expenditure control. Auditing and accounting (Table KF6)
6724 Public debts. Securities. Bonds (Table KF6)
Particular sources of revenue
6730 State and local taxation (Table KF6)
Other sources of revenue
6733 Federal grants-in-aid (Table KF6)
Federal payments in lieu of real property taxes see KF6761.3.P8
State finance
6735 General. Administration (Table KF6)
Jurisdiction. Limitations on state taxing power
6736 General (Table KF6)
6738.A-Z Particular taxes and classes of taxpayers, A-Z
6738.B2 Banks (Table KF7)
Extractive industries see KF6738.M56
6738.F3 Federal employees (Table KF7)
6738.F35 Federal government (Table KF7)
6738.I5 Interstate commerce (Table KF7)
6738.M56 Mining. Extractive industries. Severance tax (Table KF7)

Public finance
State and local finance
State finance
Jurisdiction. Limitations on state taxing power
Particular taxes and classes of taxpayers, A-Z --
Continued
Severance tax see KF6738.M56

6740	Budget. Expenditure control. Auditing and accounting (Table KF6)
6742	Investment of public funds (Table KF6)
6744	Public debts. Securities. Bonds (Table KF6)
	Particular sources of revenue
	Taxation
6750	General (Table KF6)
	Particular taxes
6752	Income tax (Table KF6)
6753	Payroll deduction. Withholding tax (Table KF6)
6755	Corporation tax (Table KF6)
6758	Estate and death taxes (Table KF6)
	Property taxes. Taxation of capital
6759	General (Table KF6)
6759.5	Assessment (Table KF6)
	Real property taxes
	Ad valorem taxes upon real estate
	Including works on both state and local taxation
6760	General (Table KF6)
6760.5	Assessment. Land valuation (Table KF6)
	Particular kinds of land, tax-exempt lands, special modes of taxation
6761	Charitable, religious, educational, and other nonprofit organizations
6761.A1	General (Table KF7)
6761.A3-Z	Particular kinds, A-Z
6761.C4	Church lands (Table KF7)
6761.S3	School lands (Table KF7)
6761.3.A-Z	Other, A-Z
6761.3.F2	Farm land (Table KF7)
6761.3.F6	Forest land. Forest yield taxes (Table KF7)
6761.3.H6	Homesteads (Table KF7)
6761.3.P8	Public lands. Federally-owned real property. Federal payments in lieu of taxation. Shared revenue (Table KF7)
	Business taxes. Business property taxes. Licenses
6763	General (Table KF6)
	Particular lines of business
6763.4	Insurance companies (Table KF6)

Public finance
State and local finance
State finance
Particular sources of revenue
Taxation
Particular taxes
Property taxes. Taxation of capital
Business taxes. Business property taxes.
Licenses
Particular lines of business -- Continued
6763.7 Railroads (Table KF6)
6763.9.A-Z Other, A-Z
6763.9.C4 Chain stores (Table KF7)
Extractive industries see KF6763.9.M54
6763.9.M54 Mining. Extractive industries. Severance tax (Table KF7)
Severance tax see KF6763.9.M54
Personal property taxes
Ad valorem taxes upon personal property. Including works on both state and local taxation
6765 General (Table KF6)
Intangible property
6765.3 General (Table KF6)
6765.4 Mortgages (Table KF6)
6765.5.A-Z Other, A-Z
6765.5.S4 Securities. Stocks, bonds, etc. (Table KF7)
6765.8.A-Z Other personal property, A-Z
6765.8.A4 Aircraft (Table KF7)
6765.8.C65 Computer programs. Computer software (Table KF7)
6765.8.M3 Machinery. Equipment (Table KF7)
Excise taxes. Sales taxes. Use taxes
6767 General (Table KF6)
6768.A-Z By commodity, transaction, etc., A-Z
Automobiles see KF6768.M6
6768.C66 Computer services (Table KF7)
6768.E43 Electronic commerce. Internet sales (Table KF7)
Gambling see KF6768.W2
Horse racing see KF6768.W2
Internet sales see KF6768.E43
6768.M25 Mail-order business (Table KF7)
6768.M3 Metal ores (Table KF7)
6768.M57 Motor fuels (Table KF7)
6768.M6 Motor vehicles (Table KF7)
6768.W2 Wagering. Horse racing (Table KF7)

Public finance
State and local finance
State finance
Particular sources of revenue -- Continued

6769.A-Z	Other sources of revenue, A-Z
	Local finance
6770	General (Table KF6)
6772	Budget. Expenditure control. Auditing and accounting (Table KF6)
6775	Local government debts. Municipal bonds (Table KF6)
	Particular sources of revenue
	Taxation
6780	General. Tax powers of municipalities (Table KF6)
	Particular taxes
6782	Income tax (Table KF6)
	Property taxes
6784	Real property tax (Table KF6)
6785	Special assessments (Table KF6)
	Retail sales tax. Excise taxes
6788	General (Table KF6)
6789.A-Z	By commodity, A-Z
6789.M6	Motor vehicles (Table KF7)
6790.A-Z	Other sources of revenue, A-Z
6790.I55	Impact fees (Table KF7)
	Particular kinds of local jurisdiction
6793	Counties (Table KF6)
6794	Cities (Table KF6)
6795	Special districts (Table KF6)
	Particular types of districts are classed with subject, individual districts under the jurisdiction from which they derive their authority
	School districts see KF4127
	National defense. Military law
7201-7210	Comprehensive. General (Table KF2)
	Wartime and emergency legislation
	For war labor disputes see KF3444+
	For economic controls see KF5901+
7220	General (Table KF6)
7221	18th and 19th centuries. Early 20th century (Table KF6)
7222	1916-1939 (Table KF6)
	1939-1945
7224	General (Table KF6)
7224.5	Japanese American internment (Table KF6)
7225	1945- (Table KF6)
	The military establishment. Armed Forces
7250	General (Table KF6)
7252	Organization and administration. Department of Defense

National defense. Military law
The military establishment. Armed Forces -- Continued
Armed Forces
Comprehensive. General
General works see KF7252
Conscription. Draft. Selective Service

7263	General (Table KF6)
	Deferment. Exemptions. Disqualification
7265	General (Table KF6)
7266.A-Z	Particular groups, A-Z
7266.A4	Agricultural occupations. Farm labor (Table KF7)
7266.C6	Conscientious objectors (Table KF7)
7268.A-Z	Special topics, A-Z
7268.A5	Aliens (Table KF7)
7268.L6	Loyalty-security groups (Table KF7)

Personnel. Services

7270	General (Table KF6)
7271	Enlistment. Recruiting (Table KF6)
7272	Discharge (Table KF6)
7273	Education and training (Table KF6)
	Academies. Schools. Courses of instruction
7273.5	General (Table KF6)
7273.55.A-Z	Particular schools, A-Z
	Pay, allowances, benefits
7274	General (Table KF6)
7275	Retirement pensions (Table KF6)
	War veterans' pensions see KF7701+
7276	Disability pensions and benefits (Table KF6)
7277	Service insurance. Indemnity (Table KF6)
7278	Housing. Barracks (Table KF6)
7279	Medical care (Table KF6)
7280	Uniform regulations. Wearing of decorations and medals (Table KF6)
	Service regulations only
	Cf. KF5154 Military decorations and awards
7285	Officers (Table KF6)
	Including appointments, promotions, retirement
7287	Enlisted personnel (Table KF6)
7288	Reserves (Table KF6)
7289	Women's services (Table KF6)
	Militia, National Guard (Army) see KF7330
	Militia, National Guard (Air Force) see KF7430
7291	Civilian personnel (Table KF6)
7295.A-Z	Special services, A-Z
7296	Equipment. Weapons. Plants (Table KF6)
7298	Hospitals (Table KF6)

Particular branches of service

National defense. Military law
The military establishment. Armed Forces
Armed Forces
Particular branches of service -- Continued
Army
Organization. Administration. Department of the Army

7305	General (Table KF6)
	Particular offices
7307	Judge Advocate General (Table KF6)
7307.5.A-Z	Other, A-Z
	Personnel. Services
7310	General (Table KF6)
7311	Enlistment. Recruiting (Table KF6)
7312	Discharge (Table KF6)
	Education and training
7313	General (Table KF6)
	Academies. Schools. Courses of instruction
7313.5	General (Table KF6)
7313.55.A-Z	Particular schools, A-Z
7313.55.J8	Judge Advocate General's School (Table KF7)
	Pay, allowances, benefits
7314	General (Table KF6)
7315	Retirement pensions (Table KF6)
	War veterans' pensions see KF7701+
7316	Disability pensions and benefits (Table KF6)
7317	Service insurance. Indemnity (Table KF6)
7318	Housing. Barracks (Table KF6)
7319	Medical care (Table KF6)
7320	Uniform regulations. Wearing of decorations and medals (Table KF6)
	Service regulations only
	Cf. KF5154 Military decorations and awards
7325	Officers (Table KF6)
	Including appointments, promotions, retirement
7327	Enlisted personnel (Table KF6)
7328	Reserves (Table KF6)
7329	Women's services (Table KF6)
7330	Militia. National Guard (Table KF6)
	Including works on the National Guard (Army and Air Force) in general
7331	Civilian personnel (Table KF6)
7335.A-Z	Special services, A-Z
7335.E5	Corps of Engineers (Table KF7)
7335.Q2	Quartermaster Corps (Table KF7)
7335.S4	Signal Corps (Table KF7)
7335.S85	Surgeon General's Office (Table KF7)

National defense. Military law
The military establishment. Armed Forces
Armed Forces
Particular branches of service
Army -- Continued

7336	Equipment. Weapons. Plants (Table KF6)
7338	Hospitals (Table KF6)

Navy
Organization. Administration. Department of the Navy

7345	General (Table KF6)
	Particular offices
7347	Judge Advocate General (Table KF6)
7347.5.A-Z	Other, A-Z
	Personnel. Services
7350	General (Table KF6)
7351	Enlistment. Recruiting (Table KF6)
7352	Discharge (Table KF6)
	Education and training
7353	General (Table KF6)
	Academies. Schools. Courses of instruction
7353.5	General (Table KF6)
7353.55.A-Z	Particular schools, A-Z
	Pay, allowances, benefits
7354	General (Table KF6)
7355	Retirement pensions (Table KF6)
	War veterans' pensions see KF7701+
7356	Disability pensions and benefits (Table KF6)
7357	Service insurance. Indemnity (Table KF6)
7358	Housing. Barracks (Table KF6)
7359	Medical care (Table KF6)
7360	Uniform regulations. Wearing of decorations and medals (Table KF6)
	Service regulations only
	Cf. KF5154 Military decorations and awards
7365	Officers (Table KF6)
	Including appointments, promotions, retirement
7367	Enlisted personnel (Table KF6)
7368	Reserves (Table KF6)
7369	Women's services (Table KF6)
7371	Civilian personnel (Table KF6)
7375.A-Z	Special services, A-Z
7375.M3	Medical Department (Table KF7)
7376	Equipment. Weapons. Plants (Table KF6)
7378	Hospitals (Table KF6)
	Marine Corps
7385	Organization. Administration (Table KF6)
	Personnel. Services

National defense. Military law
The military establishment. Armed Forces
Armed Forces
Particular branches of service
Marine Corps
Personnel. Services -- Continued

7390	General (Table KF6)
7390.1	Enlistment. Recruiting (Table KF6)
7391	Uniform regulations. Wearing of decorations and medals (Table KF6)
7395	Officers (Table KF6)
	Including appointments, promotions, retirement

Air Force
Organization. Administration. Department of the Air Force

7405	General (Table KF6)
	Particular offices
7407	Judge Advocate General (Table KF6)
7407.5.A-Z	Other, A-Z
	Personnel. Services
7410	General (Table KF6)
7411	Enlistment. Recruiting (Table KF6)
7412	Discharge (Table KF6)
	Education and training
7413	General (Table KF6)
	Academies. Schools. Courses of instruction
7413.5	General (Table KF6)
7413.55.A-Z	Particular schools, A-Z
	Pay, allowances, benefits
7414	General (Table KF6)
7415	Retirement pensions (Table KF6)
	War veterans' pensions see KF7701+
7416	Disability pensions and benefits (Table KF6)
7417	Service insurance. Indemnity (Table KF6)
7418	Housing. Barracks (Table KF6)
7419	Medical care (Table KF6)
7420	Uniform regulations. Wearing of decorations and medals (Table KF6)
	Service regulations only
	Cf. KF5154 Military decorations and awards
7425	Officers (Table KF6)
	Including appointments, promotions, retirement
7427	Enlisted personnel (Table KF6)
7428	Reserves (Table KF6)
7429	Women's services (Table KF6)
7430	Air National Guard
7431	Civilian personnel (Table KF6)

National defense. Military law
The military establishment. Armed Forces
Armed Forces
Particular branches of service
Air Force
Personnel. Services -- Continued

Number	Description
7435.A-Z	Special services, A-Z
7436	Equipment. Weapons. Plants (Table KF6)
7438	Hospitals (Table KF6)
	Coast Guard
7445	Organization. Administration (Table KF6)
	Personnel. Services
7450	General (Table KF6)
7451	Enlistment. Recruiting (Table KF6)
7452	Discharge (Table KF6)
	Education and training
7453	General (Table KF6)
	Academies. Schools. Courses of instruction
7453.5	General (Table KF6)
7453.55.A-Z	Particular schools, A-Z
	Pay, allowances, benefits
7454	General (Table KF6)
7455	Retirement pensions (Table KF6)
	War veterans' pensions see KF7701+
7456	Disability pensions and benefits (Table KF6)
7457	Service insurance. Indemnity (Table KF6)
7458	Housing. Barracks (Table KF6)
7459	Medical care (Table KF6)
7460	Uniform regulations. Wearing of decorations and medals (Table KF6)
	Service regulations only
	Cf. KF5154 Military decorations and awards
7465	Officers (Table KF6)
	Including appointments, promotions, retirement
7467	Enlisted personnel (Table KF6)
7468	Reserves (Table KF6)
7469	Women's services (Table KF6)
7471	Civilian personnel (Table KF6)
7475.A-Z	Special services, A-Z
7476	Equipment. Weapons. Plants (Table KF6)
7478	Hospitals (Table KF6)
	Auxiliary services during war or emergency
	Merchant Marine
7485	Organization. Administration (Table KF6)
	Personnel. Services
7488	General (Table KF6)
	Pay, allowances, benefits

National defense. Military law
The military establishment. Armed Forces
Auxiliary services during war or emergency
Merchant Marine
Personnel. Services
General
Pay, allowances, benefits -- Continued

7488.5	General (Table KF6)
7488.7	Service insurance. Indemnity (Table KF6)
7590	Military discipline (Table KF6)
7595	Law enforcement. Criminal investigation (Table KF6)
7596	Provost Marshall General (Table KF6)
	Military criminal law and procedure
7601-7610	General. Comprehensive (Table KF2)
	Criminal law
7615	General (Table KF6)
7618.A-Z	Particular offenses, A-Z
7618.D3	Desertion. Absence without leave (Table KF7)
	Criminal procedure. Military justice
7620	General (Table KF6)
	Courts-martial
7625	General (Table KF6)
7628	Evidence (Table KF6)
	Particular branches of service
	Army
7633	Legislative documents
	General courts-martial. Orders. By department
7633.99	Serials
7634	Monographs. By date of publication
7636	Judge Advocates General's opinions
7640.A3	Official Judge Advocates General's manuals. By date
7640.A7-Z	General works
	Including evidence
	Trials
7641	Collections
7642.A-Z	Particular trials. By defendant, A-Z
	Navy
7646-7652	General (Table KF4)
7652.A-Z	Particular trials. By defendant, A-Z
	Marine Corps
7654	General (Table KF6)
	Trials
7654.3	Collections
7654.5.A-Z	Particular trials. By defendant, A-Z
	Air Force
7657	General (Table KF6)

National defense. Military law
The military establishment. Armed Forces
Military criminal law and procedure
Criminal procedure. Military justice
Courts-martial
Particular branches of service
Air Force -- Continued

Call Number	Description
7657.5.A-Z	Particular trials. By defendant, A-Z
7659	Coast Guard (Table KF6)
7661	Military commissions (Table KF6)
	Cf. KF5063 Martial law
7665	Appellate procedure (Table KF6)
7667	Court of Military Appeals (Table KF6)
7669	Military criminal justice abroad. Jurisdiction. Status of forces agreements (Table KF6)
	Execution of sentence. Penalties. Punishment
7675	Military prisons (Table KF6)
7677	Flogging (Table KF6)
7679	Probation and parole (Table KF6)
7680	Criminal status of members of the Armed Forces. Civil law relating to soldiers, sailors, airmen, etc. (Table KF6)
	For legal assistance to servicemen see KF337.5.A7
	For re-employment rights see KF3460
	For suffrage see KF4894
	Cf. KF5353 Retired military personnel (Civil service)
	Medals, decorations of honor, etc. (General)
	see KF5154
	For service regulations, see KF7280, (Armed Forces), KF7320, (Army), KF7360, (Navy), KF7420, (Air Force), KF7460, (Coast Guard)
	Other defense and intelligence agencies
7682	General (Table KF6)
7683.A-Z	Particular agencies, A-Z
7683.C3	Central Intelligence Agency (Table KF7)
7685	Civil defense (Table KF6)
7695.A-Z	Other topics, A-Z
7695.A7	Atomic warfare (Table KF7)
	Defense research and development see KF4280.D3
7695.S3	Security classification (Table KF7)
	War veterans
7701-7710	General. Pensions (Table KF2)
7711	Administration and procedure. Veterans Administration (Table KF6)
7713	Court of Veterans Appeals (Table KF6)
	Soldiers' homes
7716	General (Table KF6)
7717.A-Z	Particular homes. By city, A-Z

National defense. Military law
War veterans -- Continued
By period
18th and 19th centuries, early 20th century
General. Revolution

7721	Pensions (Table KF6)
7722	Other benefits (Table KF6)
	Civil War
7724	Pensions (Table KF6)
7725	Other benefits (Table KF6)
7726	Spanish American War (Table KF6)
7728	Other events (Table KF6)
	1916-1939
7731	Pensions (Table KF6)
7732	Other benefits (Table KF6)
	1939-1945
7735	General. Pensions (Table KF6)
7737	Survivors' benefits (Table KF6)
7739.A-Z	Other benefits, A-Z
7739.E3	Education. Training. Readjustment aid. GI Bill of Rights (Table KF7)
	Employment priority see KF3460
7739.F5	Financial assistance. Loans (Table KF7)
7739.H6	Housing aid (Table KF7)
7739.M3	Medical care (Table KF7)
7739.M35	Veterans' hospitals (Table KF7)
7745-7749	1945-
7745	General. Pensions (Table KF6)
7747	Survivors' benefits (Table KF6)
7749.A-Z	Other benefits, A-Z
7749.E3	Education. Training. Readjustment aid. GI Bill of Rights (Table KF7)
	Employment priority see KF3460
7749.F5	Financial assistance. Loans (Table KF7)
7749.H6	Housing aid (Table KF7)
	Medical care
7749.M3	General (Table KF7)
7749.M35	Veterans' hospitals (Table KF7)
7755.A-Z	Particular groups and classes, A-Z
	Indians
	General. Collective
	Federal law
	General
8201.A1	Bibliography

KF UNITED STATES (GENERAL) KF

Indians
General. Collective
Federal law
General -- Continued

Call Number	Description
8201.A3	Periodicals
	Class here periodicals consisting primarily of informative materials (newsletters, bulletins, etc.)
	For periodicals consisting predominantly of legal articles, regardless of subject matter and jurisdiction, see K1+
8201.A55	Legislative documents
8202	Treaties. By date
	Statutes
8202.8	Serials
8203	Monographs. By date
8203.36	Collections of summaries of cases ("Digests" of cases decided by courts or regulatory agencies). By editor or title
8203.5	Regulations. By date
8203.6	Encyclopedias. Law dictionaries
8204	Rulings. By date
8204.5	Casebooks. Readings
	General works
8205.A2	Collected papers and essays. Symposia
8205.A7-.Z8	Treatises. Monographs
8205.Z9	Compends. Outlines
8205.Z95	Works on comparative and uniform state and local law
	Land laws see KF5660+
8208	Cases. Claims (Table KF6)
	Including works on the Indian Claims Commission
8210.A-Z	Other topics, A-Z
	Acknowledgement of tribes by the Federal government see KF8210.R32
8210.A53	Aged. Older Indians (Table KF7)
8210.A57	Antiquities (Table KF7)
	Including human remains
	Casinos see KF8210.G35
8210.C4	Child support (Table KF7)
8210.C45	Children (Table KF7)
8210.C5	Civil rights (Table KF7)
	Including non-discrimination
8210.C6	Commerce (Table KF7)
8210.C7	Criminal law (Table KF7)
	Including conflict of laws and jurisdiction
8210.E3	Education (Table KF7)
8210.G35	Gambling. Casinos (Table KF7)
	Government purchasing and procurement see KF8210.P8

Indians
General. Collective
Federal law
Other topics, A-Z -- Continued
Human remains see KF8210.A57
8210.I57 Intellectual property (Table KF7)
8210.J8 Jurisdiction (Table KF7)
8210.M43 Medical care (Table KF7)
8210.N37 Natural resources (Table KF7)
Older Indians see KF8210.A53
8210.P7 Probate law and practice. Wills (Table KF7)
8210.P8 Public contracts. Government purchasing and procurement (Table KF7)
Racism see KF8210.C5
8210.R32 Recognition of tribes by the Federal government (Table KF7)
8210.R37 Religious liberty (Table KF7)
8210.R4 Revenue sharing (Table KF7)
8210.S84 Suffrage (Table KF7)
8210.T3 Taxation (Table KF7)
8210.T6 Trust funds (Table KF7)
Including tribal trust funds
Tribal law
8220 General (Table KF6)
8221 Organic laws
8224.A-Z Special topics, A-Z
8224.C6 Courts. Procedure (Table KF7)
8224.L2 Land tenure (Table KF7)
8225 Administration. Office of Indian Affairs. Bureau of Indian Affairs (Table KF6)
8225.5 Courts of Indian Offenses (Table KF6)
8228.A-Z Particular groups or tribes, A-Z
Under each:
.xA2-.xA3 *Federal law*
Including treaties, statutes, regulations
.xA2-.xA29 *Serials*
.xA3 *Monographs. By date of publication*
.xA4-.xA5 *Tribal law*
Including treaties, constitutions, statutes
.xA4-.xA49 *Serials*
.xA5 *Monographs. By date of publication*
.xA6-.xZ *General works*
For Cutter numbers see E99.A+

KF UNITED STATES (GENERAL) KF

Courts. Procedure

American Judicature Society see KF294.A4

8700	Administration of justice. Organization of the judiciary (Table KF6, modified)
8700.A16	Society publications
8700.A17	Congresses and conferences. By date
8700.A19	Directories
	Department of Justice, Attorney General see KF5106+
	History see KF350+
	Judicial statistics see KF180+
	Judicial councils. Judicial conference
8705	General (Table KF6)
8707	State judicial councils
8709	Judicial impact statements
	Court organization and procedure
8711-8720	General (Table KF2)
	Special aspects
	Conduct of court proceedings. Decorum
8725	General (Table KF6)
8726	Broadcasting of court proceedings (Table KF6)
	Including television or radio broadcasting
8727	Congestion and delay (Table KF6)
8729	Foreign judgments (Table KF6)
8731	Judicial assistance (Table KF6)
	For judicial assistance in criminal matters see KF9760
	Letters rogatory see KF8956
	Administration and management
8732	General (Table KF6)
8732.5	Finance (Table KF6)
8732.7	Office equipment and supplies (Table KF6)
	Records management
8733	General (Table KF6)
8733.3	Court records on microfilm (Table KF6)
8733.5	Printing and filing of briefs and other records (Table KF6)
8733.7	Security measures (Table KF6)
8734	Rulemaking power (Table KF6)
8735	State and federal jurisdiction (Table KF6)
8736	State courts (Table KF6)
8737	Local courts (Table KF6)
	Particular courts
	Supreme Court
8741-8742	General. History (Table KF5)
	Biography of justices
8744	Collective

KF UNITED STATES (GENERAL) KF

Courts. Procedure
Court organization and procedure
Particular courts
Supreme Court
General. History
Biography of justices -- Continued

8745.A-Z Individual justices, A-Z

Under each:

.xA3 *Autobiography*

If necessary to expand because of translations or more than one entry, use .xA3-.xA39

.xA4-.xA49 *Letters. Correspondence*

.xA4 *General collections. By date of publication*

.xA41-.xA49 *Collections of letters to particular individuals, by correspondent (alphabetically)*

> *Correspondence on a particular subject is classed with the subject*

.xA5-.xZ *Biography*

Including nominations and appointments

8748 Criticism

For decisions on particular subject, see subject Cf. KF379+ Jurisprudence

Courts of appeals. Circuit courts of appeals

8750 General (Table KF6)

By circuit

8750.5 District of Columbia Circuit (Table KF6)

> Class here works published after August 1, 1970 For works published before July 29, 1970, see KFD1712

8751 Federal Circuit (Table KF6)

8752 Other circuits. By number (Table KF6)

District courts. Circuit courts

8754 General (Table KF6 modified)

8754.A72 Court records. By initial date of period covered

8755.A-Z By district, A-Z

> Subarrange each by Table KF7 modified as follows: .xA7 Court records. By period or date; .xA72-.xZ9 General works. Treatises

8755.D56 District Court for the District of Columbia (Table KF7 modified)

> Class here works published after August 1, 1970 For works published before July 29, 1970, see KFD1716

KF UNITED STATES (GENERAL) KF

Courts. Procedure
Court organization and procedure
Particular courts
District courts. Circuit courts
By district, A-Z
District Court for the District of Columbia -- Continued
8755.D56A6 Court records. By period or date
8755.D56A7-.D56Z9 General works. Treatises
8757 Older courts
Cf. KF350+ History
Courts of special jurisdiction
8759 General (Table KF6)
8760.A-Z Court of Claims
For reports see KF125.C5+
For procedure see KF9070
8760.A25 Legislative documents. By date
8760.A3 Statutes. By date
Court rules see KF9070.A459
8760.A5 Dockets. Calendars. By date
8760.A7 Administration and organization. Regulations. By date
8760.A8-.A89 Official reports and monographs
8760.A9-Z Treatises. Monographs
8764 Court of Claims and Patent Appeals (Table KF6)
For reports see KF125.C8+
For patent litigation see KF3155+
For customs procedures see KF6676+
Commerce Court see KF2184
8768.A-Z Consular courts
8768.A1 General (Table KF7)
8768.A5-Z By region or country, A-Z
e.g.
8768.C4 China (Table KF7)
Customs Court see KF6698
Domestic relations courts see KF505.5
Emergency Court of Appeals see KF6037.5+
Housing courts see KF595
Mental health courts see KF3828.5
Probate courts see KF765+
8769 Small claims courts (Table KF6)
Judicial officers. Court employees
8770 General (Table KF6)
Directories see KF8700.A19
8771 Administrative offices. Clerks of court (Table KF6)
Judges
8775 General (Table KF6)
8776 Appointment. Tenure. Retirement (Table KF6)
8777 Salaries. Pensions. Survivors' benefits (Table KF6)

Courts. Procedure
Court organization and procedure
Judicial officers. Court employees
Judges -- Continued

8778	Rating (Table KF6)
8779	Discipline. Judicial ethics (Table KF6)
	Procedures for removal. Impeachment
8781	General (Table KF6)
8782.A-Z	Particular cases. By respondent, A-Z
	Continuing education for judges see KF276
	Recall see KF4884
8785	State court judges (Table KF6)
8786	Local court judges (Table KF6)
8788	Lay judges (Table KF6)
	Government representatives. Department of Justice representatives
	For Attorney General see KF5106+
8790	General (Table KF6)
8792	United States commissioners/magistrates. Commissioners of circuit courts (Table KF6, modified)
8792.A595	Registers
8792.5	Solicitors General (Table KF6)
8793	United States attorneys (Table KF6)
8794	United States marshals (Table KF6)
	Referees, masters in chancery see KF8986
	Referees in bankruptcy see KF1530.R35
8795	Attorneys (Table KF6)
	Legal aid societies see KF336+
	Guardians ad litem see KF553
8797	Notaries (Table KF6)
8798	Sheriffs (Table KF6)
8799	Constables (Table KF6)
8800	Justices of the peace (Table KF6)
8802	Coroners. Medical examiners (Table KF6)
	Cf. RA1001+ Medical jurisprudence
	Medical evidence see KF8964
8805	Court reporters (Table KF6)
	For technique of law reporting see KF255
8806	Translators (Table KF6)
8806.5	Law clerks (Table KF6)
8807	Other (Table KF6)
	Civil procedure
	General
	Including common law and equity
8810	Bibliography. Surveys of legal research

KF UNITED STATES (GENERAL) KF

Courts. Procedure
Civil procedure
General -- Continued

8810.5 Periodicals
Class here periodicals consisting primarily of informative materials (newsletters, bulletins, etc.)
For periodicals consisting predominantly of legal articles see K1+

8811 Legislative documents. By date
Statutes
Collections

8815.A19-.A199 Serials
8815.A2 Monographs. By date of publication
8815.A3-.A319 Particular acts
Arrange chronologically, by means of successive Cutter numbers, according to date of original enactment or revision of law
Under each:
.xA15 *Compilations of legislative histories*
.xA2 *Unannotated texts. By date of publication*
.xA3-.xZ *Annotated editions. Commentaries. By author of commentary or annotations*

Court rules
General. Comprehensive
Collections

8816.A19-.A199 Serials
8816.A2 Monographs. By date of publication
8816.A23 Citators to rules
8816.A25 Drafts. By date
8816.A3-.A319 Particular rules
Arrange chronologically, by means of successive Cutter numbers, according to date of adoption or revision of rules
Under each:
.xA15 *Compilations of legislative histories. By date of publication*
.xA2 *Unannotated texts. By date of publication*
.xA3-.xZ7 *Annotated editions. Commentaries. By author of commentary or annotations*
.xZ8-.xZ89 *Digests*

District courts

8820 General
Collections

KF UNITED STATES (GENERAL) KF

Courts. Procedure
Civil procedure
General
Court rules
District courts
General
Collections -- Continued

8820.A19-.A199	Serials
8820.A2	Monographs. By date of publication
8820.A23	Citators to rules
8820.A25	Drafts. By date
8820.A3-.A319	Particular rules

Arrange chronologically, by means of successive Cutter numbers, according to date of adoption or revision of rules

Under each:

.xA15	*Compilations of legislative histories. By date of publication*
.xA2	*Unannotated texts. By date of publication*
.xA3-.xZ7	*Annotated editions. Commentaries. By author of commentary or annotations*
.xZ8-.xZ89	*Digests*

8821.A-Z	Particular courts. By district, A-Z

Under each:

	Collections
.xA19-.xA199	*Serials*
.xA2	*Monographs. By date of publication*
	Particular rules
.xA3	*Unannotated texts. By date of publication*
.xA5-.xZ49	*Annotated editions.*
	Commentaries. By author of commentary or annotations
.xZ5	*Indexes. By date of publication*

8821.D5	District Court for the District of Columbia

Class here works published after August 1, 1970
For works published before July 29, 1970, see KFD1729.5

Chancery rules, equity rules see KF8851.A5+
Admiralty rules see KF1111.A4+
Court of Claims see KF9070.A459
Courts of Appeals see KF9052.A458+
Supreme Court see KF9056

Courts. Procedure
Civil procedure
General -- Continued

Call Number	Subject
8830	Reports of decisions (Table KF31)
	e.g. Federal rules decisions
8835	Encyclopedias
8836	Form books
8837	Looseleaf services
8839	Casebooks
	General works
8840.A2	Collected papers and essays
8840.A5-Z	Treatises. Monographs
8841	Compends
8845	Nisi prius procedure
8851-8855	Equity practice and procedure (Table KF3, modified)
	Court rules
8851.A5	Unannotated. By date
8851.A6-Z	Annotated
8858	Jurisdiction. Venue (Table KF6)
8860	Removal of causes (Table KF6)
8861	Disqualification of judges (Table KF6)
	Action
8863	General
8863.A3	Forms
8863.A5-Z	Treatises. Monographs
8865	Process and service (Table KF6)
	Pleading and motions
8866-8870	General. Pleading (Table KF3)
8875	Motions (Table KF6)
8876	Special pleadings (Table KF6)
	Defenses and objections (Exceptions)
8881	Limitation of actions (Table KF6)
8882	Lis pendens (Table KF6)
8885	Counterclaim and cross claim (Table KF6)
8887	Frivolous suits (Table KF6)
8888	Confession of judgment (Table KF6)
	Parties
8890	General (Table KF6)
8891	Special aspects
	United States as party see KF9065+
8893	Joinder of claims and remedies (Table KF6)
8894	Joinder of parties (Table KF6)
8895	Interpleader (Table KF6)
8896	Class action. Aggregate litigation (Table KF6)
8896.5	Citizen suits (Table KF6)
	Pretrial procedure
	General. Deposition and discovery. Interrogatories

Courts. Procedure
Civil procedure
Pretrial procedure
General. Deposition and discovery. Interrogatories --
Continued

Call Number	Description
8900.A1	Bibliography
8900.A15	Periodicals
	Class here periodicals consisting primarily of informative materials (newsletters, bulletins, etc.)
	For periodicals consisting predominantly of legal articles, regardless of subject matter and jurisdiction see K1+
8900.A3	Forms
8900.A4	Casebooks. Readings
8900.A5-Z	Treatises. Monographs
8902.A-Z	Special topics, A-Z
	For settlement see KF9084
8902.E42	Electronic discovery
	Trial
8910	General
	Trial practice. Trial tactics
8911-8915	General (Table KF3)
8918	Moot court cases
8920	Cross-examination
8922	Forensic psychology
8923	Opening statements (Table KF6)
8924	Summation. Closing argument (Table KF6)
8925.A-Z	Particular types of cases or claims, A-Z
8925.A9	Aviation accidents (Table KF7)
8925.B84	Building and construction contracts (Table KF7)
	Business see KF8925.C55
	Child abuse (Civil proceedings) see KF8925.C45
8925.C45	Child welfare (Table KF7)
	Including non-criminal child abuse
	Civil RICO actions see KF9375
8925.C5	Civil rights (Table KF7)
	Including claims for damages resulting from state action or government misconduct
8925.C55	Commercial. Business (Table KF7)
	Construction contracts see KF8925.B84
8925.C58	Contracts (Table KF7)
8925.C6	Corporations (Table KF7)
8925.D36	Damages (Table KF7)
	Disability insurance see KF8925.S63
8925.D5	Discrimination (Table KF7)
8925.E4	Emigration and immigration (Table KF7)

Courts. Procedure
Civil procedure
Trial
Trial practice. Trial tactics
Particular types of cases or claims, A-Z -- Continued

Call Number	Subject
8925.E5	Environmental actions (Table KF7)
	Cf. KF8925.T69 Toxic torts
	Immigration see KF8925.E4
	Intellectual property see KF2983
8925.I57	Insurance (Table KF7)
8925.L33	Labor law (Table KF7)
8925.L5	Libel and slander (Table KF7)
8925.M3	Malpractice (Table KF7)
8925.N4	Negligence (Table KF7)
8925.N45	Negotiable instruments (Table KF7)
	Non-criminal child abuse see KF8925.C45
8925.P4	Personal injuries (Table KF7)
8925.P7	Products liability (Table KF7)
8925.P8	Public contracts (Table KF7)
8925.R4	Real property (Table KF7)
	Slander see KF8925.L5
8925.S63	Social security. Disability insurance (Table KF7)
8925.S7	Stockholder suits (Table KF7)
8925.T38	Tax shelters (Table KF7)
8925.T67	Torts (Table KF7)
	Cf. KF8925.T69 Toxic torts
8925.T69	Toxic torts (Table KF7)
8925.T7	Traffic accidents. Traffic violations. Drunk driving (Table KF7)
	Jury trial of right, trial by court see KF8975
	Evidence
	Cf. KF1530.E87 Bankruptcy
	Cf. KF9421 Evidence tampering
8931-8935	General (Table KF3)
8936	Special aspects
	Burden of proof
8939	General (Table KF6)
8940.A-Z	Special topics, A-Z
8940.P7	Presumptions. Judicial notice. Prima-facie evidence (Table KF7)
8940.P75	Proof of foreign law (Table KF7)
	Particular claims or actions
	For works on evidence before such courts of special jurisdiction as are classed with a particular subject, see the respective subject; e.g., Evidence before probate courts, see KF765
8944	Torts. Negligence. Res ipsa loquitur (Table KF6)

Courts. Procedure
Civil procedure
Trial
Evidence -- Continued
Particular kinds

Number	Description
8946	Circumstantial (Table KF6)
	For techniques of identification see HV8073+; RA1001+
	Cf. KF9666.5 Criminal evidence
	Documentary
8947	General (Table KF6)
8947.5	Electronic evidence. Digital evidence (Table KF6)
8948	Parol evidence. Aliunde (Table KF6)
	Witnesses
8950	General (Table KF6)
8952	Subpoena (Table KF6)
8954	Oath (Table KF6)
8956	Letters rogatory (Table KF6)
	Cf. KF8731 Judicial assistance
	Contempt of court see KF9415
	Privileged (confidential) communications
8958	General (Table KF6)
8959.A-Z	Particular relationships, A-Z
8959.A7	Attorney and client (Table KF7)
8959.C6	Confessional. Penitential communications (Table KF7)
8959.P4	Physician and patient (Table KF7)
8959.P7	Press (Table KF7)
8959.S6	Social worker and client (Table KF7)
8959.5.A-Z	Particular means of communication, A-Z
8959.5.T4	Telegrams (Table KF7)
	Expert evidence. Expert witnesses
8961	General (Table KF6)
	Particular kinds
8962	Lie detectors. Polygraph examinations (Table KF6)
8963	Identification of persons. Fingerprints. Blood grouping. Body measurements, etc.
8964	Medical evidence. Medical witnesses
8965	Psychiatric and psychological evidence (Table KF6)
8966	Computer animation evidence (Table KF6)
8967	Demonstrative evidence (Table KF6)
8968	Photographic evidence (Table KF6)
	Particular groups of expert witnesses
8968.15	Accountants (Table KF6)
8968.19	Business appraisers (Table KF6)

KF UNITED STATES (GENERAL) KF

Courts. Procedure
Civil procedure
Trial
Evidence
Particular kinds
Expert evidence. Expert witnesses
Particular groups of expert witnesses -- Continued

8968.23	Economists (Table KF6)
8968.25	Engineers (Table KF6)
8968.54	Linguists (Table KF6)
	Medical personnel see KF8964
	Mental health personnel see KF8965
8968.65	Real estate appraisers (Table KF6)
8968.66	Scientists (Table KF6)
8968.7	Social workers (Table KF6)
8968.75	Statisticians (Table KF6)
8968.77	Surveyors (Table KF6)
	Presumptions, judicial notice see KF8940.P7
	Admissibility and exclusion of evidence
8969	Hearsay (Table KF6)
	Jury and jurors
8971-8972	General (Table KF5)
	Special aspects
8975	Jury trial of right (Table KF6)
8977	Women jurors (Table KF6)
8979	Selection. Jury commissions (Table KF6)
8980	Ethics (Table KF6)
8982	Special verdicts and findings (Table KF6)
8984	Instructions to juries (Table KF6)
	For collected instructions see KF213.A+
	For individual instructions see KF389
8986	Special masters. Referees. Auditors. Examiners (Table KF6)
	Judgment
8990	General (Table KF6)
8992	Res judicata. Estoppel by judgment
8995	Costs. Fees. In forma pauperis (Table KF6)
	Legal aid see KF336+
8999	Summary judgment (Table KF6)
9000	Declaratory judgments (Table KF6)
9002	New trials (Table KF6)
	Recall of judgment see KF4884
	Remedies and special proceedings
9010	General (Table KF6)
9011	Habeas corpus (Table KF6)
9014	Injunctions. Provisional remedies (Table KF6)
	Labor injunctions see KF3435

KF UNITED STATES (GENERAL) KF

Courts. Procedure
Civil procedure
Remedies and special proceedings -- Continued
Interpleader see KF8895
9016 Receivers in equity (Table KF6)
Receivers in bankruptcy see KF1530.R3
Possessory actions, ejectment see KF652+
Replevin see KF720
Execution of judgment
9025 General (Table KF6)
9026 Attachment. Garnishment (Table KF6)
9029.A-Z Exemptions, A-Z
9029.L4 Life insurance proceeds (Table KF7)
9029.W2 Wages (Table KF7)
Extraordinary remedies
Including older remedies
9035 General (Table KF6)
Particular remedies
9036 Quo warranto
9037 Mandamus
Habeas corpus see KF9011
9038 Coram nobis
9039 Imprisonment for debt
Appellate procedure
9050 General (Table KF6)
Courts of Appeals
9052 General (Table KF6 modified)
Court rules
9052.A458 Serials
9052.A459 Monographs. By date
9052.5 District of Columbia Circuit (Table KF6 modified)
Class here works published after August 1, 1970
For works published before July 29, 1970, see
KFD1758
9052.5.A459 Court rules. By date
9053 Federal Circuit (Table KF6 modified)
9053.A459 Court rules. By date
9054 By circuit (1st, 2nd, etc.)
Under each Circuit Court of Appeals:
.A4 Court rules. By date
.A7-.Z8 Treatises. Monographs
.Z9 Compends. Outlines
Supreme Court
9056 Court rules
Collections
9056.A19-.A199 Serials
9056.A2 Monographs. By date of publication

Courts. Procedure
Civil procedure
Remedies and special proceedings
Appellate procedure
Courts of Appeals
Supreme Court
Court rules
Collections -- Continued

9056.A23	Citators to rules
9056.A25	Drafts. By date
9056.A3-.A319	Particular rules

Arrange chronologically, by means of successive Cutter numbers, according to date of adoption or revision of rules

Under each:

.xA15	*Compilations of legislative histories. By date of publication*
.xA2	*Unannotated texts. By date of publication*
.xA3-.xZ7	*Annotated editions. Commentaries. By author of commentary or annotations*
.xZ8-.xZ89	*Digests*

9057	Appeals (Table KF6)
9058	Certiorari (Table KF6)

Litigation with the United States as a party
For suability of the United States for torts see KF1321
For suability of states see KF1322

9065	General (Table KF6)
9066.A-Z	Special proceedings or topics, A-Z
9066.A5	Antitrust cases. Procedure under the Expediting Act of 1903 (Table KF7)
9070	Court of Claims (Table KF6, modified)
	For organization of Court of Claims see KF8760.A+
9070.A459	Court rules. By date

Proceedings relating to particular branches of the law or special subjects, or governed by special rules.
Noncontentious (ex-parte) jurisdiction
Cf. KF9066.A+ Litigation with the United States

9075	General

Admiralty see KF1111+
Bankruptcy see KF1527+
Condemnation procedure see KF5599
Copyright see KF3080
Military service claims see KF7711
Probate see KF765+
Tort claims procedure see KF1246+

Courts. Procedure
Civil procedure
Proceedings relating to particular branches of the law or special subjects ... Noncontentious (ex-parte) jurisdiction -- Continued
Workers' compensation see KF3611+
Judicial assistance see KF8731

9084	Negotiated settlement. Compromise (Table KF6)
	Including alternative dispute resolution
	Arbitration and award. Commercial arbitration
	For specific types of commercial or other arbitration, see the topic, e.g. KF1070 (Securities), KF902 (Construction contracts), KF505 (Domestic relations)
9085	General (Table KF6)
9086	American Arbitration Association
	Criminal law
	Cf. KF7601+ Military criminal law and procedure
	Cf. KF9771+ Juvenile criminal law and procedure
9201-9220	General. Comprehensive (Table KF1)
9223	Administration of criminal justice. Reform of criminal law, enforcement, and procedure (Table KF6)
	Special aspects
9223.4	Speedy trial
9223.5	Crime and publicity. "Trial by newspaper" (Table KF6)
	Cf. KF9415+ Contempt of court
	Punishment and penalties
9225	General (Table KF6)
	For theory and philosophy of criminal punishment, see subclass K, Criminal law, and Penology
	Cf. HV6001+ Criminology
9226	Habitual criminals. Recidivists
9227.A-Z	Particular penalties, A-Z
9227.C2	Capital punishment (Table KF7)
	Cf. subclass K
	Forfeitures, political disabilities see KF9747
	Loss of citizenship see KF4718
	Penal institutions see KF9730+
	Criminology
	see HV6001+ subclass K
	General principles
9230	Criminal jurisdiction (Conflict of criminal law) (Table KF6)
	Burden of proof see KF9660+
	Criminal liability
9235	General (Table KF8)
9236	Culpability. Mens rea. Criminal negligence (Table KF6)
9236.5	Criminal liability of juristic persons (Table KF6)
	Exemption from liability. Defenses

Criminal law
General principles
Criminal liability
Exemption from liability. Defenses -- Continued

Call Number	Topic
9240	General (Table KF6)
	Particular defenses
9241-9242	Insanity (Table KF5)
9243	Drunkenness (Table KF6)
9243.5	Poverty (Table KF6)
9244	Entrapment (Table KF6)
9244.5	Racism (Table KF6)
9245	Double jeopardy (Table KF6)
	Justification
9245.8	General
9246	Self-defense. Self-protection
9248	Other

Particular offenses
Federal statutory law and common-law offenses in general, including comparative state law
For criminal law of a particular state, see that state
General. Comprehensive

Call Number	Topic
9300.A3	Statutes. By date of publication
9300.A35	Indexes
9300.A8-Z	Treatises. Monographs
	Offenses against the person
9304	General (Table KF6)
	Homicide
9305	General (Table KF6)
9306	Murder
9309	Infanticide
9312	Lynching (Table KF6)
9315	Abortion. Procuring miscarriage (Table KF6)
	Class here works on the criminal aspects of abortion
	For works on the regulation of abortion see KF3771
9320	Assault and battery (Table KF6)
9322	Conjugal violence. Wife abuse. Husband abuse (Table KF6)
9323	Child abuse (Table KF6)
9324	Elder abuse (Table KF6)
9324.5	Stalking (Table KF6)
	Sexual offenses
9325	General (Table KF6)
	Including works on legal implications of sexual behavior in general
	Particular kinds
	Unnatural sexual intercourse
9327	General (Table KF6)

Criminal law
Particular offenses
Offenses against the person
Sexual offenses
Particular kinds
Unnatural sexual intercourse -- Continued

9328.A-Z	Particular offenses, A-Z
9328.B3	Bestiality (Table KF7)
9328.S6	Sodomy (Table KF7)
9329	Rape (Table KF6)
	Child molesting see KF9323
	Offenses against personal liberty
9332	Kidnapping. Abduction (Table KF6)
	For parental kidnapping see KF547+
9335	Peonage. Slavery (Table KF6)
9338	Shanghaiing (Table KF6)
9345	Libel. Slander. Defamation (Table KF6)
	Offenses against property
	Including works on white collar crime and offenses against the economic order in general
9350	General (Table KF6)
9351	Corporate corruption and bribery (Table KF6)
	Thievery
9352	Larceny (Table KF6)
9354	Theft of use (Table KF6)
9358	Receiving stolen goods (Table KF6)
9359	Intellectual property crimes (Table KF6)
	Including criminal violation of copyright, patent and trademark laws
9360	Embezzlement
	Fraud. False pretenses
9365	General (Table KF6)
	Particular
9367	Fraud by forgery. Bad checks (Table KF6)
9368	Insurance fraud (Table KF6)
9369	Securities fraud (Table KF6)
9370	Mail fraud (Table KF6)
9371	Automobile repair fraud (Table KF6)
	Threats. Extortion. Blackmail
9372	General (Table KF6)
9375	Racketeering. Organized crime (Table KF6)
	Including civil RICO actions
9377	Arson (Table KF6)
9379	Other
	Crimes against the government. Political crimes
9390	General (Table KF6)
	Particular

Criminal law
Particular crimes
Crimes against the government. Political crimes
Particular -- Continued

9392	Treason (Table KF6)
9394	Espionage (Table KF6)
9395	Sabotage (Table KF6)
9395.5	Criminal syndicalism (Table KF6)
9397	Sedition. Subversive activities (Table KF6)
9399	Other

Crimes against the public administration

9405	Contempt of Congress (Table KF6)
9409	Corruption and bribery (Table KF6)
	Cf. KF9351 Corporate corruption and bribery
9410	Violation of conflict-of-interest laws (Table KF6)

Offenses against the administration of justice

9415	Contempt of court (Table KF6)
9419	Judicial corruption (Table KF6)
9420	Perjury. Subornation of perjury (Table KF6)
9421	Evidence tampering (Table KF6)
9422	Escape from legal custody (Table KF6)

Offenses against public safety

9425	Crimes on the high seas (Table KF6)
9428	Riot (Table KF6)
9430	Terrorism (Table KF6)
	Sabotage see KF9395
	Traffic violation, drunk driving see KF2231

Crimes against public order and morality
Including crimes without victims

9434	General (Table KF6)
9435	Adultery (Table KF6)
9436	Bigamy (Table KF6)
9440	Gambling. Lotteries (Table KF6)
9444	Obscenity (Table KF6)
9445	Contraceptive devices (Table KF6)
	Cf. KF3766 Birth control
9448	Prostitution. Procuring (Table KF6)
	Including history ("white slave traffic")
9449	Human trafficking (Table KF6)
	Class here works on coerced transportation, transfer, or abduction of persons, especially women and children, for the purpose of exploitation.
	Including, but not limited to, forced prostitution or other forms of sexual exploitation, forced labor, child labor, debt bondage, practices similar to slavery, or removal of organs.

Criminal law
Particular crimes
Crimes against public order and morality -- Continued
9449.5 Human smuggling (Table KF6)
Class here works on smuggling of migrants by land, sea, and air in order to obtain a financial or other material benefit of the illegal entry.
9450 Vagrancy (Table KF6)
9452 Drunkenness (Table KF6)
Offenses against public property, public finance, and currency
9455 Counterfeiting. Forgery (Table KF6)
Customs crimes, smuggling see KF6699
9456 Illicit liquor traffic (Table KF6)
Tax evasion see KF6334
Offenses committed through the mail
9460 General. Postal offenses (Table KF6)
9461.A-Z Particular offenses, A-Z
Gambling see KF9440
Lotteries see KF9440
Mail fraud see KF9370
Obscenity see KF9444
Threats, extortion, blackmail see KF9372+
9479 Conspiracy (Table KF6)
Criminal procedure
9601-9620 General (Table KF1)
Administration of criminal justice see KF9223
Arrest and commitment. Rights of suspects
9625 General (Table KF6)
Habeas corpus see KF9011
9630 Searches and seizures (Table KF6)
9632 Bail. Pretrial release (Table KF6)
9635 Extradition. Interstate rendition (Table KF6)
Right to speedy trial see KF9223.4
9640 Indictment. Information. Public prosecutor (Table KF6)
9642 Grand jury (Table KF6)
For collected charges see KF213.A+
For individual charges see KF389
Arraignment. Preparation for trial
9645 General (Table KF6)
9646 Right to counsel. Public defenders (Table KF6, modified)
9646.A15 Directories. Periodicals
9650 Discovery (Table KF6)
9654 Procedure without trial. Plea bargaining. Pleas of guilty. Nolo contendere (Table KF6)
Trial
9655 General (Table KF8)

KF UNITED STATES (GENERAL) KF

Criminal procedure
Trial -- Continued

9656	Trial practice. Trial tactics (Table KF6)
9657	Moot court cases
9658	Cross-examination
	Evidence. Burden of proof
9660	General (Table KF8)
	Admission of evidence
9662	General (Table KF6)
9664	Confession (Table KF6)
9665	Informers (Table KF6)
9666	Lie detectors. Polygraph examinations (Table KF6)
9666.5	Means of identification. Fingerprints, footprints, toothprints, etc. (Table KF6) Including DNA fingerprinting
9667	Physical examinations. Blood tests, urine tests, etc. (Table KF6)
9668	Self-incrimination. Entrapment (Table KF6)
9670	Wiretapping. Electronic listening and recording devices (Table KF6)
	Witnesses
9672	General (Table KF6)
9673	Child witnesses (Table KF6)
9674	Expert evidence. Expert witnesses (Table KF6)
9677	Circumstantial evidence (Table KF6)
9678	Exculpatory evidence (Table KF6)
9680	Jury (Table KF6)
	Instructions to jury. Directed verdict
9682	General (Table KF6) For collected instructions see KF213.A+ For individual instructions see KF389
9685	Judgment. Sentence (Table KF6)
9688	New trials (Table KF6)
9690	Appeals. Appellate procedure (Table KF6)
	Special proceedings, extraordinary remedies see KF9010+
9695	Pardon (Table KF6)
(9701-9710)	Proceedings before juvenile courts see KF9771+
	Execution of sentence For history of punishment in the United States see KF9225
(9725)	Capital punishment see KF9227.C2
9728	Corrections (Table KF6)
	Imprisonment Cf. KF337.5.P7 Legal services for prisoners
9730	Prison administration. Prison discipline (Table KF6)

Criminal procedure
Execution of sentence
Imprisonment -- Continued

9731	Prisoners (Table KF6)
9733	Prison labor. Prison industries (Table KF6)
	Particular types of penal or correctional institutions
	Penitentiaries. Prisons
9735	General (Table KF6)
9736.A-Z	Particular institutions, A-Z
	Reformatories
9737	General (Table KF6)
9738.A-Z	Particular institutions, A-Z
	Prisons for women
9741	General (Table KF6)
9742.A-Z	Particular institutions, A-Z
	Juvenile detention homes see KF9825
9745	Fines (Table KF6)
9747	Forfeitures. Political disabilities (Table KF6)
	Loss of citizenship see KF4718
9750	Probation. Parole (Table KF6, modified)
9750.A155	Directories. By date
9750.5	Rehabilitation (Table KF6)
9750.7	Work release of prisoners (Table KF6)
9751	Criminal registration (Table KF6)
9754	Indeterminate sentence
9756	Judicial error. Compensation for judicial error
9760	Judicial assistance in criminal matters
	Extradition see KF9635
	Victims of crimes
9763	General (Table KF6)
	Compensation to victims of crimes see KF1328+
	Parties to actions in torts see KF1313
	Military criminal law and procedure see KF7601+
	Juvenile criminal law and procedure. Administration of juvenile justice
9771-9780	General (Table KF2)
	Juvenile courts
9786-9795	General (Table KF2 modified)
9787.9	Directories. By date
9797	Records management
	Criminal law
9800	General (Table KF6)
9802	Status offenders (Table KF6)
	Criminal procedure
9810	General (Table KF6)
9812	Trial of juveniles in adult courts (Table KF6)
9813	Right to counsel. Public defenders (Table KF6)

Juvenile criminal law and procedure. Administration of juvenile justice
Criminal procedure -- Continued
Trial

9815	General (Table KF6)
9817	Prosecution (Table KF6)
9820	Judgment. Sentence (Table KF6)
9822	Appeals. Appellate procedure (Table KF6)
	Execution of sentence
	Imprisonment
9825	Juvenile detention homes (Table KF6)
9827	Probation (Table KF6)

KFA UNITED STATES (ALABAMA) KFA

1-599	United States (Alabama) (Table KFA-KFZ modified)
	Law reports and related materials
45-45.9	Supreme Court (Table KF31 modified)
45	Reports
	Official series and predecessors
45.A19 1820	Minor
45.A19 1827	Stewart
45.A19 1831	Stewart and Porter
45.A19 1834	Porter
45.A2	Alabama Reports
45.A3-.A39	Unofficial series
45.A4	Defunct publications. By editor
45.A4S4	Shepard's Select cases
45.A4S5	Smith's Condensed reports
	Lower courts
 47-47.9	Various courts (Table KF31 modified)
47	Reports
47.A3-.A39	Unofficial series
47.A32	Alabama reporter (1977-)
48-48.9	Court of Appeals (Table KF31 modified)
48	Reports
48.A2	Official series

KFA UNITED STATES (ALASKA) KFA

1201-1799	United States (Alaska) (Table KFA-KFZ modified)
	Law reports and related materials
1245-1245.9	Supreme Court (Table KF31 modified)
1245	Reports
	Official editions
1245.A19	Alaska Federal Reports
1245.A2	Alaska Reports
1245.A3-.A39	Unofficial current series
1245.A33	Alaska Reporter 2d ser. (West, 1963-)

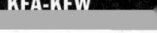

KFA UNITED STATES (ARIZONA) KFA

2401-2999	United States (Arizona) (Table KFA-KFZ modified)
	Law reports and related materials
2445-2445.9	Supreme Court (Table KF31 modified)
2445	Reports
	Official series
2445.A2 v. 1-13	Arizona reports (Territory, 1866-1911)
2445.A2 v. 14	Arizona reports (1911-)
	Lower courts
	Court of Appeals
2448-2448.9	General (Table KF31 modified)
2448	Reports
	Unofficial series
2448.A3	Arizona appeals reports (1965-)

KFA UNITED STATES (ARKANSAS) KFA

3601-4199	United States (Arkansas) (Table KFA-KFZ modified)
	Law reports and related materials
3645-3645.9	Supreme Court (Table KF31 modified)
3645	Reports
	Official series
3645.A2	Arkansas reports, (1837-)
3645.A4	Defunct publications
3645.A4A7	Arkansas law reporter (1911-1916)
	17 v.
3645.A4L3	Law reporter (1919-1944 [?])

KFC UNITED STATES (CALIFORNIA) KFC

United States (California)

1 Bibliography

Legislative documents

5 Collections. Serials

Bills

6 Collections

7 Digests

8 Calendars

Committee documents

Hearings

10.A-Z Joint. By committee or subcommittee, A-Z, and initial date of hearings

Senate

10.2.A-Z Serials. By committee or subcommittee, A-Z Subarrange by title

10.3.A-Z Monographs. By committee or subcommittee, A-Z, and initial date of hearing

10.4.A-Z Assembly. By committee or subcommittee, A-Z, and initial date of hearing

Reports

Class here only those reports issued to accompany specific bills when they are reported out of a committee to its parent legislative body after hearings have been held and/or the committee has considered and made its recommendations on the bill in question. Class other types of reports emanating from a legislative commitee with the appropriate topic.

Joint

10.6.A-Z Serials. By committee or subcommittee, A-Z Subarrange by title

10.62.A-Z Monographs. By committee or subcommittee, A-Z, and date of original publication

Senate

10.7.A-Z Serials. By committee or subcommittee, A-Z Subarrange by title

10.72.A-Z Monographs. By committee or subcommittee, A-Z, and date of original publication

Assembly

10.8.A-Z Serials. By committee or subcommittee, A-Z Subarrange by title

10.82.A-Z Monographs. By committee or subcommittee, A-Z, and date of original publication

Other legislative documents

12 Index to the proceedings

History of bills and resolutions. Legislation passed or vetoed

14 Serials

KFC UNITED STATES (CALIFORNIA) KFC

Legislative documents
Other legislative documents
History of bills and resolutions. Legislation passed or vetoed -- Continued

14.2	Monographs. By date of session or of initial session
16	Legislative digests
19	Governors' messages. By date
20	Other materials relating to legislative history

Statutes and administrative regulations
Session laws
Serial

25.A2-.A29	Official editions
	Arrange chronologically
25.A3-Z	Unofficial editions. By publisher or editor, A-Z
25.2	Monographs. By date of session or of initial session

Codification. Revision of statutes

27.A-Z	Code commissions. Revision committees. By committee, A-Z

Under each:

.xA15-.xA159	*General serials*
.xA2	*Organic acts. By date*
.xA3-.xA35	*Reports*
.xA3-.xA34	*Serials*
.xA35	*Monographs. By date*
.xA4	*Notes. By date*
.xA5	*Draft revisions. By date*
.xA8	*Other. By date*

For commissions or committees limited to a specific subject, see the subject

27.5	History. Criticism
28	Legislative Council reports and recommendations

General compilations of statutes

Since the state of California has enacted separate codes instead of a general code, the Library of Congress has elected to class as a set under KFC30.5 each unofficial comprehensive edition consisting of the several codes

Including "codes of law," "Codified statutes," "General statutes," "Revised statutes,", etc.

29	Serial compilations

KFC UNITED STATES (CALIFORNIA) KFC

Statutes and administrative regulations

General compilations of statutes -- Continued

30 Monographic compilations. By date of enactment, revision (re-enactment), or officially designated date of codification

Under each:

.A2-.A29	*Official editions (with or without annotations)*
	Arrange chronologically
.A3-.Z	*Unofficial editions*
.A3-.A39	*Unannotated texts*
	Arrange chronologically
.A4-.A49	*Annotated texts*
	Arrange chronologically
.A5-.Z	*Commentaries*
	By author

30.5.A-Z Comprehensive publishers' compilations. By publisher or editor, A-Z

Under each (except KFC30.5.W4 West's annotated California code):

.xA1-.xA29	*Serials*
.xA3-.xZ4	*Individual codes. By date*
	For volumes or sets containing more than one code, arrange by first named code, e.g. KFC30.5.D4M5 1943, Deering's California codes: Military and veterans code
.xZ5	*Supplements (not conforming to individual volumes or sets). By date*
	e.g. KFC30.5.P6Z5 1902, Pomeroy's supplement to Code of civil procedure, Civil code, and Penal code
.xZ6	*Indexes. By date*

For other compilations of statutes on a particular subject, see the subject

30.5.W4 West's annotated California code

31.A-Z Selective compilations. By editor, A-Z

For selective compilations of statutes on a particular subject, see the subject

Administrative regulations

Proclamations and executive orders

34.A2 Serials

Statutes and administrative regulations
Administrative regulations
Proclamations and executive orders -- Continued

35 General compilations of administrative regulations.
Administrative codes. By date of enactment, revision
(reenactment), or officially designated date of
codification
Under each:
.A2-.A29 *Official editions (with or without annotations)*
Arrange chronologically
.A3-.Z *Unofficial editions*
.A3-.A39 *Unannotated texts*
Arrange chronologically
.A4-.A49 *Annotated texts*
Arrange chronologically
.A5-.Z *Commentaries*
By author

36 California Administrative Register
38 Digests of statutes and/or administrative regulations
39 Citators to statutes and/or administrative regulations
40 Indexes to statutes and/or administrative regulations
Law reports and related materials
For reports relating to a particular subject, and for reports of
courts of limited jurisdiction other than those listed below, see
the subject
Supreme Court
Official series
45.A2 California Reports (1850-1934)
220 v.
45.A22 California Reports, 2d (1934-)
45.A3-.A39 Unofficial series, current
45.A4-Z Abridged, selected, defunct publications
45.C3 California Decisions (1890-1940)
100 v.
45.C35 California unreported cases (1855-1910)
7 v.
45.L3 Late political decisions of the Supreme Court (1855)
1 v.
45.O7 Opinions of the Supreme Court (Union editions)
45.R3 Radland. Unwritten decisions (1878-1879)
1 v.
45.1 Digests
45.2 Citators. Tables of cases overruled, etc.
45.4 Conversion tables. Blue books

Law reports and related materials
Supreme Court -- Continued

45.6 General indexes
For indexes relating to a particular publication, reporter system, or digest (e. g. descriptive word indexes), see that publication

45.9 Records and briefs. By citation or docket number
Lower courts
Including Supreme Court and lower courts, and California cases decided in Federal courts, combined
For federal courts in California see KF128.A+

47 Reports
47.1 Digests
47.2 Citators. Tables of cases overruled, etc.
47.4 Conversion tables. Blue books
47.6 General indexes
For indexes relating to a particular publication, reporter system, or digest (e. g. descriptive word indexes), see that publication

47.9 Records and briefs. By citation or docket number
Intermediate appellate courts. District Courts of Appeal
Official series and predecessors

48.A19 Labatt (1857-1858)
2 v.

48.A2 California Appellate Reports (1905-1934)
140 v.

48.A212 California Appellate Reports, 2d (1934-)
48.A3-.A39 Unofficial series
48.A4A-.A4Z Abridged, selected, defunct publications
By editor

48.C3 California appellate decisions (1905-1940)
103 v.
(An advance publication, probably temporary, and not to be cataloged)

48.C32 California Appellate decisions supplement
48.1 Digests
48.2 Citators. Tables of cases overruled, etc.
48.4 Conversion tables. Blue books
48.6 General indexes
For indexes relating to a particular publication, reporter system, or digest (e. g. descriptive word indexes), see that publication

48.9 Records and briefs. By citation or docket number
Trial courts
Collective. Various courts

51 Reports
51.1 Digests

KFC UNITED STATES (CALIFORNIA) KFC

Law reports and related materials
Trial courts
Collective. Various courts -- Continued

51.2	Citators. Tables of cases overruled, etc.
51.4	Conversion tables. Blue books
51.6	General indexes
	For indexes relating to a particular publication, reporter system, or digest (e. g. descriptive word indexes), see that publication
51.9	Records and briefs. By citation or docket number
52.A-Z	Particular courts, A-Z

Under each:

.x	*Reports*
.x1	*Digests*
.x2	*Citators. Tables of cases overruled, etc.*
.x3	*Conversion tables. Blue books*
.x4	*General indexes*
	For indexes relating to a particular publication, reporter system, or digest (e. g. descriptive word indexes), see that publication
.x6	*Records and briefs. By citation or docket number*

57	Digests of various reports
59	Citators to various reports
62	Collections of unreported cases
	By editor
66	Law dictionaries. Words and phrases
67	Uniform state laws
	Class here general works only
	For uniform state laws on a particular subject, see the subject
68	Form books
	Class here general works only
	For form books on a particular subject, see the subject
<69>	Periodicals
70	Yearbooks. Judicial (including criminal) statistics
	Class here only publications issued annually, containing information, statistics, etc. about the year just past
	Other publications appearing yearly are classed as periodicals in K1+
	Directories see KF192.A+
74	Legal research. Legal bibliography
	Methods of bibliographic research and of how to find the law. State law only
	For general works see KF240

KFC UNITED STATES (CALIFORNIA) KFC

74.5	Information services. Information centers
75	Legal composition and draftsmanship
	For general works see KF250+
	For legislative draftsmanship see KFC724
	The legal profession. Practice of law
	General works see KF297+
76	Admission to the bar (Table KF9)
	Legal ethics. Discipline. Disbarment
76.5.A2	General (Table KF7)
76.5.A6-Z	Particular cases. By attorney
77	Law office management. Attorneys' and legal secretaries' handbooks, manuals, etc., of state law
77.5.A-Z	Special topics, A-Z
77.5.F43	Fees (Table KF7)
77.5.G7	Group arrangements (Table KF7)
78	History
79	Law reform. Criticism
	General and comprehensive works
80	Treatises
81	Minor and popular works
82	Examination aids
84.A-Z	Works for particular groups of users, A-Z
84.B87	Businesspeople
84.E58	Entertainers
87	Conflict of laws (Table KF9)
100.A-Z	Concepts applying to several branches of law, A-Z
100.C66	Computers (Table KF7)
100.D3	Damages (Table KF7)
	Deadlines see KFC100.T54
100.N6	Notice. Legal advertising (Table KF7)
100.R43	Recording and registration (Table KF7)
	Cf. KFC113 Persons
	Cf. KFC172 Real property
100.T54	Time. Deadlines (Table KF7)
	Private law in general, works on the law of the Civil code see KFC80+
	Persons
	General. Status. Capacity and disability
	Natural persons
108	General
109	Civil status. Name
	Capacity and disability
110	General (Table KF9)
111.A-Z	Particular groups of persons, A-Z
111.A34	Aged. Older people (Table KF7)
111.H35	Handicapped. People with disabilities (Table KF7)

KFC UNITED STATES (CALIFORNIA) KFC

Persons
General. Status. Capacity and disability
Natural persons
Capacity and disability
Particular groups of persons, A-Z -- Continued
111.I5 Insane persons. Persons of unsound mind (Table KF7)
111.M5 Minors (Table KF7)
Older people see KFC111.A34
People with disabilities see KFC111.H35
111.W6 Women (Table KF7)
112 Conservatorship (Table KF9)
Cf. KFC134 Guardian and ward
113 Recording and registration. Registers of births, marriages, and deaths. Vital statistics. Birth and death certificates (Table KF9)

Domestic relations. Family law
115 General (Table KF9)
Domestic relations courts. Conciliation courts
116 General (Table KF9)
116.6.A-Z Local courts. By country, A-Z
Marriage. Husband and wife
120 General (Table KF9)
123 Invalid and voidable marriages. Nullity
Property relationships
124 General (Table KF9)
125.A-Z Particular modes of property relationships, A-Z
125.C6 Community property (Table KF7)
126 Divorce. Separation (Table KF9)
128 Unmarried couples
129 Same-sex marriage. Civil unions (Table KF9)
Including quasi-marital relationships
Parent and child
130 General (Table KF9)
132 Adoption (Table KF9)
133 Support. Desertion and nonsupport (Table KF9)
134 Guardian and ward (Table KF9)
Cf. KFC112 Conservatorship
Property
138 General. Ownership (Table KF9)
Real property. Land law
140 General (Table KF9)
140.5 Special aspects and relationships
Land tenure
141 General (Table KF9)
Ownership
144 General

KFC UNITED STATES (CALIFORNIA) KFC

Property
Real property. Land law
Land tenure
Ownership -- Continued

144.3	Community associations of property owners (Table KF9)
144.5	Horizontal property. Housing condominium (Table KF9)
	Tenancy. Leaseholds. Landlord and tenant
145	General (Table KF9)
	Rent control see KFC837.5.R4
147.A-Z	Particular kinds, A-Z
147.C6	Commercial leases (Table KF7)
147.G7	Ground leases. Building leases (Table KF7)
	Future estates and interests in land
150	General. Limitations
151	Worthier title
	Concurrent ownership
	Including works on concurrent ownership in both real and personal property
155	General (Table KF9)
157	Joint tenancy (Table KF9)
158	Partition (Table KF9)
162	Riparian rights. Water rights (Table KF9)
163	Actions to recover the possession of land. Ejectment (Table KF9)
163.5	Easements (Table KF9)
164	Covenants running with the land. Restrictive covenants (Table KF9)
	Transfer of rights in land
166	General (Table KF9)
167	Government grants (Table KF9)
	Transfer inter vivos
169	General. Vendor and purchaser (Table KF9)
	Conveyances. Title investigation. Abstracts
170	General. Deeds (Table KF9)
171	Title investigation. Abstracts (Table KF9)
172	Registration. Torrens system (Table KF9)
173	Description of land. Surveying (Table KF9)
	Mortgages
175	General (Table KF9)
177.A-Z	Special topics, A-Z
177.F6	Foreclosure (Table KF7)
180	Personal property (Table KF9)
	Trusts and trustees
188	General (Table KF9)
194.A-Z	Special topics, A-Z
194.L35	Land trusts (Table KF7)

KFC UNITED STATES (CALIFORNIA) KFC

Trusts and trustees
Special topics, A-Z -- Continued

194.L58	Living trusts (Table KF7)
195	Estate planning (Table KF9)
	Succession upon death
200	General (Table KF9)
201	Testate succession. Wills (Table KF9)
	Probate law and practice. Probate courts
205	General (Table KF9)
205.5.A-Z	Particular courts. By county, etc., A-Z
210	Administration of decedents' estates. Execution of wills. Personal representatives (Table KF9)
	Contracts
215	General and comprehensive works (Table KF8) General principles
223	Breach of contract. Remedies (Table KF9)
	Government contracts. Public contracts
224	General. Purchasing and procurement (Table KF9)
224.3	Construction and building contracts (Table KF9)
	Particular contracts
225	Comprehensive. Commercial law. Mercantile transactions (Table KF9)
	Contract for work and labor (Contract for services). Independent contractors
228	General (Table KF9)
229	Mechanics' liens (Table KF9)
230.A-Z	Particular types, A-Z
230.B8	Building and construction (Table KF7)
235	Sale of goods
	Negotiable instruments
245	General (Table KF9)
246	Bills of exchange (Table KF9)
248	Checks (Table KF9)
	Banking
250	General (Table KF9)
	Particular kinds of banks
253	Mortgage banks (Table KF9)
253.5	Mortgage bonds (Table KF9)
254	Building and loan associations (Table KF9)
255.A-Z	Other, A-Z
256.A-Z	Special topics, A-Z
256.C56	Collecting of accounts. Collection laws (Table KF7)
256.E8	Escrow business (Table KF7)
256.R43	Record keeping (Table KF7)
	Loan of money
260	General (Table KF9)
261	Interest. Usury (Table KF9)

Contracts
Particular contracts
Loan of money -- Continued

262 Consumer credit. Small loans. Finance charges (Table KF9)

265 Suretyship. Guaranty (Table KF9)
Secured transactions

266 General (Table KF9)
Particular transactions

267 Conditional sale. Installment sale. Lease purchase (Table KF9)
Marketing of securities. Investments. Stock-exchange transactions

270 General (Table KF9)
For issuing of securities see KFC350
Investment trusts. Investment companies. Mutual funds

272 General (Table KF9)

273 Real estate investment trusts (Table KF9)
Insurance
Including regulation of insurance business
For taxation see KFC879.A+

290 General. Insurance business. Agents. Brokers (Table KF9)
Particular branches
Personal insurance

292 Life (Table KF9)

293.A-Z Other, A-Z

293.H42 Health (Table KF7)
Cf. KFC591+ Social insurance

295 Property insurance (Table KF9)
Casualty insurance

297 General liability (Table KF9)

298.A-Z Particular risks, A-Z
Automobile

298.A8 General

298.A86 Uninsured motorist

298.M3 Malpractice (Table KF7)

298.P64 Pollution (Table KF7)

300 Suretyship, guaranty, title insurance. Bonding (Table KF9)

308 Reinsurance (Table KF9)

309 Restitution. Quasi contracts. Unjust enrichment (Table KF9)
Torts (Extracontractual liability)

310 General. Liability. Damages (Table KF9)
Particular torts
Torts in respect to the person

311 Personal injuries (Table KF9)

KFC UNITED STATES (CALIFORNIA) KFC

Torts (Extracontractual liability)
Particular torts
Torts in respect to the person -- Continued

312 Violation of privacy (Table KF9)
313 Torts in respect to reputation. Libel. Slander (Table KF9)
Negligence

315 General (Table KF9)
316 Contributory negligence. Last clear chance (Table KF9)
317 Malpractice (Table KF9)
320.A-Z Particular types of accidents or cases of negligence, A-Z
320.A8 Automobile accidents (Table KF7)
320.L3 Landslides (Table KF7)
320.L52 Liability for condition and use of land (Table KF7)
Strict liability. Liability without fault

321 General (Table KF9)
Products liability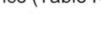

323.A3 General (Table KF7)
323.A5-Z By product, A-Z
323.5 Environmental damages (Table KF9)
Parties to actions in torts
Corporations

324 Municipal corporations (Table KF9)
326 Personal representatives (Table KF9)
327 Public officers and government employees (Table KF9)
328 School districts (Table KF9)
330 Joint tortfeasors (Table KF9)
Liability for torts of others. Vicarious liability

331 General (Table KF9)
332 Government torts (Table KF9)
333.5 Compensation to victims of crimes. Reparation (Table KF9)
334 Assistance in emergencies. Good Samaritan laws (Table KF9)
For medical emergency assistance see KFC546.A+
Agency

335 General (Table KF9)
336 Power of Attorney (Table KF9)
Associations
Comprehensive. Associations in general
Including business enterprises in general, regardless of form of organization

337 General (Table KF9)
337.5.A-Z Special topics, A-Z
337.5.A8 Auditing (Table KF7)
337.5.F5 Finance (Table KF7)
Unincorporated associations

338 General (Table KF9)
Business associations. Partnership

339 General (Table KF9)

KFC UNITED STATES (CALIFORNIA) KFC

Associations
Unincorporated associations
Business associations. Partnership -- Continued
339.5 Limited partnership (Table KF9)
Including limited liability companies and private companies
Corporations. Juristic persons
340 General (Table KF9)
Nonprofit corporations
342 General (Table KF9)
Business corporations
345 General (Table KF9)
348 Incorporation. Corporate charters and bylaws (Table KF9)
350 Corporation finance. Capital. Dividends. Issuing of securities (Table KF9)
353 Shares and shareholders' rights. Stock transfers (Table KF9)
357.A-Z Particular types of corporations, A-Z
357.C55 Close corporations (Table KF7)
357.C6 Cooperative societies (Table KF7)
359 Consolidation and merger (Table KF9)
Insolvency and bankruptcy. Creditors' rights
364 General (Table KF9)
Bankruptcy
365 General. Procedure (Table KF9)
366.A-Z Special topics, A-Z
367 Debtors' relief (Table KF9)
Including composition
Regulation of industry, trade, and commerce. Occupational law
375 General. Comprehensive. Trade regulation. Control of trade practices. Consumer protection (Table KF9)
377 Monopolies. Antitrust laws (Table KF9)
379 Small business (Table KF9)
Weights and measures. Containers
382 General. Standards (Table KF9)
By product
Fruit and vegetables
383 General (Table KF9)
383.5.A-Z Particular fruits or vegetables, A-Z
383.5.A6 Apples (Table KF7)
383.5.C2 Canned fruit (Table KF7)
384.A-Z Other products, A-Z
384.B48 Beverages (Table KF7)
Primary production. Extractive industries
Agriculture. Forestry
385 General (Table KF9)

KFC UNITED STATES (CALIFORNIA) KFC

Regulation of industry, trade, and commerce. Occupational law Primary production. Extractive industries Agriculture. Forestry -- Continued

386	Conservation of agricultural and forest lands. Soil conservation. Field irrigation. Erosion control (Table KF9)
387	Control of agricultural pests, plant diseases, and predatory animals. Weed control. Plant quarantine (Table KF9)
389	Distribution of seed grain, fertilizer, etc. (Table KF9)
390	Farm producers' and marketing cooperatives (Table KF9)
	Marketing. Market forecasts
391	General (Table KF9)
391.5.A-Z	Particular commodities, A-Z
391.5.O44	Olives (Table KF7)
391.5.P3	Peaches (Table KF7)
391.5.P34	Pears (Table KF7)
391.5.P55	Plums (Table KF7)
391.5.P78	Prunes (Table KF7)
391.5.R34	Raisins (Table KF7)
391.5.T65	Tomatoes (Table KF7)
	Livestock industry and trade. Cattle raising
393	General (Table KF9)
393.5	Cattle brands. Brand inspection (Table KF9)
394	Poultry industry (Table KF9)
396	Forestry. Timber laws (Table KF9)
397	Viticulture (Table KF9)
397.5	Aquaculture (Table KF9)
398	Fishery (Table KF9)
	Mining. Quarrying
400	General (Table KF9)
	Nonferrous metals
403	General (Table KF9)
403.5.A-Z	Particular metals, A-Z
403.5.M3	Mercury (Table KF7)
	Petroleum. Oil and gas
405	General (Table KF9)
406	Conservation. Interstate compacts (Table KF9)
408	Submerged land legislation. Tidal oil (Table KF9)
410	Oil and gas leases (Table KF9)
410.7.A-Z	Particular oil fields, reserves, etc., A-Z
	Manufacturing industries
412.A2	General (Table KF7)
412.A3-Z	By product
412.B56	Biotechnology industries (Table KF7)
412.F8	Furniture (Table KF7)
412.H68	Household appliances (Table KF7)

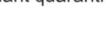

KFC UNITED STATES (CALIFORNIA) KFC

Regulation of industry, trade, and commerce. Occupational law -- Continued

Food processing industries

415 General (Table KF9)

Agricultural products

416 General (Table KF9)

417.A-Z Particular products, A-Z

417.T6 Tobacco products (Table KF7)

Meat and poultry products

418 General (Table KF9)

419 Poultry products. Eggs and egg products (Table KF9)

421 Dairy industry. Dairy products industry. Milk production and distribution (Table KF9)

424 Construction and building industry. Contractors (Table KF9)

Trade and commerce

430 General (Table KF9)

437 Retail trade (Table KF9)

Price maintenance. Competition

439 General (Table KF9)

442 Franchises (Table KF9)

444.A-Z Particular products, A-Z

444.A88 Automobiles (Table KF7)

444.M63 Mobile homes (Table KF7)

Service trades

445 General. Licensing (Table KF9)

446.A-Z Particular trades, A-Z

446.A87 Automobile repair shops (Table KF7)

446.B3 Barbers (Table KF7)

446.B4 Beauty shops (Table KF7)

446.C6 Collection agencies (Table KF7)

446.D4 Detectives (Table KF7)

446.E5 Employment agencies (Table KF7)

446.H6 Hotels. Restaurants (Table KF7)

446.I5 Insect exterminators (Table KF7)

446.L2 Laundries. Cleaners. Linen supply (Table KF7)

Life care communities see KFC446.O43

446.O43 Old age homes. Life care communities (Table KF7)

446.R3 Real estate agents (Table KF7)

446.U6 Undertakers (Table KF7)

448 Warehouses (Table KF9)

Public utilities

455 General (Table KF9)

455.1 Public Utilities Commission (Table KF9)

Power supply

Cf. KFC818 Energy conservation in buildings

456 General (Table KF9)

Electricity

KFC UNITED STATES (CALIFORNIA) KFC

Regulation of industry, trade, and commerce. Occupational law
Public utilities
Power supply
Electricity -- Continued

459	General. Comprehensive (Table KF9)
462	Rate-making (Table KF9)
465	Gas (Table KF9)
468	Water (Table KF9)
468.8.A-Z	Other sources of power, A-Z
468.8.G46	Geothermal resources (Table KF7)
468.8.S65	Solar energy (Table KF7)

Transportation and communication

469	General. Comprehensive (Table KF9)
469.5	Ratemaking (Table KF9)

Road traffic. Automotive transportation

470	General. Motor vehicle laws (Table KF9)
472	Safety equipment. Weight restrictions (Table KF9)
474	Registration. Title transfer (Table KF9)
474.5	Drivers' licenses (Table KF9)
475	Safety responsibility laws. Compulsory insurance (Table KF9)
476.A-Z	Particular vehicles, A-Z
476.M68	Motorcycles (Table KF7)
476.T65	Trailers (Table KF7)
476.T7	Trucks (Table KF7)
477	Traffic regulation and enforcement. Traffic violations. Drunk driving (Table KF9)

Carriage of passengers and goods

480	General (Table KF9)
482	Rate-making (Table KF9)
483	Freight. Freight claims (Table KF9)
486.A-Z	Special topics, A-Z
486.T7	Trip leasing (Table KF7)

Railroads

490	General. Corporate structure. Regulation of industry (Table KF9)
492	Railroad lands. Land grants. Rights of way (Table KF9)

Operation of railroads

497	Rates and rate-making. Freight (Table KF9)
499.A-Z	Particular railroads and railroad companies, A-Z
	Including litigation, decisions, rulings, etc.
501	Local transit. Streetcar lines. Subways (Table KF9)

Aviation. Commercial aviation. Air carriers

510	General (Table KF9)
511	Air traffic rules. Air safety (Table KF9)
512	Airports (Table KF9)

Water transportation. Navigation and shipping

Regulation of industry, trade, and commerce. Occupational law
Transportation and communication
Water transportation. Navigation and shipping -- Continued

Call Number	Description
520	General. Comprehensive (Table KF9)
	Ships
521	General (Table KF9)
	Safety regulations
522	General. Inspection (Table KF9)
524.A-Z	Particular types of vessels, A-Z
524.P5	Pleasure craft. Yachts (Table KF7)
526	Navigation and pilotage (Table KF9)
	Harbors and ports
530	General (Table KF9)
531.A-Z	Particular ports, A-Z
535	Press law (Table KF9)
	Telecommunication
540	General. Comprehensive (Table KF9)
541	Telegraph. Teletype (Table KF9)
543	Radio and television broadcasting (Table KF9)
	The professions
545	General. Licensing (Table KF9)
545.5	Professional corporations (Table KF9)
	Particular professions
546.A-Z	The health professions, A-Z
	For medical legislation see KFC615+
546.A1-.A13	General. Physicians (Table KF16)
546.A28-.A283	Acupuncturists (Table KF16)
546.C4-.C43	Chiropractors (Table KF16)
546.D3-.D33	Dentists (Table KF16)
546.P6-.P63	Podiatrists (Table KF16)
546.P7-.P73	Psychologists (Table KF16)
546.Q2-.Q23	Quacks (Table KF16)
546.5.A-Z	Auxiliary professions, A-Z
546.5.M4-.M43	Medical technologist (Table KF16)
546.5.N8-.N83	Nurses (Table KF16)
	Occupational therapists see KFC546.5.T54+
546.5.O6-.O63	Optometrists (Table KF16)
546.5.P4-.P43	Pharmacists (Table KF16)
	Physical therapists see KFC546.5.T54+
546.5.P48-.P483	Physicians' assistants (Table KF16)
546.5.T54-.T543	Therapists, Physical. Occupational therapists (Table KF16)
547.A-Z	Other professions, A-Z
547.A3-.A33	Accountants. Auditors (Table KF16)
547.A7-.A73	Architects (Table KF16)
547.E6-.E63	Engineers (Table KF16)
547.V3-.V33	Veterinarians (Table KF16)

KFC UNITED STATES (CALIFORNIA) KFC

550	Intellectual property. Patents. Trademarks (Table KF9)
553	Unfair competition (Table KF9)
	Social legislation
555	General (Table KF9)
	Labor law
556	General (Table KF9)
	Management-labor relations
557	General (Table KF9)
	Labor unions
560	General (Table KF9)
560.5	Open and closed shop. Right-to-work laws (Table KF9)
	Collective bargaining. Collective labor agreements
561	General (Table KF9)
562.A-Z	Particular industries and occupations, A-Z
562.A35	Agriculture (Table KF7)
562.C66	Construction industry (Table KF7) 
562.P8	Public employees (Table KF7)
562.T4	Teachers (Table KF7)
	Labor disputes
564	General (Table KF9)
565	Arbitration. Conciliation. Factfinding boards (Table KF9)
	Labor standards
570	General (Table KF9)
	Employment and dismissal
571	General (Table KF9)
	Discrimination in employment and its prevention
572	General (Table KF9)
573.A-Z	Particular groups, A-Z
573.H34	Handicapped. People with disabilities (Table KF7)
	People with disabilities see KFC573.H34
573.W65	Women (Table KF7)
	Wages. Minimum wage
575	General
	Types of wages. Mode of remuneration
575.3	Annual wage. Guaranteed wage (Table KF9)
575.5	Overtime payments. Night differentials (Table KF9)
575.6	Nonwage payments. Fringe benefits (Table KF9)
576	Hours of labor. Night work (Table KF9)
577	Vacations. Holidays. Leaves of absence (Table KF9)
	Protection of labor. Labor hygiene and safety
579	General (Table KF9)
580	Child labor (Table KF9)
581	Women labor (Table KF9)
	Labor hygiene and safety. Hazardous occupations.
	Safety regulations
584	General (Table KF9)

Social legislation
Labor law
Protection of labor. Labor hygiene and safety
Labor hygiene and safety. Hazardous occupations.
Safety regulations -- Continued

Code	Description
586.A-Z	By industry and type of labor, A-Z
586.B8	Building industry (Table KF7)
586.E9	Excavation (Table KF7)
586.L8	Lumbering (Table KF7)
586.M5	Mining (Table KF7)
586.S4	Shipbuilding (Table KF7)
586.W5	Window cleaning (Table KF7)
586.W6	Wood-using industries (Table KF7)
587.A-Z	By machinery, equipment, etc., A-Z
589.A-Z	Labor law of particular industries or types of employment, A-Z
589.A4	Agriculture (Table KF7)
589.R45	Rental housing (Table KF7)
589.W38	Water agencies (Table KF7)

Social insurance

Code	Description
590	General (Table KF9)

Particular branches
Health insurance

Code	Description
591	General (Table KF9)
591.5.A-Z	Particular groups, A-Z
591.5.P65	Poor (Table KF7)
	Including Medicaid and Medi-Cal

Workers' compensation

Code	Description
592	General (Table KF9)
592.1	Industrial Accident Commission (Table KF9)
592.2	Workmen's Compensation Appeals Board (Table KF9)
594.A-Z	Particular industries and groups of employees, A-Z
594.M5	Mining (Table KF7)
595	Social security. Retirement. Old age and disability pensions. Survivors' benefits (Table KF9)
596	Unemployment insurance (Table KF9)

Public welfare. Public assistance

Code	Description
600	General (Table KF9)
600.2	Public institutions (Table KF9)
601	Social work. Social workers (Table KF9)

Particular groups

Code	Description
602	Women (Table KF9)

Children. Child welfare. Youth services
Including children with disabilities or retarded children

Code	Description
603	General (Table KF9)
603.5	Foster home care (Table KF9)

KFC UNITED STATES (CALIFORNIA) KFC

Social legislation
Public welfare. Public assistance
Particular groups -- Continued

604	Older people (Table KF9)
	People with disabilities. Vocational rehabilitation
605	General (Table KF9)
605.3	Blind (Table KF9)
	Children see KFC603+
605.6	Homeless persons (Table KF9)
608.A-Z	Special topics, A-Z
608.D6	Domicile requirements (Table KF7)
608.5	Disaster relief (Table KF9)
609	Birth control. Family planning. Population control (Table KF9)
	Cf. KFC1121 Abortion (Criminal law)
	Public health. Sanitation
	Including environmental pollution
610	General (Table KF9)
611	Disposal of the dead. Burial and cemetery laws (Table KF9)
612	Water pollution. Drainage (Table KF9)
612.6	Drinking water standards. Fluoridation (Table KF9)
	Contagious, infectious, and other diseases
613	General. Reporting (Table KF9)
613.5.A-Z	Particular diseases, A-Z
613.5.A53	AIDS (Disease) (Table KF7)
613.5.C3	Cancer (Table KF7)
613.5.T8	Tuberculosis (Table KF7)
613.9.A-Z	Particular measures, A-Z
613.9.M67	Mosquito abatement (Table KF7)
614	Air pollution. Control of smoke, noxious gases, etc. (Table KF9)
614.5.A-Z	Other public health hazards and measures, A-Z
614.5.N64	Noise control (Table KF7)
614.5.R43	Refuse disposal (Table KF7)
	Medical legislation
615	General (Table KF9)
	Health facilities and services. Hospitals
617	General (Table KF9)
617.3	Liability (Table KF9)
619.A-Z	Other health services, A-Z
619.A25	Abortion services (Table KF7)
619.H65	Home care services (Table KF7)
619.N8	Nursing homes (Table KF7)
619.S3	Schools. School health services (Table KF7)
619.5.A-Z	Special topics, A-Z
619.5.D43	Death, Definition of (Table KF7)
	Hospital records see KFC619.5.R43
619.5.I53	Informed consent (Table KF7)

Medical legislation
Special topics, A-Z -- Continued
Living wills see KFC619.5.R5
Natural death see KFC619.5.R5
619.5.R43 Medical records. Hospital records. Records management (Table KF7)
Records management see KFC619.5.R43
619.5.R5 Right to die. Natural death. Living wills (Table KF7)
620 The mentally ill (Table KF9)
Veterinary law. Veterinary hygiene
623 General (Table KF9)
623.5 Quarantine (Table KF9)
627 Prevention of cruelty to animals (Table KF9)
Food. Drugs. Cosmetics
630 General. Comprehensive (Table KF9)
632 Drug law. Narcotics. Cosmetics (Table KF9)
Alcoholic beverages. Liquor control
635 General (Table KF9)
636.A-Z Particular products, A-Z
636.B4 Beer (Table KF7)
636.W5 Wine (Table KF7)
Public safety
640 General (Table KF9)
640.5 Weapons. Firearms. Munitions (Table KF9)
Hazardous articles and processes
641 General (Table KF9)
641.5.A-Z Particular products and processes, A-Z
641.5.A69 Asbestos (Table KF7)
641.5.A7 Atomic power. Radiation (Table KF7)
641.5.E9 Explosives (Table KF7)
641.5.H39 Hazardous wastes (Table KF7)
641.5.I6 Inflammable materials. Fireworks (Table KF7)
Nuclear energy see KFC641.5.A7
641.5.P6 Poisons. Toxic substances (Table KF7)
641.5.P63 Pesticides. Herbicides (Table KF7)
644 Fire prevention and control (Table KF9)
Control of social activities
645 Sports. Prizefighting. Horse racing (Table KF9)
646 Lotteries. Games of chance. Gambling (Table KF9)
647.A-Z Other, A-Z
647.A58 Amusements (Table KF7)
Exhibitions see KFC647.F34
647.F34 Fairs. Exhibitions (Table KF7)
Education
Education in general. Public education
School government and finance

KFC UNITED STATES (CALIFORNIA) KFC

Education
Education in general. Public education
School government and finance -- Continued

648	General (Table KF9)
	Including works treating of educational law comprehensively
649	School districts. School boards (Table KF9)
650	School lands (Table KF9)
	Finance
651	General (Table KF9)
	Support of related activities
652	School transportation (Table KF9)
	Students. Compulsory education
654	General (Table KF9)
654.5	Right to education. Admission. Discrimination and segregation (Table KF9)
	Teachers
658	General. Tenure (Table KF9)
659	Qualifications. Certification (Table KF9)
660	Salaries, pensions, etc. (Table KF9)
	Elementary and secondary education
662	General (Table KF9)
663	Pre-elementary education. Kindergartens (Table KF9)
	Curricula. Courses of instruction
664	General (Table KF9)
664.5.A-Z	Particular subjects, A-Z
664.5.L34	Language instruction (Table KF7)
	Including bilingual instruction
665.A-Z	Particular types of students, A-Z
665.E9	Exceptionally gifted students (Table KF7)
665.H3	Handicapped. People with disabilities (Table KF7)
	People with disabilities see KFC665.H3
666	Higher education. Colleges and universities (Table KF9)
	Science and the arts. Research
670	General (Table KF9)
	Libraries
675	General. Library development (Table KF9)
676.A-Z	Particular libraries, A-Z
678	Public law (Table KF9)
	Constitutional law
	Sources
679	General. Comprehensive. Collections
680	Particular constitutions. By date of constitution
	Subarrange each by Table KF40
	Including rejected proposals for new constitution. By date of referendum
681	History

KFC UNITED STATES (CALIFORNIA) KFC

Constitutional law -- Continued

682	General. Comprehensive (Table KF9)
	Separation of powers. Delegation of powers
685	General (Table KF9)
686	Conflict of interests. Incompatibility of offices. Ethics in government (Table KF9)
	Structure of government. Jurisdiction
690	General (Table KF9)
693	Submerged lands (Table KF9)
694	Public policy. Police power (Table KF9)
	Individual and state
	Civil and political rights
695	General (Table KF9)
696	Sex discrimination (Table KF9)
696.5.A-Z	Particular constitutional guarantees, A-Z
696.5.D83	Due process of law (Table KF7)
	Control of individuals
	Aliens
698	General (Table KF9)
699.A-Z	Particular ethnic groups, A-Z
699.C4	Chinese (Table KF7)
699.J2	Japanese (Table KF7)
	Internal security. Control of subversive activities
701	General (Table KF9)
702.A-Z	Particular groups, A-Z
702.C6	Communists (Table KF7)
	Church and state
705	General. Religious corporations (Table KF9)
706.A-Z	Special topics, A-Z
	Organs of the government
	The people
708	Initiative and referendum. Plebiscite (Table KF9)
709	Recall (Table KF9)
	Election law
710	General (Table KF9)
	Suffrage
711	General (Table KF9)
712.A-Z	Particular groups of voters, A-Z
712.S6	Soldiers (Table KF7)
713	Registration. Qualifications. Educational tests. Poll tax requirements (Table KF9)
714	Election districts. Apportionment. Gerrymandering (Table KF9)
715	Primaries (Table KF9)
717.A-Z	Special topics, A-Z
717.C35	Campaign expenditures (Table KF7)
	The legislative branch

KFC UNITED STATES (CALIFORNIA) KFC

Constitutional law
Organs of the government
The legislative branch -- Continued

720	General. Legislative power (Table KF9)
	The legislature
721	General. Organization (Table KF9)
722	Rules and procedure (Table KF9)
	The legislative process
723	General (Table KF9)
724	Bill drafting (Table KF9)
724.5	Legislative Counsel Bureau (Table KF9)
725	Lobbying (Table KF9)
	Legal status of legislators
726	General (Table KF9)
727	Salaries, pensions, etc. (Table KF9)
	The executive branch
740	General. Executive power (Table KF9)
	The Governor
741	General (Table KF9)
742	Powers and duties (Table KF9)
744	Impeachment (Table KF9)
745	Executive departments (Table KF9)
746.A-Z	Particular offices or positions, A-Z
	Attorney General's Office see KFC746.J86
746.J86	Department of Justice. Attorney General's Office (Table KF7)
747.A-Z	Special topics, A-Z
747.P82	Public meetings (Table KF7)
	State civil service see KFC760+
	Local government
750	General (Table KF9)
	Municipal government. Municipal services
752	General. Municipal corporations (Table KF9)
753	Municipal powers and services beyond corporate limits (Table KF9)
758	County government. County charters (Table KF9)
759	Special districts. Public authorities (Table KF9)
	Civil service. Government officials and employees
	State civil service
760	General. Qualifications for employment (Table KF9)
	Conditions and restrictions of employment. Employment discipline
763	General (Table KF9)
763.5	Loyalty-security program (Table KF9)
	Tenure and remuneration
768	General (Table KF9)
769	Salaries (Table KF9)

KFC UNITED STATES (CALIFORNIA) KFC

Civil service. Government officials and employees
State civil service
Tenure and emuneration -- Continued

770	Retirement. Pensions (Table KF9)
774	Municipal civil service (Table KF9)
	Police and power of the police
778	General (Table KF9)
778.5.A-Z	Special topics, A-Z
778.5.P74	Private police (Table KF7)
	Administrative organization. Administrative law and procedure
779	History
780	General (Table KF9)
781	Legislative functions. Rule-making power. Regulations.
	Admission of attorneys and rules of practice (Table KF9)
782	Judicial functions. Procedure. Administrative tribunals (Table KF9)
782.5	Hearing examiners (Table KF9)
	Public property. Public restraints on private property
785	General (Table KF9)
786	Conservation of natural resources (Table KF9)
	Roads
787	General. Highway law (Table KF9)
787.3	Highway finance (Table KF9)
787.5	Express highways. Parkways (Table KF9)
788	Roadside protection. Rights of way (Table KF9)
788.5	Foot trails (Table KF9)
	Water resources. Watersheds. Rivers. Lakes. Water courses
790	General. Water districts (Table KF9)
791	State water rights (Table KF9)
792.A-Z	Particular inland waterways and channels, A-Z
793	Canals
	Flood control. Levees. Dams
795	General (Table KF9)
795.5.A-Z	Particular dams, bodies of water, districts, etc., A-Z
796.A-Z	Particular bodies of water, water districts, etc., A-Z
799	Weather control. Meteorology. Weather stations (Table KF9)
800	Eminent domain (Table KF9)
	Public land law
802	General (Table KF9)
	Reclamation. Irrigation. Drainage
803	General (Table KF9)
804.A-Z	Special types of land, A-Z
804.A7	Arid lands (Table KF7)
804.3	Shore protection. Coastal zone management (Table KF9)
	State parks and forests. Wilderness preservation
805	General (Table KF9)
806	Game, bird, and fish protection (Table KF9)

KFC UNITED STATES (CALIFORNIA) KFC

Public property. Public restraints on private property --
Continued
Land grants

808	General (Table KF9)
809.A-Z	Particular claims. By claimant, A-Z
	Regional and city planning. Zoning. Building
810	General (Table KF9)
	Land use. Zoning. Land subdivision
811	General (Table KF9)
811.7	Solar access zoning. Shade control (Table KF9)
	Building laws
813	General (Table KF9)
814.A-Z	Particular types of buildings, A-Z
814.M6	Mobile homes (Table KF7)
816	Plumbing. Pipe fitting (Table KF9)
818	Heating and ventilating. Air conditioning (Table KF9)
	Including energy conservation provisions
819.A-Z	Other topics, A-Z
819.E44	Electric installations (Table KF7)
819.H35	Handicapped, Provisions for. People with disabilities, Provisions for (Table KF7)
	People with disabilities, Provisions for see KFC819.H35
820	Housing. Slum clearance. City redevelopment (Table KF9)
	Government property
825	General (Table KF9)
826	Records management (Table KF9)
827	Access to public records. Freedom of information (Table KF9)
832	Public works (Table KF9)
	Government measures in time of war, national emergency, or economic crisis. Emergency economic legislation
834	General (Table KF9)
	By period
	1945-
837	General (Table KF9)
	Rationing. Price control. Profiteering
837.3	General (Table KF9)
837.5.A-Z	By commodity or service, A-Z
837.5.R4	Rent control (Table KF7)
	Public finance
840	General (Table KF9)
841	Money. Currency. Coinage (Table KF9)
842	Budget. Government expenditures (Table KF9)
	Expenditure control. Public auditing and accounting
845	General (Table KF9)
847	Investment of public funds (Table KF9)
849	Public debts. Loans. Bond issues (Table KF9)

Public finance -- Continued
State revenue

856	General (Table KF9)

Particular sources of revenue

Taxation

860	General (Table KF9)
861	Tax saving. Tax planning (Table KF9)

Tax administration and procedure

863	General (Table KF9)
864	Double taxation (Table KF9)

Tax collection

865	General (Table KF9)
865.5	Delinquency (Table KF9)
866	Procedure. Tax courts. Remedies. Tax appeals (Table KF9)
868	Exemption (Table KF9)

Particular taxes

Income tax

870	General (Table KF9)
870.3	Payroll deduction. Withholding tax (Table KF6)
870.5	Tax credits (Table KF9)
871	Community property of husband and wife (Table KF9)
873	Income of nonprofit organizations, nonprofit corporations, foundations, endowments, pension trust funds (Table KF9)

Income of business organizations

874	General (Table KF9)
874.5	Partnerships (Table KF9)

Juristic persons. Corporations

875	General. Corporation income tax (Table KF9)
877	Surtaxes. Excess profits tax (Table KF9)
878	Small business corporations (Table KF9)
879.A-Z	Particular lines of corporate business, A-Z
879.B2	Banks (Table KF7)
879.F67	Forestry (Table KF7)
879.I5	Insurance (Table KF7)
879.R2	Railroads (Table KF7)
879.R48	Resource recovery facilities (Table KF7)

Property taxes. Taxation of capital

880	General (Table KF9)
880.5	Tax valuation (Table KF9)
881	Real property taxes (Table KF9)
881.5	Land valuation. Real property assessment (Table KF9)
881.8.A-Z	Special topics, A-Z
881.8.F67	Forest land. Forest yield taxes (Table KF7)

Public finance
State revenue
Particular sources of revenue
Taxation
Particular taxes
Property taxes. Taxation of capital
Real property taxes
Special topics, A-Z -- Continued
Gas-producing properties see KFC881.8.O34
881.8.O34 Oil- and gas-producing properties (Table KF7)
886 Corporate franchises (Special franchises).
Corporate stock (Table KF9)
Other taxes on capital and income
Estate, inheritance, and gift taxes
894 General (Table KF9)
895 Estate tax. Inheritance tax (Table KF9)
Excise taxes. Taxes on transactions
898 General (Table KF9)
899 Retail sales taxes (Table KF9)
899.5 Use taxes (Table KF9)
900.A-Z Particular commodities, services, transactions, A-Z
900.A5 Alcoholic beverages. Liquor taxes (Table KF7)
900.A8 Automobile licenses (Table KF7)
900.A9 Aviation. Air user taxes (Table KF7)
900.C37 Carbonated beverages (Table KF7)
Gambling see KFC900.W34
900.M6 Mortgages (Table KF7)
900.M67 Motor fuels. Gasoline (Table KF7)
900.M68 Motor vehicles (Table KF7)
900.T62 Tobacco and tobacco products (Table KF7)
900.W34 Wagering. Gambling (Table KF7)
902.A-Z Other sources of revenue, A-Z
902.F3 Federal grants-in-aid (Table KF7)
Local finance
905 General. State and local jurisdiction (Table KF9)
Particular sources of revenue
Taxation
910 General. Tax power of municipalities. State and local
tax jurisdiction and taxation (Table KF9)
912.A-Z Particular taxes, A-Z
912.B8 Business taxes (Table KF7)
912.P7 Property taxes (Table KF7)
912.R3 Real property tax (Table KF7)
912.R37 Retail sales taxes (Table KF7)
914 Other sources of revenue (Table KF9)
917.A-Z Particular kinds of local jurisdiction, A-Z
917.C5 Cities (Table KF7)

KFC UNITED STATES (CALIFORNIA) KFC

Public finance -- Continued

919	Claims (Table KF9)
	Military law
920	General. Comprehensive (Table KF9)
927	State militia. National Guard (Table KF9)
	Military criminal law and procedure
930	General. Comprehensive (Table KF9)
	Criminal procedure. Military justice
931	General (Table KF9)
932	Courts-martial (Table KF9)
934	Civil defense (Table KF9)
	War veterans
935	General. Pensions (Table KF9)
	By period
935.3	1916-1939 (Table KF9)
935.5	1944- (Table KF9)
940	Indians (Table KF9)
	Courts. Procedure
950	Administration of justice. Organization of the judiciary (Table KF9 modified)
	For history see KFC78
950.A19	Directories
951	Judicial councils. Judicial conference (Table KF9)
	Court organization and procedure
955	General (Table KF9)
955.5	Conduct of court proceedings. Decorum (Table KF9)
956	Congestion and delay (Table KF9)
	Administration and management
958	General (Table KF9)
958.5	Finance. Accounting (Table KF9)
	Particular courts
960	Supreme Court (Table KF9)
964	Intermediate appellate courts: District Courts of Appeal (Table KF9)
	Trial courts
	Chancery courts see KFC997
	County courts: Superior Courts
968	Collective (Table KF9)
969.A-Z	Particular courts. By county, A-Z
	Under each:
	.A7 *Court records*
	By initial date of period covered
	.A8-Z *Treatises. Monographs*
	Minor courts
	Municipal courts
970	Collective (Table KF9)

KFC UNITED STATES (CALIFORNIA) KFC

Courts. Procedure
Court organization and procedure
Particular courts
Minor courts
Municipal courts -- Continued

971.A-Z Particular courts. By city, A-Z
Under each:
.A7 *Court records*
By initial date of period covered
.A8-Z *Treatises. Monographs*

975 Justice courts. Township, police, etc., courts (Table KF9)

976 Small claims courts (Table KF9)
Judicial officers. Court employees

979 General (Table KF9)
Judges

980 General (Table KF9)
Impeachment

983 General (Table KF9)

984.A-Z Particular cases. By respondent, A-Z

985.A-Z Other, A-Z

985.C5 Clerks of court. Administrative officers (Table KF7)

985.C6 Court reporters (Table KF7)

985.J8 Justices of the peace (Table KF7)

985.N6 Notaries (Table KF7)

985.S4 Sheriffs (Table KF7)
Civil procedure
General

990 Legislation

990.A17 Legislative documents. By date
Statutes
Collections

990.A19-.A199 Serials

990.A2 Monographs. By date of publication

990.A3-.A319 Particular acts
Arrange chronologically, by means of successive Cutter numbers, according to date of original enactment or revision of law
Under each:
.xA15 Compilations of legislative histories
.xA2 Unannotated texts. By date of publication
.xA3-.xZ Annotated editions. Commentaries. By author of commentary or annotations
Court rules

992 General. Trial courts

KFC UNITED STATES (CALIFORNIA) KFC

Courts. Procedure
Civil procedure
General
Legislation
Court rules
General. Trial courts -- Continued
Collections

992.A19-.A199	Serials
992.A2	Monographs. By date of publication
992.A23	Citators to rules
992.A25	Drafts. By date
992.A3-.A319	Particular rules

Arrange chronologically, by means of successive Cutter numbers, according to date of adoption or revision of rules

Under each:

.xA15	*Compilations of legislative histories. By date of publication*
.xA2	*Unannotated texts. By date of publication*
.xA3-.xZ7	*Annotated editions. Commentaries. By author of commentary or annotations*
.xZ8-.xZ89	*Digests*

993.A-Z	Particular courts, A-Z

Under each:

.A2	*Collections*
	By date of publication
.A3-.Z49	*Particular rules*
.A3	*Unannotated texts*
	By date of publication
.A5-.Z49	*Annotated editions. Commentaries By author of commentary or annotations*
.Z5	*Indexes*
	By date of publication

Courts of intermediate appeals see KFC1078+
Supreme Court see KFC1081

995	General works (Table KF8)
997	Equity practice and procedure. Chancery courts (Table KF9)

Action

1003	General (Table KF9)
1004.A-Z	Special topics, A-Z
1004.P75	Process (Table KF7)

Pleading and motions

Courts. Procedure
Civil procedure
Pleading and motions -- Continued

1010	General. Pleading (Table KF9)
1012	Motions (Table KF9)
1013	Defenses and objections (Exceptions) (Table KF9)
1015	Lis pendens (Table KF9)
	Parties
1016	General (Table KF9)
1016.5	Joinder of parties. Coordination of actions (Table KF9)
1017	Class action (Table KF9)
	Pre-trial procedure
1020	General. Deposition and discovery. Interrogatories (Table KF9)
1021.A-Z	Special topics, A-Z
1021.E42	Electronic discovery
	Settlement see KFC1093
	Trial. Trial practice. Trial tactics
1025	General (Table KF9)
1028.A-Z	Particular types of cases or claims, A-Z
	Damages see KFC1028.T67
1028.E9	Eviction
1028.L33	Labor law
1028.M34	Malpractice
1028.P4	Personal injuries
1028.T67	Torts. Damages
	Evidence
1030	General (Table KF9)
	Burden of proof
1031	General (Table KF9)
1032	Presumptions. Judicial notice. Prima-facie evidence (Table KF9)
	Particular kinds of evidence
1038	Documentary (Table KF9)
	Witnesses
1040	General (Table KF9)
1040.5	Subpoena (Table KF9)
	Privileged (Confidential) communications
1041	General (Table KF9)
1041.5.A-Z	Particular relationships, A-Z
1041.5.H8	Husband and wife (Table KF7)
1042	Expert evidence. Expert witnesses (Table KF9)
1043	Hearsay (Table KF9)
	Jury and jurors
1045	General (Table KF9)

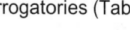

KFC UNITED STATES (CALIFORNIA) KFC

Courts. Procedure
Civil procedure
Trial. Trial practice. Trial tactics
Jury and jurors -- Continued

1047	Instructions to juries (Table KF9)
	For collected instructions see KF213.A+
	For individual instructions see KF389
	Judgment
1050	General
1051	Costs. Fees. In forma pauperis (Table KF9)
1052	Summary judgment (Table KF9)
	Remedies and special proceedings
1061	Habeas corpus (Table KF9)
1062	Injunctions. Provisional remedies (Table KF9)
1063	Receivers in equity (Table KF9)
	Execution of judgment
1065	General (Table KF9)
1066	Attachment. Garnishment (Table KF9)
1070	Extraordinary remedies (Table KF9)
	Appellate procedure
1075	General (Table KF9)
	Intermediate appeals
1078	General (Table KF9)
1080.A-Z	Particular courts, A-Z
	Under each:
	.A4-.Z Court rules
	.A4 Collections
	.A42-.Z Particular rules
	.A42 Unannotated texts
	By date of publication
	.A43-.Z Annotated editions.
	Commentaries
1081	Appeals to State Supreme Court (Table KF9)
	Proceedings relating to particular branches of the law or special subjects, or governed by special laws.
	Noncontentious (ex-parte) jurisdiction
1088	Adoption (Table KF9)
	Bankruptcy see KFC365+
1089	Lunacy (Table KF9)
	Probate see KFC205+
1093	Negotiated settlement. Compromise (Table KF9)
1094	Arbitration and award. Commercial arbitration (Table KF9)
	Criminal law
	Cf. KFC930+ Military criminal law and procedure
	Cf. KFC1195+ Juvenile criminal law and procedure
1100	General. Comprehensive (Table KF9)

KFC UNITED STATES (CALIFORNIA) KFC

Criminal law -- Continued
Administration of criminal justice. Reform of criminal law, enforcement, and procedure

1102	General (Table KF9)
1102.4	Speedy trial (Table KF9)
1102.5	Crime and publicity. Trial by newspaper (Table KF9)
	Cf. KFC1141 Contempt of court
	Punishment and penalties
1104	General (Table KF9)
1108.A-Z	Particular penalties, A-Z
1108.C2	Capital punishment (Table KF7)
	General principles
	Criminal liability
1110	General (Table KF9)
1115	Exemption from liability. Defenses (Table KF9)
	Particular defenses
1116	Insanity (Table KF9)
	Particular offenses
	Offenses against the person
1121	Abortion. Procuring miscarriage (Table KF9)
	Cf. KFC609 Birth control
1121.4	Family violence (Table KF9)
1121.5	Child abuse (Table KF9)
1122	Sexual offenses (Table KF9)
	Offenses against property
	Including works on white collar crime and offenses against the economic order in general
1128	General (Table KF9)
1131	Thievery. Larceny (Table KF9)
1131.5	Theft of use (Table KF9)
1132	Threats. Extortion. Blackmail (Table KF9)
1133	Racketeering. Organized crime (Table KF9)
1134	Arson (Table KF9)
	Offenses against government and public order. Political offenses
1137	General (Table KF9)
	Particular
1139	Criminal syndicalism. Sabotage (Table KF9)
	Offenses against the administration of justice
1141	Contempt of court (Table KF9)
	Offenses against public safety
1145	Riot
1145.5	Offenses against public convenience and morality. Crimes without victims (Table KF9)
	Criminal procedure
1155	General (Table KF9)
1156	Arrest and commitment. Rights of suspects (Table KF9)

KFC UNITED STATES (CALIFORNIA) KFC

Criminal procedure -- Continued

Number	Description
1157	Searches and seizures (Table KF9)
1157.7	Extradition. Interstate rendition (Table KF9)
1158	Indictment. Information. Public prosecutor (Table KF9)
1159	Grand jury (Table KF9)
	For collected charges see KF213.A+
	For individual charges see KF389
	Arraignment. Preparation for trial
1160	General (Table KF9)
1160.4	Right to counsel. Public defenders (Table KF9)
1160.5	Discovery (Table KF9)
1161	Procedure without trial. Plea bargaining. Pleas of guilty. Nolo contendere (Table KF9)
	Trial
1162	General (Table KF9)
	Evidence. Burden of proof
1165	General (Table KF9)
	Admission of evidence
1166	General (Table KF9)
1167	Confession (Table KF9)
1168	Wiretapping. Electronic listening and recording devices (Table KF9)
	Particular types of evidence
1169	Witnesses
1169.3.A-Z	Other, A-Z
1171	Instructions to jury. Directed verdict (Table KF9)
	For collected instructions see KF213.A+
	For individual instructions see KF389
1172	Sentence (Table KF9)
1174	Appeals. Appellate procedure (Table KF9)
1176	Pardon (Table KF9)
(1177)	Proceedings before juvenile courts see KFC1195+
	Execution of sentence
1179	Corrections
	Imprisonment
1180	General (Table KF9)
1181	Prison administration. Prison discipline (Table KF9)
1181.5	Prisoners (Table KF9)
	Particular types of penal or correctional institutions
	Reformatories
1186.A1	General
1186.A5-Z	Particular institutions, A-Z
	Juvenile detention homes see KFC1198.6
1190	Probation. Parole (Table KF9)
1190.5	Criminal registration (Table KF9)

KFC UNITED STATES (CALIFORNIA) KFC

Criminal procedure
Execution of sentence -- Continued

1194	Cancellation of records of arrest, conviction, etc. (Table KF9)
1194.5	Victims of crimes (Table KF9)
	Juvenile criminal law and procedure. Administration of juvenile justice
1195	General (Table KF9)
1196	Juvenile courts (Table KF9)
	Criminal procedure
1198	General (Table KF9)
	Execution of sentence
	Imprisonment
1198.6	Juvenile detention homes (Table KF9)
1198.8	Probation and parole (Table KF9)
1199.A-Z	Particular counties, A-Z
	Subarrange each by Table KF10C and Table KF10D modified as follows: .x2C6 = County government and services
<1199.5.A-Z>	Particular cities, A-Z
	see KFX

KFC UNITED STATES (COLORADO) KFC

Call Number	Description
1801-2399	United States (Colorado) (Table KFA-KFZ modified)
	Law reports and related materials
1845-1845.9	Supreme Court (Table KF31 modified)
1845	Reports
	Official series
1845.A2	Colorado reports (1864-)
1845.A3-.A39	Unofficial series
1845.A32	Colorado reporter
1845.A33	Colorado reporter (2d)
1845.A4A-.A4Z	Abridged, selected, defunct publications
1845.C6	Colorado reports (Chicago, Callaher, 1864-1932)
	91 v.

KFC UNITED STATES (CONNECTICUT) KFC

Call Number	Description
3601-4199	United States (Connecticut) (Table KFA-KFZ modified)
	Law reports and related materials
3645-3645.9	Supreme Court (Table KF31 modified)
3645	Reports
	Official series and predecessors
3645.A19 1802	Day (1802-1813)
	5 v.
3645.A2	Connecticut Reports (1814-)
3645.A3-.A39	Unofficial series
3645.A4	Abridged, selected, defunct
3645.A4C6	Connecticut Reports, v. 1-35 (2d ed.) Albany, Gould,
	1848-1904
	Lower courts
3647-3647.9	Various courts (Table KF31 modified)
3647	Reports
3647.A19 1785	Kirby (1785-1788) 
	1 v. 1789
3647.A19 1785a	Kirby (1785-1788)
	1 v. 1898
3647.A19 1785b	Kirby Suppl.
	1 v. 1933
3647.A19 1785c	Kirby (1785-1788)
	1 v. 1986
3647.A19 1789	Root (1789-1798)
	2 v. 1798-1802
	Official series
3647.A2	Connecticut supplement (1935-)
3647.A3-.A39	Unofficial series
3647.A3	Connecticut Reporter (1962-)
3647.A33	Connecticut docket (1987-)
	Appellate courts
3648-3648.9	Superior Court. Appellate Court (Table KF31 modified)
3648	Reports
3648.A19 1772	Superior Court: Wm Samuel Johnson Diary (1772-
	1773)
	1 v. 1942
3648.A2	Appellate Court: Connecticut appellate reports (1985-
	)

KFD UNITED STATES (DELAWARE) KFD

1-599	United States (Delaware) (Table KFA-KFZ modified)
	Law reports and related materials
45-45.9	Supreme Court (Table KF31 modified)
45	Reports
	Official series and predecessors
	Separate editions of nominative reports making up
	Delaware reports
	After Storey, separate editions are continued in Delaware reporter
	Old series
45.A19 1832	Harrington (1832-1854)
45.A19 1855	Houston (1855-1892)
45.A19 1893	Marvel (1893-1897)
45.A19 1897	Pennewill (1898-1909)
45.A19 1909	Boyce (1909-1920)
45.A19 1919	W.W. Harrington (1919-1939)
45.A19 1939	Terry (1939-1958)
45.A19 1958	Storey
	New series
45.A2 v. 1-v. 5	Harrington 5 v.
45.A2 v. 6-v. 14	Houston 9 v.
45.A2 v. 15-v. 16	Marvel 2 v.
45.A2 v. 17-v. 23	Pennewill 7 v.
45.A2 v. 24-v. 30	Boyce 7 v.
45.A2 v. 31-v. 39	W.W. Harrington 9 v.
45.A2 v. 40-v. 50	Terry 11 v.
45.A2 v. 51-v. 59	Storey 9 v.
	Lower courts
47-47.9	Various courts (Table KF31 modified)
47	Reports
	Official series
47.A2	Delaware chancery reports (1814-1968)
	Continued in Delaware reporter
47.A4	Defunct publications
47.A4B6	Boorstin's Delaware cases (1792-1830)
	3 v.
	Unofficial series
47.D4	Delaware reporter (1969-)

KFD UNITED STATES (DISTRICT OF COLUMBIA) KFD

Call Number	Description
1201-1799	United States (District of Columbia) (Table KFA-KFZ modified) Law reports and related materials
1245-1245.9	Court of last resort (Supreme Court, U.S. Court of Appeals for the District of Columbia Circuit, etc.) (Table KF31 modified)
1245	Reports
	Official series and predecessors
	New series
1245.A19	Hayward and Hazelton 2 v.
1245.A19 1-6 D.C.	Cranch 6 v.
1245.A19 6-7 D.C.	District of Columbia 2 v.
1245.A19 8-10 D.C.	MacArthur 3 v.
1245.A19 11 D.C.	MacArthur and Mackey 1 v.
1245.A19 12-20 D.C.	Mackey
1245.A19 21 D.C.	Tucker and Clephane 1 v.
	Old series
1245.A19 1801	Cranch, 1801-1840
1245.A19 1840	Hayward and Hazelton, 1843-1863
1245.A19 1863	District of Columbia, 1863-1872
1245.A19 1873	MacArthur, 1873-1879
1245.A19 1879	MacArthur and Mackey, 1879-1880
1245.A19 1880	Mackey
1245.A19 1892	Tucker and Clephane, 1892-1893
1245.A2	D.C. Court of Appeals and U.S. Court of Appeals for D.C. (1892-)
1245.A3-.A39	Unofficial series
1245.A4A-.A4Z	Abridged, selected, defunct
1245.A4A43	Additional cases, 1901
	1 v.
1245.A4M3	McCormick (Supreme Court, N.S., 1933-1935)
	2 v.
1245.A4W3	Washington Law reporter

KFF UNITED STATES (FLORIDA) KFF

1-599	United States (Florida) (Table KFA-KFZ modified)
	Law reports and related materials
45-45.9	Supreme Court (Table KF31 modified)
45	Reports
45.A2	Official series (1846-1948)
	160 v.
	Discontinued with v. 160. Entry to be closed. Continued as Florida cases in Southern Reporter, 2d, p. 581
	Lower courts
	Trial courts
51-51.9	Collective (Table KF31 modified)
51	Reports
51.A3	Florida supplement (1952-)
	50 v.
51.A32	Florida supplement second (1983-)

KFG UNITED STATES (GEORGIA) KFG

Call Number	Description
1-599	United States (Georgia) (Table KFA-KFZ modified)
	Law reports and related materials
45-45.9	Supreme Court (Table KF31 modified)
45	Reports
	Official series and predecessors
45.A19 1805	Charlton, T.U.P. (1805-1811)
	1 v.
45.A19 1811	Charlton, R.M. (1811-1837)
	1 v.
45.A19 1820	Gault, Joseph (1820-1846)
	1 v.
45.A19 1830	Dudley (1830-1833)
	1 v. (2 pts.)
45.A19 1842	Georgia decisions (1842-1843)
	1 v.
45.A2	Georgia reports (1846-)
	Supplement to v. 33 (1864)
45.A3-.A39	Unofficial series
45.A32	Georgia reports. Reprint edition
45.A33	Georgia reports annotated, Charlton, -65 Georgia (1903-)
45.A4A-.A4Z	Abridged, selected, defunct
45.A4G3	Georgia Law Reporter (1885-1886)
	Lower courts
47-47.9	General. Various courts (Table KF31 modified)
47	Reports
47.A2	Official series
47.A3-.A39	Unofficial series
	Intermediate appellate courts
48-48.9	Court of Appeals (Table KF31 modified)
48	Reports
	Official series
48.A2	Georgia Appeals reports

KFH UNITED STATES (HAWAII) KFH

1-599	United States (Hawaii) (Table KFA-KFZ modified)
	Law reports and related materials
45-45.9	Supreme Court (Table KF31 modified)
45	Reports
	Official series
45.A2	Hawaii Reports, 1847/56-
	Lower courts
47-47.9	Various courts (Table KF31 modified)
47	Reports
47.A4A-.A4Z	Abridged, selected, defunct
47.A4P6	Poepoe (1849-1889)
	1 v.
	Intermediate appellate courts
48-48.9	Court of Appeals (Table KF31 modified)
48	Reports
	Official series
48.A2	Hawaii appellate reports (1981-)

KFI UNITED STATES (IDAHO) KFI

1-599	United States (Idaho) (Table KFA-KFZ modified)
	Law reports and related materials
45-45.9	Supreme Court (Table KF31 modified)
45	Reports
	Official series
45.A2	Idaho reports (1866-)
45.A4A-.A4Z	Defunct publications. By editor, A-Z
45.A4C8	Cummins (1866-1867)
	1 v.

KFI UNITED STATES (ILLINOIS) KFI

Call Number	Description
1201-1799	United States (Illinois) (Table KFA-KFZ modified)
	Law reports and related materials
1245-1245.9	Supreme Court (Table KF31 modified)
1245	Reports
	Official series and predecessors
	Separate editions of nominative reports making up vols. 1-10 of Illinois reports
1245.A19 1819	Breese (1819-1831) 1 v. (Old series)
	.A2 v. 1 (New series)
1245.A19 1832	Scammon (1832-1843) 4 v. (Old series)
	.A2 v. 2-5 (New series)
1245.A19 1844	Gilman (1844-1849) 4 v. (Old series)
	.A2 v. 6-10 (New series)
1245.A2 v. 11-415	Illinois reports (1850-1945) 415 v.
1245.A2 1945-	Illinois reports (2d ser.)
1245.A4A-.A4Z	Defunct publications
1245.A4B55	Blackwell (1819-1841)
	1 v.
1245.A4F6	Forman (1832-1838)
	1 v.
1245.A4R4	Reports (no reporter) (Dec. Term 1832)
	1 v.
1245.A4U5	Underwood (1832-1857)
	17 v.
	Lower courts
1247-1247.9	Various courts (Table KF31 modified)
1247	Reports
	Unofficial series
1247.A3	Illinois decisions (1936-)
1247.A32	Illinois decisions (1962-)
1247.A34	West's Illinois decisions, (1976-)
1247.A4A-.A4Z	Defunct publications
1247.A4M3	Matthew's Illinois Circuit Court reports (1905-1912)
	4 v.
	Intermediate appellate courts
1248-1248.9	Appellate Court (Table KF31 modified)
1248	Reports
	Official series
1248.A2 1877	Illinois Appellate Court reports (1877-1954)
	351 v.
1248.A2 1954	Illinois Appellate Court reports, 2d ser. (1954-1973)
	133 v.
1248.A2 1972	Illinois Appellate Court reports, 3d ser. (1972-)
	Court of Claims
1254.5	Reports
	Official series
1254.5.A2	Reports (1889-)

KFI UNITED STATES (INDIANA) KFI

3001-3599	United States (Indiana) (Table KFA-KFZ modified)
	Law reports and related materials
3045-3045.9	Supreme Court (Table KF31 modified)
3045	Reports
	Official series and predecessors
3045.A19 1817	Blackford 1817-1847
	8 v.
3045.A19 1848	Smith 1848-1849
	1 v.
3045.A2	Supreme Court reports, 1848-
	Lower courts
3047-3047.9	Various courts (Table KF31 modified)
3047	Reports
3047.A3-.A39	Unofficial series
	Appellate courts
3048-3048.9	General. Collective (Table KF31 modified)
3048	Reports
	Official series
3048.A2	Indiana appellate reports (1890-)

KFI UNITED STATES (IOWA) KFI

4201-4799	United States (Iowa) (Table KFA-KFZ modified)
	Law reports and related materials
4245-1245.9	Supreme Court (Table KF31 modified)
4245	Reports
	Official series and predecessors
4245.A19 1838	Bradford (1838-1841) 3 v. in 1
4245.A19 1839	Morris (1839-1846) 1 v.
4245.A19 1847	Greene (1847-1854) 4 v.
4245.A2	Iowa reports (1855-)
4245.A4A-.A4Z	Abridged, selected, defunct
4245.A4C6	Iowa reports, edited by Cole (1874-1881) 8 v.
4245.A4C61	Iowa reports, edited by Cole (1892) 8 v.

KFK UNITED STATES (KANSAS) KFK

1-599	United States (Kansas) (Table KFA-KFZ modified)
	Law reports and related materials
45-45.9	Supreme Court (Table KF31 modified)
45	Reports
	Official series and predecessors
45.A19	McCahon (1858-1868)
45.A2	Kansas reports (1862-)
	Lower courts
	Intermediate appellate courts
48-48.9	Court of Appeals (Table KF31 modified)
48	Reports
	Official series
48.A21	Kansas appeals reports (1895-1902) 10 v.
48.A22	Kansas Court of Appeals reports, second (1977-)

KFK UNITED STATES (KENTUCKY) KFK

1201-1799	United States (Kentucky) (Table KFA-KFZ modified)
	Law reports and related materials
1245-1245.9	Court of Appeals (Table KF31 modified)
1245	Reports
	Official series and predecessors
	Separate editions of nominative reports making up vols.
	1-77 of Kentucky Reports
1245.A19 1785	Hughes (1785-1801) 1 v. (Old series)
	.A2 v. 1 (New series)
1245.A19 1801	Sneed (1801-1805) 1 v. (Old series)
	.A2 v. 2 (New series)
1245.A19 1805	Hardin (1805-1808) 1 v. (Old series)
	.A2 v. 3 (New series)
1245.A19 1808	Bibb (1808-1817) 4 v. (Old series)
	.A2 v. 4-7 (New series)
1245.A19 1817	Marshall, A.K. (1817-1821) 3 v. (Old series)
	.A2 v. 8-10 (New series)
1245.A19 1822	Littell (1822-1824) 5 v. (Old series)
	.A2 v. 11-15 (New series)
1245.A19 1824	Monroe, T.B. (1824-1828) 7 v. (Old series)
	.A2 v. 17-23 (New series)
1245.A19 1829	Marshall, J.J. (1829-1832) 7 v. (Old series)
	.A2 v. 24-30 (New series)
1245.A19 1833	Dana (1833-1840) 9 v. (Old series)
	.A2 v. 31-39 (New series)
1245.A19 1840	Monroe, Ben (1840-1857) 18 v. (Old series)
	.A2 v. 40-57 (New series)
1245.A19 1858	Metcalfe (1858-1863) 4 v. (Old series)
	.A2 v. 58-61 (New series)
1245.A19 1863	Duvall (1863-1866) 2 v. (Old series)
	.A2 v. 62-63 (New series)
1245.A19 1866	Bush (1866-1879) 14 v. (Old series)
	.A2 v. 64-77 (New series)
1245.A2	Kentucky reports (Discontinued, v. 314). Continued in
	"Kentucky cases," South Western Reporter, 2d
	ser., v. 238, p. 844 78-314 v.
	Unofficial series
1245.A31	Kentucky decisions (1886-1928)
1245.A32	Kentucky decisions (1928-)
1245.A4A-.A4Z	Abridged, selected, defunct
1245.A4K4	Kentucky opinions (1864-1886) 13 v.
	Lower courts
1247-1247.9	Various courts (Table KF31 modified)
1247	Reports
1247.A4A-.A4Z	Abridged, selected, defunct
1247.A4K4	Kentucky reporter (1881-1908)
1247.A4L5	Littell's Selected cases (1795-1821)

KFL UNITED STATES (LOUISIANA) KFL

Call Number	Description
1-599	United States (Louisiana) (Table KFA-KFZ modified)
	Law reports and related materials
45-45.9	Supreme Court (Table KF31 modified)
45	Reports
	Official series and predecessors
45.A19 1809	Orleans term reports (Martin) (1809-1812) 2 v.
45.A19 1813	Louisiana term reports (Martin) (1813-1823) 10 v.
45.A19 1823	Louisiana term reports (Martin) New series (1823-1830) 8 v.
45.A19 1830	Louisiana Supreme Court Reports (Miller and Curry) (1833-1841) 19 v.
45.A19 1846	Louisiana Annual (Supreme Court) (1846-1900) 52 v.
45.A2	Louisiana reports 100 vols. in 55 books (1809-1900) and vol. 104 (There are no vols. 101-103, because separate reports up to reprint totaled 103 vols.)
45.A21	Louisiana reports (1897-1903) 9 v.
45.A4A-.A4Z	Abridged, selected, defunct
45.A4H2	Harrison, Condensed reports (1809-1830) 4 v.
45.A4M3	Manning's unreported cases (1877-1880) 1 v.
45.A4M4	Martin's reports (1809-1830) 10 v.
	Lower courts
	Intermediate appellate courts
48-48.9	Court of Appeals (Table KF31 modified)
48	Reports
48.A19 1881	McGloin (1881-1884) 2 v.
48.A19 1885	Gunby's reports (Circuit Court of Appeals) (1885) 1 v.
48.A2	Court of Appeals Reports (1924-1932) 19 v. (Discontinued)
49.A-Z	Particular appellate courts, A-Z
49.O7	Orleans Parish (1903-1917) 14 v.
49.O73	Orleans Parish, Peltier's decisions (1917-)
	Succession upon death
148.A-Z	Special topics, A-Z
148.L4	Legitime (Table KF7)
	Local government
432	Parish government (Table KF9)

KFM UNITED STATES (MAINE) KFM

1-599	United States (Maine) (Table KFA-KFZ modified)
	Law reports and related materials
45-45.9	Supreme Court (Table KF31 modified)
45	Reports
	Official series and predecessors
	Separate editions of nominative reports making up vols.
	1-12 of Maine reports
45.A19 1820	Greenleaf (1820-1832) 9 v. (Old series)
	.A2 v. 1-9 (New series)
45.A19 1833	Fairfield (1833-1835) 3 v. (Old series)
	.A2 v. 10-12 (New series)
45.A2	Maine reports (1836-1965) 161 v.
	v. 13-161
45.A21	Maine reporter (1966-)

KFM UNITED STATES (MARYLAND) KFM

1201-1799	United States (Maryland) (Table KFA-KFZ modified)
	Law reports and related materials
1245-1245.9	Court of Appeals (Table KF31 modified)
1245	Reports
	Official series and predecessors
1245.A19 1658	Harris and McHenry (General Court) (1658-1799) 4 v.
1245.A19 1800	Harris and Johnson (General Court and Court of Appeals) (1800-1826) 7 v.
1245.A19 1826	Harris and Gill (1826-1829) 2 v.
1245.A19 1829	Gill and Johnson (1829-1842) 12 v.
1245.A19 1843	Gill and Miller (1843-1851) 9 v.
1245.A195 1811	Bland (Chancery) (1811-1832) 3 v.
1245.A195 1847	Maryland Chancery decisions (1847-1854) 4 v.
1245.A2	Maryland Reports (1851-)
1245.A3-.A39	Unofficial series
1245.A3	Maryland reporter (1942-)
1245.A4A-.A4Z	Abridged, selected, defunct
1245.A4P7	Proceedings (1695-1729) 1 v.
	Lower courts
	Intermediate appellate courts
1248-1248.9	Court of Special Appeals (Table KF31 modified)
1248	Reports
	Official series
1248.A2	Maryland appellate reports (1967-)

KFM UNITED STATES (MASSACHUSETTS) KFM

Call Number	Description
2401-2999	United States (Massachusetts) (Table KFA-KFZ modified)
	Law reports and related materials
2445-2445.9	Supreme Judicial Court (Table KF31 modified)
2445	Reports
	Official series and predecessors
	Separate editions of nominative reports making up vols.
	1-100 of Massachusetts Reports
2445.A19 1804	Williams (1804-1805) 1 v. (Old series)
	.A2 v. 1 (New series)
2445.A19 1806	Tyng (1806-1822) 16 v.
	.A2 v. 2-17 (New series)
2445.A19 1822	Pickering (1822-1839) 24 v.
	.A2 v. 18-41 (New series)
2445.A19 1840	Metcalf (1840-1844) 13 v.
	.A2 v. 42-54 (New series)
2445.A19 1848	Cushing (1848-1853) 12 v.
	.A2 v. 55-66 (New series)
2445.A19 1854	Gray (1854-1860) 16 v.
	.A2 v. 67-82 (New series)
2445.A19 1861	Allen (1861-1867) 14 v.
	.A2 v. 83-96 (New series)
2445.A19 1867	Browne (1867-1872) 13 v.
	.A2 v. 97-100 (New series)
2445.A2	Massachusetts Reports (1873-) v. 101-
2445.A3-.A39	Unofficial series
2445.A32	Massachusetts decisions (1885-)
2445.A33	Massachusetts decisions (2d) (West, 1936-)
	Lower courts
	Intermediate appellate courts
2448-2448.9	Appeals Court (Table KF31 modified)
2448	Reports
	Official series
2448.A22	Massachusetts Appeals Court reports (1972/1974-)
	Other courts
2451-2451.9	Collective (Table KF31 modified)
2451	Reports
2451.A4A-.A4Z	Abridged, selected, defunct
2451.A4M36	Massachusetts appellate decisions (1941-1978) 59 v.
2451.A4M37	Massachusetts appellate decisions (1942-)

KFM UNITED STATES (MICHIGAN) KFM

4201-4799	United States (Michigan) (Table KFA-KFZ modified)
	Law reports and related materials
4245-4245.9	Supreme Court (Table KF31 modified)
4245	Reports
	Official series and predecessors
4245.A19 1805	Blume (1805-1836) 6 v.
4245.A19 1843	Douglass (1943-1847) 2 v.
4245.A195 1836	Harrington's Chancery (1836-1842) 1 v.
4245.A195 1842	Walker's Chancery (1842-1845) 1 v.
4245.A2	Michigan reports (1847-)
4245.A3-.A39	Unofficial series
4245.A3	Michigan reports, annotated (1878-)
	Courts. Procedure
	Court organization and procedure
	Particular courts
	Trial courts: County courts. District courts. Superior courts
4715	Collective (Table KF6 modified)
4715.A545	Court records. By initial date of period covered
4715.5	Circuit court commissioners (Table KF6)

KFM UNITED STATES (MINNESOTA) KFM

5401-5999	United States (Minnesota) (Table KFA-KFZ modified)
	Law reports and related materials
5445-5445.9	Supreme Court (Table KF31 modified)
5445	Reports
	Official series
5445.A2	Minnesota reports (1851-)
5445.A3-.A39	Unofficial series
5445.A3	Minnesota law reports (1982-)

KFM UNITED STATES (MISSISSIPPI) KFM

6601-7199	United States (Mississippi) (Table KFA-KFZ modified)
	Law reports and related materials
6645-6645.9	Supreme Court (Table KF31 modified)
6645	Reports
	Official series and predecessors
	Separate editions of nominative reports making up vols.
	1-22 of Mississippi Reports
6645.A19 1818	Walker (1818-1832) 1 v. (Old series)
	.A2 v. 1 (New series)
6645.A19 1834	Howard (1834-1843) 7 v. (Old series)
	.A2 v. 2-8 (New series)
6645.A19 1843	Smedes and Marshall (1843-1850) 14 v. (Old series)
	.A2 v. 9-22 (New series)
6645.A2	Mississippi reports to June 30, 1966
	v. 23
6645.A21	Mississippi Reporter
	County civil service. County officials
7037	County civil service. County officials (Table KF9)
7037.8.A-Z	Particular offices or positions, A-Z
7037.8.C5	Chancery clerks (Table KF7)

KFM UNITED STATES (MISSOURI) KFM

7801-8399	United States (Missouri) (Table KFA-KFZ modified)
	Law reports and related materials
7845-7845.9	Supreme Court (Table KF31 modified)
7845	Reports
	Official series
7845.A2	Missouri reports (1821-1956) 365 v.
	Discontinued. Continued in Missouri Cases, S.W.
	Reporter, 2d ser. v. 295, p. 825
	Lower courts
7847-7847.9	Various courts (Table KF31 modified)
7847	Reports
	Official series
7847.A2	Missouri decisions (S.W. Reporter)
	Appellate courts
7848-7848.9	General (Table KF31 modified)
7848	Reports
	Official series
7848.A2	Missouri appeal reports (1876-1952 (?)) 241 v. (?)
	Discontinued. Continued in Missouri Cases, S.W.
	Reporter, 2d ser. v. 252, p. 96

KFM UNITED STATES (MONTANA) KFM

9001-9599	United States (Montana) (Table KFA-KFZ modified)
	Law reports and related materials
9045-9045.9	Supreme Court (Table KF31 modified)
9045	Reports
	Official series
9045.A2	Montana reports (1868-)

KFN UNITED STATES (NEBRASKA) KFN

1-599	United States (Nebraska) (Table KFA-KFZ modified)
	Legislative documents
	Committee documents
	Hearings
	Committees of the unicameral legislature
10.8.A-Z	Serials. By committee or subcommittee, A-Z
	Subarrange by title
11	Monographs. By committee or subcommittee, A-Z, and initial date of hearings
(11.3.A-Z)	This number not used
(11.4.A-Z)	This number not used
	Reports
	Reports of the unicameral legislature and its committees
11.58	General
	Individual committees and subcommittees
11.6.A-Z	Serials. By committee or subcommittee, A-Z
	Subarrange by title
11.62.A-Z	Monographs. By committee or subcommittee, A-Z, and date of original publication
	Upper house (not applicable for Nebraska)
(11.7.A-Z)	This number not used
(11.72.A-Z)	This number not used
	Lower house (not applicable for Nebraska)
(11.8.A-Z)	This number not used
(11.82.A-Z)	This number not used
	Law reports and related materials
45-45.9	Supreme Court (Table KF31 modified)
45	Reports
	Official series
45.A2	Nebraska reports (1860-)
45.A4	Defunct publications
45.A4N4	Nebraska reports (unofficial) (1901-1904)
	5 v.
	Lower courts
	Court of Appeals
48-48.9	General (Table KF31 modified)
48	Reports
	Official series
48.A2	Decisions of the Nebraska Court of Appeals (1992-)

KFN UNITED STATES (NEVADA) KFN

601-1199	United States (Nevada) (Table KFA-KFZ modified)
	Law reports and related materials
645-645.9	Supreme Court (Table KF31 modified)
645	Reports
	Official series
645.A2	Nevada reports (1865-)

KFN UNITED STATES (NEW HAMPSHIRE) KFN

1201-1799	United States (New Hampshire) (Table KFA-KFZ modified)
	Law reports and related materials
1245-1245.9	Supreme Court (Table KF31 modified)
1245	Reports
	Official series and predecessors
1245.A19 1802	Smith (1802-1816) 1 v.
1245.A2	New Hampshire reports (1816-)
1245.A3-.A39	Unofficial series
1245.A3	Supreme court reporter (1984-)

KFN UNITED STATES (NEW JERSEY) KFN

1801-2399	United States (New Jersey) (Table KFA-KFZ modified)
	Law reports and related materials
1845-1845.9	Supreme Court (Table KF31 modified)
1845	Reports
	Official series and predecessors
	Separate editions of nominative reports making up vols.
	1-137 of New Jersey Law Reports
1845.A19 1790	Coxe (1790-1795) 1 v. (Old series)
	.A2 v. 1 (New series)
1845.A19 1796	Halsted (1796-1804) 2 v. (Old series)
1845.A19 1806	Pennington (1806-1813) 2 v. (Old series)
	.A2 v. 2-3 (New series)
1845.A19 1816	Southard (1816-1820) 2 v. (Old series)
	.A2 v. 4-5 (New series)
1845.A19 1821	Halsted (1821-1831) 2 v. (Old series)
1845.A19 1831	Greene, J.S. (1831-1836) 3 v. (Old series)
	.A2 v. 13-15 (New series)
1845.A19 1837	Harrison (1837-1842) 4 v. (Old series)
	.A2 v. 16-19 (New series)
1845.A19 1842	Spencer (1842-1846) 1 v.
	.A2 v. 20 (New series)
1845.A19 1847	Zabriskie (1847-1855) 4 v. (Old Series)
	.A2 v. 21-24 (New series)
1845.A19 1855	Dutcher (1855-1862) 5 v. (Old series)
	.A2 v. 25-29 (New series)
1845.A19 1862	Vroom, P.D. (1862-1872) 6 v. (Old series)
	.A2 v. 30-35 (New series)
1845.A19 1872	Vroom, G.D.W. (1872-1914) 50 v.
	.A2 v. 36-85 (New series)
1845.A19 1914	Gummere (1914-1921) 41 v. (Old series)
	.A2 v. 86-125 (New series)
1845.A19 1940	Abbott (1940-1948) 10 v. (Old series)
	.A2 v. 126-137 (New series)
1845.A2	Halstead (1796-1804; 1821-1831) 7 v.
	v. 6-12
1845.A21	New Jersey Reports (Supreme Court) (1948-)
	Lower courts
	Intermediate appellate courts
1848-1848.9	Equity and New Jersey Superior Court (Table KF31 modified)
1848	Reports
	Equity Reports
1848.A19 1830	Saxton (1830-1832) 1 v. (Old series)
	.A2 v. 1 (New series)
1848.A19 1834	Green (1834-1845) 3 v. (Old series)
	.A2 v. 2-4 (New series)

Law reports and related materials
Lower courts
Intermediate appellate courts
Equity and New Jersey Superior Courts
Reports
Equity Reports -- Continued

1848.A19 1845	Halsted (1845-1853) 4 v. (Old series)
	.A2 v. 5-8 (New series)
1848.A19 1852	Stockton (1852-1858) 3 v. (Old series)
	.A2 v. 9-11 (New series)
1848.A19 1856	Beasley (1856-1861) 2 v. (Old series)
	.A2 v. 12-13 (New series)
1848.A19 1861	McCarter (1861-1863) 2 v. (Old series)
	.A2 v. 14-15 (New series)
1848.A19 1862	Green, C.E. (1862-1876) 12 v. (Old series)
	.A2 v. 16-27 (New series)
1848.A19 1877	Stewart (1877-1889) 18 v. (Old series)
	.A2 v. 28-45 (New series)
1848.A19 1889	Dickinson (1889-1904) 21 v. (Old series)
	.A2 v. 46-66 (New series)
1848.A19 1904	Robbins (1904-1905) 4 v. (Old series)
	.A2 v. 67-70 (New series)
1848.A19 1906	Buchanan (1906-1916) 15 v. (Old series)
	.A2 v. 71-85 (New series)
1848.A19 1916	Stockton (1916-1927) 16 v. (Old series)
	.A2 v. 86-101 (New series)
1848.A19 1926	Backes (1926-1942) 41 v. (Old series)
	.A2 v. 102-142 (New series)
1848.A21	New Jersey Superior Court Reports (1948-)
	Various courts
1851-1851.9	Collective (Table KF31 modified)
1851	Reports
1851.A2	New Jersey Miscellaneous Reports

KFN UNITED STATES (NEW MEXICO) KFN

3601-4199	United States (New Mexico) (Table KFA-KFZ modified)
	Law reports and related materials
3645-KFM3645.9	Supreme Court (Table KF31 modified)
3645	Reports
	Official series and predecessors
	Separate editions of nominative reports making up vols.
	1-5 of New Mexico reports
3645.A19 1852	Gildersleeve (1852-1883) (Old series)
	.A2 v. 1-2 (New series)
3645.A19 1883	Gildersleeve (1883-1889, Bancroft-Whitney ed.) 2 v.
	(Old series)
	.A2 v. 3-4 (New series)
3645.A19 1883a	Gildersleeve (1883-1889, reprint, E.W. Stephens) 2 v.
	(Old series)
3645.A19 1883b	Johnson (1883-1889) 2 v. (Old series)
3645.A19 1888	Gildersleeve (1888-1891) 1 v.
	.A2 v. 5 (New series)
3645.A2	New Mexico reports (1891-)

KFN UNITED STATES (NEW YORK) KFN

United States (New York)

5001	Bibliography
	Legislative documents
5005	Collections. Serials
	Bills
5006	Collections
5008.A-Z	Calendars. By committee, A-Z
	Committee documents
	Hearings
	Joint
5009.A-Z	Serials. By committee or subcommittee, A-Z
	Subarrange by title
5010.A-Z	Monographs. By committee or subcommittee, A-Z, and initial date of hearings
	Senate
5010.2.A-Z	Serials. By committee or subcommittee, A-Z
	Subarrange by title
5010.3.A-Z	Monographs. By committee or subcommittee, A-Z, and initial date of hearings
	Assembly
5010.35.A-Z	Serials. By committee or subcommittee, A-Z
	Subarrange by title
5010.4.A-Z	Monographs. By committee or subcommittee, A-Z, and initial date of hearings
	Reports
	Class here only those reports issued to accompany specific bills when they are reported out of a committee to its parent legislative body after hearings have been held and/or the committee has considered and made its recommendations on the bill in question. Class other types of reports emanating from a legislative commitee with the appropriate topic.
	Joint
5010.6.A-Z	Serials. By committee or subcommittee, A-Z
	Subarrange by title
5010.62.A-Z	Monographs. By committee or subcommittee, A-Z, and date of original publication
	Senate
5010.7.A-Z	Serials. By committee or subcommittee, A-Z
	Subarrange by title
5010.72.A-Z	Monographs. By committee or subcommittee, A-Z, and date of original publication
	Assembly
5010.8.A-Z	Serials. By committee or subcommittee, A-Z
	Subarrange by title
5010.82.A-Z	Monographs. By committee or subcommittee, A-Z, and date of original publication

KFN UNITED STATES (NEW YORK) KFN

Legislative documents -- Continued

5013 Debates. Proceedings

History of bills and resolutions. Legislation passed or vetoed

5014 Serials

5014.2 Monographs. By date of session or of initial session

Other legislative documents

5019 Governors' messages. By date

Statutes and administrative regulations. Session laws

Serials

5025.A2-.A29 Official editions

Arrange chronologically

5025.A3-Z Unofficial editions. By publisher or editor, A-Z

5025.2 Monographs. By date of session or of initial session

Codification. Revision of statutes

5027.A-Z Code commissions. Revisions committees. By committee, A-Z

Under each:

.xA15-.xA159	*General serials*
.xA2	*Organic acts. By date*
.xA3-.xA34	*Reports (Serials)*
.xA35	*Monographs. By date*
.xA4	*Notes. By date*
.xA5	*Draft revisions. By date*
.xA8	*Other. By date*

For commissions or committees limited to a specific topic, see the topic

5027.5 History. Criticism

General compilations of statutes

Including "Codes of law," "Codified statutes." "General statutes," "Revised statutes," etc.

5029 Serial compilations

5030 Monographic compilations. By date of enactment, revision (reenactment), or officially designated date of codification

Under each:

.A2-.A29	*Official editions (with or without annotations)*
	Arrange chronologically
.A3-.Z	*Unofficial editions*
.A3-.A39	*Unannotated texts*
	Arrange chronologically
.A4-.A49	*Annotated texts*
	Arrange chronologically
.A5-.Z	*Commentaries. By author*

5030.5.A-Z Selective compilations. By editor, A-Z

Compilations of statutes on a particular subject are classed with that subject

Statutes and administrative regulations -- Continued

5035 General compilations of administrative regulations. Administrative codes. By date of enactment, revision (reenactment), or officially designated date of codification

Under each:

Code	Description
.A2-.A29	*Official editions (with or without annotations)*
	Arrange chronologically
.A3-.Z	*Unofficial editions*
.A3-.A39	*Unannotated texts*
	Arrange chronologically
.A4-.A49	*Annotated texts*
	Arrange chronologically
.A5-.Z	*Commentaries. By author*

5036 New York State register

5038 Digests of statutes

5039 Citators to statutes

Citators to both reports and statutes are classed with citators to reports

5040 Indexes to statutes

Law reports and related materials

For reports relating to a particular subject, and for reports of courts of limited jurisdiction other than those listed below, see subject

Courts of last resort

Reports

Supreme Court (1777-1846) and Court for the Trial of Impeachments and Correction of Errors

Call Number	Description
5045.A15 1791	Coleman (1791-1800) 1 v.
5045.A15 1794	Coleman and Caines' (1794-1805) 1 v.
5045.A15 1796	Caines' (1796-1805) 2 v.
5045.A15 1799	Johnson's cases (1799-1803) 3 v.
5045.A15 1803	Caines's N.Y. Term Reports (1803-1805) 3 v.
5045.A15 1806	Johnson's Reports (1806-1823) 20 v.
5045.A15 1823	Cowen (1823-1829) 9 v.
5045.A15 1828	Wendell (1828-1844) 26 v.
5045.A15 1841	Hill (1841-1844) 4 v.
5045.A15 1842	Hill & Denio Supp., (Lalor) (1842-1844) 1 v.
5045.A15 1845	Denio (1845-1848) 5 v.
5045.A152	Coleman's Coleman & Caines' [etc.] 4 v. in 1
	Reprinted edition., Diossy, 1883 (1794-1809)
5045.A155	N.Y. Common Law Reports, v.1-17 plus Index

Court of Chancery

Call Number	Description
5045.A16 1814	Johnson's Chancery (1814-1823) 7 v.
5045.A16 1823	Hopkin's (1823-1826) 1 v.
5045.A16 1824	Lansing's Select Cases (1824-1826) 1 v.
5045.A16 1828	Paige (1828-1845) 11 v.

Law reports and related materials
Courts of last resort
Reports
Court of Chancery -- Continued

Call Number	Description
5045.A16 1831	Edwards (1831-1850) 4 v.
5045.A16 1839	Hoffman (1839-1840) 1 v.
5045.A16 1839a	Clarke (1839-1841) 1 v.
5045.A16 1841	Saratoga Chancery Sentinel (1841-1847) 6 in 1
5045.A16 1843	Sandford's Chancery (1843-1847) 4 v.
5045.A16 1845	Barbour's Chancery (1845-1848) 3 v.
5045.A165	N.Y. Chancery Reports Annotated Reprint (1814-1847)

Court of Appeals
Official series and predecessors

5045.A19 1847	Comstock (1847-1851) 4 v. (old style) .A2 v. 1-4 (new style)
5045.A19 1851	Selden (1851-1854) 6 v. .A2 v. 5-10
5045.A19 1854	Kernan (1854-1856) 4 v. .A2 v. 11-14
5045.A2 v. 15-	New York Reports
5045.A3-.A39	Unofficial series
5045.A32	N.Y. State Reporter (1886-1896) 75 v.
5045.A33	N.Y. Supplement (1888-1937) 300 v.
5045.A333	N.Y. Supplement, 2d ser. (1938 to date)
5045.A4A-.A4Z	Abridged, select, defunct. By editor or title
5045.A4A2	New York Court of Appeals Reports (Reprint) (1847-1888) 22 v.
5045.A4A3	Abbott (1850-1869) 4 v.
5045.A4H6	Howard (1847-1848) 1 v.
5045.A4K4	Keyes (1863-1868) 1 v.
5045.A4S4	Selden's Notes (1852-1854) 1 v.
5045.A4S5	Silvernail (1886-1892) 4 v.
5045.A4Y3	Yates' Select cases (1809) 1 v.
5045.1	Digests
5045.2	Citators. Tables of cases overruled, etc.
5045.4	Conversion tables. Blue books
5045.6	General indexes

For indexes relating to a particular publication, reporter system, or digest (e. g., descriptive word indexes), see that publication

5045.9	Records and briefs. By citation or docket number

Lower courts
General. Various courts
Including Courts of Appeals and lower courts, and New York decisions of federal courts, combined
For federal courts in New York see KF128.A+

5047	Reports

Law reports and related materials
Lower courts
General. Various courts -- Continued

Call Number	Description
5047.1	Digests
5047.2	Citators. Tables of cases overruled, etc.
5047.4	Conversion tables. Blue books
5047.6	General indexes
	For indexes relating to a particular publication, reporter system, or digest (e. g. descriptive word indexes), see that publication
5047.9	Records and briefs. By citation or docket number

Intermediate appellate courts. Supreme Court and Appellate Divisions (1847-)

Official series and predecessors

Call Number	Description
5048.A19 1847	Barbour's Supreme Court (1847-1877) 67 v.
5048.A19 1869	Lansing's Supreme Court (1869-1873) 7 v.
5048.A19 1873	Thompson and Cook (1873-1875) 6 v.
5048.A19 1874	Hun (1874-1895) 92 v.
5048.A2	Appellate Division Reports (1896-)
5048.A4A-.A4Z	Others. By editor or title
5048.A4E3	Edmonds' Select Cases (1834-1853) 2 v.
5048.A4L6	Lockwood's Reversed Cases (1799-1847) 1 v.
5048.A4S5	Silvernail's Supreme Court reports (1889-1890) 5 v.
5048.1	Digests
5048.2	Citators. Tables of cases overruled, etc.
5048.4	Conversion tables. Blue books
5048.6	General indexes
	For indexes relating to a particular publication, reporter system, or digest (e. g. descriptive word indexes), see that publication
5048.9	Records and briefs. By citation or docket number
5049.A-Z	Particular courts or appellate divisions, A-Z
	Subarrange each by Table KF32

Trial courts

Collective

Official series

Call Number	Description
5051.A2	Miscellaneous Reports (1892-)
5051.A4A-.A4Z	Others (abridged, select, defunct, etc.). By editor or title
5051.A4A5	Anthon's Nisi prius cases (1893)
	Cf. N.Y. Superior Court Reports, v. 61 (Jones & Spencer, v. 29), p. xxxiii
5051.1	Digests
5051.2	Citators. Tables of cases overruled, etc.
5051.4	Conversion tables. Blue books

KFN UNITED STATES (NEW YORK) KFN

Law reports and related materials
Lower courts
Trial courts
Collective -- Continued

5051.6	General indexes
	For indexes relating to a particular publication, reporter system, or digest (e. g. descriptive word indexes), see that publication
5051.9	Records and briefs. By citation or docket number
5052.A-Z	Individual trial courts, A-Z
	Subarrange each by Table KF32
5052.C6-.C66	Common pleas (Table KF32 modified)
5052.C6	Reports
5052.C6 1802	Livingston. Judicial opinions (1802) 1 v.
5052.C6 1850	Smith, E.D. (1850-1858) 4 v.
5052.C6 1855	Hilton (1855-1860) 2 v.
5052.C6 1859	Daly (1859-1891) 16 v.
5057	Digest of various reports
5059	Citators to various reports
5061	General indexes. Indexes to various publications
5065	Encyclopedias
5067	Uniform state laws
	Class here general works only
	Uniform state laws on a particular subject are classed with the subject
5068	Form books
	Class here general works only
	Form books on a particular subject are classed with the subject
<5069>	Periodicals
5070	Yearbooks. Judicial (including criminal) statistics
	Class here only publications issued annually, containing information, statistics, etc., about the year just past
	Other publications appearing yearly are classed as periodicals in K1+
	Directories see KF192.A+
	Legal research. Legal bibliography
5074	General
5074.5	Systems of citation
5075	Legal composition and draftsmanship
	For general works see KF250+
	For legislative draftsmanship see KFN5724
5075.5	Law reporting
	The legal profession. Practice of law
	General works see KF297+
5076	Admission to the bar (Table KF9)
	Legal ethics. Discipline. Disbarment
5076.5.A2	General (Table KF7)

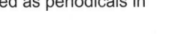

KFN UNITED STATES (NEW YORK) KFN

The legal profession. Practice of law
Legal ethics. Discipline. Disbarment -- Continued

5076.5.A6-Z	Particular cases. By attorney
5077	Law office management. Attorneys' and legal secretaries' handbooks, manuals, etc., of state law
5077.5.A-Z	Special topics, A-Z
5078	History
5078.5	Law reform. Criticism
	General and comprehensive works
5079	Collections
5080	Treatises
5081	Minor and popular works
5082	Examination aids
5083	Individual addresses and essays
5084.A-Z	Works for particular groups of users, A-Z
5084.B87	Businesspeople
5084.P78	Psychotherapists
5084.W6	Women
5084.5.A-Z	Works on diverse aspects of a particular subject and falling within several branches of the law, A-Z
5084.5.P6	Poverty. Legal protection of the poor. Handbooks for legal services (Table KF7)
5085	Equity (Table KF8)
5087	Conflict of laws (Table KF9)
	General principles and concepts
5091	Statutory construction and interpretation
5092	Codification
5100.A-Z	Concepts applying to several branches of the law, A-Z
5100.A8	Authentication. Acknowledgments. Certification (Table KF7)
5100.D2	Damages (Table KF7)
5100.L5	Limitations of actions (Table KF7)
	Cf. KFN6015 Procedure
5100.N6	Notice. Legal advertising (Table KF7)
5100.T5	Time (Computation of time) (Table KF7)
	Cf. KFN6004 Procedure
	Persons
	General. Status. Capacity and disability
	Natural persons
5108	General
5109	Civil status. Name
	Capacity and disability
5110	General (Table KF9)
5111.A-Z	Particular groups of persons, A-Z
5111.A33	Aged. Older people (Table KF7)
5111.H36	Handicapped. People with disabilities (Table KF7)
5111.I5	Insane persons. Persons of unsound mind (Table KF7)

KFN UNITED STATES (NEW YORK) KFN

Persons
General. Status. Capacity and disability
Natural persons
Capacity and disability
Particular groups of persons, A-Z -- Continued
5111.M5 Minors (Table KF7)
Older people see KFN5111.A33
People with disabilities see KFN5111.H36
5111.W6 Women (Table KF7)
Corporations see KFN5340+
Domestic relations. Family law
5115 General (Table KF9)
Family Court
Including superseded courts, e.g. Children's Courts
5116 General. Collective (Table KF9)
Local courts
5116.5 New York City (Table KF9)
Including superseded courts, e.g., Domestic Relations
Court, Children's Court, Girl's Term Court
For statistics see KFX2007.5.D6
5116.6.A-Z By county, A-Z
For statistics see KFN6199.A+
Marriage. Husband and wife
5120 General (Table KF9)
5121 Certificates. Premarital examinations (Table KF9)
5122 Performance of marriage. Civil and religious celebration (Table KF9)
5124 Property relationships (Table KF9)
Divorce. Separation
5126 General (Table KF9)
5126.5 Relationship between civil and religious divorces (Table KF9)
5127 Separate maintenance. Alimony (Table KF9)
Parent and child
5130 General. Support (Table KF9)
5131 Legitimacy. Illegitimacy. Legitimation. Paternity (Table KF9)
5132 Adoption (Table KF9)
5134 Guardian and ward (Table KF9)
Property
5138 General. Ownership (Table KF9)
Real property. Land law
5140 General (Table KF9)
Land tenure
Ownership and possession
5141 General
5142 Horizontal property. Housing condominium (Table KF9)

KFN UNITED STATES (NEW YORK) KFN

Property
Real property. Land law
Land tenure
Ownership and possession -- Continued

5145	Tenancy. Leaseholds. Landlord and tenant. Rent (Table KF9)
5149	Other interests
5150	Future estates and interests in land
	Concurrent ownership
	Including works on concurrent ownership in both real and personal property
5155	General (Table KF9)
	Tenancy by the entirety
5156	General (Table KF9)
5157	Housing cooperatives (Table KF9)
5158	Partition (Table KF9)
5160	Estates and interests arising from marriage. Dower
	Rights and interests incident to ownership and possession. Rights and duties of adjoining landowners
5161	General (Table KF9)
5162	Riparian rights. Water rights (Table KF9)
5163	Restraints on alienation (Table KF9)
	Transfer of rights in land
5166	General (Table KF9)
5167	Government grants (Table KF9)
	Transfer inter vivos
5169	General. Vendor and purchaser (Table KF9)
	Conveyances. Title investigation. Abstracts
5170	General. Deeds (Table KF9)
5171	Title investigation. Abstracts (Table KF9)
5172	Registration. Torrens system (Table KF9)
5174.A-Z	Other modes of transfer, A-Z
	Mortgages
5175	General (Table KF9)
5177.A-Z	Special topics, A-Z
5177.F6	Foreclosure (Table KF7)
	Personal property
5180	General (Table KF9)
	Ownership and possession
	Acquisition of property
5181	General (Table KF9)
	Original acquisition
5182	Treasure troves. Lost articles (Table KF9)
5185	Transfer (Table KF9)
5186.A-Z	Other topics, A-Z
	Trusts and trustees

KFN UNITED STATES (NEW YORK) KFN

Trusts -- Continued

5188	General (Table KF9)
5189	Charitable trusts (Table KF9)
5190	Cy pres doctrine (Table KF9)
5193	Trust companies (Table KF9)
5194.A-Z	Special topics, A-Z
5194.S63	Spendthrift trusts (Table KF7)
5195	Estate planning (Table KF8)

Succession upon death

5200	General (Table KF9)

Testate succession. Wills

5201	General (Table KF9)
5202.A-Z	Special topics, A-Z
5202.E5	Election (Table KF7)

Collected wills

5203	General
5203.2.A-Z	By county, etc., A-Z

Particular wills see KF759.A+

5205	Probate law and practice. Surrogates' courts (Table KF9)

For probate records see KFN5969.A+

5208	Intestate succession (Table KF9)
5210	Administration of decedents' estates. Execution of wills. Personal representatives (Table KF9)

Contracts

5215	General. Comprehensive (Table KF8)

General principles

Formation of contract

5217	Consideration
5218	Formalities. Written contract. Contract under seal. Statute of frauds
5221	Assignment of contracts. Subrogation
5222	Void and voidable contracts. Unlawful contracts. Mistake. Duress. Fraud (Table KF9)

Government contracts. Public contracts. Purchasing and procurement

5224	General (Table KF9)
5224.3	Construction and building contracts (Table KF9)

Particular contracts

5225	Comprehensive. Commercial law. Mercantile transactions (Table KF9)

Contract for work and labor (Contract for services). Independent contractors

5228	General (Table KF9)
5229	Mechanics' liens (Table KF9)
5230.A-Z	Particular types, A-Z
5230.B8	Building and construction (Table KF7)

Sale of goods

Contracts
Particular contracts
Sale of goods -- Continued

Number	Description
5235	General (Table KF9)
	Documents of title
5237	General (Table KF9)
5237.5	Bills of lading (Table KF9)
5237.6	Warehouse receipts (Table KF9)
5239	Rights of unpaid seller. Resale. Rescission (Table KF9)
	Contracts involving bailments
5240	General (Table KF9)
5241.A-Z	Particular contracts, A-Z
5241.I5	Innkeeper and guest (Table KF7)
	Negotiable instruments
5245	General (Table KF9)
	Bills of exchange
5246	General (Table KF9)
5247.A-Z	Special topics, A-Z
5247.A2	Acceptance. Protests (Table KF7)
5248	Checks (Table KF9)
	Banking
5250	General (Table KF9)
	Particular kinds of banks
5252	Savings banks (Table KF9)
5253	Agricultural credit banks (Table KF9)
5254.A-Z	Other, A-Z
5254.B8	Building and loan associations (Table KF7)
5254.F67	Foreign and international banks (Table KF7)
5256.A-Z	Particular banking transactions, A-Z
5256.C65	Collecting of accounts. Collection laws (Table KF7)
	Collection laws see KFN5256.C65
5256.D3	Deposits (Table KF7)
5256.L3	Letters of credit (Table KF7)
5259.A-Z	Particular banks, A-Z
	Loan of money
5260	General (Table KF9)
5261	Interest. Usury (Table KF9)
5262	Consumer credit. Small loans. Industrial banks. Morris plan. Finance charges (Table KF9)
5265	Suretyship. Guaranty (Table KF9)
	For suretyship insurance see KFN5300+
	For bonding see KFN5301
	Secured transactions
5266	General (Table KF9)
	Particular transactions
5266.5	Chattel mortgages (Table KF9)

KFN UNITED STATES (NEW YORK) KFN

Contracts
Particular contracts
Secured transactions
Particular transactions -- Continued

5267	Conditional sale. Installment sale. Lease purchase (Table KF9)
5268	Liens (Table KF9)

Marketing of securities. Investments. Stock-exchange transactions

5270	General (Table KF9)
	For issuing of securities see KFN5350
5272	Stockbrokers (Table KF9)
5273	Investment trusts. Investment companies. Mutual funds (Table KF9)

Commodity exchanges. Produce exchanges

5275.A1	General. Futures trading (Table KF9)
5275.A3-Z	Particular commodities
5275.C6	Cotton (Table KF7)

Carriers. Carriage of goods and passengers

5278	General

Carriage by sea. Maritime law. Admiralty

5279	General (Table KF9)
5280	Admiralty proceedings (Table KF9)
5281.A-Z	Special topics, A-Z
5281.C4	Charter parties (Table KF7)

Maritime labor law. Merchant mariners

5284	General (Table KF9)

Social insurance

5285	General (Table KF9)
5286	Unemployment insurance (Table KF9)
5287	Ocean marine insurance (Table KF9)

Insurance
Including regulation of insurance business
For taxation see KFN5879.A+

5290	General. Insurance business. Agents. Brokers (Table KF9)

Particular branches
Personal insurance

5292	Life (Table KF9)
5293.A-Z	Other, A-Z
5293.H43	Health (Table KF7)
	Cf. KFN5591+ Social insurance

Property insurance

5295.A1	General (Table KF7)
5295.A2-Z	Particular hazards
5295.F5	Fire (Table KF7)
	Ocean marine insurance see KFN5287

Contracts
Particular contracts
Insurance
Particular branches -- Continued
Casualty insurance

Number	Description
5297	General liability (Table KF9)
5298.A-Z	Particular risks, A-Z
5298.A8-.A89	Automobile (Table KF7)
5298.A8	General
5298.A84	No-fault
5298.A86	Uninsured motorist
5298.A88	Unsatisfied judgment funds
5298.E5	Employers' liability (Table KF7)
5298.G68	Government risks (Table KF7)
5298.M35	Malpractice (Table KF7)

Suretyship. Guaranty. Title insurance

Number	Description
5300	General (Table KF9)
5301	Bonding (Table KF9)
5302	Mortgage. Mortgage guaranty (Table KF9)
5303	Title insurance (Table KF9)

Torts (Extracontractual liability)

Number	Description
5310	General. Liability. Damages (Table KF9)

Particular torts
Torts in respect to the person

Number	Description
5311	Personal injuries (Table KF9)
5312	Violation of privacy (Table KF9)
5313	Torts in respect to reputation. Libel. Slander (Table KF9)

Negligence

Number	Description
5315	General (Table KF9)
5316	Contributory negligence. Last clear chance (Table KF9)
5317	Malpractice (Table KF9)
5320.A-Z	Particular accidents or cases of negligence, A-Z
5320.A8	Automobile accidents (Table KF7)
5320.B8	Building accidents (Table KF7)
5320.L5	Liability for condition and use of land (Table KF7)
5320.S5	Sidewalk accidents (Table KF7)

Strict liability. Liability without fault

Number	Description
5321	General (Table KF9)

Products liability

Number	Description
5323.A3	General (Table KF7)
5323.A5-Z	By product, A-Z

Parties to actions in torts
Corporations

Number	Description
5324	Municipal corporations (Table KF9)
5325	Nonprofit corporations (Table KF9)
5328	School districts (Table KF9)
5330	Joint tortfeasors (Table KF9)

KFN UNITED STATES (NEW YORK) KFN

Torts (Extracontractual liability) -- Continued
Liability for torts of others. Vicarious liability

5332	General (Table KF9)
5332.4	Employers' liability (Table KF9)
5332.6	Government torts (Table KF9)
5333.5	Compensation to victims of crimes. Reparation (Table KF9)
	Agency
5335	General (Table KF9)
5336	Power of attorney (Table KF9)
	Associations
	Comprehensive. Associations in general
	Including business enterprises in general, regardless of form of organization
5337	General (Table KF9)
5337.5.A-Z	Special topics, A-Z
	Unincorporated associations
5338	General (Table KF9)
	Business associations. Partnership
5339	General (Table KF9)
5339.5	Limited partnership (Table KF9)
	Including limited liability companies and private companies
	Corporations
5340	General (Table KF9)
	Nonprofit corporations
5342	General (Table KF9)
5343	Foundations. Endowments (Table KF9)
5343.5	Fundraising (Table KF9)
	Business corporations
5345	General (Table KF9)
5346	Government regulation and control. Licensing (Table KF9)
5347	Foreign corporations (Table KF9)
5348	Incorporation. Corporate charters and bylaws. Promoters (Table KF9)
5349	Directors. Officers (Table KF9)
5350	Corporation finance. Capital. Dividends. Issuing of securities (Table KF9)
	Shares and shareholders' rights. Stock transfers
5353	General (Table KF9)
	Stockholders' meetings
5354	General (Table KF9)
5355	Proxy rules (Table KF9)
5357.A-Z	Particular types of corporations, A-Z
5357.C5	Close corporations (Table KF7)
5359	Consolidation and merger (Table KF9)
	Insolvency and bankruptcy. Creditors' rights
5364	General (Table KF9)

KFN UNITED STATES (NEW YORK) KFN

Insolvency and bankruptcy. Creditors' rights -- Continued
Bankruptcy

5365	General. Procedure (Table KF9)
5366.A-Z	Special topics, A-Z
5366.D5	Discharge (Table KF7)
5366.F7	Fraudulent conveyances (Table KF7)
5366.P7	Priority of claims (Table KF7)
	Debtors' relief
5367	General. Composition. Receivership to avoid bankruptcy (Table KF9)
	Corporate reorganization
5368	General (Table KF9)
5369.A-Z	Particular types of corporations or lines of business, A-Z
5369.R2	Railroads (Table KF7)
5370	Assignments for benefit of creditors (Table KF9)
5371	Bulk transfers (Table KF9)
	Regulation of industry, trade, and commerce. Occupational law
5375	General. Comprehensive (Table KF9)
5377	Monopolies. Antitrust laws (Table KF9)
5379	Small business (Table KF9)
5382	Weights and measures. Containers (Table KF9)
	Primary production. Extractive industries
	Agriculture. Forestry
5385	General (Table KF9)
5387	Control of agricultural pests, plant diseases, and predatory animals. Weed control. Plant quarantine (Table KF9)
5390	Farm producers' and marketing cooperatives (Table KF9)
	Dairy industry see KFN5421
5396	Forestry. Timber laws (Table KF9)
	Mining. Quarrying
5400	General (Table KF9)
	Petroleum. Oil and gas
5404	General (Table KF9)
5410	Oil and gas leases (Table KF9)
	Manufacturing industries
5412.A2	General (Table KF7)
5412.A3-Z	By product, A-Z
5412.C55	Clothing (Table KF7)
	Food processing industries
5415	General (Table KF9)
5418	Meat and poultry industry (Table KF9)
5419	Poultry products. Eggs and egg products (Table KF9)
5421	Dairy industry. Dairy products industry. Milk production and distribution (Table KF9)
5424	Construction and building industry. Contractors (Table KF9)
	Trade and commerce

KFN UNITED STATES (NEW YORK) KFN

Regulation of industry, trade, and commerce. Occupational law
Trade and commerce -- Continued

5430	General (Table KF9)
	Import trade
5434	General (Table KF9)
5435.A-Z	Particular commodities, A-Z
5435.F5	Flaxseed (Table KF7)
5435.S2	Salt (Table KF7)
	Retail trade
5437	General (Table KF9)
5438	Licensing (Table KF9)
5439	Sunday legislation (Table KF9)
5440	Unfair trade practices (Table KF9)
5441	Franchises (Table KF9)
5444.A-Z	Particular products, A-Z
5444.A95	Automobiles (Table KF7)
	Service trades
5445	General. Licensing (Table KF9)
5446.A-Z	Particular trades, A-Z
5446.C6	Collection agencies (Table KF7)
5446.D39	Day care centers. Nursery schools (Table KF7)
5446.E5	Employment agencies (Table KF7)
5446.H6	Hotels. Restaurants (Table KF7)
	Cf. KFN5241.I5 Innkeeper and guest
	Nursery schools see KFN5446.D39
5446.R3	Real estate agents (Table KF7)
5446.U6	Undertakers (Table KF7)
	Warehouses
5448	General (Table KF9)
5449	Cold storage (Table KF9)
	Public utilities
5455	General. Regulation. Finance (Table KF9)
	Power supply
5457	General (Table KF9)
5457.1	Public service commissions (Table KF9)
	Electricity
5459	General. Comprehensive (Table KF9)
5460	Corporate structure. Holding companies (Table KF9)
5464.A-Z	Particular companies, A-Z
5468.8.A-Z	Other sources of power, A-Z
5468.8.R44	Refuse as fuel (Table KF7)
5468.8.S6	Solar energy (Table KF7)
	Transportation and communication
	Including state-owned and municipal services
5469	General. Comprehensive (Table KF9)
	Road traffic. Automotive transportation
5470	General. Motor vehicle laws (Table KF9)

KFN UNITED STATES (NEW YORK) KFN

Regulation of industry, trade, and commerce. Occupational law
Transportation and communication
Road traffic. Automotive transportation -- Continued

5472	Safety equipment. Weight restrictions (Table KF9)
5474	Registration. Title transfer (Table KF9)
5475	Driver education (Table KF9)
5476.A-Z	Particular vehicles, A-Z
5476.T7	Trucks (Table KF7)
5477	Traffic regulation and enforcement. Traffic violations. Drunk driving (Table KF9)
5478	Highway safety. Traffic signs. Grade crossings. Railroad crossings (Table KF9)
	Carriage of passengers and goods
5480	General (Table KF9)
5482	Passenger carriers. Bus lines (Table KF9)
5483	Taxicabs (Table KF9)
5485.A-Z	Special topics, A-Z
	Railroads
5490	General. Corporate structure. Regulation of industry (Table KF9)
5492	Railroad lands. Land grants. Right of way (Table KF9)
	Operation of railroads
5494	Railroad safety. Railroad sanitation (Table KF9)
5495	Full crew laws. Length of trains (Table KF9)
	Rates and rate-making
5497	General. Freight (Table KF9)
5498.A-Z	Particular commodities, A-Z
5498.D7	Dry goods (Table KF7)
5499.A-Z	Individual railroads and railroad companies, A-Z
	Including litigation, decisions, rulings, etc.
	Local transit
5502	General (Table KF9)
5503	Electric railroads. Streetcar lines. Subways (Table KF9)
5504.A-Z	Other types of land transportation, A-Z
5504.C2	Cable cars. Ski lifts (Table KF7)
	Aviation
5510	General. Commercial aviation. Air carriers (Table KF9)
5511	Air traffic rules. Air worthiness (Table KF9)
5512	Airports (Table KF9)
5513	Pilots. Crews. Ground personnel (Table KF9)
	Water transportation. Navigation and shipping
5520	General. Comprehensive (Table KF9)
	Ships
5521	General (Table KF9)
	Safety regulations
5522	General. Inspection (Table KF9)
5524.A-Z	Particular types of vessels, A-Z

Regulation of industry, trade, and commerce. Occupational law
Transportation and communication
Water transportation. Navigation and shipping
Ships
General
Safety regulations
Particular types of vessels, A-Z -- Continued

Call Number	Topic
5524.M6	Motor boats (Table KF7)
5524.P5	Pleasure craft. Yachts
	Navigation and pilotage
5526	General (Table KF9)
	Particular waterways
	Canals
5528	General (Table KF9)
5529.A-Z	Particular canals, A-Z
	Harbors and ports
5530	General (Table KF9)
5531.A-Z	Particular ports, A-Z
5534	Shipping laws. Water carriers (Table KF9)
5535	Press law (Table KF9)
	Telecommunication
5540	General. Comprehensive (Table KF9)
5541	Telegraph. Teletype (Table KF9)
5542	Telephone (Table KF9)
	Including radio telephone
5544.A-Z	Particular companies, A-Z
	The professions
5545	General. Licensing (Table KF9)
5545.5	Professional corporations (Table KF9)
	Particular professions
5546.A-Z	The health professions, A-Z
5546.A1-.A13	General. Physicians (Table KF16)
5546.D3-.D33	Dentists (Table KF16)
5546.P73-.P733	Psychologists (Table KF16)
5546.5.A-Z	Auxiliary professions, A-Z
5546.5.A36-.A363	Acupuncturists (Table KF16)
5546.5.C48-.C483	Chiropractors (Table KF16)
5546.5.H6-.H63	Hospital auxiliaries (Table KF16)
5546.5.N8-.N83	Nurses (Table KF16)
	Occupational therapists see KFN5546.5.T5+
5546.5.P4-.P43	Pharmacists (Table KF16)
	Physical therapists see KFN5546.5.T5+
5546.5.P63-.P633	Podiatrists (Table KF16)
5546.5.P73-.P733	Psychologists (Table KF16)
5546.5.T5-.T53	Therapists, Physical. Occupational therapists (Table KF16)
5547.A-Z	Other, A-Z

Regulation of industry, trade, and commerce. Occupational law
The professions
Particular professions
Other, A-Z -- Continued

5547.A3-.A33	Accountants. Auditors (Table KF16)
5547.E54-.E543	Engineers (Table KF16)
	Lawyers see KF297+; KFN5077
5547.S85-.S853	Surveyors (Table KF16)
5547.V46-.V464	Veterinarians (Table KF16)
	Intellectual property. Patents. Trademarks
5550	General (Table KF9)
5552	Trademarks (Table KF9)
5553	Unfair competition
	Social legislation
5555	General (Table KF9)
	Labor law
5556	General (Table KF9)
	Management-labor relations
5557	General (Table KF9)
5557.1	State Labor Boards (Table KF9)
	Labor unions
5560	General (Table KF9)
	Collective bargaining. Collective labor agreements
5561	General (Table KF9)
5562.A-Z	Particular industries and occupations, A-Z
5562.C6	Construction industry (Table KF7)
5562.F6	Food industry and trade (Table KF7)
	Government employees see KFN5562.P8
5562.H6	Hospitals (Table KF7)
5562.P8	Public employees (Table KF7)
5562.T4	Teachers (Table KF7)
5562.T7	Trucking industry (Table KF7)
	Labor disputes
5564	General (Table KF9)
5565	Arbitration. Conciliation. Fact-finding boards (Table KF9)
5566	Strikes. Boycotts. Picketing (Table KF9)
5567	Labor injunctions (Table KF9)
5568.A-Z	By industry or occupation, A-Z
	Government employees see KFN5568.P8
5568.P8	Public employees (Table KF7)
	Labor standards
5570	General. Labor conditions (Table KF9)
	Employment and dismissal
5571	General (Table KF9)
	Discrimination in employment and its prevention
5572	General (Table KF9)

Social legislation
Labor law
Labor standards
Employment and dismissal
Discrimination in employment and its prevention --
Continued

5573.A-Z	Particular groups, A-Z
5573.A4	Aged. Older people (Table KF7)
5573.H34	Handicapped. People with disabilities (Table KF7)
	People with disabilities see KFN5573.H34
5573.W64	Women (Table KF7)
5575	Wages. Minimum wage (Table KF9)
5576	Hours of labor. Night work (Table KF9)
5577	Vacations. Holidays. Leaves of absence (Table KF9)
	Protection of labor. Labor hygiene and safety
5579	General (Table KF9)
5580	Child labor (Table KF9)
5581	Woman labor (Table KF9)
	Labor hygiene and safety. Hazardous occupations.
	Safety regulations
5584	General (Table KF9)
5585	Factory inspection (Table KF9)
5586.A-Z	By industry and type of labor, A-Z
5586.A7	Atomic industry (Table KF7)
5586.C65	Construction industry (Table KF7)
	Social insurance
5590	General (Table KF9)
	Particular branches
5591	Health insurance (Table KF9)
	Workers' compensation
5592	General (Table KF9)
5593	Occupational diseases (Table KF9)
5594.A-Z	Particular industries and groups of employees
5594.C6	Construction industry (Table KF7)
	Social security. Retirement. Old age and disability
	pensions. Survivors' benefits
5595	General (Table KF9)
5595.5	Contributions. Social security taxes (Table KF9)
5596	Unemployment insurance (Table KF9)
	Public welfare. Public assistance
5600	General (Table KF9)
5600.2	Public institutions (Table KF9)
5600.5	Social workers (Table KF9)
	Particular groups
5602	Women (Table KF9)
	Children. Child welfare. Youth services
	Including children with disabilities or retarded children

Social legislation
Public welfare. Public assistance
Particular groups
Children. Child welfare. Youth services -- Continued

5603	General (Table KF9)
5603.5	Foster home care (Table KF9)
5604	Older people (Table KF9)
	People with disabilities. Vocational rehabilitation
5605	General (Table KF9)
5605.3	Blind (Table KF9)
	Children see KFN5603+
5605.5	Deaf-mute (Table KF9)
5606.A-Z	Other, A-Z
	Particular relief measures
5607	Medical aid (Table KF9)
5608.A-Z	Special topics, A-Z
5608.D6	Domicile requirements (Table KF7)
5608.5	Disaster relief (Table KF9)
	Public health. Sanitation
	Including environmental pollution
5610	General (Table KF9)
5610.1	Boards of health (Table KF9)
5611	Disposal of the dead. Burial and cemetery laws (Table KF9)
5612	Water pollution. Drainage (Table KF9)
5613	Contagious, infectious, and other diseases (Table KF9)
5613.5.A-Z	Particular diseases, A-Z
5613.5.A36	AIDS (Disease) (Table KF7)
5614	Air pollution. Control of smoke, noxious gases, etc. (Table KF9)
5614.5.A-Z	Other public health hazards and measures, A-Z
5614.5.N64	Noise control (Table KF7)
5614.5.R43	Refuse disposal (Table KF7)
	Cf. KFN5641.3 Hazardous waste disposal
5614.5.S48	Sewage disposal (Table KF7)
	Medical legislation
5615	General (Table KF9)
	Hospitals and other medical institutions
5617	General (Table KF9)
5619.A-Z	Other health services, A-Z
	Ambulance service see KFN5619.E43
5619.A46	Ambulatory medical care (Table KF7)
5619.E43	Emergency medical services. Ambulance service (Table KF7)
5619.N8	Nursing homes (Table KF7)
5619.S3	Schools. School health services (Table KF7)
5619.5.A-Z	Special topics, A-Z
5619.5.C37	Cardiopulmonary resuscitation (CPR) (Table KF7)

KFN UNITED STATES (NEW YORK) KFN

Medical legislation
Special topics, A-Z -- Continued

Call Number	Description
5619.5.D4	Death, Definition of (Table KF7)
5619.5.D62	Do-not-resuscitate orders (Table KF7)
5619.5.D64	Donation of organs, tissues, etc. (Table KF7)
5619.5.G45	Medical genetics (Table KF7)
5619.5.I53	Informed consent (Table KF7)
	Living wills see KFN5619.5.R54
	Natural death see KFN5619.5.R54
5619.5.R43	Medical records. Hospital records. Records management (Table KF7)
5619.5.R54	Right to die. Natural death. Living wills (Table KF7)
5620	The mentally ill (Table KF9)
5621.A-Z	Disorders of character, behavior, and intelligence, A-Z
5621.A5	Alcoholism (Table KF7)
	Including works on the treatment and rehabilitation of alcoholics in the criminal justice system

Veterinary laws. Veterinary hygiene

5623	General (Table KF9)
	Particular measures
5623.5	Quarantine (Table KF9)
5624.A-Z	Particular animal diseases and causative agents, A-Z
5627	Prevention of cruelty to animals (Table KF9)

Food. Drugs. Cosmetics

5630	General. Comprehensive (Table KF9)
5631	Food law (Table KF9)
5632	Drug laws. Narcotics. Cosmetics (Table KF9)

Alcoholic beverages. Liquor control

5635	General (Table KF9)
5637.A-Z	Particular products, A-Z
5637.W56	Wine (Table KF7)
5638.A-Z	Special topics, A-Z
5638.L38	Local option (Table KF7)

Public safety

5640	General (Table KF9)
5640.5	Weapons. Firearms. Munitions (Table KF9)

Hazardous articles and processes

5641	General (Table KF9)
5641.3	Hazardous waste disposal (Table KF9)
5641.5.A-Z	Particular products or processes, A-Z
5641.5.A85	Atomic power. Radiation (Table KF7)
5641.5.L42	Lead (Table KF7)
	Nuclear energy see KFN5641.5.A85
	Radiation see KFN5641.5.A85

Fire prevention and control

5644	General (Table KF9)
5644.5	Fire departments. Fire fighters (Table KF9)

KFN UNITED STATES (NEW YORK) KFN

Control of social activities

5645	Sports. Prizefighting. Horse racing (Table KF9)
5646	Lotteries. Games of chance. Gambling (Table KF9)
	Education
	Education in general. Public education
	School government and finance
5648	General (Table KF9)
	Including works treating of educational law comprehensively
5649	School districts. School boards (Table KF9)
5650	School lands (Table KF9)
5650.5	Extracurricular use of school buildings (Table KF9)
	Finance
5651	General (Table KF9)
	Support of related activities
5652	School transportation (Table KF9)
	Students. Compulsory education
5654	General (Table KF9)
5655	Religious and patriotic observances. Bible reading. Religious instruction. School prayers. Flag salute (Table KF9)
	Teachers
5658	General. Tenure (Table KF9)
5659	Qualifications. Certification (Table KF9)
5660	Salaries, pensions, etc. (Table KF9)
	Elementary and secondary education
5662	General (Table KF9)
	Curricula. Courses of instruction
5664	General (Table KF9)
5664.5.A-Z	Particular subjects, A-Z
5664.5.L37	Law (Table KF7)
5664.5.V63	Vocational education (Table KF7)
5665.A-Z	Particular types of students, A-Z
5665.P4	Physically handicapped. Students with disabilities (Table KF7)
	Students with disabilities see KFN5665.P4
	Higher education
5666	General (Table KF9)
5666.5	Finance (Table KF9)
5666.55	Student aid. Scholarships (Table KF9)
5668	Professional education. Professional schools (Table KF9)
5669.A-Z	Particular colleges and universities, A-Z
	Science and the arts. Research
5670	General (Table KF9)
	The arts
	Performing arts
5671	General (Table KF9)

KFN UNITED STATES (NEW YORK) KFN

Science and the arts. Research
The arts
Performing arts -- Continued
Motion pictures

5672	General (Table KF9)
5672.5	Censorship (Table KF9)
5674	Museums and galleries (Table KF9)
5675	Libraries (Table KF9)

Constitutional law
Sources

5679	General. Comprehensive. Collections
5680	Particular constitutions. By date of constitution
	Subarrange each by Table KF40
	Including rejected proposals for new constitution. By date of referendum
5681	History
5682	General. Comprehensive (Table KF9)
5683	Amending process

Separation of powers. Delegation of powers

5685	General (Table KF9)
5686	Conflict of interests. Incompatibility of offices. Ethics in government (Table KF9)
5687	Judicial review of legislative acts (Table KF9)

Structure of government. Jurisdiction

5690	General (Table KF9)
5692	Interstate cooperation (Table KF9)

Individual and state
Civil and political rights and liberties

5695	General (Table KF9)
5696.A-Z	Particular groups, A-Z
5696.A4	African Americans (Table KF7)
5696.5.A-Z	Particular constitutional guarantees, A-Z
5696.5.S6	Freedom of speech (Table KF7)

Control of individuals

5698	Aliens (Table KF9)

Internal security. Control of subversive activities

5701	General (Table KF9)
5702.A-Z	Particular groups, A-Z
5702.C6	Communists (Table KF7)

Church and state

5705	General. Religious corporations (Table KF9)
5706.A-Z	Special topics, A-Z
5706.C4	Church property (Table KF7)

Organs of government
The people

5709	Recall (Table KF9)

Election law

Constitutional law
Organs of government
The people
Election law -- Continued

5710	General (Table KF9)
	Suffrage
5711	General (Table KF9)
5712.A-Z	Particular groups of voters, A-Z
5712.S6	Soldiers (Table KF7)
5712.W6	Women (Table KF7)
5713	Registration. Qualifications. Educational tests. Poll tax requirements (Table KF9)
5714	Election districts. Apportionment. Gerrymandering (Table KF9)
5715	Primaries (Table KF9)
5716	Corrupt practices. Illicit political activities (Table KF9)
	The legislative branch
5720	General. Legislative power (Table KF9)
	The legislature
5721	General. Organization (Table KF9)
5722	Rules and procedure (Table KF9)
5722.5	Power and duties (Table KF9)
	Including sunset reviews of government programs
	The legislative process
5723	General (Table KF9)
5724	Bill drafting (Table KF9)
	Legal status of legislators
5726	General (Table KF9)
5726.5	Parliamentary immunity (Table KF9)
5728	Contested elections (Table KF9)
	Upper chamber (Senate)
5730	General (Table KF9)
5731	Rules and procedure (Table KF9)
	Lower chamber (Assembly)
5735	General (Table KF9)
5736	Rules and procedure
	The executive branch
5740	General. Executive power (Table KF9)
	The Governor
5741	General (Table KF9)
5742	Powers and duties (Table KF9)
5744	Impeachment (Table KF9)
	Executive departments
5745	General (Table KF9)
5746.A-Z	Particular offices or positions, A-Z
5746.L38	Department of Law (Table KF7)
5747.A-Z	Special topics, A-Z

KFN UNITED STATES (NEW YORK) KFN

Constitutional law
Organs of government
The executive branch
Executive departments
Special topics, A-Z -- Continued
5747.P83 Public meetings (Table KF7)
State civil service see KFN5760+
5749 State emblem. Flag. Seal. Seat of government (Table KF9)
Local government
5750 General (Table KF9)
Municipal government. Municipal services
5752 General. Municipal corporations (Table KF9)
5753 Municipal powers and services beyond corporate limits (Table KF9)
5754 Local laws (Collective)
5758 County government. County charters (Table KF9)
5758.5 Minor communities. Villages (Table KF9)
Civil service. Government officials and employees. State civil service
5760 General. Qualifications for employment (Table KF9)
5760.1 Civil service commissions (Table KF9)
5763 Conditions and restrictions of employment. Employment discipline (Table KF9)
5764 Impeachment. Discipline (Table KF9)
5764.5 Court for the Trial of Impeachments (Table KF9)
Types and modes of employment
5765 Veterans' preference (Table KF9)
Tenure and remuneration
5768 General (Table KF9)
5769 Salaries (Table KF9)
5770 Retirement. Pensions (Table KF9)
5771.A-Z Particular positions, A-Z
Municipal civil service
5774 General (Table KF9)
5775 Salaries (Table KF9)
5776.A-Z Particular offices or positions, A-Z
5776.P64 Police (Table KF7)
5778 Police and power of the police (Table KF9)
Administrative organization. Administrative law and procedure
5780 General (Table KF9)
5782 Judicial functions. Procedure. Administrative tribunals. Hearing examiners (Table KF9)
Public property. Public restraints on private property
5785 General (Table KF9)
Roads
5787 General. Highway law (Table KF9)
5788 Express highways. Parkways (Table KF9)

KFN UNITED STATES (NEW YORK) KFN

Public property. Public restraints on private property --
Continued
Water resources. Watersheds. Rivers. Lakes. Water courses

5790	General. Water districts (Table KF9)
5792.A-Z	Particular inland waterways and channels, A-Z
	Canals
5793	General (Table KF9)
5794.A-Z	Particular canals, A-Z
	Subarrange each by Table KF6
5796.A-Z	Particular bodies of water, water districts, etc., A-Z
5800	Eminent domain (Table KF9)
	Public land law
5802	General (Table KF9)
	State parks and forests. Wilderness preservation
5805	General (Table KF9)
5806	Game, bird, and fish protection (Table KF9)
	Regional and city planning. Zoning. Building
5810	General (Table KF9)
5811	Land use. Zoning. Land subdivision (Table KF9)
	Building laws
5813	General (Table KF9)
5814.A-Z	Particular types of buildings, A-Z
5814.S3	School buildings (Table KF7)
5816	Plumbing. Pipe fitting (Table KF9)
5818	Heating and ventilating. Air conditioning (Table KF9)
5819.A-Z	Other topics, A-Z
5819.H35	Handicapped, Provisions for. People with disabilities, Provisions for (Table KF7)
	People with disabilities, Provisions for see KFN5819.H35
5820	Housing. Slum clearance. City redevelopment (Table KF9)
	Government property
5825	General (Table KF9)
5826	Records management (Table KF9)
5827	Access to public records. Freedom of government information (Table KF9)
	Land real property
5828	General (Table KF9)
	Particular properties
5829	Government buildings (Table KF9)
5830.A-Z	Other. By place, name of plant, etc., A-Z
	Government measures in time of war, national emergency, or economic crisis. Emergency economic legislation
5834	General (Table KF9)
	By period
	1920-1939
	In case of doubt, prefer classification with subject

KFN UNITED STATES (NEW YORK) KFN

Government measures in time of war, national emergency, or economic crisis. Emergency economic legislation
By period
1920-1939 -- Continued

5835	General (Table KF9)
	Rationing, Price control. Profiteering
5835.3	General (Table KF9)
5835.5.A-Z	By commodity or service, A-Z
	1945-
	In case of doubt, prefer classification with subject
5837	General (Table KF9)
	Rationing. Price control. Profiteering
5837.3	General (Table KF9)
5837.5.A-Z	By commodity or service, A-Z
	Public finance
5840	General (Table KF9)
5841	Money. Currency. Coinage (Table KF9)
5842	Budget. Government expenditures (Table KF9)
	Expenditure control. Public auditing and accounting
5845	General (Table KF9)
5846	Comptroller. Board of Comptrollers (Table KF9)
	Particular departments
	see administration or name of department under subject
5847	Investment of public funds (Table KF9)
5849	Public debts. Loans. Bond issues (Table KF9)
	State revenue
	History
5850	General
	Older sources of revenue
5851	Fees and fines (Table KF9)
	War-time finance
5853	World War I (Table KF9)
5854	World War II (Table KF9)
5855	Later (Table KF9)
5856	General. Comprehensive (Table KF9)
	Particular sources of revenue
	Taxation
5860	General (Table KF9)
5861	Tax saving. Tax planning (Table KF9)
	Tax administration and procedure
5863	General (Table KF9)
5865	Tax collection (Table KF9)
5866	Procedure. Practice. Tax courts. Remedies. Tax appeals (Table KF9)
5868	Exemption (Table KF9)
5869	Criminal law. Tax evasion (Table KF9)
	Particular taxes

Public finance
State revenue
Particular sources of revenue
Taxation
Particular taxes -- Continued
Income tax

5870	General (Table KF9)
	Income. Exemptions
5872	Tax-exempt securities. Government bonds (Table KF9)
5873	Payroll deduction. Withholding tax (Table KF9)
5873.5.A-Z	Other topics, A-Z
5873.5.T37	Tax credits (Table KF7)
	Income of business organizations
5874	General (Table KF9)
	Juristic persons. Corporations
5875	General. Corporation income tax (Table KF9)
5877	Surtaxes. Excess profits tax (Table KF9)
5878.5	Domestic international sales corporations (Table KF9)
5879.A-Z	Particular lines of corporate business, A-Z
5879.B2	Banks (Table KF7)
5879.M6	Motion picture industry (Table KF7)
	Property taxes. Taxation of capital
5880	General (Table KF9)
5881	Real property taxes (Table KF9)
5881.5	Land valuation. Real property assessment (Table KF9)
5881.7	Exemptions (Table KF9)
5881.8.A-Z	Special topics, A-Z
5881.8.F67	Forest land. Forest yield taxes (Table KF7)
5882	Real estate transactions (Table KF9)
	Business taxes. Licenses
5884	General (Table KF9)
5885.A-Z	Particular lines of business, A-Z
5885.D2	Dairies (Table KF7)
5885.I5	Insurance (Table KF7)
	Milk trade see KFN5885.D2
5886	Corporate franchises (Special franchises). Corporate stock (Table KF9)
	Personal property taxes
5888	General (Table KF9)
5888.5	Exemptions (Table KF9)
	Intangible property
5890.A1	General (Table KF7)
5890.A3-Z	Particular kinds
5890.B6	Bonds and securities (Table KF7)

Public finance
State revenue
Particular sources of revenue
Taxation
Particular taxes
Property taxes. Taxation of capital
Personal property taxes
Intangible property
Particular kinds -- Continued
5890.M6 Mortgages (Table KF7)
5892.A-Z Other personal property, A-Z
Other taxes on capital and income
Estate, inheritance, and gift taxes
5894 General (Table KF9)
5895 Estate tax. Inheritance tax (Table KF9)
Excise taxes. Taxes on transactions
5898 General (Table KF9)
5899 Retail sales taxes (Table KF9)
5900.A-Z Particular commodities, services, transactions, A-Z
5900.A5 Alcoholic beverages. Liquor taxes (Table KF7)
5900.A8 Automobile licenses (Table KF7)
5900.L8 Luxury articles (Table KF7)
5900.M6 Motor fuels. Gasoline (Table KF7)
5900.S7 Stock-exchange transactions (Table KF7)
5900.T7 Transportation (Table KF7)
5902.A-Z Other sources of revenue, A-Z
5902.F3 Federal grants-in-aid (Table KF7)
5902.F33 Fees (Table KF7)
Local finance
5905 General (Table KF9)
5906 Relationship of state and local taxation (Table KF9)
5908 Budget. Expenditure control. Auditing and accounting (Table KF9)
Particular sources of revenue
Taxation
5910 General. Tax power of municipalities. State and local tax jurisdiction and taxation (Table KF9)
5912.A-Z Particular taxes, A-Z
5912.P7 Property taxes (Table KF7)
5912.R3 Real property tax (Table KF7)
5912.R37 Retail sales tax (Table KF7)
5914 Other sources of revenue
Military law
5920 General. Comprehensive (Table KF9)
War-time and emergency legislation
5921 General (Table KF9)
5922 18th and 19th centuries. Early 20th century (Table KF9)

KFN UNITED STATES (NEW YORK) KFN

Military law

War-time and emergency legislation -- Continued

5924	1939-1945 (Table KF9)
	State militia. National Guard
5927	General (Table KF9)
	Enlistment. Recruiting
5928	General (Table KF9)
5929.A-Z	Special topics, A-Z
5929.A5	Aliens (Table KF7)
5929.C6	Convicts (Table KF7)
	Military criminal law and procedure
5930	General. Comprehensive (Table KF9)
	Criminal procedure. Military justice
5931	General (Table KF9)
5932	Courts-martial (Table KF9)
5935	War veterans. Pensions
5940	Indians (Table KF9)
	Courts. Procedure
	Administration of justice. Organization of the judiciary
5950	General (Table KF9 modified)
5950.A19	Directories
	History see KFN5078
5951	Judicial councils. Judicial conference (Table KF9)
	Court organization and procedure
5955	General (Table KF9)
5955.5	Conduct of court proceedings. Decorum (Table KF9)
5956	Congestion and delay (Table KF9)
5957	Foreign judgments. Judicial assistance (Table KF9)
	Administration and management
5958	General (Table KF9)
5958.5	Finance. Accounting (Table KF9)
	Particular courts
5960	Court of Appeals (Table KF9)
	Intermediate appellate courts
5964	Collective. Appellate divisions of Supreme Court (Table KF9)
5965.A-Z	Particular courts, A-Z
	Trial courts
	Chancery courts see KFN5997
	County courts. District courts. Superior courts. Circuit courts
5968	Collective (Table KF9)
5969.A-Z	Particular courts. By county, A-Z
	Under each:
	.A7 *Court records*
	By period or date
	.A8-Z *Treatises. Monographs*

KFN UNITED STATES (NEW YORK) KFN

Courts. Procedure
Court organization and procedure
Particular courts -- Continued
Minor courts
Municipal courts

5970	Collective (Table KF9)
5971.A-Z	Particular courts. By city, A-Z

Under each:

.A7	*Court records*
	By period or date
.A8-Z	*Treatises. Monographs*

5974	Court of Claims (Table KF9)
5975	Justices of the Peace. Magistrates' courts (Table KF9)
5976	Small claims courts (Table KF9)

Judicial officers. Court employees

5979	General (Table KF9)

Judges

5980	General (Table KF9)

Impeachment

5983	General (Table KF9)
5984.A-Z	Particular cases. By respondent, A-Z
5984.5.A-Z	Special topics, A-Z
5984.5.D57	Discipline. Judicial ethics (Table KF7)
	Judicial ethics see KFN5984.5.D57
5984.5.S24	Salaries, pensions, etc. (Table KF7)
5985.A-Z	Other, A-Z
5985.A65	Attendants (Table KF7)
5985.A7	Attorneys (Table KF7)
5985.C5	Clerks of court. Administrative officers (Table KF7)
5985.C65	Constables (Table KF7)
5985.C66	Coroners. Medical examiners (Table KF7)
	Court attendants see KFN5985.A65
5985.C68	Court reporters (Table KF7)
5985.L2	Law clerks (Table KF7)
5985.N6	Notaries (Table KF7)
5985.S4	Sheriffs (Table KF7)

Civil procedure
General
Legislation

5990.A17	Legislative documents. By date

Statutes
Collections

5990.A19-.A199	Serials
5990.A2	Monographs. By date of publication

Courts. Procedure
Civil procedure
General
Legislation
Statutes -- Continued

5990.A3-.A319 Particular acts

Arrange chronologically, by means of successive Cutter numbers, according to date of original enactment or revision of law

Under each:

.xA15	*Compilations of legislative histories*
.xA2	*Unannotated texts. By date of publication*
.xA3-.xZ	*Annotated editions. Commentaries. By author of commentary or annotations*

Court rules
General. Trial courts
Collections

5992.A19-.A199	Serials
5992.A2	Monographs. By date of publication
5992.A23	Citators to rules
5992.A25	Drafts. By date
5992.A3-.A319	Particular rules

Arrange chronologically, by means of successive Cutter numbers, according to date of adoption or revision of rules

Under each:

.xA15	*Compilations of legislative histories. By date of publication*
.xA2	*Unannotated texts. By date of publication*
.xA3-.xZ7	*Annotated editions. Commentaries. By author of commentary or annotations*
.xZ8-.xZ89	*Digests*

KFN UNITED STATES (NEW YORK) KFN

Courts. Procedure
Civil procedure
General
Legislation
Court rules -- Continued

5993.A-Z Particular courts, A-Z

Under each:

Code	Description
.A19-.A2	*Collections*
.A19-.A199	*Serials*
.A2	*Monographs. By date of publication*
.A3-.Z49	*Particular rules*
.A3	*Unannotated texts. By date of publication*
.A5-.Z49	*Annotated editions.*
	Commentaries. By author of commentary or annotations
.Z5	*Indexes. By date of publication*

Courts of intermediate appeals see KFN6078+
Court of Appeals see KFN6081

5994-5994.9 Reports of decisions (Table KF31 modified)

5994 Reports

5994.A19 1844 Howard and Howard N.S. (1844-1884); (1884-1886) 70 v.

5994.A19 1848 Code Reporter (1848-1851) 3 v.

5994.A19 1850 Code Reports, N.S. (1850-1852)

5994.A19 1854 Abbott's Practice Cases (1854-1865) 19 v.

5994.A19 1865 Abbott's Practice Cases, N.S. (1865-1875) 16 v.

5994.A19 1876 Abbott's New Cases (1876-1894) 32 v.

5994.A19 1881 Civil Procedure Reports (1881-1907) 40 v.

5994.A19 1908 Civil Procedure Reports, N.S. (1908-1913) 4 v.

5994.A4A-.A4Z Other, defunct. By editor or title

5995 General works (Table KF8)

5997 Equity practice and procedure. Chancery courts (Table KF9)

5998 Jurisdiction. Venue (Table KF9)

5999 Removal or causes (Table KF9)

Action

6003 Process and service (Table KF9)

6004 Time. Deadlines (Table KF9)

For computation of time see KFN5100.T5

Pleading and motions

6010 General. Pleading (Table KF9)

6012 Motions (Table KF9)

Defenses and objections (Exceptions)

6015 Limitation of actions (Table KF9)

6016 Lis pendens (Table KF9)

Courts. Procedure
Civil procedure
Pleading and motions -- Continued

Number	Topic
6018	Counterclaim and cross claim (Table KF9)
	Parties
6019	Class action (Table KF9)
	Pretrial procedure
6020	General. Deposition and discovery. Interrogatories (Table KF9)
6021.A-Z	Special topics, A-Z
6021.B5	Bill of particulars (Table KF7)
6021.E42	Electronic discovery (Table KF7)
	Settlement see KFN6093
	Trial. Trial practice. Trial tactics
6025	General (Table KF9)
6028.A-Z	Particular types of cases or claims, A-Z
6028.C6	Contracts
6028.M35	Malpractice
6028.P4	Personal injuries
6028.S74	Stockholder suits
	Evidence
6030	General (Table KF9)
	Burden of proof
6031	General (Table KF9)
6032	Presumptions. Judicial notice. Prima-facie evidence (Table KF9)
	Particular claims or actions
6035	Torts. Negligence. Res ipsa loquitur (Table KF9)
	Particular kinds of evidence
6038	Documentary (Table KF9)
6040	Witnesses (Table KF9)
	Jury and jurors
6045	General
6047	Instructions to juries (Table KF9)
	For collected instructions see KF213.A+
	For individual instructions see KF389
6049	Special masters. Referees. Auditors. Examiners (Table KF9)
	Judgment
6050	General (Table KF9)
6051	Costs. Fees. In forma pauperis (Table KF9)
6052	Summary judgment (Table KF9)
6053	Declaratory judgment (Table KF9)
	Remedies and special proceedings
6060	General (Table KF9)
6062	Injunctions. Provisional remedies (Table KF9)
6063	Receivers in equity (Table KF9)

KFN UNITED STATES (NEW YORK) KFN

Courts. Procedure
Civil procedure
Remedies and special proceedings -- Continued
Execution of judgment

6065	General (Table KF9)
6066	Attachment. Garnishment (Table KF9)
	Extraordinary remedies
6070	General (Table KF9)
	Particular remedies
6071	Imprisonment for debt (Table KF9)
	Appellate procedure
6075	General (Table KF9)
	Intermediate appeals
6078	General (Table KF9)
6080.A-Z	Particular courts. By appellate district, A-Z

Under each:

.A4-.Z	*Court rules*
.A4	*Collections. By date of publication*
.A42-.Z	*Particular rules*
.A42	*Unannotated texts. By date of publication*
.A43-.Z	*Annotated editions. Commentaries*

6081	Court of Appeals (Table KF9)
6084	Writ of error (Table KF9)
	Litigation with the state as a party
6086	Court of Claims (Table KF9)
6093	Negotiated settlement. Compromise (Table KF9)
6094	Arbitration and award. Commercial arbitration (Table KF9)
	Criminal law
	Cf. KFN5930+ Military criminal law and procedure
	Cf. KFN6195+ Juvenile criminal law and procedure
6100	General. Comprehensive (Table KF9)
	Administration of criminal justice. Reform of criminal law, enforcement, and procedure
6102	General (Table KF9)
6102.5	Crime and publicity. Trial by newspaper (Table KF9)
	Cf. KFN6141 Contempt of court
	Punishment and penalties
6104	General (Table KF9)
6105	Habitual criminals. Recidivists (Table KF9)
6108.A-Z	Particular penalties, A-Z
6108.C3	Capital punishment (Table KF7)
6108.F67	Forfeitures. Political disabilities (Table KF7)
	Political disabilities see KFN6108.F67
	General principles
	Criminal liability

KFN UNITED STATES (NEW YORK) KFN

Criminal law
General principles
Criminal liability -- Continued

6110	General (Table KF9)
6111	Culpability. Mens rea (Table KF9)
	Exemption from liability. Defenses
6115	General (Table KF9)
	Particular defenses
6116	Insanity (Table KF9)
	Particular offenses
	Offenses against the person
6121	Abortion. Procuring miscarriage (Table KF9)
6121.4	Family violence (Table KF9)
6121.5	Child abuse. Child molesting. Sexual abuse of children (Table KF9)
	Sexual offenses
6122	General (Table KF9)
6124.A-Z	Particular offenses, A-Z
	Child molesting see KFN6121.5
6124.R34	Rape (Table KF7)
6126	Libel. Slander. Defamation (Table KF9)
	Offenses against property
6131	Larceny (Table KF9)
6131.5	Fraud. False pretenses (Table KF9)
6132	Threats. Extortion. Blackmail (Table KF9)
6133	Racketeering. Organized crime (Table KF9)
6134	Malicious mischief (Table KF9)
	Offenses against government and public order. Political offenses
6137	General (Table KF9)
	Particular
6138	Sedition. Subversive activities
	Offenses against the administration of justice
6141	Contempt of court (Table KF9)
6142	Perjury. Subornation of perjury (Table KF9)
	Offenses against public safety
6145	Terrorism (Table KF9)
	Offenses against public convenience and morality
6146	Gambling. Lotteries (Table KF9)
6147	Obscenity (Table KF9)
	Offenses against public property, public finance, and currency
6149	Counterfeiting. Forgery (Table KF9)
	Criminal procedure
6155	General (Table KF9)
6156	Arrest and commitment. Rights of suspects (Table KF9)
6157	Searches and seizures (Table KF9)

KFN UNITED STATES (NEW YORK) KFN

Criminal procedure -- Continued

6157.6	Bail (Table KF9)
6158	Indictment. Information. Public prosecutor (Table KF9)
6159	Grand jury (Table KF9)
	For collected charges see KF213.A+
	For individual charges see KF389
6160	Arraignment. Right to counsel. Public defenders (Table KF9)
	Trial
6162	General (Table KF9)
	Evidence. Burden of proof
6165	General (Table KF9)
	Admission of evidence
6166	General (Table KF9)
6167	Means of identification. Fingerprints, footprints, toothprints, etc. (Table KF9)
6168	Wiretapping. Electronic listening and recording devices (Table KF9)
	Particular types of evidence
6169	Witnesses (Table KF9)
6169.3.A-Z	Other, A-Z
6169.3.E8	Expert evidence. Expert witnesses (Table KF7)
6170	Jury (Table KF9)
6171	Instructions to jury. Directed verdict (Table KF9)
	For collected instructions see KF213.A+
	For individual instructions see KF389
6172	Judgment. Sentence (Table KF9)
6173	Costs (Table KF9)
(6177)	Proceedings before juvenile courts
	see KFN6195+
	Execution of sentence
6179	Corrections (Table KF9)
	Imprisonment
6180	General (Table KF9)
6181	Prison administration. Prison discipline (Table KF9)
6181.5	Prisoners (Table KF9)
6182	Prison labor. Prison industries (Table KF9)
	Particular types of penal or correctional institutions
	Reformatories
6186.A1	General
6186.A5-Z	Particular institutions, A-Z
	Juvenile detention homes see KFN6198.6
6188	Fines (Table KF9)
6189	Restitution (Table KF9)
6190	Probation. Parole (Table KF9)
6191	Indeterminate sentence (Table KF9)
	Juvenile criminal law and procedure. Administration of juvenile justice

Juvenile criminal law and procedure. Administration of juvenile justice -- Continued

6195	General (Table KF9)
6196	Juvenile courts (Table KF9)
	Cf. KFN5116+ Family court
	Criminal law
6197	General (Table KF9)
6197.5	Status offenders (Table KF9)
	Criminal procedure
6198	General (Table KF9)
	Execution of sentence
	Imprisonment
6198.6	Juvenile detention homes (Table KF9)
6199.A-Z	Particular counties, A-Z
	Subarrange each by Table KF10C and Table KF10D modified as follows: .x2C6 = County government and services
	Bronx County see KFX2095.2
	Kings County see KFX2095.4
	New York County see KFX2095
	Queens County see KFX2095.6
	Richmond County see KFX2095.8
<6199.5.A-Z>	Particular cities, A-Z
	For particular cities, see KFX

KFN UNITED STATES (NORTH CAROLINA) KFN

7401-7999 United States (North Carolina) (Table KFA-KFZ modified) Law reports and related materials

7445-7445.9 Supreme Court (Table KF31 modified)

7445 Reports

Call Number	Description
7445.A19 1778	Martin (1778-1797) 1 v. (Old series) .A2 v. 1 (New series)
7445.A19 1789	Haywood (1789-1806) 2 v. (Old series) .A2 v. 2-3 (New series)
7445.A19 1798	Taylor (1798-1802) 1 v. (Old series)
7445.A19 1800	Cameron & Norwood (1800-1804) 1 v. (Old series)
7445.A19 1804	Murphey (1804-1819) 3 v. (Old series) .A2 v. 5-7 (New series)
7445.A19 1813	Carolina Law Repository (1813-1816) 2 v. (Old series) .A2 v. 4 (New series)
7445.A19 1816	Term Reports (1816-1818) 1 v. (Old series)
7445.A19 1820	Hawks (1820-1826, J. Gales & Son ed.) 4 v. (Old series) .A2 v. 8-11 (New series)
7445.A19 1820a	Hawks (1820-1826, Turner and Hughes ed.) 4 v.
7445.A19 1826	Devereux's Law (1826-1834) 4 v. (Old series) .A2 v. 12-15 (New series)
7445.A19 1826a	Devereux's Equity (1826-1834) 2 v. (Old series) .A2 v. 16-17 (New series)
7445.A19 1834	Devereux & Battle's Law (1834-1839) 4 v. (Old series) .A2 v. 18-20 (New series)
7445.A19 1834a	Devereux & Battle's Equity (1834-1839) 2 v. (Old series) .A2 v. 21-22 (New series)
7445.A19 1840	Iredell's Law (1840-1852) 13 v. (Old series) .A2 v. 23-35 (New series)
7445.A19 1840a	Iredell's Equity (1840-1852) 8 v. (Old series) .A2 v. 36-43 (New series)
7445.A19 1852	Busbee's Law (1852-1853) 1 v. (Old series) .A2 v. 44 (New series)
7445.A19 1852a	Busbee's Equity (1852-1853) 1 v. (Old series) .A2 v. 45 (New series)
7445.A19 1853	Jones' Law (1853-1862) 8 v. (Old series) .A2 v. 46-53 (New series)
7445.A19 1853a	Jones' Equity (1853-1863) 6 v. (Old series) .A2 v. 54-59 (New series)
7445.A19 1863	Winston (1863-1864) 2 v. (Old series) .A2 v. 60 (New series)
7445.A19 1866	Phillips' Law (1866-1868) 1 v. (Old series) .A2 v. 61 (New series)
7445.A19 1866a	Phillips' Equity (1866-1868) 1 v. (Old series) .A2 v. 62 (New series)
7445.A2	North Carolina Reports (1868-) v. 63-

KFN UNITED STATES (NORTH DAKOTA) KFN

8601-9199	United States (North Dakota) (Table KFA-KFZ modified)
	Including the Dakota Territory
	Law reports and related materials
8645-8645.9	Supreme Court (Table KF31 modified)
8645	Reports
8645.A2	North Dakota Supreme Court Reports (1890-195-) 77 v.
	Discontinued. Continued in North Dakota Cases, N.W.
	Reporter, 2d ser. v. 60, p. 202
	Lower courts
8647-8647.9	Various courts (Table KF31 modified)
8647	Reports
	Unofficial current series
8647.A32	North Dakota law reports

KFO UNITED STATES (OHIO) KFO

1-599 United States (Ohio) (Table KFA-KFZ modified)
Law reports and related materials
45-45.9 Supreme Court (Table KF31 modified)
45 Reports
Official series
45.A2 Ohio reports (1821-1852) 20 v.
45.A22 Ohio state reports (1852-1964) 177 v.
45.A23 Ohio official reports (1964-). 1964- bound with Ohio appeals and Ohio miscellaneous
45.A4A-.A4Z Abridged, selected, defunct
45.A4H3 Hammond's reports (Corey & Fairbank, and Lodge & L'Hommedieu, 1833) (1821-1826) 1 v.
45.A4H32 Hammond's reports (G.D. Emerson, 1850-1852) (1821-1836) 7 v.
45.A4H35 Hammond's condensed reports (1821-1826) 1 v.
45.A4H36 Hammond's condensed reports (Wilcox) (1821-1831) 1 v.
45.A4O3 Ohio reports, century ed. (1821-1852) 20 v.
45.A4O32 Ohio reports extra annotated (1821-1852) 20 v.
45.A4O4 Ohio state reports, century ed. (1852-1899) 60 v.
45.A4O42 Ohio state reports extra annotated (1852-1912) 84 v.
45.A4O45 Ohio Supreme Court decisions (unreported cases) (1889-1899) 1 v.
45.A4W5 Wilcox's condensed reports, v. 1-4 (1821-1831) 1 v.
45.A4W52 Wilcox's condensed reports, v. 5 (1831-1832) 1 v.
45.A4W53 Wilcox's condensed reports, v. 6-7 (1833-1836) 1 v.
45.A4W7 Wright (1831-1834) 1 v.
Lower courts
47-47.9 Various courts (Table KF31 modified)
47 Reports
47.A2-.A29 Official series
47.A22 Ohio miscellaneous reports (West, 1992-)
Unofficial current series
47.A32 Ohio opinions (1932-)
47.A33 Ohio bar reports (1982-)
47.A4A-.A4Z Abridged, selected, defunct
47.A4A4 American law record: reprint of decisions of Ohio courts (below Supreme Court) (1872-1887) 1 v.
47.A4C53 Cincinnati daily court bulletin, Warden's weekly law and bank bulletin, the Cincinnati law gazette: reprint of decisions of Ohio courts (below Supreme Court) (1857-1859) 1 v.
47.A4C55 Cleveland law record, Cleveland law reporter, Cleveland law register: reprint of decisions of Ohio court (below Supreme Court) (1855-1893) 1 v.
47.A4C6 Cleveland law reporter (1878-1879) 2 v.

KFO UNITED STATES (OHIO) KFO

Law reports and related materials
Lower courts
Various courts
Reports
Abridged, selected, defunct -- Continued

47.A4C62 Cleveland law reporter (1878-1879) 2 v. Reprint edition (1977)

47.A4O35 Ohio decisions reprint (1840-1855) 13 v.
Vol. 1, Western law journal; vol. 2, Western law monthly; vol. 3, Weekly law gazette; Daily law and bank bulletin; American law register; Ohio law journal; vol. 4, Cleveland law record; Cleveland law reporter; vol. 5-6, American law record; vol. 7-11, Weekly law bulletin; vol. 12, Handy's reports; Disney's reports; vol. 13, Disney's reports; Cincinnati Superior Court reporter

47.A4O36 Ohio law abstract (1923-1964) 95 v.
Superseded by Ohio miscellaneous (1964- bound with Ohio official reports)

47.A4O37 Ohio law reporter (1903-1934) 40 v.

47.A4P6 Pollack, Ohio unreported judicial decisions (1807-1823) 1 v.

Intermediate appellate courts

48-48.9 General. Collective (Table KF31 modified)

48 Reports
Official series

48.A2 Ohio appellate reports (1913-1964) 120 v.
1964- bound with Ohio official reports

48.A4A-.A4Z Abridged, selected, defunct

48.A4O35 Ohio Circuit Court reports (1885-1901) 22 v.

48.A4O36 Ohio Circuit Court reports, new series, and Ohio Courts of Appeals reports (1903-1922) 32 v.

48.A4O37 Ohio Circuit decisions and Ohio Circuit Court decisions (1885-1918) 35 v.

District courts. Superior courts. Courts of common pleas

51-51.9 Collective (Table KF31 modified)

51 Reports

51.A4A-.A4Z Abridged, selected, defunct

51.A4O34 Ohio decisions (Ohio lower decisions) (1894-1896) 3 v.

51.A4O35 Ohio decisions (1894-1921) 32 v.

51.A4O36 Ohio nisi prius reports (1893-1901) 8 v.

51.A4O37 Ohio nisi prius reports, new series (1902-1934) 32 v.

51.A4T3 Tappan (1816-1819) 1 v.

52.A-Z Particular courts. By county, etc., A-Z

52.C5 Cincinnati

KFO UNITED STATES (OHIO) KFO

Law reports and related materials
Lower courts
District courts. Superior courts. Courts of common pleas
Particular courts. By county, etc., A-Z
Cincinnati -- Continued

52.C5D5	Disney (1854-1859) 2 v.
52.C5H3	Handy (1854-1856) 2 v.
52.C5H6	Hosea (1903-1907) 1 v.
52.C5T3	Taft & Storer (1870-1873) 2 v.
52.M6	Montgomery County
52.M6G6	Dayton reports, 3 Ohio miscellaneous decisions (Gotschall) (1865-1873) 1 v.

Courts. Procedure
Court organization and procedure
Particular courts
Minor courts
Mayors' courts
Including civil proceedings

520	Collective (Table KF9)
520.5.A-Z	Particular courts. By country, etc., A-Z

KFO UNITED STATES (OKLAHOMA) KFO

Call Number	Description
1201-1799	United States (Oklahoma) (Table KFA-KFZ modified)
	Law reports and related materials
1245-1245.9	Supreme Court (Table KF31 modified)
1245	Reports
	Official series
1245.A2	Oklahoma reports (1890-1953) 208 v.
	Discontinued. Continued in Oklahoma Decisions, Pacific Reporter, 2d ser. v. 258, p. 1189
	Unofficial series
1245.A32	Oklahoma appellate court reporter (1916-)
	Lower courts
1247-1247.9	Various courts (Table KF31 modified)
1247	Reports
	Official series
1247.A2	Oklahoma decisions

KFO UNITED STATES (OREGON) KFO

2401-2999	United States (Oregon) (Table KFA-KFZ modified)
	Law reports and related materials
2445-2445.9	Supreme Court (Table KF31 modified)
2445	Reports
	Official series
2445.A2	Oregon reports (1853-)
2445.A4A-.A4Z	Defunct publications
2445.A4A5	Annotated Oregon reports (1853-1882) 10 v.
	Lower courts
	Intermediate appellate courts
2448-2448.9	Court of Appeals (Table KF31 modified)
2448	Reports
	Official series
2448.A22	Reports (1969-)

KFP UNITED STATES (PENNSYLVANIA) KFP

1-599	United States (Pennsylvania) (Table KFA-KFZ modified)
	Law reports and related materials
45-45.9	Supreme Court (Table KF31 modified)
45	Reports
	Official series and predecessors
45.A19 1754	Dallas (1754-1806) 4 v.
45.A19 1791	Yeats (1791-1808) 4 v.
45.A19 1799	Binney (1799-1814) 6 v.
45.A19 1814	Sergeant & Rawle (1814-1828) 17 v.
45.A19 1828	Rawle (1828-1835) 5 v.
45.A19 1829	Penrose & Watts (1829-1832) 3 v.
45.A19 1832	Watts (1832-1840) 10 v.
45.A19 1835	Wharton (1835-1841) 6 v.
45.A19 1841	Watts & Sergeant (1841-1845) 9 v.
45.A195	Pennsylvania Supreme Court reports (1754-1845) 65 v.
45.A2	Pennsylvania state reports (1845-)
45.A4A-.A4Z	Abridged, selected, defunct
45.A4A4	Alden's condensed reports (1754-1844) 3 v.
45.A4G7	Grant's cases (1814-1863) 3 v.
45.A4M6	Monaghan (1888-1890) 2 v.
45.A4P4	Pennsylvania law series (1894-1896) 3 v.
45.A4P45	Pennypacker (1881-1884) 4 v.
45.A4S3	Sadler (1885-1888) 10 v.
45.A4W3	Walker (1855-1885) 4 v.
	Lower courts
47-47.9	Various courts (Table KF31 modified)
47	Reports
	Unofficial current series
47.A32	Pennsylvania reporter (1938-)
47.A4A-.A4Z	Abridged, selected, defunct
47.A4B7	Brightly nisi prius reports (1809-1851) 1 v.
47.A4C3	Campbell's legal gazette reports (1869-1872) 1 v.
47.A4C55	Clark, Pennsylvania law journal reports (1842-1852) 5 v.
47.A4C6	Common pleas reporter (1879-1887) 4 v.
47.A4F6	Foster's Legal chronicle reports (1873-1875) 3 v.
47.A4L4	Legal opinion (1870-1873) 5 v.
47.A4P4	Pennsylvania law record (1879-1880) 3 v.
47.A4W4	Weekly notes of cases (1874-1899) 44 v.
	Intermediate appellate courts
48-48.9	Superior Court (Table KF31 modified)
48	Reports
	Official series
48.A2	Reports (1895-)
	Other courts, A-Z
	Subarrange each by Table KF32
49.A2-.A26	Commonwealth Court (Table KF32 modified)

KFP UNITED STATES (PENNSYLVANIA) KFP

Law reports and related materials
Lower courts
Intermediate appellate courts
Other courts, A-Z
Commonwealth Court -- Continued
49.A2 Reports (1970-)
District courts. Courts of common pleas
51-51.9 Collective (Table KF31 modified)
51 Reports
51.A4A-.A4Z Abridged, selected, defunct
51.A4A3 Addison (1791-1799) 1 v.
51.A4D5 District reports (1892-1921) 30 v.
51.A4D55 District and county reports (1921-)
51.A4L4 Lehigh Valley law reporter (1885-1887) 2 v.
51.A4P4 Pennsylvania county court reports (1885-1921) 50
v.
52.A-Z Particular courts. By county, etc., A-Z
52.A3 Adams County
52.A3A3 Adams County legal journal (1959-)
52.B4 Beaver County
52.B4B4 Beaver County legal journal (1939-)
52.B45 Berks County
52.B45B4 Berks County law journal (1908-)
52.B45W6 Woodward's decisions (1861-1874) 2 v.
52.B55 Blair County
52.B55B53 Blair County law reporter (1898-1903) 2 v.
52.B55B54 Blair law reports, 2d ser. (1940-1947) 2 v.
52.B55B55 Blair County legal bulletin, (1938-)
52.B8 Bucks County
52.B8B8 Bucks County law reporter (1951-)
52.B85 Butler County
52.B85B8 Butler County legal journal (1959-)
52.C3 Cambria County
52.C3C28 Cambria County law journal reports (1917-1928) 1 v.
52.C3C3 Cambria County reports (1929-) 1 v.
52.C37 Carbon County
52.C37C3 Carbon County law journal (1970 [?]-)
52.C4 Centre County
52.C4C4 Centre County legal journal (1960-)
52.C48 Chester County
52.C48C48 Chester County reports (1879-1885, 1947-)
52.C7 Crawford County
52.C7C7 Crawford County legal journal (1960-)
52.C8 Cumberland County
52.C8C8 Cumberland law journal (1950-)
52.D3 Dauphin County
52.D3D3 Dauphin County reports (1897-) 2 v.

Law reports and related materials
Lower courts
District courts. Courts of common pleas
Particular courts. By county, etc., A-Z
Dauphin County -- Continued

52.D3P3	Pearson (1850-1880) 2 v.
52.D4	Delaware County
52.D4D4	Delaware County reports (1881-)
52.D4D42	Delaware County legal journal (1949-)
52.E7	Erie County
52.E7E7 1919	Erie County law journal (1919-1945) 27 v.
52.E7E7 1945	Erie County legal journal (1945-)
52.F3	Fayette County
52.F3F3	Fayette legal journal (1938-)
52.F7	Franklin County
52.F7F7	Franklin County legal journal (1977-)
52.L3	Lackawanna County
52.L3L28	Lackawanna bar (1878) 1 v.
52.L3L29	Lackawanna bar reports (1906) 1 v.
52.L3L3	Lackawanna jurist (1888-)
52.L3L33	Lackawanna legal news (1895-1903) 8 v.
52.L3L34	Lackawanna legal record (1878-1879) 1 v.
52.L3W5	Wilcox, Lackawanna County reports (1887-1889) 1 v.
52.L35	Lancaster County
52.L35L28	Lancaster bar (1869-1883) 15 v.
52.L35L3	Lancaster law review (1883-)
52.L38	Lawrence County
52.L38L3	Lawrence law journal (1941-)
52.L39	Lebanon County
52.L39D6	The Docket (1897-1898) 2 v.
52.L39L4	Lebanon County legal journal (1946-)
52.L4	Lehigh County
52.L4L4	Lehigh County law journal (1903-)
52.L8	Luzerne County
52.L8L74	Luzerne law journal (1881) 1 v.
52.L8L75	Luzerne law times (Old series) (1873-1878) 6 v.
52.L8L76	Luzerne law times (New series) (1879-1885) 7 v.
52.L8L77	Luzerne legal observer (1860-1864) 4 v.
52.L8L78	Luzerne legal register (1872-1886) 14 v.
52.L8L8	Luzerne legal register reports (1882-)
52.L9	Lycoming County
52.L9L9	Lycoming County reporter (1947-)
52.M4	Mercer County
52.M4M4	Mercer County law journal (1953-)
52.M5	Mifflin County
52.M5M5	Mifflin County legal journal (1961-)
52.M6	Monroe County

KFP UNITED STATES (PENNSYLVANIA) KFP

Law reports and related materials
Lower courts
District courts. Courts of common pleas
Particular courts. By county, etc., A-Z
Monroe County -- Continued

52.M6M6	Monroe legal reporter (1938-)
52.M65	Montgomery County
52.M65M6	Montgomery County law reporter (1885-)
52.N6	Northampton County
52.N6N6	Northampton County reporter (1887-)
52.N65	Northumberland County
52.N65N58	Northumberland County legal news (1888-1889) 1 v.
52.N65N6	Northumberland legal journal (1913-) 1 v.
52.P48	Philadelphia
52.P48A8	Ashmead (1808-1841) 2 v.
52.P48B7	Brewster (1856-1873) 4 .v
52.P48B75	Browne (1801-1814) 2 v.
52.P48M5	Miles (1835-1841) 2 v.
52.P48O4	Olwine's law journal (1849-1850) 1 v.
52.P48P3	Parson's select equity cases (1842-1851) 2 v.
52.P48P48	Philadelphia reports (1850-1891) 20 v.
52.P5	Pittsburgh
52.P5P5	Pittsburgh legal journal (1853-)
52.P5P52	Pittsburgh reports (1853-1873) 3 v.
52.S3	Schuylkill County
52.S3L4	Legal record reports (1879-1882) 2 v.
52.S3S28	Schuylkill register (1933-1945) 10 v.
52.S3S3	Schuylkill legal record (1879-)
52.S6	Somerset County
52.S6S6	Somerset legal journal (1920-)
52.S8	Susquehanna County
52.S8S8	Susquehanna legal chronicle (1878-1879) 1 v.
52.W3	Washington County
52.W3W3	Washington County reports (1920-)
52.W4	Westmoreland County
52.W4W4	Westmoreland County law journal (1911-)
52.Y6	York County
52.Y6Y6	York legal record (1880-)

Succession upon death
Testate succession. Wills. Probate law and practice
For probate records see KFP516.A+

144	General. Orphans' Courts (Table KF9)

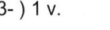

KFP UNITED STATES (PENNSYLVANIA) KFP

Succession upon death
Testate succession. Wills. Probate law and practice --
Continued

144.1.A-Z Particular Orphans' Courts. By county, A-Z
Under each:
.A4 *Court rules. By date of publication*
.A545 *Court records. By initial date of period covered*
.A65 *Form books*
.A8-.Z *Treatises. Monographs*

Contracts
Particular contracts

184 Carriers. Carriage of goods and passengers (Table KF9)

184.5 Maritime carriers. Admiralty (Table KF9)

Social legislation
Labor law
Labor-management relations. Labor unions. Collective labor agreements

332 General (Table KF9)

332.1 Pennsylvania Labor Relations Board (Table KF9)

Constitutional law
Individual and state
Civil and political rights

411 General (Table KF9)

411.3 Human Relations Commission (Table KF9)

Municipal civil service. City officials

436.8.A-Z Particular offices or positions, A-Z

436.8.B8 Burgesses. Mayors of boroughs (Table KF7)

Courts. Procedure
Court organization and procedure
Particular courts

512 Supreme Court (Table KF9)

Intermediate appellate courts

513 Superior Court (Table KF9)

Trial courts: District Courts. Courts of Common Pleas

515 Collective

516.A-Z Particular courts. By county, A-Z
Subarrange each by Table KF7 modified as follows: .A7
= Court records. By initial date of period covered

Minor courts
Municipal courts

518.3 Municipal Court of Philadelphia (Table KF9)

518.5 Allegheny County Court (Table KF9)

KFP UNITED STATES (PENNSYLVANIA) KFP

Courts. Procedure
Court organization and procedure
Particular courts
Minor courts
Municipal courts -- Continued
519.A-Z Other courts. By city, etc., A-Z
Under each:
.A7 *Court records. By initial date of period covered*
Collected wills, etc., see KFA-KFZ144.8
Magistrates. Aldermen. Justices of the Peace
520 Collective
520.5.A-Z Particular courts. By county, etc., A-Z
Civil procedure
General
Legislation
Court rules
General. Trial courts
Collections
529.A19-.A199 Serials
529.A2 Monographs. By date of publication
529.A23 Citators to rules
529.A25 Drafts. By date
529.A3-.A319 Particular rules
Arrange chronologically, by means of successive Cutter numbers, according to date of adoption or revision of rules
Under each:
.xA15 *Compilations of legislative histories. By date of publication*
.xA2 *Unannotated texts. By date of publication*
.xA3-.xZ7 *Annotated editions. By author of commentary or annotations*
.xZ8-.xZ89 *Digests*

KFP UNITED STATES (PENNSYLVANIA) KFP

Courts. Procedure
Civil procedure
General
Court rules

529.5.A-Z Particular courts, A-Z
Under each:

Collections
.xA19-.xA199 *Serials*
.xA2 *Monographs. By date of publication*
Particular rules
.xA3 *Unannotated texts. By date of publication*
.xA5-.xZ49 *Annotated editions. Commentaries. By author of commentary or annotations*
.xZ5 *Indexes. By date of publication*

Superior Court see KFP556
Supreme Court see KFP558
Pleading and motions

535.8 Defenses and objections. Affidavits of defense
Remedies and special proceedings
Appellate procedure
Intermediate appeals

556 Appeals to Superior Court (Table KF9)

(557) This number not used

558 Appeals to Supreme Court (Table KF9)

KFR UNITED STATES (RHODE ISLAND) KFR

1-599	United States (Rhode Island) (Table KFA-KFZ modified)
	Law reports and related materials
45-45.9	Supreme Court (Table KF31 modified)
45	Reports
	Official series
45.A2	Rhode Island reports (1828-)
	Defunct publications
45.A4	Rhode Island reports (1828-1908) 28 v.
	Reprinted by Bogartz, 1909-1910
45.A42	Rhode Island reports, 2d ed., 2 v.
	Lower courts
47-47.9	Various courts (Table KF31 modified)
47	Reports
47.A4A-.A4Z	Defunct publications
47.A4L3	Rhode Island law record
	Trial courts
51-51.9	Superior Court (Table KF31 modified)
51	Reports
51.A19 1917	Rhode Island Superior Court rescripts (1917-1919) 2 v.
51.A19 1924	Rhode Island decisions (1924-1935) 12 v.

KFS UNITED STATES (SOUTH CAROLINA) KFS

1801-2399	United States (South Carolina) (Table KFA-KFZ modified)
	Law reports and related materials
1845-1845.9	Supreme Court (Earlier: Court of Appeals) (Table KF31 modified)
1845	Reports
	Law reports (1783-1868)
1845.A19 1783	Bay (1783-1804) 2 v.
1845.A19 1793	Brevard & Treadway (1793-1816) 5 v.
1845.A19 1817	Nott & McCord (1817-1818) 2 v.
1845.A19 1821	McCord (1821-1828) 4 v.
1845.A19 1823	Harper (1823-1830) 1 v.
1845.A19 1828	Bailey (1828-1832) 2 v.
1845.A19 1833	Hill (1833-1837) 2 v.
1845.A19 1836	Riley (Law and Equity) (1836-1837) 1 v.
1845.A19 1837	Dudley (1837-1838) 1 v.
1845.A19 1838	Rice (1838-1839) 1 v.
1845.A19 1839	Cheves (1839-1840) 1 v.
1845.A19 1840	McMullan (1840-1842) 2 v.
1845.A19 1842	Speers (1842-1844) 2 v.
1845.A19 1844	Richardson (1844-1846) 2 v.?
1845.A19 1846	Strobhart (1846-1850) 5 v.
1845.A19 1850	Richardson (1850-1868) 13 v.?
	Equity reports (1784-1868)
1845.A195 1784	De Saussure (1784-1817) 4 v.
1845.A195 1824	Harper (1824) 1 v.
1845.A195 1825	McCord (1825-1827) 2 v.
1845.A195 1830	Bailey (1830-1831) 1 v.
1845.A195 1831	Richardson's Cases (1831-1832) 1 v.
1845.A195 1833	Hill (1833-1837)
1845.A195 1837	Dudley (1836-1837) 1 v.
1845.A195 1838	Rice (1837-1838) 1 v.
1845.A195 1839	Cheves (1839-1840) 1 v.
1845.A195 1840	McMullen (1840-1842) 1 v.
1845.A195 1842	Speers (1842-1844) 1 v.
1845.A195 1844	Richardson (1844-1846) 1 v.?
1845.A195 1846	Strobhart (1846-1850) 4 v.
1845.A195 1850	Richardson (1850-1868)
	For vol. 12, see .A19 1850
1845.A2	South Carolina Reports (1868-)
1845.A3	South Carolina Reports, Annotated ed., abridged v. 1-25 (1783-1840) 38 v. West., 1922 (continued by S.C. cases in South Eastern Reporter?)

KFS UNITED STATES (SOUTH DAKOTA) KFS

3001-3599	United States (South Dakota) (Table KFA-KFZ modified)
	Law reports and related materials
3045-3045.9	Supreme Court (Table KF31 modified)
3045	Reports
	Official series
3045.A2	South Dakota reports (1890-)

KFT UNITED STATES (TENNESSEE) KFT

1-599 United States (Tennessee) (Table KFA-KFZ modified)
Law reports and related materials

45-45.9 Supreme Court (Table KF31 modified)

45 Reports
Official series and predecessors
Separate editions of nominative reports making up vols.
1-164 of Tennessee reports

45.A19 1791 Overton (1791-1817) 2 v. (Old series)
.A2 v. 1-2 (New series)

45.A19 1811 Cooke (1811-1814) 1 v. (Old series)
.A2 v. 3 (New series)

45.A19 1814 Cooke (1814) 1 v. (Old series)
.A2 v. 3A (New series)

45.A19 1816 Haywood (1816-1818) 3 v. (Old series)
.A2 v. 4-6 (New series)

45.A19 1818 Yerger (1818-1837) 10 v. (Old series)
.A2 v. 9-18 (New series)

45.A19 1821 Peck (1821-1824) 1 v. (Old series)
.A2 v. 7 (New series)

45.A19 1825 Martin & Yerger (1825-1828) 1 v.
.A2 v. 8 (New series)

45.A19 1838 Meigs (1838-1851) 1 v. (Old series)
.A2 v. 19 (New series)

45.A19 1839 Humphreys (1839-1851) 11 v. (Old series)
.A2 v. 20-30 (New series)

45.A19 1851 Swan (1851-1853) 2 v. (Old series)
.A2 v. 31-32 (New series)

45.A19 1853 Sneed (1853-1858) 5 v. (Old series)
.A2 v. 33-37 (New series)

45.A19 1858 Head (1858-1859) 3 v. (Old series)
.A2 v. 38-40 (New series)

45.A19 1860 Coldwell (1860-1870) 7 v. (Old series)
.A2 v. 41-47 (New series)

45.A19 1870 Heiskell (1870-1874) 12 v. (Old series)
.A2 v. 48-59 (New series)

45.A19 1872 Baxter (1872-1878) 9 v. (Old series)
.A2 v. 60-68 (New series)

45.A19 1878 Lea (1878-1886) 16 v. (Old series)
.A2 v. 69-84 (New series)

45.A19 1886 Pickle (1886-1902) 24 v. (Old series)
.A2 v. 85-108 (New series)

45.A19 1902 Cates (1902-1913) 19 v. (Old series)
.A2 v. 109-127 (New series)

45.A19 1913 Thompson (1913-1926) 26 v. (Old series)
.A2 v. 128-153 (New series)

45.A19 1925 Smith (1925-1932) 11 v. (Old series)
.A2 v. 154-164 (New series)

KFT UNITED STATES (TENNESSEE) KFT

Law reports and related materials
Supreme Court
Reports
Official series and predecessors -- Continued

45.A2	Tennessee reports (1931-)
	Unofficial current series
45.A34	Tennessee decisions (S.W. Reporter)
45.A4A-.A4Z	Abridged, selected, defunct
45.A4L4	Legal reporter (1877-1879)
45.A4S5	Shannon's unreported cases (1847-1894)
45.A4T5	Thompson's unreported cases (1847-1869)
	Lower courts
	Intermediate appellate courts
48-48.9	General. Collective (Table KF31 modified)
48	Reports
	Official series and predecessors
48.A19 1901	Court of Chancery Appeals. Wright (1901-1904) 2 v.
48.A19 1910	Court of Civil Appeals. Higgins (1910-1918) 8 v.
48.A2	Court of Appeals. Reports (1925-)
48.A4A-.A4Z	Defunct publications
48.A4W4	Chancery Appeals decisions (1895-1901) 7 v. (West, 1953)
	Trial courts
52.A-Z	Particular courts, A-Z
	Subarrange each by Table KF32
52.C47-.C476	Chancery Court (7th Division) (Table KF32 modified)
52.C47	Reports
52.C47A19 1872	Cooper (1872-1878) 3 v.

KFA-KFW

KFT UNITED STATES (TEXAS) KFT

Call Number	Description
1201-1799	United States (Texas) (Table KFA-KFZ modified)
	Law reports and related materials
1245-1245.9	Supreme Court (Table KF31 modified)
1245	Reports
	Official series
1245.A2	Texas reports (1846-)
1245.A34	Texas Supreme Court journal (1957-)
1245.A4A-.A4Z	Abridged, selected, defunct
1245.A4K5	King's conflicting civil cases (1840-1911) 3 v.
	Lower courts
1247-1247.9	Various courts (Table KF31 modified)
1247	Reports
1247.A4A-.A4Z	Defunct publications
1247.A4T4	Texas court reporter (1900-1908) 20 v.
	Intermediate appellate courts
1248-1248.9	General. Collective (Table KF31 modified)
1248	Reports
	Official series and predecessors
1248.A19 1876	Texas civil cases of Court of Appeals (1876-1892) 4 v.
1248.A2	Texas civil appeals reports (1892-1911) 63 v.

KFU UNITED STATES (UTAH) KFU

1-599	United States (Utah) (Table KFA-KFZ modified)
	Law reports and related materials
45-45.9	Supreme Court (Table KF31 modified)
45	Reports
	Official series
45.A2	Utah reports (1855-)
45.A3-.A39	Unofficial series
45.A32	Utah reporter (Pacific reporter) (West, 1975-)

KFV UNITED STATES (VERMONT) KFV

1-599	United States (Vermont) (Table KFA-KFZ modified)
	Law reports and related materials
45-45.9	Supreme Court (Table KF31 modified)
45	Reports
	Official series and predecessors
45.A19 1789	Chipman, N. (1789-1791) 1 v.
45.A19 1789a	Chipman, D. (1789-1824) 1 v.
45.A19 1800	Tyler (1800-1803) 2 v.
45.A19 1815	Brayton (1815-1819) 1 v.
45.A19 1825	Aikens (1825-1828) 2 v.
45.A2	Vermont reports (1826-)

KFV UNITED STATES (VIRGINIA) KFV

2401-2999	United States (Virginia) (Table KFA-KFZ modified)
	Law reports and related materials
2445-2445.9	Supreme Court of Appeals (Table KF31 modified)
2445	Reports
	Official series and predecessors
	Separate editions of nominative reports making up vol.
	1-74 of Virginia reports
2445.A19 1728	Virginia colonial decisions (1728-1753) 2 v.
2445.A19 1730	Jefferson (1730-1740, 1768-1772) 1 v.
2445.A19 1789	Virginia Cases, Criminal (1789-1826) 2 v. (Old series)
	.A2 v. 3-4 (New series)
2445.A19 1790	Washington (1790-1796) 2 v. (Old series)
	.A2 v. 1-2 (New series)
2445.A19 1797	Call (1797-1825) 6 v. (Old series)
	.A2 v. 5-10 (New series)
2445.A19 1806	Hening & Munford (1806-1810) 4 v. (Old series)
	.A2 v. 11-14 (New series)
2445.A19 1810	Munford (1810-1820) 6 v.
	.A2 v. 15-20 (New series)
2445.A19 1820	Gilmer (1820-1821) 1 v. (Old series)
	.A2 v. 21 (New series)
2445.A19 1821	Randolph (1821-1828) 6 v. (Old series)
	.A2 v. 22-27 (New series)
2445.A19 1829	Leigh (1829-1842) 12 v. (Old series)
	.A2 v. 28-39 (New series)
2445.A19 1842	Robinson (1842-1844) 2 v. (Old series)
	.A2 v. 40-41 (New series)
2445.A19 1844	Grattan (1844-1880) 33 v. (Old series)
	.A2 v. 42-74 (New series)
2445.A2	Virginia reports (1880-)
2445.A4A-.A4Z	Abridged, selected, defunct
2445.A4P3	Patton & Heath, Special Court of Appeals (1855-1857)
	2 v.
2445.A4V45	Virginia reports, annotated (1730-1880) 26 v.
2445.A4V48	Virginia decisions (unreported) (1870-1900) 2 v.
2445.A4V49	Virginia Supreme Court reporter
2445.A4V5	Virginia appeals (1907-1926) 35 v.
	Lower courts
2447-2447.9	Various courts (Table KF31 modified)
2447	Reports
2447.A4A-.A4Z	Abridged, selected, defunct
2447.A4M57	Miscellaneous Virginia law reports (1784-1809) 1 v.
	Appellate courts
2448-2448.9	General. Collective (Table KF31 modified)
2448	Reports
	Official series
	Court of Appeals

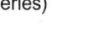

KFV UNITED STATES (VIRGINIA) KFV

Law reports and related materials
Lower courts
Appellate courts
General. Collective
Reports
Official series
Court of Appeals -- Continued
2448.A2 Reports (1985-)
2448.A4A-.A4Z Defunct publications
2448.A4W9 Wythe's Chancery (High Court of Chancery)

KFW UNITED STATES (WASHINGTON) KFW

1-599	United States (Washington) (Table KFA-KFZ modified)
	Law reports and related materials
45-45.9	Supreme Court (Table KF31 modified)
45	Reports
	Official series and predecessors
45.A19 1854	Washington Territory reports (1854-1888) 3 v.
45.A195	Washington Territory reports. Reprint ed. (New series) (1854-1888) 3 v.
45.A2	Washington reports (1890-1939) 200 v.
45.A21	Washington reports, 2d ser. (1939-)
	Lower courts
	Intermediate appellate courts
48-48.9	Court of Appeals (Table KF31 modified)
48	Reports
	Official series
48.A2	Washington appellate reports (1969-)

KFW UNITED STATES (WEST VIRGINIA) KFW

1201-1799	United States (West Virginia) (Table KFA-KFZ modified)
	Law reports and related materials
1245-1245.9	Supreme Court of Appeals (Table KF31 modified)
1245	Reports
	Official series
1245.A2	West Virginia reports (1864-)

KFW UNITED STATES (WISCONSIN) KFW

2401-2999	United States (Wisconsin) (Table KFA-KFZ modified)
	Law reports and related materials
2445-2445.9	Supreme Court (Table KF31 modified)
2445	Reports
	Official series and predecessors
2445.A19 1839	Pinney (1839-1852) 3 v.
2445.A19 1842	Burnett (1842-1843) 1 v.
2445.A19 1849	Chandler (1849-1852) 4 v.
2445.A2	Wisconsin reports (1853-)
2445.A3-.A39	Unofficial reports
2445.A33	Wisconsin reporter (N.W. reporter) (West, 1962-)
2445.A4A-.A4Z	Abridged, selected, defunct
2445.A4D5	Dixon & Ryan (1859-1878) 1 v.

KFW UNITED STATES (WYOMING) KFW

4201-4799	United States (Wyoming) (Table KFA-KFZ modified)
	Law reports and related materials
4245-4245.9	Supreme Court (Table KF31 modified)
4245	Reports
	Official series
4245.A2	Wyoming reports (1870-1959) 80 v.
4245.A21	Wyoming reporter (1959-)

UNITED STATES (CITIES)

United States (Cities)

Cities are subarranged according to Tables 10A (20 nos.), 10B (1 no.), or 10C (Cutter numbers)

1004.A	A to Akron
	Subarrange each by Table KF10C
1005	Akron, Ohio (Table KF10B)
1006.A	Akron to Alameda
	Subarrange each by Table KF10C
1007	Alameda, California (Table KF10B)
1009.A	Alameda to Albany
	Subarrange each by Table KF10C
1011-1029	Albany, New York (Table KF10A)
1031.A	Albany to Alexandria
	Subarrange each by Table KF10C
1034	Alexandria, Virginia (Table KF10B)
1035.A	Alexandria to Allegheny
	Subarrange each by Table KF10C
1041-1059	Allegheny, Pennsylvania (Table KF10A)
1061.A	Allegheny to Altoona
	Subarrange each by Table KF10C
1065	Altoona, Pennsylvania (Table KF10B)
1066.A	Altoona to Annapolis
	Subarrange each by Table KF10C
1067	Annapolis, Maryland (Table KF10B)
1068.A	Annapolis to Atlanta
	Subarrange each by Table KF10C
1071-1089	Atlanta, Georgia (Table KF10A)
1091.A	Atlanta to Auburn
	Subarrange each by Table KF10C
1092	Auburn, New York (Table KF10B)
1093.A	Auburn to Augusta
	Subarrange each by Table KF10C
1095	Augusta, Georgia (Table KF10B)
1096.A	Augusta to Austin
	Subarrange each by Table KF10C
1097	Austin, Texas (Table KF10B)
1098.A-.B	Austin to Baltimore
	Subarrange each by Table KF10C
1101-1119	Baltimore, Maryland (Table KF10A)
1121.B	Baltimore to Bangor
	Subarrange each by Table KF10C
1122	Bangor, Maine (Table KF10B)
1123.B	Bangor to Berj
	Subarrange each by Table KF10C
1124.B	Berkeley to Binghamton
	Subarrange each by Table KF10C
1125	Binghamton, New York (Table KF10B)

KFX UNITED STATES (CITIES) KFX

Number	Description
1126.B	Binghamton to Birmingham
	Subarrange each by Table KF10C
1128	Birmingham, Alabama (Table KF10B)
1129.B	Birmingham to Boston
	Subarrange each by Table KF10C
1131-1149	Boston, Massachusetts (Table KF10A)
1151.B	Boston to Bridgeport
	Subarrange each by Table KF10C
1153	Bridgeport, Connecticut (Table KF10B)
1154.B	Bridgeport to Brockton
	Subarrange each by Table KF10C
1155	Brockton, Massachusetts (Table KF10B)
1156.B	Brockton to Brooklyn
	Subarrange each by Table KF10C
1161-1179	Brooklyn, New York (Table KF10A)
1181 .B	Brooklyn to Brunswick
	Subarrange each by Table KF10C
1186	Brunswick, Georgia (Table KF10B)
1187.B	Brunswick to Buffalo
	Subarrange each by Table KF10C
1191-1209	Buffalo, New York (Table KF10A)
1211.B-.C	Buffalo to Cambridge
	Subarrange each by Table KF10C
1213	Cambridge, Massachusetts (Table KF10B)
1214.C	Cambridge to Camden
	Subarrange each by Table KF10C
1215	Camden, New Jersey (Table KF10B)
1216.C	Camden to Canton
	Subarrange each by Table KF10C
1217	Canton, Ohio (Table KF10B)
1218.C	Canton to Charleston
	Subarrange each by Table KF10C
1219	Charleston, South Carolina (Table KF10B)
1220.C	Charleston to Charlestown
	Subarrange each by Table KF10C
1223	Charlestown, Massachusetts (Table KF10B)
1224.C	Charlestown to Chelsea
	Subarrange each by Table KF10C
1227	Chelsea, Massachusetts (Table KF10B)
1228.C	Chelsea to Chicago
	Subarrange each by Table KF10C
1231-1249	Chicago, Illinois (Table KF10A)
1251.C	Chicago to Chillicothe, Missouri
	Subarrange each by Table KF10C
1255	Chillicothe, Ohio (Table KF10B)
1256.C	Chillicothe, Texas to Cincinnati, Iowa
	Subarrange each by Table KF10C

KFX UNITED STATES (CITIES) KFX

1261-1279	Cincinnati, Ohio (Table KF10A)
1281.C	Cincinnati to Cleveland, North Carolina
	Subarrange each by Table KF10C
1291-1309	Cleveland, Ohio (Table KF10A)
1311.C	Cleveland, Oklahoma to Cohoes
	Subarrange each by Table KF10C
1313	Cohoes, New York (Table KF10B)
1314.C	Cohoes to Colorado
	Subarrange each by Table KF10C
1315	Colorado Springs, Colorado (Table KF10B)
1316.C	Colorado Springs to Columbia
	Subarrange each by Table KF10C
1317	Columbia, South Carolina (Table KF10B)
1319.C	Columbia to Columbus
	Subarrange each by Table KF10C
1321-1339	Columbus, Ohio (Table KF10A)
1341.C	Columbus to Covington
	Subarrange each by Table KF10C
1342	Covington, Kentucky (Table KF10B)
1343.C-.D	Covington to Dallas
	Subarrange each by Table KF10C
1344	Dallas, Texas (Table KF10B)
1345.D	Dallas to Dayton
	Subarrange each by Table KF10C
1346	Dayton, Ohio (Table KF10B)
1347.D	Dayton to Decatur
	Subarrange each by Table KF10C
1348	Decatur, Illinois (Table KF10B)
1349.D	Decatur to Denver
	Subarrange each by Table KF10C
1351-1369	Denver, Colorado (Table KF10A)
1371.D	Denver to Des Moines
	Subarrange each by Table KF10C
1373	Des Moines, Iowa (Table KF10B)
1374.D	Des Moines to Detroit
	Subarrange each by Table KF10C
1381-1399	Detroit, Michigan (Table KF10A)
1401.D	Detroit to Duluth
	Subarrange each by Table KF10C
1402	Duluth, Minnesota (Table KF10B)
1403.D-.E	Duluth to Easton
	Subarrange each by Table KF10C
1404	Easton, Pennsylvania (Table KF10B)
1405.E	Easton to Elizabeth
	Subarrange each by Table KF10C
1406	Elizabeth, New Jersey (Table KF10B)

KFX UNITED STATES (CITIES) KFX

Code	Description
1407.E	Elizabeth to Erie
	Subarrange each by Table KF10C
1411	Erie, Pennsylvania (Table KF10B)
1412.E	Erie to Evansville
	Subarrange each by Table KF10C
1415	Evansville, Indiana (Table KF10B)
1416.E-.F	Evansville to Fall River
	Subarrange each by Table KF10C
1421-1439	Fall River, Massachusetts (Table KF10A)
1443.F	Fall River to Fort Wayne
	Subarrange each by Table KF10C
1445	Fort Wayne, Indiana (Table KF10B)
1446.F-.G	Fort Wayne to Galveston
	Subarrange each by Table KF10C
1448	Galveston, Texas (Table KF10B)
1449.G	Galveston to Grand Forks
	Subarrange each by Table KF10C
1451	Grand Forks, North Dakota (Table KF10B)
1452.G	Grand Forks to Grand Rapids
	Subarrange each by Table KF10C
1453	Grand Rapids, Michigan (Table KF10B)
1454.G-.H	Grand Rapids to Harrisburg
	Subarrange each by Table KF10C
1455	Harrisburg, Pennsylvania (Table KF10B)
1456.H	Harrisburg to Hartford
	Subarrange each by Table KF10C
1461-1479	Hartford, Connecticut (Table KF10A)
1481.H	Hartford to Haverhill
	Subarrange each by Table KF10C
1482	Haverhill, Massachusetts (Table KF10B)
1483.H	Haverhill to Hoboken
	Subarrange each by Table KF10C
1485	Hoboken, New Jersey (Table KF10B)
1486.H	Hoboken to Holyoke
	Subarrange each by Table KF10C
1491-1509	Holyoke, Massachusetts (Table KF10A)
1511.H	Holyoke to Houston
	Subarrange each by Table KF10C
1515	Houston, Texas (Table KF10B)
1516.H-.I	Houston to Indianapolis
	Subarrange each by Table KF10C
1521-1539	Indianapolis, Indiana (Table KF10A)
1543.I-.J	Indianapolis to Jacksonville
	Subarrange each by Table KF10C
1544	Jacksonville, Florida (Table KF10B)
1545	Jacksonville, Illinois (Table KF10B)

KFX UNITED STATES (CITIES) KFX

1546.J	Jacksonville to Jefferson City
	Subarrange each by Table KF10C
1547	Jefferson City, Missouri (Table KF10B)
1549.J	Jefferson City to Jersey City
	Subarrange each by Table KF10C
1551-1569	Jersey City, New Jersey (Table KF10A)
1571.J	Jersey City to Joliet
	Subarrange each by Table KF10C
1572	Joliet, Illinois (Table KF10B)
1573.J	Joliet to Joplin
	Subarrange each by Table KF10C
1574	Joplin, Missouri (Table KF10B)
1575.J-.K	Joplin to Kalamazoo
	Subarrange each by Table KF10C
1576	Kalamazoo, Michigan (Table KF10B)
1577.K	Kalamazoo to Kansas City
	Subarrange each by Table KF10C
1579	Kansas City, Kansas (Table KF10B)
1581-1599	Kansas City, Missouri (Table KF10A)
1601.K-.L	Kansas City to Lancaster
	Subarrange each by Table KF10C
1602	Lancaster, Pennsylvania (Table KF10B)
1603.L	Lancaster to Lawrence
	Subarrange each by Table KF10C
1605	Lawrence, Massachusetts (Table KF10B)
1608.L	Lawrence to Lem
	Subarrange each by Table KF10C
1611.L	Len to Lincoln
	Subarrange each by Table KF10C
1613	Lincoln, Nebraska (Table KF10B)
1614.L	Lincoln to Little Rock
	Subarrange each by Table KF10C
1615	Little Rock, Arkansas (Table KF10B)
1619.L	Little Rock to Los Angeles
	Subarrange each by Table KF10C
1621-1639	Los Angeles, California (Table KF10A)
1721.L	Los Angeles to Louisville
	Subarrange each by Table KF10C
1731-1749	Louisville, Kentucky (Table KF10A)
1751.L	Louisville to Lowell
	Subarrange each by Table KF10C
1761-1779	Lowell, Massachusetts (Table KF10A)
1781.L	Lowell to Lynn
	Subarrange each by Table KF10C
1791-1809	Lynn, Massachusetts (Table KF10A)
1811.L-.M	Lynn to McKeesport
	Subarrange each by Table KF10C

KFX UNITED STATES (CITIES) KFX

1812	McKeesport, Pennsylvania (Table KF10B)
1813.M	McKeesport to Madison
	Subarrange each by Table KF10C
1814	Madison, Wisconsin (Table KF10B)
1815.M	Madison to Manchester
	Subarrange each by Table KF10C
1816	Manchester, New Hampshire (Table KF10B)
1817.M	Manchester to Marquette
	Subarrange each by Table KF10C
1818	Marquette, Michigan (Table KF10B)
1819.M	Marquette to Memphis
	Subarrange each by Table KF10C
1821-1839	Memphis, Tennessee (Table KF10A)
1841.M	Memphis to Middletown
	Subarrange each by Table KF10C
1845	Middletown, Connecticut (Table KF10B)
1846.M	Middletown to Mill
	Subarrange each by Table KF10C
1848.M	Mill to Milwaukee
	Subarrange each by Table KF10C
1851-1869	Milwaukee, Wisconsin (Table KF10A)
1871.M	Milwaukee to Minneapolis
	Subarrange each by Table KF10C
1881-1899	Minneapolis, Minnesota (Table KF10A)
1901.M	Minneapolis to Mobile
	Subarrange each by Table KF10C
1905	Mobile, Alabama (Table KF10B)
1906.M	Mobile to Montgomery
	Subarrange each by Table KF10C
1907	Montgomery, Alabama (Table KF10B)
1909.M-.N	Montgomery to Nashville
	Subarrange each by Table KF10C
1911-1929	Nashville, Tennessee (Table KF10A)
1935.N	Nashville to New Bedford
	Subarrange each by Table KF10C
1943	New Bedford, Massachusetts (Table KF10B)
1944.N	New Bedford to New Haven
	Subarrange each by Table KF10C
1945	New Haven, Connecticut (Table KF10B)
1948.N	New Haven to New Orleans
	Subarrange each by Table KF10C
1951-1969	New Orleans, Louisiana (Table KF10A)
1971.N	New Orleans to New York
	Subarrange each by Table KF10C
2001-2099	New York City
2001	Bibliography
2002	Documents (Collections. Serials)

New York City -- Continued
Ordinances and local laws. Charters

Call Number	Description
2003.A1	Serials
2003.A3	Other collections. By date
2003.A4	Charter. By date
2003.A7A-.A7Z	Digests of ordinances and local laws
2003.A8A-.A8Z	Indexes to ordinances and local laws
	Law reports of courts under city jurisdiction
2005	General (Table KF31)
	Particular courts
2005.95	Surrogate's Courts
<2006>	Periodicals
	Yearbooks. Judicial statistics. Surveys of local administration of justice
2007	General
2007.3	Criminal statistics
2007.35	Juvenile crime
	Cf. KFX2007.5.D6 Family Court statistics
2007.5.A-Z	Other, A-Z
2007.5.D6	Domestic relations
	Including statistics on both domestic relations and juvenile delinquency related to the jurisdiction of the Family Court and its predecessors
2007.5.L33	Labor injunctions
2010	The legal profession. Works on local law practice
	Cf. KF334.A+ Local bar associations, lawyers, clubs, etc.
	Legal aid see KF337.A+
	Lawyer referral services see KF338.A+
	City government
2015	General (Table KF12)
2015.5	Election law (Table KF12)
2016	Legislative functions. The City Council (Table KF12)
	Executive functions
2017	General (Table KF12)
2017.3	The Mayor (Table KF12)
2017.4	Executive departments and administrative agencies (Table KF12)
	Civil service
2017.5.A2	General (Table KF12)
2017.5.A3-Z	Special topics, A-Z
2017.7	Police (Table KF12)
	Judicial functions. City court organization and procedure
2018	General (Table KF12)

New York City
City government
Judicial functions. City court administration and procedure - - Continued
Particular courts
Under each:

Code	Description
.A4	*Rules of practice*
.A45-.A459	*Miscellaneous documents*
.A5-.Z8	*General works*
.Z9A-.Z9Z	*Special topics*
.Z9C6	*Court sites and buildings*

2018.3 Civil courts
2018.4 Criminal courts
2018.5 Probate courts (Surrogate's courts). Probate procedure
2018.7 Magistrates' courts
Court officials and employees
2020.A2 General
2020.A3-Z Particular, A-Z
2020.C58 Coroners. Medical examiners
2020.C6 Corporation counsel. City attorneys
2020.J8 Judges
2020.M37 Marshals
2020.S5 Sheriffs
2020.5 Tort liability (Table KF12)
2022 Real property (Table KF12)
Municipal services. Municipal police power. Regulation of industry, trade, and individuals
2024 General (Table KF12)
Municipal franchises. Licensing. Control of industry, trade, and professions
2025 General. Corporations (Table KF12)
Food processing industry
2029.A2 General
2029.A3-Z Particular products, A-Z
2030 Construction and building industry (Table KF12)
Trade and commerce
2031 General
Banking
2031.3.A2 General
2031.3.A3-.Z8 Particular kinds of banks and banking transactions, A-Z
2031.3.S2 Savings banks
2031.3.T7 Trust companies
2031.3.Z9A-.Z9Z Individual banks. By name, A-Z
2031.5 Loan of money. Interest. Usury (Table KF12)
Secured transactions
2031.6.A2 General

KFX UNITED STATES (CITIES) KFX

New York City
Municipal services. Municipal police power. Regulation of industry, trade, and individuals
Municipal franchises. Licensing. Control of industry, trade, and professions
Trade and commerce
Secured transactions -- Continued

2031.6.A3-Z	Particular kinds of security, A-Z
2031.6.M4	Mechanics' liens
2031.8	Marketing of securities and commodities (Table KF12)
	Public utilities
2033	General (Table KF12)
2033.5.A-Z	Particular, A-Z
	Transportation
2034	General. Local transit (Table KF12)
2034.5.A-Z	Particular types of carriers, A-Z
2034.5.A8	Autobuses
2034.5.S7	Streetcars
2034.5.S8	Subway railroads
2035	Road traffic. Traffic regulations (Table KF12)
2038	Telecommunication (Table KF12)
	Retail trade
2041.A2	General
2041.A3-Z	Particular products
2041.5.A-Z	Services trades, A-Z
2042.A-Z	Professions, A-Z
2042.E58	Entertainers
	Social legislation. Labor relations. Public welfare
2045.A2	General
2045.A3-Z	Particular groups, A-Z
2045.C4	Children
2045.E37	Educational personnel
	Government employees see KFX2045.P8
2045.P8	Public employees
2045.S3	Sailors
2045.W5	Widows
2045.5.A-Z	Special topics, A-Z
	Public health
2048	General (Table KF12)
2048.3	Hospitals. Asylums. Nursing homes (Table KF12)
2048.5	Medical regulations (Table KF12)
2050	Food. Drugs. Cosmetics (Table KF12)
2051	Liquor (Table KF12)
	Public safety
2055	General (Table KF12)
	Road traffic, motor vehicle regulation see KFX2035
2056	Air traffic. Airports (Table KF12)

KFX UNITED STATES (CITIES) KFX

New York City
Public safety -- Continued

2057	Water transportation (Table KF12)
2060	Fire prevention. Fire department (Table KF12)
	Electric conduits see KFX2080.5
2061	Explosives (Table KF12)
2062	Accident prevention (Table KF12)
	Public order and morality
2064	General (Table KF12)
2064.5	Prostitution (Table KF12)
2065	Education (Table KF12)
2067	Science and the arts. Museums, galleries, libraries (Table KF12)
2068	Civil and political rights and liberties (Table KF12)
	Public property
2070	General (Table KF12)
2071	Roads. Streets. Expressways (Table KF12)
2072	Water resources and waterways (Table KF12)
2074	Public works (Table KF12)
2075	Eminent domain. Condemnation procedure (Table KF12)
2076	Public land law. Parks (Table KF12)
2079	City planning and redevelopment. Zoning (Table KF12)
2080	Building (Table KF12)
2080.3	Plumbing (Table KF12)
2080.5	Electric conduits and installations (Table KF12)
2081	Housing (Table KF12)
2083	City property (Table KF12)
	Economic emergency legislation
2085.A2	General
2085.A3-Z	Special topics, A-Z
2085.R3	Rent control
	Public finance
2089	General (Table KF12)
2089.5	Public debts. Bond issues (Table KF12)
	Taxation
2090	General (Table KF12)
2091.A-Z	Particular taxes, A-Z
2091.C6	Corporations
2091.P7	Property taxes
	Local offenses (Violations of ordinances) and administration of criminal justice
2093	General (Table KF12)
2094	Administration of penal institutions. Parole (Table KF12)
	Particular boroughs
2095	Manhattan (New York County)
2095.2	The Bronx (Bronx County)
2095.4	Brooklyn (Kings County)

New York City
Particular boroughs -- Continued
Queens (Queens County)
Richmond (Richmond County)
Metropolitan area government. Interstate agencies
General (Table KF12)
Transportation and communication. Port of New York Authority (Table KF12)
Social legislation. Labor law. Waterfront Commission of New York Harbor (Table KF12)
Public health. Sanitation. Interstate Sanitation Commission (Table KF12)
Liquor control, New York Alcoholic Beverage Control Board see KFX2051
Public property. Public land. Land use (Table KF12)
New York to Newark
Subarrange each by Table KF10C
Newark, New Jersey (Table KF10B)
Newark to Norfolk
Subarrange each by Table KF10C
Norfolk, Virginia (Table KF10B)
Norfolk to North
Subarrange each by Table KF10C
North Adams to Oakland
Subarrange each by Table KF10C
Oakland, California (Table KF10B)
Oakland to Omaha
Subarrange each by Table KF10C
Omaha, Nebraska (Table KF10B)
Omaha to Paterson
Subarrange each by Table KF10C
Paterson, New Jersey (Table KF10B)
Paterson to Pawtucket
Subarrange each by Table KF10C
Pawtucket, Rhode Island (Table KF10B)
Pawtucket to Peoria
Subarrange each by Table KF10C
Peoria, Illinois (Table KF10B)
Peoria to Philadelphia
Subarrange each by Table KF10C
Philadelphia, Pennsylvania (Table KF10A)
Philadelphia to Pittsburgh
Subarrange each by Table KF10C
Pittsburgh, Pennsylvania (Table KF10A)
Pittsburgh to Pittsfield
Subarrange each by Table KF10C
Pittsfield, Massachusetts (Table KF10B)

KFX		KFX
2095.6	Queens (Queens County)	
2095.8	Richmond (Richmond County)	
2096	General (Table KF12)	
2096.4	Transportation and communication. Port of New York Authority (Table KF12)	
2096.6	Social legislation. Labor law. Waterfront Commission of New York Harbor (Table KF12)	
2096.7	Public health. Sanitation. Interstate Sanitation Commission (Table KF12)	
2096.8	Public property. Public land. Land use (Table KF12)	
2101.N	New York to Newark	
2102	Newark, New Jersey (Table KF10B)	
2103.N	Newark to Norfolk	
2105	Norfolk, Virginia (Table KF10B)	
2106.N	Norfolk to North	
2107.N-.O	North Adams to Oakland	
2108	Oakland, California (Table KF10B)	
2109.O	Oakland to Omaha	
2111	Omaha, Nebraska (Table KF10B)	
2112.O-.P	Omaha to Paterson	
2113	Paterson, New Jersey (Table KF10B)	
2114.P	Paterson to Pawtucket	
2115	Pawtucket, Rhode Island (Table KF10B)	
2116.P	Pawtucket to Peoria	
2118	Peoria, Illinois (Table KF10B)	
2119.P	Peoria to Philadelphia	
2121-2139	Philadelphia, Pennsylvania (Table KF10A)	
2141.P	Philadelphia to Pittsburgh	
2151-2169	Pittsburgh, Pennsylvania (Table KF10A)	
2171.P	Pittsburgh to Pittsfield	
2172	Pittsfield, Massachusetts (Table KF10B)	

KFX UNITED STATES (CITIES) KFX

2173.P	Pittsfield to Portland
	Subarrange each by Table KF10C
2175	Portland, Maine (Table KF10B)
2176.P	Portland, Michigan to Portland, North Dakota
	Subarrange each by Table KF10C
2178	Portland, Oregon (Table KF10B)
2179.P	Portland to Providence
	Subarrange each by Table KF10C
2181-2199	Providence, Rhode Island (Table KF10A)
2201.P-.Q	Providence to Quincy
	Subarrange each by Table KF10C
2202	Quincy, Illinois (Table KF10B)
2203.Q-.R	Quincy to Reading
	Subarrange each by Table KF10C
2205	Reading, Pennsylvania (Table KF10B)
2209.R	Reading to Richmond
	Subarrange each by Table KF10C
2211-2299	Richmond, Virginia (Table KF10A)
2231.R	Richmond to Rochester
	Subarrange each by Table KF10C
2241-2259	Rochester, New York (Table KF10A)
2261.R	Rochester to Rockland
	Subarrange each by Table KF10C
2262	Rockland, Maine (Table KF10B)
2263.R-.S	Rockland to Saginaw
	Subarrange each by Table KF10C
2264	Saginaw, Michigan (Table KF10B)
2265.S	Saginaw to St. Joseph
	Subarrange each by Table KF10C
2266	St. Joseph, Missouri (Table KF10B)
2277.S	St. Joseph to St. Louis
	Subarrange each by Table KF10C
2281-2299	St. Louis, Missouri (Table KF10A)
2301.S	St. Louis to St. Paul
	Subarrange each by Table KF10C
2311-2329	St. Paul, Minnesota (Table KF10A)
2331.S	St. Paul to Salem
	Subarrange each by Table KF10C
2334	Salem, Massachusetts (Table KF10B)
2335.S	Salem to Salt Lake
	Subarrange each by Table KF10C
2337	Salt Lake City, Utah (Table KF10B)
2338.S	Salt Lake to San Antonio
	Subarrange each by Table KF10C
2341	San Antonio, Texas (Table KF10B)
2342.S	San Antonio to San Diego
	Subarrange each by Table KF10C

KFX UNITED STATES (CITIES) KFX

2343	San Diego, California (Table KF10B)
2344.S	San Diego to San Francisco
	Subarrange each by Table KF10C
2351-2369	San Francisco, California (Table KF10A)
2371.S	San Francisco to Savannah
	Subarrange each by Table KF10C
2374	Savannah, Georgia (Table KF10B)
2375.S	Savannah to Scranton
	Subarrange each by Table KF10C
2376	Scranton, Pennsylvania (Table KF10B)
2377.S	Scranton to Seattle
	Subarrange each by Table KF10C
2379	Seattle, Washington (Table KF1B)
2381.S	Seattle to Shz
	Subarrange each by Table KF10C
2382.S	Si to Somerville
	Subarrange each by Table KF10C
2383	Somerville, Massachusetts (Table KF10B)
2384.S	Somerville to Springfield
	Subarrange each by Table KF10C
2385	Springfield, Illinois (Table KF10B)
2386.S	Springfield, Kentucky to Springfield, Maine
	Subarrange each by Table KF10C
2388	Springfield, Massachusetts (Table KF10B)
2391	Springfield, Missouri (Table KF10B)
2393.S	Springfield to Steubenville
	Subarrange each by Table KF10C
2394	Steubenville, Ohio (Table KF10B)
2396.S	Steubenville to Superior
	Subarrange each by Table KF10C
2398	Superior, Wisconsin (Table KF10B)
2399.S	Superior to Syracuse
	Subarrange each by Table KF10C
2401-2419	Syracuse, New York (Table KF10A)
2421.S-.T	Syracuse to Tacoma
	Subarrange each by Table KF10C
2422	Tacoma, Washington (Table KF10B)
2423.T	Tacoma to Taunton
	Subarrange each by Table KF10C
2425	Taunton, Massachusetts (Table KF10B)
2426.T	Taunton to Terre Haute
	Subarrange each by Table KF10C
2427	Terre Haute, Indiana (Table KF10B)
2428.T	Terre Haute to Toledo
	Subarrange each by Table KF10C
2431-2449	Toledo, Ohio (Table KF10A)

KFX UNITED STATES (CITIES) KFX

2451.T	Toledo to Topeka
	Subarrange each by Table KF10C
2453	Topeka, Kansas (Table KF10B)
2455.T	Topeka to Trenton
	Subarrange each by Table KF10C
2456	Trenton, New Jersey (Table KF10B)
2458.T	Trenton to Troy
	Subarrange each by Table KF10C
2459	Troy, New York (Table KF10B)
2501.T-.U	Troy to Utica
	Subarrange each by Table KF10C
2502	Utica, New York (Table KF10B)
2503.U-.W	Utica to Washington
	Subarrange each by Table KF10C
	Washington, D.C. see KFD1201+
2531.W	Washington to Waterbury
	Subarrange each by Table KF10C
2535	Waterbury, Connecticut (Table KF10B)
2536.W	Waterbury to Wheeling
	Subarrange each by Table KF10C
2538	Wheeling, West Virginia (Table KF10B)
2541.W	Wheeling to Wichita
	Subarrange each by Table KF10C
2542	Wichita, Kansas (Table KF10B)
2543.W	Wichita to Wilkes-Barre
	Subarrange each by Table KF10C
2545	Wilkes-Barre, Pennsylvania (Table KF10B)
2546.W	Wilkes-Barre to Wilmington
	Subarrange each by Table KF10C
2548	Wilmington, Delaware (Table KF10B)
2549.W	Wilmington to Winston
	Subarrange each by Table KF10C
2551	Winston-Salem, North Carolina (Table KF10B)
2554.W	Winston to Wom
	Subarrange each by Table KF10C
2558.W	Won to Worcester
	Subarrange each by Table KF10C
2561-2579	Worcester, Massachusetts (Table KF10A)
2581.W-.Y	Worcester to Yonkers
	Subarrange each by Table KF10C
2583	Yonkers, New York (Table KF10B)
2584.Y	Yonkers to Youngstown
	Subarrange each by Table KF10C
2585	Youngstown, Ohio (Table KF10B)
2586.Y	Youngstown to Ypsilanti
	Subarrange each by Table KF10C
2588	Ypsilanti, Michigan (Table KF10B)

KFX UNITED STATES (CITIES) KFX

2589.Y-Z	Ypsilanti to Zanesville
	Subarrange each by Table KF10C
2591	Zanesville, Ohio (Table KF10B)
2593.Z	Zanesville to ZZ
	Subarrange each by Table KF10C

KFZ UNITED STATES (NORTHWEST TERRITORY) KFZ

1801-2399 United States (Northwest Territory) (Table KFA-KFZ)

KFZ UNITED STATES (CONFEDERATE STATES OF AMERICA) KFZ

8601-9199 United States (Confederate States of America) (Table KFA-KFZ)

KFZ UNITED STATES (TERRITORIES) KFZ

United States (Territories)
- Canal Zone
  - see KGH9001+
- Guam
  - see KVQ1+
- Pacific Islands Trust Territory
  - see KWE1+
- Puerto Rico
  - see KGV1+
- Ryukyu Islands and other Pacific islands under U.S. control
  - see KNX2935.O64
- Samoa
  - see KWW1+
- Virgin Islands
  - see KGZ1+

KF1 TABLE OF FORM DIVISIONS (20 NOS.) KF1

Number	Description
1	Bibliography
(1.5)	Surveys of legal research
	The Library of Congress discontinued use of this form subdivision in 2007
	see KF1 2 or KF1 19.A7+
2	Periodicals
	Class here periodicals consisting primarily of informative materials (newsletters, bulletins, etc.) relating to a particular subject, and annuals containing information about the year past, such as statistics, etc.
	For periodicals consisting predominantly of legal articles, regardless of subject matter and jurisdiction, see K1+
(2.5)	Yearbooks. Statistics
	The Library of Congress discontinued use of this form subdivision in 2007
	see KF1 2
(3)	Society publications
	The Library of Congress discontinued use of this form subdivision in 2007
	see KF1 2 or KF1 19.A7+
(4)	Congresses and conferences
	The Library of Congress discontinued use of this form subdivision in 2007
	see KF1 19.A2
<5>	Congressional hearings and reports
	see KF25
	Other legislative documents
(5.2)	Bills
	The Library of Congress discontinued use of this form subdivision in 2007
	see KF1 5.6
(5.4)	Presidential messages
	The Library of Congress discontinued use of this form subdivision in 2007
	see KF1 5.6
(5.5)	Other (staff reports, research reports, memoranda, individual testimony, etc.)
	The Library of Congress discontinued use of this form subdivision in 2007
	see KF1 5.6
5.6	Staff reports, research reports, memoranda, individual testimony, bills, Presidential messages, executive branch legislative proposals, etc.
5.8	Compilations of legislative histories (documents) other than those relating to a particular act. By date of publication
	Statutes. Regulations. Rules of practice
	Federal legislation

Statutes. Regulations. Rules of practice
Federal legislation -- Continued
Statutes
Collections. Compilations
Including collections consisting of both statutes and regulations, of comparative state statutes, and of federal and state statutes

5.99 Serials. Loose-leaf editions

6 Monographs. By date of publication

(6.5-.599) Particular acts
The Library of Congress discontinued use of this span of numbers in 2007
see KF1 6.6<date>

6.6<date> Particular acts
Arrange chronologically by appending the four-digit year of original enactment or total revision of the law to this number and deleting any trailing zeros. If more than one law is enacted in a single year, append a lowercase letter to the year (b, c, d, etc.) for each subsequent law

Under each:

	Legislative history
.A15	*Compilations of documents. Treatises. By date of publication*
(.A16)	*Treatises see .A15, above*
	Texts
	Including official editions, with or without annotations, and annotated editions and commentaries
(.A19)	*Serials*
	Serial editions are classed in the number for Serials under "Collections. Compilations," above
.A2	*Monographs. By date of publication*
(.A5-.Z)	*Annotated editions.*
	Commentaries. By author of commentary or annotations see .A2, above

Including collections consisting of an individual act and its associated regulations

Regulations. Rules of practice

KF1 TABLE OF FORM DIVISIONS (20 NOS.) KF1

Statutes. Regulations. Rules of practice
Federal legislation
Regulations. Rules of practice -- Continued
Collections. Compilations
For collections consisting of an individual act and its associated regulations see KF1 6.6<date>
For collections consisting of both statutes and regulations see KF1 5.99+

6.99 Serials
Including serial editions of individual regulations

7 Monographs. By date of publication

(7.5-.529) Particular regulations or rules of practice (or groups of regulations or rules adopted as a whole)
The Library of Congress discontinued use of this span of numbers in 2007
see KF1 7.53

7.53 Particular regulations or rules of practice (or groups of regulations or rules adopted as a whole). By date of adoption or promulgation
Including official editions, annotated editions, and commentaries
For rules of practice before a separately classed agency, see the issuing agency
For serials see KF1 6.99

(8) Digests of statutes and regulations
The Library of Congress discontinued use of this form subdivision in 2007
see KF1 8.8

(8.3) Citators for statutes and regulations
The Library of Congress discontinued use of this form subdivision in 2007
see KF1 8.8

(8.5) Indexes to federal statutes and regulations
The Library of Congress discontinued use of this form subdivision in 2007
see KF1 8.8

(8.7) Collections of summaries of federal legislation
The Library of Congress discontinued use of this form subdivision in 2007
see KF1 8.8

8.8 Finding aids for statutes and regulations
Including digests, citators, indexes, and summaries
Class citators for both cases and legislation with citators for court decisions or decisions of regulatory agencies

Comparative and uniform state and local legislation. Interstate compacts

Statutes. Regulations. Rules of practice
Comparative and uniform state and local legislation. Interstate compacts -- Continued
Collections. Selections
For collections of state laws see KF1 5.99+

9.A15	Serials
9.A2	Monographs. By date of publication
9.4	Particular interstate compacts. By date of adoption
(9.5-.529)	Particular uniform state laws
	The Library of Congress discontinued use of this span of numbers in 2007
	see KF1 9.53
9.53	Particular uniform state laws. By date of adoption
	Including drafts, amendments, annotated texts, unannotated texts, and commentaries
	For serials see KF1 9.A15
9.6.A-Z	History and criticism
	Court decisions
	Reports
10.A2	Serials
10.A5-Z	Monographs
10.3	Digests of reports (Case finders)
10.5	Citators
	Including citators for both cases and statutes
10.7	Indexes
<10.8>	Individual cases. By date
	see KF223+ and KF228.A+
	Decisions of regulatory agencies. Rulings
	Reports
12.A2	Serials
12.A5-Z	Monographs
12.3	Digests of reports (Case finders)
12.5	Citators
12.7	Indexes
(14.A-Z)	Collections of summaries of cases ("Digests" of cases decided by courts or regulatory agencies)
	The Library of Congress discontinued use of this form subdivision in 2007
	see KF1 10.3 or KF1 12.3
(14.5)	Encyclopedias
	The Library of Congress discontinued use of this form subdivision in 2007
	see KF1 17
15	Looseleaf services
	Not further subarranged by date of publication
16	Form books
17	Dictionaries. Encyclopedias

KF1 TABLE OF FORM DIVISIONS (20 NOS.) KF1

(18) Casebooks. Readings
The Library of Congress discontinued use of this form subdivision in 2007
see KF1 19.A7+
General works

(19.A1) Collections. Monographic series
The Library of Congress discontinued use of this form subdivision in 2007
see KF1 2 or KF1 19.A7+

19.A2 Congresses. Symposia. Collected papers, addresses, and essays

(19.A3-.A49) Official reports and monographs
The Library of Congress discontinued use of this form subdivision in 1994
see KF1 2 or KF1 19.A7+

19.A7-Z Treatises. Monographs

(19.3) Compends. Outlines
The Library of Congress discontinued use of this form subdivision in 2007
see KF1 19.85

(19.5) Examination aids
The Library of Congress discontinued use of this form subdivision in 2007
see KF1 19.85

(19.6) Popular works
The Library of Congress discontinued use of this form subdivision in 2007
see KF1 19.85

(19.8.A-Z) Works for particular classes of users, A-Z
The Library of Congress discontinued use of this form subdivision in 2007
see KF1 19.85

19.85 Examination aids. Popular works
Including compends, outlines, and works for particular classes of users

(19.9.A-Z) Foreign language treatises
The Library of Congress discontinued use of this form subdivision in 2007
see KF1 19.A7+

(20) Works on comparative and uniform state and local law
The Library of Congress discontinued use of this form subdivision in 2007
see KF1 19.A7+ or KF1 19.85
Where numbers for comparative state law have been established, prefer those numbers, e.g. KF5390, State civil service; KF6720+ State and local finance; KF6735+ State finance

KF1 TABLE OF FORM DIVISIONS (20 NOS.) KF1

<20.Z99A-.Z99Z> Works on the law of individual states. By state, A-Z Optional arrangement for law libraries using this classification

KF2 TABLE OF FORM DIVISIONS (10 NOS.) KF2

1 Bibliography
(1.5) Surveys of legal research
The Library of Congress discontinued use of this form subdivision in 2007
see KF2 2 or KF2 9.A7+
2 Periodicals
Class here periodicals consisting primarily of informative materials (newsletters, bulletins, etc.) relating to a particular subject, and annuals containing information about the year past, such as statistics, etc.
For periodicals consisting predominantly of legal articles, regardless of subject matter and jurisdiction, see K1+
(2.1) Yearbooks. Statistics
The Library of Congress discontinued use of this form subdivision in 2007
see KF2 2
(2.3) Society publications
The Library of Congress discontinued use of this form subdivision in 2007
see KF2 2 or KF2 9.A7+
(2.5) Congresses and conferences
The Library of Congress discontinued use of this form subdivision in 2007
see KF2 9.A2
<3> Congressional hearings and reports
see KF25
Other legislative documents
(3.2) Bills. By date
The Library of Congress discontinued use of this form subdivision in 2007
see KF2 3.6
(3.4) Presidential messages. By date
The Library of Congress discontinued use of this form subdivision in 2007
see KF2 3.6
(3.5) Other (staff reports, research reports, memoranda, individual testimony, etc.)
The Library of Congress discontinued use of this form subdivision in 2007
see KF2 3.6
3.6 Staff reports, research reports, memoranda, individual testimony, bills, Presidential messages, executive branch legislative proposals, etc.
3.8 Compilations of legislative histories (documents) other than those relating to a particular act. By date of publication
Statutes. Regulations. Rules of practice
Federal legislation

Statutes. Regulations. Rules of practice
Federal legislation -- Continued
Statutes
Collections. Compilations
Including collections consisting of both statutes and regulations, of comparative state statutes, and of federal and state statutes

3.99 Serials. Loose-leaf editions

4 Monographs. By date of publication

(4.5-.579) Particular acts
The Library of Congress discontinued use of this span of numbers in 2007
see KF2 4.58<date>

4.58<date> Particular acts
Arrange chronologically by appending the four-digit year of original enactment or total revision of the law to this number and deleting any trailing zeros. If more than one law is enacted in a single year, append a lowercase letter to the year (b, c, d, etc.) for each subsequent law
Under each:

Legislative history

.A15 *Compilations of documents. Treatises. By date of publication*

(.A16) *Treatises see .A15, above*

Texts

Including official editions, with or without annotations, and annotated editions and commentaries

(.A19) *Serials*

Serial editions are classed in the number for Serials under "Collections. Compilations," above

.A2 *Monographs. By date of publication*

(.A5-.Z) *Annotated editions. Commentaries. By author of commentary or annotations see .A2, above*

Including collections consisting of an individual act and its associated regulations

Regulations. Rules of practice

Statutes. Regulations. Rules of practice
Federal legislation
Regulations. Rules of practice -- Continued
Collections. Compilations
For collections consisting of both statutes and regulations see KF2 3.99+
For collections consisting of an individual act and its associated regulations see KF2 4.58<date>

4.599 Serials

4.6 Monographs. By date

(4.7-.719) Particular regulations or rules of practice (or groups of regulations or rules adopted as a whole)
The Library of Congress discontinued use of this span of numbers in 2007
see KF2 4.72

4.72 Particular regulations or rules of practice (or groups of regulations or rules adopted as a whole). By date of adoption or promulgation
Including official editions, annotated editions, and commentaries
For rules of practice before a separately classed agency, see the issuing agency
For serials see KF2 4.599

(4.73) Digests of statutes and regulations
The Library of Congress discontinued use of this form subdivision in 2007
see KF2 4.79

(4.75) Citators for statutes and regulations
The Library of Congress discontinued use of this form subdivision in 2007
see KF2 4.79

(4.77) Indexes to federal statutes and regulations
The Library of Congress discontinued use of this form subdivision in 2007
see KF2 4.79

4.78 Collections of summaries of federal legislation
The Library of Congress discontinued use of this form subdivision in 2007
see KF2 4.79

4.79 Finding aids for statutes and regulations
Including digests, citators, indexes, and summaries
Class citators for both cases and legislation with citators for court decisions or decisions of regulatory agencies
Comparative and uniform state and local legislation. Interstate compacts
Collections. Selections
For collections of state laws see KF2 3.99+

Statutes. Regulations. Rules of practice
Comparative and uniform state and local legislation. Interstate compacts
Collections. Selections -- Continued

4.8.A15	Serials
4.8.A2	Monographs. By date of publication
4.814	Particular interstate compacts. By date of adoption
(4.82-.839)	Particular uniform state laws
	The Library of Congress discontinued use of this span of numbers in 2007
	see KF2 4.84
4.84	Particular uniform state laws. By date of adoption
	Including drafts, amendments, annotated texts, unannotated texts, and commentaries
	For serials see KF2 4.8.A15
4.85	History and criticism

Court decisions
Reports

5.A2	Serials
5.A5-Z	Monographs
5.3	Digests of reports (Case finders)
5.5	Citators
	Including citators for both cases and statutes
5.7	Indexes
<5.8>	Individual cases. By date
	see KF223+ and KF228.A+

Decisions of regulatory agencies. Rulings
Reports

6.A2	Serials
6.A5-Z	Monographic collections
6.2	Digests of reports (Case finders)
6.25	Citators
6.28	Indexes
(6.3.A-Z)	Collections of summaries of cases ("Digests" of cases decided by courts or regulatory agencies). By editor or title, A-Z
	The Library of Congress discontinued use of this form subdivision in 2007
	see KF2 5.3 or KF2 6.2
6.4	Encyclopedias
	The Library of Congress discontinued use of this form subdivision in 2007
	see KF2 7.5
6.5	Looseleaf services
	Not further subarranged by date of publication
7	Form books
7.5	Dictionaries. Encyclopedias

KF2 TABLE OF FORM DIVISIONS (10 NOS.) KF2

(8)	Casebooks. Readings
	The Library of Congress discontinued use of this form subdivision in 2007
	see KF2 9.A7+
	General works
(9.A1)	Collections. Monographic series
	The Library of Congress discontinued use of this form subdivision in 2007
	see KF2 2 or KF2 9.A7+
9.A2	Congresses. Symposia. Collected papers and essays
(9.A3-.A49)	Official reports and monographs
	The Library of Congress discontinued use of this form subdivision in 1994. After 1994, official reports and monographs are classed as periodicals or general works
9.A7-Z	Treatises. Monographs
10	Compends. Outlines
(10.Z95)	Works on comparative and uniform state and local law
	The Library of Congress discontinued use of this form subdivision in 2007
	see KF2 9.A7+
	Where numbers for comparative state law have been established, prefer those numbers, e.g. KF5390, State civil service; KF6720+ State and local finance; KF6735+ State finance
<10.Z99A-.Z99Z>	Works on the law of individual states. By state, A-Z
	Optional arrangement for law libraries using this classification

TABLES

KF3 TABLE OF FORM DIVISIONS (5 NOS.) KF3

1.A1	Bibliography
1.A3	Periodicals
	Class here periodicals consisting primarily of informative materials (newsletters, bulletins, etc.) relating to a particular subject, and annuals containing information about the year past, such as statistics, etc.
	For periodicals consisting predominantly of legal articles, regardless of subject matter and jurisdiction, see K1+
	Statutes. Regulations. Rules of practice
	Federal legislation
	Statutes
	Including collections consisting of both statutes and regulations, of comparative state statutes, and of federal and state statutes
1.4	Serials. Loose-leaf editions
1.5	Monographs. By date of publication
	Regulations. Rules of practice
	For collections consisting of both statutes and regulations, and for collections consisting of an individual act and its associated regulations see KF3 1.4+
1.7.A-Z	Serials
1.8	Monographs. By date of publication
	Comparative and uniform state and local legislation. Interstate compacts
	Collections. Selections
	For collections of state laws see KF3 1.4+
2.A15	Serials
2.A2	Monographs. By date of publication
2.114	Particular interstate compacts. By date of adoption
(2.2-.239)	Particular uniform state laws
	The Library of Congress discontinued use of this span of numbers in 2007
	see KF3 2.24
2.24	Particular uniform state laws. By date of adoption
	For serials see KF3 2.A15
2.25	History and criticism
	Court decisions
2.4	Digests of reports (Case finders)
<2.5>	Individual cases. By date
	see KF223+ and KF228.A+
(2.8.A-Z)	Collections of summaries of cases ("Digests" of cases decided by courts or regulatory agencies). By editor or title, A-Z
	The Library of Congress discontinued use of this form subdivision in 2007
	see KF3 2.4

KF3 TABLE OF FORM DIVISIONS (5 NOS.) KF3

(3) Encyclopedias

The Library of Congress discontinued use of this form subdivision in 2007

see KF3 3.5

3.1 Form books

3.5 Dictionaries. Encyclopedias

(4) Casebooks. Readings

The Library of Congress discontinued use of this form subdivision in 2007

see KF3 5.A7+

General works

(5.A1) Collections. Monographic series

The Library of Congress discontinued use of this form subdivision in 2007

see KF3 1.A3 or KF3 5.A7+

5.A2 Congresses. Symposia. Collected papers and essays

(5.A3-.A49) Official reports and monographs

The Library of Congress discontinued use of this form subdivision in 1994. After 1994, official reports and monographs are classed as periodicals or general works

5.A7-.Z8 Treatises. Monographs

5.Z9 Compends. Outlines

(5.Z95) Works on comparative and uniform state and local law

The Library of Congress discontinued use of this form subdivision in 2007

see KF3 5.A7+

Where numbers for comparative state law have been established, prefer those numbers, e.g. KF5390, State civil service; KF6720+ State and local finance; KF6735+ State finance

<5.Z99A-.Z99Z> Works on the law of individual states. By state, A-Z

Optional arrangement for law libraries using this classification

TABLES

KF4 TABLE OF FORM DIVISIONS (5 NOS.) KF4

1.A1	Bibliography
(1.A2)	Surveys of legal research
	The Library of Congress discontinued use of this form division in 2007
	see KF4 1.A3 or KF4 5.A7+
1.A3	Periodicals
	Class here periodicals consisting primarily of informative materials (newsletters, bulletins, etc.) relating to a particular subject, and annuals containing information about the year past, such as statistics, etc.
	For periodicals consisting predominantly of legal articles, regardless of subject matter and jurisdiction, see K1+
(1.A32)	Yearbooks. Statistics
	The Library of Congress discontinued use of this form division in 2007
	see KF4 1.A3
(1.A35)	Society publications
	The Library of Congress discontinued use of this form division in 2007
	see KF4 1.A3 or KF4 5.A7+
(1.A4)	Congresses and conferences. By date
	The Library of Congress discontinued use of this form division in 2007
	see KF4 5.A2
<1.A5>	Congressional hearings and reports
	see KF25
	Other legislative documents
(1.A52)	Bills. By date
	The Library of Congress discontinued use of this form division in 2007
	see KF4 1.A56
(1.A54)	Presidential messages. By date
	The Library of Congress discontinued use of this form division in 2007
	see KF4 1.A56
(1.A55)	Other (staff reports, research reports, memoranda, individual testimony, etc.)
	The Library of Congress discontinued use of this form division in 2007
	see KF4 1.A56
1.A56	Staff reports, research reports, memoranda, individual testimony, bills, Presidential messages, executive branch legislative proposals, etc.
1.A58	Compilations of legislative histories (documents) other than those relating to a particular act. By date of publication
	Statutes. Regulations. Rules of practice
	Federal legislation

Statutes. Regulations. Rules of practice
Federal legislation -- Continued
Statutes
Collections. Compilations
Including collections consisting of both statutes and regulations, of comparative state statutes, and of federal and state statutes

1.9	Serials. Loose-leaf editions
2	Monographs. By date of publication
(2.1-.129)	Particular acts
	The Library of Congress discontinued use of this span of numbers in 2007
	see KF4 2.13<date>
2.13<date>	Particular acts
	Arrange chronologically by appending the four-digit year of the original enactment or total revision of the law to this number and deleting any trailing zeros. If more than one law is enacted in a single year, append a lowercase letter to the year (b, c, d, etc.) for each subsequent law
	Under each:
	Legislative history
	.A15 — *Compilations of documents. Treatises. By date of publication*
	(.A16) — *Treatises see .A15, above*
	Texts
	Including official editions, with or without annotations, and annotated editions and commentaries
	(.A19) — *Serials*
	Serial editions are classed in the number for Serials under "Collections. Compilations," above
	.A2 — *Monographs. By date of publication*
	(.A5-.Z) — *Annotated editions. Commentaries. By author of commentary or annotations see .A2, above*
	Including collections consisting of an individual act and its associated regulations
	Regulations. Rules of practice

Statutes. Regulations. Rules of practice
Federal legislation
Regulations. Rules of practice -- Continued
Collections. Compilations
For collections consisting of both statutes and regulations see KF4 1.9+
For collections consisting of an individual act and its associated regulations see KF4 2.13<date>

2.19	Serials
2.2	Monographs. By date
(2.25-.269)	Particular regulations or rules of practice (or groups of regulations or rules adopted as a whole)
	The Library of Congress discontinued use of this span of numbers in 2007
	see KF4 2.27
2.27	Particular regulations or rules of practice (or groups of regulations or rules adopted as a whole). By date of adoption or promulgation
	Including official editions, annotated editions, and commentaries
	For rules of practice before a separately classed agency, see the issuing agency
	For serials see KF4 2.19
	Indexes to federal statutes and regulations
(2.278)	Serials
	The Library of Congress discontinued use of this form division in 2007
	see KF4 2.3
(2.28)	Monographs. By date
	The Library of Congress discontinued use of this form division in 2007
	see KF4 2.3
2.29	Collections of summaries of federal legislation
	The Library of Congress discontinued use of this form division in 2007
	see KF4 2.3
2.3	Finding aids for statutes and regulations
	Including digests, citators, indexes, and summaries
	Class citators for both cases and legislation with citators for court decisions or decisions of regulatory agencies
	Comparative and uniform state and local legislation. Interstate compacts
	Collections. Selections
2.5.A15	Serials
2.5.A2	Monographs. By date
2.54	Particular interstate compacts. By date of adoption

KF4 TABLE OF FORM DIVISIONS (5 NOS.) KF4

Statutes. Regulations. Rules of practice
Comparative and uniform state and local legislation. Interstate compacts -- Continued

(2.6-.629)	Particular uniform state laws
	The Library of Congress discontinued use of this span of numbers in 2007
	see KF4 2.63
2.63	Particular uniform state laws. By date of adoption
	Including drafts, amendments, annotated texts, unannotated texts, and commentaries
	For serials see KF4 2.5.A15
2.65	History and criticism
	Court decisions
	Reports
3.A2	Serials
3.A5-Z	Monographic collections
3.1	Digests of reports (Case finders)
3.15	Citators
	Including citators for both cases and statutes
3.2	Indexes
<3.25>	Individual cases. By date
	see KF223+ and KF228.A+
	Decisions of regulatory agencies
	Reports
3.3.A2	Serials
3.3.A5-Z	Monographic collections
3.32	Digest of reports (Case finders)
3.34	Citators
3.35	Indexes
(3.36.A-Z)	Collections of summaries of cases ("Digests" of cases decided by courts or regulatory agencies). By editor or title, A-Z
	The Library of Congress discontinued use of this form division in 2007
	see KF4 3.1 or KF4 3.32
3.4	Looseleaf services
	Not further subarranged by date of publication
3.5	Form books
3.6	Dictionaries
(4)	Casebooks. Readings
	The Library of Congress discontinued use of this form division in 2007
	see KF4 5.A7+
	General works
(5.A1)	Collections. Monographic series
	The Library of Congress discontinued use of this form division in 2007
	see KF4 1.A3 or KF4 5.A7+

TABLES

KF4 TABLE OF FORM DIVISIONS (5 NOS.) KF4

General works -- Continued

5.A2	Congresses. Symposia. Collected papers and essays
(5.A3-.A49)	Official reports and monographs
	The Library of Congress discontinued use of this form subdivision in 1994. After 1994, official reports and monographs are classed as periodicals or general works
5.A7-.Z8	Treatises. Monographs
5.Z9	Compends. Outlines
(5.Z95)	Works on comparative and uniform state and local law
	The Library of Congress discontinued use of this form division in 2007
	see KF4 5.A7+
	Where numbers for comparative state law have been established, prefer those numbers, e.g. KF5390, State civil service; KF6720+ State and local finance; KF6735+ State finance
<5.Z99A-.Z99Z>	Works on the law of individual states. By state, A-Z
	Optional arrangement for law libraries using this classification

KF5 TABLE OF FORM DIVISIONS (2 NOS.) KF5

1.A1	Bibliography
1.A15	Periodicals
	Class here periodicals consisting primarily of informative materials (newsletters, bulletins, etc.) relating to a particular subject, and annuals containing information about the year past, such as statistics, etc.
	For periodicals consisting predominantly of legal articles, regardless of subject matter and jurisdiction, see K1+
(1.A152)	Yearbooks. Statistics
	The Library of Congress discontinued use of this form division in 2007
	see KF5 1.A15
(1.A16)	Society publications
	The Library of Congress discontinued use of this form division in 2007
	see KF5 1.A15 or KF5 2.A7+
(1.A17)	Congresses and conferences
	The Library of Congress discontinued use of this form division in 2007
	see KF5 2.A5
<1.A2>	Congressional hearings and reports
	see KF25
	Other legislative documents
	Including staff reports, research reports, memoranda, individual testimony, bills, Presidential messages, executive branch legislative proposals, etc.
1.A25	Monographs. By date of publication
	Statutes. Regulations. Rules of practice
	Federal legislation
	Statutes
	Collections. Compilations
	Including collections consisting of both statutes and regulations, of comparative state statutes, and of federal and state statutes
1.A29	Serials. Loose-leaf editions
1.A3	Monographs. By date of publication
(1.A31-.A328)	Particular acts
	The Library of Congress discontinued use of this span of numbers in 2007
	see KF5 1.A328<date>

Statutes. Regulations. Rules of practice
Federal legislation
Statutes -- Continued

1.A328<date> Particular acts

Arrange chronologically by appending the four-digit year of the original enactment or total revision of the law to this number and deleting any trailing zeros. If more than one law is enacted in a single year, append a lowercase letter to the year (b, c, d, etc.) for each subsequent law

Under each:

	Legislative history
.xA15	*Compilations of documents. Treatises. By date of publication*
(.xA16)	*Treatises see .A15, above*
	Texts
	Including official editions, with or without annotations, and annotated editions and commentaries
(.xA19)	*Serials*
	Serial editions are classed in the number for Serials under "Collections. Compilations," above
.xA2	*Monographs. By date of publication*
(.xA5-.xZ)	*Annotated editions.*
	Commentaries. By author of commentary or annotations see .A2, above

Including collections consisting of an individual act and its associated regulations

Regulations. Rules of practice

Collections. Compilations

For collections consisting of both statutes and regulations see KF5 1.A29+

For collections consisting of an individual act and its associated regulations see KF5 1.A328<date>

1.A329 Serials

1.A33 Monographs. By date

(1.A35-.A369) Particular regulations or rules of practice (or groups of regulations or rules adopted as a whole)

The Library of Congress discontinued use of this span of numbers in 2007

see KF5 1.A369

KF5 TABLE OF FORM DIVISIONS (2 NOS.) KF5

Statutes. Regulations. Rules of practice
Federal legislation
Regulations. Rules of practice -- Continued

1.A369	Particular regulations or rules of practice (or groups of regulations or rules adopted as a whole). By date of adoption or promulgation
	For rules of practice before a separately classed agency, see the issuing agency
	For serials see KF5 1.A329
	Indexes to federal statutes and regulations
(1.A3697)	Serials
	The Library of Congress discontinued use of this form division in 2007
	see KF5 1.A38
(1.A3698)	Monographs. By date
	The Library of Congress discontinued use of this form division in 2007
	see KF5 1.A38
(1.A37-.A379)	Collections of summaries of federal legislation
	The Library of Congress discontinued use of this form division in 2007
	see KF5 1.A38
1.A38	Finding aids for statutes and regulations
	Including digests, citators, indexes, and summaries
	Class citators for both cases and legislation with citators for court decisions or decisions of regulatory agencies
	Comparative and uniform state and local legislation. Interstate compacts
	Collections. Selections
1.A39	Serials
1.A4	Monographs. By date of publication
1.A414	Particular interstate compacts. By date of adoption
(1.A42-.A439)	Particular uniform state laws
	The Library of Congress discontinued use of this span of numbers in 2007
	see KF5 1.A44
1.A44	Particular uniform state laws. By date of adoption
	Including drafts, amendments, annotated texts, unannotated texts, and commentaries
	For serials see KF5 1.A39
1.A45	History and criticism
	Court decisions
	Reports
(1.A5-.A519)	Serials
	The Library of Congress discontinued use of this span of numbers in 2007
	see KF5 1.A519

KF5 TABLE OF FORM DIVISIONS (2 NOS.) KF5

Court decisions

Reports -- Continued

1.A519	Serials
1.A52	Monographic collections
1.A53	Digests of reports (Case finders)
1.A535	Citators
	Including citators for both cases and statutes
1.A54	Indexes
<1.A545>	Individual cases. By date
	see KF223+ and KF228.A+

Decisions of regulatory agencies. Rulings

Reports

(1.A6-.A619)	Serials
	The Library of Congress discontinued use of this span of numbers in 2007
	see KF5 1.A619
1.A619	Serials
1.A62	Monographic collections
1.A65	Digests of reports (Case finders)
1.A67	Citators
1.A69	Indexes
(1.A75A-.A75Z)	Collections of summaries of cases ("Digests" of cases decided by courts or regulatory agencies). By editor or title, A-Z
	The Library of Congress discontinued use of this form division in 2007
	see KF5 1.A53 or KF5 1.A65
1.A8	Looseleaf services
	Not further subarranged by date of publication
2.A3	Form books
2.A35	Dictionaries. Encyclopedias
(2.A4)	Casebooks. Readings
	The Library of Congress discontinued use of this form division in 2007
	see KF5 2.A7+

General works

(2.A45)	Collections. Monographic series
	The Library of Congress discontinued use of this form division in 2007
	see KF5 1.A15 or KF5 2.A7+
2.A5	Congresses. Symposia. Collected papers and essays
(2.A6-.A69)	Official reports and monographs
	The Library of Congress discontinued use of this form subdivision in 1994. After 1994, official reports and monographs are classed as periodicals or general works
2.A7-.Z8	Treatises. Monographs

KF5 TABLE OF FORM DIVISIONS (2 NOS.) KF5

General works -- Continued

(2.Z9) Compends. Outlines

The Library of Congress discontinued use of this form division in 2007

see KF5 2.A7+

(2.Z95) Works on comparative and uniform state and local law

The Library of Congress discontinued use of this form division in 2007

see KF5 2.A7+

Where numbers for comparative state law have been established, prefer those numbers, e.g. KF5390, State civil service; KF6720+ State and local finance; KF6735+ State finance

<2.Z99A-.Z99Z> Works on the law of individual states. By state, A-Z

Optional arrangement for law libraries using this classification

KF6 TABLE OF FORM DIVISIONS (1 NO.) KF6

Call Number	Description
.A1	Bibliography
.A15	Periodicals
	Class here periodicals consisting primarily of informative materials (newsletters, bulletins, etc.) relating to a particular subject, and annuals containing information about the year past, such as statistics, etc.
	For periodicals consisting predominantly of legal articles, regardless of subject matter and jurisdiction, see K1+
(.A152)	Yearbooks. Statistics
	The Library of Congress discontinued use of this form subdivision in 2007
	see KF6 .A15
(.A16)	Society publications
	The Library of Congress discontinued use of this form subdivision in 2007
	see KF6 .A15 or KF6 .A9+
(.A17)	Congresses and conferences
	The Library of Congress discontinued use of this form subdivision in 2007
	see KF6 .A75
<.A2>	Congressional hearings and reports
	see KF25
	Other legislative documents
.A23	Serials
(.A24-.A249)	Serials
	The Library of Congress discontinued use of this span of numbers in 2007
	see KF6 .A23
.A25	Monographs. By date of publication
	Statutes. Regulations. Rules of practice
	Federal legislation
	Statutes
	Collections. Compilations
	Including collections consisting of both statutes and regulations, of comparative state statutes, and of federal and state statutes
.A29	Serials. Loose-leaf editions
.A3	Monographs. By date of publication
(.A31-.A328)	Particular acts
	The Library of Congress discontinued use of this span of numbers in 2007
	see KF6 .A328<date>

Statutes. Regulations. Rules of practice
Federal legislation
Statutes -- Continued

.A328<date>	Particular acts

Arrange chronologically by appending the four-digit year of original enactment or total revision of the law to this number and deleting any trailing zeros. If more than one law is enacted in a single year, append a lowercase letter to the year (b, c, d, etc.) for each subsequent law

Under each:

	Legislative history
.xA15	*Compilations of documents.*
	Treatises. By date of
	publication
(.xA16)	*Treatises see .xA15, above*
	Texts
	Including official editions, with
	or without annotations, and
	annotated editions and
	commentaries
(.xA19)	*Serials*
	Serial editions are classed in
	the number for Serials
	under "Collections.
	Compilations," above
.xA2	*Monographs. By date of*
	publication
(.xA5-.xZ)	*Annotated editions.*
	Commentaries. By author of
	commentary or annotations see
	.xA2, above

Including collections consisting of an individual act and its associated regulations

Regulations. Rules of practice

Collections. Compilations

For collections consisting of both statutes and regulations see KF6 .A29+

For collections consisting of an individual act and its associated regulations see KF6 .A328<date>

.A329	Serials
.A33	Monographs. By date of publication
(.A35-.A369)	Particular regulations or rules of practice (or groups of regulations or rules adopted as a whole)
	The Library of Congress discontinued use of this span of numbers in 2007
	see KF6 .A369

Statutes. Regulations. Rules of practice
Federal legislation
Regulations. Rules of practice -- Continued

.A369 Particular regulations or rules of practice (or groups of regulations or rules adopted as a whole). By date of adoption or promulgation
Including official editions, annotated editions, and commentaries
For rules of practice before a separately classed agency, see the issuing agency
For serials see KF6 .A329

(.A3692-.A3694) Digests of statutes and regulations
The Library of Congress discontinued use of this form subdivision in 2007
see KF6 .A38

Indexes to federal statutes and regulations

(.A3697) Serials
The Library of Congress discontinued use of this form subdivision in 2007
see KF6 .A38

(.A3698) Monographs. By date
The Library of Congress discontinued use of this form subdivision in 2007
see KF6 .A38

(.A37-.A379) Collections of summaries of federal legislation
The Library of Congress discontinued use of this form subdivision in 2007
see KF6 .A38

.A38 Finding aids for statutes and regulations
Including digests, citators, indexes, and summaries
Class citators for both cases and legislation with citators for court decisions or decisions of regulatory agencies

Comparative and uniform state and local legislation. Interstate compacts

Collections. Selections
For collections of state laws see KF6 .A29+

.A39 Serials

.A4 Monographs. By date of publication

.A414 Particular interstate compacts. By date of adoption

.A42-.A439 Particular uniform state laws
The Library of Congress discontinued use of this span of numbers in 2007
see KF6 .A44

.A44 Particular uniform state laws. By date of adoption
Including drafts, amendments, annotated texts, and commentaries
For serials see KF6 .A39

KF6 TABLE OF FORM DIVISIONS (1 NO.) KF6

Statutes. Regulations. Rules of practice
Comparative and uniform state and local legislation. Interstate compacts -- Continued

.A45	History and criticism
	Court decisions
	Reports
(.A5-.A519)	Serials
	The Library of Congress discontinued use of this span of numbers in 2007
	see KF6 .A519
.A519	Serials
.A52	Monographic collections
.A53	Digests of reports (Case finders)
.A535	Citators
	Including citators for both cases and statutes
.A54	Indexes
<.A545>	Individual cases. By date
	see KF223+ and KF228.A+
	Decisions of regulatory agencies. Rulings
	Reports
(.A55-.A559)	Serials
	The Library of Congress discontinued use of this span of numbers in 2007
	see KF6 .A559
.A559	Serials
.A56	Monographic collections
.A57	Digests of reports (Case finders)
.A575	Citators
.A58	Indexes
(.A59A-.A59Z)	Collections of summaries of cases ("Digests" of cases decided by courts or regulatory agencies). By editor or title, A-Z
	The Library of Congress discontinued use of this form subdivision in 2007
	see KF6 .A53 or KF6 .A57
.A6	Looseleaf services
	Not further subarranged by date of publication
.A65	Form books
.A68	Dictionaries
(.A7)	Casebooks. Readings
	The Library of Congress discontinued use of this form subdivision in 2007
	see KF6 .A9+
	General works
(.A73)	Collections. Monographic series
	The Library of Congress discontinued use of this form subdivision in 2007
	see KF6 .A15 or KF6 .A9+

KF6 TABLE OF FORM DIVISIONS (1 NO.) KF6

General works -- Continued

.A75 Congresses. Symposia. Collected papers and essays

(.A8-.A89) Official reports and monographs

The Library of Congress discontinued use of this form subdivision in 1994

see KF6 .A15 or KF6 .A9+

.A9-.Z8 Treatises. Monographs

(.Z9) Compends. Outlines

The Library of Congress discontinued use of this form subdivision in 2007

see KF6 .A9+ or numbers for examination aids, popular works, etc., under individual topics

(.Z95) Works on comparative and uniform state and local law

The Library of Congress discontinued use of this form subdivision in 2007

see KF6 .A9+

Where numbers for comparative state law have been established, prefer those numbers, e.g. KF5390 State civil service; KF6720+ State and local finance; KF6735+ State finance

<.Z99A-.Z99Z> Works on the law of individual states. By state, A-Z

Optional arrangement for law libraries using this classification

KF7 TABLE FOR TOPICS REPRESENTED BY CUTTER NUMBERS KF7

Book numbers for works arranged by author are constructed by means of successive Cutter numbers

.xA15-.xA199	Periodicals
	Including gazettes, bulletins, circulars, etc.
.xA2	Legislative documents. By date
	Treaties. Statutes. Statutory orders (Collective or individual)
.xA29-.xA299	Serials
.xA3	Monographs. By date
	Cases. Decisions (Collective or individual)
.xA515-.xA519	Serials
.xA52	Monographs. By date
.xA7-.xZ9	General works. Treatises

KF8 TABLE OF FORM DIVISIONS UNDER SINGLE-NUMBER CAPTIONS FOR GENERAL WORKS KF8

Call Number	Description
.A1	Serial publications. Collections
.A2	Congresses. Symposia. Collected papers and essays
(.A3-.A6)	Official reports and monographs
	The Library of Congress discontinued use of this form subdivision in 1994
	see KF8 .A1 or KF8 .A75+
.A65	Form books
(.A7)	Casebooks. Readings
	The Library of Congress discontinued use of this form subdivision in 2007
	see KF8 .A75+
.A75-.Z8	Treatises. Monographs
(.Z9)	Compends. Examination aids. Popular works
	The Library of Congress discontinued use of this form subdivision in 2007
	see KF8 .A75+ or numbers for examinations, popular works, etc., under individual topics

KF9 TABLE OF FORM DIVISIONS FOR STATE LAW (1 NO.) KF9

.A1	Bibliography
.A15	Periodicals
	Class here periodicals consisting primarily of informative materials (newsletters, bulletins, etc.) relating to a particular subject, and annuals containing information about the year past, such as statistics, etc.
	For periodicals consisting predominantly of legal articles, regardless of subject matter and jurisdiction, see K1+
(.A152)	Yearbooks. Statistics
	The Library of Congress discontinued use of this form subdivision in 2007
	see KF9 .A15
(.A16)	Society publications
	The Library of Congress discontinued use of this form subdivision in 2007
	see KF9 .A15 or KF9 .A9+
(.A17)	Congresses and conferences
	The Library of Congress discontinued use of this form subdivision in 2007
	see KF9 .A75
<.A2>	Legislative hearings and reports
	The Library of Congress does not class legislative hearings and reports by topic. They are classed under "Committee documents" at the beginning of the schedule for each state, e.g. KFC10+ (California); KFN5010+ (New York); KFA10.8- KFA11.82 (Alabama); etc.
	Other legislative documents
(.A24-.A249)	Serials
	The Library of Congress discontinued use of this span of numbers in 2007
	see KF9 .A249
.A249	Serials
.A25	Monographs. By date of publication
	Statutes. Regulations. Rules of practice
	State legislation
	Statutes
	Collections. Compilations
	Including collections consisting of both statutes and regulations, of state and local legislation, and of comparative local legislation
.A29	Serials. Loose-leaf editions
.A3	Monographs. By date of publication
(.A33-.A349)	Particular acts
	The Library of Congress discontinued use of this span of numbers in 2007
	see KF9 .A35<date>

TABLE OF FORM DIVISIONS FOR STATE LAW (1 NO.)

Statutes. Regulations. Rules of practice
State legislation
Statutes -- Continued

.A35<date> Particular acts

> Arrange chronologically by appending the four-digit year of original enactment or total revision of the law to this number and deleting any trailing zeros. If more than one law is enacted in a single year, append a lowercase letter to the year (b, c, d, etc.) for each subsequent law

Under each:

	Legislative history
.xA15	*Compilations of documents. Treatises. By date of publication*
(.xA16)	*Treatises see .xA15, above*
	Texts
	Including official editions, with or without annotations, and annotated editions and commentaries
(.xA19)	*Serials*
	Serial editions are classed in the number for Serials under "Collections. Compilations," above
.xA2	*Monographs. By date of publication*
(.xA5-.xZ)	*Annotated editions.*
	Commentaries. By author of commentary or annotations see KF9 .xA2, above

Including collections consisting of an individual act and its associated regulations

Regulations. Rules of practice
Collections. Compilations

> For collections consisting of both statutes and regulations see KF9 .A29+
> For collections consisting of an individual act and its associated regulations see KF9 .A35<date>

.A39 Serials

.A4 Monographs. By date of publication

(.A43-.A449) Particular regulations or rules of practice (or groups of regulations or rules adopted as a whole)

> The Library of Congress discontinued use of this span of numbers in 2007
> see KF9 .A449

KF9 TABLE OF FORM DIVISIONS FOR STATE LAW (1 NO.) KF9

Statutes. Regulations. Rules of practice
State legislation
Regulations. Rules of practice -- Continued

.A449 Particular regulations or rules of practice (or groups of regulations or rules adopted as a whole). By date of adoption or promulgation
Including official editions, annotated editions, and commentaries
For rules of practice before a separately classed agency, see the issuing agency
For serials see KF9 .A39

(.A45-.A454) Digests of statutes and regulations
The Library of Congress discontinued use of this form subdivision in 2007
see KF9 .A48

Indexes to statutes and regulations

(.A455-.A459) Serials
The Library of Congress discontinued use of this form subdivision in 2007
see KF9 .A48

(.A46) Monographs. By date of publication
The Library of Congress discontinued use of this form subdivision in 2007
see KF9 .A48

(.A47-.A479) Collections of summaries of state legislation
The Library of Congress discontinued use of this form subdivision in 2007
see KF9 .A48

.A48 Finding aids for statutes and regulations
Including digests, citators, indexes, and summaries
Class citators for both cases and legislation with citators for court decisions or decisions of regulatory agencies

(.A49) Comparative local legislation (Collections, extracts, summaries). By date of publication
The Library of Congress discontinued use of this form subdivision in 2007.
see KF9 .A29+

Court decisions
Reports

(.A5-.A519) Serials
The Library of Congress discontinued use of this span of numbers in 2007
see KF9 .A519

.A519 Serials

.A52 Monographic collections

.A53 Digests of reports (Case finders)

KF9 TABLE OF FORM DIVISIONS FOR STATE LAW (1 NO.) KF9

Court decisions -- Continued

.A535	Citators
	Including citators for both cases and statutes
.A54	Indexes
<.A545>	Individual cases. By date
	see KF223+ and KF228.A+
	Decisions of regulatory agencies. Rulings
	Reports
(.A55-.A559)	Serials
	The Library of Congress discontinued use of this span of numbers in 2007
	see KF9 .A559
.A559	Serials
.A56	Monographic collections
.A57	Digests of reports (Case finders)
.A575	Citators
.A58	Indexes
(.A59A-.A59Z)	Collections of summaries of cases ("Digests" of cases decided by courts or regulatory agencies). By editor or title, A-Z
	The Library of Congress discontinued use of this form subdivision in 2007
	see KF9 .A53 or KF9 .A57
.A6	Looseleaf services
	Not further subarranged by date of publication
.A65	Form books
.A68	Dictionaries
(.A7)	Casebooks. Readings
	The Library of Congress discontinued use of this form subdivision in 2007
	see KF9 .A9+
	General works
(.A73)	Collections. Monographic series
	The Library of Congress discontinued use of this form subdivision in 2007
	see KF9 .A15 or KF9 .A9+
.A75	Congresses. Symposia. Collected papers and essays
(.A8-.A89)	Official reports and monographs
	The Library of Congress discontinued use of this form subdivision in 1994
	see KF9 .A15 or KF9 .A9+
.A9-.Z8	Treatises. Monographs
(.Z9)	Compends. Outlines
	The Library of Congress discontinued use of this form subdivision in 2007
	see KF9 .A9+ or numbers for examination aids, popular works, etc., under individual topics

KF10A TABLE OF DIVISIONS UNDER CITIES (20 NOS.) KF10A

Documents

For documents relating to a particular subject, see that subject

1.A2	Serials
1.A3	Monographs. By agency and date of publication

Collections of charters, ordinances, and local laws

1.A5	Serials
1.A6	Monographs. By date of publication

Including codes of ordinances

Local law reports. Collections of decisions and rulings

For decisions and rulings relative to a particular subject, see that subject

2.A2	Serials
2.A3	Monographs. By date of publication

Yearbooks. Statistics. Surveys of local administration of justice

General

3	Serials
3.2	Monographs. By date of publication
3.3.A-Z	Special topics, particular courts, A-Z

Under each:

.xA1-.xA19 — *Serials*

.xA2-.xZ — *Monographs. By date of publication*

3.5	General works. Local legal history

Particular subjects

City government

4	General (Table KF12)
4.1.A-Z	Special topics, A-Z

Court organization and procedure see KF10A 4.1.J83

4.1.E4	Election law (Table KF13)
4.1.J83	Judicial functions. Court organization and procedure (Table KF13)
4.1.T6	Tort liability of municipal corporations (Table KF13)

Municipal services

5	General (Table KF12)
5.1.A-Z	Particular services, A-Z

Regulation of industry, trade, individuals

6	General (Table KF12)
6.1.A-Z	Particular industries, groups, etc., A-Z

Social legislation. Labor relations. Public welfare

8	General (Table KF12)
8.1.A-Z	Special topics, A-Z
8.1.C64	Collective labor agreements (Table KF13)

Public health

9	General (Table KF12)
9.1.A-Z	Special topics, A-Z
9.1.A3	Air pollution (Table KF13)

Public safety

10	General (Table KF12)

KF10A TABLE OF DIVISIONS UNDER CITIES (20 NOS.) KF10A

Particular subjects

Public safety -- Continued

10.1.A-Z	Special topics, A-Z
	Education
11	General (Table KF12)
11.1.A-Z	Special topics, A-Z
11.1.S34	School integration (Table KF13)
11.1.S7	Students. Compulsory education (Table KF13)
11.5	Civil and political rights and liberties (Table KF12)
	Public property. City planning and redevelopment. Zoning. Building
12	General (Table KF12)
12.1.A-Z	Special topics, A-Z
12.1.E4	Electric installations (Table KF13)
12.1.E42	Eminent domain (Table KF13)
12.1.P5	Plumbing (Table KF13)
	Public finance
14	General (Table KF12)
	Taxation
15	General (Table KF12)
15.5.A-Z	Particular taxes, A-Z
15.5.P7	Property taxes (Table KF13)
15.8.A-Z	Special topics, A-Z
	Local offenses (Violations of ordinances) and administration of criminal justice. Municipal correctional institutions. Parole
17	General (Table KF12)
17.3.A-Z	Particular correctional institutions, A-Z
17.4.A-Z	Particular offenses and special topics, A-Z
17.4.B3	Bail (Table KF13)
17.4.H6	Homicide (Table KF13)
17.4.P8	Public defenders (Table KF13)
18	Juvenile criminal law and procedure. Administration of juvenile justice (Table KF12)
19.A-Z	Particular districts, wards, etc., A-Z
	Metropolitan area government
19.4	General (Table KF12)
19.5.A-Z	Particular subjects, A-Z
19.5.F5	Finance. Taxation (Table KF13)
19.5.P9	Public health. Sanitation (Table KF13)
19.5.T72	Transportation and communication (Table KF13)

KF10B TABLE OF DIVISIONS UNDER CITIES (1 NO.) KF10B

Documents

For documents relating to a particular subject, see that subject

1.A2	Serials
1.A25	Monographs. By agency and date of publication
	Collections of charters, ordinances, and local laws
1.A3	Serials
1.A35	Monographs. By date of publication
	Including codes of ordinances
	Local law reports. Collections of decisions and rulings
	For decisions and rulings relative to a particular subject, see that subject
1.A4	Serials
1.A45	Monographs. By date of publication
	Yearbooks. Statistics. Surveys of local administration of justice
	General
1.A6	Serials
1.A62	Monographs. By date of publication
1.A63A-.A63Z	Special topics, particular courts, A-Z
	Under each:
	.x1-.x19 *Serials*
	.x2-.x9 *Monographs. By date of publication*
1.A65	General works. Local legal history
	Particular subjects
1.1	City government (Table KF12)
1.15	Municipal services (Table KF12)
1.3	Regulation of industry, trade, individuals (Table KF12)
1.4	Social legislation. Labor relations. Public welfare (Table KF12)
1.45	Public health (Table KF12)
1.5	Public safety (Table KF12)
1.6	Education (Table KF12)
1.65	Civil and political rights and liberties (Table KF12)
1.7	Public property. City planning and redevelopment. Zoning. Building (Table KF12)
	Public finance
1.8	General (Table KF12)
1.85	Taxation (Table KF12)
1.89	Local offenses (Violations or ordinances) and administration of criminal justice. Municipal correctional institutions. Parole (Table KF12)
1.895	Juvenile criminal law and procedure. Administration of juvenile justice (Table KF12)
1.9.A-Z	Particular districts, wards, etc., A-Z
	Metropolitan area government
1.94	General (Table KF12)
1.95.A-Z	Particular subjects, A-Z
1.95.F5	Finance. Taxation (Table KF13)
1.95.P9	Public health. Sanitation (Table KF13)

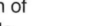

Metropolitan area government
Particular subjects, A-Z -- Continued
1.95.T72 Transportation and communication (Table KF13)

KF10C TABLE OF DIVISIONS UNDER CITIES OR COUNTIES REPRESENTED BY CUTTER NUMBERS (GENERAL) KF10C

Documents

For documents relating to a particular subject, see that subject

.xA2-.xA24	Serials
.xA25-.xA29	Monographs. By agency and date of publication
	Collections of charters, ordinances, and local laws
.xA3-.xA34	Serials
.xA35	Monographs. By date of publication
	Including codes of ordinance
.xA36-.xA369	Digests, indexes, etc. of local laws
	Local law reports. Collections of decisions and rulings
	Decisions and rulings relating to a particular subject are classed with that subject
.xA4-.xA44	Serials
.xA45	Monographs. By date of publication
	Yearbooks. Statistics. Surveys of local administration of justice
.xA6-.xA62	Serials
.xA63	Monographs. By date of publication
	General works. Local legal history
.xA8-.xA84	Sources
.xA85-.xZ	Treatises. Monographs
.x2A-.x2Z	Particular subjects
	see Table KF10D .x2A+

KF10D TABLE OF DIVISIONS UNDER CITIES OR COUNTIES REPRESENTED BY CUTTER NUMBERS (PARTICULAR SUBJECTS) KF10D

Call Number	Subject
.x2A-.x2Z	Particular subjects, A-Z
	Each subject subarranged alphabetically by author
	Building see KF10D .x2Z62+
	City government see KF10D .x2G62+
	City planning and redevelopment see KF10D .x2Z62+
.x2C56-.x2C569	Civil and political rights
.x2C572-.x2C5729	Civil procedure
.x2C62-.x2C629	Correctional and penal institutions
	Cosmetics see KF10D .x2F62+
.x2C72-.x2C729	Criminal offenses (Violations of local law) and local administration of justice
.x2D65-.x2D659	Domestic relations
	Drugs see KF10D .x2F62+
.x2E42-.x2E429	Education. Teachers. Schools
.x2F52-.x2F529	Finance. Taxation
.x2F62-.x2F629	Food. Cosmetics. Drugs
.x2G62-.x2G629	Government
.x2H32-.x2H329	Health regulations
.x2H52-.x2H529	Highway law
.x2I52-.x2I529	Indians
.x2L32-.x2L329	Land titles
.x2L352-.x2L3529	Landlord and tenant
	Local and metropolitan transit see KF10D .x2T62+
.x2M82-.x2M829	Municipal services
	Penal institutions see KF10D .x2C62+
.x2P42-.x2P429	Persons
.x2P62-.x2P629	Power supply
	Public finance, taxation see KF10D .x2F52+
	Public health see KF10D .x2H32+
.x2P92-.x2P929	Public safety
	Public welfare see KF10D .x2S62+
	Schools see KF10D .x2E42+
.x2S47-.x2S479	Service trades
.x2S62-.x2S629	Social legislation. Public welfare
	Taxation see KF10D .x2F52+
	Teachers see KF10D .x2E42+
	Tenant see KF10D .x2L352+
.x2T582-.x2T5829	Traffic regulation
.x2T62-.x2T629	Transportation. Local and metropolitan transit
.x2W32-.x2W329	Water resources and waterways
	Waterways see KF10D .x2W32+
.x2Z62-.x2Z629	Zoning. Building. City planning and redevelopment

KF11 TABLE FOR PARTICULAR LAW SCHOOLS KF11

Catalogs, bulletins
    see KF270

Notation	Description
.xA2-.xA29	Outlines of study, teachers' manuals, etc.
.xA3	Registers. By date
.xA4-.xA49	Yearbooks
	Directories of alumni and students
.xA5-.xA59	General
.xA6-.xA69	By class
	Classes arranged chronologically
	Alumni associations
.xA7-.xA79	Periodicals (Official organs)
.xA8	Yearbooks
.xA83-.xA839	Directories
.xA84	Reports. By date
.xA85-.xZ	History and general works
.x2A-.x2Z	Other associations (Friends, etc.)
.x25	Faculty
	Faculty divided like alumni associations
.x28	Students
.x3A3	Class yearbooks
.x3A4-.x3A49	Law clubs
	Administration
.x3A5-.x3A59	General works
.x3A6-.x3A69	Board of overseers
	Dean's reports
.x3A695-.x3A699	Serials
.x3A7	Individual reports. By date
.x3A8-.x3Z	Special topics (Administration), A-Z
	History. General works
.x4A4-.x4A49	Periodicals (i.e. official organs or student newspapers)
	For law journals, see K1+
.x4A5-.x4Z5	Treatises. Monographs
.x4Z6-.x4Z69	Addresses, essays, lectures
.x5A-.x5Z4	Special topics, A-Z
.x5C4	Chairs, lectureships
.x5Z5-.x5Z59	Anniversaries, special celebrations, etc.
	Including programs, collected addresses, etc.
.x5Z6	Collected graduation, exercise addresses. By date

KF12 LAW OF THE UNITED STATES -- SUBARRANGEMENT OF PARTICULAR SUBJECTS UNDER CITIES (1 NO.) KF12

Code	Description
.A1-.A19	Legislative documents
	Legislation
.A195-.A199	Serials
.A2	Monographs. By date
.A4-.A49	Decisions. By court, agency, etc.
.A7-.A79	Miscellaneous documents
.A8-.Z	General works. Treatises. Monographs

KF13 LAW OF THE UNITED STATES -- SUBARRANGEMENT OF PARTICULAR SUBJECTS UNDER CITIES (CUTTER NO.) KF13

.xA1-.xA19	Legislative documents
	Legislation
.xA195-.xA199	Serials
.xA2	Monographs. By date
.xA4-.xA49	Decisions. By court, agency, etc.
.xA7-.xA79	Miscellaneous documents
.xA8-.xZ	General works. Treatises. Monographs

KF14 TABLE FOR GOVERNMENT MEASURES IN TIME OF WAR, NATIONAL EMERGENCY, ETC. KF14

1	General (Table KF6)
2	Military requisitions from civilians (Table KF6)
4	Control of manpower. Relief of manpower shortage (Table KF6)
	For general works, see KF3546
5	Control of unemployment. Youth training (Table KF6)
7	Enemy property. Alien property. International trade (Table KF6)
8	General moratorium (Table KF6)
	Strategic materials. Stockpiling
9	General (Table KF6)
10.A-Z	By commodity, A-Z
	Rationing
13	General (Table KF6)
14.A-Z	By commodity or service, A-Z
14.F6	Food (Table KF7)
	Price control. Profiteering
17	General (Table KF6)
17.5	Procedure (Table KF6)
18.A-Z	By commodity or service, A-Z
	For wage control, see KF3492
18.P4	Petroleum products (Table KF7)
18.R3	Rent (Table KF7)
	Industrial priorities and allocations
21	General (Table KF6)
22.A-Z	By industry or commodity, A-Z
22.H6	Housing (Table KF7)
22.P82	Public utilities (Table KF7)
24	War damage compensation. Foreign claims settlements (Table KF6)
25	Other (Table KF6)

KF15 TABLE FOR PROFESSIONS (ONE NUMBER) KF15

0	General (Table KF6)
0.1	Licensing. Certification (Table KF6)
0.2	Professional ethics (Table KF6)
0.3	Malpractice. Liability (Table KF6)

KF16 TABLE FOR PROFESSIONS (FOUR CUTTER NUMBERS) KF16

.x	General (Table KF7)
.x1	Licensing. Certification (Table KF7)
.x2	Professional ethics (Table KF7)
.x3	Malpractice. Liability (Table KF7)

KF17 TABLE FOR FOOD PROCESSING INDUSTRIES (ONE NUMBER) KF17

0	General. Comprehensive (Table KF6)
0.1	Trade practices. Antitrust and antimonopoly measures. Price policy (Table KF6)
0.2	Economic assistance. Price supports. Surpluses (Table KF6)
0.3	Sanitation. Plant inspection (Table KF6)
0.4	Standards. Grading (Table KF6)
0.5	Products inspection (Table KF6)
	Cf. KF3878 Food adulteration
0.7.A-Z	Particular companies, A-Z

KF18 TABLE FOR LIVESTOCK INDUSTRY (ONE NUMBER) KF18

Number	Description
0	General. Comprehensive (Table KF6)
0.1	Trade practices. Trade regulations (Table KF6)
0.2	Prices. Consumer protection (Table KF6)
0.3	Economic assistance. Price supports. Surpluses (Table KF6)
0.4	Sanitation. Product inspection (Table KF6)
	For meat inspection, see KF1911
	Standards and grading
	see KF1726
0.8.A-Z	Special topics, A-Z

KF19 TABLE FOR BODIES OF WATER (CUTTER NUMBER) KF19

Call Number	Description
.xA15-.xA199	Periodicals
	Including gazettes, bulletins, circulars, etc.
.xA35-.xA39	Interstate compacts
.xA5-.xA7	Other documents
.xA8-.xZ	Treatises. Monographs

KF20 TABLE OF JOINT CONGRESSIONAL COMMITTEES (FOR HEARINGS) KF20

Code	Description
.A34	Adequacy and Use of Phosphate Resources of the United States
.A8	Atomic Energy
	Subcommittees
.A827	Agreements for Cooperation
.A836	Communities
.A838	Dormitory Rental Situation at Oak Ridge, Tenn.
.A842	Energy
.A844	Environment and Safety
.A853	Leasing of Certain Department Store Facilities in Oak Ridge, Tenn
.A854	Legislation
.A859	Military Applications
.A8713	Radiation
.A872	Raw Materials
	Research and Development see KF20 .A874
.A874	Research, Development, and Radiation
.A876	Review the Liquid Metal Fast Breeder Reactor
.A877	Security
.C66	Congressional Operations
.D4	Defense Production
	Subcommittees
.D455	Materials Availability
.D467	Deficit Reduction (Joint Select Committee)
.D47	Deficit Reduction (Temporary Joint Committee)
.D48	Determine What Employment May be Furnished Federal Prisoners
.E2	Economic
	Subcommittees
.E222	Agricultural Policy
.E224	Agriculture and Transportation
.E2248	Automation and Energy Resources
.E226	Consumer Economics
.E229	Defense Procurement
.E2314	Economic Goals and Intergovernmental Policy
.E2315	Economic Goals and International Policy
.E232	Economic Growth
	Economic Growth and Stabilization see KF20 .E232
.E235	Foreign Economic Policy
.E237	Economic Resources and Competitiveness
	Economic Resources, Competitiveness, and Security Economics see KF20 .E237
.E2387	Economic Stabilization
.E239	Economic Statistics
.E243	Economy in Government
.E244	Education and Health
.E245	Energy

TABLE OF JOINT CONGRESSIONAL COMMITTEES (FOR HEARINGS)

Economic

Subcommittees -- Continued

Code	Subject
.E2465	Federal Procurement and Regulation
.E247	Fiscal and Intergovernmental Policy
	Fiscal Policy see KF20 .E247
.E248	Foreign Economic Policy
.E249	General Credit Control and Debt Management
.E252	Inter-American Economic Relationships
.E253	International Economics
.E255	International Exchange and Payments
.E257	International Trade, Finance, and Security Economics
.E2587	Investment
.E259	Investment, Jobs, and Prices
.E263	Low-Income Families
.E265	Monetary and Fiscal Policy
.E2653	Monetary, Credit, and Fiscal Policies
.E266	National Security Economics
.E267	Priorities and Economy in Government
.E2675	Profits
.E274	Technology and National Security
.E276	Trade, Productivity, and Economic Growth
.E277	Urban Affairs
	Economic Report see KF20 .E2
.F43	Federal Aid in the Construction of Post Roads
.F67	Forestry
.G6	Government Organization
.H37	Harriman Geographic Code System
.H39	Hawaii
.H68	Housing
.I56	Interior Department and Forestry Service
.I57	Internal Revenue Taxation
.I58	Interstate and Foreign Commerce
.L33	Labor-Management Relations
.L5	Library
.M46	Membership in Federal Reserve System
.M87	Muscle Shoals
.N38	National Economic Committee
.N39	Navajo-Hopi Indian Administration
.N67	Northern Pacific Railroad Land Grants
.O7	Organization of Congress
.P33	Pacific Coast Naval Bases
.P4	Pearl Harbor Attack
.P664	Postage on Second-Class Mail Matter and Compensation for Transportation of Mail
.P665	Postal Rates
.P67	Postal Salaries

KF20 TABLE OF JOINT CONGRESSIONAL COMMITTEES (FOR HEARINGS) KF20

Code	Committee
.P7	Printing
.P8	Public Works
.R428	Readjustment of Service Pay
.R43	Reduction of Nonessential Federal Expenditures
.R46	Reorganization of the Administrative Branch of the Government.
.R87	Rural Credits
	Subcommittees
.R876	Personal Rural Credits
.S54	Short-Time Rural Credits
.T385	Tax Evasion and Avoidance
.T39	Taxation
.T46	Tennessee Valley Authority
.V48	Veterans' Affairs
.W37	Washington Metropolitan Problems

KF21 TABLE OF SENATE STANDING COMMITTEES (FOR KF21 HEARINGS)

.A3	Aeronautical and Space Sciences
	Subcommittees
.A323	Aerospace Technology and National Needs
.A324	Governmental Organization for Space Activities
.A325	NASA Authorization
.A327	Upper Atmosphere
	Agriculture see KF21 .A35
	Agriculture and Forestry see KF21 .A35
.A35	Agriculture, Nutrition and Forestry
	Subcommittees
.A3532	Acreage Allotments and Conservation Payments
.A3533	Agricultural Credit
	Agricultural Credit and Rural Electrification see KF21 .A3533
.A35332	Agricultural Exports
.A35334	Agricultural Production and Stabilization of Prices
	Agricultural Production, Marketing, and Stabilization of Prices see KF21 .A35334
	Agricultural Research and General Legislation see KF21 .A3534
.A3534	Agricultural Research, Conservation, Forestry, and General Legislation
.A35343	Agriculture
.A35345	Allocation of REA Funds
.A35348	Commodity Credit Corporation
.A3535	Conservation and Forestry
.A3536	Domestic and Foreign Marketing and Product Promotion
.A3537	Domestic and Foreign Marketing, Inspection, and Plant and Animal Health
.A3542	Energy, Science, and Technology
.A3543	Environment, Soil Conservation, and Forestry
.A35455	Farm Credit Administration
.A3546	Farm Program Administration
.A3547	Federal Crop Insurance
.A3548	Food Supply
.A3549	Foreign Agricultural Policy
	Forestry, Conservation, and Rural Revitalization see KF21 .A3534
.A3553	Forestry, Water Resources, and Environment
.A3555	H. R. 3800
.A3556	Interest Rates
.A35564	Introduction of Sisal and Manila Hemp and the Production of Binding Twine
	Marketing, Inspection, and Product Promotion see KF21 .A3536
.A3558	Nomination of Don Paarlberg
.A3559	Nutrition

TABLE OF SENATE STANDING COMMITTEES (FOR HEARINGS)

Agriculture, Nutrition and Forestry
Subcommittees -- Continued
Nutrition and Investigations see KF21 .A3559
Production and Price Competitiveness see KF21 .A35334

.A3567	Research, Nutrition, and General Legislation
.A3569	Rice
.A3574	Rural Development
.A3575	Rural Development, Oversight, and Investigations
.A357532	S. 1331
.A357533	S. 1397
.A3575335	S. 1636
.A357534	S. 2110
.A357535	S. 2434
.A357536	S. 2835
.A3575364	S. 2925
.A357537	S. 3333
.A35754	S. Res. 142
.A357543	S. Res. 158, Corn and Wheat
.A357546	Senate Joint Resolution 29
.A357549	Senate Joint Resolution 66
.A35755	Senate Resolution 36
.A35756	Senate Resolution 197
.A35758	Soil and Water Conservation
	Soil and Water Conservation, Forestry and Environment see KF21 .A35758
.A3576	Soil Conservation and Forestry
.A6	Appropriations
	Subcommittees
	Agriculture and Related Appropriations see KF21 .A643
.A643	Agriculture, Rural Development, and Related Agencies
.A644	Agriculture, Rural Development, Food and Drug Administration, and Related Agencies
.A645	Commerce, Justice, Science, and Related Agencies
	Commerce, Justice, State, the Judiciary and Related Agencies see KF21 .A659
.A646	Control of Foot-And-Mouth Disease
.A6463	Defense
.A6465	Deficiencies
.A646515	Deficiencies and Supplementals
.A6466	Department of the Interior, Environment, and Related Agencies
	Departments of Labor, Health and Human Services, Education, and Related Agencies see KF21 .A653
	Departments of State, Justice, and Commerce, the Judiciary, and Related Agencies see KF21 .A659
	Dept. of Defense see KF21 .A6463

KF21 TABLE OF SENATE STANDING COMMITTEES (FOR HEARINGS) KF21

Appropriations
Subcommittees -- Continued
Dept. of Homeland Security see KF21 .A6483
Dept. of the Interior and Related Agencies see KF21 .A652
Dept. of the Treasury, U.S. Postal Service, and General Government Appropriations see KF21 .A662
Dept. of Transportation and Related Agencies see KF21 .A66

Code	Subject
.A64675	Diplomatic and Consular Appropriation Bill
.A6468	District of Columbia
.A64687	Energy and Water, and Related Agencies
.A6469	Energy and Water Development
.A64693	Ex Officio Members from Committee on Post Office Department and Civil Service Appropriations
.A64694	Financial Services and General Government
.A64695	Foreign Assistance and Related Programs
	Foreign Operations see KF21 .A647
.A647	Foreign Operations, Export Financing, and Related Programs
.A6473	Fortifications Bill
.A6475	Government Corporations
.A6483	Homeland Security
	Housing and Urban Development, Space, Science, Veterans, and Certain Other Independent Agencies see KF21 .A6486
.A6486	HUD-Independent Agencies
.A6516	Independent Offices
.A652	Interior and Related Agencies
	Labor, and Health, Education, and Welfare, and Related Agencies see KF21 .A653
.A653	Labor, Health and Human Services, Education, and Related Agencies
.A654	Legislative Branch
.A655	Military Construction
.A6553	Military Construction and Veterans Affairs, and Related Agencies
.A657	Public Works
.A658	Speculation in Commodity Markets
.A6586	State, Foreign Operations, and Related Programs
.A659	State, Justice, and Commerce, the Judiciary, and Related Agencies
	Transportation see KF21 .A66
.A6597	Transportation and Housing and Urban Development, and Related Agencies
.A66	Transportation and Related Agencies

Appropriations
Subcommittees -- Continued
Transportation, Treasury, and General Government, and
Related Agencies see KF21 .A662
.A6615 Transportation. Treasury, the Judiciary, Housing and Urban
Development, and Related Agencies
Treasury and General Government see KF21 .A662
.A662 Treasury and General Government, and Related Agencies
Treasury, Postal Service, and General Government see
KF21 .A662
Treasury, U.S. Postal Service, and General Government
Appropriations see KF21 .A662
.A666 VA-HUD-Independent Agencies
.A668 War Department
.A7 Armed Services
Subcommittees
.A743 Air Support, Close
.A7432 AirLand
.A7433 AirLand Forces
.A7435 Arms Control
Center for Naval Analyses see KF21 .A759
Close Air Support see KF21 .A743
.A744 Coalition Defense and Reinforcing Forces
.A745 Consider H.R. 15728
.A7452 Conventional Forces and Alliance Defense
.A7453 Defense Acquisition Policy
.A7454 Defense Industry and Technology
.A7455 Defense Procurement Matters, Task Force on Selected
.A746 Drug Abuse in the Military
.A748 Electronic Battlefield
.A749 Emerging Threats and Capabilities
Force Requirements and Personnel see KF21 .A7548
.A754 General Legislation
.A7543 General Procurement
.A7544 H.R. 2460
.A7545 H.R. 5555
.A7546 Investigations
.A75475 M-16 Rifle
.A7548 Manpower and Personnel
.A755 Military Construction
.A756 Military Construction and Stockpiles
.A7565 Military Pay
.A758 National Stockpile and Naval Petroleum Reserves
.A759 Naval Analyses, Center for
.A76 Nuclear Deterrence, Arms Control, and Defense Intelligence
.A763 Officer Grade Limitations

TABLE OF SENATE STANDING COMMITTEES (FOR HEARINGS)

Armed Services
Subcommittees -- Continued

Code	Topic
.A764	Pacific Study Group
.A765	Personnel
.A766	Preparedness
.A767	Preparedness Investigating
.A7672	Preparedness Subcommittee No. 6
.A7677	Procurement
.A768	Procurement Policy and Reprogramming
.A769	Pro Forma
.A77	Projection Forces and Regional Defense
	Readiness see KF21 .A7717
.A7717	Readiness and Management Support
.A772	Readiness, Sustainability, and Support
.A7723	Real Estate and Military Construction
.A773	Research and Development
.A774	Reserve General Officer Promotions
.A777	Sea Power and Force Projection
.A778	Strategic
	Strategic and Theater Nuclear Forces see KF21 .A779
.A7784	Strategic Arms Limitation Talks
	Strategic Forces see KF21 .A778
.A779	Strategic Forces and Nuclear Deterrence
.A785	Survivor Benefits
.A7855	Tactical Air Power
.A7857	Tactical Warfare
.A786	Thailand Servicemen's Club Activities
.A787	Treatment of Deserters from Military Service
.A788	Volunteer Armed Force and Selective Service
.A92	Audit and Control the Contingent Expenses
.B3	Banking and Currency
	Subcommittees
.B318	Agricultural, Finance, Farm Mortgages, and Related Matters
.B322	Banking
.B323	Coffee Prices
.B325	Coinage and Philippine Currency
.B3253	Coinage and Related Matters
.B3257	Community Facilities
.B326	Controls of Meat and Alcoholic Beverage Grains
.B33	Currency and Coinage
.B343	Federal Reserve
.B344	Federal Reserve Matters
.B345	Financial Institutions
.B347	Full Employment
.B35	H. R. 6776
.B3517	Home Loan Bank and Related Matters

KF21 TABLE OF SENATE STANDING COMMITTEES (FOR KF21 HEARINGS)

Banking, Housing, and Urban Affairs Subcommittees -- Continued

Code	Subject
.B35175	Home Mortgages, etc.
.B352	Housing
.B3527	Housing and Rents
.B353	Housing and Urban Affairs
.B355	International Finance
.B364	Monetary Policy, Banking, and Deposit Insurance
.B367	Production and Stabilization
.B37	Reconstruction Finance Corporation
.B3712	Reconstruction Finance Corporation Matters
.B3714	Rubber
.B3715	Rubber and Tin
.B3718	S. 6
.B372	Securities
.B3724	Securities and Exchange
.B373	Securities, Insurance, and Banking
.B374	Senate Bill 1
.B375	Small Business
.B378	Sugar
.B39	Banking, Housing, and Urban Affairs Subcommittees
.B3939	Consumer Affairs
.B3942	Consumer Credit
.B39424	Consumer and Regulatory Affairs
.B394245	Economic Policy
.B39425	Economic Stabilization
.B39428	Federal Credit Programs
	Financial Institutions see KF21 .B3943
.B3943	Financial Institutions and Consumer Affairs
.B3944	Financial Institutions and Regulatory Relief
.B39445	Financial Services and Technology
.B3945	Housing and Transportation
	Housing and Urban Affairs see KF21 .B3945
	Housing Opportunity and Community Development see KF21 .B3945
.B39452	Housing, Transportation, and Community Development
.B39453	HUD/MOD Rehab Investigation
.B39454	HUD Oversight and Structure
.B39456	Insurance
.B3946	International Finance
.B3947	International Finance and Monetary Policy
	International Trade and Finance see KF21 .B3946
.B3948	Minting and Coinage
.B395	Production and Stabilization
	Rural Housing see KF21 .B3953

KF21 TABLE OF SENATE STANDING COMMITTEES (FOR HEARINGS) KF21

Banking and Currency
Subcommittees -- Continued

Code	Subject
.B3953	Rural Housing and Development
	Securities see KF21 .B3954
.B3954	Securities and Investment
.B3956	Securities, Insurance, and Investment
.B3958	Security and International Trade and Finance
.B3962	Small Business
.B8	Budget
	Subcommittees
.B83	Control of Federal Credit
.B835	Education Task Force
.B84	Industrial Growth and Productivity
.B86	Synthetic Fuels
.B873	Temporary Task Force on Federal Credit
.C4	Census
.C45	Civil Service
	Subcommittees
.C454	S. 564
.C457	S. 2666 and S. 2674
.C47	Civil Service and Retrenchment
.C5	Claims
	Subcommittees
.C526	Senate Joint Resolution 177
.C55	Coast and Insular Survey
.C6	Commerce
	Subcommittees
.C626	Automobile Marketing Practices
.C628	Aviation
.C6288	Cancer Research
.C629	Civil Aviation
.C632	Commerce, Department of
.C634	Communications
.C636	Consumer
	Department of Commerce see KF21 .C632
.C645	Energy, Natural Resources, and the Environment
.C6455	Environment
.C646	Federal Power Commission Procedures
.C6462	Fisheries, Forest Products, Minerals, and Land Surveys
.C64625	Flood Control
.C6463	Foreign Commerce
.C6464	Foreign Commerce and Tourism
.C647	Freight Car Shortage
.C648	H. R. 15455
.C652	Merchant Marine
.C654	Merchant Marine and Fisheries

TABLE OF SENATE STANDING COMMITTEES (FOR HEARINGS)

Commerce

Subcommittees -- Continued

Code	Subject
.C663	Oceanography
.C665	Oceans and Atmosphere
.C667	Oil and Natural Gas Production and Distribution
.C672	Rivers and Harbors
.C6733	S. 5
.C6735	S. 314
.C67355	S. 599
.C67364	S. 1651
.C6737	S. 1944
.C6738	S. 2414
.C6739	S. 3170
.C67394	S. 3290
.C674	S.J. Res. 159
.C675	S. Res. 146 (74th Congress)
.C677	Science, Technology, and Commerce
.C679	Senate Bill 1963
.C6795	Senate Joint Resolution 209
.C68	Senate Resolution 294
.C686	Stabilization
.C687	Study Textile Industry
.C688	Surface Transportation
.C689	Transportation on the Great Lakes-St. Lawrence Seaway
.C6893	Unemployment Bills
.C69	Commerce, Science, and Transportation Subcommittees
.C692	Aviation
.C69215	Aviation Operations, Safety, and Security
.C6923	Business, Trade, and Tourism
.C6925	Communications
.C69254	Communications, Technology, and the Internet
.C6926	Competitiveness, Innovation, and Export Promotion
	Consumer see KF21 .C693
.C6928	Consumer Affairs and Product Safety
.C693	Consumer Affairs, Foreign Commerce, and Tourism
.C69315	Consumer Affairs, Product Safety, and Insurance
.C69317	Consumer Protection, Product Safety, and Insurance
	Consumers see KF21 .C693
.C6932	Disaster Prevention and Prediction
.C6933	Fisheries and the Coast Guard
	Foreign Commerce and Tourism see KF21 .C695
.C69335	Global Climate Change and Impacts
.C6934	Interstate Commerce, Trade, and Tourism
.C6935	Manufacturing and Competitiveness
.C694	Merchant Marine

KF21 TABLE OF SENATE STANDING COMMITTEES (FOR KF21 HEARINGS)

Commerce, Science, and Transportation
Subcommittees -- Continued

Code	Committee/Subcommittee
.C695	Merchant Marine and Tourism
.C696	National Ocean Policy Study
.C6965	Oceans and Fisheries
.C6966	Oceans, Atmosphere, and Fisheries
.C69664	Oceans, Atmosphere, Fisheries, and Coast Guard
.C6967	Oceans, Fisheries, and Coast Guard
.C6969	Science and Space
.C69696	Science, Technology, and Innovation
.C697	Science, Technology, and Space
.C6976	Space, Aeronautics, and Related Sciences
.C698	Surface Transportation
.C699	Surface Transportation and Merchant Marine
.C69914	Surface Transportation and Merchant Marine Infrastructure, Safety, and Security
.C6993	Technology, Innovation, and Competitiveness
.C6995	Trade, Tourism, and Economic Development
.D4	Democratic Policy
.D5	District of Columbia
	Subcommittees
.D528	Business and Commerce
.D532	Business, Commerce, and Judiciary
.D538	Education and Labor
.D542	Excise and Liquor Legislation
.D545	Fiscal Affairs
.D549	H.R. 3838
.D5496	Home Rule and Reorganization
.D5498	Housing
.D5516	Incorporations
.D552	Insurance and Banks
.D555	Judiciary
.D562	Metropolitan Area Problems
.D567	Parks and Highways
.D5678	Public Health
.D568	Public Health, Education, Welfare, and Safety
.D5684	Public Health, Hospitals, and Charities
.D5687	Rental Investigation
.D56876	S. 223
.D56878	S. 2074
.D5688	S. 3843
.D5689	S. 4661
.D56894	S. 4973
.D569	S. Res. 358
.D574	Streets and Avenues
.D585	Wire Tapping in the District of Columbia

KF21 TABLE OF SENATE STANDING COMMITTEES (FOR KF21 HEARINGS)

Code	Description
.E3	Education and Labor
	Subcommittees
.E314	Employees' Compensation
.E316	H. R. 6128
.E322	Health
.E3224	Health and Education
.E325	Post-Defense Planning
.E3282	S. 180
.E3283	S. 591
.E3284	S. 619
.E32843	S. 637
.E3285	S. 1109
.E32857	S. 1305
.E3286	S. 1456 and S. 1510
.E32863	S. 1620
.E32865	S. 1770 and S. 2085
.E32867	S. 1920
.E3287	S. 1970
.E3288	S. 2412
.E32887	S. 3230
.E3289	S. 3390
.E33	Senate Resolution 266
.E55	Energy and Natural Resources
	Subcommittees
.E5523	Energy
.E5525	Energy and Mineral Resources
.E5527	Energy Conservation and Regulation
	Energy Conservation and Supply see KF21 .E553
.E5528	Energy Production and Regulation
.E553	Energy Production and Supply
.E5535	Energy Regulation
.E5536	Energy Regulation and Conservation
.E554	Energy Research and Development
.E5542	Energy Research, Development, Production, and Regulation
.E5543	Energy Resources and Materials Production
	Forests and Public Land Management see KF21 .E5583
.E5554	Minerals Resources Development and Production
.E5555	National Parks
	National Parks, Historic Preservation, and Recreation see KF21 .E5583
.E5556	Natural Resources Development and Production
.E5558	Oversight and Investigations
.E556	Parks and Recreation
	Parks, Historic Preservation, and Recreation see KF21 .E5583
.E5565	Parks, Recreation, and Renewable Resources

Energy and Natural Resources
Subcommittees -- Continued
Public Lands and Forests see KF21 .E5583
.E5578 Public Lands and Reserved Water
.E558 Public Lands and Resources
.E5583 Public Lands, National Parks, and Forests
.E5584 Public Lands, Reserved Water, and Resource Conservation
.E5586 Renewable Energy, Energy Efficiency, and Competitiveness
.E559 Water and Power
.E6 Environment and Public Works
Subcommittees
Clean Air and Nuclear Regulation see KF21 .E66
.E623 Clean Air and Nuclear Safety
.E625 Clean Air, Climate Change, and Nuclear Safety
.E626 Clean Air, Wetlands, and Climate Change
.E627 Clean Air, Wetlands, Private Property, and Nuclear Safety
Clean Water, Fisheries, and Wildlife see KF21 .E63
Drinking Water, Fisheries, and Wildlife see KF21 .E63
Fisheries, Wildlife, and Drinking Water see KF21 .E63
.E63 Fisheries, Wildlife, and Water
.E645 Environmental Pollution
.E647 Environmental Protection
.E65 Hazardous Wastes and Toxic Substances
.E66 Nuclear Regulation
.E666 Private Sector and Consumer Solutions to Global Warming and Wildlife Protection
.E674 Regional and Community Development
.E675 Resource Protection
.E677 Superfund and Environmental Oversight
.E6772 Superfund and Waste Management
Superfund, Ocean, and Water Protection see KF21 .E647
Superfund, Recycling, and Solid Waste Management see KF21 .E647
.E6774 Superfund, Toxics, Risk and Waste Management
Superfund, Waste Control, and Risk Assessment see KF21 .E647
.E678 Toxic Substances and Environmental Oversight
Toxic Substances, Environmental Oversight, Research and Development see KF21 .E65
Toxic Substances, Research, and Development see KF21 .E65
.E679 Transportation
Transportation and Infrastructure see KF21 .E685
Transportation, Infrastructure, and Nuclear Safety see KF21 .E685

KF21 TABLE OF SENATE STANDING COMMITTEES (FOR KF21 HEARINGS)

Environment and Public Works
Subcommittees -- Continued

Code	Description
.E68	Transportation Safety, Infrastructure Security, and Water Quality
.E683	Water Resources
.E685	Water Resources, Transportation, and Infrastructure
	Water Resources, Transportation, Public Buildings, and Economic Development see KF21 .E685
.E9	Expenditures in the Executive Departments
	Subcommittees
.E935	Fidelity Bond Bills
.E945	Intergovernmental Relations
.E95	Investigations
.E968	Reorganization
.E97	Surplus Property
.F5	Finance
	Subcommittees
	Administration of the Internal Revenue Code see KF21 .F55385
	Deficits, Debt Management, and International Debt see KF21 .F54
.F54	Deficits, Debt Management, and Long-term Economic Growth
.F5436	Economic Growth, Employment, and Revenue Sharing
.F5525	Energy
.F5526	Energy and Agricultural Taxation
.F5527	Energy and Foundations
.F55274	Energy, Natural Resources, and Infrastructure
.F5528	Estate and Gift Taxation
.F553	Financial Markets
.F5534	Foundations
.F5535	H. R. 2959
.F5536	H. R. 5529
.F5538	Health
.F55382	Health Care
	Health Care for Low-Income Families see KF21 .F55382
.F55383	Health for Families and the Uninsured
.F55385	Internal Revenue Code, Administration of
.F55388	International Debt
.F5539	International Finance and Resources
.F554	International Trade
.F555	International Trade, Customs, and Global Competitiveness
	Long-term Growth and Debt Reduction see KF21 .F54
.F558	Medicare and Long-Term Care
.F56	Oversight of the Internal Revenue Service
	Private Pension Plans see KF21 .F565

KF21 TABLE OF SENATE STANDING COMMITTEES (FOR HEARINGS) KF21

Finance

Subcommittees -- Continued

Code	Subject
.F565	Private Pension Plans and Employee Fringe Benefits
.F5653	Private Retirement Plans and Oversight of the Internal Revenue Service
.F566	Public Assistance
	Revenue Sharing see KF21 .F567
.F567	Revenue Sharing, Intergovernmental Revenue Impact, and Economic Problems
.F5675	S. 2079
.F56754	S. 2620
.F5676	Savings, Pensions, and Investment Policy
.F568	Social Security
.F5683	Social Security and Family Policy
.F5684	Social Security and Income Maintenance Programs
.F5685	Social Security, Pensions, and Family Policy
	State Taxation of Interstate Commerce see KF21 .F572
.F5687	Tariff
	Taxation see KF21 .F5693
.F5693	Taxation and IRS Oversight
.F5694	Taxation and Debt Management
.F5695	Taxation and Debt Management Generally
.F572	Taxation of Interstate Commerce, State
.F576	Tourism and Sugar
.F579	Undervaluation
.F58	Unemployment and Related Problems
.F582	Unemployment Compensation, Revenue Sharing, and Economic Problems
.F584	Veterans' Legislation
.F59	Fisheries
.F6	Foreign Relations

Subcommittees

Code	Subject
.F625	African Affairs
.F626	American Republics Affairs
.F627	Arms Control, International Law, and Organization
.F628	Arms Control, International Organizations, and Security Agreements
	Arms Control, Oceans, and International Environment see KF21 .F6286
.F6286	Arms Control, Oceans, International Operations, and Environment
.F629	Canadian Affairs
.F6315	Central Asia and South Caucasus
.F633	Claims Legislation
.F6337	Commercial Relations with China
.F634	Commercial Treaties and Consular Conventions

Foreign Relations
Subcommittees -- Continued

Code	Subject
.F6344	Constitution of the International Labor Organization Instrument of Amendment
.F635	Disarmament
.F6354	East Asian and Pacific Affairs
.F63544	Economic and Social Affairs
.F6355	European Affairs
.F63555	Expanded International Information and Education Program
.F6356	Fisheries Conventions
.F6357	Foreign Assistance
.F636	Foreign Assistance and Economic Policy
.F6364	Foreign Economic Policy
.F637	Foreign Service
	Foreign Service Information Office Corps see KF21 .F644
.F639	Genocide Convention
.F6415	Great Lakes Basin
.F6417	Great Lakes Fisheries Convention
.F643	Human Rights Conventions
.F644	Information Office Corps, Foreign Service
.F6447	International Claims Settlement Act of 1949
.F645	International Complex
.F6455	International Convention on the Prevention and Punishment of the Crime of Genocide
.F646	International Development and Foreign Assistance, Economic Affairs, and International Environmental Protection
.F648	International Economic Policy
.F649	International Economic Policy, Export and Trade Promotion
	International Economic Policy, Oceans, and Environment see KF21 .F649
	International Economic Policy, Trade, Oceans, and Environment see KF21 .F649
.F655	International Grains Agreement
	International Operations see KF21 .F657
.F656	International Operations and Organizations, Democracy, and Human Rights
.F6564	International Operations and Organizations, Human Rights, Democracy, and Global Women's Issues
.F657	International Operations and Terrorism
.F658	International Organization Affairs
.F6583	International Organization and Disarmament Affairs
.F6586	International Wheat Agreement
.F6588	Level of Rainy Lake Convention
.F659	Multinational Corporations
.F6618	Near East and Africa

KF21 TABLE OF SENATE STANDING COMMITTEES (FOR HEARINGS) KF21

Foreign Relations
Subcommittees -- Continued

Code	Subject
.F6619	Near Eastern and South and Central Asian Affairs
.F662	Near Eastern and South Asian Affairs
.F6622	Nominations
.F66225	North American Regional Broadcasting Agreement and the Mexican Broadcasting Agreement
.F6623	Ocean Space
.F6625	Oceans and International Environment
.F663	Overseas Information Programs
.F6633	Revision of the United Nations Charter
	Saint Lawrence Seaway see KF21 .F668
.F6635	Senate Concurrent Resolution 22
.F6637	Senate Joint Resolution 104
.F665	Senate Resolution 50
.F666	South Asian Affairs
.F668	St. Lawrence Seaway
.F669	State Department Organization and Public Affairs
.F673	Tax Conventions
.F68	Technical Assistance Programs
	Terrorism, Narcotics, and International Communications see KF21 .F685
.F685	Terrorism, Narcotics, and International Operations
.F69	United Nations Charter
.F693	United States Foreign Aid to Europe
.F695	United States Security Agreements and Commitments Abroad
.F6955	Vienna Convention
.F696	War Powers
	Western Hemisphere Affairs see KF21 .F697
	Western Hemisphere and Peace Corps Affairs see KF21 .F697
.F6967	Western Hemisphere, Peace Corps, and Global Narcotic Affairs
	Western Hemisphere, Peace Corps, and Narcotics Affairs see KF21 .F697
.F697	Western Hemisphere, Peace Corps, Narcotics, and Terrorism
.F7	Forest Reservations and the Protection of Game
.G6	Government Operations
	Subcommittees
.G634	Budgeting, Management, and Expenditures
.G644	Executive Reorganization
.G6443	Executive Reorganization and Government Research
.G6444	Federal Procurement

KF21 TABLE OF SENATE STANDING COMMITTEES (FOR KF21 HEARINGS)

Government Operations

Subcommittees -- Continued

Code	Description
.G6445	Federal Spending Practices, Efficiency, and Open Government
.G645	Federal Surplus Property
.G646	Foreign Aid Expenditures
.G648	Government Research
.G653	Impoundment of Funds
.G655	Intergovernmental Relations
.G658	Investigations
.G6583	Legislative Program
.G65845	National Policy Machinery
.G6585	National Security and International Operations
.G65855	Oversight Procedures
.G6586	Privacy and Information Systems
.G65867	Reorganization
.G6587	Reorganization and International Organizations
.G6588	Reorganization, Research, and International Organizations
.G659	Reports, Accounting, and Management
.G6594	S. 5
.G668	Government Reform and Oversight

Subcommittees

.G6685	National Economic Growth, Natural Resources, and Regulatory Affairs
.G67	Governmental Affairs

Subcommittees

	Civil Service and General Services see KF21 .G6724
.G6724	Civil Service, Post Office, and General Services
.G6725	Congressional Operations and Oversight
.G6726	Consumer and Environmental Affairs
.G6728	Energy, Nuclear Proliferation, and Federal Services
.G6729	Energy, Nuclear Proliferation, and Government Processes
.G673	Federal Expenditures, Research, and Rules
.G67313	Federal Services, Post Office, and Civil Service
.G67315	Federal Spending, Budget, and Accounting
.G6732	Federal Spending Practices and Open Government
.G6733	Financial Management and Accountability
.G67333	Financial Management, the Budget, and International Security
	General Services, Federalism, and the District of Columbia see KF21 .G6735
	Government Efficiency, Federalism, and the District of Columbia see KF21 .G6735
.G6734	Government Information and Regulation
.G6735	Governmental Efficiency and the District of Columbia
.G6737	Information Management and Regulatory Affairs

KF21 TABLE OF SENATE STANDING COMMITTEES (FOR KF21 HEARINGS)

Governmental Affairs

Subcommittees -- Continued

Code	Description
.G6738	Intergovernmental Relations
.G6739	International Security, Proliferation, and Federal Services
.G674	Investigations
.G676	Oversight of Government Management
	Oversight of Government Management and the District of Columbia see KF21 .G6735
	Oversight of Government Management, Restructuring, and the District of Columbia see KF21 .G6735
.G6763	Oversight of Government Management, the Federal Workforce, and the District of Columbia
.G6765	Post Office and Civil Service
	Regulation and Government Information see KF21 .G6734
.G677	Reports, Accounting, and Management
	Health, Education, Labor, and Pensions see KF21 .L27
.H6	Homeland Security
.H63	Homeland Security and Governmental Affairs
	Subcommittees
.H6314	Contracting Oversight
.H6316	Disaster Recovery
.H632	Federal Financial Management, Government Information, and International Security
.H6323	Federal Financial Management, Government Information, Federal Services, and International Security
.H633	Financial Management, Government Information, and International Security
.H634	Investigations
.H636	Oversight of Government Management, the Federal Workforce, and the District of Columbia
.H637	State, Local, and Private Sector Preparedness and Integration
.H8	Human Resources
	Subcommittees
.H823	Aging
.H825	Alcoholism and Drug Abuse
.H83	Child and Human Development
.H838	Education, Arts, and Humanities
.H84	Employment, Poverty, and Migratory Labor
.H842	Handicapped
.H845	Health and Scientific Research
.H855	Labor
.I4	Immigration
.I42	Impeachment Trial

KF21 TABLE OF SENATE STANDING COMMITTEES (FOR KF21 HEARINGS)

.I45 Indian Affairs

Class here hearings of the Committee on Indian Affairs held during the period 1820-1976 and after March 1993. Class hearings of the Select Committee on Indian Affairs held during the period 1977-March 1993 in KF26.5.I4.

Subcommittees

.I454	S. 1786
.I457	Senate Resolution 79
.I46	Industrial Expositions
.I5	Interior and Insular Affairs

Subcommittees

.I525	Energy Research and Water Resources
.I526	Environment and Land Resources
.I527	Indian Affairs
.I528	Integrated Oil Operations
.I529	Irrigation and Reclamation
.I532	Legislative Oversight
.I534	Minerals, Materials, and Fuels
.I539	Outer Continental Shelf
.I542	Parks and Recreation
.I547	Public Lands
.I5475	S. 1357 and H.R. 3795
.I5477	S. 1407
.I548	Territories and Insular Affairs
.I549	Water and Power Resources
.I5496	Interoceanic Canals
.I55	Interstate and Foreign Commerce

Subcommittees

.I55115	Automobile Marketing
.I5512	Automobile Marketing Practices
.I55124	Aviation
.I5513	Communications
.I5515	Domestic Land and Water Transportation
.I5516	Export Controls and Policies
.I5517	Freight Car Shortage
.I55175	H. R. 3505
.I55178	International Air Agreements
.I5518	Joint Resolution 72
.I55185	Maritime Subsidy Program
.I5519	Merchant Marine and Fisheries
.I55193	Merchant Marine and Maritime Matters
.I55195	No. 1--Surface Transportation
.I55196	No. 2, Communications
.I55197	No. 3, Aviation
.I55198	No. 4, Water Transportation
.I552	No. 5, Fisheries and Wildlife

TABLE OF SENATE STANDING COMMITTEES (FOR HEARINGS)

Interstate and Foreign Commerce
Subcommittees -- Continued

Code	Subject
.I5523	No. 6, Business and Consumer Interests
.I5536	Oil and Coal Shortage
.I554	Oil Shortage
.I5547	S. 211
.I5548	S. 236
.I55483	S. 238
.I55487	S. 734 and S. 1028
.I5549	S. 777 and S. 1255
.I55492	S. 1446
.I55495	S. 2041 and S. 2226
.I55497	S. 2801
.I55498	S. 3358
.I555	S. Res. 111
.I559	Surface Transportation
.I5596	Textile Industry
.I5597	Transportation and Communication
.I58	Interstate Commerce
	Subcommittees
.I582	Certain Railroad Labor Legislation
.I587	H. R. 4816
.I5873	H. R. 7121
.I5875	H. R. 10598
.I5882	International Communications
.I5885	Nomination of J. Halden Alldredge
.I589	S. 18
.I58913	S. 758
.I58917	S. 799
.I58918	S. 874, S. 1633, and S. 1813
.I58919	S. 1085
.I5892	S. 1335
.I58922	S. 1489
.I58924	S. 1639
.I58926	S. 1915, S. 1990, and S. 2294
.I589265	S. 2047
.I58927	S. 2444
.I589272	S. 2445
.I58928	S. 2610
.I58929	S. 3798
.I5893	S. 3875
.I5895	S. J. Res. 22, S. J. Res. 32, H. J. Res. 101, and H. R. 4146
.I58952	S. Res. 71
.I58953	Senate Joint Resolution 58
.I58954	Senate Joint Resolution 147
.I58956	Senate Resolution 146

TABLE OF SENATE STANDING COMMITTEES (FOR HEARINGS)

Interstate Commerce

Subcommittees -- Continued

.I58957	Senate Resolution 185
.I5896	Senate Resolution 286
.I5897	Senate Resolution 297
.I7	Irrigation and Reclamation
	Subcommittees
.I725	Application of the Verde River Irrigation and Power District for the Use of Power Sites on the Verde River, Ariz.
.I745	S. 555
.I75	Senate Resolution 295
.J8	Judiciary
	Subcommittees
.J823	Administrative Practice and Procedure
.J832	Administration of the Internal Security Act and Other Internal Security Laws
.J8325	Administration of the Trading with the Enemy Act
.J8327	Administrative Oversight and the Courts
.J833	Administrative Practice and Procedure
.J834	Agency Administration
.J8345	Amendments to the Displaced Persons Act
.J8347	Antitrust and Monopoly
	Antitrust and Monopoly Legislation see KF21 .J835
.J835	Antitrust, Business Rights, and Competition
.J8352	Antitrust, Competition Policy, and Consumer Rights
	Antitrust, Monopolies, and Business Rights see KF21 .J835
	Antitrust, Monopoly, and Business Rights see KF21 .J835
.J8354	Bankruptcy
.J8357	Citizens and Shareholders Rights and Remedies
	Constitution see KF21 .J8359
.J8358	Constitution, Civil Rights, and Property Rights
.J8359	Constitution, Federalism, and Property Rights
.J836	Constitutional Amendments
.J837	Constitutional Rights
.J8374	Corrections and Rehabilitation
	Courts see KF21 .J8376
.J8376	Courts and Administrative Practice
.J83765	Crime and Drugs
.J83767	Crime, Corrections, and Victims' Rights
	Criminal Justice see KF21 .J8377
.J8377	Criminal Justice Oversight
.J8378	Criminal Law
.J838	Criminal Laws and Procedures
.J84	Cyclamates
.J842	Emigration of Refugees and Escapees
.J843	FBI Oversight

KF21 TABLE OF SENATE STANDING COMMITTEES (FOR HEARINGS) KF21

Judiciary

Subcommittees -- Continued

Code	Subject
.J844	Federal Charters, Holidays, and Celebrations
.J849	H. R. 3592
.J8493	H. R. 4044
.J8495	H. R. 5138
.J8497	H. R. 8574 and S. 3084
.J8499	Human Rights and the Law
	Immigration see KF21 .J8525
.J852	Immigration and Naturalization
	Immigration and Refugee Affairs see KF21 .J8525
.J8525	Immigration and Refugee Policy
.J8526	Immigration, Border Security, and Citizenship
.J8528	Immigration, Refugees, and Border Security
.J855	Improvements in Judicial Machinery
.J8552	Improvements in the Federal Criminal Code
.J8553	Incorporation Bills
.J8554	Intellectual Property
.J8556	Jurisprudence and Governmental Relations
.J856	Juvenile Delinquency
.J8565	Juvenile Justice
.J8568	Legislation on Judicial and Congressional Salaries
.J857	Limitations on Contracted and Delegated Authority
	National Penitentiaries see KF21 .J865
.J8578	Nomination of Robert H. Jackson
.J858	Nominations
.J863	Patents, Copyrights, and Trademarks
	Patents, Trademarks, and Copyrights see KF21 .J863
.J865	Penitentiaries, National
.J867	Penitentiaries and Corrections
	Problems Connected with Emigration of Refugees and Escapees see KF21 .J842
	Problems Connected with Refugees and Escapees see KF21 .J869
.J869	Refugees and Escapees, Problems Connected with
.J87	Regulatory Reform
.J872	Representation of Citizen Interests
.J872115	S. 42, S. 1352, and S. 1465
.J87212	S. 87
.J87215	S. 215
.J8723	S. 575
.J8724	S. 1008
.J8725	S. 1033
.J872514	S. 1114 and S. 2609
.J872516	S. 1120
.J872519	S. 1322

Judiciary
Subcommittees -- Continued

Code	Subject
.J87252	S. 1362
.J87253	S. 1477
.J87254	S. 1578
.J87255	S. 1842
.J87256	S. 1910
.J872567	S. 1978
.J87257	S. 1981
.J87258	S. 2054
.J87259	S. 2441 and H. R. 7420
.J8726	S. 3529
.J8727	S. 3752
.J8728	S. 6221
.J87285	S. J. Res. 1, 10, 12, 21, and 82
.J872854	S. J. Res. 15 and S. J. Res. 289
.J872856	S. J. Res. 65
.J87286	S. J. Res. 84
.J872868	S. J. Res. 191
.J8729	S. J. Res. 220
.J87292	S. Res. 92
.J87293	S. Res. 116
.J87294	S. Res. 206
.J873	Security and Terrorism
.J8733	Senate Joint Resolution 5
.J8735	Senate Joint Resolution 35
.J87356	Senate Joint Resolution 52
.J8736	Senate Joint Resolution 61
.J874	Separation of Powers
.J8745	Technology and the Law
.J8746	Technology, Terrorism, and Government Information
.J87465	Terrorism and Homeland Security
	Terrorism, Technology, and Government Information see KF21 .J8746
.J8747	Terrorism, Technology, and Homeland Security
.J879	Tris Hearing Panel
.J885	War Claims Act Amendments
	Youth Violence see KF21 .J8565
.L27	Labor and Human Resources
	Subcommittees
.L2716	Aging
.L2717	Aging, Family, and Human Services
.L272	Alcoholism and Drug Abuse
.L2725	Bioterrorism and Public Health Preparedness
.L273	Child and Human Development
.L2733	Children and Families

TABLE OF SENATE STANDING COMMITTEES (FOR HEARINGS)

Labor and Human Resources
Subcommittees -- Continued

	Children, Family, Drugs, and Alcoholism see KF21 .L2733
.L2734	Disability Policy
.L27347	Education and Early Childhood Development
.L2735	Education, Arts, and Humanities
	Employment and Productivity see KF21 .L2737
.L2736	Employment and Training
.L27364	Employment and Workplace Safety
.L2737	Employment, Poverty, and Migratory Labor
	Employment, Safety, and Training see KF21 .L2736
.L2738	Family and Human Services
.L2739	Handicapped
.L274	Health and Scientific Research
.L2753	Investigations and General Oversight
.L276	Labor
.L278	Public Health
	Public Health and Safety see KF21 .L278
.L2783	Retirement and Aging
.L2784	Retirement Security and Aging
.L279	Substance Abuse and Mental Health Services
.L3	Labor and Public Welfare
	Subcommittees
.L334	Aging
.L3346	Alcoholism and Narcotics
.L3347	Alleviation of Juvenile Delinquency
.L337	Arts and Humanities
.L339	Bilingual Education
.L342	Children and Youth
.L3423	Civil Rights
.L34235	Construction of Educational Facilities
.L3425	Disability Compensation
.L343	Education
.L345	Employment, Manpower, and Poverty
.L346	Employment, Poverty, and Migratory Labor
.L347	Establishment of a Commission on Ethics in Government
.L348	Evaluation and Planning of Social Programs
.L3486	Fair Labor Standards Act Amendments
.L3488	Federal Advisory Commission on the Arts
.L3515	Handicapped
.L352	Handicapped Workers
.L354	Health
.L3543	Health Legislation
.L3547	Hospital Construction and Local Public Health Units
.L355	Human Resources
.L3556	Indian Education

TABLE OF SENATE STANDING COMMITTEES (FOR HEARINGS)

Labor and Public Welfare
Subcommittees -- Continued

Code	Subject
.L356	International Health, Education, and Labor Programs
.L359	Juvenile Delinquency
.L363	Labor
.L3634	Labor and Labor-Management Relations
.L3637	Legislation Affecting the Food and Drug Administration
.L3655	Migratory Labor
.L367	National Science Foundation
.L368	National Service Corps
.L369	Poverty
.L3695	Problems of the Aged and Aging
.L373	Railroad Retirement
.L377	S. 3626
.L383	Science
.L389	Unemployment
.L392	Utilization of Scientific Manpower
.L393	Veterans' Administration Policies With Respect to Hospital Administration
.L394	Veterans' Affairs
.L3945	Vocational Rehabilitation of the Physically Handicapped
.L397	Youth Conservation Corps
.L5	Library
.M3	Manufactures
	Subcommittees
.M328	S. 174 and 262
.M33	S. Res. 163
.M5	Military Affairs
	Subcommittees
.M53	Contract Termination
.M545	H. R. 3755
.M572	S. 1682
.M573	S. 1695
.M5735	S. 2710
.M574	S. 3837
.M575	Scrap Iron and Steel
.M5755	Surplus Property
.M576	Technological Mobilization
.M578	War Contracts
.M579	War Mobilization
.M58	Mines and Mining
	Subcommittees
.M5846	S. 1476
.M585	S. 2420
.N3	Naval Affairs
	Subcommittees

Naval Affairs
Subcommittees -- Continued

Code	Entry
.N35	S. 3980
.N36	Senate Resolution 70
.N365	Senate Resolution 200
.P16	Pacific Islands and Porto Rico
.P2	Patents
	Subcommittees
.P25	H. R. 82
.P3	Pensions
.P4	Philippines
.P6	Post Office and Civil Service
	Subcommittees
.P634	Census and Statistics
.P637	Civil Service
.P638	Compensation and Employment Benefits
.P642	Federal Employees Compensation
.P643	Health Benefits and Life Insurance
.P648	Insurance
.P6555	No. 4
.P656	No. 5
.P659	Post Office
.P662	Postal Affairs
.P664	Postal Operations
.P666	Postal Policy
.P668	Postal Rates
.P674	Retirement
.P68	Post Offices and Post Roads
.P6815	Longevity Bills
.P685	Printing
.P69	Privileges and Elections
	Subcommittees
.P694	S. Res. 278
.P697	Senate Resolution 97
.P698	Senate Resolutions 467 and 485
.P72	Public Buildings and Grounds
.P74	Public Health and National Quarantine
.P748	Public Lands
	Subcommittees
.P7485	Indian Affairs
.P7487	Senate Resolution 98
.P7488	Territories and Insular Affairs
.P75	Public Lands and Surveys
	Subcommittees
.P755	S. Res. 291
.P756	S. Res. 347

KF21 TABLE OF SENATE STANDING COMMITTEES (FOR KF21 HEARINGS)

Public Lands and Surveys Subcommittees -- Continued

Code	Description
.P758	Senate Resolutions 147 and 312
.P8	Public Works
	Subcommittees
.P822	Accelerated Public Works
.P825	Air and Water Pollution
.P827	Disaster Relief
.P828	Economic Development
.P836	Environmental Pollution
.P838	Environmental Science and Technology
.P846	Flood Control: Rivers and Harbors
.P85	Materials Policy
.P866	Public Buildings and Grounds
.P867	Public Roads
.P868	Roads
.P872	Transportation
.P878	Water Resources
.R45	Relations with Cuba
.R77	Rules
.R8	Rules and Administration
	Subcommittees
.R83	Amendments to Rule XXII
.R843	Computer Services
.R844	Consider the Appointment of Female Pages
.R849	Consider the Reimbursement of Actual Travel Expense of Senators
.R855	Library
.R867	Privileges and Elections
.R87	Rules
.R885	Smithsonian Institution
.R888	Standing Rules of the Senate
.S6	Small Business
	Subcommittees
.S634	Advocacy and the Future of Small Business
.S635	Competition and Antitrust Enforcement
.S6354	Competitiveness and Economic Opportunity
.S637	Entrepreneurship and Special Problems Facing Small Business
	Export Expansion see KF21 .S6377
.S6377	Export Expansion and Agricultural Development
.S638	Export Promotion and Market Development
	Government Contracting and Paperwork Reduction see KF21 .S647
.S646	Government Procurement
.S647	Government Regulation and Paperwork

TABLE OF SENATE STANDING COMMITTEES (FOR HEARINGS)

Small Business

Subcommittees -- Continued

Innovation and Technology see KF21 .S648

.S648	Innovation, Technology, and Productivity
.S664	Price Discrimination and the Basing-Point System
.S667	Productivity and Competition
.S6676	Retailing, Distribution, and Marketing Practices
.S668	Rural Economy and Family Farming
.S67	Small Business: Family Farm
.S685	Urban and Minority-Owned Business Development
.S687	Urban and Rural Economic Development
	Small Business and Entrepreneurship see KF21 .S6
.T38	Territories
.T4	Territories and Insular Affairs
	Subcommittees
.T42	S. 3577
.T45	S. Res. 309 (77th Congress)
.T5	Territories and Insular Possessions
.V4	Veterans' Affairs
	Subcommittees
.V433	Cemeteries and Burial Benefits
.V435	Compensation and Pension
	Compensation and Pensions see KF21 .V435
.V454	Health and Hospitals
.V457	Health and Readjustment
.V464	Housing and Insurance
.V465	Housing, Insurance, and Cemeteries
.V474	Readjustment, Education, and Employment
.W6	Woman Suffrage

KF22 TABLE OF SENATE SELECT AND SPECIAL COMMITTEES (FOR HEARINGS) KF22

Code	Topic
.A25	Affairs in the Indian Territory
.A3	Aging
	Subcommittees
.A344	Consumer Interests of the Elderly
.A347	Employment and Retirement Incomes
.A348	Federal and State Activities
.A349	Federal, State, and Community Services
	Frauds and Misrepresentations Affecting the Elderly see KF22 .A344
.A353	Health of the Elderly
.A354	Housing for the Elderly
.A355	Involuntary Relocation of the Elderly
.A356	Long-Term Care
.A366	Nursing Homes
.A384	Retirement and the Individual
.A386	Retirement Income
.A43	Air and Ocean Mail Contracts
.A46	Alleged Executions Without Trial in France
	American Small Business, Problems of see KF22 .P73
.A86	Atomic Energy
.A88	Attorney General
.B36	Bankruptcy and Receivership Proceedings and the Administration of Justice in United States Courts
.B87	Bureau of Internal Revenue
.C44	Censure Charges
.C46	Centralization of Heavy Industry in the United States
.C48	Charges Against Senator Burton K. Wheeler of Montana
.C57	Circumstances Connected with the Removal of the Northern Cheyennes from the Sioux Reservation to the Indian Territory
.C58	Civil Service Laws
.C64	Conditions in the American Merchant Marine
.C643	Conduct of the Excise Board of the District of Columbia
.C65	Conservation of Wild Life Resources
.C66	Contribution Investigation
.C76	Crop Insurance
.D4	Deepwater Ports Legislation
.E4	Election of William Lorimer
.E6	Equal Educational Opportunity
.E87	Ethics
.E96	Expenditures in Senatorial Primary and General Elections
.F37	Farm Labor and Conditions in the West
.F67	Foreign Aid Program
.F84	Fuel Situation in the Middle West
.G37	Gasoline and Fuel-Oil Shortages
.G6	Government Organization

KF22 TABLE OF SENATE SELECT AND SPECIAL KF22 COMMITTEES (FOR HEARINGS)

Governmental Operations with Respect to Intelligence Activities see KF22 .I5

Code	Subject
.H34	Haiti and Santo Domingo
.I355	Illegal Appointments and Dismissals in the Civil Service
.I364	Impeachment Trial Committee on the Articles against Judge Alcee L. Hastings
.I367	Impeachment Trial Committee on the Articles against Judge Walter L. Nixon, Jr.
.I37	Improper Activities in the Labor or Management Field
.I4	Indian Affairs
	Class here hearings of the Select Committee on Indian Affairs held during the period 1977-March 1993. Class hearings of the Committee on Indian Affairs held during the period 1820-1976 and after March 1993 in KF26.I45.
	Subcommittees
.I435	Investigations
.I5	Intelligence
	Subcommittees
.I553	Intelligence and the Rights of Americans
.I557	Secrecy and Disclosure
	International Narcotics Control Caucus see KF22 .N37
.L34	Law Enforcement Undercover Activities of Components of the Dept. of Justice
.L6	Lobbying Activities
.M85	Munitions Industry
.N37	Narcotics Control, International
.N374	National Defense Program
	National Ocean Policy Study see KF22 .O3
.N38	National Water Resources
.N56	Nine-Foot Channel from the Great Lakes to the Gulf of Mexico
.N8	Nutrition and Human Needs
.O3	Ocean Policy Study, National
.O4	Official Conduct
.O43	Old-age Pension System
.O74	Organization of Congress
.O75	Organized Crime in Interstate Commerce
.P4	Petroleum Resources
.P55	Political Activities, Lobbying, and Campaign Contributions
.P57	Post-office Leases
.P58	Post-War Economic Policy and Planning
.P6	POW/MIA Affairs
.P68	Presidential and Senatorial Campaign Expenditures
.P7	Presidential Campaign Activities
.P72	Presidential Campaign Expenditures
.P73	Problems of American Small Business
.P735	Production, Transportation, and Marketing of Wool

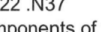

KF22 TABLE OF SENATE SELECT AND SPECIAL COMMITTEES (FOR HEARINGS) KF22

Code	Description
.P75	Propaganda or Money Alleged to Have Been Used by Foreign Governments to Influence United States Senators
.P8	Public School System of the District of Columbia
.R38	Reconstruction and Production
.R4	Reforestation
.R46	Reorganization of the Courts of the United States and Reform Judicial Procedure
.S54	Secret Military Assistance to Iran and Nicaraguan Opposition
.S58	Senate Committee System
.S582	Senatorial Campaign Expenditures
.S583	Senatorial Campaign Expenditures, 1946
.S585	Ship-purchase Bill
.S59	Silver
.S6	Small Business
	Subcommittees
.S62	Daytime Broadcasting
.S622	Economic Development, Marketing, and the Family Farmer
.S623	Environmental, Rural and Urban Economic Development
.S624	Financing and Investment
.S625	Government Procurement
.S627	Government Regulation
	Government Regulation and Paperwork see KF22 .S627
	Government Regulation and Small Business Advocacy see KF22 .S627
.S65	Manpower
.S654	Military Procurement
.S655	Mobilization and Procurement
	Monopoly see KF22 .S658
.S658	Monopoly and Anticompetitive Practices
.S664	Price Discrimination and the Basing-Point System
.S667	Relations of Business with Government
.S672	Retailing, Distribution, and Fair Trade Practices
.S674	Retailing, Distribution, and Marketing Practices
.S676	Rubber
.S682	Science and Technology
.S685	Taxation
.S686	Taxation, Financing, and Investment
.S693	Urban and Rural Economic Development
.S698	Space and Astronautics
.S7	Standards and Conduct
.S75	Street Railway Conditions in the District of Columbia
.S87	Survey of Land and Water Policies of the United States
.T39	Taxation of Governmental Securities and Salaries
.T4	Termination of the National Emergency
.U52	Unemployment and Relief
.U54	Unemployment Insurance

TABLE OF SENATE SELECT AND SPECIAL COMMITTEES (FOR HEARINGS)

.U56	Unemployment Problems
.U59	United States Tariff Commission
.V4	Veterans' Bureau
.W34	Wages and Prices of Commodities
.W55	Wild Life Resources
.Y43	Year 2000 Technology Problem

KF23 TABLE OF HOUSE STANDING COMMITTEES (FOR KF23 HEARINGS)

.A3 Agriculture

Subcommittees

.A32	Appropriations
	Conservation and Credit see KF23 .A3226
.A3226	Conservation, Credit, and Rural Development
.A3227	Conservation, Credit, Energy, and Research
	Conservation, Credit, Rural Development, and Research see KF23 .A345
.A32273	Conservation, Energy, and Forestry
	Cotton see KF23 .A3228
.A3228	Cotton, Rice, and Sugar
.A3326	Dairy and Poultry
.A33262	Dairy Products
.A33265	Department Investigations, Oversight, and Research
.A33273	Department Operations and Nutrition
.A33275	Department Operations, Investigations and Oversight
	Department Operations, Nutrition, and Foreign Agriculture see KF23 .A33276
.A332755	Department Operations, Oversight, and Credit
.A332757	Department Operations, Oversight, Dairy, Nutrition, and Forestry
.A33276	Department Operations, Oversight, Nutrition, and Forestry
.A33277	Department Operations, Research, and Foreign Agriculture
.A332775	Departmental Operations
.A3328	Departmental Oversight
.A33283	Departmental Oversight and Consumer Relations
	Domestic Marketing and Consumer Relations see KF23 .A3336
.A3336	Domestic Marketing, Consumer Relations, and Nutrition
.A3338	Environment, Credit, and Rural Development
.A337	Equipment, Supplies, and Manpower
.A343	Family Farms and Rural Development
	Family Farms, Rural Development, and Special Studies see KF23 .A344
.A3433	Food Shortages
.A3434	Foot-and-Mouth Disease
.A3436	Foreign Agricultural Operations
	Foreign Agriculture and Hunger see KF23 .A33277
	Forestry, Resource Conservation, and Research see KF23 .A377
.A3438	Forests
.A344	Forests, Family Farms, and Energy
	General Farm Commodities see KF23 .A345
.A3446	General Farm Commodities and Risk Management
.A345	General Farm Commodities, Resource Conservation, and Credit

KF23 TABLE OF HOUSE STANDING COMMITTEES (FOR HEARINGS) KF23

Agriculture

Subcommittees -- Continued

Code	Subject
.A355	Grain Elevator Bankruptcy
.A357	Horticulture and Organic Agriculture
.A362	Legislation to Extend the Commodity Food Distribution Authority
.A364	Livestock
	Livestock and Feed Grains see KF23 .A365
.A365	Livestock and Grains
.A366	Livestock and Horticulture
	Livestock, Dairy, and Poultry see KF23 .A366
.A3667	Nutrition and Horticulture
.A367	Oilseeds and Rice
	Peanuts and Tobacco see KF23 .A3864
.A369	Poultry
.A374	Research and Extension
.A377	Resource Conservation, Research, and Forestry
	Risk Management and Specialty Crops see KF23 .A379
.A379	Risk Management, Research, and Specialty Crops
.A3796	Rural Development
.A3797	Rural Development, Biotechnology, Specialty Crops, and Foreign Agriculture
.A3799	Rural Development, Research, Biotechnology, and Foreign Agriculture
.A3817	Specialty Crops and Foreign Agriculture Programs
.A382	Specialty Crops and Natural Resources
.A383	Specialty Crops, Rural Development, and Foreign Agriculture
.A386	Tobacco
.A3864	Tobacco and Peanuts
.A3869	Wheat
.A387	Wheat, Soybeans, and Feed Grains
.A43	Alcoholic Liquor Traffic
.A6	Appropriations
	Subcommittees
.A627	Agricultural Department
.A628	Agriculture and Related Agencies
.A632	Agriculture--Environmental and Consumer Protection Appropriations
	Agriculture, Rural Development, and Related Agencies see KF23 .A628
	Agriculture, Rural Development, Food and Drug Administration, and Related Agencies see KF23 .A628
.A6323	Appropriations for Treasury and Post Office Departments
.A6324	Civil Functions and Military Construction
	Commerce, Justice, and State, the Judiciary, and Related Agencies see KF23 .A6327

KF23 TABLE OF HOUSE STANDING COMMITTEES (FOR HEARINGS) KF23

Appropriations

Subcommittees -- Continued

Code	Description
.A63245	Commerce, Justice, Science, and Related Agencies
.A6325	Deficiencies
.A63253	Deficiencies and Army Civil Functions
.A632535	Deficiency Appropriations
.A6326	Department of Commerce
.A63266	Department of the Army Appropriations
.A63267	Department of Transportation
.A6327	Departments of Commerce, Justice, and State, the Judiciary, and Related Agencies
	Departments of Labor, and Health, Education, and Welfare, and Related Agencies see KF23 .A652
	Departments of Labor, Health and Human Services, Education, and Related Agencies see KF23 .A653
	Departments of State, Justice, Commerce, the Judiciary, and Related Agencies Appropriations see KF23 .A664
.A6328	Departments of Transportation, and Housing and Urban Development, and Related Agencies
	Departments of Transportation and Treasury, and Independent Agencies Appropriations see KF23 .A669
.A6329	Departments of Transportation, Treasury, HUD, the Judiciary, District of Columbia, and Independent Agencies Appropriations
	Departments of Treasury, and Post Office, and Executive Office of the President see KF23 .A674
.A633	Dept. of Defense
	Dept. of the Interior and Related Agencies see KF23 .A6484
	Dept. of Transportation and Related Agencies Appropriations see KF23 .A667
.A6335	District of Columbia Appropriations
.A64	Energy and Water Development
.A644	Financial Services and General Government
.A645	Flood Stricken Areas
.A646	Foreign Operations and Related Agencies (1968?-1978)
.A6463	Foreign Operations and Related Agencies (1981-1987)
.A64633	Foreign Operations and Related Agencies Appropriations
.A64634	Foreign Operations Appropriations
	Foreign Operations, Export Financing, and Related Programs see KF23 .A646
.A64636	General Government Matters
.A6464	Government Corporations Appropriations
.A6465	Homeland Security
.A6466	HUD-Independent Agencies
.A647	HUD-Space-Science
.A6473	HUD-Space-Science-Veterans

KF23 TABLE OF HOUSE STANDING COMMITTEES (FOR HEARINGS) KF23

Appropriations

Subcommittees -- Continued

.A6478	Independent Offices
.A648	Independent Offices and Dept. of Housing and Urban Development
.A6484	Interior and Related Agencies
.A64846	Interior Department
.A6485	Interior, Environment, and Related Agencies
.A652	Labor, and Health, Education, and Welfare, and Related Agencies
.A653	Labor, Health and Human Services, Education, and Related Agencies
.A654	Legislative
	Legislative Branch Appropriations see KF23 .A654
.A655	Military Construction Appropriations
.A6552	Military Construction, Veterans Affairs, and Related Agencies
.A6554	Military Quality of Life and Veterans Affairs, and Related Agencies
.A656	National Security
.A657	Navy Department
.A6576	Pension Appropriation Bill
.A658	Public Works
.A6583	Public Works Appropriations
.A662	Rural Development, Agriculture, and Related Agencies
.A663	Science, State, Justice, and Commerce, and Related Agencies
.A6635	State, Foreign Operations, and Related Programs
.A6637	State, Justice, and Commerce Departments Appropriations
.A6638	State, Justice, Commerce, and Labor Departments Appropriations
.A6639	State, Justice, Commerce, and the Judiciary Appropriations
.A664	State, Justice, Commerce, the Judiciary, and Related Agencies Appropriations
.A667	Transportation and Related Agencies Appropriations
.A669	Transportation and Treasury, and Independent Agencies Appropriations
.A673	Treasury and Post Office
.A674	Treasury, and Post Office, and Executive Office of the President
.A676	Treasury, Postal Service, and General Government Appropriations
	VA, HUD, and Independent Agencies see KF23 .A6466
.A678	War Department
.A6783	War Department Civil Functions
.A7	Armed Services
	Subcommittees

KF23 TABLE OF HOUSE STANDING COMMITTEES (FOR HEARINGS) KF23

Armed Services

Subcommittees -- Continued

Call Number	Topic
.A733	Acquisition Policy Panel
.A734	Air and Land Forces
	Alleged Drug Abuse in the Armed Services see KF23 .A738
.A7354	Arms Control and Disarmament
	Arms Control and Disarmament (Special Panel of the Procurement and Military Nuclear Systems Subcommittee) see KF23 .A7657
	Army Procurement of the M561, Gama Goat see KF23 .A7635
.A73547	Business Challenges within the Defense Industry
.A7355	Capability of the National Guard to Cope with Civil Disturbances
	Civil Defense Panel see KF23 .A7533
.A7356	Commercial Air Transportation for Service Personnel While on Authorized Leave
.A7357	Composition of the Fleet and Block Obsolescence of Naval Vessels
.A7358	Construction of Military Hospital Facilities
.A736	Defense Acquisition Reform
.A7362	Defense Activities
.A73625	Defense Agencies
.A7363	Defense Burdensharing Panel
.A7364	Defense (Department of) Energy Resources and Requirements
.A73643	Defense Financial Management and Auditability Reform
.A73647	Defense Policy Panel
.A7365	Defense Procurement Procedures
	Department of Defense Energy Resources and Requirements see KF23 .A7364
	Department of Energy Reorganization see KF23 .A7395
	Dept. of Energy, Defense Nuclear Facilities Panel see KF23 .A739
.A7366	Development and Procurement of New Combat and Tactical Vehicles by the Department of the Army
.A7367	Disciplinary Problems in the U.S. Navy
.A737	Draft
.A738	Drug Abuse in the Armed Services
.A7386	Emerging Threats and Capabilities
.A739	Energy (Dept. of), Defense Nuclear Facilities Panel
.A7395	Energy (Department of) Reorganization
.A7397	Enlisted Promotion Policy Review
.A74	Environmental Restoration Panel
.A743	Exchanges and Commissaries

Armed Services
Subcommittees -- Continued

Code	Description
.A744	Future Uses of Defense Manufacturing and Technology Resources Panel
.A745	Grace Commission Panel
.A746	Human Relations
	Indian Ocean Forces Limitation and Conventional Arms Transfer Limitation, Panel on see KF23 .A749
.A748	Intelligence
.A749	Intelligence and Military Application of Nuclear Energy
	Including the Panel on the Strategic Arms Limitation Talks and the Comprehensive Test Ban Treaty and the Panel on Indian Ocean Forces Limitation and Conventional Arms Transfer Limitation
.A752	Investigating
.A753	Investigations
.A7533	Civil Defense Panel
.A7535	Nonappropriated Fund Panel
.A7537	Small Business Panel
.A755	Investigations, Special
.A763	M-16 Rifle Program
.A7635	M561, Gama Goat, Army Procurement of the
.A7636	Merchant Marine
.A7637	Middle East
.A76377	Military Acquisition
.A763775	Military Airlift
.A7638	Military Application of Nuclear Energy
.A7639	Military Commitments to Europe, U.S.
.A76392	Military Compensation
.A763945	Military Dental Care
.A76395	Military Education
	Military Forces and Personnel see KF23 .A763984
.A76397	Military Installations and Facilities
.A76398	Military Personnel
.A763984	Military Personnel and Compensation
	Military Procurement see KF23 .A76377
	Military Readiness see KF23 .A7659
	Military Research and Development see KF23 .A7668
	Moral, Welfare, and Recreation Panel see KF23 .A7659
.A763986	Morale, Welfare, and Recreation, Special Oversight Panel on
.A764	My Lai Incident
.A76416	National Military Airlift
.A7642	NATO Standardization, Interoperability, and Readiness
.A7643	Naval Vessels to Foreign Countries, Transfer of
.A7644	Navy Training Activities on the Island of Vieques, Status of
.A76444	No. 2

Armed Services
Subcommittees -- Continued
No. 6

Call Number	Subject
.A76445	No. 6
.A7645	Nonappropriated Fund Activities within the Department of Defense
	Nonappropriated Fund Panel see KF23 .A7535
.A765	North Atlantic Treaty Organization Commitments
.A7654	Nuclear Weapons Safety
.A7655	Number 1, Number 2, Number 3, Number 4, Number 5
.A7656	Oversight and Investigations
.A76567	Procurement
.A7657	Procurement and Military Nuclear Systems
	Including the Special Panel on Arms Control and Disarmament
.A76575	Procurement Practices of the Department of Defense
.A7658	Projection Forces Subcommittee
.A76584	Proposed Undersea Warfare Laboratory, Los Alamitos, Calif.
.A7659	Readiness
	Including the Morale, Welfare, and Recreation Panel and the Special Operations Panel
.A766	Relocation of the U.S. Army Intelligence School from Fort Holabird to Fort Huachuca
.A7668	Research and Development
	Research and Technology see KF23 .A7668
.A767	Retired-Pay Revisions
.A768	Seapower
.A7684	Seapower and Expeditionary Forces
.A7687	Seapower and Projection Forces
.A769	Seapower and Strategic and Critical Materials
.A769115	Service Academies
	Sinking of the U.S.S. Guitaro see KF23 .A785
	Small Business Panel see KF23 .A7537
	Special Investigations see KF23 .A755
	Special Operations Panel (of the Readiness Subcommittee) see KF23 .A7659
	Status of Navy Training Activities on the Island of Vieques see KF23 .A7644
	Strategic Arms Limitation Talks and the Comprehensive Test Ban Treaty, Panel on see KF23 .A749
.A77	Strategic Defense Initiative
.A772	Strategic Forces
.A774	Supplemental Service Benefits
.A778	Survivors' Benefits
.A779	Tactical Air and Land Forces
.A7793	Tactical Air Support
.A78	Technology Transfer
.A7822	Terrorism

Armed Services
Subcommittees -- Continued

Code	Description
.A7824	Terrorism, Unconventional Threats, and Capabilities
.A7827	Total Force
	Transfer of Naval Vessels to Foreign Countries see KF23 .A7643
.A783	Transportation
	U.S. Military Commitments to Europe see KF23 .A7639
.A785	U.S.S. Guitaro, Sinking of the
.A787	U.S.S. Pueblo
.A788	Utilization of Manpower in the Military
.A789	Utilization of Military Manpower
.A7894	Utilization of Naval Shipyard Facilities
.B3	Banking and Currency
	Subcommittees
.B325	Bank Supervision and Insurance
.B333	Consumer Affairs
.B339	Domestic and International Monetary Effect of Energy and Other Natural Resource Pricing
.B342	Domestic Finance
.B3426	H.R. 3082 and Other Bills to Provide Loans Through Reconstruction Finance Corporation
.B343	Home Financing Practices and Procedures
.B344	Housing
.B346	International Finance
.B348	International Trade
.B36	No. 1
.B362	No. 2
.B363	No. 3
.B364	No. 4
.B375	Small Business
.B387	Urban Growth
.B3874	Urban Mass Transportation
	Banking and Financial Services see KF23 .B5
.B39	Banking, Currency, and Housing
	Subcommittees
.B3913	Automobile Industry
.B392	Consumer Affairs
.B393	Domestic and International Monetary Effect of Energy and other Natural Resource Pricing
.B395	Domestic Monetary Policy
.B3955	Economic Stabilization
	General Oversight and Renegotiation see KF23 .B3985
.B3967	Historic Preservation and Coinage
.B397	Housing and Community Development
.B3974	International Development Institutions and Finance

Banking, Currency, and Housing
Subcommittees -- Continued

Code	Description
.B3985	Oversight and Renegotiation, General
.B5	Banking, Finance, and Urban Affairs
	Subcommittees
.B514	Capital Markets and Government Sponsored Enterprises
	Capital Markets, Insurance, and Government Sponsored Enterprises see KF23 .B515
.B515	Capital Markets, Securities, and Government Sponsored Enterprises
.B52	City
	Community Investment, Task Force on see KF23 .B5464
.B535	Consumer Affairs
.B536	Consumer Affairs and Coinage
.B5364	Consumer Credit and Insurance
.B5368	Domestic and International Monetary Policy
	Domestic and International Monetary Policy, Trade, and Technology see KF23 .B5368
.B537	Domestic Monetary Policy
.B5373	Domestic Monetary Policy and Technology
	Domestic Monetary Policy, Technology, and Economic Growth see KF23 .B5368
.B538	Economic Growth and Credit Formation
.B542	Economic Stabilization
	Financial Institutions and Consumer Credit see KF23 .B5364
.B544	Financial Institutions Supervision, Regulation, and Deposit Insurance
.B54423	Examination, Audit, and Review Task Force
.B54426	Resolution Trust Corporation Task Force
	Financial Institutions Supervision, Regulation, and Insurance see KF23 .B544
.B54428	General Oversight and Investigations
.B5443	General Oversight and Renegotiation
.B545	Historic Preservation and Coinage
	Homeownership, Task Force on see KF23 .B5466
.B546	Housing and Community Development
.B5464	Task Force on Community Investment
.B5466	Task Force on Homeownership
.B5467	Task Force on Rental Housing
	Housing and Community Opportunity see KF23 .B546
.B5468	Insurance, Housing, and Community Opportunity
.B54685	International Competitiveness of United States Financial Institutions
.B547	International Development, Finance, Trade, and Monetary Policy

Banking, Finance, and Urban Affairs
Subcommittees -- Continued
International Development Institutions and Finance see KF23 .B547

.B548 International Finance, Trade, and Monetary Policy
International Monetary Policy and Trade see KF23 .B5368

.B55 International Trade, Investment, and Monetary Policy
Oversight and Investigations see KF23 .B54428

.B575 Policy Research and Insurance
Rental Housing, Task Force on see KF23 .B5467

.B8 Budget
Task Forces

.B83 AIDS
Budget Process see KF23 .B842

.B842 Budget Process (1998-)

.B8422 Budget Process, Reconciliation, and Enforcement

.B8423 Capital Resources and Development

.B8424 Community and Natural Resources

.B8425 Community and Physical Resources
Community Development and Natural Resources see KF23 .B8424

.B843 Community Resources and General Government

.B8438 Defense and International Affairs

.B8439 Defense, Foreign Policy, and Space

.B844 Distributive Impacts of Budget and Economic Policies

.B8447 Economic Policy

.B84475 Economic Policy and Growth

.B8448 Economic Policy and Productivity

.B8449 Economic Policy, Projections, and Revenues

.B845 Economic Projections

.B8453 Education and Employment

.B8454 Energy and Technology

.B8455 Energy and the Environment

.B8457 Enforcement, Credit, and Multiyear Budgeting

.B846 Entitlements, Uncontrollables, and Indexing

.B8464 Federalism/State-Local Relations

.B847 Government Efficiency

.B8478 Health

.B8479 Homeless and Housing

.B84795 Housing and Infrastructure

.B848 Human and Community Resources

.B849 Human Resources

.B85 Human Resources and Block Grants

.B852 Income Security

.B853 Inflation

.B855 International Finance and Trade

KF23 TABLE OF HOUSE STANDING COMMITTEES (FOR HEARINGS) KF23

Budget

Task Forces -- Continued

Code	Description
.B858	Legislative Savings
.B869	National Security and International Affairs
.B87	National Security and Veterans
.B873	National Security Programs
.B876	Physical Resources
.B878	Social Security
.B879	State and Local Government
.B882	Tax Expenditures and Off-Budget Agencies
.B883	Tax Expenditures and Tax Policy
.B884	Tax Expenditures, Government Organization, and Regulation
.B885	Tax Policy
.B887	Transportation, Research and Development, and Capital Resources
.B89	Urgent Fiscal Issues
.C46	Census
.C5	Civil Service
.C55	Claims
.C64	Coinage, Weights, and Measures
	Commerce see KF23 .E55
.D48	Disposition of Executive Papers
.D5	District of Columbia
	Subcommittees
.D533	Bicentennial Affairs, the Environment, and the International Community
.D535	Business, Commerce and Fiscal Affairs
.D536	Business, Commerce and Taxation
.D537	Commerce, Housing, and Transportation
.D5374	Crime and Law Enforcement
.D5378	Economic Development and Regional Affairs
.D538	Education
.D5384	Education, Labor, and Social Services
.D539	Fiscal Affairs
.D5392	Fiscal Affairs and Health
.D5393	Government Affairs and Budget
.D5395	Fiscal and Government Affairs
.D53955	Food Storage and Prices
.D5396	Government Affairs and Budget
.D542	Government Operations
.D543	Government Operations and Metropolitan Affairs
.D545	Health, Education, Recreation
.D5455	Home Rule and Reorganization
.D546	Housing and Youth Affairs
.D553	Insurance and Banking
.D555	Investigating

KF23 TABLE OF HOUSE STANDING COMMITTEES (FOR HEARINGS) KF23

District of Columbia

Subcommittees -- Continued

Code	Description
.D557	Judiciary
.D558	Judiciary and Education
	Judiciary, Manpower, and Education see KF23 .D558
.D562	Labor, Social Services, and the International Community
.D563	Metropolitan Affairs
.D5644	No. 1, 2, 3, 4, 5
.D56442	No. 6
.D5655	Parks and Playgrounds
.D5665	Police and Firemen
.D5675	Public Health, Hospitals, and Charities
.D568	Public Health, Welfare, Housing and Youth Affairs
.D5687	Public School Standards and Conditions, and Juvenile Delinquency in the District of Columbia
.D569	Public Utilities
.D5693	Public Utilities, Insurance, and Banking
.D573	Revenue and Financial Affairs
.D585	Special Select Subcommittee
.D586	Streets and Traffic
.D587	Taxation
.D588	Traffic, Streets, and Highways
.D59	Utility Preparedness
	Economic and Educational Opportunities see KF23 .E3
.E28	Education
	Education and Labor see KF23 .E3
.E3	Education and the Workforce

Subcommittees

Code	Description
.E315	21st Century Competitiveness
.E332	Agricultural Labor
.E33213	Aid for Blind Children
.E33215	Allocation of Scarce Materials for School Construction
.E3322	Antipoverty in the District of Columbia (Task Force)
.E33225	Assistance and Rehabilitation of the Physically Handicapped
.E332255	Assistance to School Districts Affected by Federal Activities
.E33226	Assistance to Schools in Federally Impacted Areas
.E3324	Coal Mine Safety
.E33245	Communism in New York City Distributive Trades
.E33247	Communist Infiltration of Maritime and Fisheries Unions
.E3325	Compensation, Health, and Safety
.E3326	De Facto School Segregation
.E3327	Discrimination Against Women
.E33278	Early Childhood, Elementary, and Secondary Education
.E3328	Early Childhood, Youth, and Families
.E3329	Economic Opportunity
.E333	Education (General Subcommittee)

KF23 TABLE OF HOUSE STANDING COMMITTEES (FOR HEARINGS) KF23

Education and the Workforce

Subcommittees -- Continued

Code	Description
.E335	Education (Select Subcommittee)
.E336	Education (Special Subcommittee)
.E33635	Education Reform
.E3364	Elementary, Secondary, and Vocational Education
	Employer-Employee Relations see KF23 .E347
.E3366	Employment Opportunities
.E337	Equal Opportunities
.E3374	Fair Employment Practice Act
.E3375	Federal Activities in Education
.E337528	Federal Aid for Library Service in Rural Areas
.E33753	Federal Aid to School Construction
.E3376	Fine Arts Programs in Colleges
.E338	General Education
.E339	Handicapped
.E3394	Health and Safety
.E3395	Health, Employment, Labor, and Pensions
.E3396	Healthy Families and Communities
.E33967	Higher Education and Workforce Training
.E3397	Higher Education, Lifelong Learning, and Competitiveness
.E34	Human Resources
.E3415	Impact of Imports and Exports on American Employment
.E3418	International Education
.E342	International Labor Organization (Task Force)
.E343	Labor (General Subcommittee)
.E345	Labor (Select Subcommittee)
.E346	Labor (Special Subcommittee)
.E3465	Labor-Management Disputes in Michigan, Indiana, Ohio
.E347	Labor-Management Relations
.E348	Labor Standards
.E349	Labor Standards, Occupational Health, and Safety
.E35	Library Service in Rural Areas
.E352	Manpower, Compensation, and Health and Safety
.E354	Minimum Wages in Certain Territories, Possessions, and Oversea Areas of the United States
.E3545	National Labor Relations Board
.E356	No. 1, 2
.E3564	No. 4, Wages and Hours of Labor - Labor Statistics and Labor Standards
.E3566	No. 6 - Welfare
.E367	Oversight and Investigations
.E368	Oversight of Education Programs
.E369	Postsecondary Education
	Postsecondary Education and Training see KF23 .E3694
.E3694	Postsecondary Education, Training, and Life-long Learning

Education and the Workforce
Subcommittees -- Continued

Code	Subject
.E372	Poverty
.E3722	Promote the Education of the Blind
.E3726	Safety and Compensation
.E3727	Safety in Longshore and Harbor Work
.E37285	Secondary Boycott of Crowley's Milk Co., Inc.
.E37286	Secondary Boycott of Philan, Inc.
.E373	Select Education
.E374	Shared-Time Education
.E376	Special Education
.E377	State Committees on Education Beyond the High School
.E3775	Steamship Unions
.E378	Strikes and Racketeering in the Detroit Area
.E3784	Strikes and Racketeering in the Kansas City Area
.E382	Unemployment and the Impact of Automation
	Twenty-first Century Competitiveness see KF23 .E315
.E386	War on Poverty Program
.E387	Welfare and Pension Funds
.E39	Workforce Protections
.E48	Election of President, Vice-President, and Representatives in Congress.
.E5	Elections
	Elections No. 1 see KF23 .E5
	Elections No. 2 see KF23 .E5
.E55	Energy and Commerce
	Subcommittees
	Commerce, Consumer Protection, and Competitiveness see KF23 .E5515
.E5514	Commerce, Manufacturing, and Trade
.E5515	Commerce, Trade, and Consumer Protection
	Commerce, Trade, and Hazardous Materials see KF23 .E5515
.E552	Commerce, Transportation, and Tourism
.E5522	Communications and Technology
.E5523	Communications, Technology, and the Internet
.E5524	Energy and Air Quality
.E5525	Energy and Environment
	Energy and Power see KF23 .E5524
.E5526	Energy Conservation and Power
.E5527	Environment and Hazardous Materials
.E55273	Environment and the Economy
	Finance and Hazardous Materials see KF23 .E5515
.E5528	Fossil and Synthetic Fuels
.E553	Health
	Health and the Environment see KF23 .E553

Energy and Commerce
Subcommittees -- Continued

Code	Description
.E5546	Oversight and Investigations
	Telecommunications and Finance see KF23 .E555
.E555	Telecommunications and the Internet
	Telecommunications, Consumer Protection, and Finance see KF23 .E555
	Telecommunications, Trade, and Consumer Protection see KF23 .E555
.E5585	Transportation and Hazardous Materials
	Transportation, Tourism, and Hazardous Materials see KF23 .E5585
.E5588	U.S.-Pacific Rim Trade
.E559	U.S. Trade with China
.E57	Expenditures in the Department of Agriculture
.E572	Expenditures in the Department of Commerce and Labor
.E575	Expenditures in the Department of Justice
.E58	Expenditures in the Executive Departments
	Subcommittees
.E5812	Civil Service Commission
.E58125	Executive and Legislative Reorganization
.E58127	Federal Relations with International Organizations.
.E5813	Government Operations
.E5814	H. R. 8127
.E5815	Inter-Governmental Relations
.E5818	Military Housing Construction in Alaska
.E58184	Procurement and Buildings
.E581845	Public Accounts
.E58185	Publicity and Propaganda
.E58187	State Department
.E5819	Viers Mill Village Veterans' Housing Project, Montgomery County, Md.
.E584	Expenditures in the Interior Department
.E585	Expenditures in the Navy Department
.E586	Expenditures in the Post-Office Department
.E587	Expenditures in the State Department
.E588	Expenditures in the Treasury Department
.E59	Expenditures in the War Department
.E593	Expenditures on Public Buildings
	Financial Services see KF23 .B5
.F55	Flood Control
.F58	Food Shortages
.F6	Foreign Affairs
	Subcommittees
.F625	Africa
.F627	Africa and Global Health

KF23 TABLE OF HOUSE STANDING COMMITTEES (FOR KF23 HEARINGS)

Foreign Affairs

Subcommittees -- Continued

.F636 Arms Control, International Security, and Science
.F638 Asia and the Pacific
.F639 Asia, the Pacific, and the Global Environment
Asian and Pacific Affairs see KF23 .F638
Economic Policy, Trade, and Environment see KF23 .F6465
.F642 Europe
.F64214 Europe and the Middle East
.F643 Far East and the Pacific
.F644 Foreign Economic Policy
.F6445 H. J. Res. 112, 113, and 114
.F645 Human Rights and International Organizations
.F646 Inter-American Affairs
.F6465 International Economic Policy and Trade
.F6467 International Narcotics Control
.F647 International Operations
.F648 International Organizations
International Organizations and Movements see KF23 .F648
.F64814 International Organizations, Human Rights, and Oversight
.F6482 International Political and Military Affairs
.F64825 International Security and Scientific Affairs
International Security, International Organizations, and
Human Rights see KF23 .F645
.F64827 Middle East and South Asia
.F64828 Mutual Security Programs
.F6483 National Security Policy and Scientific Developments
.F6485 Near East
.F64853 Near East and South Asia
.F648535 No. 5
.F64856 Review of Foreign Aid Programs
.F64857 Settlement of Intercustodial Conflicts Involving Enemy
Property
.F64859 Southwestern Border Projects
.F6486 State Department Organization and Foreign Operations
.F6489 Terrorism, Nonproliferation, and Trade
.F6492 Western Hemisphere
Western Hemisphere Affairs see KF23 .F6492
Government Operations see KF23 .G6
.G6 Government Reform
Subcommittees
.G616 Antiracketeering
.G617 Assigned Power and Land Problems
.G626 Census
Civil Service see KF23 .G63
.G63 Civil Service and Agency Organization

Government Reform

Subcommittees -- Continued

Code	Committee Name
.G634	Commerce, Consumer, and Monetary Affairs
.G636	Conservation and Natural Resources Subcommittee
.G638	Conservation, Energy, and Natural Resources Subcommittee
.G64	Criminal Justice, Drug Policy, and Human Resources
.G644	District of Columbia
.G646	Donable Property
	Employment and Housing see KF23 .G653
.G653	Employment, Housing, and Aviation
.G654	Energy and Resources
	Energy Policy, Natural Resources, and Regulatory Affairs see KF23 .G6685
.G655	Environment, Energy, and Natural Resources
.G659	Executive and Legislative Reorganization
.G65917	Federal Workforce and Agency Organization
.G6592	Federalism and the Census
.G6594	Foreign Operations and Government Information
.G6596	Foreign Operations and Monetary Affairs
.G662	Government Activities
.G6626	Government Activities and Transportation
	Government Efficiency and Financial Management see KF23 .G6627
.G6627	Government Efficiency, Financial Management and Intergovernmental Relations
.G66278	Government Information
.G6628	Government Information and Individual Rights
.G6629	Government Information, Justice, and Agriculture
.G66292	Government Management, Finance, and Accountability
.G66293	Government Management, Information, and Technology
	Human Resources see KF23 .G663
	Human Resources and Intergovernmental Relations see KF23 .G663
.G662936	Human Rights and Wellness
.G66294	Information, Justice, Transportation, and Agriculture
.G663	Intergovernmental Relations
.G664	Intergovernmental Relations and Human Resources
.G6645	International Operations
.G665	Invasion of Privacy
.G667	Legal and Monetary Affairs
.G6674	Legislation and Military Operations
.G6676	Legislation and National Security
.G6678	Manpower and Housing
.G668	Military Operations
.G6685	National Economic Growth, Natural Resources, and Regulatory Affairs

KF23 TABLE OF HOUSE STANDING COMMITTEES (FOR KF23 HEARINGS)

Government Reform

Subcommittees -- Continued

.G6687	National Security, Emerging Threats, and International Relations
.G6688	National Security, International Affairs, and Criminal Justice
.G6689	National Security, Veterans Affairs, and International Relations
.G669	Natural Resources and Power
.G6698	Postal Reform & Oversight
.G67	Postal Service
.G6733	Public Works and Resources
.G6734	Racketeering
.G6735	Regulatory Affairs
.G6737	Reorganization
.G674	Research and Technical Programs
.G676	Special Studies
.G677	Special Task Force
	Technology and Procurement Policy see KF23 .G66293
.G679	Technology, Information Policy, Intergovernmental Relations, and the Census
.G682	Water Resources and Power
	Government Reform and Oversight see KF23 .G6
.H57	Homeland Security
	Subcommittees
.H5716	Border, Maritime, and Global Counterterrorism
.H5725	Economic Security, Infrastructure Protection, and Cybersecurity
.H5728	Emergency Communications, Preparedness and Response
.H573	Emergency Preparedness, Science, and Technology
.H5733	Emerging Threats, Cybersecurity, and Science and Technology
.H575	Intelligence, Information Sharing, and Terrorism Risk Assessment
.H5753	Investigations
.H576	Management, Integration, and Oversight
.H5764	Management, Investigations, and Oversight
.H577	Prevention of Nuclear and Biological Attack
.H578	Transportation Security and Infrastructure Protection
	House Administration see KF23 .H6
.H6	House Oversight
	Subcommittees
.H643	Campaign Finance Reform
.H6432	Capitol Security
.H6436	Contested Election in the 13th Congressional District of Florida (Task Force)

KF23 TABLE OF HOUSE STANDING COMMITTEES (FOR KF23 HEARINGS)

House Oversight

Subcommittees -- Continued

Code	Description
.H644	Contested Election in the 46th Congressional District of California (Task Force)
.H6443	Contracts
.H645	Elections (Subcommittee)
.H646	Elections (Task Force)
.H647	Enrolled Bills and Library
.H648	Federal Printing and Paperwork
.H652	Information and Computers
.H653	Investigation of the House Post Office
.H655	Libraries and Memorials
.H6553	Library
	Library and Memorials see KF23 .H655
.H656	Office Systems
.H6565	Personnel and Police
	Printing see KF23 .H657
.H657	Procurement and Printing
.I4	Immigration and Naturalization
	Subcommittees
.I427	Naturalization and Citizenship
.I428	Salaries in the Immigration Service
.I45	Indian Affairs
	Subcommittees
.I454	General Bills
.I46	Industrial Arts and Expositions
.I49	Insular Affairs
	Subcommittees
.I497	Political, Economic, and Social Conditions in Puerto Rico
.I5	Interior and Insular Affairs
	Subcommittees
.I514	Bonneville Power Administration
.I518	Energy and the Environment
.I519	Energy and Mineral Resources
.I522	Environment
.I524	Fisheries, Wildlife, and Oceans
.I525	General Oversight and Alaska Lands
.I5253	General Oversight and California Desert Lands
.I526	General Oversight and Investigations
	General Oversight, Northwest Power, and Forest Management see KF23 .I526
.I5269	Indian (Special Subcommittee)
.I527	Indian Affairs
.I5274	Indian Affairs (Special Subcommittee)
.I528	Indian Affairs and Public Lands
	Insular Affairs see KF23 .I5283

Interior and Insular Affairs
Subcommittees -- Continued

Code	Description
.I5282	Insular Affairs, Oceans, and Wildlife
.I5283	Insular and International Affairs
.I529	Irrigation and Reclamation
.I536	Mines and Mining
.I5362	Mining and Natural Resources
.I5363	Mining, Forest Management, and Bonneville Power Administration
.I5364	National Parks
.I5365	National Parks and Insular Affairs
	National Parks and Public Lands see KF23 .I5365
.I537	National Parks and Recreation
.I5373	National Parks, Forests, and Public Lands
	Native American Affairs see KF23 .I5377
.I5377	Native American and Insular Affairs
.I538	Oversight and Investigations
.I544	Public Lands
.I546	Special Investigations
.I547	Territorial and Insular Affairs
.I5473	Water and Power
.I5474	Water and Power Resources
.I548	Internal Security
.I549	International Relations
	Subcommittees
.I54914	Africa
.I549143	Africa, Global Human Rights and International Operations
	Asia and the Pacific see KF23 .I54915
	Asian and Pacific Affairs see KF23 .I54915
.I54915	East Asia and the Pacific
.I54916	Europe
.I54917	Europe and Emerging Threats
	Europe and the Middle East see KF23 .I54916
.I5492	Future Foreign Policy Research and Development
.I54922	Inter-American Affairs
.I54923	International Development
	International Economic Policy see KF23 .I54924
.I54924	International Economic Policy and Trade
.I5493	International Operations
.I54934	International Operations and Human Rights
.I5494	International Organizations
.I54944	International Political and Military Affairs
.I54947	International Resources, Food, and Energy
.I5495	International Security and Scientific Affairs
.I54957	International Terrorism and Nonproliferation
.I5496	International Terrorism, Nonproliferation, and Human Rights

TABLE OF HOUSE STANDING COMMITTEES (FOR HEARINGS)

International Relations
Subcommittees -- Continued

.I5497	International Trade and Commerce
.I5498	Investigations
.I54984	Middle East and Central Asia
.I54985	Middle East and South Asia
.I54986	Oversight and Investigations
.I5499	Western Hemisphere
.I55	Interstate and Foreign Commerce Subcommittees
.I5525	Aviation
.I5529	Bridge
.I5536	Commerce and Finance
.I55363	Commerce and Trade
.I5537	Communications
.I5538	Communications and Power
.I554	Consumer Protection and Finance
.I55415	Dept. of Health, Education, and Welfare
.I5542	Energy and Power
.I55422	Federal Communications Commission
.I55423	Federal Power
.I55425	Federal Trade Commission
.I55428	Health and Safety
.I55429	Health and Science
.I5543	Health and the Environment
.I5544	Investigate Power Failures
.I5545	Investigations
.I55455	Land Grants
.I55457	Legislative Oversight
.I5546	Light-House Establishment
.I55465	Merchant Marine and Fisheries
.I5547	Oversight and Investigations
.I5549	Petroleum
.I555	Petroleum and Federal Power
.I5554	Petroleum Investigation
.I5563	Public Health
.I5567	Public Health and Environment
.I55677	Public Health and Safety
.I5568	Public Health and Welfare
.I5569	Public Health, Science, and Commerce
.I5572	Railroads
.I55725	Regulatory Agencies
.I5575	Securities
.I55755	Securities and Exchange Commission
.I558	Traffic Safety
.I5585	Transportation

Interstate and Foreign Commerce
Subcommittees -- Continued

Code	Description
.I5587	Transportation and Aeronautics
.I5589	Transportation and Commerce
.I559	Transportation and Communications
.I5594	War Claims Act and Trading with the Enemy Act
.I57	Invalid Pensions
.I7	Irrigation and Reclamation
.I73	Irrigation of Arid Lands
.J8	Judiciary

Subcommittees

Code	Description
.J832	Administrative Law and Governmental Relations
.J836	Antitrust Task Force
.J84	Bankruptcy and Reorganization
.J847	Civil and Constitutional Rights
.J849	Civil Rights
	Civil Rights and Constitutional Rights see KF23 .J847
.J854	Claims and Governmental Relations
.J856	Commercial and Administrative Law
.J8563	Competition Policy and Antitrust Laws
.J8565	Constitution
.J8567	Constitution, Civil Rights, and Civil Liberties
.J8568	Courts and Competition Policy
	Courts and Intellectual Property see KF23 .J857
	Courts, Civil Liberties, and the Administration of Justice see KF23 .J857
	Courts, Intellectual Property, and the Administration of Justice see KF23 .J857
.J857	Courts, the Internet, and Intellectual Property
.J858	Crime
.J8584	Crime and Criminal Justice
.J8588	Crime, Terrorism, and Homeland Security
.J859	Criminal Justice
.J862	Economic and Commercial Law
	Immigration and Claims see KF23 .J8645
	Immigration, Border Security, and Claims see KF23 .J8645
.J864	Immigration, Citizenship, and International Law
.J8643	Immigration, Citizenship, Refugees, Border Security, and International Law
.J8645	Immigration, Refugees, and International Law
	Intellectual Property and Judicial Administration see KF23 .J857
	International Law, Immigration, and Refugees see KF23 .J8645
.J865	Judicial Impeachment
.J8663	Monopolies and Commercial Law

Judiciary

Subcommittees -- Continued

Code	Description
.J8664	Monopoly Power
.J8665	No. 3
.J8666	Number 1, 2, 3, 4, 5
.J869	Patents, Trade-marks, and Copyrights
.J8697	Presidential Inability
.J872	Reapportionment
.J873	Reform of Federal Criminal Laws
.J875	State Taxation of Interstate Commerce
.J878	Submerged Lands
.J883	Telecom and Antitrust
.L3	Labor

Subcommittees

Code	Description
.L33	Aid to the Physically Handicapped
.L36	No. 1
.L53	Library
.M4	Merchant Marine and Fisheries

Subcommittees

Code	Description
.M418	Alaskan Fisheries
.M42	Alaskan Problems
.M433	Coast Guard
.M434	Coast Guard and Navigation
.M436	Coast Guard, Coast and Geodetic Survey, and Navigation
.M4364	Coast Guard, Coast and Geodetic Survey, and Public Health Service
.M437	Conservation of Wildlife Resources
.M439	Environment and Natural Resources
.M445	Fisheries and Wildlife Conservation
.M447	Fisheries and Wildlife Conservation and the Environment
.M453	Fisheries Management
.M4538	Fuel Shortage
.M455	Inland Waterways and Fresh-Water Fisheries
.M457	Lighthouse Service
.M4574	Marine Insurance
.M4575	Maritime Affairs
.M458	Maritime Education and Training
.M464	Merchant Marine
.M466	Merchant Marine in Overseas Aviation
.M469	No. 1
.M4692	No. 2--Shellfish and Salt Water Fisheries
.M4693	No. 3--Panama Canal
.M4694	No. 4 on Miscellaneous Affairs

Oceanography see KF23 .M473

Oceanography and the Great Lakes see KF23 .M473

Merchant Marine and Fisheries
Subcommittees -- Continued
Oceanography, Great Lakes, and the Outer Continental Shelf
see KF23 .M473

.M473	Oceanography, Gulf of Mexico, and the Outer Continental Shelf
.M474	Oversight and Investigations
.M475	Panama Canal
.M4755	Panama Canal/Outer Continental Shelf
.M4757	Production in Shipbuilding Plants
.M4759	Salt-Water Fish and Shellfish Problems
.M476	Shipyard Profits
.M477	Shortage of Steel
.M48	Merchant Marine, Radio, and Fisheries
.M55	Military Affairs
	Subcommittees
.M553	Draft Deferment
.M5544	No. 1
.M5545	No. 5
.M5547	No. 8
.M555	No. 11
.M556	Procurement, Material & Personnel
.M557	Real Estate
.M56	Militia
.M57	Mines and Mining
	National Security see KF23 .A7
	Natural Resources see KF23 .I5
.N3	Naval Affairs
	Subcommittees
.N336	Conduct and Administration of Naval Affairs
.O94	Oversight and Government Reform
	Subcommittees
.O942	Domestic Policy
.O9425	Federal Workforce, Postal Service, and the District of Columbia
.O943	Government Management, Organization, and Procurement
.O944	Information Policy, Census, and National Archives
.O946	National Security and Foreign Affairs
.P3	Patents
	Subcommittees
.P33	Compulsory Licensing of Patents
.P335	Copyrights
.P344	Phosphate Rock Process Patents
.P348	Trade-Marks
.P46	Pensions
.P6	Post Office and Civil Service

Post Office and Civil Service -- Continued

Subcommittees

Code	Description
.P632	Census and Population
.P634	Census and Statistics
.P6345	Census, Statistics, and Postal Personnel
.P635	Civil Service
.P6355	Civil Service Commission and Personnel Programs
.P636	Compensation
.P638	Compensation and Employee Benefits
.P644	Employee Benefits
.P6445	Employee Ethics and Utilization
.P645	Employee Political Rights and Intergovernmental Programs
.P6452	H.R. 1935 and H.R. 5379
.P6453	H.R. 1939 and S. 971
.P64536	H.R. 4569
.P64538	H.R. 4808
.P6454	H.R. 4817
.P64545	H.R. 5179
.P6455	H.R. 7032 and Related Bills
.P6456	Human Resources
.P646	Investigations
.P652	Manpower
.P653	Manpower and Civil Service
.P656	Manpower Utilization
	Manpower Utilization and Departmental Personnel Management see KF23 .P656
	Oversight and Investigations see KF23 .P646
.P666	Position Classification
.P6663	Post Office and Postal Operations Subcommittee
.P6664	Postal Facilities and Mail
.P6665	Postal Facilities and Modernization
.P6667	Postal Facilities, Mail, and Labor Management
.P667	Postal Operations
.P6674	Postal Operations and Services
.P6677	Postal Personnel and Modernization
.P668	Postal Rates
.P672	Postal Service
.P6725	Presidential Pay Recommendations
.P6727	Quadrennial Pay Commission Task Force
.P673	Retirement and Employee Benefits
.P674	Retirement, Insurance, and Health Benefits
.P7	Post Office and Post Roads
	Subcommittees
.P7169	No. 1
.P717	No. 1, Salaries and allowances
.P7173	No. 2

KF23 TABLE OF HOUSE STANDING COMMITTEES (FOR KF23 HEARINGS)

Post Office and Post Roads
Subcommittees -- Continued

Code	Description
.P7175	No. 2, Classification of Mails and Postage Rates
.P718	No. 2, Offenses Against the Postal Service
.P719	No. 3, Post Office Quarters and Facilities
.P7194	No. 4
.P7195	No. 4, Air-Mail Service
.P72	No. 5. Special Postal Service
.P7215	No. 6, Air Mail Service
.P7217	No. 6, First and Second Class Mail, Domestic
.P722	No. 7, Air Mail Service
.P7225	No. 7, Rural Mail
.P7228	No. 8, Special Postal Services (Registry, Money Orders, Special Delivery, Collect on Delivery, Insurance)
.P724	No. 10, Railway Mail Service
.P725	No. 12--Railroad Mail Service
.P73	Printing
.P738	Private Land Claims
	Public Buildings and Grounds see KF23 .P8
.P76	Public Lands
	1805-1946: Committee on the Public Lands; 1946-1951: Committee on Public Lands
	Subcommittees
.P765	Indian Affairs
.P7655	Irrigation and Reclamation
.P766	Mines and Mining
.P767	No. 4 - Mines and Mining
.P768	Territorial and Insular Possessions
.P8	Public Works
	Subcommittees
.P823	Alaska Exposition for 1967
.P826	Appalachia
.P828	Appalachian Regional Development
.P829	Areas of Destruction of Hurricane Betsy
.P832	Conservation and Watershed Development
.P835	Economic Development
.P836	Economic Development Programs
.P838	Energy
.P843	Federal-Aid Highway Program
.P846	Flood Control
.P8463	Flood Control and Internal Development
.P855	Investigations and Oversight
.P857	Investigations and Review
.P864	Montana Flood Damage
.P868	Public Buildings and Grounds
.P872	Real Property Acquisition

KF23 TABLE OF HOUSE STANDING COMMITTEES (FOR HEARINGS) KF23

Public Works

Subcommittees -- Continued

.P874	Rivers and Harbors
.P876	Roads
.P887	Transportation
.P889	Water Resources
.P889	Watershed Development
.P896	Public Works and Transportation
	Subcommittees
.P89624	Aviation
.P89627	Coast Guard and Maritime Transportation
.P8963	Economic Development
	Economic Development, Public Buildings, and Emergency Management see KF23 .P8964
	Economic Development, Public Buildings, Hazardous Materials, and Pipeline Transportation see KF23 .P8964
	Ground Transportation see KF23 .P8966
	Highways and Transit see KF23 .P896317
.P896317	Highways, Transit, and Pipelines
.P89632	Investigations and Oversight
.P89634	Investigations and Review
.P89636	Oversight and Review
.P89637	Oversight, Investigations, and Emergency Management
	Public Buildings and Economic Development see KF23 .P8964
.P8964	Public Buildings and Grounds
.P8965	Railroads
.P89653	Railroads, Pipelines, and Hazardous Materials
.P8966	Surface Transportation
	Water Resources see KF23 .P8968
.P8968	Water Resources and Environment
.R25	Railways and Canals
.R34	Reform in the Civil Service
.R38	Resources
	Subcommittees
.R3845	Endangered Species
.R3846	Energy and Mineral Resources
.R38467	Fisheries and Oceans
.R3847	Fisheries Conservation, Wildlife, and Oceans
	Fisheries, Wildlife, and Oceans see KF23 .R3847
.R3848	Forests and Forest Health
.R3849	Improving the National Environmental Policy Act
.R385	Indian Trust Fund Management
.R38527	National Parks
	National Parks and Public Lands see KF23 .R3853
	National Parks, Forests, and Public Lands see KF23 .R3853

Resources
Subcommittees -- Continued

Code	Description
.R3853	National Parks, Recreation, and Public Lands
.R3854	Native American & Insular Affairs
.R387	Private Property Rights
.R3885	Salvage Timber and Forest Health
.R3886	Updating the National Environmental Policy Act
.R3887	Water and Power
.R3888	Water and Power Resources
.R389	Wetlands
.R4	Revision of the Laws
.R5	Rivers and Harbors
.R6	Roads
.R8	Rules

Subcommittees

Code	Description
.R827	Broadcasting
.R84	Federal Spending Limitation Proposals
.R873	Legislative and Budget Process
.R87317	Legislative Procedure
	Legislative Process see KF23 .R873
.R8733	Legislative Reorganization
.R8737	Rules of the House
.R874	Rules and Organization of the House

Science see KF23 .S39

Code	Description
.S3	Science and Astronautics

Subcommittees

Code	Description
.S334	Advanced Research and Technology
.S335	Aeronautics and Space Technology
.S336	Applications and Tracking and Data Acquisition
.S338	Earth Sciences
.S339	Energy
.S343	H.R. 10771
.S345	International Cooperation in Science and Space
.S348	Investigating Subcommittee
.S353	Manned Space Flight
.S356	NASA Oversight
.S357	National Bureau of Standards
.S3578	No. 1
.S358	No. 3
.S383	Science, Research, and Development
.S384	Selection of Astronauts
.S385	Space Science and Applications
.S386	Space Sciences
.S39	Science and Technology

Subcommittees

Science and Technology
Subcommittees -- Continued

Code	Description
.S3917	Advanced Energy Technologies and Energy Conservation Research, Development, and Demonstration
.S392	Aviation and Transportation R. & D
.S3924	Basic Research
.S3927	Domestic and International Scientific Planning, Analysis, and Cooperation
.S393	Domestic and International Scientific Planning and Analysis
	Energy see KF23 .S3935
	Energy and Environment see KF23 .S3935
.S3934	Energy Development and Applications
.S3935	Energy Research and Development
.S3936	Energy Research and Production
.S394	Energy Research, Development and Demonstration
.S395	Environment
.S396	Environment and the Atmosphere
.S3965	Environment, Technology, and Standards
.S397	Fossil and Nuclear Energy Research, Development and Demonstration
.S3973	International Scientific Cooperation
.S3975	Investigations and Oversight
.S3978	Natural Resources, Agriculture Research, and Environment
.S398	Natural Resources and Environment
	Research see KF23 .S3924
.S3984	Research and Science Education
	Science see KF23 .S399
.S3987	Science Policy
.S399	Science, Research, and Technology
	Space see KF23 .S3995
.S3995	Space and Aeronautics
	Space Science and Applications see KF23 .S3995
	Technology see KF23 .S39957
.S39955	Technology and Competitiveness
.S39956	Technology and Innovation
.S39957	Technology, Environment, and Aviation
.S3996	Technology Policy
	Transportation, Aviation, and Communications see KF23 .S3997
.S3997	Transportation, Aviation, and Materials
	Transportation, Aviation, and Weather see KF23 .S3997
	Science, Space, and Technology see KF23 .S39
.S6	Small Business
	Subcommittees
.S63	Access to Equity Capital and Business Opportunities
.S633	Activities of Regulatory Agencies

Small Business
Subcommittees -- Continued

Code	Description
.S6335	Antitrust and Restraint of Trade Activities Affecting Small Business
.S6337	Antitrust, Consumers, and Employment
.S6338	Antitrust, Impact of Deregulation, and Privatization
.S634	Antitrust, the Robinson-Patman Act, and Related Matters
.S635	Capital, Investment, and Business Opportunities
.S636	Commodities and Services
.S6363	Contracting and Technology
.S6365	Development of Rural Enterprises, Exports, and the Environment
.S6367	Empowerment
.S637	Energy and Agriculture
.S638	Energy and Environment
.S6384	Energy, Environment, and Safety Issues Affecting Small Business
.S639	Energy, Environment, Safety and Research
.S6392	Environment and Employment
.S6393	Environment and Labor
	Export Opportunities and Special Small Business Problems see KF23 .S6395
.S6395	Exports, Tax Policy, and Special Problems
	Exports, Tourism, and Special Problems see KF23 .S6395
.S6396	Finance and Tax
.S6397	General Oversight
.S64	General Oversight and Minority Enterprise
.S6414	General Oversight and the Economy
.S642	Government Procurement and International Trade
	Government Programs see KF23 .S644
.S644	Government Programs and Oversight
.S6443	Impact of Telephone Costs
.S646	Investigations and Oversight
	Minority Enterprise and General Oversight see KF23 .S65
.S65	Minority Enterprise, Finance, and Urban Development
.S665	Procurement, Exports, and Business Opportunities
	Procurement, Innovation, and Minority Enterprise Development see KF23 .S67
.S67	Procurement, Taxation, and Tourism
	Procurement, Tourism, and Rural Development see KF23 .S67
	Regulation and Business Opportunities see KF23 .S675
	Regulation and Paperwork see KF23 .S675
	Regulation, Business Opportunities, and Energy see KF23 .S675

KF23 TABLE OF HOUSE STANDING COMMITTEES (FOR KF23 HEARINGS)

Small Business

Subcommittees -- Continued

Regulation, Business Opportunities, and Technology see KF23 .S675

.S672	Regulations and Healthcare
.S673	Regulations, Health Care, and Trade
.S675	Regulatory Reform and Oversight
	Regulatory Reform and Paperwork Reduction see KF23 .S675
.S6755	Rural and Urban Entrepreneurship
.S6756	Rural Development, Entrepreneurship, and Trade
.S6757	Rural Enterprises, Agriculture, and Technology
.S6758	Rural Enterprises, Business Opportunities, and Special Small Business Problems
.S676	Rural Enterprises, Exports, and the Environment
.S6814	SBA and SBIC Authority and General Small Business Problems
.S6815	SBA and SBIC Authority, Minority Enterprise, and General Small Business Problems
.S6816	SBA and SBIC Legislation
	SBA and the General Economy see KF23 .S6815
.S6818	SBA Oversight and Minority Enterprise
.S6819	SBA, the General Economy, and Minority Enterprise Development
.S686	Special Small Business Problems
.S688	Tax, Access to Equity Capital, and Business Opportunities
.S6883	Tax, Finance, and Exports
.S689	Taxation and Finance
	Workforce, Empowerment, and Government Programs see KF23 .S6367
.S7	Standards of Official Conduct
.T4	Territories
	Transportation and Infrastructure see KF23 .P896
.U5	Un-American Activities
	Subcommittees
.U52	Legislation
.U55	United States Steel Corporation
.V4	Veterans' Affairs
	Subcommittees
.V422	Administration
.V4224	Administration and Finance in the Veterans' Administration Benefits see KF23 .V43
.V424	Cemeteries
.V426	Cemeteries and Burial Benefits
.V4275	Codification of Title 38
.V428	Compensation and Pensions

KF23 TABLE OF HOUSE STANDING COMMITTEES (FOR HEARINGS) KF23

Veterans' Affairs

Subcommittees -- Continued

Code	Description
.V429	Compensation, Pension, and Insurance
.V43	Compensation, Pension, Insurance, and Memorial Affairs
.V4315	Disability Assistance and Memorial Affairs
.V432	Economic Opportunity
.V433	Education and Training
	Education, Training, and Employment see KF23 .V436
.V43593	Education, Training, and Rehabilitation
.V436	Education, Training, Employment, and Housing
	Health see KF23 .V444
.V443	Hospitals
.V444	Hospitals and Health Care
	Housing see KF23 .V446
.V446	Housing and Memorial Affairs
.V455	Insurance
.V456	Insurance Bills
.V457	Intermediate Care
.V459	Medical Facilities and Benefits
.V46	Oversight (Special Oversight Subcommittee)
.V4613	Oversight (Special Select Committee on Oversight)
.V462	Oversight and Investigations
.V463	Philippines
.V464	Review WASP Bills
.V466	San Fernando Veterans' Administration Hospital Disaster
.V466148	Spanish War
.V46615	Spanish War Veterans
	Special Investigations see KF23 .V462
.W27	War Claims
	Subcommittees
.W276	No. 1
.W28	Water Power
.W3	Ways and Means
	Subcommittees
.W316	Administration of Internal Revenue Laws
.W32	Administration of the Social Security Laws
.W33	Customs and Tariff
.W34	Employee Fringe Benefits
.W3414	Excise Tax Technical and Administrative Problems
.W3415	Extension of Social Security to Puerto Rico and the Virgin Islands
.W342	Foreign Trade Policy
.W344	Health
	Human Resources see KF23 .W3464
.W3443	Income Security and Family Support
.W3446	Miscellaneous Revenue Measures

TABLE OF HOUSE STANDING COMMITTEES (FOR HEARINGS)

Ways and Means

Subcommittees -- Continued

Code	Subcommittee
.W3448	Narcotics
.W345	Oversight
.W346	Public Assistance
.W3464	Public Assistance and Unemployment Compensation
.W3468	Select Revenue Measures
.W347	Social Security
.W3475	Tariffs and Foreign Trade
.W348	Trade
.W349	Unemployment Compensation
.W3493	Unemployment Insurance
.W57	Woman Suffrage
.W6	World War Veterans' Legislation

Subcommittees

Code	Subcommittee
.W638	General Legislation
.W64	Hospitals
.W65	Insurance

TABLE OF HOUSE SELECT AND SPECIAL COMMITTEES (FOR HEARINGS)

KF24 — KF24

Code	Topic
.A24	Acts of Executive Agencies Beyond the Scope of Their Authority
.A3	Aging
	Subcommittees
.A344	Federal, State, and Community Services
.A355	Health and Long-Term Care
.A358	Housing and Consumer Interests
.A36	Human Services
.A374	Retirement Income and Employment
.A377	Rural Elderly (Task Force)
.A46	American Retail Federation
.A47	American Sugar Refining Co. and Others
.A8	Assassinations
.A84	Astronautics and Space Exploration
.C3	Campaign Expenditures
.C46	Certain Charges under House Resolution 543
.C468	Charges Against Two Members of the House of Representatives
.C47	Charges Made by Dr. William A. Wirt
.C48	Children, Youth, and Families
.C57	Committees
.C59	Commodity Transactions
.C6	Communist Aggression
	Subcommittees
.C615	Latin America
.C63	Communist Propaganda in the United States
.C64	Conservation of Wildlife Resources
.C65	Covert Arms Transactions with Iran
.C7	Crime
.D57	Disposition of Surplus Property
.D574	Distribution of House Rooms
.E3	Educational Programs Under GI Bill
.E32	Educational, Training, and Loan Guaranty Programs Under GI Bill
.E54	Energy
.E544	Energy Independence and Global Warming
.E8	Ethics
.E95	Expenditures in the War Department
	Subcommittees
.E956	No. 2 (Camps)
.E97	Export Control
.F37	Farm Security Administration
.F43	Federal Communications Commission
.F57	Fiscal Relations Between the United States and the District of Columbia
.F66	Food Shortages
.G68	Government Hospital for the Insane
.G685	Government Research

TABLE OF HOUSE SELECT AND SPECIAL COMMITTEES (FOR HEARINGS)

Code	Topic
.H58	Homeland Security
	Subcommittees
.H582	Cybersecurity, Science, and Research & Development
.H583	Emergency Preparedness and Response
.H5837	Infrastructure and Border Security
.H584	Intelligence and Counterterrorism
.H587	Rules
.H59	House Resolution 288
.H6	House Restaurant
.H8	Hunger
	Subcommittees
.H83	Domestic Task Force
.H85	International Task Force
.I5	Intelligence
	Subcommittees
.I53	Intelligence Community Management
.I54	Legislation
.I55	Oversight
.I56	Program and Budget Authorization
	Interstate Migration of Destitute Citizens see KF24 .N35
.I77	Irrigation
.K38	Katyn Forest Massacre
.L63	Lobby Investigation
.L632	Lobbying Activities
.M36	Management and Control of the House Restaurant
.M5	Missing Persons in Southeast Asia
.N3	Narcotics Abuse and Control
.N35	National Defense Migration
.N36	National Defense Program in Its Relation to Small Business of the United States
.N365	National Disabled Soldiers' League (Inc.)
.N37	National Labor Relations Board
.N38	National Security League
.O38	Official Conduct of George W. English, United States District Judge, Eastern District of Illinois
.O42	Old-Age Pension Organizations
.O58	Operations of the United States Air Services
.O6	Operations, Policies, and Affairs of the United States Shipping Board and Emergency Fleet Corporation
.O8	Outer Continental Shelf
.P33	Page Board on Education for Congressional Pages
.P67	Population
.P68	Post-War Economic Policy and Planning
	Subcommittees
.P684	Foreign Trade and Shipping
.P69	Post-war Military Policy

TABLE OF HOUSE SELECT AND SPECIAL COMMITTEES (FOR HEARINGS)

Code	Description
.P694	Preparation for and Response to Hurricane Katrina
.P7	Professional Sports
.P85	Pulp and Paper Investigation
.P87	Purchase of Danish Islands
.R39	Readjustment of Service Pay
.R42	Real Estate Bondholders' Reorganizations
.R43	Reform in the Civil Service
.S6	Small Business
	Subcommittees
.S633	Activities of Regulatory Agencies
.S636	Environmental Problems Affecting Small Business
	Government Procurement see KF24 .S647
.S647	Government Procurement and International Trade
	Minority Small Business Enterprise see KF24 .S654
.S654	Minority Small Business Enterprise and Franchising
.S657	No. 1
.S658	No. 2
.S659	No. 3
.S6593	No. 4 on Distribution Problems
.S676	Special Small Business Problems
.S67622	Urban Areas
.S6763	Social Security and Women (Task Force)
.S67633	Speaker's Commission on Pages
.S87	Survivors Benefits
.T39	Tax-Exempt Foundations and Comparable Organizations
.U17	U.S. Shipping Board Operations
.U528	Un-American Activities (1934)
.U53	Un-American Activities (1938-1944)
.U825	Use of Chemicals in Food Products
.U83	Use of Chemicals in Foods and Cosmetics
.V53	Victor L. Berger
.V67	Voting Irregularities of August 2, 2007
.W36	Water Power
.W42	Welfare and Education of Congressional Pages
.W43	Welfare Reform
	A subcommittee of the Committee on Agriculture, Committee on Education and Labor, and Committee on Ways and Means

KF25 TABLE OF JOINT CONGRESSIONAL COMMITTEES (FOR REPORTS) KF25

	Affairs of the District of Columbia see KF25 .D57
.A8	Atomic Energy
.C64	Conduct of the War
.C65	Conference Committees
.C66	Congressional Operations
.D57	District of Columbia, Affairs of
.E2	Economic
	Subcommittees
.E242	Economy in Government
.E252	International Exchange and Payments
.E257	Priorities and Economy in Government
.I5	Internal Revenue Taxation
.P67	Postage on Second-Class Mail Matter and Compensation for Transportation of Mail
.P7	Printing
.R28	Reconstruction
.T4	Tennessee Valley Authority

KF26 TABLE OF SENATE STANDING COMMITTEES (FOR REPORTS) KF26

Code	Committee/Subcommittee
.A3	Aeronautical and Space Sciences
.A33	NASA Authorization
	Agriculture and Forestry see KF26 .A35
.A35	Agriculture, Nutrition, and Forestry
	Subcommittees
.A3545	Environment, Soil Conservation, and Forestry
.A3565	Rural Development
.A6	Appropriations
.A7	Armed Services
	Subcommittees
.A735	Close Air Support
.A737	Drug Abuse in the Military
.A745	Electronic Battlefield
.B3	Banking and Currency
.B39	Banking, Housing, and Urban Affairs
	Subcommittees
.B3954	Securities
.B8	Budget
.C6	Commerce
	Subcommittees
.C654	Merchant Marine and Fisheries
.C69	Commerce, Science, and Transportation
.D5	District of Columbia
.E3	Education and Labor
.E55	Energy and Natural Resources
.E58	Environment and Public Works
.F5	Finance
.F6	Foreign Relations
	Subcommittees
.F684	United States Security Agreements and Commitments Abroad
.G6	Government Operations
	Subcommittees
.G648	Executive Reorganization and Government Research
.G655	Intergovernmental Relations
.G658	Investigations
.G68	Governmental Affairs
	Subcommittees
.G684	Investigations
	Health, Education, Labor and Pensions see KF26 .L27
.H65	Homeland Security and Governmental Affairs
	Subcommittees
.H654	Investigations
.I45	Indian Affairs
.I5	Interior and Insular Affairs
	Subcommittees

KF26 TABLE OF SENATE STANDING COMMITTEES (FOR REPORTS) KF26

Interior and Insular Affairs
Subcommittees -- Continued

Code	Description
.I546	Outer Continental Shelf
.I548	Public Lands
	Interstate Commerce see KF26 .I55
.I55	Interstate and Foreign Commerce
.J8	Judiciary
	Subcommittees
.J826	Antitrust and Monopoly
.J834	Constitutional Amendments
.J836	Constitutional Rights
.J845	Investigate the Administration of the Internal Security Act and Other Internal Security Laws
.J8455	Investigate Individuals Representing the Interests of Foreign Governments
.J846	Judicial Machinery, Improvements in
.J8464	Juvenile Delinquency
.J847	Revision and Codification
.J874	Separation of Powers
.L27	Labor and Human Resources
.L3	Labor and Public Welfare
	Subcommittees
.L364	Labor
.M5	Military Affairs
	Subcommittees
.M588	War Contracts
.M59	War Mobilization
.P6	Post Office and Civil Service
.P8	Public Works
	Subcommittees
.P835	Air and Water Pollution
.R8	Rules and Administration
	Subcommittees
.R836	Computer Services
.V4	Veterans' Affairs

TABLE OF SENATE SELECT AND SPECIAL COMMITTEES (FOR REPORTS)

KF27		KF27

Code	Committee
.A3	Aging
	Subcommittees
.A335	Long-Term Care
.E87	Ethics
.G7	Governmental Operations with Respect to Intelligence Activities
.I5	Intelligence
.I53	Investigate Alleged Outrages in the Southern States
.N3	National Emergencies and Delegated Emergency Powers
.O4	Official Conduct
.O7	Organization of Congress
.P7	Presidential Campaign Activities
.R4	Revision of the Laws
.S4	Senate Committee System
.S6	Small Business
.S66	Space and Astronautics
.S7	Standards and Conduct
.T4	Termination of the National Emergency

KF28 TABLE OF HOUSE STANDING COMMITTEES (FOR REPORTS) KF28

Code	Subject
.A3	Agriculture
.A6	Appropriations
.A7	Armed Services
	Subcommittees
.A725	Air Defense of Southeastern United States
	Alleged Drug Abuse in the Armed Forces see KF28 .A739
.A728	Antisubmarine Warfare
.A7285	Armed Services Investigating
.A7288	Army Procurement of the M561, Gama Goat
.A729	Army Tank Program
.A7315	Commercial Air Transportation for Service Personnel While on Authorized Leave
.A732	Defense Aspects of the Equal Employment Opportunity Program
.A7324	Defense Communications
.A733	Dept. of Defense Worldwide Communications Subcommittee
.A734	Disciplinary Problems in the U.S. Navy
.A735	Disturbances on Military Bases
.A739	Drug Abuse in the Armed Forces, Alleged
.A746	Exchanges and Commissaries
	Intelligence and Military Application of Nuclear Energy
.A7626	MBFR Panel
.A7627	Panel on Indian Ocean Forces Limitation and Conventional Arms Transfer Limitation
.A763	Panel on the Strategic Arms Limitation Talks and the Comprehensive Test Ban Treaty
.A7637	Investigate the Sinking of the U.S.S. Guitarro
.A764	Investigations
.A766	M-16 Rifle Program
.A773	Military Airlift
.A7732	National Defense Posture
.A774	Nato Standardization, Interoperability, and Readiness
.A7744	North Atlantic Treaty Organization Commitments
.A776	Proposed Disposal of U.S. Naval Academy Dairy Farm
.A778	Real Estate
.A779	Recruiting and Retention of Military Personnel
.A7795	Relocation of the U.S. Army Intelligence School from Fort Holabird to Fort Huachuca
.A78	Retired-Pay Revisions
.A782	Seapower
.A784	Supplemental Service Benefits
.A786	Special Investigations
.A788	Survivors' Benefits
.A7884	Transfer of Naval Vessels to Foreign Countries
.A7885	Transportation
.A7887	U.S.S. Pueblo

KF28 TABLE OF HOUSE STANDING COMMITTEES (FOR REPORTS) KF28

Armed Services
Subcommittees -- Continued

Code	Description
.A789	Utilization of Manpower in the Military
.B3	Banking and Currency
	Subcommittees
.B345	Domestic Finance
.B354	Home Financing Practices and Procedures
.B356	Housing
.B375	Small Business
.B5	Banking, Finance, and Urban Affairs
.B8	Budget
.C5	Claims
.C66	Commerce and Manufactures
.D5	District of Columbia
	Subcommittees
.D533	Investigate Crime and Law Enforcement in the District of Columbia
.E3	Education and Labor
	Subcommittees
.E332	Education (General Subcommittee)
.E333	Education (Select Subcommittee)
.E345	Labor
.E347	Labor-Management Relations
.E35	Merit Pay
.E36	Education and the Workforce
.E44	Elections
.E55	Energy and Commerce
	Subcommittees
.E552	Oversight and Investigations
.F55	Financial Services
.F6	Foreign Affairs
	Subcommittees
.F642	Europe
.F645	Foreign Economic Policy
.F655	International Organizations and Movements
.F663	National Security Policy and Scientific Developments
.F665	Near East
.F669	State Department Organization and Foreign Operations
	Government Operations see KF28 .G6
.G6	Government Reform
	Subcommittees
.G636	Conservation and Natural Resources
.G642	Foreign Operations and Government Information
.G65	Government Information, Justice, and Agriculture
.G677	Special Studies
	Government Reform and Oversight see KF28 .G6

KF28 TABLE OF HOUSE STANDING COMMITTEES (FOR REPORTS) KF28

Code	Committee/Subcommittee
.H57	Homeland Security
.H6	House Administration
	Subcommittees
.H638	Electrical and Mechanical Office Equipment
.H653	Legislative Service Organizations
.I45	Indian Affairs
.I5	Interior and Insular Affairs
	Subcommittees
.I525	Mines and Mining
.I53	Internal Security
	Subcommittees
.I534	Loyalty-Security
.I54	International Relations
.I55	Interstate and Foreign Commerce
	Subcommittees
.I5535	Commerce and Finance
.I555	Investigations
.J8	Judiciary
	Subcommittees
.J848	H. Res. 920
.J853	Immigration, Citizenship, and International Law
.J8666	Number 1, 2, 3, 4, 5
.M4	Merchant Marine and Fisheries
	Subcommittees
.M436	Coast Guard, Coast and Geodetic Survey, and Navigation
.M45	Military Affairs
.N38	Natural Resources
.O94	Oversight and Government Reform
.P3	Patents
.P39	Payment of Pensions, Bounty and Back Pay
.P6	Post Office and Civil Service
	Subcommittees
.P634	Census and Statistics
.P642	Investigations
.P645	Manpower and Civil Service
.P647	Manpower Utilization
	Post Office and Post Roads see KF28 .P6
.P8	Public Works
	Subcommittees
.P845	Flood Control and Internal Development
.P896	Public Works and Transportation
.R37	Resources
.R4	Revision of the Laws
.R73	Roads and Canals
.R8	Rules
	Subcommittees

KF28 TABLE OF HOUSE STANDING COMMITTEES (FOR REPORTS) KF28

Rules

Subcommittees -- Continued

Code	Committee/Subcommittee
.R854	Legislative Reorganization
	Science see KF28 .S39
.S3	Science and Astronautics
	Subcommittees
.S33	Advanced Research and Technology
.S333	Aeronautics and Space Technology
.S339	Energy
.S378	International Cooperation in Science and Space
.S382	Science, Research, and Development
.S384	Space Science and Applications
.S39	Science and Technology
.S6	Small Business
	Subcommittees
.S672	Activities of Regulatory Agencies
.S678	Special Small Business Problems
.S7	Standards of Official Conduct
.T4	Territories
.U5	Un-American Activities
.V4	Veterans' Affairs
.W3	Ways and Means

TABLE OF HOUSE SELECT AND SPECIAL COMMITTEES (FOR REPORTS)

Code	Topic
.A5	Alleged Corruptions in Government
.A8	Assassinations
.C3	Campaign Expenditures
.C7	Crime
.D57	District of Columbia
.G37	Gardiner Investigation
.G6	Government Research
.I53	Intelligence
.I55	Interstate Migration of Destitute Citizens
.M35	Matthew Patterson
.M78	Mount Pleasant, N.Y.
.N37	National Defense
.N38	National Labor Relations Board
.N4	New Orleans Riots
.O8	Outer Continental Shelf
.P68	Post Office Department
.P694	Preparation for and Response to Hurricane Katrina
.P7	Professional Sports
.R35	Relief of Persons Imprisoned for Debt
.R37	Revisal and Unfinished Business
.S6	Small Business
	Subcommittees
.S633	Activities of Regulatory Agencies
.S645	Government Procurement
.S664	Minority Small Business Enterprise
.S676	Small Business Problems in Smaller Towns and Urban Areas
.U5	United States Involvement in Southeast Asia
.V67	Voting Irregularities of August 2, 2007
.W55	William Hill

KF30 TABLE FOR TRADE AGREEMENTS AND TARIFFS ON PARTICULAR COMMODITIES (CUTTER NUMBER) KF30

.xA1-.xA7	General. By date
.xA8-.xZ	By country, A-z

TABLE FOR LAW REPORTS AND RELATED MATERIALS (1 NUMBER)

0	Reports
0.1	Digests
0.2	Citators. Tables of cases overruled, etc.
0.4	Conversion tables. Blue books
0.6	General indexes
	For indexes relating to a particular publication, reporter system, or digest (e.g. descriptive-word indexes), see the publication
0.7	Dockets of cases pending
0.9	Records and briefs

KF32 TABLE FOR LAW REPORTS AND RELATED MATERIALS (CUTTER NUMBER) KF32

.x	Reports
.x1	Digests
.x2	Citators. Tables of cases overruled, etc.
.x3	Conversion tables. Blue books
.x4	General indexes
	For indexes relating to a particular publication, reporter system, or digest (e.g. descriptive-word indexes), see the publication
.x5	Dockets of cases pending
.x6	Records and briefs

KF33 TABLE FOR LAW SOCIETIES (CUTTER NUMBER) KF33

.xA1-.xA4	Proceedings. Annual reports
.xA5-.xA6	Official monographs
.xA7-.xZ	Other monographs. By author, A-Z

KF34 TABLE FOR COLLECTIVE LABOR DISPUTES, BY INDUSTRY (2 CUTTER NUMBERS) KF34

.x	General (Table KF7)
.x1A-.x1Z	Particular cases. By employer, A-Z

KF35 TABLE FOR SOURCES OF POWER (1 NUMBER) KF35

Number	Description
0	General. Comprehensive (Table KF6)
0.1	Federal, state, and local jurisdiction (Table KF6)
0.2	Corporate structure. Holding companies. Antitrust measures (Table KF6)
0.3	Finance (Table KF6)
0.4	Valuation. Accounting (Table KF6)
0.5	Ratemaking (Table KF6)
0.6	Operation (Table KF6)
0.65	Liability (Table KF6)
0.8.A-Z	Particular companies, A-Z
	Subarrange each by Table KF7

KF36 TABLE FOR SOURCES OF POWER (7 CUTTER NUMBERS) KF36

.x	General. Comprehensive (Table KF7)
.x1	Federal, state, and local jurisdiction (Table KF7)
.x2	Corporate structure. Holding companies. Antitrust measures (Table KF7)
.x3	Finance (Table KF7)
.x4	Valuation. Accounting (Table KF7)
.x5	Ratemaking (Table KF7)
.x6	Operation (Table KF7)
.x65	Liability (Table KF7)
.x7A-.x7Z	Particular companies, A-Z

KF37 TABLE FOR ELECTRONIC DATA PROCESSING, BY SUBJECT (2 CUTTER NUMBERS) KF37

1	Federal law
2	Collective state law

KF38 TABLE FOR ELECTRONIC DATA PROCESSING, BY KF38
SUBJECT (2 SUCCESSIVE CUTTER NUMBERS)

.x Federal law
.x2 Collective state law

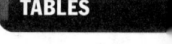

KF39 TABLE FOR SUBARRANGEMENT OF BIOGRAPHY (CUTTER NUMBER) KF39

.xA3	Autobiography. By date
	Letters. Correspondence
.xA4	General collections. By date of publication
.xA41-.xA49	Collections of letters to particular individuals, by correspondent (alphabetically)
	For correspondence on a particular subject, see the subject
.xA5-.xZ	Biography and criticism

KF40 TABLE FOR SUBARRANGEMENT OF STATE CONSTITUTIONS (1 NUMBER) KF40

Call Number	Description
.A15	Collections
(.A18-.A189)	Documents of revision commission
	The Library of Congress discontinued use of this span of numbers in 2009
	see KF40 .A19
.A19	Documents of revision commission. By date
	Class with existing constitution
(.A2-.A229)	Proceedings. Debates
	The Library of Congress discontinued use of this span of numbers in 2009
	see KF40 .A23
.A23	Proceedings. Debates
(.A25-.A259)	Preliminary drafts of new constitution
	The Library of Congress discontinued use of this span of numbers in 2009
	see KF40 .A26
.A26	Preliminary drafts of new constitution. By date
	Class with existing constitution
(.A28-.A2849)	Miscellaneous documents
	The Library of Congress discontinued use of this span of numbers in 2009
	see KF40 .A2849
.A2849	Miscellaneous documents
.A285	Contemporary criticism. Private proposals and drafts
.A29	Works on the legislative history (origin and making) of the constitution
	Texts of the constitution
.A295	Serials
	Monographs
(.A3-.A399)	Official editions (with or without annotations)
	The Library of Congress discontinued use of this span of numbers in 2009
	see KF40 .A399
.A399	Official editions (with or without annotations). By date
	Unofficial editions
(.A4-.A59)	Unannotated texts
	The Library of Congress discontinued use of this span of numbers in 2009
	see KF40 .A59
.A59	Unannotated texts. By date
.A6	Annotated texts. Commentaries
	Amendments
.A7	Collective

KF40 TABLE FOR SUBARRANGEMENT OF STATE CONSTITUTIONS (1 NUMBER) KF40

Amendments -- Continued

.A8-.A899 Particular amendments

Arrange chronologically, by means of successive Cutter numbers, according to date of adoption or rejection

Under each amendment:

.A2-.A39	*Texts*
.A4-.A59	*Official reports and monographs*
.A6-.Z	*General works*

For works on particular amendments, see the subject

KFA-KFZ UNITED STATES - STATES AND TERRITORIES KFA-KFZ

Table of subject subdivisions for the Law of the States (except California and New York) and territories of the United States

1	Bibliography
	Legislative documents
	Bills
6	Collections
7	Digests
8.A-Z	Calendars. By committee, A-Z
9	Debates
10	Indexes
	Committee documents
	Hearings
	Joint
10.8.A-Z	Serials. By committee or subcommittee, A-Z
	Subarrange by title
11	Monographs. By committee or subcommittee and initial date of hearings
11.3.A-Z	Upper house. By committee or subcommittee, A-Z, and initial date of hearings
11.4.A-Z	Lower house. By committee or subcommittee, A-Z, and initial date of hearings
	Reports
	Class here only those reports issued to accompany specific bills when they are reported out of a committee to its parent legislative body after hearings have been held and/or the committee has considered and made its recommendations on the bill in question. Class other types of reports emanating from a legislative commitee with the appropriate topic.
	Joint
11.58	General
	Individual committees and subcommittees
11.6.A-Z	Serials. By committee or subcommittee, A-Z
	Subarrange by title
11.62.A-Z	Monographs. By committee or subcommittee, A-Z, and date of original publication
	Upper house
11.7.A-Z	Serials. By committee or subcommittee, A-Z
	Subarrange by title
11.72.A-Z	Monographs. By committee or subcommittee, A-Z, and date of original publication
	Lower house
11.8.A-Z	Serials. By committee or subcommittee, A-Z
	Subarrange by title
11.82.A-Z	Monographs. By committee or subcommittee, A-Z, and date of original publication
12	Index to proceedings

KFA-KFZ UNITED STATES - STATES AND TERRITORIES KFA-KFZ

Legislative documents -- Continued

History of bills and resolutions. Legislation passed or vetoed

15	Serials
15.2	Monographs. By date of session or of initial session

Journals

18	Serials
18.2	Monographs. By date of session or of initial session
18.5	Indexes
19	Governors' messages. By date

Class here messages relating to legislation
For governor's messages in general, see J87

20	Other

Statutes and administrative regulations

Statutes

Session laws

25.A-Z	Serials

Under each:

.A2-.A29	*Official editions. Arrange chronologically*
.A3-.Z	*Unofficial editions. By publisher or editor*

25.2	Monographs. By date of session or of initial session
25.5	Digests of session laws. By date of session

Class here monographs only
For serials see KFA-KFZ 38

Codification. Revision of statutes

27.A-Z	Code commissions. Revision committees. By committee, A-Z

Under each:

.xA15-.xA159	*General serials*
.xA2	*Organic acts. By date*
	Reports
.xA3-.xA34	*Serials*
.xA35	*Monographs. By date*
.xA4	*Notes. By date*
.xA5	*Draft revisions. By date*
.xA8	*Other. By date*

For commissions or committees limited to a specific subject, see the subject

28	Code revision bills

General compilations of statutes

Including "codes of law," "codified statutes," "general statutes," "revised statutes," etc.

29	Serials

Including codes republished on a regular basis and cataloged as serials

KFA-KFZ UNITED STATES - STATES AND TERRITORIES KFA-KFZ

Statutes and administrative regulations

Statutes

General compilations of statutes -- Continued

30 Monographs. By date of enactment, revision (re-enactment), officially designated date of codification, or date of first publication

Under each:

.A2-.A29 *Official editions (with or without annotations)*

Arrange chronologically

.A4-.A49 *Unofficial editions (with or without annotations)*

Arrange chronologically

30.5.A-Z Selective compilations of statutes. By editor or compiler, A-Z

For compilations of statutes on a particular subject, see the subject

31 Supplemental services

Digests, citators, indexes, etc. see KFA-KFZ 38

Administrative regulations

Proclamations and executive orders

34.A2 Serials

34.A5 Monographs. By date

34.A55 Indexes. By date

Comprehensive collections of administrative regulations. Administrative codes

34.5 Serials

Including compilations republished on a regular basis and cataloged as serials

35 Monographs. By date of enactment, revision (re-enactment), officially designated date of codification, or date of first publication

Under each:

.A2-.A29 *Official editions (with or without annotations)*

Arrange chronologically

.A4-.A49 *Unofficial editions (with or without annotations)*

Arrange chronologically

35.5.A-Z Selective compilations of administrative regulations. By editor or compiler, A-Z

For compilations of administrative regulations on a particular subject, see the subject

36 Registers. Supplementary services

Digests, citators, indexes, etc. see KFA-KFZ 38

38 Digests of statutes and/or administrative regulations

39 Citators to statutes and/or administrative regulations

40 Indexes to statutes and/or administrative regulations

TABLES

KFA-KFZ UNITED STATES - STATES AND TERRITORIES KFA-KFZ

Statutes and administrative regulations -- Continued

41	Other bibliographic aids. Tables of popular names, etc. By date of publication
	Law reports and related materials
45-45.9	Highest court of appeals. Supreme Court (Table KF31)
	Lower courts
47-47.9	General. Various courts (Table KF31)
	Including highest court and lower courts, and state cases decided by federal courts, combined
	Intermediate appellate courts. Courts of Appeals
48-48.9	General. Collective (Table KF31)
	Including reports of the only intermediate appellate court of a state
49.A-Z	Particular courts, A-Z
	Subarrange each by Table KF32
	Trial courts (County, district, superior, circuit courts)
51-51.9	Collective (Table KF31)
	Including reports of the only intermediate appellate court of a state
52.A-Z	Particular courts. By county, etc., A-Z
	Subarrange each by Table KF32
	Minor courts
53.A-Z	Municipal courts. By city, etc., A-Z
	Subarrange each by Table KF32
54	Other
	Court of Claims
54.5	Reports
54.51	Digests
54.52	Citators. Tables of cases overruled, etc.
54.54	Conversion tables. Blue books
54.56	General indexes
54.57	Dockets of cases pending
54.59	Records and briefs
55.A-Z	Regional and local reports, A-Z
	Subarrange each by Table KF32
57	Digests of various reports
59	Citators to various reports
60	Other auxiliary publications
	e.g. Conversion tables, chronological tables, tables of popular names of cases
61	General indexes. Indexes to various publications
65	Encyclopedias
66	Law dictionaries
	Including "Words and phrases"
67	Uniform state laws
68	Form books
<69>	Periodicals

KFA-KFZ UNITED STATES - STATES AND TERRITORIES KFA-KFZ

70	Yearbooks
	Class here only publications issued annually, containing information, statistics, etc. about the year just past
	Judicial statistics
71	General
	Criminal statistics
71.5	General
71.55	Juvenile crime
	Directories
	see KF192.A+
72	Congresses
75	Legal research. Legal bibliography. Legal draftsmanship
	Class here works on state law only
	For general works, see KF240+
	Cf. KFA-KFZ 421.5.B5 Legislative draftsmanship
	Cf. KFA-KFZ 441.D35 Drafting of administrative regulations
75.5	Electronic data processing. Information retrieval
	The legal profession. Practice of law
	For general works, see KF297+
76	Admission to the bar (Table KF9)
	Legal ethics, discipline, disbarment
76.5.A2	General (Table KF7)
76.5.A6-Z	Particular cases. By attorney
77	Law office management. Attorneys' and legal secretaries' handbooks, manuals, etc. of state law
77.5.A-Z	Special topics, A-Z
77.5.A38	Advertising
77.5.A95	Automation
77.5.F4	Fees
77.5.G7	Group arrangements. Prepaid legal services
77.5.I57	Insurance
77.5.M37	Marketing of legal services
	History
78	General
78.8.A-Z	Special topics, A-Z
78.8.W5	Witchcraft trials
79	Law reform. Criticism
	General and comprehensive works
80	Treatises
81	Individual essays. Addresses. Examination aids. Aids for particular groups of users
82.A-Z	Works for particular groups of users, A-Z
82.B87	Businesspeople (Table KF7)
82.C65	College students (Table KF7)
84.5.A-Z	Works on diverse aspects of a particular subject and falling within several branches of the law, A-Z
84.5.A45	Animals (Table KF7)

KFA-KFZ UNITED STATES - STATES AND TERRITORIES KFA-KFZ

General and comprehensive works
Works on diverse aspects of a particular subject and falling within several branches of the law, A-Z -- Continued

84.5.C65	Computers (Table KF7)
84.5.D63	Dogs (Table KF7)
84.5.H67	Horses (Table KF7)
84.5.P7	Poverty. Legal protection of the poor. Handbooks for legal services (Table KF7)
84.5.S95	Swimming pools (Table KF7)
85	Equity
87	Conflict of laws (Table KF9)
	General principles and concepts
88.5	Statutory construction and interpretation
89	Conflicting decisions
90.A-Z	Principles and concepts applying to several branches of the law, A-Z
90.C6	Codification
90.D3	Damages
90.F6	Form requirements. Formalities
90.L5	Limitation of actions
90.T5	Time. Notice. Deadlines
	Private law, works on the law of the Civil code see KFA-KFZ 80+
	Natural persons
	General. Status. Capacity
91.A1	General (Table KF7)
91.A25-Z	Particular groups of persons, A-Z
91.A3	Aged. Older people (Table KF7)
91.H3	Handicapped. People with disabilities (Table KF7)
91.I5	Insane persons. Persons of unsound mind (Table KF7)
91.M5	Minors (Table KF7)
	Older people see KFA-KFZ 91.A3
	People with disabilities see KFA-KFZ 91.H3
91.W6	Women (Table KF7)
92	Conservatorships (Table KF9)
	Cf. KFA-KFZ 106+ Guardian and ward
93	Recording and registration. Registers of births, marriages, deaths. Vital statistics. Birth and death certificates (Table KF9)
	Domestic relations
94	General. Comprehensive (Table KF9)
	Domestic relations courts. Children's courts
94.5	General. Collective (Table KF9)
94.6.A-Z	Local courts. By county, A-Z
	For statistics see KFA-KFZ 599.A+
	Marriage
95	General (Table KF9)
95.5	Invalid and nullifiable marriages (Table KF9)

Natural persons
Domestic relations
Marriage -- Continued
Husband and wife
Cf. KFA-KFZ 567.W53 Wife abuse

96	Status of married women (Table KF9)
97	Marital property relationships (Table KF9)
100	Divorce. Separation (Table KF9)
102	Unmarried couples (Table KF9)
103	Same-sex marriages. Civil unions (Table KF9)
	Including quasi-marital relationships

Parent and child
Cf. KFA-KFZ 567.C5 Child abuse

104	General (Table KF9)
104.4	Illegitimate children (Table KF9)
104.5	Adoption (Table KF9)
	Parental rights and duties. Property of minors. Custody
104.6	General (Table KF9)
104.8	Support. Desertion and nonsupport (Table KF9)

Guardian and ward
Cf. KFA-KFZ 92 Conservatorships

106	General (Table KF9)
107	Guardians ad litem (Table KF9)

Property

110	General (Table KF9)
110.5	Right of property
	Real property. Land law
112	General (Table KF9)
112.5	Alien landownership (Table KF9)
	Land tenure
	Ownership and possession
114.A1	General (Table KF7)
114.A5-Z	Special topics, A-Z
	Community associations of property owners see KFA-KFZ 114.H66
114.C6	Condominium (Table KF7)
114.H66	Homeowners' associations. Community associations of property owners (Table KF7)
	Tenancy
117	General. Leaseholds. Landlord and tenant (Table KF9)
117.3	Commercial leases (Table KF9)
	Including both real and personal property
117.5	Farm tenancy (Table KF9)
119	Future estates and interests in land. Limitations (Table KF9)
120	Concurrent ownership. Joint tenancy. Tenancy by the entirety (Table KF9)

Property

Real property. Land law

Land tenure -- Continued

121	Possessory actions. Ejectment (Table KF9)
122	Restraints on alienation (Table KF9)
123.A-Z	Special topics, A-Z
123.B6	Boundaries. Fences (Table KF7)
123.D6	Dower. Curtesy (Table KF7)
123.F57	Fixtures (Table KF7)
123.P2	Partition (Table KF7)
123.S8	Subsoil rights (Table KF7)
123.W2	Water rights. Riparian rights (Table KF7)
124	Easements (Table KF9)
125	Covenants running with the land. Restrictive covenants (Table KF9)
	Transfer of rights in land
126	General. Vendor and purchaser. Real estate transactions (Table KF9)
127	Conveyancing. Title investigation. Deeds. Registration (Table KF9)
127.3	Settlement costs (Table KF9)
127.5	Description of land. Surveying (Table KF9)
128.A-Z	Other modes of transfer, A-Z
128.A3	Adverse possession (Table KF7)
128.J8	Judicial process or decree. Judicial sales (Table KF7)
128.T2	Tax deeds (Table KF7)
	Mortgages
130	General (Table KF9)
130.5.A-Z	Special topics, A-Z
130.5.D58	Discrimination in mortgage loans (Table KF7)
130.5.F6	Foreclosure (Table KF7)
130.5.R48	Reverse mortgages (Table KF7)
	Personal property
134	General (Table KF9)
134.5.A-Z	Special topics, A-Z
134.5.D47	Detinue (Table KF7)
134.5.F8	Future interests (Table KF7)
134.5.R4	Replevin (Table KF7)
	Trusts and trustees
137	General (Table KF9)
138	Trust companies (Table KF9)
139.A-Z	Special topics, A-Z
139.A25	Accounting (Table KF7)
139.C4	Charitable trusts (Table KF7)
139.C9	Cy pres doctrine (Table KF7)
139.L3	Land trusts (Table KF7)
139.L54	Life insurance trusts (Table KF7)

KFA-KFZ UNITED STATES - STATES AND TERRITORIES KFA-KFZ

Trusts and trustees
Special topics, A-Z -- Continued
139.L57 Living trusts (Table KF7)
Massachusetts trusts, business trusts see KFA-KFZ 207.7
140 Estate planning (Table KF9)
Succession upon death
142 General (Table KF9)
Testate succession. Wills. Probate law and practice. Probate courts
For probate records see KFA-KFZ 516.A+
144 General (Table KF9)
144.2.A-Z Particular courts. By county, etc., A-Z
144.5.A-Z Special topics, A-Z
144.5.A25 Accounting (Table KF7)
144.5.C65 Contested wills (Table KF7)
144.5.C67 Costs. Fees (Table KF7)
Collected wills
144.8.A1 General
144.8.A3-Z By county, etc., A-Z
Particular wills
see KF759
146 Intestate succession (Table KF9)
147 Administration of decedents' estates. Execution of wills. Personal representatives (Table KF9)
148.A-Z Special topics, A-Z
148.U6 Unclaimed estates (Table KF7)
Contracts
General principles
150 General works (Table KF9)
151.A-Z Special topics, A-Z
151.B74 Breach of contract (Table KF7)
151.F7 Fraud (Table KF7)
151.5 Government contracts. Public contracts. Purchasing and procurement (Table KF9)
Particular contracts
152 Comprehensive. Commercial law (Table KF9)
Contract of service. Master and servant
154 General (Table KF9)
154.5.A-Z Special topics, A-Z
154.5.A6 Apprentices (Table KF7)
Contract for work and labor (Contract for services). Independent contractors
155 General (Table KF9)
155.5 Mechanics' liens (Table KF9)
155.8.A-Z Particular types of contracts, A-Z
155.8.B8 Building and construction (Table KF7)
155.8.C65 Computer contracts (Table KF7)

Contracts
Particular contracts -- Continued
Sale of goods

156	General (Table KF9)
156.5.A-Z	Documents of title, A-Z
156.5.A2	General
156.5.B5	Bills of lading (Table KF7)
156.5.W3	Warehouse receipts (Table KF7)
156.7.A-Z	Special topics, A-Z
156.7.C6	Conditions and warranties. Implied warranties
	Contracts involving bailments
159	General (Table KF9)
159.5.A-Z	Particular contracts, A-Z
159.5.H57	Hire of goods (Table KF7)
159.5.P3	Parking of vehicles (Table KF7)
	Including airplanes
	Public contracts see KFA-KFZ 151.5
	Negotiable instruments
	General. Bills of exchange
160	General. Comprehensive (Table KF9)
160.5.A-Z	Special topics, A-Z
161	Checks (Table KF9)
161.5.A-Z	Other, A-Z
161.5.M67	Money orders (Table KF7)
161.5.P7	Promissory notes (Table KF7)
	Banking
165	General (Table KF9)
166.A-Z	Particular kinds of banks, A-Z
166.A4	Agricultural credit banks (Table KF7)
166.B8	Building and loan associations (Table KF7)
166.C6	Cooperative banks. Credit unions (Table KF7)
	Credit unions see KFA-KFZ 166.C6
166.M67	Mortgage banks (Table KF7)
166.S2	Saving banks (Table KF7)
167.A-Z	Particular banking transactions, A-Z
167.C6	Collecting of accounts. Collection laws (Table KF7)
	For collection agencies see KFA-KFZ 282.C64
167.D44	Deposits and accounts (Table KF7)
	Including deposit insurance
167.E43	Electronic funds transfer (Table KF7)
167.E8	Escrow business (Table KF7)
	Investment services see KFA-KFZ 167.S43
167.L47	Letters of credit (Table KF7)
167.R43	Record keeping (Table KF7)
167.S43	Securities processing. Investment services (Table KF7)
168.A-Z	Particular banks, A-Z
169	Foreign-exchange brokerage (Table KF9)

Contracts
Particular contracts -- Continued
Loan of money

170	General. Interest. Usury (Table KF9)
171	Consumer credit. Small loans. Finance charges (Table KF9)
174	Suretyship. Guaranty (Table KF9)
	For suretyship insurance, bonding see KFA-KFZ 192.S8
	Secured transactions
175	General (Table KF9)
176.A-Z	Particular transactions, A-Z
176.C4	Chattel mortgages (Table KF7)
176.C6	Conditional sale. Installment sale (Table KF7)
176.L5	Liens (Table KF7)
176.T7	Trust receipts (Table KF7)
	Marketing of securities. Investments. Stock exchanges
	For issuing of securities see KFA-KFZ 214.A1+
179	General (Table KF9)
179.5.A-Z	Special topics, A-Z
179.5.B7	Brokers (Table KF7)
179.5.I5	Investment trusts. Investment companies. Mutual funds (Table KF7)
179.5.L4	Legal investments. Trust investments (Table KF7)
	Commodity exchanges. Produce exchanges
180.A1	General (Table KF9)
180.A5-Z	Particular commodities, A-Z
	Subarrange each by Table KF7
184	Carriers. Carriage of goods and passengers (Table KF9)
	Insurance
185	General. Insurance business. Agents. Brokers (Table KF9)
	For taxation see KFA-KFZ 477.5.I6
	Insurance fraud see KFA-KFZ 568.I57
	Particular branches
	Personal insurance
	Life insurance
186	General (Table KF9)
186.5.A-Z	Special topics, A-Z
186.5.V3	Variable contracts. Variable annuities (Table KF7)
187.A-Z	Other, A-Z
187.H4	Health (Table KF7)
	Cf. KFA-KFZ 341+ Social insurance
	Property insurance 
188	General (Table KF9)
189.A-Z	Special. By risk, A-Z
189.A8	Aviation (Table KF7)
189.F5	Fire (Table KF7)
	Casualty insurance

Contracts
Particular contracts
Insurance
Particular branches
Casualty insurance -- Continued

191.A1	General liability (Table KF7)
191.A4	Automobile (Table KF7)
191.A43	Uninsured motorist (Table KF7)
191.A44	Unsatisfied judgment funds (Table KF7)
191.A46	No-fault (Table KF7)
191.A5-Z	Other risks
191.G67	Government risks (Table KF7)
191.M2	Malpractice (Table KF7)
191.P64	Pollution (Table KF7)
191.P75	Products liability (Table KF7)
192.A-Z	Other, A-Z
192.S8	Suretyship. Bonding (Table KF7)
193.A-Z	Particular types of insurance, A-Z
193.B87	Business insurance (Table KF7)
193.C74	Credit insurance (Table KF7)
193.F7	Fraternal insurance. Friendly societies (Table KF7)
193.T5	Title insurance (Table KF7)
193.5	Reinsurance (Table KF9)
194	Restitution. Quasi contracts. Unjust enrichment (Table KF9)
	Torts
195	General. Liability. Damages (Table KF9)
	Particular torts
	Negligence
196	General. Liability for accidents. Contributory negligence. Last clear chance (Table KF9)
196.2	Malpractice (Table KF9)
196.3.A-Z	Particular accidents or cases of negligence, A-Z
196.3.A78	Attractive nuisance (Table KF7)
196.3.A8	Automobile accidents (Table KF7)
196.3.B8	Building accidents (Table KF7)
196.3.L3	Liability for condition and use of land (Table KF7)
	Attractive nuisance see KFA-KFZ 196.3.A78
	Building accidents see KFA-KFZ 196.3.B8
196.3.P5	Playground accidents. Public recreation (Table KF7)
196.3.S65	Sports accidents (Table KF7)
196.3.S7	Streetcar accidents (Table KF7)
197.A-Z	Other torts, A-Z
197.D25	Death by wrongful act (Table KF7)
197.D27	Deceit. Fraud (Table KF7)
197.D3	Defamation. Libel and slander (Table KF7)
197.D65	Domestic relations. Family violence (Table KF7)
	Family violence see KFA-KFZ 197.D65

KFA-KFZ UNITED STATES - STATES AND TERRITORIES KFA-KFZ

Torts
Particular torts
Other torts, A-Z -- Continued

197.I5	Damage resulting from intoxication. Dramshop acts (Table KF7)
197.P3	Personal injuries (Table KF7)
197.P7	Violation of privacy (Table KF7)
197.T67	Tortious interference (Table KF7)
	Including interference with business relationships and interference with contractual relationships
197.T73	Trespass (Table KF7)
197.5	Strict liability. Liability without fault (Table KF9)
197.6	Damage caused by animals (Table KF9)
197.7	Products liability (Table KF9)
197.8	Environmental damages (Table KF9)
198.A-Z	Parties to action in torts, A-Z
198.C5	Corporations (Table KF7)
198.M8	Municipalities (Table KF7)
198.P37	Parks. Recreation departments (Table KF7)
198.P8	Public officers (Table KF7)
	Recreation departments see KFA-KFZ 198.P37
198.S3	School districts (Table KF7)
199.A-Z	Special topics, A-Z
199.E45	Employers' liability (Table KF7)
199.G6	Government liability (Table KF7)
199.J6	Joint tortfeasors (Table KF7)
199.L44	Lender liability (Table KF7)
199.V64	Volunteers' liability (Table KF7)
200	Compensation to victims of crimes. Reparation (Table KF9)
201	Assistance in emergencies. Good Samaritan laws (Table KF9)
	Agency
202	General (Table KF9)
203	Power of attorney (Table KF9)
	Associations
	Comprehensive. Associations in general
	Including business enterprises in general, regardless of form of organization
205	General (Table KF9)
205.5.A-Z	Special topics, A-Z
205.5.B8	Business records. Record keeping and retention (Table KF7)
	Unincorporated associations
206	General (Table KF9)
206.5.A-Z	Particular types of associations, A-Z
206.5.C5	Clubs (Table KF7)
	Business associations. Partnership
207	General (Table KF9)

KFA-KFZ UNITED STATES - STATES AND TERRITORIES KFA-KFZ

Associations
Unincorporated associations
Business associations. Partnership -- Continued

207.5	Limited partnership (Table KF9)
	Including limited liability companies and private companies
207.7	Massachusetts trusts. Business trusts (Table KF9)
208.A-Z	Special topics, A-Z
	Corporations
210	General (Table KF9)
211	Nonprofit corporations. Foundations. Endowments (Table KF9)
	Business corporations
213	General (Table KF9)
213.5	Incorporation. Corporate charters and bylaws. Promoters (Table KF9)
	Management
213.6	General (Table KF9)
	Boards of directors. Officers
213.7	General (Table KF9)
213.8	Remuneration, salaries, pensions (Table KF9)
	Finance. Issuing of securities
214.A1	General (Table KF7)
214.A2-Z	Special topics, A-Z
214.A23	Accounting. Auditing. Financial statements (Table KF7)
	Auditing see KFA-KFZ 214.A23
	Financial statements see KFA-KFZ 214.A23
215.A-Z	Other topics, A-Z
215.C55	Close corporations (Table KF7)
215.C65	Consolidation and merger (Table KF7)
215.D55	Dissolution. Liquidation (Table KF7)
215.F6	Foreign corporations (Table KF7)
	Liquidation see KFA-KFZ 215.D55
	Merger see KFA-KFZ 215.C65
215.M5	Minority stockholders (Table KF7)
215.S5	Shares and shareholders' rights. Stock transfers (Table KF7)
	Stock transfers see KFA-KFZ 215.S5
218	Cooperative societies (Table KF9)
	Insolvency and bankruptcy. Creditors' rights
220	General (Table KF9)
	Bankruptcy
221	General (Table KF9)
222.A-Z	Special topics, A-Z
222.F7	Fraudulent conveyances (Table KF7)
	Debtors' relief
224	General. Composition (Table KF9)
	Corporate reorganization

KFA-KFZ UNITED STATES - STATES AND TERRITORIES KFA-KFZ

Insolvency and bankruptcy. Creditors' rights
Debtors' relief
Corporate reorganization -- Continued

225.A1	General (Table KF7)
225.A5-Z	Particular types of corporations or lines of business
225.F35	Farms (Table KF7)
225.R2	Railroads (Table KF7)
226.A-Z	Other topics, A-Z
226.A7	Assignments for the benefit of creditors (Table KF7)
228	Economic policy. Economic planning. Economic development (Table KF9)
	For economic emergency legislation see KFA-KFZ 463+
	Regulation of industry, trade, and commerce. Occupational law
230	General and comprehensive works. Trade regulation. Control of trade practices. Consumer protection (Table KF9)
231	Monopolies. Antitrust laws (Table KF9)
234	Small business (Table KF9)
	Weights and measures. Containers
235.A1	General (Table KF7)
235.A5-Z	By product
235.F7	Fruits and vegetables (Table KF7)
	Primary production. Extractive industries
	Agriculture. Forestry. Horticulture
239	General. Soil conservation (Table KF9)
239.1	State Department of Agriculture (Table KF9)
240	Control of plant diseases, pests, and predatory animals. Weed control, etc. (Table KF9)
242	Economic legislation. Farm producers' organizations. Cooperatives (Table KF9)
	Marketing regulations
244.A1	General (Table KF7)
244.A5-Z	By product
244.E3	Eggs (Table KF7)
244.G7	Grain (Table KF7)
244.O54	Onions (Table KF7)
244.P35	Peanuts (Table KF7)
244.P58	Potatoes (Table KF7)
244.P6	Poultry (Table KF7)
244.S4	Seeds (Table KF7)
244.S66	Soybeans (Table KF7)
244.T63	Tobacco (Table KF7)
244.W38	Watermelons (Table KF7)
246	Livestock industry. Cattle-raising industry (Table KF9)
247	Poultry-raising industry (Table KF9)
	Dairy industry see KFA-KFZ 272.D2
249	Forestry and timber laws (Table KF9)
250	Horticulture (Table KF9)

Regulation of industry, trade, and commerce. Occupational law
Primary production. Extractive industries
Agriculture. Forestry. Horticulture -- Continued

251	Viticulture (Table KF9)
252	Citrus fruit industry (Table KF9)
253	Aquaculture (Table KF9)
254	Fishery (Table KF9)
	Mining. Quarrying
255	General (Table KF9)
255.5	Strip mining (Table KF9)
256	Coal (Table KF9)
256.5	Peat (Table KF9)
	Nonferrous metals
257.A1	General (Table KF7)
257.A5-Z	Particular metals, A-Z
257.U7	Uranium (Table KF7)
	Petroleum. Oil and gas
258.A1	General (Table KF7)
258.A5-Z	Special topics, A-Z
	Inspection see KFA-KFZ 258.S7
258.L4	Leases (Table KF7)
258.R43	Refineries (Table KF7)
258.S7	Standards. Inspection (Table KF7)
258.S8	Submerged land legislation. Tidal oil (Table KF7)
259.A-Z	Other nonmetallic minerals and gases, A-Z
259.P45	Phosphate (Table KF7)
	Manufacturing industries
265	General (Table KF9)
	Chemical industries
267.A1	General (Table KF7)
267.A5-Z	Particular products
267.F4	Fertilizer (Table KF7)
	Textiles and textile products
269.A1	General (Table KF9)
269.A5-Z	Particular textiles and textile products, A-Z
	Individual types of manufacture
271.A-Z	Consumer products. Light industries, A-Z
271.B56	Biotechnology industries (Table KF7)
271.B64	Book industries and trade (Table KF7)
271.C4	Clocks and watches (Table KF7)
271.F8	Furniture (Table KF7)
	Food processing industries
272.A1	General (Table KF7)
272.A5-Z	Particular products
272.D2	Dairy products. Milk production and distribution (Table KF7)
272.M35	Maple products (Table KF7)

Regulation of industry, trade, and commerce. Occupational law
Food processing industries
Particular products -- Continued

272.M42	Meat and poultry products (Table KF7)
275	Construction and building industry. Contractors (Table KF9)
	Trade and commerce
	Wholesale trade
280.A1	General (Table KF7)
280.A5-Z	Particular products, A-Z
	Subarrange each by Table KF7
	Retail trade
281.A1	General (Table KF7)
281.A5-Z	Special topics, A-Z
281.A82	Auctions (Table KF7)
	Canvassing see KFA-KFZ 281.P43
281.D57	Direct selling (Table KF7)
281.F55	Flea markets (Table KF7)
281.F7	Franchises (Table KF7)
281.P2	Pawnbrokers (Table KF7)
281.P43	Peddling. Canvassing (Table KF7)
281.S8	Sunday legislation (Table KF7)
281.T7	Trading stamps (Table KF7)
281.U5	Unit pricing (Table KF7)
281.V45	Vending stands (Table KF7)
281.5.A-Z	Particular products, A-Z
281.5.A8	Automobiles (Table KF7)
281.5.C54	Cigarettes (Table KF7)
281.5.D7	Drugs. Pharmaceutical products (Table KF7)
281.5.G76	Groceries (Table KF7)
281.5.H42	Hearing aids (Table KF7)
281.5.M63	Mobile homes (Table KF7)
	Pharmaceutical products see KFA-KFZ 281.5.D7
	Services and trades
	Including licensing
282.A1	General (Table KF7)
282.A5-Z	Particular services and trades, A-Z
	Air conditioning industry see KFA-KFZ 282.H43
282.A82	Asbestos abatement contractors and industries (Table KF7)
282.A9	Automotive maintenance and repair industry (Table KF7)
	Including service stations
282.B37	Barbers (Table KF7)
282.B4	Beauty shops (Table KF7)
282.C35	Camps (Table KF7)
282.C37	Caterers (Table KF7)
282.C44	Cemeteries (Table KF7)
	Cleaners see KFA-KFZ 282.L38

Regulation of industry, trade, and commerce. Occupational law
Trade and commerce
Service trades
Particular trades -- Continued

Call Number	Description
282.C64	Collection agencies (Table KF7)
	For collection laws see KFA-KFZ 167.C6
282.D3	Day care centers. Nursery schools (Table KF7)
282.D47	Detectives. Private investigators (Table KF7)
282.E4	Electricians (Table KF7)
282.E43	Electrologists (Table KF7)
282.E45	Elevator industry (Table KF7)
282.E55	Employment agencies (Table KF7)
	Foster homes for adults see KFA-KFZ 282.G75
282.G75	Group homes for adults. Foster homes for adults (Table KF7)
282.H34	Halfway houses (Table KF7)
282.H43	Heating and air conditioning industry (Table KF7)
282.H58	Horseshoers (Table KF7)
282.H6	Hotels. Restaurants (Table KF7)
282.I5	Insect exterminators. Pest control operators (Table KF7)
282.L38	Laundries. Cleaners. Linen supply (Table KF7)
	Life care communities see KFA-KFZ 282.O4
	Linen supply see KFA-KFZ 282.L38
282.M37	Marinas (Table KF7)
282.M66	Motion picture theaters (Table KF7)
282.O4	Old age homes. Life care communities (Table KF7)
	Pest control operators see KFA-KFZ 282.I5
282.P55	Plumbers (Table KF7)
	Private investigators see KFA-KFZ 282.D47
282.R33	Radio and television service technicians (Table KF7)
282.R4	Real estate agents (Table KF7)
282.R45	Rest homes (Table KF7)
282.T37	Tattoo establishments (Table KF7)
	Cf. KFA-KFZ 329.T55+ Licensing of tattoo artists
	Television service technicians see KFA-KFZ 282.R33
282.T68	Trailer camps (Table KF7)
282.T7	Travel agents (Table KF7)
282.U5	Undertakers (Table KF7)
284	Warehouses
	Public utilities
285	General (Table KF9)
285.1	Public service commissions (Table KF9)
	Power supply. Energy policy
286	General (Table KF9)
287	Electricity (Table KF9)
288	Gas (Table KF9)
289	Water (Table KF9)

Regulation of industry, trade, and commerce. Occupational law
Public utilities
Power supply. Energy policy -- Continued

290	Atomic power (Table KF9)
291.A-Z	Other, A-Z
291.G37	Gasohol (Table KF7)
291.G45	Geothermal resources (Table KF7)
291.R4	Refuse as fuel (Table KF7)
291.S64	Solar energy (Table KF7)
	Transportation and communication
295	General (Table KF9)
	Road traffic. Automotive transportation
296	General (Table KF9)
	Motor vehicle laws
297	General (Table KF9)
297.2	Safety equipment. Weight restrictions (Table KF9)
297.4	Registration. Title transfer (Table KF9)
297.6	Drivers' licenses (Table KF9)
297.62	Driver education (Table KF9)
297.7	Safety responsibility laws. Financial responsibility laws. Compulsory insurance (Table KF9)
297.75.A-Z	Particular vehicles, A-Z
297.75.B53	Bicycles (Table KF7)
297.75.M67	Motorcycles (Table KF7)
297.75.S64	Snowmobiles. All terrain vehicles (Table KF7)
297.75.T7	Trailers (Table KF7)
297.8	Traffic regulations and enforcement. Traffic violations. Drunk driving. Parking rules (Table KF9)
297.85	Traffic courts (Table KF9)
297.9	Highway safety. Traffic signs. Grade crossings. Railroad crossings (Table KF9)
297.94	School buses (Table KF9)
298	Car pools. Van pools (Table KF9)
	Motor carriers
299	General. Rate-making (Table KF9)
299.5.A-Z	Special topics, A-Z
299.5.C3	Charter parties (Table KF7)
300.A-Z	Particular types of motor carriers, A-Z
300.B86	Buses (Table KF7)
300.L56	Limousines (Table KF7)
300.T3	Taxicabs (Table KF7)
300.T78	Trucks (Table KF7)
	Railroads
301	General. Regulation of industry. Corporate structure (Table KF9)
301.3	Railroad lands (Table KF9)
	Operation of railroads

Regulation of industry, trade, and commerce. Occupational law
Transportation and communication
Railroads
Operation of railroads -- Continued

301.5	Safety and sanitation (Table KF9)
301.6	Rate-making (Table KF9)
301.7	Liability (Table KF9)
301.9.A-Z	Particular railroad companies, A-Z
303	Local transit. Streetcar lines. Subways (Table KF9)
303.5	Pipelines (Table KF9)
304.A-Z	Other land transportation, A-Z
304.C2	Cable cars. Ski lifts (Table KF7)
	Aviation
305	General (Table KF9)
305.2	Air traffic rules. Air safety (Table KF9)
305.5	Airports (Table KF9)
305.8	Aviation personnel (Table KF9)
	Water transportation. Navigation and shipping
308	General (Table KF9)
	Ships
308.1	General (Table KF9)
308.5.A-Z	Particular types of vessels, A-Z
308.5.M67	Motor boats (Table KF7)
308.5.T35	Tank vessels (Table KF7)
	Canals
309.A1	General (Table KF7)
309.A5-Z	Particular canals, A-Z
	Subarrange each by Table KF7
310.A-Z	Particular waterways, A-Z
	Harbors and ports
312.A1	General
312.A5-Z	Particular ports
314	Shipping. Water carriers (Table KF9)
316	Press law (Table KF9)
	Telecommunication
318	General (Table KF9)
318.3	Telegraph (Table KF9)
318.5	Telephone (Table KF9)
318.6	Radio and television broadcasting (Table KF9)
	Including public broadcasting
318.9.A-Z	Particular companies, A-Z
	The professions
	Including occupations
325	General. Licensing (Table KF9)
325.5	Professional corporations (Table KF9)
	Health professions
	For medical legislation see KFA-KFZ 360+

Regulation of industry, trade, and commerce. Occupational law
The professions
Health professions -- Continued
General. Physicians

326	General (Table KF9)
326.1	Licensing. Certification (Table KF9)
326.2	Professional ethics (Table KF9)
326.3	Malpractice. Liability (Table KF9)
326.5.A-Z	Other, A-Z
326.5.A25-.A253	Acupuncturists (Table KF16)
	Audiologists see KFA-KFZ 326.5.S64+
326.5.C4-.C43	Chiropractors (Table KF16)
326.5.D38-.D383	Dental hygienists (Table KF16)
326.5.D4-.D43	Dentists (Table KF16)
326.5.D53-.D533	Dietitians. Nutritionists (Table KF16)
326.5.F35-.F353	Faith healers (Table KF16)
326.5.G94-.G943	Gynecologists. Obstetricians (Table KF16)
326.5.M38-.M383	Massage therapists (Table KF16)
326.5.M43-.M433	Medical technologists (Table KF16)
326.5.M53-.M533	Midwives (Table KF16)
326.5.N38-.N383	Naturopaths (Table KF16)
326.5.N8-.N83	Nurses (Table KF16)
	Nurses, Practical see KFA-KFZ 326.5.P66+
326.5.N85-.N853	Nursing home administrators (Table KF16)
	Nutritionists see KFA-KFZ 326.5.D53+
	Obstetricians see KFA-KFZ 326.5.G94+
	Occupational therapists see KFA-KFZ 326.5.T5+
326.5.O6-.O63	Optometrists (Table KF16)
326.5.O78-.O783	Orthopedists (Table KF16)
326.5.O8-.O83	Osteopaths (Table KF16)
326.5.P4-.P43	Pharmacists (Table KF16)
326.5.P45-.P453	Physicians' assistants (Table KF16)
	Physical therapists see KFA-KFZ 326.5.T5+
326.5.P62-.P623	Podiatrists (Table KF16)
326.5.P66-.P663	Practical nurses (Table KF16)
326.5.P73-.P733	Psychologists. Psychiatrists. Psychotherapists (Table KF16)
326.5.P83-.P833	Public health personnel (Table KF16)
326.5.R47-.R473	Respiratory therapists (Table KF16)
326.5.S64-.S643	Speech therapists. Audiologists (Table KF16)
326.5.T5-.T53	Therapists, Physical. Occupational therapists (Table KF16)
329.A-Z	Other professions, A-Z
	For lawyers, see KFA-KFZ 76+ (State law); KF297+ (General)
329.A25-.A253	Accountants (Table KF16)
329.A7-.A73	Architects (Table KF16)
329.E6-.E63	Engineers (Table KF16)

KFA-KFZ UNITED STATES - STATES AND TERRITORIES KFA-KFZ

Regulation of industry, trade, and commerce. Occupational law
The professions
Other professions, A-Z -- Continued

329.F55-.F553	Financial planners (Table KF16)
329.F67-.F673	Foresters (Table KF16)
329.G45-.G453	Geologists (Table KF16)
329.I58-.I583	Interior decorators (Table KF16)
329.I59-.I593	Interpreters for the deaf (Table KF16)
329.L35-.L353	Landscape architects (Table KF16)
329.S88-.S883	Surveyors (Table KF16)
329.T55-.T553	Tattoo artists (Table KF16)
329.V48-.V483	Veterinarians (Table KF16)
330	Intellectual and industrial property. Patents and trademarks
	Social legislation
	Labor law
	Including works on both labor law and social insurance
331	General (Table KF9)
	Labor-management relations. Labor unions. Collective labor agreements
332	General (Table KF9)
332.5	Open and closed shop. Right to work laws (Table KF9)
332.8.A-Z	Particular industries and occupations, A-Z
332.8.A35	Agriculture (Table KF7)
	Government employees see KFA-KFZ 332.8.P77
332.8.H6	Hospitals (Table KF7)
332.8.L8	Lumber trade (Table KF7)
332.8.P77	Public employees (Table KF7)
332.8.T4	Teachers (Table KF7)
	Labor disputes. Strikes. Picketing. Labor injunctions. Arbitration. Conciliation
333	General (Table KF9)
333.8.A-Z	Particular industries and occupations, A-Z
333.8.A34	Agriculture (Table KF7)
333.8.P8	Public employees (Table KF7)
333.8.P83	Public utilities (Table KF7)
333.8.T4	Teachers (Table KF7)
	Labor standards. Employment. Wages
334	General (Table KF9)
334.5.A-Z	Special topics, A-Z
334.5.C65	Covenants not to compete (Table KF7)
334.5.D5	Discrimination in employment (Table KF7)
334.5.E55	Employment and dismissal (Table KF7)
	Holidays see KFA-KFZ 334.5.V32
	Leaves of absence see KFA-KFZ 334.5.V32
334.5.M55	Minimum wage (Table KF7)
334.5.O93	Overtime (Table KF7)
334.5.P4	Pension and retirement plans (Table KF7)

KFA-KFZ UNITED STATES - STATES AND TERRITORIES KFA-KFZ

Social legislation
Labor law
Labor standards. Employment. Wages
Special topics, A-Z -- Continued
334.5.V32 Vacations. Holidays. Leaves of absence (Table KF7)
Labor hygiene and safety
335 General (Table KF9)
335.3 Women (Table KF9)
335.5 Children (Table KF9)
335.6 Home labor (Table KF9)
335.7 Apprentices. Learners (Table KF9)
336.A-Z Particular industries or type of labor, A-Z
336.C6 Construction industry (Table KF7)
336.E45 Electric power plants (Table KF7)
Logging see KFA-KFZ 336.S38
336.M5 Mining (Table KF7)
336.P46 Petroleum and oil industry (Table KF7)
336.P67 Poultry industry. Poultry plants (Table KF7)
336.S38 Sawmills. Logging. Woodworking industries (Table KF7)
336.T4 Telecommunication (Table KF7)
Woodworking industries see KFA-KFZ 336.S38
338.A-Z Labor law of particular industries or types of employment, A-Z
338.A4 Agriculture (Table KF7)
338.H42 Health facilities (Table KF7)
Social insurance
340 General (Table KF9)
Particular branches
Health insurance
Cf. KFA-KFZ 187.H4 Personal insurance
341 General (Table KF9)
341.5.A-Z Particular industries or groups, A-Z
341.5.A34 Aged. Older people. Medicare (Table KF7)
Medicaid see KFA-KFZ 341.5.P65
Medicare see KFA-KFZ 341.5.A34
Older people see KFA-KFZ 341.5.A34
341.5.P65 Poor (Table KF7)
Including Medicaid
341.7.A-Z Particular services and benefits, A-Z
341.7.R46 Renal disease program
Workers' compensation
342 General (Table KF9)
342.5 Occupational diseases (Table KF9)
342.8.A-Z Particular cases, A-Z
344 Social security. Retirement. Old age and disability pensions. Survivors' benefits (Table KF9)
345 Unemployment insurance (Table KF9)

Social legislation -- Continued
Public welfare. Public assistance

349	General (Table KF9)
	For abatement of nuisance see KFA-KFZ 378+
349.1	Boards of public welfare (Table KF9)
349.2	Public institutions (General). Departments of public institutions (Table KF9)
349.5	Social workers (Table KF9)
349.8	Maternal and infant welfare (Table KF9)
350.A-Z	Particular groups, A-Z
350.A35	Aged. Older people (Table KF7)
350.B5	Blind (Table KF7)
350.C4	Children (Table KF7)
	Including children with disabilities or retarded children and foster home care
350.H3	Handicapped. People with disabilities (Table KF7)
350.H65	Homeless persons (Table KF7)
	Including sheltered housing
	Older people see KFA-KFZ 350.A35
	People with disabilities see KFA-KFZ 350.H3
351.A-Z	Special topics, A-Z
351.D6	Domicile requirements (Table KF7)
351.E53	Energy assistance. Home heating (Table KF7)
351.F66	Food stamp program (Table KF7)
	Home heating see KFA-KFZ 351.E53
351.V6	Vocational rehabilitation (Table KF7)
352	Disaster relief (Table KF9)
353	Birth control. Family planning. Population control (Table KF9)
	Cf. KFA-KFZ 567.A2 Abortion (Criminal law)
	Public health. Sanitation
	Including environmental pollution
	Cf. KFA-KFZ 459.8.H43 Building laws
354	General (Table KF9)
	For abatement of nuisances see KFA-KFZ 378+
354.1	Public health boards (Table KF9)
355	Burial and cemetery laws (Table KF9)
	Cf. KFA-KFZ 282.C44 Trade regulation
356	Water pollution and drainage (Table KF9)
356.1	Water pollution control agency (Table KF9)
356.6	Drinking water standards. Fluoridation (Table KF9)
	Contagious, infectious, and other diseases
357	General. Reporting (Table KF9)
357.8.A-Z	Particular diseases, A-Z
357.8.A35	AIDS (Disease) (Table KF7)
357.8.A48	Alzheimer's disease (Table KF7)
357.8.B5	Diseases causing blindness (Table KF7)
357.8.C35	Cancer (Table KF7)

Public health. Sanitation
Contagious, infectious, and other diseases
Particular diseases, A-Z -- Continued

357.8.P45	Phenylketonuria (Table KF7)
357.8.T83	Tuberculosis (Table KF7)
357.8.V46	Venereal diseases (Table KF7)
357.9.A-Z	Particular measures, A-Z
357.9.I44	Immunization. Vaccination (Table KF7)
	Vaccination see KFA-KFZ 357.9.I44
	Air pollution
358	General (Table KF9)
358.3	Tobacco smoking (Table KF9)
359.A-Z	Other public health hazards and measures, A-Z
	Hazardous waste disposal see KFA-KFZ 380.H39
359.M65	Molds. Toxigenic fungi (Table KF7)
359.N6	Noise control (Table KF7)
359.R3	Refuse disposal (Table KF7)
359.S4	Sewage disposal (Table KF7)
	Toxigenic fungi see KFA-KFZ 359.M65
	Medical legislation
360	General (Table KF9)
360.5	Patients' rights (Table KF9)
	Hospitals and other medical institutions
361	Hospitals (Table KF9)
363.A-Z	Other health services, A-Z
363.A25	Abortion services (Table KF7)
	Ambulance service see KFA-KFZ 363.E43
363.A43	Ambulatory medical care (Table KF7)
363.B55	Blood banks (Table KF7)
363.C45	Child health services (Table KF7)
363.E43	Emergency medical services. Ambulance service (Table KF7)
363.H65	Home health services (Table KF7)
363.L3	Laboratories, Medical (Table KF7)
363.N8	Nursing homes (Table KF7)
363.R44	Rehabilitation centers (Table KF7)
363.S3	Schools. School health services (Table KF7)
365	The mentally ill (Table KF9)
366.A-Z	Disorders of character, behavior, and intelligence, A-Z
366.A42	Alcoholism (Table KF7)
	Including works on the treatment and rehabilitation of alcoholics in the criminal justice system
366.N35	Narcotic addiction. Drug addiction (Table KF7)
367.A-Z	Special topics, A-Z
367.D4	Death, Definition of (Table KF7)
367.D65	Donation of organs, tissues, etc. (Table KF7)
367.D78	Drug administration (Table KF7)

KFA-KFZ UNITED STATES - STATES AND TERRITORIES KFA-KFZ

Medical legislation

Special topics, A-Z -- Continued

367.H86	Human reproductive technology (Table KF7)
367.I5	Informed consent (Table KF7)
	Living wills see KFA-KFZ 367.R53
	Natural death see KFA-KFZ 367.R53
	Organ donations see KFA-KFZ 367.D65
367.R4	Medical records. Hospital records. Records management (Table KF7)
367.R53	Right to die. Natural death. Living wills (Table KF7)
	Tissue donation see KFA-KFZ 367.D65
	Veterinary law and hygiene
368	General (Table KF9)
368.5.A-Z	Particular measures, A-Z
368.5.Q3	Quarantine (Table KF7)
369.A-Z	Particular animal diseases and causative agents, A-Z
369.B7	Brucellosis (Table KF7)
369.R33	Rabies (Table KF7)
369.T8	Tuberculosis (Table KF7)
370	Prevention of cruelty to animals. Animal experimentation (Table KF9)
	Food. Drugs. Cosmetics
372	General. Food law (Table KF9)
372.5.A-Z	Particular food products, A-Z
372.5.D34	Dairy products (Table KF7)
372.5.F5	Flour (Table KF7)
372.5.F78	Fruit juices (Table KF7)
373	Drugs. Cosmetics (Table KF9)
	Narcotics
374	General (Table KF9)
374.5.A-Z	Particular narcotics, A-Z
374.5.M3	Marijuana (Table KF7)
	Alcohol. Alcoholic beverages. Prohibition
375	General (Table KF9)
375.5.A-Z	Particular products, A-Z
375.5.B44	Beer. Malt liquors (Table KF7)
	Malt liquors see KFA-KFZ 375.5.B44
375.5.W56	Wine (Table KF7)
376.A-Z	Special topics, A-Z
376.D75	Drinking age (Table KF7)
376.L6	Local option (Table KF7)
	Public safety
378	General (Table KF9)
	Including abatement of nuisances in general
379	Weapons. Firearms (Table KF9)
	Hazardous articles and processes. Product safety
380.A1	General (Table KF7)

Public safety
Hazardous articles and processes. Product safety -- Continued

380.A5-Z	Particular articles and processes, A-Z
380.A7	Ammonia (Table KF7)
380.A75	Asbestos (Table KF7)
380.A8	Atomic power. Radiation (Table KF7)
380.E9	Explosives. Propellant actuated devices (Table KF7)
380.H39	Hazardous wastes (Table KF7)
380.I6	Inflammable materials. Fireworks (Table KF7)
380.L32	Lead (Table KF7)
380.L5	Liquefied petroleum gas (Table KF7)
380.P4	Pesticides (Table KF7)
	Accident prevention
380.5.A1	General (Table KF7)
380.5.A5-Z	Special topics
380.5.G32	Gas containers and equipment (Table KF7)
380.5.S7	Steam boilers (Table KF7)
381	Fire prevention (Table KF9)
	Control of social activities
381.5	General works (Table KF9)
382	Vacationing. Recreation (Table KF9)
	Including campgrounds, hostels, outdoor swimming facilities, etc.
384	Sports. Prizefighting. Horse racing (Table KF9)
385	Lotteries. Games of chance. Gambling (Table KF9)
386.A-Z	Other, A-Z
386.A47	Amusements (Table KF7)
386.D6	Dog racing (Table KF7)
	Exhibitions see KFA-KFZ 386.F35
386.F35	Fairs. Exhibitions (Table KF7)
	Education
	School government. School finance
390	General (Table KF9)
	Including works treating educational law comprehensively
390.3	School districts. School boards (Table KF9)
390.5	School superintendents (Table KF9)
390.7	School lands (Table KF9)
391.A-Z	Special topics, A-Z
391.C57	Charter schools (Table KF7)
391.F3	Federal aid (Table KF7)
391.P45	Personal records (Table KF7)
391.S7	State aid (Table KF7)
391.T7	Transportation of pupils. School safety patrols (Table KF7)
	Students. Compulsory education. School attendance
392	General (Table KF9)
392.2	Right to education. Admission. Discrimination and segregation (Table KF9)
392.3	Educational tests and measurements (Table KF9)

Education
Students. Compulsory education. School attendance --
Continued

Number	Topic
392.5	Student records (Table KF9)
392.6	School discipline. Tort liability of school boards and staff for disciplinary actions (Table KF9)
392.7	Religious and patriotic observances. Bible reading. Religious instruction. School prayers. Flag salute (Table KF9)
	Teachers
393	General. Certification. Tenure (Table KF9)
393.5	Salaries, pensions, etc. (Table KF9)
	Elementary and secondary education
395	General (Table KF9)
395.25	Evaluation and selection of instructional materials (Table KF9)
395.26	Curricula. Courses of instruction (Table KF9)
395.3	Language instruction (Table KF9) Including bilingual education
395.4	Physical education (Table KF9)
395.5	Vocational education (Table KF9)
395.7.A-Z	Other special courses, A-Z
395.7.L38	Law (Table KF7)
395.9.A-Z	Particular types of students, A-Z
395.9.H3	Handicapped. Students with disabilities (Table KF7)
395.95	Private education. Private schools (Table KF9)
395.97	Domestic education. Home schools (Table KF9)
	Higher education. Colleges and universities
396	General. Finance (Table KF9)
396.5.A-Z	Individual colleges and universities, A-Z
	Science and the arts. Research
398	General (Table KF9)
398.2.A-Z	Particular branches and subjects, A-Z
398.2.B54	Biotechnology (Table KF7)
398.2.I53	Industrial research (Table KF7)
398.2.O25	Oceanography (Table KF7)
	Performing arts
398.5	General. Theater (Table KF9)
398.7	Motion pictures (Table KF9)
398.8	Museums and galleries (Table KF9)
398.9	Historic buildings and monuments. Archaeological sites (Table KF9) Including preservation of cultural property
	Libraries and archives
399	General (Table KF9)
399.5.A-Z	Particular libraries, A-Z
	Constitutional law
	Sources

KFA-KFZ UNITED STATES - STATES AND TERRITORIES KFA-KFZ

Constitutional law
Sources -- Continued

400	General. Comprehensive. Collections
400.5	Colonial charters. By date of charter
	Under each:
	.A3-.A39 Texts
	.A6-.Z General works
401	Particular constitutions. By date of constitution
	Subarrange each by Table KF40
	Including rejected proposals for new constitution. By date of referendum
	History
401.5	General works
401.6.A-Z	Special topics, A-Z
	For history of a particular subject of constitutional law, see that subject
	Admission to the union see KFA-KFZ 401.6.S8
401.6.S55	Slavery
401.6.S8	Statehood. Admission to the Union
402	General principles (Table KF9)
403	Amending process (Table KF9)
	Separation of powers. Delegation of powers
405	General (Table KF9)
406	Conflict of interests (General). Incompatibility of offices. Ethics in government (Table KF9)
407	Judicial review of legislative acts (Table KF9)
	Structure of government. Jurisdiction
409	General (Table KF9)
410.A-Z	Special topics, A-Z
410.C3	Capital and capitol (Table KF7)
410.I6	Interstate compacts (Table KF7)
410.S8	Submerged lands (Table KF7)
	Individual and state
	Civil and political rights
411	General (Table KF9)
411.5.A-Z	Particular groups, A-Z
411.5.A34	African Americans (Table KF7)
411.5.H56	Hispanic Americans (Table KF7)
411.5.H64	Homosexuals. Gays (Table KF7)
	Negroes see KFA-KFZ 411.5.A34
411.7	Sex discrimination (Table KF9)
	Discrimination in mortgage loans see KFA-KFZ 130.5.D58
412.A-Z	Particular civil rights, A-Z
412.P47	Petition, Freedom of (Table KF7)
412.R45	Religion and conscience, Freedom of (Table KF7)
413	Political parties (Table KF7)
	Control of individuals

Constitutional law
Individual and state
Control of individuals -- Continued

414	General. Aliens (Table KF9)
414.5	Identification. Registration (Table KF9)
	Including identification cards
	Internal security. Subversive activities
415	General (Table KF9)
416.A-Z	Particular groups, A-Z
416.C65	Communists (Table KF7)
417	Church and state. Religious corporations (Table KF9)
	Organs of government
	The people
419	Initiative and referendum (Table KF9)
	Election law
420	General (Table KF9)
420.3	Primaries (Table KF9)
420.6	Local elections (Table KF9)
420.85.A-Z	Special topics, A-Z
420.85.A2	Absentee voting (Table KF7)
420.85.A6	Apportionment. Election districts (Table KF7)
420.85.C2	Campaign expenditures (Table KF7)
	Literacy tests see KFA-KFZ 420.85.R4
420.85.R4	Registration. Qualifications. Educational tests. Poll tax requirements (Table KF7)
420.85.S9	Suffrage (Table KF7)
420.85.V6	Voting machines (Table KF7)
420.9.A-Z	Other topics, A-Z
420.9.R3	Recall (Table KF7)
	The legislative branch
	The legislature
421	General. Organization. Legislative process (Table KF9)
421.5.A-Z	Special topics, A-Z
421.5.B5	Bill drafting (Table KF7)
421.5.C6	Committees (Table KF7)
	Ethics see KFA-KFZ 421.5.L4
421.5.I46	Impeachment power and procedure (Table KF7)
421.5.L33	Legislative branch employees (Table KF7)
421.5.L35	Legislative service agencies. Revisors of statutes, etc. (Table KF7)
421.5.L4	Legislators. Legal status of legislators. Ethics (Table KF7)
421.5.L6	Lobbying (Table KF7)
421.5.O85	Oversight (Table KF7)
421.5.P7	Printing (Table KF7)
421.5.R8	Rules and procedures (Table KF7)
421.5.S65	Special and local legislation (Table KF7)

KFA-KFZ UNITED STATES - STATES AND TERRITORIES KFA-KFZ

Constitutional law
Organs of government
The legislative branch
The legislature
Special topics, A-Z -- Continued

421.5.S95	Sunset reviews of government programs (Table KF7)
421.5.V46	Veto, Legislative (Table KF7)
	Contested elections
	Cases
	Upper chamber
421.7	General (Table KF9)
421.72.A-Z	Particular cases. By incumbent, A-Z
	Lower chamber
421.8	General (Table KF9)
421.82.A-Z	Particular cases. By incumbent, A-Z
422	Upper chamber (Senate) (Table KF9)
423	Lower chamber (Assembly) (Table KF9)
	The executive branch
425	General. Executive power (Table KF9)
426	The Governor. Lieutenant Governor (Table KF9)
	Powers and duties
426.3	General (Table KF9)
426.35.A-Z	Particular powers, A-Z
426.35.V45	Veto power (Table KF7)
	Impeachment
426.4	General (Table KF9)
426.45	Particular cases. By governor
	Including proposed impeachments
426.5	Legal status. Disability. Succession (Table KF9)
	Executive departments
427	General (Table KF9)
427.5.A-Z	Particular offices or positions, A-Z
427.5.A8	Attorneys general (Table KF7)
	For opinions of attorneys general see KFA-KFZ 440.A55+
427.5.P8	Public advocates (Table KF7)
427.5.S4	Secretary of State (Table KF7)
427.8.A-Z	Special topics, A-Z
427.8.P8	Public meetings (Table KF7)
427.8.R46	Reorganization (Table KF7)
	State civil service see KFA-KFZ 435+
428	Judiciary. Judicial power (Table KF6)
429	State emblem. Flag. Seal. Seat of government (Table KF9)
	Local government
430	General (Table KF9)
	Municipal government. Municipal corporations
431	General works (Table KF9)

Local government

Municipal government. Municipal corporations -- Continued

431.3	Municipal powers and services beyond corporate limits (Table KF9)
431.5	City charters and ordinances (Collections) (Table KF9)
431.6	City councils (Table KF9)
431.7	Mayors (Table KF9)
431.9.A-Z	Special topics, A-Z
431.9.A5	Annexation (Table KF7)
431.9.H6	Home rule (Table KF7)
431.9.R4	Referendum (Table KF7)
432	County government (Table KF9)
432.5	Minor communities. Townships. Villages (Table KF9)
433	Special districts. Public authorities (Table KF9)
	State civil service. State officials
435	General (Table KF9)
435.15	Civil service commissions (Table KF9)
435.3	Performance rating (Table KF9)
435.5	Tenure and remuneration. Salaries. Pensions (Table KF9)
435.6	Travel regulations (Table KF9)
435.8.A-Z	Particular offices or positions, A-Z
435.8.S7	State police (Table KF7)
	Municipal civil service. City officials
	Including local government officials in general
436	General (Table KF9)
436.5	Tenure and remuneration. Salaries. Pensions (Table KF9)
436.8.A-Z	Particular offices or positions, A-Z
436.8.C55	City attorneys. Corporation counsel. Town counsel (Table KF7)
436.8.P64	Police (Table KF7)
436.8.S4	Selectmen (Table KF7)
436.8.T6	Town clerks. City clerks (Table KF7)
	County civil service. County officials
437	General (Table KF9)
437.5	Tenure and remuneration. Salaries. Pensions (Table KF9)
437.8.A-Z	Particular offices or positions, A-Z
437.8.A7	County attorneys (Table KF7)
437.8.C55	County clerks (Table KF7)
439	Police and power of the police (Table KF9)
	Administrative organization. Administrative law and procedure
440	General. Regulatory agencies (Table KF9 modified)
	Attorneys General's opinions
	Reports
440.A559	Serials
440.A56	Monographic collections. By date of publication
	Prefer subject
441.A-Z	Special topics, A-Z

KFA-KFZ UNITED STATES - STATES AND TERRITORIES KFA-KFZ

Administrative organization. Administrative law and procedure
Special topics, A-Z -- Continued

441.D35	Drafting of administrative regulations (Table KF7)
441.H4	Hearing examiners (Table KF7)
441.O5	Ombudsman (Table KF7)
	Sunset reviews of government programs see KFA-KFZ 421.5.S95
	Public property. Public restraints on private property
442	General (Table KF9)
443	Conservation laws (Table KF9)
	Roads. Highway law
444	General (Table KF9)
444.5	Highway finance (Table KF9)
444.6	Roadside protection. Rights of way (Table KF9)
	Including restrictions on signboards, advertising, etc.
444.8	Foot trails (Table KF9)
444.9.A-Z	Particular roads, A-Z
445	Bridges. Tunnels (Table KF9)
	Water resources. Watersheds. Lakes. Water courses
446	General. Water rights. Water districts (Table KF9)
	Waterways. Rivers. Canals
447	General (Table KF9)
447.5.A-Z	Particular waterways, A-Z
447.8	Flood control. Levees. Dams (Table KF9)
448.A-Z	Particular bodies of water, water districts, etc., A-Z
	Water supply
449	Wells (Table KF9)
449.5	Weather control. Meteorology. Weather stations
450	Eminent domain (Table KF9)
	Public land law. Reclamation. Irrigation. Drainage
451	General (Table KF9)
451.2	Rights-of way across public lands (Table KF9)
451.5	Arid lands (Table KF9)
451.7	Swamps. Marshes. Wetlands (Table KF9)
451.8	Shore protection. Beaches (Table KF9)
	State preserves. State parks and forests. Wilderness preservation
452	General (Table KF9)
452.5	Recreation areas (Table KF9)
	Game, bird, and fish protection and refuge
453	General (Table KF9)
453.5.A-Z	Particular animals, A-Z
453.8.A-Z	Particular refuges, A-Z
453.9.A-Z	Particular preserves, parks, etc., A-Z
454	Homesteads (Table KF9)
455	Land grants (Table KF9)
455.5.A-Z	Particular claims. By claimant, A-Z

Public property. Public restraints on private property -- Continued
Regional and city planning. Zoning. Land subdivision. Building

458	General (Table KF9)
458.3	Real estate development (Table KF9)
	Cf. KFA-KFZ 282.R4 Real estate agents
458.7	Solar access zoning. Shade control (Table KF9)
	Particular land uses and zoning controls
458.75	Child care services (Table KF9)
458.8	Sex-oriented businesses (Table KF9)
458.9	Rural and agricultural uses (Table KF9)
458.92.A-Z	Other land uses and zoning controls, A-Z
458.92.G75	Group homes (Table KF7)
458.92.H65	Home-based businesses (Table KF7)
	Building laws
459.A1	General (Table KF7)
459.A5-Z	Particular types of buildings, A-Z
459.C65	Commercial buildings (Table KF7)
459.C67	Court buildings (Table KF7)
459.H6	Hotels, restaurants, taverns, etc. (Table KF7)
459.M6	Mobile homes (Table KF7)
	Nursing homes see KFA-KFZ 363.N8
459.P7	Prefabricated buildings (Table KF7)
459.S3	School buildings (Table KF7)
459.3	Plumbing, pipe fitting, etc. (Table KF9)
	Wells see KFA-KFZ 449
459.5	Electric installations (Table KF9)
459.6	Gas installations (Table KF9)
459.7	Elevators (Table KF9)
459.75	Heating and ventilating. Air conditioning (Table KF9)
459.8.A-Z	Other topics, A-Z
459.8.H35	Handicapped, Provisions for. People with disabilities, Provisions for (Table KF7)
459.8.H43	Health regulations. Sanitation (Table KF7)
	Sanitation see KFA-KFZ 459.8.H43
459.9	Structures other than buildings. Billboards (Table KF9)
	Housing. City redevelopment. Slum clearance
460	General (Table KF9)
460.5.A-Z	Special topics, A-Z
460.5.D5	Discrimination (Table KF7)
460.5.F5	Finance (Table KF7)
460.5.H68	Housing authorities (Table KF7)
	Government property
462	General (Table KF9)
462.5.A-Z	Particular properties, A-Z
462.5.A97	Automobiles. Motor vehicles (Table KF7)
462.5.L34	Land and real property (Table KF7)
	Motor vehicles see KFA-KFZ 462.5.A97

KFA-KFZ UNITED STATES - STATES AND TERRITORIES KFA-KFZ

Public property. Public restraints on private property
Government property
Particular properties, A-Z -- Continued

462.5.P8	Public records (Table KF7)
	Real property see KFA-KFZ 462.5.L34
462.6.A-Z	Special topics, A-Z
462.6.A25	Access to public records. Freedom of information (Table KF7)
462.6.S87	Surplus property (Table KF7)
462.8	Public works (Table KF9)
	Government measures in time of war, national emergency, or economic crisis. Emergency economic legislation
	By period
	In case of doubt, prefer classification with subject
	1914-1939
463	General (Table KF9)
	Rationing. Price control. Profiteering
463.3	General (Table KF9)
463.5.A-Z	By commodity or service, A-Z
463.5.R3	Rent control (Table KF7)
	1939-
464	General (Table KF9)
	Rationing. Price control. Profiteering
464.3	General (Table KF9)
464.5.A-Z	By commodity or service, A-Z
464.5.R3	Rent control (Table KF7)
	Public finance
465	General (Table KF9)
466	Money. Currency. Coinage (Table KF9)
	Budget. Expenditure control. Public auditing
467	General (Table KF9)
467.3	Public depositories (Table KF9)
467.5	Investment of public funds (Table KF9)
468	Public debts. Loans. Bond issues (Table KF9)
	State revenue
469	General. History (Table KF9)
	Taxation
	Including works on both state and local taxation
470	General (Table KF9)
470.5	Tax saving. Tax planning (Table KF9)
470.8	Tax expenditures (Table KF9)
	Administration. Procedure. Collection. Enforcement
471	General (Table KF9)
471.5	Remedies. Tax courts. Tax appeals (Table KF9)
471.9.A-Z	Special topics, A-Z
471.9.C65	Confidentiality of returns (Table KF7)
471.9.D4	Delinquency (Table KF7)

Public finance
State revenue
Taxation
Administration. Procedure. Collection. Enforcement
Special topics, A-Z -- Continued

471.9.F6	Foreclosure. Tax sales (Table KF7)
471.9.L5	Tax liens (Table KF7)
	Tax exemption
472	General (Table KF9)
473	Tax incentives (Table KF9)
	Particular taxes
	Income tax
	Income tax in general. Personal income tax
475	General (Table KF9)
475.5.A-Z	Special topics, A-Z
475.5.D58	Taxation in divorce. Divorce settlements (Table KF7)
475.5.N6	Nonwage payments. Fringe benefits (Table KF7)
475.5.T35	Tax credits (Table KF7)
475.5.T78	Trusts (Table KF7)
475.5.W5	Withholding tax (Table KF7)
475.7	Income of nonprofit organizations, nonprofit corporations, foundations, endowments, pension trust funds (Table KF9)
	Income of business organizations
476	General (Table KF9)
	Corporation income tax
477	General (Table KF9)
477.5.A-Z	Particular lines of corporate business, A-Z
477.5.B35	Banks (Table KF7)
477.5.H67	Hospitality industry (Table KF7)
	Including hotels and restaurants
	Hotels see KFA-KFZ 477.5.H67
477.5.I6	Insurance (Table KF7)
477.5.M54	Mining. Petroleum (Table KF7)
	Petroleum see KFA-KFZ 477.5.M54
477.5.P8	Public utilities (Table KF7)
	Restaurants see KFA-KFZ 477.5.H67
	Property taxes. Taxation of capital
478	General. Assessment (Table KF9)
	Real property
479	General (Table KF9)
479.3	Special assessments (Table KF9)
479.5	Real estate transactions (Table KF9)
479.8.A-Z	Special topics, A-Z
479.8.E9	Exemptions (Table KF7)
479.8.F37	Farm land (Table KF7)

Public finance
State revenue
Taxation
Particular taxes
Property taxes. Taxation of capital
Real property
Special topics, A-Z -- Continued

479.8.F58	Foreclosure. Tax sales (Table KF7)
479.8.F6	Forest land. Forest yield taxes (Table KF7)
	Tax sales see KFA-KFZ 479.8.F58
	Business taxes. Licenses
480	General (Table KF9)
	Severance tax see KFA-KFZ 480.5.M5
480.5.A-Z	Particular lines of business, A-Z
480.5.A35	Agricultural land (Table KF7)
480.5.B3	Banks (Table KF7)
	Extractive industries see KFA-KFZ 480.5.M5
480.5.M5	Mining. Extractive industries. Severance tax (Table KF7)
480.5.R4	Retail trade (Table KF7)
480.8	Corporate franchises. Corporate stock (Table KF9)
	Personal property taxes
481	General (Table KF9)
	Intangible property
481.5.A1	General (Table KF7)
481.5.A3-Z	Particular kinds
481.5.B6	Bonds and securities (Table KF7)
481.5.M6	Mortgages (Table KF7)
481.7.A-Z	Other personal property, A-Z
481.7.C65	Computer programs. Software (Table KF7)
481.7.R34	Railroads (Table KF7)
	Software see KFA-KFZ 481.7.C65
	Other taxes on capital and income
482	Estate, inheritance, and gift taxes (Table KF9)
482.5.A-Z	Other, A-Z
482.5.E4	Emergency transportation tax [New Jersey only] (Table KF7)
	Excise taxes. Taxes on transactions
483	General (Table KF9)
484	Retail sales tax (Table KF9)
484.5	Use taxes (Table KF9)
485.A-Z	Taxes on particular commodities, services, transactions, etc., A-Z
485.A34	Admissions. Amusements (Table KF7)
485.A5	Alcoholic beverages. Liquor taxes (Table KF7)
	Amusements see KFA-KFZ 485.A34
	Gambling see KFA-KFZ 485.W34

Public finance
State revenue
Taxation
Particular taxes
Excise taxes. Taxes on transactions
Taxes on particular commodities, services,
transactions, etc., A-Z -- Continued

485.M6	Motor fuels (Table KF7)
485.M62	Motor vehicles (Table KF7)
	Real property see KFA-KFZ 479.5
485.T44	Telecommunication facilities. Telegraph. Telephone (Table KF7)
	Telegraph see KFA-KFZ 485.T44
	Telephone see KFA-KFZ 485.T44
485.T6	Tobacco and tobacco products (Table KF7)
485.W34	Wagering. Gambling (Table KF7)
486	Stamp duties
487.A-Z	Other sources of revenue, A-Z
487.F3	Federal grants-in-aid (Table KF7)
487.F33	Fees (Table KF7)
487.L5	Licenses (Table KF7)
	Local finance
488	General (Table KF9)
488.5	Budget. Expenditure control. Auditing (Table KF9)
489	Municipal debts. Loans. Municipal bonds (Table KF9)
	Particular sources of revenue
	Taxation
490	General. State and local jurisdiction (Table KF9)
490.5	Procedure. Enforcement (Table KF9)
491.A-Z	Particular taxes, A-Z
491.A8	Automobile trailer taxes. Mobile home taxes (Table KF7)
491.B8	Business taxes. Business property taxes. Licenses (Table KF7)
491.I5	Income tax (Table KF7)
491.L4	Levee taxes (Table KF7)
491.P7	Property taxes (Table KF7)
491.R4	Real property taxes (Table KF7)
491.R44	Special assessment (Table KF7)
491.8	Other sources of revenue
492.A-Z	Particular kinds of local jurisdictions, A-Z
492.C5	Cities (Table KF7)
492.C6	Counties (Table KF7)
	Military law
495	General. Comprehensive (Table KF9)
496	War and emergency legislation (Table KF9)
497	State militia. National Guard (Table KF9)

KFA-KFZ UNITED STATES - STATES AND TERRITORIES KFA-KFZ

Military law -- Continued

499	Military criminal law and procedure. Courts-martial (Table KF9)
501	Civil defense (Table KF9)
	War veterans
502	General. Pensions. Bonuses (Table KF9)
	By period
502.5	18th and 19th centuries (Table KF9)
502.6	1916-1939 (Table KF9)
502.8	1945- (Table KF9)
	Indians
505	General (Table KF9)
505.5.A-Z	Particular groups, tribes, etc., A-Z
505.6.A-Z	Special topics, A-Z
505.6.A44	Alcohol. Alcoholic beverages. Prohibition (Table KF7)
	Citizenship, Tribal see KFA-KFZ 505.6.T74
505.6.C5	Civil rights (Table KF7)
505.6.C57	Claims (Table KF7)
505.6.C59	Constitutional law (Table KF7)
505.6.C6	Courts. Procedure (Table KF7)
505.6.C84	Cultural property (Table KF7)
505.6.E3	Education (Table KF7)
	Enrollment, Tribal see KFA-KFZ 505.6.T74
505.6.G35	Gambling on Indian reservations (Table KF7)
	Games of chance see KFA-KFZ 505.6.L67
505.6.H85	Hunting and fishing rights (Table KF7)
505.6.L67	Lotteries. Games of chance (Table KF7)
505.6.M66	Motor vehicles (Table KF7)
505.6.P7	Probate (Table KF7)
	Prohibition see KFA-KFZ 505.6.A44
505.6.T38	Taxation (Table KF7)
505.6.T74	Tribal citizenship. Tribal enrollment (Table KF7)
505.6.W38	Water rights (Table KF7)
	Courts. Procedure
508	Administration of justice. Organization of the judiciary (Table KF9, modified)
508.A19	Directories
	History see KFA-KFZ 78+
509	Judicial councils (Table KF9)
	Court organization and procedure
510	General (Table KF9)
510.5.A-Z	Special topics, A-Z
510.5.A3	Administration and management (Table KF7)
510.5.C6	Conduct of court proceedings. Decorum (Table KF7)
510.5.C65	Congestion and delay (Table KF7)
	Particular courts
512	Court of last resort (Supreme court) (Table KF9)
	Intermediate appellate courts

Courts. Procedure
Court organization and procedure
Particular courts
Intermediate appellate courts -- Continued

513	Collective (Table KF9)
514.A-Z	Particular courts, A-Z
	Trial courts: County courts. District courts. Superior courts
	For chancery courts see KFA-KFZ 531
515	Collective (Table KF9, modified)
515.A545	Court records. By initial date of period covered
516.A-Z	Particular courts. By county, etc., A-Z
	Subarrange each by Table KF7 modified as follows: .A7 = Court records. By initial date of period covered
	For collected wills, etc. see KFA-KFZ 144.8.A1+
	Minor courts
517	General (Table KF9)
	Municipal courts
518	Collective (Table KF9)
519.A-Z	Particular courts. By city, etc., A-Z
	Subarrange each by Table KF7 modified as follows: .A7 = Court records. By initial date of period covered
	For collected wills, etc. see KFA-KFZ 144.8.A1+
	Justices of the peace. Magistrates' courts
	Including civil proceedings
	For criminal proceedings, summary conviction see KFA-KFZ 583.5
520	Collective (Table KF9)
520.5.A-Z	Particular courts. By county, etc., A-Z
	Small claims courts
521	Collective (Table KF9)
521.5.A-Z	Particular courts. By county, etc., A-Z
522	Court of Claims (Table KF9)
524.A-Z	Various courts in the same locality. By city, county, etc., A-Z
	Judicial officers. Court employees
524.5	General (Table KF9)
	Directories see KFA-KFZ 508.A19
	Judges
525	General (Table KF9)
525.5.A-Z	Special topics, A-Z
525.5.A6	Appointment. Tenure. Retirement (Table KF7)
525.5.D5	Discipline. Judicial ethics (Table KF7)
525.5.E3	Education (Table KF7)
525.5.I4	Impeachment (Table KF7)
525.5.N6	Nominations. Judicial selection (Table KF7)
	Pensions see KFA-KFZ 525.5.S3
525.5.R3	Rating (Table KF7)
	Retirement see KFA-KFZ 525.5.A6

Courts. Procedure
Court organization and procedure
Judicial officers. Court employees
Judges
Special topics, A-Z -- Continued

525.5.S3	Salaries, pensions, etc. (Table KF7)
525.5.W67	Workload (Table KF7)
526.A-Z	Other, A-Z
526.A8	Attorneys (Table KF7)
526.C5	Clerks of court. Administrative officers (Table KF7)
526.C6	Constables (Table KF7)
526.C65	Coroners. Medical examiners (Table KF7)
526.C68	Court reporters (Table KF7)
	Guardians ad litem see KFA-KFZ 107
526.N6	Notaries (Table KF7)
526.S4	Sheriffs (Table KF7)
526.T72	Translators (Table KF7)
526.V5	Viewers (Table KF7)

Civil procedure
Including works on both civil and criminal procedure
General
Legislation

528.A17	Legislative documents. By date
	Statutes
	Collections
528.A19-.A199	Serials
528.A2	Monographs. By date of publication
528.A3-.A319	Particular acts
	Arranged chronologically, by means of successive Cutter numbers, according to date of original enactment or revision of law
	Under each:
	.xA15 — *Compilations of legislative histories*
	.xA2 — *Unannotated texts. By date of publication*
	.xA3-.xZ — *Annotated editions. Commentaries. By author of commentary or annotations*

Court rules
General. Comprehensive
Collections

529.A19-.A199	Serials. Loose-leaf editions
529.A2	Monographs. By date of publication
529.A23	Citators to rules
529.A25	Drafts. By date

Courts. Procedure
Civil procedure
General
Legislation
Court rules
General. Comprehensive -- Continued

529.A3-.A319 Particular rules

Arranged chronologically, by means of successive Cutter numbers, according to date of adoption or revision of rules

Under each:

.xA15	*Compilations of legislative histories. By date of publication*
.xA2	*Unannotated texts. By date of publication*
.xA3-.xZ7	*Annotated editions. By author of commentary or annotations*
.xZ8-.xZ89	*Digests*

529.5.A-Z Particular courts. By district, A-Z

Under each:

	Collections
.xA19-.xA199	*Serials*
.xA2	*Monographs. By date of publication*
	Particular rules
.xA3	*Unannotated texts. By date of publication*
.xA5-.xZ49	*Annotated editions. Commentaries. By author of commentary or annotations*
.xZ5	*Indexes. By date of publication*

For courts of intermediate appeal, see 556.A4; highest court of appeals, see 558.A4

529.8 Indexes to statutes and court rules

530 General works (Table KF8)

531 Equity practice and procedure. Chancery courts (Table KF9)

532 Jurisdiction. Venue. Removal of causes (Table KF9) Action

533 General (Table KF9)

534.A-Z Special topics, A-Z

534.P7 Process (Table KF7)

534.T5 Time. Deadlines (Table KF7)

Pleading and motions

535 General. Pleading (Table KF9)

535.8 Defenses and objections (Table KF9)

536.A-Z Special topics, A-Z

KFA-KFZ UNITED STATES - STATES AND TERRITORIES KFA-KFZ

Courts. Procedure
Civil procedure
General
Pleading and motions
Special topics, A-Z -- Continued

536.C6	Counterclaim. Cross claims (Table KF7)
536.L5	Limitation of actions (Table KF7)
536.4	Frivolous suits (Table KF9)
	Parties
536.5	General (Table KF9)
536.6.A-Z	Special topics, A-Z
536.6.C55	Class action
536.6.J6	Joinder of parties (Table KF7)
536.8	Confession of judgment (Table KF9)
	Pre-trial procedure
537	General. Deposition and discovery. Interrogatories (Table KF9)
537.5.A-Z	Special topics, A-Z
	Settlement see KFA-KFZ 560.3
	Trial. Trial practice
538	General (Table KF8)
538.4	Cross-examination (Table KF9)
539.A-Z	Particular types of cases or claims, A-Z
539.C64	Collection (Table KF7)
539.D43	Death by wrongful act (Table KF7)
539.D56	Discrimination (Table KF7)
539.E45	Eminent domain (Table KF7)
539.E49	Environmental actions (Table KF7)
539.L32	Labor law (Table KF7)
539.M34	Malpractice (Table KF7)
539.P4	Personal injuries (Table KF7)
539.P7	Products liability (Table KF7)
539.R4	Real property (Table KF7)
539.T7	Traffic accidents. Traffic violations. Drunk driving (Table KF7)
539.W6	Workers' compensation (Table KF7)
	Evidence
540	General (Table KF9)
540.3	Admission of evidence (Table KF9)
	Including motions in limine
540.4	Burden of proof. Presumptions. Prima facie evidence (Table KF9)
540.5.A-Z	Particular claims or actions, A-Z
540.5.N4	Negligence. Torts. Res ipsa loquitur (Table KF7)
	Witnesses
541	General (Table KF9)
	Privileged (confidential) communications

Courts. Procedure
Civil procedure
Trial. Trial practice
Evidence
Witnesses
Privileged (confidential) communications -- Continued

541.2	General (Table KF9)
541.3.A-Z	Particular relationships, A-Z
541.3.A77	Attorney and client (Table KF7)
541.3.P7	Press (Table KF7)
541.5	Expert evidence. Expert witnesses (Table KF9)
541.6	Hearsay (Table KF9)
541.9.A-Z	Other, A-Z
541.9.D45	Demonstrative (Table KF7)
541.9.D63	Documentary (Table KF7)
	Jury and jurors
542	General (Table KF9)
542.4	Special verdicts and findings (Table KF9)
542.6	Instructions to juries (Table KF9)
	For collected instructions see KF213.A+
	For individual instructions see KF389
	Proceedings before magistrates' courts see KFA-KFZ 520+
543	Special masters. Referees. Auditors. Examiners (Table KF9)
	Judgment
544	General (Table KF9)
545	Costs. Fees. In forma pauperis (Table KF9)
546.A-Z	Particular kinds of judgments, A-Z
546.S8	Summary judgment (Table KF7)
	Remedies and special proceedings
547	General (Table KF9)
548	Habeas corpus (Table KF9)
549	Injunctions. Provisional remedies (Table KF9)
550	Receivers in equity (Table KF9)
551	Execution of judgment. Attachment. Garnishment (Table KF9)
	Extraordinary remedies
552	General (Table KF9)
553.A-Z	Particular remedies, A-Z
553.I6	Imprisonment for debt (Table KF7)
553.M2	Mandamus (Table KF7)
553.Q52	Quo warranto (Table KF7)
	Appellate procedure
555	General (Table KF9)
	Intermediate appeals
556	General (Table KF9)

Courts. Procedure
Civil procedure
Remedies and special proceedings
Appellate procedure
Intermediate appeals -- Continued

557 By appellate district
Use KF6 for districts represented by district number, KF7
for districts represented by cutter number for name,
modified by KF9

558 Appeals to highest state court (Table KF9)

559 Litigation with the state as a party. Proceedings before Court of Claims (Table KF9)

560.A-Z Proceedings relating to particular branches of the law or special subjects. Non-contentious (ex parte) jurisdiction. By subject, A-Z

560.A3 Adoption (Table KF7)

560.L8 Lunacy (Table KF7)
Probate see KFA-KFZ 144+
Tort claims see KFA-KFZ 195+
Workers' compensation see KFA-KFZ 342+

560.3 Negotiated settlement. Compromise (Table KF9)
Including alternative dispute resolution

560.5 Arbitration and award. Commercial arbitration (Table KF9)
Criminal law
Cf. KFA-KFZ 499 Military criminal law and procedure
Cf. KFA-KFZ 595+ Juvenile criminal law and procedure

561 General. Comprehensive (Table KF9)
Administration of criminal justice. Reform of criminal law, enforcement, and procedure

562 General (Table KF9)

562.4 Speedy trial
Punishment and penalties

563 General (Table KF9)

564 Habitual criminals. Recidivists (Table KF9)

565.A-Z Particular penalties, A-Z

565.C2 Capital punishment (Table KF7)

565.F6 Forfeitures. Political disabilities (Table KF7)

565.S7 Sterilization (Table KF7)

566 General principles (Table KF9)
Criminal liability. Exemption from liability. Defenses

566.5 General (Table KF9)

566.6 Insanity (Table KF9)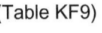
Justification

566.68 General (Table KF9)

566.7 Self-defense. Self-protection (Table KF9)
Particular offenses

566.8 General. Comprehensive (Table KF9)

Criminal law

Particular offenses -- Continued

Offenses against the person

567.A1	General (Table KF7)
567.A2-Z	Special topics, A-Z
567.A2	Abortion (Table KF7)
	Cf. KFA-KFZ 353 Birth control
567.A35	Aged abuse. Elder abuse (Table KF7)
567.C5	Child abuse. Child molesting. Sexual abuse of children (Table KF7)
567.F35	Family violence (Table KF7)
567.H6	Homicide (Table KF7)
	Older people, Abuse of see KFA-KFZ 567.A35
	Sexual abuse of children see KFA-KFZ 567.C5
567.S3	Sexual offenses (Table KF7)
567.W53	Wife abuse (Table KF7)
567.5	Libel. Slander. Defamation (Table KF9)

Offenses against property

568.A1	General (Table KF7)
568.A5-Z	Special topics, A-Z
568.A7	Arson (Table KF7)
	Blackmail see KFA-KFZ 568.T57
568.C65	Computer crimes (Table KF7)
568.C7	Credit card fraud (Table KF7)
	Extortion see KFA-KFZ 568.T57
568.F75	Fraud by forgery. Bad checks (Table KF7)
568.I57	Insurance fraud (Table KF7)
568.M2	Malicious mischief (Table KF7)
568.R3	Racketeering. Organized crime (Table KF7)
568.S43	Securities fraud (Table KF7)
568.T45	Thievery. Larceny. Shoplifting (Table KF7)
568.T57	Threats. Extortion. Blackmail (Table KF7)
569	Offenses against government and public order. Subversive activities. Sedition. Treason (Table KF9)

570.A-Z	Offenses against the administration of justice, A-Z
570.C6	Contempt of court (Table KF7)
570.5.A-Z	Offenses against public safety, A-Z
570.5.R5	Riot (Table KF7)

Offenses against public convenience and morality

571.A1	General (Table KF7)
571.A5-Z	Special topics, A-Z
571.B4	Bigamy (Table KF7)
571.D5	Disorderly conduct (Table KF7)
571.D7	Drunkenness (Table KF7)
571.G2	Gambling. Lotteries (Table KF7)
571.O2	Obscenity (Table KF7)
571.P7	Prostitution. Procuring. White slave traffic (Table KF7)

Criminal law

Particular offenses -- Continued

572.A-Z	Offenses against public property, public finance, and currency, A-Z
572.W45	Welfare fraud
574	Conspiracy (Table KF9)
	Criminal procedure
575	General (Table KF9)
576	Arrest and commitment. Rights of suspects (Table KF9)
576.5	Searches and seizures (Table KF9)
576.6	Bail (Table KF9)
576.7	Extradition. Interstate rendition (Table KF9)
577	Indictment. Information. Public prosecutor. Grand jury (Table KF9)
	For collected charges see KF213.A+
	For individual charges see KF389
578	Arraignment. Right to counsel. Public defenders (Table KF9)
578.3	Discovery (Table KF9)
578.5	Procedure without trial. Plea bargaining. Pleas of guilty. Nolo contendere (Table KF9)
	Trial
579	General (Table KF9)
	Evidence. Admission of evidence. Burden of proof
580	General (Table KF9)
580.5.A-Z	Special types of evidence and special topics, A-Z
580.5.E9	Expert evidence. Expert witnesses (Table KF7)
580.5.H4	Hearsay (Table KF7)
580.5.I4	Immunity of witnesses (Table KF7)
580.5.L5	Lie detectors. Polygraph examinations (Table KF7)
580.5.M4	Means of identification. Fingerprints, footprints, toothprints, etc. (Table KF7)
	Including DNA fingerprinting
	Polygraph examinations see KFA-KFZ 580.5.L5
580.5.W5	Wiretapping. Electronic listening and recording devices (Table KF7)
580.5.W54	Witnesses (Table KF7)
581	Jury (Table KF9)
583	Instructions to jury. Directed verdict (Table KF9)
	For collected instructions see KF213.A+
	For individual instructions see KF389
583.2	Judgment. Sentence (Table KF9)
583.4	Costs (Table KF9)
583.45	New trials (Table KF9)
583.5	Proceedings before magistrates' courts. Summary convictions (Table KF9)
584	Appeals. Appellate procedure (Table KF9)
585	Pardon (Table KF9)

Criminal procedure -- Continued

(586)	Proceedings before juvenile courts
	see KFA-KFZ 595+
	Execution of sentence. Corrections
587	General (Table KF9)
	Imprisonment. Prison administration
588	General (Table KF9)
588.5	Prisoners (Table KF9)
589	Prison labor. Prison industries (Table KF9)
590.A-Z	Particular types of penal or correctional institutions, A-Z
	Juvenile detention homes see KFA-KFZ 598.6
590.P3	Penitentiaries (Table KF7)
590.R3	Reformatories (Table KF7)
590.5.A-Z	Particular institutions, A-Z
591	Fines (Table KF9)
591.2	Forfeitures. Political disabilities (Table KF9)
592	Probation. Parole (Table KF9)
592.5	Criminal registration (Table KF9)
593	Indeterminate sentence (Table KF9)
	Victims of crimes
594	General (Table KF9)
	Compensation to victims of crimes see KFA-KFZ 200
	Juvenile criminal law and procedure. Administration of juvenile justice
595	General (Table KF9)
596	Juvenile courts (Table KF9)
	Cf. KFA-KFZ 94.5+ Domestic relations courts and children's courts
	Criminal law
597	General (Table KF9)
597.5	Status offenders (Table KF9)
	Criminal procedure
598	General (Table KF9)
598.3	Trial (Table KF9)
	Execution of sentence
	Imprisonment
598.6	Juvenile detention homes (Table KF9)
598.8	Probation. Parole (Table KF9)
599.A-Z	Law of particular counties, parishes, and other local self-government (except cities and other municipal corporations). By county, etc., A-Z
	Subarrange each by Table KF10C and Table KF10D modified as follows: .x2C6 = County government and services
<599.5.A-Z>	Particular cities, A-Z
	see KFX

INDEX

A

Abatement of nuisances: KFA-KFZ 378
Abbreviations: KF246
Abduction: KF9332
Ability grouping (Public education): KF4157
Abortion: KF9315, KFC1121, KFN6121, KFA-KFZ 567.A2
Social legislation: KF3771
Abortion services: KFC619.A25, KFA-KFZ 363.A25
Absence without leave (Military law): KF7618.D3
Absentee voting: KF4901, KFA-KFZ 420.85.A2
Abstracting and indexing systems: KF247
Abstractors, Title (Directories): KF195.T5
Abstracts of title: KF678+, KFC171, KFN5171
Abused wives (Legal services to): KF337.5.A27
Academic faculties: KF4240
Academic freedom: KF4242
Access to children
Family law: KF547+
Access to public accommodations: KF4756+
Access to public records: KF5753, KFC827, KFN5827, KFA-KFZ 462.6.A25
Accession (Personal property): KF713.A3
Accident control: KF3970+, KFX2062
Accident insurance: KF1187
Accident prevention: KFA-KFZ 380.5.A1+
Accidents, Aviation: KF1290.A9
Accidents, Building: KFN5320.B8, KFA-KFZ 196.3.B8
Accidents, Helicopter: KF1290.A9
Accidents, Marine: KF1107
Accidents, Playground: KF1290.P5
Accidents, School: KF1309, KF1310
Accidents, Sidewalk: KFN5320.S5

Accidents, Streetcar: KFA-KFZ 196.3.S7
Accidents, Traffic: KF1306.T7
Accord and satisfaction: KF830
Accountants
Expert witnesses (Civil procedure): KF8968.15
Legal handbooks: KF390.A3
Regulation of profession: KF2920, KFC547.A3+, KFN5547.A3+, KFA-KFZ 329.A25+
Accounting
Corporations: KF1446, KFA-KFZ 214.A23
Courts: KFC958.5, KFN5958.5
Decedents' estates: KF779.A3
Law office management: KF320.A2
Postal service: KF2684
Probate: KFA-KFZ 144.5.A25
Public finance
Federal: KF6231+
Local: KF6772, KFN5908
State: KF6740
State and local: KF6722
Railroads: KF2308
Telecommunication: KF2765.5
Telegraph: KF2775.5
Telephone: KF2780.5
Trusts and trustees: KFA-KFZ 139.A25
Accounts (Banking): KFA-KFZ 167.D44
Accretion: KF685.A3
Acknowledgement of Indian tribes
Federal government: KF8210.R32
Acquisition of property: KF711+
Acreage allotments: KF1705+
Action
Civil procedure: KFC1003
Actions in rem: KF560+
Actors
Collective labor agreements: KF3409.A3
Copyright: KF3076
Acupuncturists: KF2913.A28+, KFC546.A28+, KFN5546.5.A36+, KFA-KFZ 326.5.A25+
Adhesion contracts: KF809

INDEX

Adjoining landowners: KFN5161+
Administration of criminal justice: KF9223, KFC1102+, KFN6102+, KFA-KFZ 562+
Data processing: KF242.C72+
Administration of decedents' estates: KF774+, KFC210, KFN5210, KFA-KFZ 147
Administration of justice: KF384
Criminal justice: KF9223, KFC1102+, KFN6102+, KFA-KFZ 562+
Juvenile justice: KF9771+, KFC1195+, KFN6195+, KFA-KFZ 595+
Organization of the judiciary: KF8700, KFC950, KFN5950+, KFN5950, KFA-KFZ 508
Administrative agency investigations: KF5422
Administrative law: KF5401+, KFA-KFZ 440+
Legal profession: KF299.A32
Legal research: KF241.A35
Administrative lawyers (Directories): KF195.A4
Administrative organization and procedure: KF5401+, KFC779+, KFN5780+, KFA-KFZ 440+
Administrative regulations (Citators): KF78
Administrative Review, Commission on (United States House of Representatives): KF4997.A33
Administrative tribunals: KF5416+, KFC782, KFN5782
Admiralty: KF299.M37
Admiralty proceedings: KF1111+, KFN5280
Admissibility and exclusion of evidence: KF8969+
Admission (Education): KF4151+, KFA-KFZ 392.2
Admission taxes: KF6611.A3
Admission to law school: KF285.A1+
Admission to the bar: KF302+, KF5414, KFN5076, KFA-KFZ 76

Admission to the Union
Constitutional law: KF4545.S7, KFA-KFZ 401.6.S8
Admissions (Taxation): KFA-KFZ 485.A34
Adoption
Domestic relations: KF545, KFN5132, KFA-KFZ 104.5
Procedure: KFC1088, KFA-KFZ 560.A3
Adoption proceedings: KFC1088, KFA-KFZ 560.A3
Adult education: KF4223
Adulteration of food: KF3878
Adultery: KF9435
Adventures, Joint: KF1380.5
Adverse possession: KF685.A4, KFA-KFZ 128.A3
Advertising: KF5532, KFA-KFZ 444.6
Lawyers: KF310.A3
Legal profession: KFA-KFZ 77.5.A38
Regulation: KF1348.A38
Trade regulation: KF1614+
Advertising, Legal: KF450.N6, KFN5100.N6
Advertising, Outdoor
Building laws: KF5710
Advisory opinions
Constitutional law: KF4579.A38
Affidavits of defense: KFP535.8
Affirmative action: KF4755.5
African American lawyers: KF299.A35
African American universities and colleges: KF4232
African Americans
Civil rights: KF4756+, KFN5696.A4, KFA-KFZ 411.5.A34
Discrimination: KF4756+, KFN5696.A4
Education: KF4151+
Employment: KF3464+, KFN5572+, KFA-KFZ 334.5.D5
Suffrage: KF4893
Agencies, Employment: KF2042.E5, KFC446.E5, KFN5446.E5
Agency: KF1341+, KFC335+, KFN5335+, KFA-KFZ 202+

INDEX

Agents, Real estate: KF2042.R4, KFC446.R3, KFN5446.R3

Aggregate litigation
- Civil procedure: KF8896

Aging, Select Committee on (United States House of Representatives): KF4997.A34

Aging, Special Committee on (United States Senate): KF4987.A25

Agricultural Adjustment Act: KF1691

Agricultural assistance: KF4670.A35

Agricultural commodities
- Acreage allotments: KF1705+
- Export trade: KF1990.A4
- Freight classification: KF2355.A4+
- Grading: KF1721+
- Marketing: KF1718+, KFC391+, KFA-KFZ 244.A1+
- Marketing quotas: KF1705+
- Perishables: KF1719.P3
- Price supports: KF1693+
- Processing: KF1902+, KFC416+
- Processing tax: KF6630+
- Regulation: KFC416+
- Standards: KF1721+
- Surpluses: KF1709+

Agricultural cooperatives: KF1715, KFC390, KFN5390, KFA-KFZ 242

Agricultural credit banks: KF1011, KFN5253, KFA-KFZ 166.A4

Agricultural insurance: KF1203+

Agricultural laborers
- Management-labor relations: KF3452.A3
- Military service: KF7266.A4
- Social security: KF3664.A4
- Wages: KF3505.A4
- Workers' compensation: KF3632.A4

Agricultural land
- Business taxes: KFA-KFZ 480.5.A35

Agricultural law and legislation (Electronic data processing): KF242.A45+

Agricultural machinery industry (Collective labor agreements): KF3409.A4

Agricultural marketing agreements: KF1696+

Agricultural marketing orders: KF1696+

Agricultural migrant labor: KF3580.A4

Agricultural pests, Control of: KF1687+, KFN5387, KFA-KFZ 240

Agricultural price supports: KF1692+

Agricultural production control: KF1692+

Agricultural surpluses: KF1709+

Agricultural warehouses: KF2056

Agricultural workers
- Workers' compensation: KF3632.A4

Agriculture: KF1681+, KFC385+, KFN5385+, KFA-KFZ 239+
- Collective labor agreements: KFC562.A35, KFA-KFZ 332.8.A35
- Income tax: KF6495.A47
- Labor disputes: KFA-KFZ 333.8.A34
- Labor law: KFC589.A4, KFA-KFZ 338.A4
- Wages: KF3505.A4

Agriculture and Forestry, Committee on (United States Senate): KF4987.A3

Agriculture, Committee on (United States House of Representatives): KF4997.A35

Agriculture Department (U.S.): KF1683

Agriculture, Nutrition, and Forestry, Committee on (United States Senate): KF4987.A35

AIDS (Disease): KF3803.A54, KFC613.5.A53, KFN5613.5.A36, KFA-KFZ 357.8.A35

AIDS patients
- Employment of: KF3470

Air, Carriage by: KF1093

Air carriers: KFC510+, KFN5510

Air charters: KF2446

Air conditioning
- Building laws: KF5708, KFC818, KFN5818, KFA-KFZ 459.75

Air conditioning industry
- Regulation: KFA-KFZ 282.H43

Air express: KF2447

Air Force education and training: KF7413+

INDEX

Air Force hospitals: KF7438
Air Force pay: KF7414+
Air Force pensions: KF7415
Air Force (U.S.): KF7405+
Air freight: KF2447
Air freight forwarders: KF2462
Air mail: KF2700
Air National Guard: KF7430
Air pollution: KF3812+, KFC614, KFN5614, KFA-KFZ 358+
Air safety: KF2406, KFC511, KFA-KFZ 305.2
Air traffic rules: KF2406, KFC511, KFN5511, KFX2056, KFA-KFZ 305.2
Air user taxes: KF6614.A9, KFC900.A9
Aircargo: KF2447
Aircraft
  Personal property tax: KF6765.8.A4
Airfreight: KF2447
Airlines: KF2421+
  Collective labor agreements: KF3409.A43
  Insolvency and bankruptcy: KF1535.A37
Airmail subsidies: KF2449
Airplane industry
  Collective labor agreements: KF3409.A45
  Wages: KF3505.A5
Airplane parking: KFA-KFZ 159.5.P3
Airplanes
  Products liability: KF1297.A57
Airports: KF2415+, KFC512, KFN5512, KFX2056, KFA-KFZ 305.5
Airspace: KF580
Airworthiness: KF2406, KFN5511
Alabama
  Laws: KFA1+
Alaska
  Laws: KFA1201+
Alchoholic beverages
  Import trade: KF1996.A5
Alcohol: KF3901+, KFA-KFZ 375+
  Indians: KFA-KFZ 505.6.A44
  Taxation: KF6611.A5
Alcohol, Denatured: KF3924.D3

Alcohol, Industrial (Manufacture): KF1876.A5
Alcohol production: KF3901+
Alcoholic beverages
  Advertising: KF1616.A5
  Indians: KFA-KFZ 505.6.A44
  Labeling: KF1620.A5+
  Liquor laws: KF3901+, KFC635+, KFN5635+, KFX2051, KFA-KFZ 375+
  Taxation: KF6612+, KFC900.A5, KFN5900.A5, KFA-KFZ 485.A5
Alcoholics, Treatment and rehabilitation of: KF3829.A5, KFN5621.A5
Alcoholism: KFA-KFZ 366.A42
  Medical legislation: KF3829.A5, KFN5621.A5
Alcoholism and traffic accidents: KF2231
Aleatory contracts: KF1241+
Alien landownership: KF573, KFA-KFZ 112.5
Alien property: KF564
Alien tort claims: KF1309.5
Aliens: KF4800+, KFC698+, KFN5698, KFA-KFZ 414
  Deportation: KF4842
  Income tax: KF6441
  Military service: KF7268.A5
  National Guard: KFN5929.A5
  Public welfare: KF3743
Aliens, Illegal
  Legal services to: KF337.5.I45
Alimony
  Domestic relations: KF537, KFN5127
  Income tax: KF6428.A4
All terrain vehicles (Motor vehicle laws): KF2220.S6, KFA-KFZ 297.75.S64
Allegheny County Court (Pennsylvania): KFP518.5
Alteration of checks: KF961.F6
Alternative dispute resolution: KF9084, KFA-KFZ 560.3
Aluminum industry: KF1836.A5
  Collective labor agreements: KF3409.A5

INDEX

Alzheimer's disease: KF3803.A56, KFA-KFZ 357.8.A48

Amateur radio broadcasting stations: KF2828

Ambulance chasing (Legal ethics): KF310.A4

Ambulance service: KF3826.E5, KFN5619.E43, KFA-KFZ 363.E43

Ambulatory medical care: KF3826.A45, KFN5619.A46, KFA-KFZ 363.A43

Amending and amendments
- State constitutions: KFC680, KFN5680, KFA-KFZ 401
- U.S. Constitution: KF4557+

American Arbitration Association: KF9086

American Bar Association: KF325+

American Bar Foundation: KF294.A3

American Digest: KF141

American Judicature Society: KF294.A4

American Law Institute: KF294.A5

American Patent Law Association: KF3165.A6

American State Papers: KF11

Americans abroad (Legal handbooks): KF390.A5

Amish: KF4869.A45

Ammonia: KFA-KFZ 380.A7

Ammunition
- Public safety: KF3941+
- Taxation: KF6614.A5

Amortization (Income tax): KF6386

Amusements
- Control of social activities: KF3987, KFC647.A58, KFA-KFZ 386.A47
- Taxation: KFA-KFZ 485.A34

Ancillary business activities (Legal ethics): KF310.A43

Anesthesiologists: KF2910.A5+

Anesthetists: KF2910.A5+

Anguish and fright: KF1264

Animal Industry, Bureau of (U.S.): KF1730.1

Animal products inspection: KF3806

Animal protection: KF3841+

Animal rights: KF3841+

Animal rights lawyers: KF299.A55

Animal welfare: KF3841+

Animal welfare lawyers: KF299.A55

Animals
- Cruelty to animals: KF3841+, KFC627, KFN5627, KFA-KFZ 370
- Diseases: KF3838.A+, KFN5624.A+, KFA-KFZ 369.A+
- Dissection: KF3843
- Legal aspects: KF390.5.A5, KFA-KFZ 84.5.A45
- Quarantine: KF3836.Q2, KFC623.5, KFA-KFZ 368.5.Q3
- Slaughtering: KF3844
- Tort liability: KF1293
- Transportation: KF3842
- Veterinary medicine: KF3835+, KFC623+, KFN5623+, KFA-KFZ 368+
- Vivisection: KF3843
- Wildlife protection: KF5640+, KFC806, KFN5806, KFA-KFZ 453+

Animals, Damage caused by
- Liability: KFA-KFZ 197.6

Annexation
- Municipal government: KF5315.A5, KFA-KFZ 431.9.A5

Annuities
- Income tax: KF6425

Annuities, Variable (Life insurance): KF1177.V3, KFA-KFZ 186.5.V3

Antennas
- Zoning: KF5700.5.A58

Anthem, National: KF5150

Antibiotics: KF3894.B5

Antidumping duties: KF6708.D8

Antiquities
- Indians: KF8210.A57

Antitrust aspects
- Medical legislation: KF3827.A58

Antitrust Division (Department of Justice): KF1653

Antitrust laws: KF1631+, KFC377, KFN5377, KFA-KFZ 231
- Copyright: KF3116
- Labor unions: KF3402
- Legal research: KF241.A57

INDEX

Antitrust lawyers (Directories): KF195.A57
Antitrust payments (Taxation): KF6499.D3
Antitrust recoveries (Taxation): KF6499.D3
Apiculture: KF1755
Appellate courts, Intermediate (State): KFN5048+
Court rules: KFC1078+, KFN6078+, KFA-KFZ 556+
Organization: KFC964, KFN5964+, KFA-KFZ 513+
Procedure: KFC1075+, KFN6078+, KFA-KFZ 555+
Appellate procedure: KFP555+
Civil: KF9050+, KFC1075+, KFN6075+
Civil procedure: KFA-KFZ 555+
Criminal: KF9690, KFC1174, KFA-KFZ 584
Juvenile courts: KF9822
Military: KF7665
Study and teaching: KF277.A64
Taxation: KF6324, KFC866, KFN5866, KFA-KFZ 471.5
Apples
Grading: KF1725.A6
Marketing: KF1719.A6
Standards: KF1725.A6
Weights and measures: KFC383.5.A6
Applications
Patent law: KF3125.C5
Appointment of judges: KF8776, KFA-KFZ 525.5.A6
Apportionment
Election law: KF4905, KFC714, KFN5714, KFA-KFZ 420.85.A6
Electronic data processing: KF242.A65+
Appraisal of goods (Commercial policy): KF6708.A66
Appraisals, Employee: KF3457.8
Apprentices
Apprentice contracts: KFA-KFZ 154.5.A6

Apprentices
Labor hygiene and safety: KFA-KFZ 335.7
Labor standards: KF3559
Appropriations, Committee on
United States House of Representatives: KF4997.A6
Aquaculture: KF1760, KFC397.5, KFA-KFZ 253
Arbitration
Labor disputes: KF3416+, KFC565, KFN5565, KFA-KFZ 333+
Arbitration and award: KF9085+, KFC1094, KFN6094, KFA-KFZ 560.5
Archaeological sites: KFA-KFZ 398.9
Architects: KF2925, KFC547.A7+, KFA-KFZ 329.A7+
Archives: KF4325, KFA-KFZ 399+
Arid lands: KF5616+, KFA-KFZ 451.5
Arizona
Laws: KFA2401+
Arkansas
Laws: KFA3601+
Armed Forces hospitals: KF7298
Armed Forces personnel
Legal handbooks: KF390.A67
Legal services to: KF337.5.A7
Armed Services, Committee on
United States House of Representatives: KF4997.A7
United States Senate: KF4987.A7
Army Corps of Engineers (U.S.): KF7335.E5
Army Department (U.S.): KF7305+
Army education and training: KF7313+
Army hospitals: KF7338
Army pay: KF7314+
Army pensions: KF7315
Army (U.S.): KF7305+
Arraignment: KF9645+, KFC1157, KFN6160, KFA-KFZ 578
Arrest and commitment: KF9625+, KFC1156, KFN6156, KFA-KFZ 576
Arrest records, Cancellation of: KFC1194
Arsenic: KF3964.A67

INDEX

Arson: KF9377, KFC1134, KFA-KFZ 568.A7

Art

Patent law: KF3133.A38

Art collectors (Legal handbooks): KF390.A7

Art galleries

Regulation: KF2042.A76

Artificial insemination: KF3830+

Artificial islands: KF2594

Artificial satellites in telecommunication: KF2770

Artisans (Legal handbooks): KF390.A69

Artists (Legal handbooks): KF390.A7

Artists' studios (Building laws): KF5709.3.A78

Arts and science: KF4270+, KFC670+, KFN5670+, KFX2067, KFA-KFZ 398+

Arts, The

Copyright: KF3035+

Government aid: KF4288+

Asbestos: KF3964.A73, KFC641.5.A69

Products liability: KF1297.A73

Public safety: KFA-KFZ 380.A75

Asbestos abatement contractors and industries: KFA-KFZ 282.A82

Asian Americans

Civil rights: KF4757.5.A75

Asians

Aliens: KF4848.A83

Assassination

Trials: KF221.M8

Assault and battery: KF9320

Assembly committee documents (State): KFN5010.4.A+

Assembly, Freedom of: KF4778

Assembly (Legislature): KFN5735+, KFA-KFZ 423

Assessment

Local taxation (Real property): KF6785, KFA-KFZ 491.R44

State taxation: KF6759.5

Real property: KF6760.5, KFC881.5, KFN5881.5, KFA-KFZ 479.3

Assessment insurance: KF1169.A7

Assets, Sale of

Insolvency and bankruptcy: KF1536.S34

Assignments

Bankruptcy: KF1548.A7, KFA-KFZ 226.A7

Contracts: KF814

Life insurance: KF1181.A8

Patents: KF3149

Assignments for benefit of creditors: KF1548.A7, KFN5370, KFA-KFZ 226.A7

Assistance in emergencies: KF1329+, KFC334, KFA-KFZ 201

Assisted suicide

Medical legislation: KF3827.E87

Association of Trial Lawyers of America: KF294.A8

Associations: KF1355+, KFC337+, KFN5337+, KFA-KFZ 205+

Associations, Business: KF1365+, KFC339+, KFN5339+, KFA-KFZ 207+

Associations, Unincorporated: KF1361+, KFC338+, KFN5338+, KFA-KFZ 206+

Assumpsit: KF836+

Assumption of risk (Employer's liability): KF1319.A7

Asylums: KFX2048.3

Atheism

Church and state: KF4868.A84

Athletes

Legal handbooks: KF390.A74

Athletic equipment and supplies (Products liability): KF1297.A77

Atomic damage insurance: KF1220.N8

Atomic damage (Liability): KF1220.N8

Atomic Energy Commission (U.S.): KF2138.1

Atomic Energy, Joint Committee on (U.S. Congress): KF4939.5.A8

Atomic industry

Collective labor agreements: KF3409.A7

Labor hygiene and safety: KF3574.A7, KFN5586.A7

Workers' compensation: KF3632.A7

INDEX

Atomic power
  Public safety: KF3948, KFC641.5.A7, KFN5641.5.A85, KFA-KFZ 380.A8
  Public utilities: KF2138+, KFA-KFZ 290
Atomic safety
  Labor law: KFN5586.A7
Atomic warfare: KF7695.A7
Atomic waste disposal: KF3950
Attachment and garnishment: KF9026, KFC1066, KFN6066, KFA-KFZ 551
Attendants, Court: KFN5985.A65
Attorney and client: KF311+
  Privileged communication: KF8959.A7, KFA-KFZ 541.3.A77
Attorney General (U.S.): KF5106+
Attorney General's Office (California): KFC746.J86
Attorneys: KF297+
  Admission to the bar: KF302+
Attorneys as judicial officers: KF8795, KFN5985.A7, KFA-KFZ 526.A8
Attorneys before regulatory agencies: KF5414, KFC781
Attorneys, City: KF5322, KFX2020.C6
Attorneys, County: KFA-KFZ 437.8.A7
Attorneys' fees: KF316, KFA-KFZ 77.5.F4
  Workers' compensation: KF3623.A8
Attorneys general: KFA-KFZ 427.5.A8
Attorneys General's opinions: KF5406.A6+, KFA-KFZ 440.A55+
Attorneys' handbooks, manuals, etc.: KF319, KFN5077, KFA-KFZ 77
Attorneys, Patent: KF3165.A3+
Attorneys, United States: KF8793
Attractive nuisance: KF1287.5.A8, KFA-KFZ 196.3.A78
Auction houses: KF2038.A8
Auction sales: KF920
Auctions: KFA-KFZ 281.A82
Audiologists: KF2915.S63+, KFA-KFZ 326.5.S64+
Audiovisual education: KF4209.A8
Auditing: KF1357
  Corporations: KF1446, KFC337.5.A8, KFA-KFZ 214.A23

Auditing
  Postal services: KF2684
  Public expenditures
    Federal: KF6231+
    Local: KF6772, KFN5908, KFA-KFZ 488.5
    State: KF6740, KFC845+, KFN5845+, KFA-KFZ 467+
    State and local: KF6722
Auditors (Financial advisors): KF2920, KFC547.A3+, KFN5547.A3+
Auditors (Trial practice): KF8986, KFN6049, KFA-KFZ 543
Author and publisher: KF3084
Authors (Legal handbooks): KF390.A96
Autism (Capacity and disability): KF480.5.A94
Autobuses: KFX2034.5.A8
Automatic information retrieval
  Legal research: KF242.A+
Automatic stays (Bankruptcy): KF1530.A88
Automation
  Law office management: KF320.A9, KFA-KFZ 77.5.A95
Automobile accidents: KF1290.A8, KFC320.A8, KFN5320.A8, KFA-KFZ 196.3.A8
  Financial responsibility laws: KF2219
Automobile collectors (Legal handbooks): KF390.A97
Automobile dealers: KF2036.A8
Automobile expenses (Income tax): KF6395.A96
Automobile industry
  Collective labor agreements: KF3409.A8
  Management-labor relations: KF3452.A8
  Products liability: KF1297.A8
  Wages: KF3505.A9
Automobile lawyers (Directories): KF195.A8
Automobile licenses: KF6614.A8, KFC900.A8, KFN5900.A8
Automobile litigation (Electronic data processing): KF242.A85+

Automobile racers (Legal handbooks): KF390.A98

Automobile repair fraud: KF9371

Automobile repair shops: KF2042.A8, KFC446.A87

Automobile service stations: KFA-KFZ 282.A9

Automobile trailer taxes: KFA-KFZ 491.A8

Automobiles

Import trade: KF1996.A96

Automotive equipment (Products liability): KF1297.A8

Automotive maintenance and repair industry

Regulation: KFA-KFZ 282.A9

Automotive transportation: KF2201+, KFC470+, KFN5470+, KFA-KFZ 296+

Income tax: KF6495.A8

Aviation: KF2400+, KF2400+, KFC510+, KFN5510+, KFA-KFZ 305+

Taxation: KF6614.A9, KFC900.A9

Aviation accident claims (Trial practice): KF8925.A9

Aviation accidents: KF1290.A9

Aviation, Commercial: KF2421+, KFC510+, KFN5510

Aviation industry

Insolvency and bankruptcy: KF1535.A37

Labor law: KF3580.A8

Aviation insurance: KF1194, KFA-KFZ 189.A8

Aviation personnel: KFA-KFZ 305.8

Awards, Civilian: KF5153

Awards, Military: KF5154

AWOL: KF7618.D3

B

Bad checks

Commercial law: KF961.A+

Criminal law: KF9367, KFA-KFZ 568.F75

Bail: KF9632, KF10A 17.4.B3, KFA-KFZ 576.6

Bail bonds: KF1226

Bailments

Contracts involving bailments: KF939+, KFN5240+, KFA-KFZ 159+

Personal property: KF718.A+

Bakery products

Advertising: KF1616.B33

Inspection: KF1903

Standards and grading: KF1903

Baking industry: KF1903

Baking powder: KF3879.B2

Baking powder industry: KF1944.B2

Bank deposit insurance: KF1023

Bank deposits: KF1022

Bank holding companies: KF1017

Bank insurance: KF1189.5

Bank mergers: KF1018

Bank reserves: KF1030.R35

Bank secrets: KF1030.R3

Bankhead-Jones Farm Tenant Act: KF1701

Banking: KF966+, KFC250+, KFN5250+, KFX2031.3.A+, KFA-KFZ 165+

Advertising: KF1616.B34

Banking and Currency, Committee on (United States House of Representatives): KF4997.B3

Banking, Housing and Urban Affairs, Committee on (United States Senate): KF4987.B36

Banking law (Legal research): KF241.B34

Banking lawyers (Directories): KF195.B3

Bankruptcy and insolvency: KF1501+, KFC364+, KFC365+, KFN5364+

Conflict of laws: KF418.B3

Electronic data processing: KF242.B3+

Legal research: KF241.B36

Taxation: KF6332

Bankruptcy lawyers (Directories): KF195.B35

Bankruptcy statistics: KF185.B2, KF185.E58

Banks: KF966+

Business taxes: KFA-KFZ 480.5.B3

INDEX

Banks
Corporate reorganization: KF1546.B2
Income tax: KF6495.B2, KFC879.B2, KFN5879.B2, KFA-KFZ 477.5.B35
Labor law: KF3580.B34
State taxation: KF6738.B2
Tort liability: KF1301.5.B36
Wages: KF3505.B25
Bar association journals: KF200
Bar associations, National: KF325+
Bar associations, State: KF330+
Bar associations, Student: KF288
Bar examinations: KF303
Barber supply industry: KF1893.B2
Barbers: KFC446.B3, KFA-KFZ 282.B37
Barges
Safety regulations: KF2558.B2
Barratry: KF1114.B2
Battered wives: KF337.5.A27
Battery
Criminal law: KF9320
Battery industry
Wages: KF3505.B27
Battlefields: KF4310+
Beaches: KFA-KFZ 451.8
Bean processing industry: KF1909.B3
Beauty shops: KFC446.B4, KFA-KFZ 282.B4
Beauty supply industry: KF1893.B2
Bedding (Labeling): KF1620.F83
Beef (Standards and grading): KF1726.C2
Beekeeping: KF1755
Beer
Alcoholic beverage laws: KF3924.B4, KFC636.B4, KFA-KFZ 375.5.B44
Labeling: KF1620.A53
Liquor laws: KF3924.B4, KFC636.B4, KFA-KFZ 375.5.B44
Taxation: KF6613.B3
Behavior modification (Medical legislation): KF3827.B4
Benzene: KF3964.B45
Bestiality: KF9328.B3
Beverage industry: KF1940.A+

Beverages (Containers): KF1666.B3, KFC384.B48
Bible reading in schools: KF4162, KFN5655, KFA-KFZ 392.7
Bicycles: KF2220.B5, KFA-KFZ 297.75.B53
Bigamy: KF9436, KFA-KFZ 571.B4
Bilingual ballots: KF4896.L56
Bilingual education: KF4204, KFC664.5.L34, KFA-KFZ 395.3
Bilingualism: KF4767
Bill drafting: KF4950, KFC724, KFN5724, KFA-KFZ 421.5.B5
Study and teaching: KF277.B55
Bill of Rights: KF4741+
Bill of sale: KF949
Billboards
Building laws: KF5710, KFA-KFZ 459.9
Bills
Congressional documents: KF16+
Bills of exchange: KF958+, KFC246, KFN5246+, KFA-KFZ 160+
Taxation: KF6614.B4
Bills of lading: KF925+, KFN5237.5, KFA-KFZ 156.5.B5
Ocean bills of lading: KF1109
Biography: KF354.A+
General: KF355.A+
Local bar associations: KF334.A+
State bar associations: KF332.A+
Supreme Court justices: KF8744+
Biological products: KF3894.B5
Biotechnology
Patent law: KF3133.B56
Research: KFA-KFZ 398.2.B54
Biotechnology industries: KF1893.B56, KFC412.B56, KFA-KFZ 271.B56
Bird protection: KF5640+, KFC806, KFN5806, KFA-KFZ 453+
Birds, Migratory: KF5640+, KF5640
Birth certificates: KF485, KFC113, KFA-KFZ 93
Birth control: KF3766
Legal research: KF241.B57
Social legislation: KFC609, KFA-KFZ 353

Birth registers: KFC113
Bituminous Coal Commission (U.S.): KF1830.5
Black Panthers Trial, New York, 1970-1971: KF224.B55
Blackmail: KF9372+, KFC1132, KFN6132, KFA-KFZ 568.T57
Blind persons
Education: KF4212
Public welfare: KF3739, KFC605.3, KFN5605.3, KFA-KFZ 350.B5
Blind students: KF4212
Blindness, Diseases causing: KFA-KFZ 357.8.B5
Blood banks: KF3826.B55, KFA-KFZ 363.B55
Blood grouping (Evidence): KF8963
Blue Shield (Health insurance): KF1184.G7
Board of War Communications (U.S.): KF2765.21
Boards of directors
Business corporations: KFA-KFZ 213.7+
Boards of education: KF4131
Boats: KF2536+, KFN5521+, KFA-KFZ 308.1+
Taxation: KF6614.B6
Body armor
Public safety: KF3942.B6
Body measurements (Evidence): KF8963
Bond lawyers: KF299.B65
Bonded warehouses: KF2054
Bonding: KF1225+, KFC300, KFN5301, KFA-KFZ 192.S8
Bonding of employees: KF1225
Bonds: KF1456
Bonds, Municipal: KF6775, KFX2089.5, KFA-KFZ 489
Bonus system
Labor law: KF3496
Book industries and trade: KF1893.B57, KFA-KFZ 271.B64
Bookbinding industry: KF1893.B6
Bottled water industry: KF1940.M5
Bottomry: KF1114.B6

Boundaries
Real property: KF639, KFA-KFZ 123.B6
Boycotts: KF3430+, KFN5566
Branch banking: KF1019
Brand inspection (Cattle): KF1730.8.B7, KFC393.5
Brandy (Taxation): KF6613.B7
Breach of contract: KF836+, KFC223, KFA-KFZ 151.B74
Life insurance: KF1181.B6
Breach of trust: KF745
Breast implants
Products liability: KF1297.B74
Brewery workers (Workers' compensation): KF3632.B6
Bribery
Criminal law: KF9409
Criminal trials: KF221.B74
Bridges: KF5540+, KFA-KFZ 445
Brief writing: KF251
Briefs (Printing and filing)
Courts: KF8733.5
Broadcasting (Advertising): KF1617.B7
Broadcasting of court proceedings: KF8726
Broadcasting rights (Copyright)
Art and photography: KF3060.3
Literature: KF3060.3
Music: KF3045.3
Brokers: KF1348.B7
Contracts: KFA-KFZ 179.5.B7
Brokers, Customhouse: KF6696.5
Brokers, Stock: KF1071
Brucellosis in animals: KFA-KFZ 369.B7
Brush manufacturing industry: KF1893.B7
Budget
Local finance: KF6772, KFN5908, KFA-KFZ 488.5
Public finance: KF6221+
State: KF6740, KFC842, KFN5842, KFA-KFZ 467+
State and local: KF6722

INDEX

Budget, Committee on the (United States House of Representatives): KF4997.B8

Building accidents: KFN5320.B8, KFA-KFZ 196.3.B8

Liability for: KF1287.5.B8

Building and construction industry

Collective labor agreements: KF3409.C65, KFN5562.C6

Contracts: KF901+, KFC230.B8, KFN5230.B8, KFA-KFZ 155.8.B8

Government contracts: KF865, KFC224.3, KFN5224.3

Trial practice: KF8925.B84

Income tax: KF6495.C6

Labor disputes: KF3450.C65+

Labor hygiene and safety: KF3574.C65, KFC586.B8, KFA-KFZ 336.C6

Labor law: KF3580.C6

Regulation: KF1950, KFC424, KFN5424, KFX2030, KFA-KFZ 275

Wages: KF3505.C65

Workers' compensation: KFN5594.C6

Building and loan associations: KF1009, KFC254, KFN5254.B8, KFA-KFZ 166.B8

Building cleaning industry

Labor hygiene and safety: KF3574.B84

Labor law: KF3580.B84

Building contractors: KF1950, KFC424, KFN5424

Building laws: KF5701+, KFC813+, KFN5813+, KFA-KFZ 459.A1+

Building lawyers (Directories): KF195.C58

Building leases: KF593.G7, KFC147.G7

Building (Public property): KF5691+, KFX2080, KF10D .x2Z62+

Buildings, Prefabricated

Building laws: KF5702.P74, KFA-KFZ 459.P7

Bulk transfers: KF1548.B8, KFN5371

Burden of proof

Civil procedure: KF8939+, KFC1031+, KFN6031+, KFA-KFZ 540.4

Criminal procedure: KF9660+, KFC1165+, KFN6165+, KFA-KFZ 580+

Bureau of Animal Industry (U.S.): KF1730.1

Bureau of Indian Affairs (U.S.): KF8225

Bureau of Labor Statistics (U.S.): KF3327.B8

Bureau of Mines (U.S.): KF1820.5

Bureau of Narcotics (U.S.): KF3890.1

Bureau of Navigation (U.S.): KF2566.5

Bureau of Prohibition (U.S.): KF3921

Burgesses: KFP436.8.B8

Burglary insurance: KF1200

Burial insurance: KF1188

Burial laws: KF3781, KFC611, KFN5611, KFA-KFZ 355

Burros (Wildlife protection): KF5645.H65

Bus accidents: KF1290.S7

Bus lines: KF2260, KFN5482

Buses: KFA-KFZ 300.B86

Business

Civil rights: KF4753

Business appraisers

Expert witnesses (Civil procedure): KF8968.19

Business associations: KF1365+, KFC339+, KFN5339+, KFA-KFZ 207+

Business cases

Contracts

Trial practice: KF8925.C55

Business consultants: KF390.C65

Business corporations: KF1396+, KFC345+, KFN5345+, KFA-KFZ 213+

Business insurance: KF1189.5, KFA-KFZ 193.B87

Business interruption insurance: KF1202.B8

Business licenses: KF6763+, KFN5884+, KFA-KFZ 480+

Business life insurance: KF1180.B8

Business methods
Patent law: KF3133.B87
Business organizations: KF1365+, KFC339+, KFC345+, KFN5339+, KFN5345+, KFA-KFZ 207+, KFA-KFZ 213+
Business taxes: KF6763+
Government ownership: KF1480
Income tax: KF6450+, KFC874+, KFN5874+, KFA-KFZ 476+
Licenses: KF6763+, KFN5884+, KFA-KFZ 480+
Regulation: KF1600+, KFC375+, KFN5375+, KFA-KFZ 230+
Business practices
Contracts: KF905.B87
Business records: KF1357.5
Corporations: KFA-KFZ 205.5.B8
Business relationships
Interference with: KFA-KFZ 197.T67
Business taxes: KF6763+, KFC912.B8, KFN5884+, KFA-KFZ 480+, KFA-KFZ 491.B8
Business trusts: KF1381, KFA-KFZ 207.7
Business use of home
Income tax: KF6395.B88
Businesspeople
Immigration: KF4825.B87
Legal works for: KF390.B84, KFC84.B87, KFN5084.B87, KFA-KFZ 82.B87
Butane industry
Wages: KF3505.B8
Bylaws
Corporations: KF1386.B9

C

C.I.A.: KF7683.C3
C.I.F. clause: KF934
C.O.D. shipments: KF2692.5
Cabinet, President's: KF5089+
Cable cars: KFN5504.C2, KFA-KFZ 304.C2
Cable television: KF2844
Cafeteria benefit plans: KF3517

Calendar
Regulation: KF1668
Calendars, Legislative: KF20.8+, KFC8, KFN5008.A+, KFA-KFZ 8.A+
California
Laws: KFC1+
California. Industrial Accident Commission: KFC592.1
Campaign expenditures: KF4920, KFC717.C35, KFA-KFZ 420.85.C2
Campaign funds: KF4920
Campgrounds: KFA-KFZ 382
Camps: KF2042.C35, KFA-KFZ 282.C35
Canals
Navigation and pilotage: KF2573+, KFN5528+, KFA-KFZ 309.A1+
Water courses (Public property): KF5584+, KFC793, KFN5793+, KFA-KFZ 447+
Cancellation of defense contracts: KF863+
Cancellation of records of arrest, conviction, etc.: KFC1194
Cancer: KF3803.C3, KFC613.5.C3, KFA-KFZ 357.8.C35
Cancer patients
Employment of: KF3470.5
Canned fruit (Packaging): KFC383.5.C2
Canning industry
Collective labor agreements: KF3409.C2
Labor law: KF3580.C2
Canvassing: KFA-KFZ 281.P43
Capacity and disability: KF475+, KFC110+, KFN5110+
Natural persons: KFA-KFZ 91+
Capacity to make a will: KF760.C3
Capital
Corporate finance: KF1428+, KFC350, KFN5350
Taxation: KF6525+
State taxation: KF6759+, KFC880+, KFN5880+, KFA-KFZ 478+
Capital and capitol: KFA-KFZ 410.C3
Capital gains tax: KF6566

INDEX

Capital investment
  Income tax: KF6415+
Capital punishment: KF9227.C2, KFC1108.C2, KFN6108.C3, KFA-KFZ 565.C2
Car pools (Motor vehicle laws): KF2239.5, KFA-KFZ 298
Carbon
  Air pollution: KF3812.2
Cardiologists: KF2910.C37+
Cardiopulmonary resuscitation (CPR): KFN5619.5.C37
Cardiovascular disease: KF3803.C37
Carriage by air: KF1093
Carriage by land: KF1092
Carriage by sea: KF1096+
Carriers
  Contracts: KF1091+, KFN5278+, KFP184, KFA-KFZ 184
  Regulation
    Automotive transportation: KFC480+, KFN5480+
    Railroads: KFN5494, KFA-KFZ 301.5
Carriers, Maritime: KF1096+, KFN5279+, KFP150+
Cash on delivery shipments: KF2692.5
Casinos
  Indians: KF8210.G35
Casualty insurance: KF1215+, KFC297+, KFN5297+, KFA-KFZ 191.A1+
Caterers: KFA-KFZ 282.C37
Catholic Church: KF4869.C2
Cats
  Legal aspects: KF390.5.C35
Cattle
  Standards and grading: KF1726.C2
Cattle brands: KF1730.8.B7, KFC393.5
Cattle raising: KF1730+, KFC393+, KFA-KFZ 246
CATV: KF2844
Cemeteries: KF3781, KFC611, KFN5611, KFA-KFZ 355
Cemeteries, National: KF5810
  Regulation: KFA-KFZ 282.C44

Censorship
  Constitutional law: KF4770+
  Motion pictures: KF4300, KFN5672.5
  Postal service: KF2737
  Press: KF4775
  Radio broadcasting: KF2819.C3
  School libraries: KF4219
Census: KF485
Central Intelligence Agency: KF7683.C3
Cereal products industry: KF1902+
Certificate of need
  Health facilities and hospitals: KF3825.5
Certiorari: KF9058
Chain stores
  Regulation: KF2031
  Taxation: KF6763.9.C4
Chance, Games of: KF3992, KFN5646, KFA-KFZ 385
Chancery courts: KFC997, KFN5997, KFA-KFZ 531
Charitable gifts (Income tax): KF6388
Charitable trusts: KF739+, KFN5189, KFA-KFZ 139.C4
Charter parties: KF1114.C4, KFN5281.C4, KFA-KFZ 299.5.C3
Charter schools: KF4134, KFA-KFZ 391.C57
Charters, County: KF5330
Charters, Municipal: KF5313
Chattel mortgages: KF1053+, KFN5266.5, KFA-KFZ 176.C4
Checklists of law reports: KF3
Checklists of statutes: KF2
Checks: KF960+, KFC248, KFN5248, KFA-KFZ 161
Cheese
  Taxation: KF6614.C4
Cheese industry: KF1924.C5
Chemical industries
  Collective labor agreements: KF3409.C4
  Products liability: KF1297.C4
  Regulation: KF1875+, KFA-KFZ 267.A+

INDEX

Chemicals
  Patent law: KF3133.C4
  Trade agreements: KF6669.C34
Chemists: KF2940.C45+
Chicago Board of Trade: KF1087.C55
Chicago Seven (Criminal trials): KF224.C47
Child abuse
  Criminal law: KF9323, KFC1121.5, KFN6121.5, KFA-KFZ 567.C5
Child abuse, Non-criminal (Trial practice): KF8925.C45
Child care services
  Zoning: KFA-KFZ 458.75
Child health services: KF3826.C48, KFA-KFZ 363.C45
Child labor: KF3551+, KFC580, KFN5580, KFA-KFZ 335.5
Child labor (Human trafficking): KF9449
Child molesting
  Criminal law: KFN6121.5, KFA-KFZ 567.C5
Child sexual abuse
  Reparation: KF1328.5.C45
Child support
  Indians: KF8210.C4
Child welfare (Trial practice): KF8925.C45
Child witnesses
  Criminal procedure: KF9673
Children
  Capacity and disability: KF479, KFN5111.M5, KFA-KFZ 91.M5
  Indians: KF8210.C45
  Labor law: KF3551+, KFC580, KFN5580, KFA-KFZ 335.5
  Public welfare: KF3731+, KFC603+, KFN5603+, KFX2045.C4, KFA-KFZ 350.C4
Children, Illegitimate: KF543, KFN5131, KFA-KFZ 104.4
Children of illegal aliens
  Educational law: KF4217.I46
Children of immigrants
  Educational law: KF4217.I46
Children with disabilities: KFC603+, KFN5603+, KFA-KFZ 350.C4

Children's Bureau (U.S.): KF3736
Children's Court (New York City): KFN5116.5
Children's courts (New York): KFN5116+
Chinese Americans
  Civil rights: KF4757.5.C47
Chiropractors: KF2913.C4+, KFC546.C4+, KFN5546.5.C48+, KFA-KFZ 326.5.C4+
Choses in action: KF706
Choses in possession: KF715
Christian lawyers: KF299.C47
Christian-Science healers: KF2913.C45+
Christian Scientists: KF4869.C4
Church and education: KF4124
Church and state: KF4865+, KFC705+, KFN5705+, KFA-KFZ 417
Church lands (Taxation): KF6761.C4
Church property: KF4868.C4, KFN5706.C4
Cigarette paper (Taxation): KF6614.C5
Cigarettes
  Drug laws: KF3894.T63
  Retail trade: KFA-KFZ 281.5.C54
Cigars (Taxation): KF6635
Circumstantial evidence
  Civil procedure: KF8946
  Criminal procedure: KF9677
Citizen participation (Administrative procedure): KF5415
Citizen suits: KF8896.5
Citizens band radio: KF2829
Citizenship: KF4700+
Citizenship, Loss of: KF4715+
Citizenship requirements
  Merchant mariners: KF1124
Citizenship, Tribal: KFA-KFZ 505.6.T74
Citrus fruit industry: KFA-KFZ 252
Citrus fruit processing industry: KF1909.C57
City attorneys: KF5322, KFX2020.C6, KFA-KFZ 436.8.C55
City clerks: KFA-KFZ 436.8.T6
City councils: KF5317, KFX2016, KFA-KFZ 431.6

City government: KF5304+, KFC752+, KFN5752+, KFX2015+, KFA-KFZ 431+

City planning: KF5691+, KFC810+, KFN5810+, KFX2079, KF1OD .x2Z62+, KFA-KFZ 458+

City property (New York City): KFX2083

City redevelopment: KF5721+, KFC820, KFN5820, KFX2079, KF1OD .x2Z62+, KFA-KFZ 460+

Civil Aeronautics Board (U.S.): KF2441.A55+

Civil and political rights: KF1OD .x2C56+, KFA-KFZ 411+ Indians: KFA-KFZ 505.6.C5

Civil Aviation Agency (U.S.): KF2441.A55+

Civil courts: KFX2018.3

Civil defense: KF7685, KFC934, KFA-KFZ 501

Civil divorces and religious divorces, Relationship between Domestic relations: KF536, KFN5126.5

Civil liability for racketeering: KF9375

Civil procedure: KF8810+, KFC990+, KFN5990+, KFP528+, KF1OD .x2C572+, KFA-KFZ 528+

Conflict of laws: KF418.C48

Civil RICO actions: KF9375

Civil rights: KF4741+, KFC695+, KFN5695+, KFP411+, KFX2068 Government liability: KF1325.C58 Indians: KF8210.C5 Torts: KF1306.C64 Trial practice: KF8925.C5

Civil service County: KFA-KFZ 437+ Federal: KF5336+, KF5375 Municipal: KF5393+, KFC774, KFN5774+, KFX2017.5.A2+, KFA-KFZ 436+ State: KF5390, KFC760+, KFN5760+, KFA-KFZ 435+

Civil Service Commission (U.S.): KF5338

Civil service pensions County: KFA-KFZ 437.5 Federal: KF5380 Municipal: KF5396, KFA-KFZ 436.5 State: KFC770, KFA-KFZ 435.5

Civil service salaries City: KFA-KFZ 436.5 County: KFA-KFZ 437.5 State: KFC769, KFN5769, KFN5770, KFA-KFZ 435.5

Civil unions: KF539, KFC129, KFA-KFZ 103

Civilian awards: KF5153

Civilian personnel Air Force: KF7431 Armed Forces: KF7291 Army: KF7331 Coast Guard: KF7471 Navy: KF7371

Claim drafting Patent law: KF3125.C5

Claims Indians: KFA-KFZ 505.6.C57 Public finance: KFC919

Claims against third parties (Tort liability): KF1313

Claims and remedies, Joinder of: KF8893

Claims Court (U.S.) Reports: KF125.C5+

Claims for damages resulting from government misconduct Trial practice: KF8925.C5

Claims for damages resulting from state action Trial practice: KF8925.C5

Class action Civil procedure: KF8896, KFC1017, KFN6019, KFA-KFZ 536.6.C55

Classification: KF435

Classification of civil service: KF5372

Cleaning industry Wages: KF3505.L2

Clearinghouses: KF1015

Clergy: KF4868.C44 Income tax: KF6442 Legal handbooks: KF390.C5

Clergy
Social security: KF3664.C58
Clerks
Collective labor agreements: KF3409.C5
Wages: KF3505.C5
Clerks of court: KF8771, KFC985.C5, KFN5985.C5, KFA-KFZ 526.C5
Client and social worker (Privileged communications): KF8959.S6
Client security funds
Attorney and client: KF314.C45
Climate change insurance: KF1202.C58
Climatic changes: KF3783
Clinical method (Teaching of law): KF282
Clock industry: KF1893.C5, KFA-KFZ 271.C4
Cloning, Human: KF3831
Close corporations
Corporation law: KF1466, KFC357.C55, KFN5357.C5, KFA-KFZ 215.C55
Income tax: KF6484
Closing argument: KF8924
Clothing
Taxation: KF6614.C56
Clothing industry: KFN5412.C55
Collective labor agreements: KF3409.C56
Cloture: KF4984
Clubs: KF1362.C5, KFA-KFZ 206.5.C5
Coal
Export trade: KF1990.C54
Freight classification: KF2355.C6
Taxation: KF6614.C6
Coal mining industry
Collective labor agreements: KF3409.C6
Health insurance: KF3608.C6
Labor disputes: KF3450.C6+
Labor hygiene and safety: KF3574.M53
Price fixing: KF1629.C6
Regulation: KF1826+, KFA-KFZ 256
Wages: KF3505.C6

Coal mining industry
Workers' compensation: KF3632.C6
Coast Guard education and training: KF7453+
Coast Guard hospitals: KF7478
Coast Guard pay: KF7454+
Coast Guard pensions: KF7455
Coast Guard (U.S.): KF7445+
Coastal zone management: KF5627, KFC804.3
Coastwise shipping: KF2645
Cocaine
Drug laws: KF3891.C62
Code commissions: KF56.A+, KFN5027.A+, KFA-KFZ 27.A+
California: KFC27.A+
Code of Federal Regulations: KF70.A3
Code revision bills: KF59, KFA-KFZ 28
Code revision committees: KF56.A+, KFN5027.A+, KFA-KFZ 27.A+
Codification: KF434, KFN5092, KFA-KFZ 90.C6
Statutes and administrative regulations: KF531+, KFN5027+, KFA-KFZ 27+
Coffee exchanges: KF1086.C6
Coffee trade: KF1984.C6
Coinage: KF6201+, KFC841, KFN5841, KFA-KFZ 466
Cold storage warehouses: KF2057, KFN5449
Collected wills: KFN5203+, KFA-KFZ 144.8.A1+
Collecting of accounts: KF1024, KFC256.A+, KFN5256.C65, KFA-KFZ 167.C6
Collection agencies: KF2042.C6, KFC446.C6, KFN5446.C6, KFA-KFZ 282.C64
Collection cases (Trial practice): KFA-KFZ 539.C64
Collection laws: KF1024, KFC256.A+, KFN5256.C65, KFA-KFZ 167.C6
Collective bargaining: KF3407+, KFC561+, KFN5561+

INDEX

Collective labor agreements: KF3407+, KFC561+, KFN5561+, KFP332+, KFA-KFZ 332+
Maritime unions: KF1127
Postal service: KF2670.8
Collective settlements: KF1390.C6
College students
Discipline: KF4243
Legal status: KF4243
Legal works for: KFA-KFZ 82.C65
Suffrage: KF4896.C64
Colleges and universities
Educational law: KF4225+, KFC666, KFN5666+, KFA-KFZ 396+
Tort liability: KF1303.2.C6
Collisions at sea: KF1107
Colonial charters
Constitutional law: KFA-KFZ 400.5
Color additives in food: KF3879.C64
Colorado
Laws: KFC1801+
Commemorative medals: KF5155+
Commerce and trade: KF1970+, KFC430+, KFN5430+, KFX2031+, KFA-KFZ 280+
Indians: KF8210.C6
Commerce, Committee on (United States House of Representatives): KF4997.C6
Commerce Court (U.S.): KF2184
Commerce Department (U.S.): KF1971
Commerce, Regulation of: KF1600+, KFC375+, KFN5375+, KFA-KFZ 230+
Commerce, Science, and Transportation, Committee on (United States Senate): KF4987.C6
Commercial arbitration: KF9085+, KFC1094, KFN6094, KFA-KFZ 560.5
Commercial aviation: KF2421+, KFC510+, KFN5510
Tort liability for aviation accidents: KF1290.A9
Commercial buildings
Building law: KFA-KFZ 459.C65
Commercial espionage: KF3197
Commercial law: KF871+, KFC225, KFN5225, KFA-KFZ 152

Commercial law
Cases
Trial practice: KF8925.C55
Electronic data processing: KF242.C65+
Legal research: KF241.C64
Commercial Law League of America: KF294.C6
Commercial lawyers (Directories): KF195.C57
Commercial leases: KF593.C6, KFC147.C6, KFA-KFZ 117.3
Commercial travelers: KF1348.C6
Commissioners of circuit courts: KF8792
Commitment
Criminal procedure: KF9625+, KFC1156, KFN6156, KFA-KFZ 576
Commodity Credit Corporation: KF1692.1
Commodity exchanges: KF1085+, KFN5275.A1+, KFA-KFZ 180.A1+
Common law: KF394
Common-law marriage: KF516
Common stock: KF1441+
Commonwealth Court: KFP49.A2+
Communes: KF1390.C6
Communication, Radio: KF2801+
Communications law (Legal profession): KF299.C54
Communications lawyers (Directories): KF195.C573
Communications (Legal research): KF241.C65
Communism (Criminal trials): KF221.C55
Communists: KFC702.C6, KFN5702.C6, KFA-KFZ 416.C65
Subversive activities
United States: KF4856.C6
Communities, Minor: KFN5758.5
Community antenna television: KF2844
Community associations of property owners: KF576, KFC144.3, KFA-KFZ 114.H66
Community legal services: KF336+

INDEX

Community property: KF526, KFC125.C6
- Income tax: KFC871

Community use of school facilities: KF4135

Compacts, Interstate: KF4618, KFA-KFZ 410.I6

Company unions: KF3397

Comparative negligence: KF1286

Compensation, Deferred (Income tax): KF6379

Compensation for judicial error: KF9756

Compensation to victims of crimes: KF1328+, KFC333.5, KFN5333.5, KFA-KFZ 200

Competition
- Retail trade: KF2015+, KFC439+

Competition, Unfair: KFN5553

Composition
- Debtors' relief: KF1540, KFC367, KFN5367, KFA-KFZ 224

Composition, Legal: KF250+, KFA-KFZ 75

Compromise: KF9084, KFC1093, KFN6093, KFA-KFZ 560.3

Comptroller General (U.S.): KF6236

Comptroller of the Treasury: KF1001

Compulsory education: KFC654+, KFN5654+

Compulsory insurance: KF2219

Computation of time: KF450.T5

Computer animation evidence: KF8966

Computer assisted instruction (Teaching of law): KF282.5

Computer contracts: KF905.C6, KFA-KFZ 155.8.C65

Computer crimes: KFA-KFZ 568.C65
- Insolvency and bankruptcy: KF1535.C65

Computer games
- Regulation: KF3994

Computer industry
- Income tax: KF6495.C57
- Regulation: KF1890.C6

Computer lawyers (Directories): KF195.C574

Computer networks
- Advertising: KF1617.C65

Computer programs
- Copyright: KF3024.C6
- Patent law: KF3133.C65
- Personal property tax: KFA-KFZ 481.7.C65

Computer services
- Taxation: KF6768.C66

Computerized data files
- Government property: KF5752.5

Computers: KFC100.C66
- Legal aspects: KF390.5.C6
- Sales contracts: KF915.Z93C65

Computers and privacy: KF1263.C65

Concentrated milk industry: KF1924.C6

Conciliation
- Labor disputes: KF3416+, KFC565, KFN5565

Conciliation courts: KFC116+

Conciliation (Labor disputes): KFA-KFZ 333+

Concurrent ownership: KF619+, KFC155+, KFN5155+, KFA-KFZ 120

Condemnation procedure (Public property)
- New York City: KFX2075

Conditional sale: KF1056, KFC267, KFN5267, KFA-KFZ 176.C6

Condominium: KFA-KFZ 114.C6

Condominium (Real property): KF581, KFC144.5, KFN5142

Conduct of court proceedings: KF8725+, KFC955.5, KFN5955.5, KFA-KFZ 510.5.C6

Confession
- Criminal procedure: KF9664, KFC1167

Confession of judgment: KF8888, KFA-KFZ 536.8

Confessional
- Privileged communications: KF8959.C6

Confidential communications: KF8958+, KFC1041+, KFA-KFZ 541.2+

Confidentiality of tax returns: KF6328, KFA-KFZ 471.9.C65

INDEX

Confirmation of Presidential nominations (United States Senate): KF4988.5
Confiscations (Conflict of laws): KF418.C58
Conflict of interests
  Agency: KF1346
  Constitutional law: KF4568, KFC686, KFN5686
  Congress: KF4970
  General: KFA-KFZ 406
  Criminal law: KF9410
Conflict of laws: KF410+, KFC87, KFN5087, KFA-KFZ 87
  Study and teaching: KF277.C6
Conflicting decisions: KF431, KFA-KFZ 89
Confusion (Personal property): KF713.A3
Congress and the Nation: KF49.C653
Congress, Contempt of: KF9405
Congress (U.S.): KF4935+
  Elections: KF4912.2+
Congressional committees
  Calendars: KF20.8+
  Hearings: KF24.8+
  Joint committees: KF4939+
  Organization
    House of Representatives: KF4996+
    Senate: KF4986+
  Reports: KF29.7+
Congressional daily: KF49.C57
Congressional documents: KF11+
Congressional hearings calendar: KF49.C58
Congressional index (Commerce Clearing House): KF49.C6
Congressional Information Service: KF49.C62
Congressional Operations, Joint Committee on (U.S. Congress): KF4939.5.C66
Congressional quarterly: KF49.C65
Congressional Record: KF35+
Conjugal violence: KF9322
Connecticut
  Laws: KFC3601+

Consanguinity: KF772.C6
Conscientious objectors: KF7266.C6
Conscription: KF7263+
Consent decrees: KF1657.C6
Conservation easements: KF658.C65
Conservation of natural resources: KF5505+
Conservation of water: KF5551+
Conservatorship: KF481.5, KFC112, KFA-KFZ 92
Consignment of goods: KF947
Consolidated returns (Taxation): KF6499.C58
Conspiracy
  Criminal law: KF9479, KFA-KFZ 574
  Criminal trials: KF221.C6
Constables: KF8799, KFN5985.C65, KFA-KFZ 526.C6
Constitution (United States): KF4525+
Constitutional conventions, State: KF4529+
Constitutional history: KF4541+, KFA-KFZ 401.5
Constitutional law: KF4501+, KFC679+, KFN5679+
  General: KFA-KFZ 400+
  Indians: KFA-KFZ 505.6.C59
  Legal research: KF241.C66
  State: KFP400+
Constitutional torts: KF1321
  Government employees: KF1306.C64
Constitutions, State: KF4530, KFC680, KFN5680, KFA-KFZ 401
Construction and interpretation, Statutory: KF425, KFN5091, KFA-KFZ 88.5
Construction industry
  Collective labor agreements: KFC562.C66
  Labor hygiene and safety: KFN5586.C65
Construction lawyers (Directories): KF195.C58
Construction of health facilities and hospitals: KF3825.5

Construction workers
Management-labor relations: KF3452.C6
Consular courts: KF8768.A+
Consulates: KF5780+
Consuls, Foreign: KF4694.F67
Consultants: KF2940.C66+
Civil service: KF5357
Consultants, Business (Legal handbooks): KF390.C65
Consulting contracts: KF905.C67
Consumer credit: KF1039+, KFC262, KFN5262, KFA-KFZ 171
Consumer protection: KF1600.2+, KFC375, KFA-KFZ 230
Cattle industry: KF1730.2
Contact lens industry: KF2036.E93
Contagious and infectious diseases: KF3800+, KFC613+, KFN5613, KFA-KFZ 357+
Containers: KF1665+, KFC382+, KFN5382, KFA-KFZ 235.A1+
Contempt of Congress: KF9405
Contempt of court: KF9415, KFC1141, KFN6141, KFA-KFZ 570.C6
Contested elections: KF4975+, KFN5728, KFA-KFZ 421.7+
President: KF5073+
Contested will cases: KF759.A+
Contested wills: KF769.C6, KFA-KFZ 144.5.C65
Contests (Radio broadcasting): KF2819.C64
Contingent estates: KF597
Contingent fees: KF310.C6
Contraceptive devices: KF9445
Contraceptive drug implants
Products liability: KF1297.C65
Contract for services: KF898+, KFC228+, KFN5228+, KFA-KFZ 155+
Contract for work and labor: KF898+, KFC228+, KFN5228+, KFA-KFZ 155+
Contract of service: KF894+, KFA-KFZ 154+
Contract under seal: KF810

Contractors
Building and construction industry: KF1950, KFC424, KFN5424, KFA-KFZ 275
Contractors, Independent: KF898+, KFC228+, KFN5228+, KFA-KFZ 155+
Contracts: KF801+, KFC215+, KFN5215+, KFA-KFZ 150+
Conflict of laws: KF418.C6
Insurance: KF1084.I5
Trial practice: KF8925.C58, KFN6028.C6
Contracts, Aleatory: KF1241+
Contracts, Apprenticeship: KFA-KFZ 154.5.A6
Contracts, Maritime: KF1096+
Contracts, Publishing: KF3084
Contracts through correspondence, telephone, teletype, wire, computer, etc.: KF807.5
Contracts, Unlawful: KF818.A+, KFN5222
Contracts, Variable
Life insurance: KF1177.V3, KFA-KFZ 186.5.V3
Contracts, Void and voidable: KF817+, KFN5222
Contractual relationships
Interference with: KFA-KFZ 197.T67
Contributions (Income tax): KF6388
Contributory negligence: KF1286, KFC316, KFN5316, KFA-KFZ 196
Control of individuals: KFN5698+
Control of social activities: KF3985+, KFC645+, KFN5645+, KFA-KFZ 381.5+
Control of trade practices: KF1601+, KFC375, KFA-KFZ 230
Controls on employment (Immigration law): KF4829
Conversion, Equitable
Land tenure: KF601
Conveyances: KF666+, KFC170+, KFN5170+, KFA-KFZ 127
Conveyances, Fraudulent: KFN5366.F7
Convict labor: KF9733
Cooperation, Interstate: KFN5692

Cooperative banks: KF1008, KFA-KFZ 166.C6
Cooperative education: KF4250
Cooperative societies
- Corporation law: KF1470, KFC357.C6, KFA-KFZ 218
- Income tax: KF6485
Cooperatives, Agricultural: KF1715, KFC390, KFN5390, KFA-KFZ 242
Cooperatives, Housing: KF623
Coordination of actions (Parties in civil procedure): KFC1016.5
Copper mining: KF1836.C6
Copyright: KF2986+
- Antitrust aspects: KF3116
- Income tax: KF6428.I5
Copyright infringement: KF3080
Copyright Office: KF3002+
Copyright violation crimes: KF9359
Coram nobis: KF9038
Corn
- Acreage allotments: KF1706.G73
- Marketing quotas: KF1706.G73
Corn processing industry: KF1904.C6
Coroners: KF8802, KFN5985.C66, KFX2020.C58, KFA-KFZ 526.C65
Corporate alliances: KF1380.6+
Corporate charters and bylaws: KF1420, KFC348, KFN5348, KFA-KFZ 213.5
Corporate corruption and bribery (Criminal law): KF9351
Corporate franchises (Taxation): KF6558, KFC886, KFN5886, KFA-KFZ 480.8
Corporate legal departments: KF1425
Corporate practice of law: KF6495.L4
Corporate reorganization
- Insolvency and bankruptcy: KF1544+, KFN5368+, KFA-KFZ 225.A1+
- Taxation: KF6499.C6
Corporate stock (Taxation): KF6558, KFC886, KFN5886, KFA-KFZ 480.8
Corporation cases (Trial practice): KF8925.C6

Corporation finance: KF1428+, KFC350, KFN5350, KFA-KFZ 214.A1+
Corporation law (Legal research): KF241.C67
- Electronic data processing: KF242.C67+
Corporation lawyers: KF299.I5, KFX2020.C6, KFA-KFZ 436.8.C55
- Directories: KF195.C6
Corporations: KF1384+, KFC340+, KFN5340+
- Conflict of laws: KF418.C64
- General: KFA-KFZ 210+
- Income tax: KF6455+, KFC875+, KFN5875, KFX2091.C6, KFA-KFZ 477+
- Tort liability: KF1301+, KFC324+, KFN5324+, KFA-KFZ 198.C5
Corporations, Business: KF1396+, KFC345+, KFN5345+
Corporations, Foreign: KF1419, KFN5347
Corporations, Government: KF1480
Corporations, Publicly chartered: KF1359.A1+
Corporations, Religious: KF4865, KFC705, KFN5705, KFA-KFZ 417
Corporations, Small business (Taxation): KF6491
Corps of Engineers (U.S. Army): KF7335.E5
Correctional institutions: KF9735+, KF1OD .x2C62+, KFA-KFZ 590.5.A+
Corrections: KF9728, KFC1179, KFN6179, KFA-KFZ 587+
Correspondence schools: KF4222
Corrupt practices
- Election law: KF4921
Corruption
- Criminal law: KF9409
Corruption, Judicial: KF9419
Cosmetics: KF3896, KFC632, KFN5632, KFX2050, KF1OD .x2F62+, KFA-KFZ 373
Cost-of-living adjustments
- Social security: KF3658.C66

INDEX

Cost-of-living adjustments
  Wages: KF3499
Costs
  Bankruptcy: KF1530.F54
  Criminal procedure: KFN6173, KFA-KFZ 583.4
  Health facilities and hospitals: KF3825.5
  Probate law: KFA-KFZ 144.5.C67
Costs, Settlement: KF681
Cotton
  Acreage allotments: KF1706.C6
  Import trade: KF1996.C6
  Marketing quotas: KF1706.C6
  Standards and grading: KF1724.C6
  Taxation: KF6614.C68
Cotton exchanges: KF1086.C65, KFN5275.C6
Cotton fabrics
  Labeling: KF1620.T33
Cotton textile industry
  Manufacture: KF1886.C6
  Wholesale trade: KF1999.C66
Cotton trade
  Commodity exchanges: KF1086.C65, KFN5275.C6
  Export: KF1990.C6
  Import: KF1990.C6
  Wholesale: KF1999.C65
Counterclaims
  Civil procedure: KF8885, KFN6018, KFA-KFZ 536.C6
Counterfeiting: KF9455, KFN6149
County attorneys: KFA-KFZ 437.8.A7
County charters: KF5330, KFC758, KFN5758
County civil service: KFA-KFZ 437+
County clerks: KFA-KFZ 437.8.C55
County government: KF5330, KFC758, KFN5758, KFA-KFZ 432
Courses of instruction
  Educational law
    Elementary and secondary education: KF4201+, KFC664+, KFA-KFZ 395.26

Court administration: KF8732+, KFC958+, KFN5958+, KFA-KFZ 510.5.A3
  Data processing: KF242.C68+
  Juvenile courts: KF9771+
  Legal profession: KF299.C6
  Study and teaching: KF277.C65
Court attendants: KFN5985.A65
Court buildings
  Building law: KF5702.C6, KFA-KFZ 459.C67
Court clerks: KF8771, KFC985.C5, KFN5985.C5, KFA-KFZ 526.C5
Court congestion and delay: KF8727, KFC956, KFN5956, KFA-KFZ 510.5.C65
Court costs: KF8995, KFC1051, KFN6051, KFA-KFZ 545
Court documents, Electronic filing of
  Bankruptcy: KF1530.E44
Court for the Trial of Impeachments (New York): KFN5764.5
Court of Appeals (Federal Circuit) (U.S.): KF3157
Court of Claims (U.S.)
  Organization: KF8760.A+, KFN5974
  Procedure: KF9070, KFN6086, KFA-KFZ 522
  Reports: KF125.C5+
Court of Customs and Patent Appeals (U.S.): KF3157, KF6698, KF8764
  Customs procedures: KF6676+
  Reports: KF125.C8+
Court of Military Appeals (U.S.): KF7667
Court of Veterans Appeals (United States): KF7713
Court officials and employees: KF8770+, KFC979+, KFN5979+, KFA-KFZ 524.5+
Court proceedings, Broadcasting of: KF8726
Court proceedings, Conduct of: KF8725+
Court records on microfilm: KF8733.3
Court reporters: KF8805, KFC985.C6, KFN5985.C68, KFA-KFZ 526.C68

INDEX

Court rules (Federal): KF8816+
- Admiralty: KF1111.A4+
- Bankruptcy proceedings: KF1527.A2+
- Chancery: KF8851.A5+
- Circuit courts of appeals: KF9052.A458+
- Courts of appeals: KF9052.A458+, KF9054
- District courts: KF8820+
  - Bankruptcy proceedings: KF1527.A4
  - Eminent domain: KF5599.A28
  - Equity: KF8851.A5+
  - Supreme Court: KF9056
    - Bankruptcy proceedings: KF1527.A3+

Court rules (State): KFC992+, KFN5992+, KFP529+, KFA-KFZ 529+
- Appellate courts, Intermediate: KFC1078+, KFN6078+, KFA-KFZ 556+
- Court of Appeals: KFN6081
- Court of Claims: KFN6086
- Court of last resort: KFA-KFZ 558
- Supreme Court: KFC1081
- Trial courts: KFC992+, KFN5992+, KFP529+, KFA-KFZ 529+

Courts (Federal)
- Criminal procedure: KF9601+
- History: KF350+
- Organization and procedure: KF8699.2+
- Civil procedure: KF8810+
- Reports: KF101+

Courts, Indian tribal: KF8224.C6

Courts-martial: KF7625+, KFC932, KFN5932, KFA-KFZ 499

Courts of appeals (Federal)
- Court rules: KF9052.A458+
- Organization: KF8750+
- Procedure: KF9052+
- Reports: KF110+

Courts of appeals (State)
- Organization: KFC964, KFN5960
- Procedure: KFN6081
- Reports: KFA-KFZ 48+

Courts of common pleas: KFP51+

Courts of common pleas
- Organization: KFP515+

Courts of last resort (State)
- Court rules: KFA-KFZ 558
- Organization: KFC960, KFN5960, KFP512, KFA-KFZ 512
- Procedure: KFC1080.A+, KFN6081

Courts (State): KFC955+, KFN5955+, KFP508+, KFA-KFZ 512+
- General
  - Organization and procedure: KF8736
  - Judges: KF8785
  - Reports: KF132+

Covenants not to compete
- Labor law: KF3463, KFA-KFZ 334.5.C65

Covenants, Restrictive: KF662, KFC164, KFA-KFZ 125

Covenants running with the land: KF661, KFC164, KFA-KFZ 125

Craftsmen (Legal handbooks): KF390.A69

Cream
- Import trade: KF1996.M5

Credit card fraud: KFA-KFZ 568.C7

Credit cards: KF1039+

Credit information, Liability for: KF1266.5.C7

Credit insurance: KF1231, KFA-KFZ 193.C74

Credit, Letters of: KF1028, KFA-KFZ 167.L47

Credit rating: KF1443

Credit rating agencies: KF1443

Credit unions: KF1008, KFA-KFZ 166.C6

Creditors' rights: KF1501+, KFC364+, KFN5364+, KFA-KFZ 220+

Crime and publicity: KF9223.5, KFC1102.5, KFN6102.5

Crime, Juvenile: KFX2007.35
- Statistics: KF184

Crimes against public order and morality: KF9434+

Crimes against the government: KF9390+

Crimes, Sex: KF9325+
Crimes, White collar: KF9350+
Crimes without victims: KF9434+, KFC1145.5
Criminal Court (New York City): KFX2018.4
Criminal investigation: KF9601+, KFC1155+, KFN6155+, KFA-KFZ 576
Military law: KF7595
Criminal jurisdiction: KF9230
Criminal law: KF9201+, KFC1100+, KFN6100+, KFA-KFZ 561+
Antitrust laws: KF1657.C7
Customs: KF6699
Data processing: KF242.C76+
Indians: KF8210.C7
Legal research: KF241.C75
Taxation: KF6334, KFN5869
Criminal law, Military: KF7601+, KFC931+, KFN5931+, KFA-KFZ 499
Criminal lawyers: KF299.C7
Criminal liability: KF9235+, KFC1110+, KFN6110+, KFA-KFZ 566.5+
Criminal negligence: KF9236
Criminal procedure: KF9601+, KFC1155+, KFN6155+, KFA-KFZ 575+
Trial: KF9655+
Criminal records, Cancellation of: KFC1194
Criminal registration: KF9751, KFC1190.5, KFA-KFZ 592.5
Criminal statistics: KF183, KFN5070, KFX2007.3, KFA-KFZ 71.5+
Criminal syndicalism: KF9395.5, KFC1139
Criminal trials: KF219+
Criminals, Sterilization of: KFA-KFZ 565.S7
Criticism: KFC79
Crop insurance: KF1204+
Cross claims
Civil procedure: KF8885, KFN6018, KFA-KFZ 536.C6
Cross-examination
Civil procedure: KF8920, KFA-KFZ 538.4
Cross-examination
Criminal procedure: KF9658
Cruelty to animals: KF3841+, KFC627, KFN5627, KFA-KFZ 370
Crushed stone industry
Labor law: KF3580.C7
Wages: KF3505.C7
Crustaceans: KF1773.S4
Cryonics (Medical legislation): KF3827.C78
Culpability
Criminal law: KF9236, KFN6111
Cultural exchanges: KF4330
Cultural property, Preservation of
Indians: KFA-KFZ 505.6.C84
Curled hair industry: KF1893.C8
Currency: KF6201+, KFC841, KFN5841, KFA-KFZ 466
Criminal law: KF9455+
Curricula
Educational law
Elementary and secondary education: KF4201+, KFC664+, KFN5664+, KFA-KFZ 395.26
Higher education: KF4245+
Curtesy: KF629, KFA-KFZ 123.D6
Custody of children: KF547+
Conflict of laws: KF418.C78
Customhouse brokers: KF6696.5
Customs administration: KF6676+
Customs Court (U.S.): KF6698
Customs crimes: KF6699
Customs duties: KF6651+
Customs duty exemptions: KF6704+
Customs Service (U.S.): KF6696
Cut-rate trade: KF2020
Cy pres doctrine: KF741, KFN5190, KFA-KFZ 139.C9

D

Dairy industry: KF1921
Regulation: KF1921+, KFC421, KFN5421, KFA-KFZ 272.D2
Taxation: KFN5885.D2
Dairy products
Food law: KFA-KFZ 372.5.D34

INDEX

Dairy products
  Standards and grading: KF1921
Dakota Territory
  Laws: KFN8601+
Damage caused by animals
  Liability: KFA-KFZ 197.6
Damage to property (Commercial aviation): KF2454
Damages: KF445+, KFC100.D3, KFN5100.D2, KFA-KFZ 90.D3
  Antitrust law: KF1657.T7
  Contracts: KF836+
  Income tax: KF6428.D36
  Taxation: KF6499.D3
  Torts: KF1246+, KFC310, KFN5310, KFA-KFZ 195
  Trial practice: KF8925.D36
Dams: KF5588+, KFC795+, KFA-KFZ 447.8
Data processing, Electronic
  Legal research: KF242.A+
Data protection: KF1263.C65
Data storage and retrieval systems
  Legal research: KF242.A+
Day care centers: KF2042.D3, KFN5446.D39, KFA-KFZ 282.D3
Day care providers
  Legal handbooks: KF390.D38
Dead, Disposal of the: KF3781, KFC611, KFN5611
Deadlines: KFC100.T54, KFA-KFZ 90.T5
Deaf-mutes
  Capacity and disability: KF480.5.D4
  Public welfare: KFN5605.5
Death
  Definition: KF3827.D4
  Succession upon: KF753+, KFC200+, KFN5200+, KFA-KFZ 142+
Death by wrongful act: KF1260, KFA-KFZ 197.D25
  Trial practice: KFA-KFZ 539.D43
Death certificates: KF485, KFC113, KFA-KFZ 93
Death on the high seas
  Merchant mariners: KF1132
Death registers: KFC113

Death, Succession upon: KFP142+
Debentures: KF1456
Debt bondage (Human trafficking): KF9449
Debt, Imprisonment for: KF9039, KFN6071, KFA-KFZ 553.I6
Debtor and creditor
  Bankruptcy: KF1501+, KFC364+, KFN5364+, KFA-KFZ 220+
  Collection of accounts: KF1024
  Conflict of laws: KF418.C6
  Execution of judgments: KF9025+, KFC1050+, KFN6050+, KFA-KFZ 544+
Debtors' relief: KF1539+, KFC367, KFN5367+, KFA-KFZ 224+
Debts of deceased person: KF779.L5
Decedents' estates: KF774+, KFC210, KFN5210, KFA-KFZ 147
  Conflict of laws: KF418.D3
  Debts: KF779.L5
  Taxation: KF6576+
Deceit: KFA-KFZ 197.D27
  Torts: KF1271
Declaration of Independence: KF4506
Declaration of war: KF4941
Decorations of honor: KF5153+
Decorum in court: KF8725+, KFC955.5, KFN5955.5, KFA-KFZ 510.5.C6, KFA-KFZ 510.5.C65
Deductions
  Income tax: KF6385+
Deeds: KF666+
Defamation
  Criminal law: KFN6126, KFA-KFZ 567.5
Defeasible fees: KF597
Defense, Civil: KF7685, KFC934, KFA-KFZ 501
Defense contracts: KF851+
Defense Department (U.S.): KF7252
Defense industries
  Regulation: KF1890.D45
Defense Mediation Board (U.S.): KF3444+
Defense research: KF4280.D3

Defenses

Criminal law: KF9240+, KFC1115, KFN6115

Defenses and objections

Civil procedure: KF8881+, KFC1013, KFN6015+, KFA-KFZ 535.8

Deferment

Military service: KF7265+

Deferred compensation (Income tax): KF6379

Definition of death

Medical legislation: KF3827.D4, KFC619.5.D43, KFN5619.5.D4, KFA-KFZ 367.D4

Delaware

Laws: KFD1+

Delegation of powers: KF4565, KFC685+, KFN5685+, KFA-KFZ 405+

Delinquency (Taxation): KFA-KFZ 471.9.D4

Demurrage

Railroad law: KF2353

Denatured alcohol: KF3924.D3

Denominational schools: KF4124

Dental care (Insurance): KF1186

Dental hygienists: KFA-KFZ 326.5.D38+

Dental specialists: KF2910.D3+

Dentists: KF2910.D3+, KFC546.D3+, KFN5546.D3+, KFA-KFZ 326.5.D4+

Department of Agriculture (U.S.): KF1683

Department of Commerce (U.S.): KF1971

Department of Defense (U.S.): KF7252

Department of Energy (U.S.): KF2120.13

Government contracts: KF869.5.E5

Department of Health, Education, and Welfare (U.S.): KF3720.5

Department of Justice (California)

Attorney General's Office: KFC746.J86

Department of Justice (U.S.): KF5106+

Department of Labor (U.S.): KF3325+

Department of Law (New York): KFN5746.L38

Department of State (U.S.): KF5110+

Department of the Air Force (U.S.): KF7405+

Department of the Army (U.S.): KF7305+

Department of the Interior (U.S.): KF5501

Department of the Navy (U.S.): KF7345+

Department of Transportation (U.S.)

Government contracts: KF869.5.T75

Department stores: KF2030

Depletion allowances (Corporation income tax): KF6481+

Deportation: KF4842

Deposit insurance: KF1023, KFA-KFZ 167.D44

Deposit of goods: KF945

Depositories, Public: KFA-KFZ 467.3

Depository libraries: KF5003

Deposits

Bailments: KF945

Banking: KF1022+, KFN5256.D3, KFA-KFZ 167.D44

Depreciation allowances

Income tax: KF6386

Desertion

Domestic relations: KF549, KFA-KFZ 104.8

Military law: KF7618.D3

Design

Law office management: KF320.L39

Design protection: KF3086

Copyright: KF3065

Patent law: KF3142

Designs and models

Copyright: KF3065

Patent law: KF3142

Detectives: KF2042.D48

Legal handbooks: KF390.D4

Regulation: KFC446.D4, KFA-KFZ 282.D47

Detention homes, Juvenile: KF9825, KFC1198.6, KFN6198.6, KFA-KFZ 598.6

Detinue (Personal property): KFA-KFZ 134.5.D47

INDEX

Development contracts: KF869
Development rights transfer (Land use): KF5698.5
Dibromopropanol phosphate: KF3964.D53
Diesel fuel
  Taxation: KF6617.D4
Dietary supplements: KF3879.D5
Dietitians: KF2915.D53+, KFA-KFZ 326.5.D53+
Digital evidence
  Civil procedure: KF8947.5
Direct selling: KF2026.5, KFA-KFZ 281.D57
Directed verdict: KF9682+, KFC1171, KFN6171
Directories
  Domestic relations lawyers: KF195.D6
  Fraternities: KF289
  General: KF190+
  Internal Revenue Service (U.S.): KF6301.A18
  Judiciary: KF8700.A19, KFA-KFZ 508.A19
  Juvenile courts: KF9771+
  Labor lawyers: KF195.L3
  Law schools: KF292.A+
  Law teachers: KF266
Lawyer disciplinary agencies: KF307
Lawyer referral services: KF338.A33+
Legal aid agencies: KF336.A4
Negligence lawyers: KF195.N4
Patent lawyers: KF3165.A3
Public defenders: KF9646.A15
Public utility lawyers: KF195.P85
Railroad lawyers: KF195.R3
Student bar associations: KF288
Disabilities, Children with: KFC603+, KFN5603+
Disabilities, People with
  Building laws: KF5709.3.H35, KFC819.H35, KFN5819.H35
  Capacity and disability: KFC111.H35, KFN5111.H36, KFA-KFZ 91.H3
  Education: KFC665.H3

Disabilities, People with
  Employment of: KFC573.H34, KFN5573.H34
  Public welfare: KFA-KFZ 350.H3
Disabilities, Students with: KFN5665.P4, KFA-KFZ 395.9.H3
Disability: KF475+, KFN5110+
  Natural persons: KFA-KFZ 91+
Disability clause
  Life insurance: KF1178.D5
Disability insurance
  Personal insurance: KF1182
Disability insurance cases
  Trial practice: KF8925.S63
Disability law
  Directories: KF195.H36
Disability pensions: KF3641+, KFC595, KFN5595+, KFA-KFZ 344
  Air Force: KF7416
  Armed Forces: KF7276
  Army: KF7316
  Coast Guard: KF7456
  Navy: KF7356
Disaster loans (Agriculture): KF1712
Disaster preparedness
  Law offices: KF320.E44
Disaster relief
  Agriculture: KF1712
  Social legislation: KF3750, KFC608.5, KFN5608.5, KFA-KFZ 352
Disbarment: KF308+, KFC76.5.A2+, KFN5076.5.A2+, KFA-KFZ 76.5.A2+
Discharge
  Air Force: KF7412
  Armed Forces: KF7272
  Army: KF7312
  Coast Guard: KF7452
  Navy: KF7352
Discharge (Bankruptcy): KF1530.D4, KFN5366.D5
Discipline
  Judges: KF8779, KFN5984.5.D57, KFA-KFZ 525.5.D5
  Legal profession: KF308+, KFC76.5.A2+, KFN5076.5.A2+, KFA-KFZ 76.5.A2+
Discipline, Labor: KF3540+

Discipline, Military: KF7590
Discipline of legislators
Congress: KF4960+
Discipline, Prison: KF9730
Disclosure requirements
Stock transfers: KF1449
Discount and discount rate: KF1026
Discount houses: KF2020
Discovery
Criminal procedure: KFA-KFZ 578.3
Discovery, Abuse of: KF1270.5
Discovery, Electronic: KF8902.E42, KFC1021.E42
Civil procedure
New York: KFN6021.E42
Discovery (Law): KF9650, KFC1160.5
Discrimination: KF4755
Constitutional law: KF4755, KFA-KFZ 411.7
Suffrage: KF4893
Trial practice: KF8925.D5, KFA-KFZ 539.D56
Discrimination in education: KF4151+, KFC654.5, KFA-KFZ 392.2
Discrimination in employment
Labor law: KF3464+, KFC572+, KFN5572+, KFA-KFZ 334.5.D5
Discrimination in housing: KF5740, KFA-KFZ 460.5.D5
Discrimination in mortgage loans: KF697.D5, KFA-KFZ 130.5.D58
Discrimination in public accommodations: KF4756+
Diseases, Contagious and infectious: KF3800+, KFC613+, KFA-KFZ 357+
Diseases, Occupational
Workers' compensation: KF3622, KFN5593, KFA-KFZ 342.5
Dismissal of employees: KF3457+, KF3471+, KFC571+, KFN5571+, KFA-KFZ 334.5.E55
Dismissal pay: KF3472
Disorderly conduct: KFA-KFZ 571.D5
Disparagement in advertising: KF3198
Disposal of the dead: KF3781, KFC611, KFN5611

Dispute resolution
Study and teaching: KF277.D57
Dispute resolution, Alternative: KFA-KFZ 560.3
Disqualification
Military service: KF7265+
Disqualification of judges: KF8861
Dissection
Animals: KF3843
Dissemination
Copyright
Art and photography: KF3060.1
Literary copyright: KF3030.1
Music: KF3045.1
Dissolution
Corporation law: KFA-KFZ 215.D55
Taxation: KF6499.D5
Distilling apparatus (Taxation): KF6614.D4
Distilling industry
Industrial alcohol: KF1876.A5
Liquor: KF3901+, KFC635+, KFN5635+, KFX2051, KFA-KFZ 375+
District courts: KFP51+
District Courts of Appeal
California: KFC964
District of Columbia
Constitutional status: KF4545.D57
Laws: KFD1201+
Divestiture
Corporation law: KF1478
Dividends
Corporation law: KF1428+, KFC350, KFN5350
Income tax: KF6417
Divorce
Conflict of laws: KF418.M2
Domestic relations: KF531+, KFC126, KFN5126+, KFA-KFZ 100
Taxation: KF6333
Divorce settlements: KF531+
Income tax: KFA-KFZ 475.5.D58
Divorced people
Insolvency and bankruptcy: KF1535.D58

INDEX

DNA fingerprinting
- Criminal law: KF9666.5, KFA-KFZ 580.5.M4

Do-not-resuscitate orders (Medical legislation): KFN5619.5.D62

Doctrine of election (Life insurance): KF1181.E5

Document preparation, Legal: KF250+

Documentary evidence
- Civil procedure: KF8947+

Documents, Legislative: KF11+, KFC5+, KFN5005+, KFA-KFZ 6+

Documents of title: KF924+, KFN5237+
- Sale of goods: KFA-KFZ 156.5.A+

Dog racing: KFA-KFZ 386.D6

Dogs
- Legal aspects: KF390.5.D6, KFA-KFZ 84.5.D63

Domain, Eminent: KF5599, KFC800, KFN5800, KFX2075, KFA-KFZ 450

Domestic education: KF4221, KFA-KFZ 395.97

Domestic employees
- Social security: KF3664.H6

Domestic international sales corporations (Taxation): KF6493, KFN5878.5

Domestic relations: KF501+, KFC115+, KFN5115+, KFX2007.5.D6, KF10D .x2D65+, KFA-KFZ 94+
- Electronic data processing: KF242.D65+
- Legal research: KF241.D65
- Torts: KFA-KFZ 197.D65

Domestic Relations Court (New York City): KFN5116.5

Domestic relations courts: KF505.5, KFC116+, KFA-KFZ 94.5+

Domestic relations lawyers
- Directories: KF195.D6
- Legal profession: KF299.D6

Domestic shipping: KF2645+

Domestics
- Labor law: KF3580.D64
- Legal handbooks: KF390.D64

Domicile
- Corporations: KF1386.D6
- Public welfare: KF3723, KFC608.D6, KFN5608.D6, KFA-KFZ 351.D6

Donation of organs, tissues, etc.
- (Medical legislation): KF3827.D66, KFN5619.5.D64, KFA-KFZ 367.D65

Double jeopardy
- Criminal liability: KF9245

Double taxation: KF6306, KFC864

Dower: KF629, KFN5160, KFA-KFZ 123.D6

Draft (Military service): KF7263+

Drafting of administrative regulations: KFA-KFZ 441.D35

Draftsmanship, Legal: KF250+, KFA-KFZ 75

Draftsmanship, Legislative: KF4950, KFN5724, KFA-KFZ 421.5.B5

Drainage
- Land reclamation: KF5615+, KFC803+, KFN5612, KFA-KFZ 451+
- Public health: KF3786+, KFC612, KFA-KFZ 356

Dramshop acts (Tort liability): KF1293.5, KFA-KFZ 197.I5

Dredging (Water courses): KF5581

Drinking age: KF3925.D74, KFA-KFZ 376.D75

Drinking water standards: KF3794, KFC612.6, KFA-KFZ 356.6

Driver education: KFN5475, KFA-KFZ 297.62

Drivers' liability insurance: KF1218, KFC298.A8, KFN5298.A8+, KFA-KFZ 191.A4
- Compulsory: KF2219, KFC475

Drivers' licenses: KF2218, KFC474.5, KFA-KFZ 297.6

Drought relief: KF1712

Drug addiction: KF3829.N2, KFA-KFZ 366.N35

Drug administration
- Medical legislation: KFA-KFZ 367.D78

Drug industry
- Manufacture: KF1879
- Retail trade: KF2036.D7

Drug laws: KF3885+, KFC632, KFN5632, KFX2050, KF10D .x2F62+, KFA-KFZ 373

Drug paraphernalia: KF3895

Drugs

- Advertising: KF1616.D78
- Labeling: KF3885
- Patent law: KF3133.D78
- Products liability: KF1297.D7
- Retail trade: KF2036.D7, KFA-KFZ 281.5.D7
- Taxation: KF6614.D7

Drunk driving: KF2231, KFC477, KFN5477, KFA-KFZ 297.8

Drunk driving claims (Trial practice): KF8925.T7, KFA-KFZ 539.T7

Drunkenness

- Criminal defense: KF9452
- Criminal liability: KF9243, KFA-KFZ 571.D7
- Tort liability: KF1293.5, KFA-KFZ 197.I5

Due process of law: KF4765, KFC696.5.D83

Dumping

- Customs administration: KF6708.D8

Duress: KF450.D85

- Contracts: KF820

Duty-free imports: KF6704+

- By commodity: KF6669.A+

Dyes and dyestuffs industry: KF1876.D9

E

Earthquake insurance: KF1202.E2

Easements: KF657+, KFC163.5, KFA-KFZ 124

East Indians

- Citizenship: KF4720.E3
- Nationality: KF4720.E3

Economic assistance

- Agriculture and forestry: KF1691+
- Cattle industry: KF1730.3

Economic Committee, Joint (U.S. Congress): KF4939.5.E36

Economic development: KFA-KFZ 228

Economic emergency legislation: KF5900+, KFX2085.A+, KFA-KFZ 463+

Economic offenses: KF9350+, KFC1128+

Economic planning: KF1570+, KFA-KFZ 228

Economic policy: KF1570+, KFA-KFZ 228

Economic sanctions: KF4678

Economics, Medical: KF2907.F3

Economics of law practice: KF315+

Economists

- Expert witnesses (Civil procedure): KF8968.23

Education: KF4101+, KFC648+, KFC648+, KFN5648+, KFN5648+, KFX2065, KFA-KFZ 390+

- Discrimination: KF4151+
- Federal aid: KF4136+, KFA-KFZ 391.F3
- Finance: KF4125+, KFC648+, KFN5648+, KFA-KFZ 390+
- Law: KF287+
- State aid: KFA-KFZ 391.S7
- Wages: KF3505.E3

Education and church: KF4124

Education and Labor, Committee on (United States House of Representatives): KF4997.E3

Education and the Workforce, Committee on United States House of Representatives: KF4997.E35

Education, Compulsory: KF4150+, KFC654+, KFN5654+, KFA-KFZ 392+

Education, Doctrine of (Life insurance): KF1181.E5

Education, Elementary and secondary: KF4195+, KFC662+, KFN5662+, KFA-KFZ 395+

Education, Higher: KF4225+, KFC666, KFN5666+, KFA-KFZ 396+

Education, International (Higher education curricula): KF4245.5.I5

Education, Legal: KF261+

Education, Medical: KF2907.E3

INDEX

Education, Office of (U.S.): KF4121
Education, Physical: KF4203
Education, Pre-elementary: KF4197
Education, Private: KF4220, KFA-KFZ 395.95
Education, Professional: KF4256+, KFN5668
Education, Public: KF4101+, KFC648+, KFN5648+
Education, Secondary: KF4195+, KFC662+, KFN5662+, KFA-KFZ 395+
Education, Vocational: KF4205+
Educational exchanges: KF4330
Educational expenses (Income tax): KF6395.E3
Educational gifts (Income tax): KF6388
Educational law and legislation
Electronic data processing: KF242.E37+
Legal research: KF241.E38
Educational, Technical: KF4208
Educational technology: KF4209.E38
Educational tests and measurements: KF4156, KFA-KFZ 392.3
Educational tests for voter registration: KF4898, KFN5713, KFA-KFZ 420.85.R4
Educational, Vocational: KFA-KFZ 395.5
Educators, Legal handbooks for: KF390.E3
Egg industry: KF1916
Eggs and egg products
Inspection: KF1916
Marketing regulations: KFA-KFZ 244.E3
Standards and grading: KF1916
Ejectment: KF652+, KFC163, KFA-KFZ 121
Elder abuse: KF9324, KFA-KFZ 567.A35
Election
Wills: KFN5202.E5
Election districts: KF4905, KFC714, KFN5714

Election law: KF241.E5, KF4885+, KFC710+, KFN5710+, KFX2015.5, KFA-KFZ 420+
Elections, Local: KF4916, KFA-KFZ 420.6
Elections, Municipal: KF4916
Electoral college
United States: KF4911
Electric appliances (Patent law): KF3133.E5
Electric controllers
Patent law: KF3159.E56
Electric industry
Collective labor agreements: KF3409.E5
Labor hygiene and safety: KF3574.E5
Electric installations
Building laws: KF5704, KFC819.E44, KF10A 12.1.E4, KFA-KFZ 459.5
Electric lamp industry
Wages: KF3505.E5
Electric machinery industry: KF1890.E4
Electric power plants (Labor hygiene and safety): KFA-KFZ 336.E45
Electric power supply (Public utilities): KF2125+, KFC459+, KFN5459+, KFA-KFZ 287
Electric railroads: KF2393, KFN5503
Tort liability: KF1290.S7
Electric utilities: KFC459+, KFN5459+, KFA-KFZ 287
Electrical engineering (Ships)
Safety regulations: KF2564.E4
Electricians: KFA-KFZ 282.E4
Electrologists: KFA-KFZ 282.E43
Electronic commerce
Income tax: KF6495.E45
Insolvency and bankruptcy: KF1535.E44
Taxation: KF6768.E43
Electronic data processing
Legal research: KF242.A+, KFA-KFZ 75.5
Electronic discovery: KF8902.E42, KFC1021.E42
Civil procedure
New York: KFN6021.E42

Electronic evidence
  Civil procedure: KF8947.5
Electronic filing of court documents
  Bankruptcy: KF1530.E44
Electronic funds transfer: KFA-KFZ 167.E43
  Banking law: KF1030.E4
Electronic game industry: KF1893.E44
Electronic information resources
  Copyright: KF3024.E44
Electronic listening and recording devices: KF9670, KFC1168, KFN6168, KFA-KFZ 580.5.W5
Electronic publishing
  Copyright: KF3024.E44
Elementary and secondary education: KF4195+, KFC662+, KFN5662+, KFA-KFZ 395+
Elevator accidents
  Liability for: KF1287.5.E45
Elevator industry
  Regulation: KFA-KFZ 282.E45
Elevators
  Building laws: KF5705, KFA-KFZ 459.7
Embassies: KF5780+
Embezzlement: KF9360
Emblem, National: KF5150
Emblem, State: KFN5749, KFA-KFZ 429
Embryonic stem cells
  Medical legislation: KF3827.S74
Emergency assistance: KF1329+, KFC334
  Medical: KF2905
Emergency Court of Appeals (U.S.): KF6037.5+
Emergency economic legislation: KFC834+, KFN5834+
Emergency management
  Law offices: KF320.E44
  Social legislation: KF3750
Emergency medical personnel: KF2915.E4+
Emergency medical services: KF3826.E5, KFN5619.E43, KFA-KFZ 363.E43
Emergency Relief Appropriation Act, 1935: KF6015.E4
Emergency transportation tax (New Jersey): KFA-KFZ 482.5.E4
Emigration
  Trial practice: KF8925.E4
Eminent domain: KF5599, KFC800, KFN5800, KFX2075, KFA-KFZ 450
  Conflict of laws: KF418.E4
  General: KF10A 12.1.E42
Eminent domain claims (Trial practice): KFA-KFZ 539.E45
Emission density zoning (Air pollution): KF3812.5.E55
Employee appraisals: KF3457.8
Employee pensions trusts: KF736.P3
Employee seniority: KF3458
Employee vacations: KF3531, KFN5577
Employees, Bonding of: KF1225
Employees Compensation Commission (U.S.): KF3626.5.A2+
Employees' inventions: KF3135+
Employees, Resignation of: KF3471+
Employers' liability: KF1316+, KFN5332.4, KFA-KFZ 199.E45
Employers' liability insurance: KFN5298.E5
Employment: KF3457+, KFC571+, KFN5571+
Employment agencies: KF2042.E5, KFC446.E5, KFN5446.E5
  Regulation: KFA-KFZ 282.E55
Employment, Free choice of: KF4769
Employment interviewing: KF3457.7
Employment (Labor law): KFA-KFZ 334.5.E55
Employment references: KF3457.6
Employment seniority: KF3458
Employment Service (U.S.): KF3676
Employment tests: KF3457.3
Endowment policies (Life insurance): KF1180.E5
Endowments
  Income tax: KFA-KFZ 475.7

INDEX

Energy and Commerce, Committee on (United States House of Representatives): KF4997.E53

Energy and Natural Resources, Committee on (United States Senate): KF4987.E54

Energy assistance (Public welfare): KFA-KFZ 351.E53

Energy conservation provisions (Building laws): KF5708, KFC818

Energy policy: KF2120+, KFA-KFZ 286+

Energy research: KF4280.E53

Energy Research and Development Administration: KF4280.E53

Engineers: KF2928, KFC547.E6+, KFN5547.E54+, KFA-KFZ 329.E6+

Expert witnesses (Civil procedure): KF8968.25

Immigration: KF4825.E53

Legal handbooks: KF390.E54

Engineers, Corps of (U.S. Army): KF7335.E5

Enlisted personnel

Air Force: KF7427

Armed Forces: KF7287

Army: KF7327

Coast Guard: KF7467

Navy: KF7367

Enrollment, Tribal: KFA-KFZ 505.6.T74

Enterprise liability: KF1300

Entertainers

Copyright: KF3076

Labor law: KF3580.S7

Legal handbooks: KF390.E57

Regulation of profession: KF2932+, KFX2042.E58

Works for: KFC84.E58

Entertainment expenses (Income tax): KF6395.T7

Entertainment lawyers: KF299.E57

Entertainment lawyers (Directories): KF195.E58

Entertainment tax: KF6611.A3

Entrapment

Criminal law: KF9244

Environment and Public Works, Committee on (United States Senate): KF4987.E57

Environmental actions (Trial practice): KF8925.E5, KFA-KFZ 539.E49

Environmental damages

Government liability: KF1325.E58

Torts: KF1298+, KFC323.5, KFA-KFZ 197.8

Environmental law

Electronic data processing: KF242.E58+

Study and teaching: KF277.E5

Environmental lawyers: KF299.E6

Directories: KF195.E6

Environmental pollution: KFN5610+

Environmental Protection Agency (Government contracts): KF869.5.E54

Epileptics (Capacity and disability): KF480.5.E6

Equal Employment Opportunity Commission (United States): KF3464.15

Equal protection of the law: KF4764

Equal time rule (Radio and television communication): KF2812

Equipment

Air Force: KF7436

Armed Forces: KF7296

Army: KF7336

Coast Guard: KF7476

Navy: KF7376

Equitable conversion

Land tenure: KF601

Equitable distribution of marital property: KF535.7

Equitable liens: KF698

Equitable ownership: KF601+

Equity: KF398+, KFN5085, KFA-KFZ 85

Civil procedure: KF8851+, KFC997, KFN5997, KFA-KFZ 531

Erosion control: KF1686, KFC386

Error, Writ of: KFN6084

Escalator accidents

Liability for: KF1287.5.E45

Escalator clause (Wages): KF3499
Escape from legal custody: KF9422
Escrow business: KF1027, KFA-KFZ 167.E8
Espionage: KF9394
Espionage, Industrial: KF3197
Estate planning: KF746+, KFC195, KFN5195, KFA-KFZ 140
  Lawyers (Directories): KF195.E75
  Tax planning: KF6576+
Estate settlement costs: KF769.E65
Estate taxes: KF6571+, KFC894+, KFN5894+, KFA-KFZ 482
Estates
  Contingent estates: KF597
  Future estates: KF604+
  Taxes: KF6571+
Estates for life
  Land tenure: KF578
Estates (Land tenure): KF577
  Curtesy: KF629, KFA-KFZ 123.D6
  Dower: KF629, KFN5160, KFA-KFZ 123.D6
  Future estates: KFC150+, KFN5150, KFA-KFZ 119
Estates, Unclaimed: KF780, KFA-KFZ 148.U6
Estoppel: KF450.E7
Estoppel by judgment: KF8992
Ethics: KFA-KFZ 421.5.L4
  Juries: KF8980
Ethics in government: KF4568, KFC686, KFN5686, KFA-KFZ 406
Ethics, Judicial: KF8779, KFN5984.5.D57, KFA-KFZ 525.5.D5
Ethics, Law student: KF287.5
Ethics, Legal: KF305+, KFC76.5.A2+, KFN5076.5.A2+, KFA-KFZ 76.5.A2+
Ethics, Select Committee on (United States Senate): KF4987.E84
Ethnic minorities
  Civil rights: KF4755
Etiquette, Legal: KF305+
Eugenics: KF3832
Euthanasia
  Medical legislation: KF3827.E87

Evaluation and selection of instructional materials: KFA-KFZ 395.25
Evaporated milk industry: KF1924.E8
Everglades National Park (Water resources): KF5590.E8
Eviction claims (Trial practice): KFC1028.E9
Evidence
  Bankruptcy: KF1530.E87
  Criminal procedure: KF9660+, KFC1165+, KFN6165+, KFA-KFZ 580+
  General and civil procedure: KF8931+, KFC1030+, KFN6030+, KFA-KFZ 540+
Evidence, Circumstantial
  Civil procedure: KF8946
Evidence, Computer animation: KF8966
Evidence, Demonstrative: KF8967, KFA-KFZ 541.9.D45
Evidence, Digital
  Civil procedure: KF8947.5
Evidence, Documentary: KFC1038, KFN6038, KFA-KFZ 541.9.D63
  Civil procedure: KF8947+
Evidence, Electronic
  Civil procedure: KF8947.5
Evidence, Hearsay
  Civil procedure: KFC1043
  Criminal procedure: KFA-KFZ 580.5.H4
Evidence, Medical: KF8964
Evidence, Photographic: KF8968
Evidence, Prima facie: KF8940.P7, KFC1032, KFN6032
Evidence, Psychiatric and psychological: KF8965
Evidence tampering: KF9421
Ex-convicts
  Employment of: KF3468
  Legal handbooks: KF390.E87
  Suffrage: KF4896.E92
Examinations, Bar: KF303
Examinations, Premarital: KF512
Examiners, Title (Directories): KF195.T5

INDEX

Examiners (Trial practice): KF8986, KFN6049, KFA-KFZ 543

Excavation Labor law: KFC586.E9

Exceptionally gifted students: KFC665.E9

Exceptions Civil procedure: KF8881+, KFC1013

Excess and surplus lines Insurance: KF1170.E94

Excess benefits Taxation: KF6614.E94

Excess profits tax: KF6471+, KFC877, KFN5877

Exchange visitors' program Immigration: KF4825.E93

Exchanges, Commodity: KF1085+, KFN5275.A1+, KFA-KFZ 180.A1+

Exchanges, Educational: KF4330

Exchanges, Produce: KF1085+, KFN5275.A1+, KFA-KFZ 180.A1+

Excise taxes Federal: KF6600+ Local: KF6788+ State: KF6767+, KFC898+, KFN5898+, KFA-KFZ 483+

Exclusions Insolvency and bankruptcy: KF1536.E93

Exculpatory evidence (Criminal procedure): KF9678

Execution of judgment: KF9025+, KFC1065+, KFN6065+, KFA-KFZ 551

Execution of sentence Criminal procedure: KF9725+, KFC1179+, KFN6179+, KFA-KFZ 587+ Juvenile criminal law: KF9825+, KFC1198.6+, KFN6198.592+, KFA-KFZ 598.6+ Military law: KF7675+

Execution of wills: KF774+, KFC210, KFN5210, KFA-KFZ 147

Executive advisory bodies: KF5125

Executive agreements: KF5057

Executive branch: KF5050+, KFC740+, KFN5740+, KFA-KFZ 425+

Executive departments: KF5101+, KFC745, KFN5745+, KFX2017.4, KFA-KFZ 427+

Executive impoundment of appropriated funds: KF4579.I4

Executive privilege (Constitutional law): KF4570

Executives (Legal handbooks): KF390.E9

Executives' liability insurance: KF1220.E83

Executors and administrators: KF774+, KFC210, KFN5210 Decedents' estates: KFA-KFZ 147

Exemption Criminal liability: KF9240+, KFC1115, KFN6115+, KFN6115, KFA-KFZ 566.5 Customs duties: KF6704+ Execution of judgment: KF9029.A+ Income tax: KF6329 Military service: KF7265+ Real property tax: KF6761+, KFA-KFZ 479.8.E9 Taxation: KF6329, KFN5868, KFA-KFZ 472+

Exemptions Insolvency and bankruptcy: KF1536.E93

Exercise personnel: KF2915.E95+

Exhibitions: KFC647.F34, KFA-KFZ 386.F35

Expatriation: KF4715

Expediting Act of 1903, Procedure under: KF9066.A5

Expenditure control Public finance Federal: KF6231+ Local: KF6772, KFN5908, KFA-KFZ 488.5 State: KF6740, KFC845+, KFN5845+, KFA-KFZ 467+ State and local: KF6722

Expenses Income tax: KF6394+

Experiments with humans in medicine: KF3827.M38

INDEX

Expert evidence
  Civil procedure: KF8961+, KFC1042, KFA-KFZ 541.5
  Criminal procedure: KF9674, KFN6169.3.E8, KFA-KFZ 580.5.E9
  Directories: KF195.E96
Explosives
  Public safety: KF3953, KFC641.5.E9, KFX2061, KFA-KFZ 380.E9
  Shipping: KF2560.E85
Export controls
  Legal research: KF241.E85
Export-Import Bank of the United States: KF1978
Export trade: KF1987+
Export trading companies: KF1988
Express companies: KF2740+
Express highways: KF5530, KFC787.5, KFN5788, KFX2071
Expulsion: KF4842
Extinguishment of debts (Income tax): KF6428.E9
Extortion: KF9372+, KFC1132, KFN6132, KFA-KFZ 568.T57
Extractive industries: KF1681+, KFC385+, KFN5385+, KFA-KFZ 239+
  Business taxes: KF6763.9.M54, KFA-KFZ 480.5.M5
  State taxation: KF6738.M56
Extracurricular school programs: KF4218
Extracurricular use of school buildings: KFN5650.5
Extradition: KF9635, KFC1157.7, KFA-KFZ 576.7
Extraordinary remedies: KF9035+, KFC1070, KFN6070+, KFA-KFZ 552+
Eyeglasses industry: KF2036.E93

F

F.O.B. clause: KF934
Facility management
  Contracts: KF905.F34
Factfinding boards
  Labor disputes: KF3427, KFC565, KFN5565

Factory inspection: KF3571, KFN5585
Faculties, Academic: KF4240
Fair Labor Standards Act: KF3481+
Fair trade legislation: KF2016+
Fairness doctrine (Radio and television communication): KF2812
Fairs: KF2026, KFC647.F34, KFA-KFZ 386.F35
Faith-based human services
  Constitutional law: KF4868.F35
Faith healers: KF2913.F3+, KFA-KFZ 326.5.F35+
Fall accidents: KF1290.S55
False pretenses: KF9365+
  Criminal law: KFN6131.5
Family Court (New York): KFN5116+
Family farm operating agreements: KF674
Family law: KF501+, KFC115+, KFN5115+
  Legal profession: KF299.D6
Family partnerships: KF1382
Family planning: KF3766, KFC609, KFA-KFZ 353
Family provisions: KF760.F2
Family violence
  Criminal law: KFC1121.4, KFN6121.4, KFA-KFZ 567.F35
  Torts: KFA-KFZ 197.D65
Farm corporations: KF1713
Farm Credit Administration (U.S.): KF1012.F2
Farm Credit Corporation (U.S.): KF1012.F2
Farm land
  Real property tax: KFA-KFZ 479.8.F37
  Taxation: KF6761.3.F2
  Tenancy: KF593.F3, KFA-KFZ 117.5
Farm Loan Commissioner (U.S.): KF1012.F2
Farm loans: KF1701
Farm marketing cooperatives: KF1715, KFC390, KFN5390, KFA-KFZ 242
Farm mortgage insurance: KF1701
Farm producers' cooperatives: KF1715, KFC390, KFN5390, KFA-KFZ 242

INDEX

Farm tenancy: KF593.F3, KFA-KFZ 117.5
Farmers
Legal handbooks: KF390.F3
Farms
Corporate reorganization: KF1546.F35, KFA-KFZ 225.F35
Federal aid to education: KF4136+, KFA-KFZ 391.F3
Federal aid to higher education: KF4234
Federal aid to transportation: KF2186
Federal and state jurisdiction
Constitutional law: KF4600+
Courts: KF8735
Taxation: KF6736+
Federal and state relations: KF4600+
Federal areas within states: KF4625
Federal Bureau of Investigation (United States): KF5108
Federal civil service: KF5336+
Federal Communications Commission: KF2765.1
Federal Deposit Insurance Company: KF1023
Federal employees
State taxation: KF6738.F3
Unemployment insurance: KF3680.F3
Workers' compensation: KF3626
Federal Farm Loan Board: KF1012.F2
Federal Farm Loan Bureau: KF1012.F2
Federal government (State taxation): KF6738.F35
Federal Maritime Board: KF1105.2
Federal Power Commission: KF2120.1
Federal Radio Commission (U.S.): KF2765.1
Federal Register: KF70.A2
Federal Reserve banks: KF981+
Federal Reserve Board: KF6219
Federal Reserve System: KF6218+
Federal Rules Decisions: KF8830
Federal Securities Act: KF1431+
Federal Security Agency: KF3650.5, KF3720.5
Federal ship mortgage insurance: KF1114.B65

Federal-state disputes: KF4612
Federal taxation: KF6271+
Federal Tort Claims Act: KF1321
Federal Trade Commission: KF1611+
Federal Transit Administration (Government contracts): KF869.5.T73
Federalist, The: KF4515
Fees
Legal profession: KFA-KFZ 77.5.F4
Probate law: KFA-KFZ 144.5.C67
Public revenue: KF6265, KFN5902.F33, KFA-KFZ 487.F33
Fees, Medical: KF2907.F3
Fees, Patent: KF3125.F3
Fellow servant rule: KF1319.F4
Fences
Real property: KF639, KFA-KFZ 123.B6
Fertilization in vitro: KF3830+
Fertilizer industry: KF1876.F3
Regulation: KFA-KFZ 267.F4
Feticide: KF9315, KFC1121, KFN6121, KFA-KFZ 567.A2
Fiber optics
Patent law: KF3159.F52
Field crops
Acreage allotments: KF1706.A+
Grading: KF1724.A+
Marketing quotas: KF1706.A+
Price supports: KF1693.A+
Standards: KF1724.A+
Field irrigation: KF1686, KFC386
Filibustering: KF4894
Filing fees
Bankruptcy: KF1530.F54
Filled milk: KF1924.F4
Filming (Copyright): KF3030.6
Finance
Business enterprises: KFC337.5.F5
Health facilities and hospitals: KF3825.5
Finance charges: KF1039+, KFC262, KFN5262, KFA-KFZ 171
Finance, Committee on (United States Senate): KF4987.F5
Finance, Court: KF8732.5, KFC958.5, KFN5958.5

INDEX

Finance, Local: KF6770+, KFC905+, KFN5905+, KFX2089+, KFX2090+, KFA-KFZ 488+

Finance, School: KF4125+, KFC648+, KFN5648+, KFA-KFZ 390+

Finance, State: KF6735+

Finance, State and local: KF6720+

Finance, Transportation: KF2186

Financial planners: KF2921, KFA-KFZ 329.F55+

Financial responsibility laws: KF2219, KFA-KFZ 297.7

Financial Services, Committee on (United States House of Representatives): KF4997.F5

Financial statements (Corporations): KF1446, KFA-KFZ 214.A23

Fine arts: KF4288

Fines (Penalties): KF9745, KFN6188, KFA-KFZ 591

Fingerprints

Criminal law: KF9666.5, KFN6167, KFA-KFZ 580.5.M4

Evidence: KF8963

Fire accidents: KF1290.F4

Fire departments: KF3976, KFN5644.5, KFX2060

Fire fighters: KF3976, KFN5644.5

Fire insurance: KF1196, KFN5295.F5, KFA-KFZ 189.F5

Fire insurance business: KF1198

Fire prevention and control: KF3975+, KFC644, KFN5644+, KFX2060, KFA-KFZ 381

Firearms

Products liability: KF1297.F55

Public safety: KF3941+, KFC640.5, KFN5640.5, KFA-KFZ 379

Taxation: KF6614.F5

Fireworks (Public safety): KF3955, KFC641.5.I6, KFA-KFZ 380.I6

Fish and Wildlife Service (U.S.): KF1770.1

Fish meal: KF3879.F5

Fish protection: KF5640+, KFC806, KFN5806, KFA-KFZ 453+

Fishery: KF1770+, KFC398, KFA-KFZ 254

Fishery products

Inspection: KF1930

Standards and grading: KF1930

Fishery products industry: KF1930+

Fishing industry: KF1771+

Fixtures

Real property: KFA-KFZ 123.F57

Flag: KF5150, KFN5749, KFA-KFZ 429

Flag salute in schools: KF4162, KFN5655, KFA-KFZ 392.7

Flavoring essences: KF3879.F55

Flaxseed trade (Import): KFN5435.F5

Flea markets: KFA-KFZ 281.F55

Flogging: KF7677

Flood control: KF5588+, KFC795+, KFA-KFZ 447.8

Flood relief (Agriculture): KF1712

Florida

Laws: KFF1+

Flour

Food law: KFA-KFZ 372.5.F5

Flour milling: KF1902

Flour trade (Wholesale): KF1999.F5

Fluoridation of water: KF3794, KFC612.6, KFA-KFZ 356.6

Food

Labeling: KF1620.F66

Food additives: KF3879.P7

Food adulteration: KF3878

Food (Advertising): KF1616.F6

Food and Drug Administration (U.S.): KF3871

Food, drugs, and cosmetics: KF3861+, KFC630+, KFN5630+, KFX2050, KF10D .x2F62+, KFA-KFZ 372+

Food law: KF3875+, KFN5631, KFA-KFZ 372+

Food preservatives: KF3879.P7

Food processing industries: KF1900+, KFC415+, KFN5415+, KFX2029.A+, KFA-KFZ 272.A1+

Collective labor agreements: KFN5562.F6

Products liability: KF1297.F6

INDEX

Food relief (Foreign assistance program): KF4670.F66
Food stamp program
Public welfare: KFA-KFZ 351.F66
Food stamp program (Public welfare): KF3745.F62
Foot trails: KF5534, KFC788.5, KFA-KFZ 444.8
Footprints
Criminal law: KF9666.5, KFN6167, KFA-KFZ 580.5.M4
Forced labor (Human trafficking): KF9449
Forced prostitution (Human trafficking): KF9449
Foreclosure
Mortgages: KF697.F6, KFC177.F6, KFN5177.F6, KFA-KFZ 130.5.F6
Real property tax: KFA-KFZ 479.8.F58
Taxation: KFA-KFZ 471.9.F6
Foreign Affairs, Committee on (United States House of Representatives): KF4997.F6
Foreign agents: KF4854
Foreign and international banks: KFN5254.F67
Foreign assistance program: KF4668+
Foreign banking: KF1030.F6
Foreign banks: KF1001.5
Foreign consuls: KF4694.F67
Foreign corporations: KF1419, KFN5347, KFA-KFZ 215.F6
Foreign-exchange brokerage: KF1033, KFA-KFZ 169
Foreign governments and employees
Tort liability: KF1309.5
Foreign investment: KF1575
Foreign investments
Income tax: KF6419
Foreign investors
Legal handbooks: KF390.B84
Foreign investors in the United States: KF6441
Foreign judgments: KF8729, KFN5957
Foreign law, Proof of: KF8940.P75
Foreign mail: KF2693

Foreign patent licensing agreements: KF3147
Foreign personal representatives (Decedents' estates): KF779.F6
Foreign propaganda: KF4854
Foreign relations: KF4650+
Foreign Relations, Committee on (United States Senate): KF4987.F6
Foreign Service (U.S.): KF5112+
Foreign students
Immigration: KF4825.S7
Forensic psychology: KF8922
Forensic science (Directories): KF195.E96
Forest fires: KF3977
Forest land
Conservation: KF1686
National forests: KF5631+
Taxation: KF6761.3.F6, KFC881.8.F67, KFN5881.8.F67, KFA-KFZ 479.8.F6
Forest Service (U.S.): KF5631.5
Forest yield taxes: KF6761.3.F6, KFC881.8.F67, KFN5881.8.F67, KFA-KFZ 479.8.F6
Foresters: KFA-KFZ 329.F67+
Forestry: KF1750, KFC385+, KFC396, KFN5385+, KFN5396, KFA-KFZ 249
Income tax: KF6495.A47
Forestry (Income tax): KFC879.F67
Forests, National: KF5631+
Forests, State: KFC805+, KFN5805+, KFA-KFZ 452+
Forfeitures
Criminal law: KFN6108.F67, KFA-KFZ 565.F6
Criminal procedure: KF9747, KFA-KFZ 591.2
Forgery
Bad checks: KF9367
Counterfeiting: KF9455, KFN6149
Fraud by forgery: KF9367
Form books: KF170, KFN5068, KFA-KFZ 68
Form requirements: KFA-KFZ 90.F6
Formalities
Contracts: KF810, KFN5218

Forwarding agents: KF2745
- Air freight: KF2462
- Ocean freight: KF2654

Foster home care (Child welfare): KF3736.5, KFC603.5, KFN5603.5, KFA-KFZ 350.C4

Foster homes for adults: KFA-KFZ 282.G75

Foundations
- Corporation law: KF1389+, KFN5343, KFA-KFZ 211
- Income tax: KF6449, KFC873, KFA-KFZ 475.7

Foundries
- Labor hygiene and safety: KF3574.F6

Franchise lawyers (Directories): KF195.F73

Franchises, Corporate (Taxation): KF6558, KFC886, KFN5886, KFA-KFZ 480.8

Franchises, Retail: KF2023, KFC442, KFN5441, KFA-KFZ 281.F7

Franking privilege: KF2734
- Congressional: KF4969.F7

Fraternal insurance: KF1238, KFA-KFZ 193.F7

Fraternal Society Law Association: KF294.F7

Fraternities, Legal (Directories): KF289

Fraud
- Contracts: KF821, KFN5222, KFA-KFZ 151.F7
- Criminal law: KF9365+, KFN6131.5
- Torts: KF1271, KFA-KFZ 197.D27

Fraud by forgery: KF9367, KFA-KFZ 568.F75

Fraudulent conveyances: KF1534, KFN5366.F7, KFA-KFZ 222.F7

Free choice of employment: KF4769

Freedom of assembly: KF4778

Freedom of conscience: KF4783, KFA-KFZ 412.R45

Freedom of employment: KF4769

Freedom of expression: KF4770+

Freedom of government information: KF5753, KFC827, KFN5827, KFA-KFZ 462.6.A25

Freedom of movement: KF4785

Freedom of petition: KF4780, KFA-KFZ 412.P47

Freedom of religion: KF4783, KFA-KFZ 412.R45
- Students and school employees: KF4162

Freedom of speech: KF4772, KFN5696.5.S6

Freedom of the press: KF4774

Freemasons: KF1362.F7

Freight: KF2190+, KFC483
- Rates: KF2346+, KFC497, KFN5497

Freight claims: KF2190+, KFC483
- Railroads: KF2372

Freight classification (Railroads): KF2346+

Freight forwarders: KF2745
- Air freight: KF2462
- Ocean freight: KF2654

Friendly societies: KF1238, KFA-KFZ 193.F7

Fright and anguish: KF1264

Fringe benefits
- Civil service: KF5385
- Labor law: KF3509+, KFC575.6
- Merchant mariners: KF1131

Fringe benefits (Nonwage payments)
- Income tax: KFA-KFZ 475.5.N6

Frivolous suits: KF8887, KFA-KFZ 536.4

Fruit and vegetables
- Acreage allotments: KF1707
- Marketing agreements: KF1697.F78
- Marketing quotas: KF1707
- Price supports: KF1694
- Standards and grading: KF1725.A1+
- Weights and measures: KFC383+

Fruit juices
- Food law: KFA-KFZ 372.5.F78

Fruit processing industry: KF1908+

Fruits and vegetables
- Weights and measures: KFA-KFZ 235.F7

Fuel consumption (Motor vehicles): KF2213

INDEX

Fuel efficiency (Motor vehicles): KF2213
Fugitive Slave Act: KF4545.S5
Fund raising (Foundations): KF1389.5, KFN5343.5
Fungi, Toxigenic
- Public health hazards: KFA-KFZ 359.M65
Fur-seal fishing: KF1773.S33
Furniture industry: KFC412.F8, KFA-KFZ 271.F8
Furniture (Labeling): KF1620.F83
Furs
- Import trade: KF1996.F8
Furs (Labeling): KF1620.F8
Future estates: KF604+, KFC150+, KFN5150, KFA-KFZ 119
Future interests
- Personal property: KFA-KFZ 134.5.F8
- Real property: KF604+, KFC150+, KFN5150, KFA-KFZ 119
Futures trading: KF1085

G

Gambling
- Contracts: KF1241
- Criminal law: KF9440, KFN6146, KFA-KFZ 571.G2
- Indians: KF8210.G35
- Regulation: KF3992, KFC646, KFN5646, KFA-KFZ 385
- Taxation: KFA-KFZ 485.W34
  - Federal: KF6636.W2
  - State: KF6768.W2, KFC900.W34
Gambling on Indian reservations: KFA-KFZ 505.6.G35
Game laws: KF5640
Game protection: KF5640+, KFC806, KFN5806, KFA-KFZ 453+
Game rights: KF649
Games of chance: KFA-KFZ 385
- Indians: KFA-KFZ 505.6.L67
Garnishment: KF9026, KFC1066, KFN6066, KFA-KFZ 551

Gas
- Public utilities: KFC465, KFA-KFZ 288
Gas containers and equipment (Public safety): KFA-KFZ 380.5.G32
Gas industry
- Mining: KF1841+, KFC405+, KFN5404+
- Public utilities: KF2130+
- Regulation: KFA-KFZ 258.A1+
Gas installations
- Building laws: KF5704.5, KFA-KFZ 459.6
Gas leases: KF1865
Gas, Natural: KF1870
Gasohol (Public utilities): KFA-KFZ 291.G37
Gasoline
- Taxation: KF6616, KFC900.M67, KFN5900.M6
Gays
- Civil and political rights: KF4754.5, KFA-KFZ 411.5.H64
- Discrimination against
  - Labor law: KF3467.5
- Legal services to: KF337.5.G38
General Accounting Office (U.S.): KF6236
General area studies (Higher education curricula): KF4245.5.I5
General Services Administration (U.S.): KF5750
General trusts: KF733
Generic drugs: KF3894.G45
Geologists: KFA-KFZ 329.G45+
Georgia
- Laws: KFG1+
Geothermal resources (Public utilities): KF2140.G45+, KFC468.8.G46, KFA-KFZ 291.G45
Geriatricians: KF2910.G45+
Gerrymandering: KF4905, KFC714, KFN5714
GI Bill of Rights: KF7739.E3, KF7749.E3
Gift taxes: KF6594, KFC894+, KFN5894+, KFA-KFZ 482

INDEX

Gifted children: KF4209.5
Gifted students: KFC665.E9
Gifts causa mortis: KF760.G4
Gifts, Charitable (Income tax): KF6388
Gifts inter vivos: KF716
Girl's Term Court (New York City): KFN5116.5
Glass fruit jars
Patent law: KF3159.G56
Global warming: KF3783
Gold clause: KF828
Gold standard (Currency): KF6211
Gold trading: KF6211
Good faith: KF450.G6
Good Samaritan laws: KF1329+, KFC334, KFA-KFZ 201
Government Affairs, Committee on (United States Senate): KF4987.G65
Government consultants: KF5357
Government contracts: KF841+
Government corporations: KF1480
Government, County: KF5330
Government expenditures: KF6221+, KFC842, KFN5842
Government grants creating rights in land: KFC167, KFN5167
Government insurance
Bank deposits: KF1023
Farm mortgages: KF1701
Mortgages, Housing: KF5737
Ship mortgages: KF1114.B65
Government, Local: KF5300+
Government misconduct, Claims for damages resulting from
Trial practice: KF8925.C5
Government, Municipal: KF5304+, KFC752+, KFN5752+, KFX2015+, KFA-KFZ 431+
Government officials and employees
Bonding: KF1225
Civil service
County: KFA-KFZ 437+
Federal: KF5336+
Municipal: KF5393+, KFC774, KFN5774+, KFA-KFZ 436+
State: KF5390, KFC760+, KFN5760+, KFA-KFZ 435+

Government officials and employees
Collective labor agreements: KF3409.P77, KFC562.P8, KFN5562.P8, KFX2045.P8, KFA-KFZ 332.8.P77
Hours of labor: KF3528.P8
Inventions: KF3136
Labor disputes: KF3450.P8+, KFA-KFZ 338.A+
Labor hygiene and safety: KF3574.G68
Labor law: KF3580.G6
Patents: KF3136
State taxation: KF6738.F3
Tort liability: KF1306.A2+, KFC327, KFA-KFZ 198.P8
Workers' compensation: KF3626
Government Operations, Committee on
United States House of Representatives: KF4997.G6
United States Senate: KF4987.G6
Government-owned business organizations: KF1480
Government-owned corporations: KF1480
Government ownership
Merchant fleet: KF2636
Railroads: KF2295
Telecommunication: KF2765.2+
Telephone: KF2780.2+
Telegraph: KF2775.2+
Government Printing Office (U.S.): KF5001
Government procurement
Indians: KF8210.P8
Government property: KF5750+, KFC825+, KFN5825+, KFA-KFZ 462+
Government purchasing
Indians: KF8210.P8
Government records (Government property): KFA-KFZ 462.5.P8
Government Reform, Committee on
United States House of Representatives: KF4997.G67
Government risks insurance: KF1220.G68, KFN5298.G68, KFA-KFZ 191.G67

INDEX

Government tort liability: KF1321+, KFC332, KFN5332.6, KFA-KFZ 199.G6

Governmental investigations: KF5422

Governmental Operations with Respect to Intelligence Activities, Select Committee to Study (United States Senate): KF4987.G63

Governors: KF5050.Z95, KFC741+, KFN5741+, KFA-KFZ 426

Governors' messages: KFC19, KFN5019, KFA-KFZ 19

Grade crossings: KF2234, KFN5478, KFA-KFZ 297.9

Grain

- Acreage allotments: KF1706.G7+
- Freight classification: KF2355.A46
- Marketing quotas: KF1706.G7+
- Marketing regulations: KF1719.G7, KFA-KFZ 244.G7
- Price supports: KF1693.G7+
- Shipping: KF2560.G6
- Standards and grading: KF1724.G7+

Grain elevators (Insolvency and bankruptcy): KF1535.G73

Grain exchanges: KF1086.G7

Grand jury: KF9642, KFC1159, KFN6159, KFA-KFZ 577

Grandparents' rights

- Domestic relations: KF548

Grants-in-aid, Federal

- State and local revenue: KF6733
- State revenue: KFN5902.F3, KFA-KFZ 487.F3

Grapefruit processing industry: KF1909.G6

Gratuities: KF3658.T5

Grazing districts: KF5630

Great Lakes (Navigation and piloting): KF2571

Grievances

- Labor law: KF3544

Groceries

- Retail trade: KF2036.G7, KFA-KFZ 281.5.G76

Grocery workers (Labor law): KF3580.G7

Ground leases: KF593.G7, KFC147.G7

Group arrangements (Prepaid services): KF310.G7, KFA-KFZ 77.5.G7

Group health insurance: KF1184.G7

Group homes

- Zoning: KF5700.5.G74, KFA-KFZ 458.92.G75

Group homes for adults: KFA-KFZ 282.G75

Group insurance: KF1169.G7

- Health insurance: KF1184.G7
- Life insurance: KF1177.G7

Group medical practice: KF2907.G7

Guaranty insurance: KF1231+, KFC300, KFN5300+

Guardian and ward: KF553+, KFC134, KFN5134, KFA-KFZ 106+

Guidance workers (Educational law): KF4192.5.G8

Gynecologists: KF2910.G94+, KFA-KFZ 326.5.G94+

H

Habeas corpus: KF9011, KFC1061, KFA-KFZ 548

Habitual criminals: KF9226, KFN6105, KFA-KFZ 564

Halfway houses: KFA-KFZ 282.H34

Hallucinogenic drugs

- Drug laws: KF3894.H34

Handbag industry: KF1893.H2

Handbooks, manuals, etc.: KF319, KFN5077, KFA-KFZ 77

Handguns (Public safety): KF3942.H3

Harbor and river improvement: KF5580+

Harbors and ports: KF2581+, KFC530+, KFN5530+, KFA-KFZ 312.A1+

Harrisburg Seven (Criminal trials): KF224.H27

Hawaii

- Laws: KFH1+

Hazardous articles and processes

- Public safety: KF3945+, KFC641+, KFN5641+, KFA-KFZ 380.A1+

Hazardous occupations: KF3566+, KFC584+, KFN5584+

Hazardous substances, Improper disposal of

- Environmental damages: KF1299.H39
- Tort liability of corporations: KF1301.H39

Hazardous waste management industry

- Labor hygiene and safety: KF3574.H39

Hazardous wastes: KF3946, KFC641.5.H39, KFN5641.3, KFA-KFZ 380.H39

Health benefits

- Civil service: KF5385
- Labor: KF3515+
- Veterans: KF7739.M3, KF7749.M3+

Health, Education, Labor, and Pensions, Committee on (United States Senate): KF4987.H4

Health facilities: KF3825+, KFC617+

- Collective labor disputes: KF3450.H4+
- Income tax: KF6495.H4
- Labor hygiene and safety: KF3574.H66
- Labor law: KF3580.H4, KFA-KFZ 338.H42

Health insurance

- Civil service: KF5385
- Coal miners: KF3608.C6
- Fringe benefits (Labor): KF3515+
- Older people: KF3608.A4
- Personal insurance: KF1183+, KFC293.H42, KFN5293.H43, KFA-KFZ 187.H4
- Railroads: KF3608.R2
- Social insurance: KF3605+, KFC591+, KFN5591, KFA-KFZ 341+

Health lawyers

- Directories: KF195.M43
- Legal profession: KF299.M43

Health maintenance organizations (Health insurance): KF1184.H4

Health professions: KF2905+, KFN5546.A+, KFA-KFZ 326+

Health regulations

- Building laws: KFA-KFZ 459.8.H43

Hearing aids

- Retail trade: KF2036.H4, KFA-KFZ 281.5.H42

Hearing examiners: KF5421, KFC782.5, KFN5782, KFA-KFZ 441.H4

Hearsay

- Civil procedure: KF8969, KFA-KFZ 541.6

Heating and ventilating

- Building laws: KF5708, KFC818, KFN5818, KFA-KFZ 459.75

Heating contracts: KF905.P5

Heating fixture industry

- Manufacture: KF1890.P5
- Wholesale trade: KF1999.P5

Heating industry

- Regulation: KFA-KFZ 282.H43

Hedge funds: KF1078.3

Heirless property: KF780

Helicopter accidents: KF1290.A9

Herbicides

- Public safety: KF3959, KFC641.5.P63

Herbs industry: KF1939

Heroin: KF3891.H4

High technology industries

- Corporate reorganization: KF1546.H35
- Income tax: KF6495.H45
- Regulation: KF1890.H53

Higher education: KF4225+, KFC666, KFN5666+, KFA-KFZ 396+

Highway conditions (Government liability): KF1325.T7

Highway finance: KF5528, KFC787.3, KFA-KFZ 444.5

Highway intersections: KF2234, KFN5478, KFA-KFZ 297.9

Highway law: KF5521+, KFC787+, KFN5787, KFA-KFZ 444+

Highway safety: KF2234, KFN5478, KFA-KFZ 297.9

Highway transport workers (Hours of labor): KF3528.H5

INDEX

Hire of goods: KF946, KFA-KFZ 159.5.H57

Hispanic Americans (Civil rights): KFA-KFZ 411.5.H56

Historic buildings and monuments: KF4310+, KFA-KFZ 398.9

Historic monuments: KF4310+

Historical documents: KF4325

Historical vessels: KF4310+

Hobbies (Income tax): KF6395.H63

Hogs (Processing tax): KF6631.H6

Hold harmless agreements: KF812.I5

Holder in due course (Bills of exchange): KF959.H6

Holding companies: KF1465

Banks: KF1017

Corporation law: KF1465

Public utilities: KFN5460

Electric utilities: KF2125+

Gas companies: KF2130+

Power utilities: KF2120+

Water supply companies: KF2133+

Railroads: KF2293

Holidays: KF3531, KFN5577, KFA-KFZ 334.5.V32

Labor law: KFC577

Home-based businesses

Zoning: KF5700.5.H65, KFA-KFZ 458.92.H65

Home care services: KFC619.H65

Home health services: KF3826.H64, KFA-KFZ 363.H65

Home heating (Public welfare): KFA-KFZ 351.E53

Home labor: KF3557, KFA-KFZ 335.6

Home rule

Municipal government: KFA-KFZ 431.9.H6

Home schools: KF4221, KFA-KFZ 395.97

Home study schools: KF4222

Homeland Security and Governmental Affairs, Committee on (United States Senate): KF4987.H65

Homeland Security, Committee on United States House of Representatives: KF4997.H66

Homeless children

Educational law: KF4217.H68

Homeless persons

Public welfare: KF3742, KFC605.6, KFA-KFZ 350.H65

Homeowners

Legal handbooks: KF390.H53

Homeowners' associations: KFA-KFZ 114.H66

Homesteads

Public land: KF5670+

Public land law: KFA-KFZ 454

Real property tax: KF6761.3.H6

Homicide: KF9305+, KF10A 17.4.H6, KFA-KFZ 567.H6

Honor, Decorations of: KF5153+

Horizontal property: KF581, KFC144.5, KFN5142

Hormones: KF3894.B5

Horse racing: KF3989, KFC645, KFN5645, KFA-KFZ 384

Taxation: KF6768.W2

Horses

Legal aspects: KF390.5.H6, KFA-KFZ 84.5.H67

Sales contracts: KF915.Z93H6

Wild horses (Protection): KF5645.H65

Horseshoers: KFA-KFZ 282.H58

Horticulture: KFA-KFZ 250

Hosiery industry: KF1886.H6

Hospital auxiliaries: KFN5546.5.H6+

Hospital lawyers (Directories): KF195.H67

Hospital records: KF3827.R4, KFC619.5.R43, KFN5619.5.R43, KFA-KFZ 367.R4

Hospitality industry

Income tax: KF6495.H67, KFA-KFZ 477.5.H67

Hospitalization insurance: KF1185

Hospitals: KF3825+, KFC617+, KFN5617+, KFX2048.3, KFA-KFZ 361

Air Force: KF7438

Armed Forces: KF7298

Army: KF7338

Coast Guard: KF7478

INDEX

Hospitals
- Collective labor agreements: KF3409.H66, KFN5562.H6, KFA-KFZ 332.8.H6
- Labor hygiene and safety: KF3574.H66
- Management-labor relations: KF3452.H6
- Navy: KF7378
- Veterans: KF7739.M35, KF7745+, KF7749.M35
- Wages: KF3505.H58
- Hostels: KFA-KFZ 382
- Hotels: KFA-KFZ 282.H6
- Income tax: KF6495.H67, KFA-KFZ 477.5.H67
- Regulation: KF2042.H6, KFC446.H6, KFN5446.H6
- Wages: KF3505.H6

Hotels, restaurants, taverns, etc.
- Building laws: KFA-KFZ 459.H6
- Regulation: KFA-KFZ 282.H6

Hours of labor: KF3525+, KFC576, KFN5576
- Children: KF3551+
- Merchant mariners: KF1131
- Women: KF3555

House Administration, Committee on (United States House of Representatives): KF4997.H68

House of Representatives (U.S.): KF4990+
- Contested elections: KF4977.A2+
- Elections: KF4914

Household appliances
- Labeling: KF1620.A6

Household appliances industry: KFC412.H68

Household employees
- Social security: KF3664.H6

Housing: KF5721+, KFC820, KFN5820, KFX2081, KFA-KFZ 460+
- Air Force: KF7418
- Armed Forces: KF7278
- Army: KF7318
- Coast Guard: KF7458

Housing
- Discrimination: KF5740, KFA-KFZ 460.5.D5
- Finance: KF5735+, KFA-KFZ 460.5.F5
- Navy: KF7358
- Veterans: KF7739.H6, KF7749.H6

Housing authorities: KFA-KFZ 460.5.H68

Housing condominium: KF581, KFC144.5, KFN5142

Housing cooperatives: KF623, KFN5157

Housing courts: KF595

Housing finance: KF5735+

Housing lawyers (Directories): KF195.H68

Housing receiverships: KF5738

Human body
- Legal aspects: KF390.5.H85

Human cloning: KF3831

Human Relations Commission (Pennsylvania): KFP411.3

Human remains
- Indians: KF8210.A57

Human reproduction: KF3760+

Human reproductive technology: KF3830+
- Medical legislation: KFA-KFZ 367.H86

Human Resources, Committee on (United States Senate): KF4987.H86

Human smuggling: KF9449.5

Human trafficking: KF9449

Humans in medical experiments: KF3827.M38

Hunting and fishing rights
- Indians: KFA-KFZ 505.6.H85
- Real property: KF649

Husband abuse: KF9322

Husband and wife
- Confidential communications: KFC1041.5.H8
- Domestic relations: KF506+, KFN5120+, KFA-KFZ 96+

Hydroelectric power
- Public utilities: KF2133+

INDEX

Hygiene, School: KF3826.S3, KFC619.S3, KFN5619.S3, KFA-KFZ 363.S3

Hygiene, Veterinary: KF3835+, KFC623+, KFN5623+, KFA-KFZ 368+

I

Ice cream industry
- Labor law: KF3580.I3
- Regulation: KF1924.I3

Ice industry
- Wages: KF3505.I3

Idaho
- Laws: KFI1+

Identification: KFA-KFZ 414.5
- Aliens: KF4840
- Foreign agents: KF4854

Identification cards: KFA-KFZ 414.5

Identification, Means of
- Criminal law: KF9666.5, KFN6167, KFA-KFZ 580.5.M4

Identification of individuals: KF4791

Identification of persons (Evidence): KF8963

Illegal aliens
- Legal services to: KF337.5.I45
- Public welfare: KF3743

Illegal aliens, Children of
- Educational law: KF4217.I46

Illegitimate children: KF543, KFN5131, KFA-KFZ 104.4

Illicit liquor traffic: KF9456

Illicit political activities (Civil service): KF5344

Illinois
- Laws: KFI1201+

Immigrants
- Legal services to: KF337.5.I45
- Public welfare: KF3743

Immigrants, Children of
- Educational law: KF4217.I46

Immigrants, Legal handbooks for: KF390.I5A+

Immigration: KF4801+
- Trial practice: KF8925.E4

Immigration and naturalization lawyers
- Directories: KF195.I45

Immigration and Naturalization Service (U.S.): KF4821

Immigration inspection: KF3807

Immigration law
- Electronic data processing: KF242.I42+

Immunity of witnesses: KFA-KFZ 580.5.I4

Immunity, Parliamentary: KF4966

Immunization
- Public health laws: KF3808+, KFA-KFZ 357.9.I44

Impact fees (Local finance): KF6790.I55

Impeachment
- Cabinet officers: KF5090+
- Civil service: KFN5764
- Governors: KFC744, KFN5744, KFA-KFZ 426.4+
- Judges: KF8781+, KFC983+, KFN5983+, KFA-KFZ 525.5.I4
- Municipal officials: KF5325.I5
- President: KF5075+

Impeachment power and procedure: KF4958, KFA-KFZ 421.5.I46

Implied warranties: KF919.C6, KFA-KFZ 156.7.C6

Import trade: KF1993+, KFN5434+

Impossibility, Supervening: KF832

Imprisonment: KF9730+, KFC1180+, KFN6180+, KFA-KFZ 588+
- Juvenile criminal law: KF9825+, KFC1198.6+, KFN6198.6+, KFA-KFZ 598.6+

Imprisonment for debt: KF9039, KFN6071, KFA-KFZ 553.I6

Improvements (Real property): KF636

In forma pauperis: KF8995, KFC1051, KFN6051, KFA-KFZ 545

In-house training (Continuing legal education): KF276.5

In rem actions: KF560+

Incentive wages: KF3496

Income averaging: KF6396.5

INDEX

Income tax
- Federal: KF6351+
- Local: KF6782, KFA-KFZ 491.I5
- State: KF6752+, KFC870+, KFN5870+, KFA-KFZ 475+

Income tax deductions: KF6385+

Income tax exemptions: KF6329

Incompatibility of offices: KF4568, KFC686, KFN5686, KFA-KFZ 406

Incontestability clause (Life insurance): KF1178.I5

Incorporation: KF1420, KFC348, KFN5348, KFA-KFZ 213.5

Indemnity against liability: KF812.I5

Independent contractors: KF898+, KFC228+, KFN5228+, KFA-KFZ 155+
- Legal handbooks: KF390.I54
- Workers' compensation: KF3632.I53

Indeterminate sentence: KF9754, KFN6191, KFA-KFZ 593

Indexes
- Statutes: KF80, KFC40, KFN5040, KFA-KFZ 40

Indian Affairs, Committee on (United States Senate): KF4987.I45

Indian lands: KF5660+

Indian trust funds: KF8210.T6

Indiana
- Laws: KFI3001+

Indians: KF8201+, KFA-KFZ 505+
- California: KFC940
- Courts: KFA-KFZ 505.6.C57
- Education: KF8210.E3, KFA-KFZ 505.6.E3
- New York (State): KFN5940

Indictment: KF9640, KFC1158, KFN6158, KFA-KFZ 577

Indirect taxes: KF6598+

Individual and state: KFP411+

Individual retirement accounts (IRAs): KF3510+
- Income tax deductions: KF6395.R35

Individuals, Control of: KFN5698+

Industrial Accident Commission (California): KFC592.1

Industrial alcohol (Manufacture): KF1876.A5

Industrial banks: KF1039+

Industrial buildings
- Building laws: KF5702.I53

Industrial designers: KF2930.I54+

Industrial espionage: KF3197

Industrial hygiene and safety: KF3566+, KFC579+, KFN5579+, KFA-KFZ 335+

Industrial lawyers: KF299.I5

Industrial property
- Electronic data processing: KF242.I46+
- Income tax: KF6428.I5

Industrial research: KF4280.I53, KFA-KFZ 398.2.I53

Industry, Regulation of: KF1600+, KFC375+, KFN5375+, KFX2024+, KFA-KFZ 230+

Industry-wide liability: KF1300

Infant welfare: KF3728

Infanticide: KF9309

Infectious diseases: KF3800+, KFC613+, KFA-KFZ 357+

Inflammable materials: KF3955, KFC641.5.I6, KFA-KFZ 380.I6

Information
- Criminal procedure: KF9640, KFC1158, KFN6158, KFA-KFZ 577

Information centers (Legal profession): KFC74.5

Information retrieval
- Legal research: KF242.A+, KFA-KFZ 75.5

Informed consent
- Medical legislation: KF3827.I5, KFC619.5.I53, KFN5619.5.I53, KFA-KFZ 367.I5

Informers
- Criminal procedure: KF9665

Infringement, Copyright: KF3080

Infringement, Patent: KF3155+

Inheritance and succession: KF753+, KFC200+, KFN5200+, KFP142+, KFA-KFZ 142+
- Conflict of laws: KF418.S82
- Electronic data processing: KF242.I5+

INDEX

Inheritance taxes: KF6571+, KFC894+, KFN5894+, KFA-KFZ 482

Initiative

Legal research: KF241.E5

Initiative and referendum: KF4881, KFC708, KFA-KFZ 419

Injunctions: KF9014, KFC1062, KFN6062, KFA-KFZ 549

Inland marine insurance: KF1192

Inland navigation: KF2566+

Inland water carriers: KF2645+

Inland water transportation: KF2645+

Innkeeper and guest: KF951, KFN5241.I5

Insane persons

Capacity and disability: KF480+, KFC111.I5, KFN5111.I5, KFA-KFZ 91.I5

Criminal liability: KF9241+, KFC1116, KFN6116, KFA-KFZ 566.6

Medical care: KF3828, KFC620, KFN5620, KFA-KFZ 365

Insect exterminators: KFC446.I5, KFA-KFZ 282.I5

Insider trading in corporate securities: KF1073.I5

Inspection

Petroleum: KFA-KFZ 258.S7

Installment land contracts: KF675

Installment sale: KF1056, KFC267, KFN5267, KFA-KFZ 176.C6

Instructions to jury: KF9682+, KFC1047, KFC1171, KFN6047, KFN6171, KFA-KFZ 583

Insulating materials

Labeling: KF1620.I58

Insurance: KF1146+, KFN5290+, KFA-KFZ 185+

Accident: KF1187

Agricultural: KF1203+

Assessment: KF1169.A7

Atomic damage: KF1220.N8

Aviation: KF1194

Bank deposit: KF1023

Burglary: KF1200

Burial: KF1188

Business interruptions: KF1202.B8

Insurance

Business life: KF1180.B8

Casualty: KF1215+, KFC297+, KFN5297+, KFA-KFZ 191.A1+

Climate change: KF1202.C58

Contracts: KF1084.I5, KFC290+

Credit: KF1231

Crop: KF1204+

Deposit: KF1023

Earthquakes: KF1202.E2

Employers' liability: KFN5298.E5

Endowment: KF1180.E5

Farm mortgage: KF1701

Fire: KF1196, KFN5295.F5

Fraternal: KF1238, KFA-KFZ 193.F7

Guaranty: KF1231+, KFC300, KFN5300+

Hospitalization: KF1185

Inland marine: KF1192

Legal profession: KF320.I56, KFA-KFZ 77.5.I57

Legal research: KF241.I58

Liability: KF1215, KFC297, KFN5297, KFA-KFZ 191.A1

Machinery: KF1212.M2

Malpractice: KF1220.M2, KFC298.M3, KFA-KFZ 191.M2

Mortgage: KF5737

Mortgage guaranty: KF1232

Multiple-line underwriting: KF1170.5

Nuclear damage: KF1220.N8

Ocean marine: KF1135+

Personal: KF1171+, KFC292+, KFN5292+, KFA-KFZ 186+

Plate glass: KF1212.P5

Pollution: KF1220.P5

Products liability: KF1220.P6

Property: KF1190+, KFC295, KFN5295.A1+, KFA-KFZ 189.A+

Robbery: KF1200

Suretyship: KF1223+, KFC300, KFN5300+, KFA-KFZ 192.S8

Theft: KF1200

Tornado: KF1207

Tort liability: KF1301.5.I58

Transportation: KF1192

Trial practice: KF8925.I57

Insurance
- Uninsured motorist: KF1218.8, KFC298.A86, KFN5298.A86, KFA-KFZ 191.A43
- Unsatisfied judgment funds: KFN5298.A88, KFA-KFZ 191.A44
- Windstorms: KF1202.W5

Insurance agents: KF1167, KFC290, KFN5290, KFA-KFZ 185

Insurance brokers: KF1167, KFC290, KFN5290, KFA-KFZ 185

Insurance companies
- Advertising: KF1616.I5
- Business taxes: KF6763.4, KFN5885.I5
- Corporate reorganization: KF1546.I5
- Income tax: KF6495.I5, KFC879.I5, KFA-KFZ 477.5.I6
- Insolvency and bankruptcy: KF1535.I58
- Regulation: KF1167, KFC290, KFN5290, KFA-KFZ 185

Insurance, Compulsory
- Armed Forces service insurance
  - Merchant Marine: KF7488+
- Automobile drivers: KF2219, KFC475, KFA-KFZ 297.7
- Farm mortgages: KF1701
- Mortgages, Housing: KF5737

Insurance fraud: KF9368, KFA-KFZ 568.I57

Insurance law (Electronic data processing): KF242.I55+

Insurance lawyers (Directories): KF195.I5

Insurance policies (Taxation): KF6614.I5

Insurance trusts: KF736.L4

Intangible property (Personal property tax): KF6765.3+, KFN5890.A1+, KFA-KFZ 481.5.A1+

Integrated bar: KF330

Intellectual property: KF2971+, KFC550, KFN5550+, KFA-KFZ 330
- Indians: KF8210.I57

Intellectual property lawyers
- Directories: KF195.I52

Intelligence, Permanent Select Committee on (United States House of Representatives): KF4997.I46

Intelligence, Select Committee on (United States Senate): KF4987.I47

Interest
- Income tax: KF6417
  - Deductions: KF6392
- Loans: KF1036, KFC261, KFN5261, KFX2031.5, KFA-KFZ 170

Interference practice (Patent law): KF3124

Interference with business relationships: KFA-KFZ 197.T67

Interference with contractual relationships: KFA-KFZ 197.T67

Interior and Insular Affairs, Committee on (United States Senate): KF4987.I5

Interior decorators: KF2930.I58+, KFA-KFZ 329.I58+

Interior Department (U.S.): KF5501

Interlocking directorates: KF1657.I57

Internal Revenue Service (U.S.)
- Taxation: KF6301+

Internal security: KF4850+, KFC701+, KFN5701+, KFA-KFZ 415+

Internal Security, Committee on (United States House of Representatives): KF4997.I48

International and municipal law: KF4581

International business transactions,
- Taxation of: KF6419

International education (Higher education curricula): KF4245.5.I5

International lawyers (Directories): KF195.I54

International Relations, Committee on (United States House of Representatives): KF4997.I5

International trade: KF1975+

International trade lawyers (Directories): KF195.I54

Internet
- Advertising: KF1617.C65

Internet and privacy: KF1263.C65

INDEX

Internet sales
  Taxation: KF6768.E43
Internists: KF2910.I56+
Interpleader: KF8895
Interpreters for the deaf
  Regulation of profession: KFA-KFZ 329.I59+
Interracial marriage: KF517
Interrogatories: KF8900.A+
Intersex people
  Capacity and disability: KF478.5
Interstate agencies (New York metropolitan area): KFX2096+
Interstate Commerce Act: KF2161+, KF2246+, KF2271+
Interstate Commerce Commission (U.S.): KF2181
  Regulations
    Motor carriers: KF2246+
Interstate commerce, Taxation of: KF6738.I5
Interstate Compact to Conserve Oil and Gas: KF1852.A415
Interstate compacts: KF4618, KFA-KFZ 410.I6
  Petroleum: KF1852+, KFC406
Interstate cooperation: KFN5692
Interstate rendition: KF9635, KFC1157.7, KFA-KFZ 576.7
Intertemporal law: KF420
Intestate succession: KF771+, KFN5208, KFA-KFZ 146
Intoxication, Damage resulting from: KFA-KFZ 197.I5
Invalid marriages: KF518, KFC123, KFA-KFZ 95.5
Inventions: KF3131+
Inventions, Employees': KF3135+
Inventions, Government employees': KF3136
Inventions, Secret: KF3128
Investment advisors: KF1072
Investment banks: KF1006
Investment companies: KF1078+, KFC272+, KFN5273, KFA-KFZ 179.5.I5
  Income tax: KF6495.I55

Investment companies, Real estate: KF1079, KFC273
Investment companies, Small business: KF1080
Investment credit (Income tax): KF6389
Investment of public funds
  Federal: KF6239
  State: KF6742, KFC847, KFN5847, KFA-KFZ 467.5
Investment services: KFA-KFZ 167.S43
  Banking: KF1030.S43
Investment trusts: KF1078+, KFC272+
Investments: KF1066+, KFC270+, KFN5270+, KFA-KFZ 179+
Investments, Legal: KF1083
Iowa
  Laws: KFI4201+
IRAs: KF3510+
Irish American lawyers: KF299.I75
Iron and steel industry
  Collective bargaining: KF3409.S7
  Labor disputes: KF3450.I7+
  Price fixing: KF1629.S7
  Regulation: KF1890.S7
  Wages: KF3505.I6
Iron ore (Freight classification): KF2355.I7
Irrigation
  Agriculture: KF1686
  Land reclamation: KF5615+, KFC803+, KFA-KFZ 451+

J

JD/MBA professionals: KF299.J35
Jewelry industry: KF1893.J3
Jewish lawyers: KF299.J4
Jews: KF4869.J3
Job security: KF3471+
Joinder of claims: KF8893
Joinder of parties: KF8894
  Civil procedure: KFC1016.5, KFA-KFZ 536.6.J6
Joinder of remedies: KF8893
Joint adventures: KF1380.5
Joint income tax returns: KF6401

Joint tenancy (Land tenure): KF620, KFC157, KFA-KFZ 120

Joint tortfeasors: KF1312, KFC330, KFN5330, KFA-KFZ 199.J6

Joint undertakings: KF1380.5

Joint ventures: KF1380.5

Joint wills: KF760.J6

Journalists: KF2750

Judge Advocate General (U.S.)
- Air Force: KF7407
- Army: KF7307
- Navy: KF7347

Judge Advocate General's School (U.S. Army): KF7313.55.J8

Judge advocates: KF299.J8

Judges: KF8775+, KFC980+, KFN5980+, KFX2020.J8
- Education: KFA-KFZ 525.5.E3
- General: KFA-KFZ 525+
- Local courts (General): KF8786
- State courts: KF8785

Judgment
- Civil procedure: KF8990+, KFC1050+, KFN6050+, KFA-KFZ 544+
- Criminal procedure: KF9685, KFN6172, KFA-KFZ 583.2
- Juvenile criminal law: KF9820
- Probate law and practice: KF769.J83

Judgment, Confession of: KF8888

Judgment, Execution of: KF9025+, KFN6065+, KFA-KFZ 551

Judgments, Foreign: KF8729

Judicial assistance: KF8731, KFN5957
- Criminal procedure: KF9760

Judicial conference: KF8705+, KFC951, KFN5951

Judicial corruption: KF9419

Judicial councils: KF8705+, KFC951, KFN5951, KFA-KFZ 509

Judicial decree
- Land transfer: KF685.J8, KFA-KFZ 128.J8

Judicial education: KF276

Judicial error, Compensation for: KF9756

Judicial ethics: KF8779, KFN5984.5.D57, KFA-KFZ 525.5.D5

Judicial impact statements: KF8709

Judicial notice: KF8940.P7, KFC1032, KFN6032

Judicial officers: KF8770+, KFC979+, KFN5979+, KFA-KFZ 508.A19, KFA-KFZ 524.5+

Judicial power: KF5130, KFA-KFZ 428

Judicial process
- Land transfer: KF685.J8, KFA-KFZ 128.J8

Judicial review of legislative acts: KF4575, KFN5687, KFA-KFZ 407

Judicial sales
- Land transfer: KF685.J8, KFA-KFZ 128.J8

Judicial statistics: KF180+, KFN5070, KFA-KFZ 71+
- New York City: KFX2007+

Judiciary: KFA-KFZ 428

Judiciary, Committee on the (United States House of Representatives): KF4997.J8

Judiciary, Committee on the (United States Senate): KF4987.J8

Jukeboxes
- Copyright, Literary: KF3030.5
- Copyright, Musical: KF3045.5

Jurisdiction
- Conflict of laws: KF413.J87
- Constitutional law: KF4600+, KFC690+, KFN5690+, KFA-KFZ 409+
- Courts: KF8858, KFN5998, KFA-KFZ 532
- Indians: KF8210.J8
- Taxation: KF6736+, KFC910, KFN5910

Jurisdiction, Criminal: KF9230

Jurisdiction, State and federal
- Courts: KF8735

Jurisprudence and philosophy of law: KF379+

Juristic persons: KF1384+, KFC340+
- Criminal liability: KF9236.5

INDEX

Juristic persons
  Income tax: KF6455+, KFC875+, KFN5875+
Jurors, Women: KF8977
Jury and jurors
  Civil procedure: KF8971+, KFC1045+, KFN6045+, KFA-KFZ 542+
  Criminal procedure: KF9680, KFN6170, KFA-KFZ 581
Jury trial of rights: KF8975
Justice courts: KFC975
Justice Department (U.S.): KF5106+
Justices of the peace: KF8800, KFC985.J8, KFN5975, KFP520+, KFA-KFZ 520+
Justification
  Criminal law: KF9245.8+, KFA-KFZ 566.68+
Juvenile courts: KF9786+, KFC1196, KFN6196, KFA-KFZ 596
  Data processing: KF242.J85+
Juvenile crime
  Statistics: KF184, KFX2007.35, KFA-KFZ 71.55
Juvenile criminal law: KF9771+, KFC1195+, KFN6195+, KFA-KFZ 595+
Juvenile criminal procedure: KF9771+, KFC1195+, KFN6195+, KFA-KFZ 595+
Juvenile detention homes: KF9825, KFC1198.6, KFN6198.6, KFA-KFZ 598.6
Juvenile lawyers (Directories): KF195.J8
Juvenile status offenders: KF9802, KFN6197.5, KFA-KFZ 597.5
Juveniles (Legal services to): KF337.5.J88

K

Kansas
  Laws: KFK1+
Kentucky
  Laws: KFK1201+

Kentucky and Virginia resolutions, 1798: KF4621
Kidnapping: KF9332
Kindergartens: KF4197, KFC663
Knitwear industry: KF1886.K5
Knives
  Public safety: KF3942.K56

L

Labeling: KF1619+
  Cotton fabrics: KF1620.T33
  Drugs: KF3885
  Hazardous substances: KF3945+
  Narcotics: KF3885
  Pharmaceutical products: KF3885
  Poisons: KF3958+
  Toxic substances: KF3958+
Labels
  Copyright: KF3072
Labor
  Civil rights: KF4754
Labor and Public Welfare, Committee on (United States Senate): KF4987.L3
Labor boycotts: KF3430+, KFN5566
Labor conditions: KF3455, KFN5570
Labor Department (U.S.): KF3325+
Labor discipline: KF3540+
Labor disputes: KF3415+, KFC564+, KFN5564+, KFA-KFZ 333+
  Arbitration: KF3416+, KFC565, KFN5565
  Conciliation: KF3416+, KFC565, KFN5565
  Maritime law: KF1130
  Merchant mariners: KF1130
  Wartime disputes: KF3444+
Labor hygiene and safety: KF3566+, KFC579+, KFN5579+, KFA-KFZ 335+
Labor injunctions: KF3435, KFN5567, KFA-KFZ 333+
  By industry: KF3448+
  Yearbooks: KFX2007.5.L33
Labor law: KF3301+, KFC556+, KFN5556+, KFP331+, KFX2096.6, KFA-KFZ 331+

INDEX

Labor law
- Legal profession: KF299.L3
- Legal research: KF241.L33
- Study and teaching: KF277.L33

Labor law cases (Trial practice): KF8925.L33, KFC1028.L33, KFA-KFZ 539.L32

Labor law, Maritime: KF1121+

Labor lawyers
- Directories: KF195.L3

Labor-management relations: KF3351+, KFC557+, KFN5557+, KFP332+, KFX2045.A2+, KFA-KFZ 332+

Labor-Management Reporting and Disclosures Act: KF3400

Labor, Prison: KF9733

Labor relations: KFX2045.A2+

Labor safety and hygiene: KF3566+, KFC579+, KFN5579+, KFA-KFZ 335+

Labor standards: KF3455+, KFC570+, KFN5570+, KFA-KFZ 334+

Labor supply: KF3546

Labor unions: KFC560+, KFN5560+, KFP332+, KFA-KFZ 332+
- Civil service
  - Federal: KF5365
  - Municipal: KF5394
- Legal profession: KF317
- Management-labor relations: KF3381+

Laboratories
- Labor hygiene and safety: KF3574.L32

Laboratories, Medical: KF3826.L3, KFA-KFZ 363.L3

Laborers, Seasonal
- Immigration: KF4824.A+

Lacquer
- Labeling: KF1620.P2

Ladders
- Products liability: KF1297.L33

Lakes: KF5551+, KFC790+, KFN5790+, KFA-KFZ 446+

Land
- Government property: KF5760+, KFC825+, KFN5828+, KFA-KFZ 462.5.L34
- Public lands: KF5601+, KFC802+, KFN5802+
- Real property (Private law): KF566+, KFC140+, KFN5140+, KFA-KFZ 112+

Land, Carriage by: KF1092

Land grant colleges: KF4230

Land grants: KF5675+, KFC808+, KFA-KFZ 455

Land reclamation: KF5615+, KFC803+, KFA-KFZ 451+

Land subdivision: KF5697+, KFC811+, KFN5811, KFA-KFZ 458+

Land surveying: KF683, KFA-KFZ 127.5

Land taxation
- Federal taxes: KF6535+

Land tenure: KF574+, KFC141+, KFN5141+, KFA-KFZ 114+
- Indian tribal law: KF8224.L2

Land transfer: KF665+, KFC166+, KFN5166+, KFA-KFZ 126+

Land trusts: KF736.L3, KFC194.L35, KFA-KFZ 139.L3

Land use: KF5697+, KFC811+, KFN5811, KFX2096+, KFA-KFZ 458+
- Government liability: KF1325.L36

Land valuation
- Real property taxes: KF6760.5, KFC881.5, KFN5881.5

Landlord and tenant: KF586+, KFC145+, KFN5145, KFX2022, KFA-KFZ 117

Landowners, Adjoining: KFN5161+

Lands
- Public lands: KFA-KFZ 451+

Landscape architects: KFA-KFZ 329.L35+

Landslide prevention
- Zoning: KF5700.5.L36

Landslides (Negligence): KFC320.L3

Language and languages: KF4280.L35

Language instruction: KF4204, KFC664.5.L34, KFA-KFZ 395.3

Larceny: KF9352, KFC1131, KFN6131, KFA-KFZ 568.T45

INDEX

Last clear chance: KF1286, KFC316, KFN5316, KFA-KFZ 196

Latin Americans
- Civil rights: KF4757.5.L38

Laundry and cleaning industry
- Regulation: KF2042.L3, KFC446.L2, KFA-KFZ 282.L38
- Wages: KF3505.L2

Law
- Higher education curricula: KF4245.5.L3

Law and literature
- Study and teaching: KF277.L38

Law as a career: KF297

Law as a course in elementary and secondary education: KF4208.5.L3, KFN5664.5.L37, KFA-KFZ 395.7.L38

Law clerks
- Court employees: KF8806.5

Law dictionaries: KF156, KFC66, KFA-KFZ 66

Law enforcement
- Military law: KF7595

Law library catalogs: KF4

Law office management: KF318+, KFC77, KFN5077, KFA-KFZ 77

Law reform: KF384, KFC79, KFN5078.5, KFA-KFZ 79
- Criminal law and procedure: KF9223, KFC1102+, KFN6102+, KFA-KFZ 562+

Law reporting: KF255, KFN5075.5

Law reports
- Checklists: KF3
- Citators: KF150, KFN5059, KFA-KFZ 59
- Collections: KF101+, KF8830, KFC45+, KFN5045+, KFP45+, KFA-KFZ 45+
- Conversion tables: KF152
- Digests: KF127, KF148.A+, KFC57
- Popular names of cases: KF152

Law school, Admission to: KF285.A1+

Law societies: KF294.A+

Law student ethics: KF287.5

Law students: KF287+

Law teachers
- Directories: KF266

Lawyer and society: KF298

Lawyer referral services: KF338.A+

Lay judges: KF8788

Layout and design
- Law office management: KF320.L39

Lead
- Product safety: KFA-KFZ 380.L32
- Safety: KFN5641.5.L42

Learners (Labor hygiene and safety): KFA-KFZ 335.7

Lease and rental services
- Wages: KF3505.L28

Lease purchase: KF1056, KFC267, KFN5267

Leaseholds: KF586+, KFC145+, KFN5145, KFA-KFZ 117

Leases
- Contracts: KF586+, KFC145+, KFN5145, KFA-KFZ 117
- Income tax: KF6428.L3
- Petroleum: KFA-KFZ 258.L4

Leases, Commercial: KF593.C6

Leather industry
- Collective labor agreements: KF3409.L3
- Wages: KF3505.L3

Leave regulations
- Civil service: KF5384
- Postal service: KF2670.56

Leaves of absence
- Labor law: KF3531, KFC577, KFN5577, KFA-KFZ 334.5.V32
- Teachers: KF4188

Legal abbreviations: KF246

Legal advertising: KF450.N6, KFN5100.N6

Legal advisors, Police: KF5399.5.L4

Legal aid: KF336+

Legal aid societies: KF336.A33+

Legal assistants: KF320.L4
- Directories: KF195.L43

Legal bibliography: KF240+, KFC74, KFN5074+, KFA-KFZ 75

Legal composition: KF250+, KFC75, KFN5075, KFA-KFZ 75

INDEX

Legal custody, Escape from: KF9422
Legal departments, Corporate: KF1425
Legal document preparation: KF250+
Legal draftsmanship: KF250+, KFC75, KFN5075, KFA-KFZ 75
Legal education: KF261+
Legal ethics: KF305+, KFC76.5.A2+, KFN5076.5.A2+, KFA-KFZ 76.5.A2+
Study and teaching: KF277.L4
Legal etiquette: KF305+
Legal fees: KFA-KFZ 77.5.F4
Attorneys' fees: KF316
Court costs: KF8995, KFC1051, KFN6051, KFA-KFZ 545
Patent fees: KF3125.F3
Legal fraternities: KF289
Legal investments: KF1083, KFA-KFZ 179.5.L4
Legal maxims: KF159
Legal profession: KF297+, KFN5075.52+, KFX2010, KFA-KFZ 76+
Legal quotations: KF159
Legal records (Law office management): KF320.R42
Legal reform: KF384
Criminal law: KF9223, KFC1102+, KFN6102+, KFA-KFZ 562+
Legal research: KF240+, KFC74, KFN5074+, KFA-KFZ 75
Legal secretaries' handbooks, manuals, etc.: KF319, KFN5077, KFA-KFZ 77
Legal service corporations: KF6495.L4
Legal Services Corporation: KF336.A2+
Legal services to Armed Forces personnel: KF337.5.A7
Legal services to the poor: KF336+
Legislative bodies: KF4933
City councils: KF5317, KFA-KFZ 431.6
State legislatures: KF4933, KFC721+, KFN5721+, KFA-KFZ 421+
U.S. Congress: KF4935+
Legislative branch employees: KF4934, KFA-KFZ 421.5.L33
Legislative calendars: KF20.8+, KFC8, KFN5008.A+, KFA-KFZ 8.A+

Legislative committees: KFA-KFZ 421.5.C6
Legislative Counsel Bureau (California): KFC724.5
Legislative documents: KF11+, KFC5+, KFN5005+, KFA-KFZ 6+
Legislative draftsmanship: KF4950, KFN5724, KFA-KFZ 421.5.B5
Legislative hearings
Congress (U.S.)
House: KF27
Joint: KF25
Senate: KF26
State legislatures: KFC10+, KFA-KFZ 10.8+
Legislative process: KF4945+, KFA-KFZ 421
Legislative reference checklist: KF49.L43
Legislative reference services: KF4952
Legislative reports
Congress (U.S.)
House: KF32
Joint: KF30
Senate: KF31
State legislatures: KFC10.6+, KFN5010.6+, KFA-KFZ 11.58+
Legislative service agencies: KFA-KFZ 421.5.L4
Legislative veto: KF4944, KFA-KFZ 421.5.V46
Legislators: KF4966+, KFC726+, KFN5726+, KFA-KFZ 421.5.L35
Legislators as lawyers: KF299.L4
Legitimacy of children: KF542, KFN5131
Legitimation of children: KF542, KFN5131
Legitime: KF760.F2, KFL148.L4
Lender liability (Tort liability): KF1301.5.B36, KFA-KFZ 199.L44
Leprosy: KF3803.L3
Lesbians
Civil and political rights: KF4754.5
Discrimination against
Labor law: KF3467.5

INDEX

Letter writing
Law office management: KF320.L48
Letters of credit: KF1028, KFN5256.L3, KFA-KFZ 167.L47
Levee taxes: KFA-KFZ 491.L4
Levees: KF5588+, KFC795+, KFA-KFZ 447.8
Liability: KF450.L5, KFC310, KFN5310
Attorney and client: KF313
Commercial aviation: KF2454+
Health facilities and hospitals: KF3825.3, KFC617.3
Legal research: KF241.T67
Products liability: KF1296+
Railroads: KF2371+, KFA-KFZ 301.7
Strict liability: KF1292+
Telecommunication: KF2765.65
Telegraph: KF2775.65
Telephone: KF2780.65
Liability, Criminal: KF9235+, KFC1110+, KFN6110+, KFA-KFZ 566.5+
Liability for aviation accidents: KF1290.A9
Liability for condition and use of land: KF1287+, KFC320.L52, KFN5320.L5, KFA-KFZ 196.3.L3
Liability for credit information: KF1266.5.C7
Liability for debts of deceased: KF779.L5
Liability for marine accidents: KF1107
Government liability: KF1325.M2
Liability for nuclear damage: KF1220.N8
Liability for playground accidents: KF1290.P5
School districts: KF1309
Teachers: KF1310
Liability for school accidents: KF1309, KF1310
Liability for sidewalk accidents: KFN5320.S5
Liability for streetcar accidents: KFA-KFZ 196.3.S7
Liability for torts of others: KF1314+, KFC331+, KFN5332+

Liability for traffic accidents: KF1306.T7
Liability insurance: KF1215, KFC297, KFN5297, KFA-KFZ 191.A1
Liability insurance, Compulsory
Automobile drivers: KF2219
Liability, Professional: KF1289
Liability without fault: KF1292+, KFC321+, KFN5321+, KFA-KFZ 197.5
Libel and slander
Criminal law: KF9345, KFN6126, KFA-KFZ 567.5
Criminal trials: KF221.L5
Torts: KF1266, KFC313, KFN5313, KFA-KFZ 197.D3
Trial practice: KF8925.L5
Liberty of speech: KF4772
Librarians: KF4316
Libraries: KF4315+, KFC675+, KFN5675, KFX2067, KFA-KFZ 399+
Labor law: KF3580.L52
Libraries, Depository: KF5003
Library catalogs
United States: KF4
Library information networks: KF4319.I5
Library, Joint Committee on the (U.S. Congress): KF4939.5.L5
Library networks: KF4319.I5
Library of Congress (U.S.): KF4317
Library surveillance: KF4858.L5
Licenses
Local revenue: KFA-KFZ 491.B8
State revenue: KF6763+, KFC912.B8, KFN5884+, KFA-KFZ 480+, KFA-KFZ 487.L5
Licensing
Business corporations: KF1418, KFN5346
Health facilities and hospitals: KF3825.1
Professions: KFN5545+, KFA-KFZ 325
Retail trade: KFN5438
Service trades: KFN5445
Services and trades: KFA-KFZ 282.A1+

Lie detectors
- Civil procedure: KF8962
- Criminal procedure: KF9666, KFA-KFZ 580.5.L5

Liens: KFN5268, KFA-KFZ 176.L5
Liens, Equitable: KF698
Liens, Maritime: KF1114.B6
Liens, Mechanics: KF899+
Liens, Railroad: KF2305
Liens, Tax: KF6316
Lieutenant governors: KFA-KFZ 426
Life care communities: KF2042.O43, KFC446.O43, KFA-KFZ 282.O4
Life insurance: KF1171+, KFC292, KFN5292, KFA-KFZ 186+
- Business life: KF1180.B8
- Civil service: KF5385
- Conflict of laws: KF418.L5
- Endowment: KF1180.E5

Life insurance companies: KF1176
Life insurance proceeds
- Exemption from execution: KF9029.L4
- Income tax: KF6428.L5

Life insurance trusts: KF736.L4, KFA-KFZ 139.L54
Lighthouse Service (U.S.): KF2588.5
Lighthouses: KF2588+
Limine, Motions in: KFA-KFZ 540.3
Limitation of actions: KF450.L55, KFA-KFZ 90.L5
- Civil procedure: KF8881, KFN5100.L5, KFA-KFZ 536.L5
- Conflict of laws: KF418.L55

Limited liability companies: KF1380, KFC339.5, KFN5339.5, KFA-KFZ 207.5
Limited partnership: KF1380, KFC339.5, KFN5339.5, KFA-KFZ 207.5
Limousines: KFA-KFZ 300.L56
Linen industry: KF1886.L4
Linen supply services: KF2042.L3, KFC446.L2, KFA-KFZ 282.L38
Linguistic minorities
- Employment: KF3466
- Suffrage: KF4896.L56

Linguistic rights: KF4767
Linguists
- Expert witnesses (Civil procedure): KF8968.54

Linseed oil
- Labeling: KF1620.P2

Liquefied petroleum gas
- Product safety: KFA-KFZ 380.L5

Liquidation
- Corporation law: KFA-KFZ 215.D55
- Taxation: KF6499.D5

Liquor: KF3901+, KFC635+, KFN5635+, KFX2051, KFA-KFZ 375+
- Criminal law: KF9456
- Taxation: KF6612+, KFC900.A5, KFN5900.A5, KFA-KFZ 485.A5

Liquor industry
- Labor law: KF3580.L5
- Liquor laws: KFA-KFZ 375+
- Products liability: KF1297.L5
- Regulation: KF3901+, KFC635+, KFN5635+, KFX2051, KFA-KFZ 375+
- Workers' compensation: KF3632.B6

Liquor laws: KF3901+, KFC635+, KFN5635+, KFX2051, KFA-KFZ 375+
Liquor taxes: KF6612+, KFC900.A5, KFN5900.A5
Liquor traffic, Illicit: KF9456
Lis pendens: KF8882, KFC1015, KFN6016
Literary copyright: KF3020+
Litigation
- Electronic data processing: KF242.P746+
- Intellectual property: KF2983

Litigation lawyers (Directories): KF195.L53
Livestock
- Standards and grading: KF1726.A1+

Livestock industry and trade: KF1730+, KFC393+, KFA-KFZ 246
Living trusts: KF734, KFC194.L58, KFA-KFZ 139.L57
Living wills: KF3827.E87, KFC619.5.R5, KFN5619.5.R54, KFA-KFZ 367.R53

INDEX

Load line: KF2556
Loan associations: KF1009, KFC254, KFA-KFZ 166.B8
Loan of money: KF1035+, KFC260+, KFN5260+, KFX2031.5, KFA-KFZ 170+
Loans, Personal: KF1039+, KFC260+, KFN5260+, KFA-KFZ 170+
Veterans: KF7739.F5, KF7749.F5
Lobbying: KF4948, KFC725, KFA-KFZ 421.5.L6
Lobbying expenses (Income tax): KF6395.L63
Lobbyists (Directories): KF195.L6
Lobster fishing: KF1773.S45
Local court judges: KF8786
Local elections: KF4916, KFA-KFZ 420.6
Local government: KF5300+, KFC750+, KFN5750+, KFA-KFZ 430+
Local government lawyers
Directories: KF195.L62
Local option
Liquor laws: KF3925.L6, KFN5638.L38, KFA-KFZ 376.L6
Local revenue: KF6780+, KFC910+, KFA-KFZ 490+
Local taxation: KF6780+, KFC910+, KFN5910+, KFX2090+, KFA-KFZ 490+
Local transit: KF2391+, KFC501, KFN5502+, KFX2034+, KFA-KFZ 303
Local transit lines (Tort liability): KF1290.S7
Logging (Labor hygiene and safety): KFA-KFZ 336.S38
Longshoremen
Labor hygiene and safety: KF3574.L6
Workers' compensation: KF3628
Los Siete de la Raza Trial, San Francisco, 1970: KF224.L64
Loss of citizenship: KF4715+
Losses (Income tax): KF6396
Lost articles: KF713.T7, KFN5182
Lost wills: KF769.L6

Lotteries
Criminal law: KF9440, KFN6146, KFA-KFZ 571.G2
Indians: KFA-KFZ 505.6.L67
Regulation: KF3992, KFC646, KFN5646, KFA-KFZ 385
Loudspeakers
Copyright: KF3030.5
Louisiana
Laws: KFL1+
Loyalty oaths
Lawyers: KF304
Teachers: KF4183
Loyalty-security groups
Armed Forces: KF7268.L6
Loyalty-security program
Civil service: KF5346, KFC763.5
Lumber
Freight classification: KF2355.L8
Lumber industry
Collective labor agreements: KFA-KFZ 332.8.L8
Legal handbooks: KF390.L8
Lumbering (Labor hygiene and safety): KFC586.L8
Lumbermen
Legal handbooks: KF390.L8
Lunacy proceedings: KFC1089, KFA-KFZ 560.L8
Lunch programs, School: KF4143
Luxury articles
Taxation: KF6614.L8, KFN5900.L8
Lynching: KF9312

M

Machine data storage and retrieval
Legal research: KF242.A+
Machine-readable bibliographic data (Literary copyright): KF3024.M32
Machinery insurance: KF1212.M2
Machinery (Personal property tax): KF6765.8.M3
Magistrates' courts: KFN5975, KFP520+, KFX2018.7, KFA-KFZ 520+
Criminal procedure: KFA-KFZ 583.5
Mail fraud: KF9370

Mail-order business
- Taxation: KF6768.M25
- Trade regulation: KF2028

Maine
- Laws: KFM1+

Malicious mischief: KFN6134, KFA-KFZ 568.M2

Malicious prosecution: KF1270

Malpractice: KF1289, KFC317, KFN5317, KFA-KFZ 196.2
- Attorney and client: KF313
- Casualty insurance: KFC298.M3, KFN5298.M35
- Legal research: KF241.M34
- Trial practice: KF8925.M3, KFC1028.M34, KFN6028.M35, KFA-KFZ 539.M34

Malpractice insurance: KF1220.M2

Malt liquors (Alcoholic beverage laws): KF3924.B4, KFA-KFZ 375.5.B44

Management
- Business corporations: KFA-KFZ 213.6+

Management-labor relations: KF3351+, KFC557+, KFN5557+, KFA-KFZ 332+

Mandamus: KF9037, KFA-KFZ 553.M2

Mandatory retirement: KF3478

Manpower controls: KF3546

Manual training
- Educational law: KF4208

Manufacturing clause (Copyright): KF3015

Manufacturing industries: KF1874+, KFC412.A2+, KFN5412.A2+, KFA-KFZ 265+

Maple products
- Food processing
  - Regulation: KFA-KFZ 272.M35

Maps
- Copyright: KF3074

Margarine
- Taxation: KF6628.O5

Margins (Security training): KF1073.M3

Marijuana: KF3891.M2, KFA-KFZ 374.5.M3

Marinas: KFA-KFZ 282.M37

Marine accidents: KF1107

Marine accidents
- Government liability: KF1325.M2

Marine Corps (U.S.): KF7385+

Marine insurance: KF1135+

Marine radio: KF2826

Marital property: KF524+, KFC124, KFN5124, KFA-KFZ 97
- Conflict of laws: KF418.M2
- Taxation
  - Estate tax: KF6590
  - Income tax: KF6400

Maritime carriers: KF1096+, KFN5279+, KFP184.5

Maritime Commission (U.S.): KF2609

Maritime contracts: KF1096+

Maritime Labor Board (U.S.): KF1130.5

Maritime labor law: KF1121+, KFN5284+

Maritime law: KF299.M37, KF1096+

Maritime lawyers (Directories): KF195.M37

Maritime liens: KF1114.B6

Maritime torts: KF1107
- Government liability: KF1325.M2

Maritime unions: KF1127

Market forecasts: KFC391+

Marketing
- Regulation: KF1348.A38

Marketing agreements, Agricultural: KF1696+

Marketing, Agricultural: KF1718+, KFC391+, KFA-KFZ 244.A1+
- By product
  - Apples: KF1719.A6
  - Peaches: KFC391.5.P3
  - Perishable products: KF1719.P3

Marketing forecasts: KF1718+

Marketing of legal services: KF316.5, KFA-KFZ 77.5.M37

Marketing of securities: KF1065.2+, KFC270+, KFN5270+, KFX2031.8, KFA-KFZ 179+

Marketing orders, Agricultural: KF1696+

Marketing quotas, Agricultural: KF1705+
- By commodity
  - Corn: KF1706.G73

Marketing quotas, Agricultural
By commodity
Cotton: KF1706.C6
Field crops: KF1706.A+
Grain: KF1706.G7+
Potatoes: KF1706.P6
Wheat: KF1706.G78
Markets: KF2026
Marking devices (Manufacturing industry): KF1893.M2
Marriage
Conflict of laws: KF418.M2
Domestic relations: KF506+, KFC120+, KFN5120+, KFA-KFZ 95+
Marriage, Common-law: KF516
Marriage, Invalid and voidable: KF518, KFA-KFZ 95.5
Marriage registers: KF485, KFC113, KFA-KFZ 93
Marriage settlements: KF529
Married women: KF521+, KFA-KFZ 96+
Marshals: KFX2020.M37
Marshals, United States: KF8794
Marshes: KF5624, KFA-KFZ 451.7
Martial arts (Legal aspects): KF390.5.M37
Martial law: KF5063
Maryland
Laws: KFM1201+
Mass media: KF2750
Mass media and privacy: KF1263.M43
Mass stipends: KF760.M2
Massachusetts
Laws: KFM2401+
Massachusetts trusts: KF1381, KFA-KFZ 207.7
Massage therapists: KFA-KFZ 326.5.M38+
Master and servant
Contract of service: KF894+
Tort liability: KF1315
Maternal and infant welfare: KF3728, KFA-KFZ 349.8
Maternal health services: KF3826.M38
Maxims: KF159
Mayors: KF5319, KFA-KFZ 431.7
Mayors of boroughs: KFP436.8.B8

Meals on wheels program (Public welfare): KF3745.M42
Measures and weights: KF1665+, KFC382+, KFN5382, KFA-KFZ 235.A1+
Meat
Inspection: KF1911
Price supports: KF1911
Standards and grading: KF1726.A1+
Surpluses: KF1911
Meat industry
Collective labor agreements: KF3409.M3
Regulation: KF1911+, KFC418+, KFN5418, KFA-KFZ 272.M42
Mechanical reproduction
Copyright
Art and photography: KF3060.1
Literary copyright: KF3030.1
Music: KF3045.1
Mechanics' liens: KF899+, KFC229, KFN5229, KFX2031.6.M4, KFA-KFZ 155.5
Mechanized information retrieval storage and retrieval systems
Legal research: KF242.A+
Medals, Commemorative: KF5155+
Medi-Cal: KFC591.5.P65
Medicaid: KF3608.P66, KFC591.5.P65, KFA-KFZ 341.5.P65
Medical and health care industry
Insolvency and bankruptcy: KF1535.M44
Medical care
Air Force: KF7419
Armed Forces: KF7279
Army: KF7319
Coast Guard: KF7459
Indians: KF8210.M43
Mentally ill: KF3828
Navy: KF7359
Older people: KF3608.A4
Study and teaching: KF277.P82
Veterans: KF7739.M3, KF7749.M3+
Medical economics: KF2907.F3
Medical education: KF2907.E3

INDEX

Medical emergency assistance: KF2905
Medical evidence: KF8964
Medical examiners: KF8802, KFN5985.C66, KFX2020.C58, KFA-KFZ 526.C65
Medical expenses (Income tax): KF6395.M3
Medical experiments with humans: KF3827.M38
Medical fees: KF2907.F3
Medical genetics: KF3827.G4
Medical legislation: KFN5619.5.G45
Medical instruments and apparatus: KF3827.M4
Products liability: KF1297.M4
Medical instruments and apparatus industry: KF3574.M43
Medical law
Legal research: KF241.M45
Medical lawyers
Directories: KF195.M43
Legal profession: KF299.M43
Medical legislation: KF3821+, KFC615+, KFN5615+, KFA-KFZ 360+
Legal research: KF241.M45
Medical personnel
Immigration: KF4825.M43
Legal handbooks: KF390.P45
Wages: KF3505.H58
Medical records: KF3827.R4, KFC619.5.R43, KFN5619.5.R43, KFA-KFZ 367.R4
Medical statistics: KF3827.S73
Medical technologists: KFC546.5.M4+, KFA-KFZ 326.5.M43+
Medical witnesses: KF8964
Medicare: KF3608.A4, KFA-KFZ 341.5.A34
Medicinal spirits: KF3924.M3
Meetings, Stockholders': KF1450+, KFN5354+
Mens rea: KF9236, KFN6111
Mental disabilities, People with
Legal services to: KF337.5.M46
Mental disabilities, Students with: KF4215

Mental disabilities, Students with Colleges and universities: KF4244.M45
Mental health courts: KF3828.5
Mental health facilities: KF3828
Mentally ill
Criminal liability: KF9241+, KFC1116, KFN6116
Employment of: KF3469
Medical care: KF3828, KFC620, KFN5620, KFA-KFZ 365
Mercantile transactions: KF871+, KFC225, KFN5225
Merchant fleet: KF2635+
Merchant marine
Services during war: KF7485+
Shipping laws: KF2601+
Merchant Marine and Fisheries, Committee on (United States House of Representatives): KF4997.M4
Merchant mariners
Employers' liability: KF1317.M3
Labor law: KF1121+, KFN5284+
Social insurance: KF1132, KFN5285+
Unemployment insurance: KFN5286
Workers' compensation: KF1132
Mercury mining: KFC403.5.M3
Mergers
Antitrust law (General): KF1654+
Banks: KF1018
Corporate reorganization: KF1544+, KFN5368+, KFA-KFZ 225.A1+
Corporation law: KF1477, KFC359, KFN5359, KFA-KFZ 215.C65
Railroads: KF2293
Taxation: KF6499.M4
Telecommunication: KF2765.3
Telegraph: KF2775.3
Telephone: KF2780.3
Merit Systems Protection Board: KF5338
Metal ores (Taxation): KF6768.M3
Meteorology: KF5594, KFC799, KFA-KFZ 449.5
Methadone: KF3891.M3
Methane industry: KF1873.M48
Methodists: KF4869.M3

INDEX

Metropolitan area government
  By city
    New York: KFX2096+
Mexican Americans
  Civil rights: KF4757.5.M4
Michigan
  Laws: KFM4201+
Microsoft Word (Computer program)
  Law office management:
    KF322.5.M53
Midwives: KF2915.M5+, KFA-KFZ
  326.5.M53+
Migrant agricultural labor: KF3580.A4
Migrant laborers' children (Education):
  KF4217.M5
Migratory birds: KF5640
Military assistance: KF4670.M54
Military awards: KF5154
Military commissions: KF7661
Military contracts: KF851+
Military criminal law: KF7601+,
  KFC930+, KFN5930+, KFA-KFZ 499
Military discipline: KF7590
Military education and training: KF7273
Military government: KF5063
Military installations: KF5800
Military justice: KF7620+, KFC931+,
  KFN5931+
Military justice lawyers
  Directories: KF195.M54
Military law: KF7201+, KFC920+,
  KFN5920+, KFA-KFZ 495+
Military lawyers: KF299.J8
Military offenses: KF7618.A+
Military pay: KF7274+
  Income tax: KF6411.M5
  Merchant Marine: KF7488.5+
Military pensions: KF7275
  Veterans: KF7701+
Military prisons: KF7675
Military procurement: KF851+
Military property: KF5845+
Military service claims: KF7711
Military service disqualifications:
  KF7265+
Military service exemptions: KF7265+
Military surplus: KF5845+

Milk
  Import trade: KF1996.M5
Milk production and distribution:
  KFC421, KFN5421
  Regulation: KFA-KFZ 272.D2
Milk products
  Inspection: KF1921
Mine safety: KF3574.M5, KFC586.M5
Mineral resources, Conservation:
  KF5508
Mineral water industry: KF1940.M5
Mines and mineral resources: KF5508
  Taxation: KF6614.M55
Minimum wage: KF3481+, KFC575+,
  KFN5575
  By industry: KF3505.A+
  Labor law: KFA-KFZ 334.5.M55
Mining
  Income tax: KF6495.M5
Mining industry: KF1801+, KFC400+,
  KFN5400+
  Business taxes: KF6763.9.M54, KFA-
    KFZ 480.5.M5
  By industry
    Aluminum: KF1836.A5
    Coal: KF1826+
      Hygiene: KF3574.M53
      Workers' compensation:
        KF3632.C6
    Copper: KF1836.C6
    Mercury: KFC403.5.M3
    Natural gas: KF1870
    Nonferrous metals: KF1835+,
      KFC403+
    Oil: KF1841+, KFC405+, KFN5404+
    Petroleum: KF1841+, KFC405+
    Platinum: KF1836.P5
    Uranium: KF1836.U6
  Employers' liability: KF1317.M5
  General: KFA-KFZ 255+
  Hygiene: KF3574.M5, KFC586.M5,
    KFA-KFZ 336.M5
  Income tax: KF6495.M5, KFA-KFZ
    477.5.M54
  Safety regulations: KF3574.M5,
    KFC586.M5, KFA-KFZ 336.M5
  State taxation: KF6738.M56

Mining industry
Workers' compensation: KFC594.M5
Minnesota
Laws: KFM5401+
Minor communities: KFN5758.5, KFA-KFZ 432.5
Minority lawyers: KF299.M56
Minority shareholders: KFA-KFZ 215.M5
Minority stockholders: KF1448.5, KFA-KFZ 215.M5
Minors
Capacity and disability: KF479, KFC111.M5, KFN5111.M5, KFA-KFZ 91.M5
Property of minors: KF547+, KFA-KFZ 104.6+
Mint regulations: KF6215
Mirror industry: KF1893.M4
Misbranding: KF1619+
Miscarriage, Induced: KF9315, KFC1121, KFN6121, KFA-KFZ 567.A2
Miscegenation: KF517
Mischief, Malicious: KFA-KFZ 568.M2
Misrepresentation
Contracts: KF821
Missing persons: KF471
Mississippi
Laws: KFM6601+
Missouri
Laws: KFM7801+
Mistake
Void and voidable contracts: KF819, KFN5222
Mobile home taxes: KFA-KFZ 491.A8
Mobile homes
Building laws: KF5702.M63, KFC814.M6, KFA-KFZ 459.M6
Retail trade: KF2036.M63, KFC444.M63, KFA-KFZ 281.5.M63
Models
Copyright: KF3065
Patent law: KF3142
Modification
Mortgages: KF697.M63
Molds: KF3964.M64

Molds
Public health hazards: KFA-KFZ 359.M65
Money: KF6201+, KFC841, KFN5841, KFA-KFZ 466
Money laundering
Banking: KF1030.R3
Money, Loan of: KF1035+, KFC260+, KFN5260+, KFX2031.5, KFA-KFZ 170+
Money orders: KFA-KFZ 161.5.M67
Monopolies: KF1631+, KFC377, KFN5377, KFA-KFZ 231
Montana
Laws: KFM9001+
Monuments, National
Public land law: KF5635+
Moot court cases
Civil procedure: KF8918
Criminal procedure: KF9657
Moot courts: KF281.A2+
Mopeds (Motor vehicle laws): KF2220.M58
Mormons: KF4869.M6
Morris plan: KF1039+, KFN5262
Mortgage banks: KF1002, KFC253, KFA-KFZ 166.M67
Mortgage foreclosure: KF697.F6
Mortgage guaranty insurance: KF1232, KFN5302
Mortgage insurance: KF5737
Mortgages
Excise tax: KFC900.M6
Modification: KF697.M63
Personal property tax: KF6765.4, KFN5890.M6, KFA-KFZ 481.5.M6
Real property: KF691+, KFC175+, KFN5175+, KFA-KFZ 130+
Restructuring: KF697.M63
Mortgages as investments: KF696
Mortgages, Chattel: KF1053+, KFA-KFZ 176.C4
Mortgages, Ship: KF1114.B6
Mosquito abatement: KF3811, KFC613.9.M67
Motels: KF2042.M6
Mothers' pensions: KF3658.M6

Motion picture industry
Collective labor agreements: KF3409.M66
Income tax: KF6495.M6, KFN5879.M6
International trade: KF1984.M6
Regulation: KF4302
Motion picture theaters: KFA-KFZ 282.M66
Motion pictures
Censorship: KF4300, KFN5672.5
Copyright: KF3070
Regulation: KF4298+, KF4302, KFN5672+, KFA-KFZ 398.7
Motions in limine: KFA-KFZ 540.3
Motions (Pleading): KF8866+, KFC1012, KFN6012, KFP535.8, KFA-KFZ 535+
Motor boats: KFA-KFZ 308.5.M67
Safety regulations: KF2558.M6, KFN5524.M6
Motor carriers: KF2246+, KFA-KFZ 299+
Motor fuels
Taxation
Federal: KF6615+
State finance: KF6768.M57, KFC900.M67, KFN5900.M6, KFA-KFZ 485.M6
Motor vehicles
Excise and sales taxes
Federal: KF6619+
Local: KF6789.M6
State: KF6768.M6, KFC900.M68, KFA-KFZ 485.M62
Government property: KFA-KFZ 462.5.A97
Indians: KFA-KFZ 505.6.M66
Insurance
Casualty: KF1218, KFC298.A8+, KFN5298.A8+, KFA-KFZ 191.A4
Property: KF1210
International trade: KF1984.A9
Product safety: KF3965.A87
Products liability: KF1297.A8

Motor vehicles
Retail trade: KF2036.A8, KFC444.A88, KFN5444.A95, KFA-KFZ 281.5.A8
Road traffic: KF2201+, KFC470+, KFN5470+, KFX2035, KFA-KFZ 296+
Trade agreements: KF6669.M6
Motorcycles
Motor vehicle laws: KFA-KFZ 297.75.M67
Road traffic: KF2220.M6, KFC476.M68
Motorists' lawyers (Directories): KF195.A8
Moving expenses (Income tax): KF6395.M68
Multiple-line underwriting (Insurance): KF1170.5
Multiple sclerosis: KF3803.M84
Municipal bonds: KF6775, KFX2089.5, KFA-KFZ 489
Municipal charters: KF5313
Municipal civil service: KF5393+, KFC774, KFN5774+, KFP436+, KFA-KFZ 436+
Municipal corporations: KF5304+, KFC752, KFN5752, KFA-KFZ 431+
Corporate reorganization: KF1546.M8
Electronic data processing: KF242.M8+
Insolvency and bankruptcy: KF1535.M85
Tort liability: KF1302.A2+, KFC324, KFN5324, KFA-KFZ 198.M8
Municipal correctional institutions
New York City: KFX2094
Municipal Court of Philadelphia: KFP518.3
Municipal courts: KFC970+, KFN5970+, KFA-KFZ 518+
Municipal debts: KFX2089.5, KFA-KFZ 489
Municipal elections: KF4916
Municipal franchises: KF5315.M78, KFX2025+

INDEX

Municipal government
- City law
  - New York City: KFX2015+
  - Federal law: KF5304+
  - State law: KFC752+, KFN5752+, KFA-KFZ 431+

Municipal government lawyers
- Directories: KF195.L62

Municipal loans: KFA-KFZ 489

Municipal ownership (Municipal government): KF5315.M8

Municipal planning: KFN5810+

Municipal services
- City law
  - New York City: KFX2024+
  - Federal law: KF5304+
  - State law: KFC752+, KFN5752+

Munitions
- Public safety: KF3941+, KFC640.5, KFN5640.5
- Shipping: KF2560.E85

Munitions trade
- Export trade: KF1990.M8
- International trade: KF1984.M8

Murder: KF9306
- Criminal trials: KF221.M8

Museums: KFX2067

Museums and galleries: KF4305, KFN5674, KFA-KFZ 398.8

Music: KF4291+

Musical copyright: KF3035+

Muslims: KF4869.M86

Mutual funds: KF1078+, KFC272+, KFN5273, KFA-KFZ 179.5.I5

Mutual security program: KF4665

N

Narcotic addiction: KF3829.N2, KFA-KFZ 366.N35

Narcotics
- Drug laws: KF3890+, KFN5632, KFA-KFZ 374+
- Taxation: KF6623+

Narcotics Abuse and Control, Committee on (United States House of Representatives): KF4997.N37

Narcotics, Bureau of (U.S.): KF3890.1

Nasciturus: KF481

National Aeronautics and Space Administration: KF4280.S7
- Government contracts: KF869.5.N3

National anthem: KF5150

National Archives: KF5755

National Association of Attorneys General: KF294.N28

National banks: KF991+

National bar associations: KF325+

National cemeteries: KF5810

National Data Center (U.S.): KF485

National defense: KF7201+

National emblem: KF5150

National forests: KF5631+

National Guard: KF7330, KFC927, KFA-KFZ 497
- Air Force: KF7430
- Army: KF7330
- New York (State): KFN5927+

National Institute of Municipal Law Officers: KF294.N38

National Labor Relations Board: KF3372

National monuments
- Public land law: KF5635+

National parks
- Public land law: KF5635+

National preserves: KF5630+

National Reporter System: KF135+

National revenue: KF6251+

National territory: KF4635

National War Labor Board (U.S.): KF3444+

Nationality and citizenship: KF4700+

Natural death: KFC619.5.R5, KFN5619.5.R54, KFA-KFZ 367.R53

Natural gas industry: KF1870

Natural persons: KF466+, KFC108+, KFN5108+, KFA-KFZ 91+

Natural resources: KFC786
- Conservation: KF5505+
- Indians: KF8210.N37
- Judicial statistics: KF185.E58
- Minerals: KF5508

INDEX

Natural resources
- Minerals
  - Oil and gas: KF1852+, KFC406, KFN5404+
  - Petroleum: KF1852+, KFC406, KFN5404+
- Soil conservation: KFC386, KFA-KFZ 239
- Water: KF5551+, KFC790+, KFN5790+

Natural Resources, Committee on (United States House of Representatives): KF4997.N38

Naturalization: KF4706+

Naturopaths: KF2913.N38+, KFA-KFZ 326.5.N38+

Navigation
- Soil conservation: KF1686

Navigation and pilotage: KF2566+, KFC526, KFN5526+

Navigation, Bureau of (U.S.): KF2566.5

Navy Department (U.S.): KF7345+

Navy education and training: KF7353+

Navy hospitals: KF7378

Navy pay: KF7354+

Navy pensions: KF7355

Navy (U.S.): KF7345+

Nazi Saboteurs Trial, Washington, D.C., 1942: KF224.N28

Nebraska
- Laws: KFN1+

Negligence: KF1276+, KFC315+, KFN5315+
- Electronic data processing: KF242.N43+
- General: KFA-KFZ 196+

Negligence claims (Trial practice): KF8925.N4, KFA-KFZ 540.5.N4

Negligence, Contributory: KF1286, KFC316, KFN5316, KFA-KFZ 196

Negligence, Criminal: KF9236

Negligence lawyers (Directories): KF195.N4

Negotiable instrument cases
- Trial practice: KF8925.N45

Negotiable instruments: KF956+, KFC245+, KFN5245+, KFA-KFZ 160+

Negotiated settlement: KF9084, KFC1093, KFN6093, KFA-KFZ 560.3

Neighboring rights: KF3075+

Neurologists: KF2910.N45+

Neutrality laws: KF4675

Nevada
- Laws: KFN601+

New Deal legislation: KF6011+

New Hampshire
- Laws: KFN1201+

New Jersey
- Laws: KFN1801+

New Mexico
- Laws: KFN3601+

New trials
- Civil procedure: KF9002
- Criminal procedure: KF9688, KFA-KFZ 583.45

New York
- Laws: KFN5001+

New York State register: KFN5036

New York Stock Exchange: KF1074.N3

Newsletters (Law office management): KF320.N48

Newspapers
- Collective labor agreements: KF3409.N3
- Labor law: KF3580.N48

Newsprint
- Import trade: KF1996.P2

Night differentials: KF3503, KFC575.5

Night work: KF3525+, KFC576, KFN5576
- Children: KF3551+
- Merchant mariners: KF1131
- Women: KF3555

Nisi prius: KF8845

No-fault automobile insurance: KF1219.5, KFN5298.A84, KFA-KFZ 191.A46

Noise control: KF3813, KFC614.5.N64, KFN5614.5.N64, KFA-KFZ 359.N6

Nolo contendere: KF9654, KFC1161, KFA-KFZ 578.5

Nominations of judges: KFA-KFZ 525.5.N6

INDEX

Non-criminal child abuse (Trial practice): KF8925.C45
Non-forfeiture clause (Life insurance): KF1178.N6
Nondiscrimination clause (Defense contracts): KF3464+
Nonferrous metal industry
- Mining: KF1835+, KFC403+
- Price fixing: KF1629.N6
- Regulation: KFA-KFZ 257.A1+
Nonmailable merchandise: KF2695+
Nonprofit corporations: KF1388+, KFC342+, KFN5342+, KFA-KFZ 211
- Contributions
  - Income tax: KF6388
  - Income tax: KF6449, KFA-KFZ 475.7
  - Social security: KF3664.N6
  - Tort liability: KF1303+
Nonprofit organizations
- Corporation law: KF1388+, KFN5342+, KFA-KFZ 211
- Income tax: KF6449, KFA-KFZ 475.7
- Labor law: KF3580.N65
- Management-labor relations: KF3452.N65
- Social security: KF3664.N6
- Tort liability: KF1303+
Nonsupport (Domestic relations): KF549, KFA-KFZ 104.8
Nonteaching school personnel: KF4192+
Nonwage payments
- Civil service: KF5385
- Income tax: KFA-KFZ 475.5.N6
- Labor law: KF3509+, KFC575.6
- Merchant mariners: KF1131
North Carolina
- Laws: KFN7401+
North Dakota
- Laws: KFN8601+
Notaries: KF8797, KFC985.N6, KFN5985.N6, KFA-KFZ 526.N6
Notice: KF450.N6, KFC100.N6, KFN5100.N6, KFA-KFZ 90.T5
Notice, Judicial: KF8940.P7, KFC1032, KFN6032
NOW accounts (Banking): KF1023.5

Nuclear materials (Export trade): KF1990.N82
Nuisances: KF1273
- Abatement of: KFA-KFZ 378
Nullity of marriage: KF518, KFC123, KFA-KFZ 95.5
Nursery schools: KF2042.D3, KFN5446.D39, KFA-KFZ 282.D3
Nurses: KF2915.N8+, KFC546.5.N8+, KFN5546.5.N8+
- Collective labor agreements: KF3409.N8
- General: KFA-KFZ 326.5.N8+
- Legal handbooks: KF390.N8
Nursing home administrators: KF2915.N84+, KFA-KFZ 326.5.N85+
Nursing homes: KF3826.N8, KFC619.N8, KFN5619.N8, KFX2048.3, KFA-KFZ 363.N8
Nutrition and Human Needs, Select Committee on (United States Senate): KF4987.N8
Nutritionists: KF2915.D53+, KFA-KFZ 326.5.D53+

O

Oath (Witnesses): KF8954
Obesity: KF3803.O24
Obesity in children: KF3803.O24
Objections
- Civil procedure: KF8881+, KFN6015+, KFA-KFZ 535.8
Obligations
- Conflict of laws: KF418.C6
Obscenity: KF9444, KFN6147, KFA-KFZ 571.O2
Obstetricians: KF2910.G94+, KFA-KFZ 326.5.G94+
Occupational diseases
- Workers' compensation: KF3622, KFN5593, KFA-KFZ 342.5
Occupational law: KF1600+, KFC375+, KFN5375+, KFA-KFZ 230+
Occupational therapists: KF2915.T45+, KFC546.5.T54+, KFN5546.5.T5+
Occupations: KFA-KFZ 325+

INDEX

Ocean bills of lading: KF1109
Ocean freight forwarders: KF2654
Ocean marine insurance: KF1135+, KFN5287
Oceanography: KF4280.O3, KFA-KFZ 398.2.O25
"Of counsel" relationships
- Prepaid services: KF310.O34
Offenses against currency: KF9455+, KFA-KFZ 572.A+
Offenses against government and public order: KFC1137+, KFN6137+, KFA-KFZ 569
Offenses against personal liberty: KF9332+
Offenses against property: KF9350+, KFC1128+, KFN6131+, KFA-KFZ 568.A1+
Offenses against public convenience and morality: KFC1145.5, KFN6146+, KFA-KFZ 571.A1+
Offenses against public finance: KF9455+, KFA-KFZ 572.A+
Offenses against public property, public finance, and currency: KF9455+, KFA-KFZ 572.A+
Offenses against public safety: KF9425+, KFC1145+, KFN6144.5+, KFA-KFZ 570.5.A+
Offenses against the administration of justice: KF9415+, KFC1141+, KFN6141+, KFA-KFZ 570.A+
Offenses against the person: KF9304+, KFC1121+, KFN6121+, KFA-KFZ 567.A1+
Offenses against the public administration: KF9405+
Offenses committed through the mail: KF9460+
Offenses, Economic: KF9350+
Offenses, Military: KF7618.A+
Office equipment and supplies
- Court administration: KF8732.7
- Law office management: KF320.O35
Office of Education (U.S.): KF4121
Office of Independent Counsel. Special prosecutors: KF5107.5

Office of Personnel Management: KF5338
Officers
- Air Force: KF7425
- Armed Forces: KF7285
- Army: KF7325
- Business corporations: KFA-KFZ 213.7+
- Coast Guard: KF7465
- Marine Corps: KF7395
- Navy: KF7365
Ohio
- Laws: KFO1+
Oil
- Processing tax: KF6631.O4
Oil and gas leases: KF1865
Oil- and gas-producing properties (Taxation): KFC881.8.O34
Oil fields
- Pooling: KF1853
- Unit operation: KF1853
Oklahoma
- Laws: KFO1201+
Old age homes: KF2042.O43, KFC446.O43, KFA-KFZ 282.O4
Old age pensions: KFN5595+
Older Indians: KF8210.A53
Older people
- Abuse of: KFA-KFZ 567.A35
- Capacity and disability: KFC111.A34, KFN5111.A33, KFA-KFZ 91.A3
- Employment: KF3465, KFN5573.A4
- Health insurance: KF3608.A4, KFA-KFZ 341.5.A34
- Legal handbooks: KF390.A4
- Legal services to: KF337.5.A33
- Public welfare: KF3737+, KFC604, KFN5604, KFA-KFZ 350.A35
- Study and teaching: KF277.A35
Oleomargarine
- Taxation: KF6628.O5
Oleomargarine industry: KF1936.O5
Oligophrenia, Phenylketonuria: KF3803.P4
Olive processing industry: KF1909.O5
Olives (Marketing): KFC391.5.O44

INDEX

Ombudsman: KF5423, KFA-KFZ 441.O5

Onions
  Marketing regulations: KFA-KFZ 244.O54

Open and closed shop: KF3394+, KFC560.5, KFA-KFZ 332.5

Open-pit mining: KFA-KFZ 255.5

Opening statements: KF8923

Ophthalmologists: KF2910.O64+

Opium
  Drug laws: KF3891.O3
  Taxation: KF6624.O6

Optical fibers
  Patent law: KF3159.F52

Optical industry (Advertising): KF1616.O6

Option: KF811

Optometrists: KF2915.O6+, KFC546.5.O6+, KFA-KFZ 326.5.O6+

Oral historians (Legal handbooks): KF390.O7

Oregon
  Laws: KFO2401+

Organized crime: KF9375, KFC1133, KFN6133, KFA-KFZ 568.R3

Orphans' Courts (Pennsylvania): KFP144.1.A+

Orthopedists: KF2910.O78+, KFA-KFZ 326.5.O78+

Osteopaths: KFA-KFZ 326.5.O8+

Outdoor advertising
  Building laws: KF5710

Outdoor swimming facilities: KFA-KFZ 382

Overseas sales: KF934

Oversight, Legislative: KFA-KFZ 421.5.O85

Overtime
  Labor law: KFA-KFZ 334.5.O93

Overtime payments: KF3503, KFC575.5

Overweight persons
  Civil rights: KF4757.5.O94

Ownership
  Personal property: KF708+, KFN5181+, KFN5181+

Ownership
  Property (General): KF560+, KFN5138
  Real property: KF575+, KFC144+, KFN5141+, KFA-KFZ 114.A1+

Ownership, Concurrent: KF619+, KFC155+, KFN5155+, KFA-KFZ 120

Oyster fishing: KF1773.S49

P

Paint
  Labeling: KF1620.P2

Paper
  Import trade: KF1996.P2

Paper (Freight classification): KF2355.P2

Paper industry
  Collective labor agreements: KF3409.P2
  Income tax: KF6495.P2
  Labor hygiene and safety: KF3574.P2

Paralegal personnel: KF320.L4
  Directories: KF195.L43

Parcel post: KF2692

Pardon: KFA-KFZ 585
  Criminal procedure: KF9695, KFC1176

Parens patriae suits: KF1657.P3

Parent and child: KF540+, KFC130+, KFN5130+, KFA-KFZ 104+

Parental kidnapping: KF547+

Parking of vehicles: KFA-KFZ 159.5.P3

Parking rules
  Traffic regulations: KF2236

Parks
  New York City: KFX2076
  Tort liability: KFA-KFZ 198.P37

Parks, National
  Public land law: KF5635+

Parks, State: KFC805+, KFN5805+, KFA-KFZ 452+

Parkways: KF5530, KFC787.5, KFN5788

Parliamentary immunity: KF4966, KFN5726.5

Parol evidence: KF8948

Parole
- Criminal procedure: KF9750, KFC1190, KFN6190, KFX2094, KFA-KFZ 592
- Juvenile criminal procedure: KFC1198.8, KFA-KFZ 598.8
- Military law: KF7679

Parties
- Civil procedure: KF8890+, KFC1016+, KFN6019+, KFA-KFZ 536.5+

Parties, Political: KF4788

Partition
- Real property: KF626, KFC158, KFN5158, KFA-KFZ 123.P2

Partnership: KF1371+, KFC339+, KFN5339+, KFA-KFZ 207+
- Income tax: KF6452, KFC874.5

Partnership, Limited: KF1380, KFA-KFZ 207.5

Passenger carriers: KF2260, KFN5482

Passenger fares
- Aviation: KF2445
- Railroads: KF2360+

Passenger ships
- Safety regulations: KF2558.P36

Passport Office (U.S.): KF4794.5

Passports: KF4794

Patent assignments: KF3149

Patent attorneys: KF3165.A3+

Patent fees: KF3125.F3

Patent infringement: KF3155+

Patent law: KF3096+, KFC550, KFN5550+, KFA-KFZ 330
- Antitrust aspects: KF3116

Patent laws and legislation
- Electronic data processing: KF242.P3+

Patent licenses: KF3145+
- Foreign licensing requirements: KF3147

Patent medicines: KF3894.P3

Patent Office (U.S.): KF3120+

Patent practice: KF3165.A3+

Patent procedure: KF3120+

Patent violation crimes: KF9359

Patents and trademarks
- Comprehensive: KF3091+, KFC550, KFN5550+, KFA-KFZ 330
- Income tax: KF6428.I5
- Patents: KF3096+
- Trademarks: KF3176+, KFN5552

Paternity: KF542, KFN5131

Patient referral: KF2907.P38

Patients' rights: KF3823, KFA-KFZ 360.5

Patriotic observances in schools: KF4162, KFN5655, KFA-KFZ 392.7

Patriotic societies: KF1359.A1+

Pawnbrokers: KF2038.P3, KFA-KFZ 281.P2

Payment at source of income
- Income tax: KF6435+

Payment (Contracts): KF827+

Payroll deductions
- Income tax: KF6436+
- State taxation: KF6753, KFC870.3, KFN5873

Pea processing industry: KF1909.P3

Peace Corps (U.S.): KF4689

Peaches (Marketing): KFC391.5.P3

Peanuts
- Marketing regulations: KFA-KFZ 244.P35

Pears (Marketing): KFC391.5.P34

Peat
- Regulation: KFA-KFZ 256.5

Peddling: KF2027, KFA-KFZ 281.P43

Pedestrian areas: KF5535

Pedestrians: KF2240

Pediatricians: KF2910.P42+

Pen industry: KF1893.P3

Penal institutions: KF9730+, KFC1180+, KFN6180+, KFX2094, KF10D .x2C62+, KFA-KFZ 588+

Penalties (Criminal law): KF9225+, KFC1104+, KFN6104+, KFA-KFZ 563+

Pencil industry: KF1893.P3

Penitential communications: KF8959.C6

Penitentiaries: KF9735+, KFA-KFZ 590.P3

INDEX

Pennsylvania
- Laws: KFP1+

Pennsylvania Labor Relations Board: KFP332.1

Pennsylvania. Municipal Court of Philadelphia: KFP518.3

Pension plans
- Labor (General): KF3510+, KFA-KFZ 334.5.P4
- Teachers: KF4185

Pension trusts: KF736.P3
- Income tax: KF6449, KFC873, KFA-KFZ 475.7

Pensions: KFC595, KFN5595+
- Agricultural laborers: KF3664.A4
- Business corporations: KFA-KFZ 213.8
- Household employees: KF3664.H6
- Income tax: KF6425
- Judges: KF8777, KFN5984.5.S24, KFA-KFZ 525.5.S3
- Legislators: KF4967, KFC727
- Non-profit organization employees: KF3664.N6
- Radio-broadcasting employees: KF3664.R2
- Railroad employees: KF3659+
- Self-employed: KF3664.S4
- Social security: KF3641+, KFA-KFZ 344
- Teachers: KF4185, KFC660, KFN5660, KFA-KFZ 393.5

Pensions, Mothers: KF3658.M6

Peonage: KF9335

People, The
- Organs of the government: KF4880.5+

People with disabilities
- Building laws: KF5709.3.H35, KFC819.H35, KFN5819.H35
- Capacity and disability: KF480+, KFC111.H35, KFN5111.H36, KFA-KFZ 91.H3
- Civil service: KF5355
- Education: KFC665.H3
- Employment of: KF3469, KFC573.H34, KFN5573.H34

People with disabilities
- Provisions for (Building laws): KFA-KFZ 459.8.H35
- Public welfare: KF3738+, KFC605+, KFN5605+, KFA-KFZ 350.H3

People with mental disabilities
- Capacity and disability: KF480+
- Legal services to: KF337.5.M46

Performance (Contracts): KF826+

Performance rating
- Civil service: KF5349, KFA-KFZ 435.3

Performing arts: KF4290+, KFN5671+, KFA-KFZ 398.5+

Performing arts lawyers: KF299.E57

Performing rights
- Copyright
  - Literary copyright: KF3030.2
  - Musical copyright: KF3045.2

Perishable agricultural products
- Marketing: KF1719.P3
- Warehouses: KF2057

Perjury: KF9420, KFN6142

Perpetuities
- Future estates: KF613
- Life insurance: KF1181.R8

Personal injuries: KF1256+, KFC311, KFN5311, KFA-KFZ 197.P3
- Commercial aviation: KF2455
- Government liability: KF1325.P3
- Master and servant: KF1315.P3
- Vicarious liability: KF1315.P3

Personal injuries lawyers
- Directories: KF195.P47

Personal injury claims (Trial practice): KF8925.P4, KFC1028.P4, KFN6028.P4, KFA-KFZ 539.P4

Personal insurance: KF1171+, KFC292+, KFN5292+, KFA-KFZ 186+

Personal property: KF701+, KFC180, KFN5180+, KFA-KFZ 134+
- Government property: KF5820+

Personal property taxes: KF6765+, KFN5888+, KFA-KFZ 481+

Personal records
- School government: KFA-KFZ 391.P45

INDEX

Personal representatives: KF774+, KFC210, KFN5210
- Decedents' estates: KFA-KFZ 147

Personnel
- Air Force: KF7410+
- Armed Forces: KF7270+
- Army: KF7310+
- Coast Guard: KF7450+
- Marine Corps: KF7390+
- Merchant marine: KF7488+
- Navy: KF7350+

Personnel records: KF3457.5

Persons: KF465+, KFC108+, KFN5108+, KFA-KFZ 91+

Persons, Juristic: KF1384+

Persons, Natural: KF466+

Persons of unsound mind
- Capacity and disability: KF480+

Pest control operators: KFA-KFZ 282.I5

Pesticides
- Public safety: KF3959, KFC641.5.P63, KFA-KFZ 380.P4

Pests (Agricultural), Control of: KF1687+, KFC387, KFN5387, KFA-KFZ 240

Pet owners (Legal handbooks): KF390.P4

Petroleum: KF3964.P47
- Import trade: KF1996.P3
- Trade agreements: KF6669.P48

Petroleum, Crude (Taxation): KF6629.P3

Petroleum in submerged lands: KF1856

Petroleum industry
- Collective labor agreements: KF3409.P3
- Income tax: KFA-KFZ 477.5.M54
- Insolvency and bankruptcy: KF1535.P48
- Labor hygiene and safety: KF3574.P3, KFA-KFZ 336.P46
- Labor law: KF3580.P3
- Regulation: KF1841+, KFC405+, KFN5404+, KFA-KFZ 258.A1+

Petroleum products
- Import trade: KF1996.P3

Petroleum trade
- International trade: KF1984.P3
- Labor hygiene and safety: KFA-KFZ 336.P46

Pharmaceutical industries: KF1879

Pharmaceutical products
- Labeling: KF3885
- Retail trade: KF2036.D7, KFA-KFZ 281.5.D7

Pharmacists: KF2915.P4+, KFC546.5.P4+, KFN5546.5.P4+, KFA-KFZ 326.5.P4+

Phenylketonuria: KF3803.P4, KFA-KFZ 357.8.P45

Phenylpyruvic oligophrenia: KF3803.P4

Philadelphia Municipal Court: KFP518.3

Philosophy and jurisprudence of law: KF379+

Phonographs
- Copyright: KF3030.5

Phonorecord industry: KF1893.P46

Phosphate
- Regulation: KFA-KFZ 259.P45

Phosphorus, White: KF3964.W4

Photographers: KF2042.P45

Photographic evidence: KF8968

Photography
- Copyright: KF3067

Physical disabilities, Students with: KF4210+
- Colleges and universities: KF4244.P58

Physical education: KF4203, KFA-KFZ 395.4

Physical fitness centers: KF2042.P49

Physical therapists: KFC546.5.T54+, KFN5546.5.T5+

Physician and patient (Privileged communications): KF8959.P4

Physician extenders (Health insurance): KF3609.R87

Physicians: KF2905+, KFC546.A1+, KFN5546.A1+, KFA-KFZ 326+
- Legal handbooks: KF390.P45

Physicians' assistants: KF2915.P45+, KFC546.5.P48+, KFA-KFZ 326.5.P45+

Picketing: KF3432, KFN5566, KFA-KFZ 333+

Picture, Unauthorized publication of: KF1263.U5

Pilotage: KF2566+, KFC526

Pipe fitting
- Building laws: KFC816, KFN5816, KFA-KFZ 459.3

Pipelines: KF2398, KFA-KFZ 303.5

Piracy
- Criminal trials: KF221.P57

PKU: KF3803.P4, KFA-KFZ 357.8.P45

Planning
- Health facilities and hospitals: KF3825.5
- Land use (Government liability): KF1325.L36

Planning, City: KF5691+, KFC810+, KFN5810+, KFA-KFZ 458+

Planning, Regional: KF5691+, KFC810+, KFN5810+, KFA-KFZ 458+

Plant diseases and pests: KF1687+, KFC387, KFN5387, KFA-KFZ 240

Plant quarantine: KF1687+, KFC387, KFN5387, KFA-KFZ 240

Plant sanitation and inspection
- Baking industry: KF1903
- Dairy producers: KF1921
- Egg producers: KF1916
- Fishery products industry: KF1930
- Fruit processing industry: KF1908
- Meat industry: KF1911
- Oil and fat industry: KF1935
- Poultry industry: KF1738
- Seafood industry: KF1930
- Sheep raising industry: KF1734
- Vegetable oil and fat industry: KF1935
- Vegetable processing industry: KF1908

Plants (Patent law): KF3133.P53

Plastics industry (Collective labor agreements): KF3409.P5

Plate glass insurance: KF1212.P5

Platinum mining: KF1836.P5

Playground accidents: KF1290.P5, KFA-KFZ 196.3.P5

Playing cards (Taxation): KF6629.P5

Plea bargaining: KF9654, KFC1161, KFA-KFZ 578.5

Pleading and motions: KF8866+, KFC1010+, KFN6010+, KFP535+, KFA-KFZ 535+

Pleasure craft
- Safety regulations: KF2558.P5, KFC524.P5, KFN5524.P5

Plebiscite: KF4881, KFC708

Plumbers: KFA-KFZ 282.P55

Plumbing
- Building laws: KF5709, KFC816, KFN5816, KF10A 12.1.P5, KFA-KFZ 459.3
- New York City: KFX2080.3

Plumbing and heating industry (Collective labor disputes): KF3450.P53+

Plumbing contracts: KF905.P5

Plumbing fixture industry
- Manufacture: KF1890.P5
- Wholesale trade: KF1999.P5

Plums (Marketing): KFC391.5.P55

Podiatrists: KF2910.P64+, KFC546.P6+, KFN5546.5.P63+, KFA-KFZ 326.5.P62+

Poisons: KF3958+, KFC641.5.P6

Police: KF5399+, KFC778+, KFN5778, KFX2017.7, KFA-KFZ 439
- Legal handbooks: KF390.P65
- Municipal civil service: KF5398.P6, KFN5776.P64, KFA-KFZ 436.8.P64

Police courts: KFC975

Police legal advisors: KF5399.5.L4

Police power: KF5399+
- Constitutional law: KF4695, KFC694

Police, State: KFA-KFZ 435.8.S7

Poliomyelitis immunization: KF3809.P6

Political crimes: KF9390+

Political disabilities
- Criminal law: KFN6108.F67
- Criminal procedure: KFA-KFZ 591.2

Political offenses: KFC1137+, KFN6137+
- Criminal trials: KF221.P6

Political parties: KF4788

INDEX

Political parties
  Constitutional law: KFA-KFZ 413
Political rights: KF4741+, KFC695+, KFN5695+, KFP411+, KFX2068
  Indians: KF8210.C5
Poll taxes (Election law): KF4898, KFC713, KFN5713, KFA-KFZ 420.85.R4
Pollution: KF3775+, KFC610+, KFN5610+, KFA-KFZ 354+
  Air: KF3812+, KFC614, KFN5614, KFA-KFZ 358+
  Casualty insurance: KFC298.P64
  Environment: KF3775
  Insurance: KF1220.P5, KFA-KFZ 191.P64
  Water: KF3786+, KFC612, KFN5612, KFA-KFZ 356
Polychlorinated biphenyls: KF3964.P64
Polychlorobiphenyls: KF3964.P64
Polygraph examinations
  Civil procedure: KF8962
  Criminal procedure: KF9666, KFA-KFZ 580.5.L5
Pooling and unit operation of oil fields: KF1853
Poor
  Health insurance: KF3608.P66, KFC591.5.P65, KFA-KFZ 341.5.P65
  Legal protection: KF390.5.P6, KFN5084.5.P6, KFA-KFZ 84.5.P7
Popular names of cases: KFA-KFZ 60
Population control: KF3766, KFC609, KFA-KFZ 353
Port of New York Authority: KFX2096.4
Portland cement (Price fixing): KF1629.P6
Ports and harbors: KF2581+, KFC530+, KFN5530+, KFA-KFZ 312.A1+
Possessory actions: KF652+, KFC163, KFA-KFZ 121
Possessory estates
  Land tenure: KF578
Post Office and Civil Service, Committee on (United States House of Representatives): KF4997.P6

Post Office Department (U.S.): KF2668+
Postal notes: KF2727
Postal offenses: KF9460
Postal rates: KF2688+, KF2730+
Postal savings: KF2725
Postal service: KF2661+
Postal unions: KF2670.8
Postmasters: KF2675+
Potatoes
  Acreage allotments: KF1706.P6
  Marketing quotas: KF1706.P6
  Marketing regulations: KFA-KFZ 244.P58
Poultry
  Marketing regulations: KFA-KFZ 244.P6
  Standards and grading: KF1726.P6
Poultry, Dressed
  Inspection: KF1915
  Price supports: KF1915
  Standards and grading: KF1915
  Surpluses: KF1915
Poultry industry: KF1738, KFC394, KFA-KFZ 247
  Labor hygiene and safety: KFA-KFZ 336.P67
Poultry inspection: KF1915
Poultry plants (Labor hygiene and safety): KFA-KFZ 336.P67
Poultry products
  Inspection: KF1915
  Price supports: KF1915
  Standards and grading: KF1915
  Surpluses: KF1915
Poultry products industry: KF1915+, KFC418+, KFN5418
Poverty
  Criminal liability: KF9243.5
  Legal works on: KF390.5.P6, KFN5084.5.P6
Power of appointment: KF607
Power of attorney: KF1347, KFC336, KFN5336
Power supply
  Public utilities: KF2120+, KFC456+, KFN5457+, KFA-KFZ 286+

Powers, Separation and delegation of: KF4565, KFC685+, KFN5685+, KFA-KFZ 405+

Practical nurses: KF2915.P73+, KFA-KFZ 326.5.P66+

Practice of law: KF300+, KFA-KFZ 76+

Pre-elementary education: KF4197

Predatory animals: KF1687+, KFC387, KFN5387, KFA-KFZ 240

Prefabricated buildings: KF5702.P74

Preferential employment: KF3458+

Veterans

Civil service: KFN5765

Preferred provider organizations (Health insurance): KF1184.P73

Preferred stock: KF1456

Pregnancy discrimination

Labor law: KF3467

Premarital examinations: KF512

Premises liability: KF1287+

Prenuptial agreements: KF529

Prepaid legal services: KFA-KFZ 77.5.G7

Presbyterians: KF4869.P7

Preservatives, Food: KF3879.P7

Preserves, State: KFA-KFZ 452+

President (U.S.): KF5051+

Election: KF4910+

Presidential Campaign Activities, Select Committee on (United States Senate): KF4987.P7

Presidential commissions: KF5125

Presidential libraries: KF4318.A1+

Presidential messages: KF47

Press

Privileged communication: KFA-KFZ 541.3.P7

Press censorship: KF4775

Press law: KF2750, KFC535, KFN5535, KFA-KFZ 316

Student publications: KF4165

Press (Privileged communications): KF8959.P7

Presumptions: KF8940.P7, KFC1032, KFN6032, KFA-KFZ 540.4

Pretrial procedure

Civil procedure: KF8900+, KFC1020+, KFN6020+, KFA-KFZ 537+

Electronic data processing: KF242.P73+

Study and teaching: KF277.P68

Pretrial release: KF9632

Prevention of accidents: KFA-KFZ 380.5.A1+

Prevention of cruelty to animals: KF3841+, KFC627, KFN5627, KFA-KFZ 370

Price control

Government measures in time of crisis

1914-1939: KFA-KFZ 463.3+

1939-: KFA-KFZ 464.3+

Price discrimination: KF1626+

Price fixing: KF1626+

Price maintenance

Retail trade: KF2015+, KFC439+

Price supports

Agriculture: KF1692+

Bakery products: KF1903

Cattle industry: KF1730.3

Dairy products: KF1921

Eggs and egg products: KF1916

Fats, Vegetable: KF1935

Field crops: KF1693.A+

Fishery products: KF1930

Fruit: KF1694

Fruit, Processed: KF1908

Grain: KF1693.G7+

Meat and meat products: KF1911

Oils and fats, Vegetable: KF1935

Rice: KF1693.G75

Rye: KF1693.G76

Seafood: KF1930

Sheep: KF1734

Sugar beets and sugar cane: KF1693.S8

Tobacco: KF1693.T6

Vegetable oils and fats: KF1935

Vegetables: KF1694

Vegetables, Processed: KF1908

Prices

Cattle industry: KF1730.2

INDEX

Prima-facie evidence: KF8940.P7, KFC1032, KFN6032
Primaries: KFC715, KFN5715, KFA-KFZ 420.3
Primary production: KF1681+, KFC385+, KFN5385+, KFA-KFZ 239+
Printing industry (Collective labor agreements): KF3409.P7
Printing inventions (Patent law): KF3133.P7
Printing, Joint Committee on (U.S. Congress): KF4939.5.P7
Printing, Legislative: KFA-KFZ 421.5.P7
Prints
Copyright: KF3072
Priority of claims
Bankruptcy: KF1532, KFN5366.P7
Prison administration: KF9730, KFC1181, KFN6181, KFX2094, KFA-KFZ 588+
Prison discipline: KF9730, KFC1181, KFN6181
Prison industries: KF9733, KFN6182, KFA-KFZ 589
Prison labor: KF9733, KFN6182, KFA-KFZ 589
Prisoners
Legal services to: KF337.5.P7
National Guard Service: KFN5929.C6
Prison administration: KF9731, KFC1181.5, KFN6181.5, KFA-KFZ 588.5
Social security: KF3664.P73
Prisons: KF9730+, KFC1180+, KFN6180+, KFX2094, KFA-KFZ 588+
Prisons for women: KF9741+
Prisons, Military: KF7675
Privacy, Violation of: KF1262+, KFA-KFZ 197.P7
Private antitrust actions: KF1657.P74
Private cars (Railroads): KF2318
Private companies: KF1380, KFC339.5, KFN5339.5, KFA-KFZ 207.5
Private education: KF4220, KFA-KFZ 395.95
Private equity funds: KF1078.5

Private investigators: KF2042.D48, KFA-KFZ 282.D47
Private police: KF5399.5.P7, KFC778.5.P74
Private property: KF562
Private property, Public restraints on: KF5500+, KFC785+
Private railroad cars: KF2318
Private schools: KF4220, KFA-KFZ 395.95
Private trusts: KF733+
Privileged communications: KF8958+, KFC1041+, KFA-KFZ 541.2+
Privilegium fori
Colonial U.S. law: KF364.P7
Prizefighting: KF3989, KFC645, KFN5645, KFA-KFZ 384
Probate accounting: KFA-KFZ 144.5.A25
Probate law and practice: KF765+, KFC205+, KFN5205, KFP144+, KFX2018.5, KFA-KFZ 144+
Indians: KF8210.P7, KFA-KFZ 505.6.P7
Probate lawyers (Directories): KF195.P7
Probate records: KF8755.A+
Probation
Criminal procedure: KF9750, KFC1190, KFN6190, KFA-KFZ 592
Juvenile criminal procedure: KF9827, KFC1198.8, KFA-KFZ 598.8
Military law: KF7679
Procedure
Legal education: KF277.P7
Procedure (Electronic data processing): KF242.P746+
Procedures for removal (Judges): KF8781+
Process
Civil procedure: KFC1004.P75
Processing of agricultural commodities (Taxation): KF6630+
Processing tax: KF6630+
Procurement lawyers
Directories: KF195.P83
Procurement, Military: KF851+

Procuring
Criminal law: KF9448
Produce exchanges: KF1085+, KFN5275.A1+, KFA-KFZ 180.A1+
Product counterfeiting: KF3197.5
Product inspection
Cattle industry: KF1730.4
Product safety: KF3945+, KFA-KFZ 380.A1+
Production control
Agriculture: KF1692+
Products liability: KF1296+, KFC323.A3+, KFN5323.A+, KFA-KFZ 197.7
Legal research: KF241.P75
Products liability claims
Trial practice: KF8925.P7, KFA-KFZ 539.P7
Products liability insurance: KF1220.P6, KFA-KFZ 191.P75
Professional associations: KF2902
Professional corporations: KF2901, KFC545.5, KFN5545.5, KFA-KFZ 325.5
Income tax: KF6495.P7
Labor law: KF3580.P74
Professional education: KF4256+, KFN5668
Professional liability: KF1289
Professional schools: KF4256+, KFN5668
Professional standards review organizations (Medicine): KF3827.P7
Professions, The: KF2900+, KFC545+, KFN5545+, KFX2042.A+, KFA-KFZ 325+
Profit sharing
Labor law: KF3496
Profiteering
Government measures in time of crisis
1914-1939: KFA-KFZ 463.3+
1939-: KFA-KFZ 464.3+
Programming (Radio broadcasting): KF2815
Prohibition: KF3901+, KFA-KFZ 375+
Indians: KFA-KFZ 505.6.A44

Promissory notes: KF962, KFA-KFZ 161.5.P7
Promoters (Business corporations): KF1420, KFN5348, KFA-KFZ 213.5
Promotions (Civil service): KF5377
Proof of foreign law: KF8940.P75
Propaganda, Subversive (through the mail): KF2738
Propellant actuated devices: KFA-KFZ 380.E9
Property: KF560+, KFC138+, KFN5138+, KFA-KFZ 110+
Property, Church: KF4868.C4
Property, Horizontal: KF581, KFC144.5, KFN5142
Property insurance: KF1190+, KFC295, KFN5295.A1+, KFA-KFZ 188+, KFA-KFZ 189.A+
Property lawyers (Directories): KF195.P75
Property, Military: KF5845+
Property, Public: KF5500+, KFC785+, KFN5785+, KFX2070+, KFA-KFZ 442+
Property taxes
Federal: KF6525+
Local: KF6784+, KFN5912.P7, KFX2091.P7, KFA-KFZ 491.P7
Local finance: KFC912.P7
State: KF6759+, KFC880+, KFN5880+, KFA-KFZ 478+
Property transfer: KF715+
Proposed impeachments (Governors): KFA-KFZ 426.4+
Proprietary drugs: KF3894.P3
Prosecution (Juvenile criminal law): KF9817
Prosecution, Malicious: KF1270
Prospective overruling: KF422
Prostitution: KFA-KFZ 571.P7
Criminal law: KF9448, KFX2064.5
Prostitution (Human trafficking): KF9449
Provisional remedies: KF9014, KFC1062, KFN6062, KFA-KFZ 549
Provost Marshall General (U.S.): KF7596

INDEX

Proxy rules (Corporation law): KF1451
Prunes (Marketing): KFC391.5.P78
Psychiatric evidence: KF8965
Psychiatric hospitals: KF3828
Psychiatrists: KF2910.P75+, KFA-KFZ 326.5.P73+
Psychological evidence: KF8965
Psychologists: KFC546.P7+, KFN5546.P73+, KFN5546.5.P73+, KFA-KFZ 326.5.P73+
Psychology, Forensic: KF8922
Psychosurgery: KF3827.P78
Psychotherapists: KF2910.P75+, KFA-KFZ 326.5.P73+
Legal works for: KFN5084.P78
Public accommodations, Access to: KF4756+
Public advocates: KFA-KFZ 427.5.P8
Public assistance: KF3720+, KFC600+, KFN5600+, KFA-KFZ 349+
Public authorities: KF5332, KFC759, KFA-KFZ 433
Public broadcasting (Regulation): KFA-KFZ 318.6
Public contracts: KF841+, KFC224+, KFN5224+, KFA-KFZ 151.5
Indians: KF8210.P8
Public contracts claims (Trial practice): KF8925.P8
Public contracts lawyers
Directories: KF195.P83
Public debts
Federal: KF6241+
Local finance: KF6775, KFX2089.5
State and local finance: KF6724
State finance: KF6744, KFC849, KFN5849, KFA-KFZ 468
Public defenders: KF9646, KFC1160.4, KFN6160, KF10A 17.4.P8, KFA-KFZ 578
Juvenile criminal law: KF9813
Public depositories: KFA-KFZ 467.3
Public domain
Copyright
Art: KF3052
Literature: KF3022
Music: KF3037

Public education: KF4101+, KFC648+, KFN5648+, KFN5648+
Public employees
Labor disputes: KFA-KFZ 333.8.P8
Public finance
Federal: KF6200+
Local: KF6770+, KFC905+, KFN5905+, KFX2089+, KFA-KFZ 488+
State: KF6735+, KFC840+, KFN5840+, KFA-KFZ 465+
Public health: KF3775+, KFC610+, KFN5610+, KFX2048+, KFX2096.7, KFA-KFZ 354+
Study and teaching: KF277.P82
Public health personnel: KFA-KFZ 326.5.P83+
Public institutions: KFC600.2, KFN5600.2, KFA-KFZ 349.2
Public interest law: KF390.5.P78
Public interest lawyers: KF299.P8
Public land law: KF5601+, KFC802+, KFN5802+, KFX2076, KFX2096.8, KFA-KFZ 451+
Public Land Office (U.S.): KF5607
Public lands (Real property taxes): KF6761.3.P8
Public law: KFC678
Electronic data processing: KF242.P8+
Public meetings (Executive departments): KF5105.5, KFC747.P82, KFN5747.P83, KFA-KFZ 427.8.P8
Public officers
Tort liability: KF1306.A2+, KFC327, KFA-KFZ 198.P8
Public order and morality (New York City): KFX2064+, KFX2064
Public policy: KF450.P8, KFC694
Public Printer (U.S.): KF5001
Public property: KF5500+, KFC785+, KFN5785+, KFX2070+, KFX2096.8, KFA-KFZ 442+
Religious observances on: KF4868.R45

Public prosecutor: KF9640, KFC1158, KFN6158, KFA-KFZ 577
Public radio: KF2824
Public records (Government property): KFA-KFZ 462.5.P8
Public recreation
Tort liability: KF1290.P5, KFA-KFZ 196.3.P5
Public relations
Practice of law: KF310.P63
Public relations law: KF390.5.P8
Public safety: KF3941+, KFC640+, KFN5640+, KFX2055+, KFA-KFZ 378+
Public sanitation: KF3775+, KFC610+, KFN5610+, KFX2096.7, KFA-KFZ 354+
Public utilities
Collective labor agreements: KF3409.P8
Corporate reorganization: KF1546.P83
Income tax: KF6495.P8, KFA-KFZ 477.5.P8
Labor disputes: KFA-KFZ 333.8.P83
Regulation: KF2076+, KFC455+, KFN5455+, KFX2033+, KFA-KFZ 285+
Public Utilities Commission (California): KFC455.1
Public utility lawyers (Directories): KF195.P85
Public welfare: KF3720+, KFC600+, KFN5600+, KFX2045.A2+, KFA-KFZ 349+
Public workers (Workers' compensation): KF3632.P8
Public works: KF5865, KFC832, KFX2074, KFA-KFZ 462.8
Public Works and Transportation, Committee on (United States House of Representatives): KF4997.P8
Publication of picture, Unauthorized: KF1263.U5
Publications (Law office management): KF320.N48

Publicly chartered corporations: KF1359.A1+
Publisher and author: KF3084
Publishing contracts: KF3084
Puerto Ricans (Citizenship): KF4720.P83
Pulp (Freight classification): KF2355.P2
Pulp industry (Income tax): KF6495.P2
Punishment: KF9225+, KFC1104+, KFN6104+, KFA-KFZ 563+
Purchasing agents (Legal handbooks): KF390.P8
Purchasing and procurement: KF841+, KFC224+, KFN5224+, KFA-KFZ 151.5
Put and call transactions: KF1073.P88
Puts: KF1073.P88

Q

Quacks: KF2913.Q2+, KFC546.Q2+
Quakers
Church and state: KF4869.Q83
Quantum meruit: KF836+
Quarantine
Animals: KF3836.Q2, KFC623.5, KFN5623.5, KFA-KFZ 368.5.Q3
Immigrants: KF3807
Plants: KF1687+
Quarrying: KF1801+, KFC400+, KFN5400+, KFA-KFZ 255+
Quartermaster Corps (U.S. Army): KF7335.Q2
Quasi contracts: KF1244, KFC309, KFA-KFZ 194
Quasi copyright: KF3075+
Quasi-marital relationships: KF539, KFC129, KFA-KFZ 103
Quitrent: KF593.Q5
Quo warranto: KFA-KFZ 553.Q52
Quotations: KF159

R

Rabies in animals: KFA-KFZ 369.R33
Racial minorities
Civil rights: KF4755

INDEX

Racism
- Criminal liability: KF9244.5

Racketeering: KF9375, KFC1133, KFN6133, KFA-KFZ 568.R3

Radiation
- Public safety: KF3948+, KF3948, KFC641.5.A7, KFN5641.5.A85, KFA-KFZ 380.A8

Radio and television receiver industry: KF1893.R2

Radio and television service technicians: KFA-KFZ 282.R33

Radio broadcasting
- Collective labor agreements: KF3409.R2
- Court proceedings: KF8726
- Regulation: KF2814+, KFC543, KFA-KFZ 318.6
- Social security: KF3664.R2

Radio broadcasting stations, Amateur: KF2828

Radio communication: KF2801+

Radio, Marine: KF2826

Radio (Patent law): KF3133.R2

Radio receiver industry: KF1893.R2

Radio receivers
- Retail trade: KF2036.T4

Radio stations: KF2810

Radioactive substances (Products liability): KF1297.R33

Radiobiology: KF4280.R2

Radiological services: KF3826.R34

Radiologists: KF2910.R33+

Radiopharmaceuticals: KF3894.R33

Radon: KF3964.R35

Railroad cars, Private: KF2318

Railroad crossings: KF2234, KFN5478, KFA-KFZ 297.9

Railroad Labor Board (U.S.): KF3448.1

Railroad lands: KF2298, KFC492, KFN5492, KFA-KFZ 301.3

Railroad lawyers (Directories): KF195.R3

Railroad liens: KF2305

Railroad safety and sanitation: KF2326+, KFN5494, KFA-KFZ 301.5

Railroads
- Collective labor agreements: KF3409.R25
- Corporate reorganization: KF1546.R2, KFN5369.R2, KFA-KFZ 225.R2
- Employer's liability: KF1317.R2+
- Freight: KF2346+, KFC497, KFN5497
- Freight claims: KF2372
- Government ownership: KF2295
- Health insurance: KF3608.R2
- Income tax: KF3528.R2, KF6495.R2, KFC879.R2
- Labor disputes: KF3448
- Labor law: KF3580.R2
- Liability: KF2371+, KFA-KFZ 301.7
- Passenger fares: KF2360+
- Pensions: KF3659+
- Personal injuries: KF2375
- Personal property tax: KFA-KFZ 481.7.R34
- Rate-making: KF2336+, KFC497, KFN5497+, KFN5497, KFA-KFZ 301.6
- Regulation: KF2271+, KFC490+, KFN5490+, KFA-KFZ 301+
- Social security: KF3659+
- State taxation: KF6763.7
- Ticket brokers: KF2366
- Unemployment insurance: KF3680.R2
- Wages: KF3505.R2
- Workers' compensation: KF3629

Railroads, Electric: KF2393, KFN5503

Railway postal employees: KF2679+

Raisin industry: KFC391.5.R34

Rape: KF9329, KFN6124.R34

Ratemaking: KF2187, KFC469.5
- Aviation: KF2445
- Motor carriers: KFA-KFZ 299
- Railroads: KF2336+, KFC497, KFN5497+, KFN5497, KFA-KFZ 301.6
- Telecommunication: KF2765.6
- Telegraph: KF2775.6
- Telephone: KF2780.6
- Water transportation: KF2615

Rates, Postal: KF2688+, KF2730+
Rating
Employment and dismissal: KF3457.8
Rating of judges: KF8778, KFA-KFZ 525.5.R3
Rationing
Government measures in time of crisis
1914-1939: KFA-KFZ 463.3+
1939-: KFA-KFZ 464.3+
Reading: KF4203.5
Real estate agents: KF2042.R4, KFC446.R3, KFN5446.R3, KFA-KFZ 282.R4
Real estate appraisers: KF8968.65
Real estate development: KF5698.3, KFA-KFZ 458.3
Real estate investment companies: KF1079, KFC273
Insolvency and bankruptcy: KF1535.R43
Real estate transactions: KFA-KFZ 126
Property taxes: KF6540, KFN5882, KFA-KFZ 479.5
Real property: KF566+, KFC140+, KFN5140+, KFX2022, KFA-KFZ 112+
Electronic data processing: KF242.P75+
Government property: KF5760+, KFN5828+, KFA-KFZ 462.5.L34
Real property cases (Trial practice): KF8925.R4, KFA-KFZ 539.R4
Real property taxes
Federal taxes affecting real property: KF6535+
Local: KF6784, KFC912.R3, KFN5912.R3, KFA-KFZ 491.R4
State: KF6760+, KFC881, KFN5881, KFA-KFZ 479+
Reapportionment
Election law: KF4905, KFC714, KFN5714, KFA-KFZ 420.85.A6
Recall: KF4884, KFC709, KFN5709, KFA-KFZ 420.9.R3
Judges: KF4884
Receivers in bankruptcy: KF1530.R3
Receivers in equity: KF9016, KFC1063, KFN6063, KFA-KFZ 550

Receiving stolen goods: KF9358
Recidivists: KF9226, KFN6105, KFA-KFZ 564
Reclamation of land: KF5615+, KFA-KFZ 451+
Recognition of Indian tribes
Federal government: KF8210.R32
Recommended legislation: KF47.5
Reconstruction Finance Corporation: KF6015.R3
Record keeping: KF1357.5
Banking: KF1030.R3, KFC256.R43, KFA-KFZ 167.R43
Corporations: KFA-KFZ 205.5.B8
Recording and registration: KFC100.R43
Persons: KFC113
Recording devices (Copyright)
Literature: KF3030.4
Music: KF3045.4
Records management
Courts: KF8733+
Government property: KF5752, KFC826, KFN5826
Hospitals: KF3827.R4, KFC619.5.R43, KFN5619.5.R43, KFA-KFZ 367.R4
Juvenile courts: KF9797
Law office management: KF320.R42
Recreation areas: KF5638, KFA-KFZ 452.5
Recreation departments (Tort liability): KFA-KFZ 198.P37
Recruiting and enlistment
Air Force: KF7411
Armed Forces: KF7271
Army: KF7311
Coast Guard: KF7451
Marine Corps: KF7390.1
Navy: KF7351
Recycling of waste: KF5510
Redistricting
Electronic data processing: KF242.A65+
Reemployment (Civil service): KF5362
Referees (Civil procedure): KF8986, KFN6049, KFA-KFZ 543

INDEX

Referendum: KF4881, KFC708, KFA-KFZ 419
- Legal research: KF241.E5
- Municipal government: KFA-KFZ 431.9.R4

Referral services, Lawyer: KF338.A+

Refineries: KFA-KFZ 258.R43

Reformatories: KF9737+, KFC1186.A1+, KFN6186.A1+, KFA-KFZ 590.R3
- Women: KF9741+

Refugees
- Immigration law: KF4836
- Legal services to: KF337.5.R4

Refuse as fuel: KFN5468.8.R44, KFA-KFZ 291.R4

Refuse disposal: KF3816.R4, KFC614.5.R43, KFN5614.5.R43, KFA-KFZ 359.R3

Regional planning: KF5691+, KFC810+, KFN5810+, KFA-KFZ 458+

Registers of births, marriages, and deaths: KFC113

Registration: KFC100.R43
- Real property: KF679, KFC172, KFN5172, KFA-KFZ 127

Registration of criminals: KF9751

Registration of individuals: KF4791, KFA-KFZ 414.5
- Aliens: KF4840
- Foreign agents: KF4854

Registration of land titles: KF679, KFC172, KFN5172, KFA-KFZ 127

Registration of motor vehicles: KF2215, KFC474, KFN5474, KFA-KFZ 297.4

Registration of voters: KF4898, KFC713, KFN5713, KFA-KFZ 420.85.R4

Regulation of commerce, industry, and trade: KF1600+, KFC375+, KFN5375+, KFX2024+, KFA-KFZ 230+

Regulatory agencies: KF2120.1, KF5406+, KFA-KFZ 440

Rehabilitation centers: KFA-KFZ 363.R44

Rehabilitation of criminals: KF9750.5

Reinsurance: KF1236, KFC308, KFA-KFZ 193.5

Relationship between civil and religious divorces
- Domestic relations: KF536, KFN5126.5

Release, Pretrial: KF9632

Religious aspects
- Constitutional law: KF4551

Religious corporations: KF4865, KFC705, KFN5705, KFA-KFZ 417

Religious discrimination
- Employment: KF3466.5

Religious divorces and civil divorces, Relationship between
- Domestic relations: KF536, KFN5126.5

Religious instruction in public schools: KF4162, KFN5655, KFA-KFZ 392.7

Religious lawyers (Directories): KF195.R44

Religious liberty
- Indians: KF8210.R37

Religious observances in schools: KF4162, KFN5655, KFA-KFZ 392.7

Religious observances on public property: KF4868.R45

Religious wills: KF760.R44

Remainders
- Future estates and interests: KF609+

Remedies
- Breach of contract: KF836+
- Civil procedure: KF9010+, KFC1061+, KFN6060+, KFA-KFZ 547+

Remedies, Joinder of: KF8893

Removal of organs (Human trafficking): KF9449

Removal, Procedures for (Judges): KF8781+

Remuneration
- Business corporations: KFA-KFZ 213.8

Renal disease program (Health insurance): KF3609.R44, KFA-KFZ 341.7.R46

Renegotiation of defense contracts: KF861+

Rent: KF586+, KFN5145

Rent control

- Government measures in time of crisis
  - 1914-1939: KFA-KFZ 463.5.R3
  - 1939-: KFA-KFZ 464.5.R3
- New York City: KFX2085.R3

Rent subsidies: KF3745.R4

Rent supplements: KF3745.R4

Rental housing

- Labor law: KFC589.R45

Renvoi: KF413.R4

Reorganization (Executive departments): KFA-KFZ 427.8.R46

Repairs

- Income tax deductions: KF6395.R3

Reparation: KF1328+, KFC333.5, KFN5333.5, KFA-KFZ 200

Replevin: KF720, KFA-KFZ 134.5.R4

Representatives, Personal: KF774+, KFC210, KFN5210

Reprinting

- Copyright
  - Art and photography: KF3060.1
  - Literary copyright: KF3030.1
  - Music: KF3045.1

Repurchase agreements: KF1029

Reputation, Torts in respect to: KF1266+, KFC313, KFN5313

Res ipsa loquitur: KF8944, KFN6035, KFA-KFZ 540.5.N4

Res judicata: KF8992

Rescission contracts: KF839, KFN5239

Research

- Science and the arts: KFA-KFZ 398+

Research and development partnership: KF1380.7

Research contracts: KF869

Research, Defense: KF4280.D3

Research, Legal: KF240+, KFN5074+, KFA-KFZ 75

Reserves

- Air Force: KF7428
- Armed Forces: KF7288
- Army: KF7328
- Coast Guard: KF7468

Reserves

- Navy: KF7368

Reserves (Banking): KF1030.R35

Residence requirements for lawyers: KF304.5

Residence requirements for municipal officials: KF5325.R46

Resignation of employees: KF3471+

Resistance welders (Manufacturing industry): KF1893.R3

Resolution Trust Corporation (Government contracts): KF869.5.R47

Resource recovery facilities (Income tax): KFC879.R48

Resources, Committee on United States House of Representatives: KF4997.R4

Respiratory therapists: KFA-KFZ 326.5.R47+

Respondeat superior doctrine: KF1253

Respondentia: KF1114.B6

Rest homes: KFA-KFZ 282.R45

Restatement of the common law: KF395.A2+

Restaurants: KFA-KFZ 282.H6

- Income tax: KF6495.H67, KFA-KFZ 477.5.H67
- Regulation: KF2042.H6, KFC446.H6, KFN5446.H6
- Wages: KF3505.H6

Restitution

- Breach of contract: KF839
- Criminal procedure: KFN6189

Restraint of trade: KF1624+

Restrictive covenants: KF662, KFC164, KFA-KFZ 125

Restructuring

- Mortgages: KF697.M63

Resulting trusts: KF742

Retail and service establishments

- Collective labor agreements: KF3409.R37

Retail franchises: KFA-KFZ 281.F7

Retail sales taxes

- Federal: KF6606

INDEX

Retail sales taxes
  Local: KF6788+, KFC912.R37, KFN5912.R37
  State: KF6767+, KFC899, KFN5899, KFA-KFZ 484
Retail trade
  Business taxes: KFA-KFZ 480.5.R4
  Insolvency and bankruptcy: KF1535.R45
  Labor hygiene and safety: KF3574.R48
  Labor law: KF3580.R3
  Legal handbooks: KF390.R4
  Management-labor relations: KF3452.R3
  Regulation: KF2005+, KFC437, KFN5437+, KFX2041.A2+, KFA-KFZ 281+
  Wages: KF3505.R3
Retarded children: KFC603+, KFN5603+, KFA-KFZ 350.C4
Retention (Law office management): KF320.R42
Retired air force personnel: KF5353
Retired army personnel: KF5353
Retired military officers: KF5353
Retired military personnel (Civil service): KF5353
Retired naval personnel: KF5353
Retired persons (Legal handbooks): KF390.A4
Retirement contributions
  Income tax deductions: KF6395.R35
Retirement of judges: KFA-KFZ 525.5.A6
Retirement pensions, Air Force: KF7415
Retirement pensions, Army: KF7315
Retirement pensions, Coast Guard: KF7455
Retirement pensions, Military: KF7275
Retirement pensions, Navy: KF7355
Retirement plans: KFA-KFZ 334.5.P4
Retroactive judicial decisions: KF422
Retroactive law: KF420
Revenue sharing
  Indians: KF8210.R4

Revenue, State: KF6750+, KFC856+, KFN5850+, KFA-KFZ 469+
Reverse mortgages: KF697.R48
  Real property law: KFA-KFZ 130.5.R48
Reversions: KF608
Revisors of statutes: KFA-KFZ 421.5.L4
Rhode Island
  Laws: KFR1+
Rice (Price supports): KF1693.G75
Ride sharing (Motor vehicle laws): KF2239.5
Right of property: KF562, KFA-KFZ 110.5
Right to counsel: KF9646, KFC1160.4, KFN6160, KFA-KFZ 578
  Juvenile criminal law: KF9813
Right to die: KF3827.E87, KFC619.5.R5, KFN5619.5.R54
  Medical legislation: KFA-KFZ 367.R53
Right to education: KF4151+, KFC654.5, KFA-KFZ 392.2
Right to resistance against government: KF4786
Right to work laws: KF3394+, KFC560.5, KFA-KFZ 332.5
Right turn on red: KF2235
Rights of suspects: KF9625+, KFC1156, KFN6156, KFA-KFZ 576
Rights of way
  Highways: KF5532, KFC788
  Public lands: KF5609, KFA-KFZ 451.2
  Railroads: KF2298, KFC492, KFN5492
  Roads: KFC788, KFA-KFZ 444.6
Riot: KF9428, KFA-KFZ 570.5.R5
Riparian rights: KF641+, KFC162, KFN5162, KFA-KFZ 123.W2
River and harbor improvement: KF5580+
Rivers
  Navigation and pilotage: KF2575+
  Water resources development: KF5551+, KFC790+, KFN5790+, KFA-KFZ 447+

INDEX

Road construction workers (Labor law): KF3580.R6
Road traffic: KF2201+, KFC470+, KFN5470+, KFX2035, KFA-KFZ 296+
Roads: KF5521+, KFC787+, KFN5787+, KFX2071, KFA-KFZ 444+
Roadside protection: KF5532, KFC788, KFA-KFZ 444.6
Robbery insurance: KF1200
Rockslide prevention
Zoning: KF5700.5.L36
Rolling stock: KF2315+
Roofs (Building laws): KF5703
Rubber
Patent law: KF3159.R83
Rubber industry: KF1890.R8
Rule against perpetuities
Future estates: KF613
Life insurance: KF1181.R8
Rule of law
Constitutional law: KF382
Rules and Administration, Committee on (United States Senate): KF4987.R85
Rules, Committee on (United States House of Representatives): KF4997.R8
Rum
Taxation: KF6613.R8
Trade agreements: KF6669.R85
Rural and agricultural uses of land: KF5700, KFA-KFZ 458.9
Rural free delivery: KF2716
Rural health services (Health insurance): KF3609.R87
Rye (Price supports): KF1693.G76

S

Sabotage: KF9395, KFC1139
Safe deposit boxes (Banking): KF1030.S2
Safety equipment
Motor vehicles: KF2212, KFC472, KFN5472, KFA-KFZ 297.2
Safety, Public: KF3941+, KFC640+, KFN5640+, KFX2055+, KFA-KFZ 378+
Safety, Railroad: KF2326+, KFN5494, KFA-KFZ 301.5
Safety regulations
Labor law: KF3566+, KFC584+, KFN5584+
Motor vehicles: KF2212, KFC472, KFN5472, KFA-KFZ 297.2
Shipping: KF2541+, KFC522+, KFN5522+
Safety responsibility laws: KF2219, KFC475, KFA-KFZ 297.7
Sailors
Public welfare: KFX2045.S3
Salaries
Business corporations: KFA-KFZ 213.8
Income tax: KF6410+
Judges: KF8777, KFN5984.5.S24, KFA-KFZ 525.5.S3
Legislators: KF4967, KFC727
Teachers: KF4185, KFC660, KFN5660, KFA-KFZ 393.5
Sale, Conditional: KF1056, KFC267, KFN5267, KFA-KFZ 176.C6
Sale of assets
Insolvency and bankruptcy: KF1536.S34
Sale of business enterprises
Taxation: KF6499.S34
Sale of goods: KF911+, KFC235, KFN5235+, KFA-KFZ 156+
Sales
Conflict of laws: KF418.S2
Sales, Overseas: KF934
Sales personnel
Legal handbooks: KF390.S2
Sales personnel, Traveling: KF1348.C6
Sales tax: KF6767+
Sales tax, Retail
Federal: KF6606
Local: KF6788+, KFC912.R37, KFN5912.R37
State: KFC899, KFN5899
Salmon fishing: KF1773.S23
Salt
Import: KFN5435.S2
Salvadorean aliens: KF4848.S26

INDEX

Salvage
  Maritime law: KF1114.S2
Same-sex marriage: KF539, KFC129, KFA-KFZ 103
Sanitation
  Building laws: KFA-KFZ 459.8.H43
  Cattle industry: KF1730.4
Sanitation, Public: KF3775+, KFC610+, KFN5610+, KFX2096.7, KFA-KFZ 354+
Sanitation, Railroad: KF2326+, KFA-KFZ 301.5
Sardine fishing: KF1773.S25
Savings accounts: KF1023.6
Savings banks: KF1004, KFN5252, KFX2031.3.S2, KFA-KFZ 166.S2
Sawmills (Labor hygiene and safety): KFA-KFZ 336.S38
Scholarships
  Educational law: KF4235, KFN5666.55
  Income tax: KF6411.S3
School accidents: KF1309
School attendance: KF4158, KFA-KFZ 392+
School boards: KF4131, KFC649, KFN5649, KFA-KFZ 390.3
School buildings
  Building laws: KF5702.S3, KFN5814.S3, KFA-KFZ 459.S3
School buses: KF2239, KFA-KFZ 297.94
School discipline: KF4159
School districts
  Educational law: KF4127, KFC649, KFN5649, KFA-KFZ 390.3
  Tort liability: KF1309, KFC328, KFN5328, KFA-KFZ 198.S3
School employees
  Collective labor agreements: KF3409.S3
  Freedom of religion: KF4162
School facilities, Community use of: KF4135
School government and finance: KF4125+, KFC648+, KFN5648+, KFA-KFZ 390+

School health services: KF3826.S3, KFC619.S3, KFN5619.S3, KFA-KFZ 363.S3
School hygiene: KF3826.S3, KFC619.S3, KFN5619.S3, KFA-KFZ 363.S3
School lands
  Educational law: KF4135, KFC650, KFN5650, KFA-KFZ 390.7
  Real property taxes: KF6761.S3
School libraries: KF4219
School lunch programs: KF4143
School prayers: KF4162, KFN5655, KFA-KFZ 392.7
School principals: KF4133, KFA-KFZ 390.5
School psychologists (Education law): KF4192.5.P8
School safety patrols: KFA-KFZ 391.T7
School sports: KF4166
School superintendents: KF4133, KFA-KFZ 390.5
School transportation: KF4141, KFC652, KFN5652, KFA-KFZ 391.T7
Schools, Correspondence: KF4222
Schools, Denominational: KF4124
Schools, Private: KF4220, KFA-KFZ 395.95
Science
  Elementary and secondary education: KF4208.5.S34
Science and Astronautics, Committee on (United States House of Representatives): KF4997.S3
Science and law
  Directories: KF195.S43
Science and Technology, Committee on (United States House of Representatives): KF4997.S34
Science and the arts: KF4270+, KFC670+, KFN5670+, KFX2067, KFA-KFZ 398+
Science as a course in elementary and secondary education: KF4208.5.S34
Science, Committee on
  United States House of Representatives: KF4997.S25

INDEX

Science lawyers
  Directories: KF195.S43
Scientific exchanges: KF4330
Scientists
  Expert witnesses (Civil procedure): KF8968.66
Scientologists: KF4869.S35
Scout leaders
  Legal handbooks: KF390.S35
Sea, Carriage by: KF1096+
Sea, Collisions at: KF1107+
Seafood
  Inspection: KF1930
  Standards and grading: KF1930
Seafood industry: KF1930+
Seal of government: KF5150, KFN5749, KFA-KFZ 429
Sealing: KF1773.S33
Seals: KF1773.S33
Seam binding industry: KF1893.S3
Searches and seizures
  Criminal procedure: KF9630, KFC1157, KFN6157, KFA-KFZ 576.5
Seasonal laborers
  Immigration: KF4824.A+
Seat of government: KF5150, KFN5749, KFA-KFZ 429
Secession of states: KF4613
Secondary education: KF4195+, KFC662+, KFN5662+, KFA-KFZ 395+
Secondary mortgage market: KF697.S43
Secondhand trade: KF2038.A1+
Secret inventions: KF3128
Secretary of State: KFA-KFZ 427.5.S4
Secured transactions: KF1046+, KFC266+, KFN5266+, KFX2031.6.A2+, KFA-KFZ 175+
Securities
  Corporation finance: KF1431+, KFC350, KFN5350, KFA-KFZ 214.A1+
  Electronic data processing: KF242.S43+
  Income tax: KF6415+
  Local finance: KF6775, KFA-KFZ 489
  Marketing: KF1066+, KFC270+, KFN5270+, KFX2031.8, KFA-KFZ 179+
  Personal property tax: KF6765.5.S4, KFN5890.B6, KFA-KFZ 481.5.B6
  State and local finance: KF6724
  State finance: KF6744, KFC849, KFN5849, KFA-KFZ 468
  Stock exchanges: KFC270+, KFN5270+, KFX2031.8, KFA-KFZ 179+
Securities and Exchange Commission (U.S.): KF1444
Securities fraud: KF9369, KFA-KFZ 568.S43
Securities Investor Protection Corporation: KF1084.I5
Securities processing: KFA-KFZ 167.S43
  Banking: KF1030.S43
Security classification: KF7695.S3
Security, Internal: KF4850+, KFC701+, KFN5701+, KFA-KFZ 415+
Security measures
  Courts: KF8733.7
Sedition
  Criminal law: KF9397, KFN6138, KFA-KFZ 569
  Criminal trials: KF221.P6
  Federal and state jurisdiction: KF4621
Seeds
  Marketing regulation: KFA-KFZ 244.S4
  Standards and grading: KF1722
Segregation (Education): KF4151+, KFC654.5, KFA-KFZ 392.2
Selective Service (U.S.): KF7263+
Selectmen: KFA-KFZ 436.8.S4
Self-defense: KF9246, KFA-KFZ 566.7
Self-employed persons
  Social security: KF3664.S4
Self-incrimination: KF9668
Self-protection: KF9246, KFA-KFZ 566.7
Senate committee documents (State): KFN5010.3.A+, KFA-KFZ 11.3.A+

INDEX

Senate (U.S.): KF4980+
  Elections: KF4913
    Contested elections: KF4976+
Seniority (Employment): KF3458+
Sentence
  Criminal procedure: KF9685, KFC1172, KFN6172, KFA-KFZ 583.2
  Juvenile criminal law: KF9820
Sentence, Indeterminate: KF9754, KFN6191, KFA-KFZ 593
Separation
  Marriage law: KF531+, KFC126, KFN5126+, KFA-KFZ 100
Separation of powers: KF4565, KFC685+, KFN5685+, KFA-KFZ 405+
Servants
  Labor law: KF3580.D64
  Legal handbooks: KF390.D64
  Social security: KF3664.H6
Service, Contract of: KF894+, KFA-KFZ 154+
Service insurance
  Air Force: KF7417
  Armed Forces: KF7277
  Army: KF7317
  Coast Guard: KF7457
  Merchant Marine: KF7488.7
  Navy: KF7357
Service stations, Automobile
  Regulation: KFA-KFZ 282.A9
Service trades: KF2041+, KFC445+, KFN5445+, KFX2041.5.A+
Services
  Regulation: KFA-KFZ 282.A1+
Services, Contract for: KF898+, KFC228+, KFN5228+, KFA-KFZ 155+
Session laws: KF50+, KFC25+, KFN5025+, KFA-KFZ 25+
Settlement costs: KF681
  Real property: KFA-KFZ 127.3
Settlement of defense contracts: KF858+
Settlements
  Income tax: KF6428.D36
Settlements, Marriage: KF529

Severance tax: KF6763.9.M54, KFA-KFZ 480.5.M5
  State taxation: KF6738.M56
Sewage disposal: KF3816.S49, KFN5614.5.S48, KFA-KFZ 359.S4
Sewing machines
  Patent law: KF3159.S43
Sex crimes
  Criminal trials: KF221.S49
Sex discrimination: KF4758, KFC696, KFA-KFZ 411.7
  Labor law: KF3467
Sex-oriented businesses
  Zoning law: KF5699, KFA-KFZ 458.8
Sexual abuse of children
  Criminal law: KFN6121.5, KFA-KFZ 567.C5
Sexual behavior
  Legal implications: KF9325+
Sexual exploitation (Human trafficking): KF9449
Sexual harassment
  Labor law: KF3467
Sexual intercourse, Unnatural: KF9327+
Sexual minorities
  Civil and political rights: KF4754.5
  Discrimination against
    Labor law: KF3467.5
Sexual offenses: KF9325+, KFC1122, KFN6122+, KFA-KFZ 567.S3
Sexual orientation discrimination
  Labor law: KF3467.5
Shade control: KF5698.7, KFC811.7, KFA-KFZ 458.7
Shanghaiing: KF9338
Shareholders' rights: KF1448+, KFC353, KFN5353+, KFA-KFZ 215.S5
Shares: KF1448+, KFC353, KFN5353+, KFA-KFZ 215.S5
Sheep raising: KF1734
Shellfish fishing: KF1773.S4+
Sheltered housing: KFA-KFZ 350.H65
Sheltered workshops (Management-labor relations): KF3452.S5

Sheriffs: KF8798, KFC985.S4, KFN5985.S4, KFX2020.S5, KFA-KFZ 526.S4

Ship mortgage insurance Government insurance: KF1114.B65 Private insurance: KF1232.5

Ship mortgages: KF1114.B6

Shipbuilding industry Labor disputes: KF3450.S4+ Labor hygiene and safety: KF3574.S4, KFC586.S4 Regulation: KF1890.S4+

Shipping: KF2601+, KFN5534, KFA-KFZ 314

Shipping Board (U.S.): KF2608

Shipping industry: KF2606+

Ships: KF2536+, KFC521+, KFN5521+, KFA-KFZ 308.1+

Ships, Historical: KF4310+

Shipyards Labor hygiene and safety: KF3574.S4

Shoe trade Wages: KF3505.S4

Shop committees: KF3542

Shop stewards: KF3542

Shoplifting: KFA-KFZ 568.T45

Shopping centers (Building laws): KF5702.S45

Shore protection: KF5627, KFC804.3, KFA-KFZ 451.8

Shorthand (Law office management): KF320.S4

Sick leave: KF3532

Sickle cell anemia: KF3803.S55

Sidewalk accidents: KFN5320.S5

Signal Corps (U.S. Army): KF7335.S4

Signboards: KF5532, KFA-KFZ 444.6

Silk Import trade: KF1996.S55

Silk industry: KF1886.S4

Silver money: KF6213

Ski lifts: KFN5504.C2, KFA-KFZ 304.C2

Slaughtering of animals: KF3844

Slavery Constitutional history: KF4545.S7, KFA-KFZ 401.6.S55

Slavery Criminal law: KF9335

Slavery (Human trafficking): KF9449

Slaves: KF482.A2+

Sleep disorders: KF3803.S62

Sleepy Lagoon Trial, Los Angeles, 1942-1943: KF224.S49

Slide fastener industry: KF1893.S5

Slip and fall accidents: KF1290.S55

Slum clearance: KF5721+, KFC820, KFN5820, KFA-KFZ 460+

Small business Investment companies: KF1080 Regulation: KF1659, KFC379, KFN5379, KFA-KFZ 234 Taxation: KF6491

Small Business Administration (U.S.): KF1659.1

Small Business, Committee on (United States House of Representatives): KF4997.S6

Small Business, Committee on (United States Senate): KF4987.S6

Small business corporations (Taxation): KF6491, KFC878

Small claims courts: KF8769, KFC976, KFN5976, KFA-KFZ 521+

Small loans: KFA-KFZ 171

Smoking Air pollution: KF3812+

Smoking, Claims for injuries from: KF1297.T63

Smuggling: KF6699

Smuggling of humans: KF9449.5

Snowmobiles (Motor vehicle laws): KF2220.S6, KFA-KFZ 297.75.S64

Social activities: KF3985+, KFC645+, KFN5645+, KFA-KFZ 381.5+

Social disabilities, Students with: KF4216

Social insurance: KF3600+, KFC590+, KFN5590+, KFA-KFZ 340+ Merchant mariners: KF1132+, KFN5285+

Social legislation: KF3300+, KFC555+, KFN5555+, KFP331+, KFX2045.A2+, KFX2096.6, KFA-KFZ 331+

INDEX

Social sciences: KF4280.S6
Social security: KF3641+, KFC595, KFN5595+, KFA-KFZ 344
Social security cases
  Trial practice: KF8925.S63
Social security taxes: KF3651+, KFN5595.5
Social service agencies (Tort liability): KF1311
Social worker and client (Privileged communications): KF8959.S6
Social workers
  Education law: KF4192.5.S63
  Expert witnesses (Civil procedure): KF8968.7
  Legal handbooks: KF390.S6
  Regulation of profession: KF3721+, KFC601, KFN5600.5, KFA-KFZ 349.5
Societies, Patriotic: KF1359.A1+
Society of Friends
  Church and state: KF4869.Q83
Sodomy: KF9328.S6
Soft drink industry: KF1940.S65
  Collective labor agreements: KF3409.S6
Software
  Personal property tax: KFA-KFZ 481.7.C65
Software industry
  Income tax: KF6495.C57
Soil banks: KF1705+
Soil conservation: KF1686, KFC386, KFA-KFZ 239
Solar access zoning (Land use): KF5698.7, KFC811.7, KFA-KFZ 458.7
Solar energy (Public utilities): KF2140.S65+, KFC468.8.S65, KFN5468.8.S6, KFA-KFZ 291.S64
Soldiers: KF7250+
  Homestead law: KF5673.S6
  Suffrage: KF4894, KFC712.S6, KFN5712.S6
Soldiers' homes: KF7716+
Solicitors General: KF8792.5
South Carolina
  Laws: KFS1801+

South Dakota
  Laws: KFS3001+
Soybeans
  Marketing regulations: KFA-KFZ 244.S66
Space exploration: KF4280.S7
Space law: KF2471+
Special districts: KF5332, KFC759, KFA-KFZ 433
Special masters (Trial practice): KF8986, KFN6049, KFA-KFZ 543
Special pleadings: KF8876
Specie: KF1030.R35
Specific performance: KF837
Speech, Freedom of: KF4772
Speech therapists: KF2915.S63+, KFA-KFZ 326.5.S64+
Speedy trial: KF9223.4, KFC1102.4, KFA-KFZ 562.4
Spendthrift trusts: KF736.S6, KFN5194.S63
Spice industry: KF1939
Spinoffs
  Corporation law: KF1478
Sports: KF3989, KFC645, KFN5645, KFA-KFZ 384
  Legal research: KF241.S66
Sports accidents: KF1290.S66, KFA-KFZ 196.3.S65
Sports physicians: KF2910.S65+
Sprinkler irrigation contractors: KF2930.S67+
Stalking (Criminal law): KF9324.5
Stamp duties: KF6645, KFA-KFZ 486
Stamped envelopes: KF2733
Standard clauses (Contracts): KF808
Standard forms (Contracts): KF808
Standard time
  Regulation: KF1668
Standards
  Petroleum: KFA-KFZ 258.S7
Standards and grading
  Agricultural commodities: KF1721+
    Apples: KF1725.A6
    Cattle: KF1726.C2
    Dairy products: KF1921
    Eggs and egg products: KF1916

Standards and grading
Agricultural commodities
Field crops: KF1724.A+
Fruit: KF1725.A1+
Livestock: KF1726.A1+
Meat: KF1726.A1+
Poultry: KF1726.P6
Poultry products: KF1915
Seeds: KF1722+
Sheep: KF1726.A1+
Vegetables: KF1725.A1+
Standards of Official Conduct, Committee on (United States House of Representatives): KF4997.S73
Star routes: KF2717
Stare decisis: KF429
Start-up expenses
Income tax: KF6395.S73
State action, Claims for damages resulting from
Trial practice: KF8925.C5
State action doctrine
Antitrust law: KF1657.S72
State aid to education: KFA-KFZ 391.S7
State and church: KF4865+, KFC705+, KFN5705+, KFA-KFZ 417
State and federal relations: KF4600+
State and local finance: KF6720+
State and local revenue (General): KF6724
State and local taxation (General): KF6730
State banks: KF1020
State bar associations: KF330+
State civil service: KF5390, KFC760+, KFN5760+, KFA-KFZ 435+
State constitutional conventions: KF4529+
State constitutions: KF4529+, KF4530, KFC680, KFN5680, KFA-KFZ 401
State court judges: KF8785
State emblem: KFN5749, KFA-KFZ 429
State executives: KF5050.Z95
State finance: KF6735+
State forests: KF5648, KFC805+, KFN5805+, KFA-KFZ 452+
State government lawyers
Directories: KF195.L62
State jurisdiction (Interstate commerce): KF1663
State legislation (Indexes): KF85, KFN5040, KFA-KFZ 40
State legislatures: KF4933, KFC721+, KFN5721+, KFA-KFZ 421+
State parks: KF5648, KFC805+, KFN5805+, KFA-KFZ 452+
State police: KFA-KFZ 435.8.S7
State preserves: KF5648, KFA-KFZ 452+
State revenue: KF6750+, KFC856+, KFN5850+, KFA-KFZ 469+
State taxation: KFC860+, KFN5860+, KFA-KFZ 470+
State trade jurisdiction: KF1663
Statehood
Constitutional history: KF4545.S7, KFA-KFZ 401.6.S8
Statistical methods (Law office management): KF320.S73
Statisticians
Expert witnesses (Civil procedure): KF8968.75
Statistics: KF180+, KFN5070, KFX2007+
Statute of frauds
Conflict of laws: KF418.S7
Contracts: KF810
Statutes
Checklists: KF2
Citators: KF78, KFA-KFZ 39
Codification: KF53+, KFN5027.A+
Compilations: KF60+, KFN5029+
Construction: KF425
Digests: KF85, KFN5038, KFA-KFZ 38
General compilations: KFA-KFZ 29+
Indexes: KF85, KFN5040, KFA-KFZ 40
Interpretation: KF425, KFN5091
Revision: KF53+, KFN5027.A+
Session laws: KF50+, KFN5025+, KFA-KFZ 25+
Statutes at large (U.S.): KF50+

INDEX

Steam boilers
  Public safety: KF3970, KFA-KFZ 380.5.S7
  Taxation: KF6633.S65
Steamboat Inspection Service (U.S.): KF2550.5
Steamboats
  Patent law: KF3159.S72
Steel
  Trade agreements: KF6669.S83
Steerage passengers
  Shipping laws: KF2625
Stem cells
  Medical legislation: KF3827.S74
Sterilization (Eugenics): KF3832
Sterilization of criminals: KFA-KFZ 565.S7
Stipends, Mass: KF760.M2
Stock, Corporate (Taxation): KF6558, KFC886, KFN5886, KFA-KFZ 480.8
Stock exchange transactions: KF1066+, KFC270+, KFN5270+
Stock-exchange transactions: KFA-KFZ 179+
Stock exchange transactions
  Taxation: KF6633.S7, KFN5900.S7
Stock exchanges: KF1066+
Stock transfers: KF1454, KFC353, KFN5353+, KFA-KFZ 215.S5
  Taxation: KF6499.S34
Stockbrokers: KF1071, KFN5272
Stockholder suits: KF8925.S7, KFN6028.S74
Stockholders' meetings: KF1450+, KFN5354+
Stockholders' rights: KF1448+, KFN5353+
Stores, Department: KF2030
Strategic alliances
  Business associations: KF1380.6+
Streetcar accidents: KF1290.S7, KFA-KFZ 196.3.S7
Streetcar lines: KF2393, KFC501, KFN5503, KFX2034.5.S7, KFA-KFZ 303
Tort liability: KF1290.S7
Streets: KFX2071

Strict liability: KF1292+, KFC321+, KFN5321+, KFA-KFZ 197.5
Strikes: KF3430+, KFN5566, KFA-KFZ 333+
Strip mining: KF1823, KFA-KFZ 255.5
Structures other than buildings
  Building laws: KF5710, KFA-KFZ 459.9
Student bar associations: KF288
Student discipline: KFA-KFZ 392.6
Student government
  Higher education: KF4243
Student personnel services: KF4248
Student publications: KF4165
Student records: KF4156.5, KFA-KFZ 392.5
Student teachers: KF4190.S8
Students
  Educational law: KF4150+, KFC654+, KFN5654+, KFA-KFZ 392+
  Freedom of religion: KF4162
  Immigration: KF4825.S7
Students, Blind: KF4212
Students, Exceptionally gifted: KFC665.E9
Students, Law: KF287+
Students' societies: KF4164
Students with disabilities: KF4210+, KFN5665.P4, KFA-KFZ 395.9.H3
Students with mental disabilities: KF4215
Students with social disabilities: KF4216
Suability of states: KF1322
Subcontracting
  Government contracts: KF869.3
  Labor law: KF3475
Subdivision of land: KF5697+, KFC811+, KFN5811, KFA-KFZ 458+
Submerged lands
  Jurisdiction: KF4627, KFC693
  Tidal oil: KF1856, KFC408, KFA-KFZ 258.S8
Subpoena: KF8952, KFC1040.5
Subprime mortgage loans: KF697.S83
Subrogation
  Contracts: KF814, KFN5221

INDEX

Subrogation
Workers' compensation: KF3623.S8
Subsidiary and parent companies: KF1465
Subsoil rights: KFA-KFZ 123.S8
Subversive activities
Constitutional law: KF4850+, KFC701+, KFN5701+, KFA-KFZ 415+
Criminal law: KF9397, KFN6138, KFA-KFZ 569
Subversive Activities Control Board (U.S.): KF4851
Subversive propaganda (through the mail): KF2738
Subway accidents: KF1290.S7
Subways: KF2393, KFC501, KFN5503, KFX2034.5.S8, KFA-KFZ 303
Tort liability: KF1290.S7
Succession, Intestate: KF771+, KFN5208, KFA-KFZ 146
Succession, Testate: KF755+, KFC201, KFN5201+, KFP144+, KFA-KFZ 144+
Succession to the Presidency: KF5082
Suffrage: KF4891+, KFC711+, KFN5711+, KFA-KFZ 420.85.S9
Indians: KF8210.S84
Soldiers: KF4894, KFC712.S6, KFN5712.S6
Women: KF4895
Sugar
Import trade: KF1996.S8
Refining: KF1907
Taxation: KF6633.S8
Sugar beets (Price supports): KF1693.S8
Sugar cane (Price supports): KF1693.S8
Sugar industry
Labor law: KF3580.S8
Price fixing: KF1629.S8
Suicide clause (Life insurance): KF1178.I5
Summary convictions: KFA-KFZ 583.5
Summary judgment
Civil procedure: KFA-KFZ 546.S8
Summation: KF8924

Sunday legislation: KF2009, KFN5439, KFA-KFZ 281.S8
Sunglasses industry: KF1893.S8
Sunset reviews of government programs: KF4943, KFN5722.5, KFA-KFZ 421.5.S95
Superior Court: KFP48+, KFP48
Pennsylvania
Organization: KFP513
Supervening impossibility: KF832
Support
Domestic relations: KFC133, KFN5130, KFA-KFZ 104.8
Income tax: KF6428.A4
Supreme Court (California)
Court rules: KFC1081
Organization: KFC960
Procedure: KFC1081
Supreme Court (New York)
Organization: KFN5964
Procedure: KFN6078+
Reports: KFN5048+
Supreme Court (Pennsylvania)
Organization: KFP512
Supreme Court (U.S.): KF8741+
Court rules: KF9056
Organization: KF8741+
Procedure: KF9056+
Reports: KF101+
Suretyship and guaranty
Contracts: KF1045, KFC265, KFN5265, KFA-KFZ 174
Insurance: KF1223+, KFC300, KFN5300+, KFA-KFZ 192.S8
Suretyship insurance: KF1223+, KFC300, KFN5300+, KFA-KFZ 192.S8
Surgeon General's Office (United States Army): KF7335.S85
Surplus agricultural commodities: KF1709+
Meat: KF1911
Poultry products: KF1915
Surplus government property: KF5840+, KFA-KFZ 462.6.S87
Military: KF5846+

INDEX

Surpluses
- Cattle industry: KF1730.3

Surrogates' courts: KFN5205, KFX2005.95

Surtaxes
- Income tax: KF6404+, KFC877, KFN5877
- Corporations: KF6471+

Surveyors: KF2940.S87+, KFN5547.S85+, KFA-KFZ 329.S88+
- Expert witnesses
- Civil procedure: KF8968.77

Surveys of local administration of justice
- New York City: KFX2007+

Survivors' benefits: KF3641+, KFC595, KFN5595+
- Judges: KF8777
- Social security: KFA-KFZ 344
- Veterans
  - 1939-1945: KF7737
  - 1945-: KF7747

Suspects, Rights of: KF9625+, KFC1156, KFN6156, KFA-KFZ 576

Susquehanna River Basin (Water resources): KF5590.S9

Swamps: KF5624, KFA-KFZ 451.7

Swimming pools
- Legal aspects: KF390.5.S9, KFA-KFZ 84.5.S95

Synthetic fuels (Public utilities): KF2140.S95+

Synthetic rubber industry: KF1876.R8

Syrups: KF3879.S9

Systems of citation: KF245, KFN5074.5

T

Tank vessels: KFA-KFZ 308.5.T35
- Safety regulations: KF2558.T2

Tariff: KF6651+

Tariff Commission (U.S.): KF6662

Tariff preferences: KF6708.P7

Tattoo artists: KFA-KFZ 329.T55+

Tattoo establishments: KFA-KFZ 282.T37

Taverns
- Wages: KF3505.H6

Tax accounting: KF6314

Tax administration: KF6300+, KFC863+, KFN5863+, KFA-KFZ 471+

Tax collection: KF6310+, KFC865+, KFN5865, KFA-KFZ 471+

Tax consultants: KF6320

Tax courts: KF6324, KFC866, KFN5866, KFA-KFZ 471.5

Tax credits (Income tax): KF6397, KFC870.5, KFN5873.5.T37, KFA-KFZ 475.5.T35

Tax deeds
- Land transfer: KF685.T2, KFA-KFZ 128.T2

Tax delinquency: KFC865.5

Tax evasion: KF6334, KFN5869

Tax-exempt lands: KF6761+

Tax exemption: KF6329, KFN5868, KFA-KFZ 472+

Tax expenditures: KF6298, KFA-KFZ 470.8

Tax foreclosure: KFA-KFZ 471.9.F6

Tax incentives: KFA-KFZ 473

Tax lawyers: KF299.T3
- Directories: KF195.T38

Tax liens: KF6316, KFA-KFZ 471.9.L5

Tax penalties: KF6321

Tax planning: KF6296+, KFC861, KFN5861, KFA-KFZ 470.5

Tax procedure: KF6300+, KFC863+, KFN5863+, KFA-KFZ 471+

Tax sales
- Land transfer: KF685.T2
- Real property tax: KFA-KFZ 479.8.F58
- State revenue: KFA-KFZ 471.9.F6

Tax saving: KF6296+, KFC861, KFN5861, KFA-KFZ 470.5

Tax shelters: KF6297.5
- Trial practice: KF8925.T38

Tax valuation: KF6528, KFC880.5

Taxation
- Business organizations: KF6450+
- Data processing: KF242.T38+
- Federal: KF6271+
- Indians: KF8210.T3, KFA-KFZ 505.6.T38

INDEX

Taxation
- Legal research: KF241.T38

Taxation, Double: KF6306, KFC864

Taxation in divorce
- Income tax: KFA-KFZ 475.5.D58

Taxation Joint Committee on (U.S. Congress): KF4939.5.T39

Taxation, Local: KFN5910+

Taxation of land
- Federal taxes: KF6535+

Taxation of real property
- Federal taxes: KF6535+

Taxes as deductions (Income tax): KF6390

Taxicabs: KF2263, KFN5483, KFA-KFZ 300.T3

Teachers
- Collective labor agreements: KF3409.T4, KFC562.T4, KFN5562.T4, KFX2045.E37, KFA-KFZ 332.8.T4
- Educational law: KF4175+, KFC658+, KFN5658+, KFA-KFZ 393+
- Labor disputes: KF3450.T43+, KFA-KFZ 333.8.T4

Teachers' assistants: KF4190.T43

Teachers' pensions: KF4185, KFC660, KFN5660, KFA-KFZ 393.5

Teachers, Student: KF4190.S8

Technical education: KF4208

Technology and law
- Directories: KF195.S43

Telecommunication: KF2761+, KFC540+, KFN5540+, KFX2038, KFA-KFZ 318+

Telecommunication facilities
- Taxation: KF6633.T3, KFA-KFZ 485.T44

Telecommunication industry
- Labor hygiene and safety: KFA-KFZ 336.T4
- Management-labor relations: KF3452.T45

Telecommunication towers
- Zoning: KF5700.5.A58

Telecommuting
- Law office management: KF320.T44

Telegrams
- Privileged communications: KF8959.5.T4

Telegraph: KF2775+, KFC541, KFN5541, KFA-KFZ 318.3
- Taxation: KF6633.T3, KFA-KFZ 485.T44

Telemarketing: KF2026.5

Telephone: KF2780+, KFN5542, KFA-KFZ 318.5
- Taxation: KF6633.T3, KFA-KFZ 485.T44

Teletype: KF2775+, KFC541, KFN5541

Television as a teaching medium: KF4209.T3

Television broadcasting: KF2840+, KFC543, KFA-KFZ 318.6
- Collective labor agreements: KF3409.R2
- Court proceedings: KF8726

Television receiver industry: KF1893.R2

Television receivers
- Retail trade: KF2036.T4

Temporary employment: KF3580.T45

Temporary lawyers: KF299.T46

Tenancy: KF585+, KFC145+, KFN5145, KFA-KFZ 117+

Tenancy by the entirety: KF621+

Tender (Payment): KF827+

Tennessee
- Laws: KFT1+

Tennessee Valley Authority: KF5590.T4

Tenure
- Civil service
  - County: KFA-KFZ 437.5
  - Federal: KF5370+
  - Municipal: KFA-KFZ 436.5
  - State: KFC768+, KFN5768+, KFA-KFZ 435.5
- Judges: KF8776, KFA-KFZ 525.5.A6
- Real property: KFX2022
- Teachers: KF4175, KFC658, KFN5658, KFA-KFZ 393

Territory, National: KF4635

Terrorism: KF9430
- Criminal law: KFN6145

INDEX

Testamentary trusts: KF735
Testate succession: KF755+, KFC201, KFN5201+, KFP144+, KFA-KFZ 144+
Texas
  Laws: KFT1201+
Textile industries
  Collective labor agreements: KF3409.T45
  Regulation: KF1881+, KFA-KFZ 269.A1+
  Textile labeling: KF1620.T3+
Theater: KF4296, KFA-KFZ 398.5
Theater buildings (Building laws): KF5702.T4
Theft insurance: KF1200
Therapists, Occupational: KF2915.T45+, KFC546.5.T54+, KFN5546.5.T5+, KFA-KFZ 326.5.T5+
Therapists, Physical: KF2915.T45+, KFC546.5.T54+, KFN5546.5.T5+, KFA-KFZ 326.5.T5+
Thievery: KF9352+, KFC1131, KFA-KFZ 568.T45
THOMAS (Computer file): KF49.T56
Threats: KF9372+, KFC1132, KFN6132, KFA-KFZ 568.T57
Ticket brokers (Railroads): KF2366
Tidal oil: KF1856, KFC408, KFA-KFZ 258.S8
Tie-ins
  Antitrust law: KF1657.T53
Timber laws: KF1750, KFC396, KFN5396, KFA-KFZ 249
Time: KF450.T5, KFC100.T54, KFN5100.T5, KFA-KFZ 90.T5
Tin industry (International trade): KF1984.T5
Tips: KF3658.T5
Title abstractors (Directories): KF195.T5
Title examiners (Directories): KF195.T5
Title insurance: KF1234, KFN5303, KFA-KFZ 193.T5
Title investigation: KF666+, KFC170+, KFC171, KFN5170+, KFN5171
  Real property: KFA-KFZ 127

Title investigators (Directories): KF195.T5
Title transfer (Motor vehicles): KF2215, KFC474, KFN5474, KFA-KFZ 297.4
Tobacco
  Advertising: KF1616.T5
  Drug laws: KF3894.T63
  Grading: KF1724.T6
  Import trade: KF1996.T6
  Price supports: KF1693.T6
  Products liability: KF1297.T63
  Standards and grading: KF1724.T6
  Taxation: KF6635, KFC900.T62, KFA-KFZ 485.T6
Tobacco industry: KF1910.T6
  Collective labor agreements: KF3409.T6
Tobacco products
  Import trade: KF1996.T6
  Marketing regulations: KFA-KFZ 244.T63
  Regulation: KFC417.T6
  Taxation: KF6635, KFC900.T62, KFA-KFZ 485.T6
Tobacco smoking
  Air pollution: KF3812.3, KFA-KFZ 358.3
Tobacco workers (Fringe benefits): KF3519.T6
Tomato processing industry: KF1909.T6
Tomatoes (Marketing): KFC391.5.T65
Toothprints
  Criminal law: KF9666.5, KFN6167, KFA-KFZ 580.5.M4
Tornado insurance: KF1207
Torrens system: KF679, KFC172, KFN5172
Tort liability, Government: KF1321+, KFC332, KFN5332+, KFA-KFZ 199.G6
Tort liability of acupuncturists: KF2913.A28+
Tort liability of buses: KF1290.S7
Tort liability of chiropractors: KF2913.C4+

INDEX

Tort liability of Christian-Science healers: KF2913.C45+

Tort liability of colleges and universities: KF1303.2.C6

Tort liability of corporations: KF1301+, KFC324, KFN5324, KFA-KFZ 198.C5

Tort liability of correctional personnel: KF1308

Tort liability of dentists and dental specialists: KF2910.D3+

Tort liability of government employees: KF1306.A2+, KFC327

Tort liability of local transit lines: KF1290.S7

Tort liability of municipal corporations: KF1302.A2+, KFC324, KFN5324, KFX2020.5, KFA-KFZ 198.M8

Tort liability of nonprofit corporations: KF1303+, KFN5325

Tort liability of nurses: KF2915.N8+

Tort liability of optometrists: KF2915.O6+

Tort liability of pharmacists: KF2915.P4+

Tort liability of public officers: KF1306.A2+

Tort liability of public officers and government employees: KFA-KFZ 198.P8

Tort liability of quacks: KF2913.Q2+

Tort liability of school boards and staff: KF4159, KFA-KFZ 392.6

Tort liability of school districts: KF1309, KFC328, KFN5325, KFA-KFZ 198.S3

Tort liability of street cars: KF1290.S7

Tort liability of subways: KF1290.S7

Tort liability of teachers: KF1310

Tort liability of the police: KF1307

Tort liability of universities and colleges: KF1303.2.C6

Tortious interference: KFA-KFZ 197.T67

Torts: KF1246+, KFC310+, KFN5310+, KFA-KFZ 195+

Conflict of laws: KF418.T6

Legal research: KF241.T67

Trial practice: KF8925.T67

Town clerks: KFA-KFZ 436.8.T6

Town counsel: KFA-KFZ 436.8.C55

Township courts: KFC975

Township government: KFA-KFZ 432.5

Toxic substances

Public safety: KF3958+, KFC641.5.P6

Toxic torts

Trial practice: KF8925.T69

Toxigenic fungi: KF3964.M64

Public health hazards: KFA-KFZ 359.M65

Toy industry: KF1893.T68

Trade agreements: KF6665+

Trade and commerce: KF1970+, KFC430+, KFN5430+, KFX2031+, KFA-KFZ 280+

Trade associations: KF1661

Trade barriers (Interstate commerce): KF1663

Trade practices: KF1601+, KFC375+, KFA-KFZ 230

Trade regulation: KF1600.2+, KFC375+, KFN5375+, KFX2024+, KFA-KFZ 230+

Trade, Restraint of: KF1624+

Trademark infringement: KF3193

Trademark violation crimes: KF9359

Trademarks: KF3176+, KFC550, KFN5550+, KFN5552, KFA-KFZ 330

Income tax: KF6428.I5

Trades

Regulation: KFA-KFZ 282.A1+

Trading in corporate securities, Insider: KF1073.I5

Trading on margin: KF1073.M3

Trading stamps: KFA-KFZ 281.T7

Trading with the enemy (International trade): KF1980

Traffic accident claims (Trial practice): KF8925.T7, KFA-KFZ 539.T7

Traffic accidents: KF1306.T7

Government liability: KF1325.T7

Traffic courts: KF2232, KFA-KFZ 297.85

Traffic regulation: KF2226+, KFC477, KFN5477, KFX2035, KFA-KFZ 297.8

Traffic signs: KF2234, KFN5478, KFA-KFZ 297.9

Traffic violation claims (Trial practice): KF8925.T7, KFA-KFZ 539.T7

Traffic violations: KF2231, KFC477, KFN5477, KFA-KFZ 297.8

Trafficking in humans: KF9449

Trailer camps: KFA-KFZ 282.T68

Trailer industry (Collective labor disputes): KF3450.T7+

Trailers (Road traffic): KF2220.T6, KFC476.T65, KFA-KFZ 297.75.T7

Transactions, Taxes on Federal: KF6600+ State: KFC898+, KFN5898+, KFA-KFZ 483+

Transfer inter vivos Land transfer: KF665+, KFC169+, KFN5169+

Transfer of land: KF664.2+, KFC166+, KFN5166+, KFA-KFZ 126+

Transfer of personal property: KF715+, KFN5185

Transfer of real property: KF664.2+

Transgender people Civil and political rights: KF4754.5 Discrimination against Labor law: KF3467.5

Transit, Local: KF2391+, KFC501, KFN5502+, KFX2034+, KFA-KFZ 303

Translating (Law office management): KF320.T73

Translation (Copyright): KF3030.7

Translators Court employees: KF8806, KFA-KFZ 526.T72

Transportation Federal aid: KF2186 Labor disputes: KF3450.T8+ Labor law: KF3580.T7 Management-labor relations: KF3452.T73 Taxation: KF6636.T7, KFN5900.T7

Transportation and communication Metropolitan area government: KFX2096.4

Transportation and communication Regulation: KF2161+, KFC469+, KFN5469+, KFX2034+, KFA-KFZ 295+

Transportation and Infrastructure, Committee on United States House of Representatives: KF4997.T7

Transportation, Automotive: KF2201+, KFC470+, KFN5470+, KFA-KFZ 296+

Transportation insurance: KF1192

Transportation lawyers (Directories): KF195.T7

Travel agents: KF2042.T75, KFA-KFZ 282.T7

Travel expenses (Income tax): KF6395.T7

Travel regulations Civil service: KF5387, KFA-KFZ 435.6

Travelers, Commercial: KF1348.C6

Traveling sales personnel: KF1348.C6

Treason: KF9392, KFA-KFZ 569 Criminal trials: KF221.P6

Treasure troves: KF713.T7, KFN5182

Treasury Department (U.S.): KF6200.5

Treaty-making power (United States President): KF5055

Trees Legal aspects: KF390.5.T73

Trespass to land: KF1272

Trespass (Torts): KFA-KFZ 197.T73

Trial Civil procedure: KFC1025+, KFN6025+, KFA-KFZ 538+ Criminal procedure: KF9655+, KFC1162+, KFN6162+, KFA-KFZ 579+ Juvenile criminal law: KF9815+, KFA-KFZ 598.3

Trial by newspaper: KF9223.5, KFC1102.5, KFN6102.5

Trial courts (Federal) Circuit courts: KF8754+ Commissioners: KF8792 Reports: KF115+ District courts: KF8754+

INDEX

Trial courts (Federal)
- District courts
  - Court rules: KF8820+
  - Reports: KF120+
  - Older courts: KF8757
- Trial courts (State)
  - Court rules: KFN5992+, KFP529+, KFA-KFZ 529+
  - Organization: KFN5968+, KFP515+, KFA-KFZ 515+
  - Reports: KFN5051+, KFA-KFZ 51+

Trial practice
- Civil procedure: KF8911+, KFC1025+, KFN6025+, KFA-KFZ 538+
- Criminal procedure: KF9656

Trial practice lawyers (Directories): KF195.L53

Trial tactics
- Civil procedure: KFC1025+, KFN6025+

Trials
- Civil: KF228+
- Courts-martial
  - Air Force: KF7657.5.A+
  - Army: KF7642.A+
  - Navy: KF7652.A+
- Criminal: KF219+
- Impeachment: KF4961.A2+

Tribal citizenship: KFA-KFZ 505.6.T74

Tribal enrollment: KFA-KFZ 505.6.T74

Tribal law, Indian: KF8220+

Tribal trust funds: KF8210.T6

Trip leasing: KF2268.T7, KFC486.T7

Tris: KF3964.D53

Trout
- Labeling: KF1620.T7

Trover: KF1274

Truancy: KF4158, KFA-KFZ 392+

Truck lines: KF2265

Trucking industry (Collective labor agreements): KF3409.T65, KFN5562.T7

Trucks (Road traffic): KF2220.T7, KFC476.T7, KFN5476.T7, KFA-KFZ 300.T78

Trust companies: KF744+, KFN5193, KFX2031.3.T7, KFA-KFZ 138
- Income tax: KF6495.T6

Trust funds, Indian tribal: KF8210.T6

Trust indentures: KF1457

Trust investments: KF1083, KFA-KFZ 179.5.L4

Trust receipts: KF1061, KFA-KFZ 176.T7

Trustees: KF744+

Trusts
- Income tax: KF6443, KFA-KFZ 475.5.T78

Trusts and trustees: KF726+, KFC188+, KFN5188+, KFA-KFZ 137+
- Conflict of laws: KF418.T7

Trusts, Charitable: KF739+, KFN5189

Trusts, General: KF733

Trusts, Land: KFA-KFZ 139.L3

Trusts, Life insurance: KF736.L4

Trusts, Living: KF734

Trusts, Private: KF733+

Trusts, Testamentary: KF735

Tuberculosis
- Public health laws: KF3803.T8, KFC613.5.T8, KFA-KFZ 357.8.T83

Tuberculosis in animals
- Veterinary law: KFA-KFZ 369.T8

Tuna fishing: KF1773.T8

Tunnels: KFA-KFZ 445

Turnover tax: KF6598+

TVA: KF5590.T4

Tying arrangements
- Antitrust law: KF1657.T53

Typewriting (Law office management): KF320.T9

U

U.S. Employment Service: KF3676

U.S. Tariff Commission: KF6662

Ultra vires
- Corporations: KF1386.U5

Umbrella industry: KF1893.U5

Un-American Activities, Committee on (United States House of Representatives: KF4997.I48

INDEX

Unauthorized practice of law: KF308+
Unauthorized publication of picture: KF1263.U5
Unborn children: KF481
Unclaimed estates: KF780, KFA-KFZ 148.U6
Underground space: KF579
Undertakers: KF2042.U5, KFC446.U6, KFN5446.U6, KFA-KFZ 282.U5
Underwriting (Insurance) Multiple-line: KF1170.5
Undue influence
Void and voidable contracts: KF820
Unemployment insurance: KF3671+, KFC596, KFN5596, KFA-KFZ 345
Merchant mariners: KFN5286
Unfair competition: KF3195+, KFC553, KFN5553
Unfair trade practices: KF1601+
Retail trade: KF2022, KFN5440
Uniform manufacturing industry: KF1893.U55
Uniform regulations
Air Force: KF7420
Armed Forces: KF7280
Army: KF7320
Coast Guard: KF7460
Marine Corps: KF7391
Navy: KF7360
Uniform state laws (General): KF165.A2+, KFN5067, KFA-KFZ 67
Unincorporated associations: KF1361+, KFC338+, KFN5338+, KFA-KFZ 206+
Uninsured motorist insurance: KF1218.8, KFC298.A86, KFN5298.A86, KFA-KFZ 191.A43
Union lists of library holdings: KF4
Union organization: KF3400+
Unions, Maritime: KF1127
Unit operation of oil fields, wells, etc.: KF1853
Unit pricing: KFA-KFZ 281.U5
United States Civil Service Commission: KF5338
United States Coast Guard: KF7445+
United States Code: KF61+
United States commissioners: KF8792

United States congressional serial set: KF12
United States Court of Appeals for the Federal Circuit: KF3157
United States Court of Military Appeals: KF7667
United States Customs Court: KF6698
United States Employees Compensation Commission: KF3626.5.A2+
United States Fish and Wildlife Service: KF1770.1
United States Foreign Service: KF5112+
United States magistrates: KF8792
United States Marine Corps: KF7385+
United States Maritime Commission: KF2609
United States marshals: KF8794
United States Revised Statutes: KF60
United States Shipping Board: KF2608
United States Warehouse Act: KF2056
Universities: KF4225+, KFC666, KFN5666+, KFA-KFZ 396+
Unjust enrichment: KF1244, KFC309, KFA-KFZ 194
Unjust enrichment tax: KF6405
Unlawful contracts: KF818.A+, KFN5222
Unmarried couples: KF538, KFC128
Unsatisfied judgment funds: KF1219, KFN5298.A88, KFA-KFZ 191.A44
Uranium mining industry: KF1836.U6
Regulation: KFA-KFZ 257.U7
Urologists: KF2910.U75+
Usage and custom: KF427
Use taxes
Federal: KF6609
State: KF6767+, KFC899.5, KFA-KFZ 484.5
Usury: KFC261
Contracts (General): KF818.U7
Loans: KF1036, KFN5261, KFX2031.5, KFA-KFZ 170
Utah
Laws: KFU1+

V

Vacationing: KFA-KFZ 382
Vacations: KF3531
- Civil service: KF5384
- Labor law: KFC577, KFN5577, KFA-KFZ 334.5.V32

Vaccination
- Public health laws: KF3808+, KFA-KFZ 357.9.I44

Vaccines: KF3894.B5
- Products liability: KF1297.V32

Vagrancy: KF9450
Value-added tax: KF6598
Van pools (Motor vehicle laws): KF2239.5, KFA-KFZ 298
Variable annuities (Life insurance): KF1177.V3, KFA-KFZ 186.5.V3
Variable contracts (Life insurance): KF1177.V3, KFA-KFZ 186.5.V3
Variable rate mortgage loans: KF697.V37
Varnish
- Labeling: KF1620.P2

VAT: KF6598
Vegetable oils and fats
- Inspection: KF1935
- Price supports: KF1935
- Standards and grading: KF1935
- Surpluses: KF1935
- Taxation
  - Excise tax: KF6627+
  - Processing tax: KF6631.O4

Vegetable oils and fats industry: KF1935+
Vegetable processing industry: KF1908+
Vending machines: KF2034
Vending stands: KFA-KFZ 281.V45
Vendor and purchaser: KF665.A15+, KFC169, KFN5169, KFA-KFZ 126
Venereal diseases: KF3803.V3, KFA-KFZ 357.8.V46
Ventures, Joint: KF1380.5
Verdict, Directed: KF9682+, KFC1171, KFN6171, KFA-KFZ 583

Vermont
- Laws: KFV1+

Vessels, Historical: KF4310+
Veterans: KF7701+, KFC935+, KFN5935, KFA-KFZ 502+
- Citizenship: KF4720.V3
- Educational assistance: KF7739.E3, KF7749.E3
- Financial assistance: KF7739.F5, KF7749.F5
- Homesteads: KF5673.S6
- Hospitals: KF7739.M35, KF7749.M35
- Nationality: KF4720.V3
- Pensions: KF7701+, KFC935+, KFN5935, KFA-KFZ 502+
  - By period: KF7721
- Preferential employment: KF3460
  - Civil service: KF5352, KFN5765

Veterans' Administration (U.S.): KF7711
Veterans' Affairs, Committee on (United States House of Representatives): KF4997.V47
Veterans' Affairs, Committee on (United States Senate): KF4987.V47
Veterinarians: KF2940.V3+, KFC547.V3+, KFN5547.V46+, KFA-KFZ 329.V48+
Veterinary hygiene: KF3835+, KFC623+, KFN5623+, KFA-KFZ 368+
Veterinary law: KF3835+, KFC623+, KFN5623+, KFA-KFZ 368+
Veterinary medicine: KF3835+
Veterinary public health: KF3835+
Veto power
- United States Governor: KFA-KFZ 426.35.V45
- United States president: KF5067

Viatical settlements: KF1177.V53
Vicarious liability: KF1314+, KFC331+, KFN5332+
Vice President (United States)
- Constitutional law: KF5085
- Election law: KF4910+

Victims of crimes: KF1313, KF9763+, KFC1194.5, KFA-KFZ 594+
Victory tax: KF6406

INDEX

Video games
  Regulation: KF3994
Video tape recorder industry: KF1893.V53
Viewers (Judicial officer): KFA-KFZ 526.V5
Village government: KFA-KFZ 432.5
Villages: KFN5758
Vinegar (Taxation): KF6636.V4
Vinyl chloride: KF3964.V46
Violation of privacy: KF1262+, KFC312, KFN5312, KFA-KFZ 197.P7
Violations of local ordinances: KFX2093+
Virginia
  Laws: KFV2401+
Virginia and Kentucky resolutions, 1798: KF4621
Visas: KF4827
Vital statistics: KF485, KFA-KFZ 93
Viticulture: KFC397, KFA-KFZ 251
Vivisection: KF3843
Vocational education: KF4205+, KFN5664.5.V63, KFA-KFZ 395.5
Vocational rehabilitation: KF3738+, KFC605+, KFN5605+, KFA-KFZ 351.V6
Void and voidable contracts: KF817+, KFN5222
Voidable marriages: KF518, KFC123
Voluntary employees' beneficiary associations: KF3517
Volunteer workers (Public welfare): KF3721.5
Volunteers' liability
  Tort liability: KFA-KFZ 199.V64
Voter registration: KF4898, KFN5713, KFA-KFZ 420.85.R4
Voting, Absentee: KF4901
Voting machines: KF4904, KFA-KFZ 420.85.V6
Voting systems: KF4904
Voting trusts: KF1452

W

Wage and Hour Laws: KF3481+

Wage control: KF3492+
Wagering
  Taxation: KFA-KFZ 485.W34
  State: KF6768.W2, KFC900.W34
Wages
  Exemption from execution: KF9029.W2
  Income tax: KF6410+
  Labor law: KF3481+, KFC575+, KFN5575, KFA-KFZ 334+
  Merchant mariners: KF1131
Waiver: KF450.W3
  Life insurance: KF1181.W2
Walter E. Meyer Research Institute of Law: KF294.W35
War and emergency powers: KF5060
War contracts: KF851+
War materiel: KF5845+
War revenue tax: KF6406
War risks
  Life insurance: KF1181.W25
  Marine insurance: KF1137
Warehouse receipts: KF930, KFN5237.6, KFA-KFZ 156.5.W3
Warehouses: KFA-KFZ 284
  Contracts: KF945
  Regulation: KF2050+, KFC448, KFN5448+
Warehouses, Agricultural: KF2056
Warehouses, Bonded: KF2054
Warranties: KF919.C6, KFA-KFZ 156.7.C6
Warranties, Implied: KF919.C6, KFA-KFZ 156.7.C6
Warranty of seaworthiness (Marine insurance): KF1136
Wartime and emergency legislation: KF7220+, KFN5921+, KFA-KFZ 496
Wartime finance: KF6251+
Wartime labor disputes: KF3444+
Wartime surtaxes: KF6406
Washington
  Laws: KFW1+
Waste disposal, Atomic: KF3950
Watch industry: KF1893.C5, KFA-KFZ 271.C4

INDEX

Water agencies
  Labor law: KFC589.W38
Water conservation: KF5551+
Water courses: KFA-KFZ 446+
Water fluoridation: KF3794
Water pollution and drainage: KF3786+, KFC612, KFN5612, KFA-KFZ 356
  Environmental damages: KF1299.W38
Water resources: KF5551+, KFC790+, KFN5790+, KFA-KFZ 446+
Water rights
  Indians: KFA-KFZ 505.6.W38
  Public property: KFC791, KFA-KFZ 446
  Real property: KF641+, KFC162, KFN5162, KFA-KFZ 123.W2
Water supply
  Public utilities law: KF2133+, KFC468, KFA-KFZ 289
Water transportation: KF2531+, KFC520+, KFN5520+, KFX2057, KFA-KFZ 308+
Waterfowl refuges: KF5643+
Watergate Trial, Washington, D.C., 1973: KF224.W33
Watermelons
  Marketing regulations: KFA-KFZ 244.W38
Watersheds: KF5551+, KFC790+, KFN5790+, KFA-KFZ 446+
Waterways
  New York City: KFX2072
Ways and Means, Committee on (United States House of Representatives): KF4997.W3
Weapons
  Air Force: KF7436
  Armed Forces: KF7296
  Army: KF7336
  Coast Guard: KF7476
  Navy: KF7376
  Public safety: KF3941+, KFC640.5, KFN5640.5, KFA-KFZ 379
Weather control: KF5594, KFC799, KFA-KFZ 449.5

Weather stations: KF5594, KFC799, KFA-KFZ 449.5
Weed control: KF1687+, KFC387, KFN5387, KFA-KFZ 240
Weight restrictions
  Motor vehicles: KF2212, KFC472, KFN5472
Weight restrictions (Automotive transportation): KFA-KFZ 297.2
Weights and measures: KF1665+, KFC382+, KFN5382, KFA-KFZ 235.A1+
Welfare fraud: KFA-KFZ 572.W45
Wells: KFA-KFZ 449
West Virginia
  Laws: KFW1201+
Wetlands: KF5624, KFA-KFZ 451.7
Wheat
  Acreage allotments: KF1706.G78
  Marketing quotas: KF1706.G78
  Processing tax: KF6631.W4
  Standards and grading: KF1724.G79
Whiskey
  Labeling: KF1620.A57
  Taxation: KF6613.W4
White collar crimes: KF9350+, KFC1128+
White collar workers
  Collective labor agreements: KF3409.W5
White phosphorus: KF3964.W4
White slave traffic: KF9448, KFA-KFZ 571.P7
Wholesale trade: KF1998+, KFA-KFZ 280.A1+
Widows
  Public welfare
    New York: KFX2045.W5
Wife abuse: KF9322, KFA-KFZ 567.W53
Wife abuse victims: KF337.5.A27
Wilderness preservation: KFC805+, KFN5805+, KFA-KFZ 452+
  Public land law: KF5635+
Wildlife protection: KF5640+
Wildlife refuges: KF5643+

INDEX

Wills: KF755+, KFC201, KFN5201+, KFP144+, KFA-KFZ 144+
- Indians: KF8210.P7

Wills, Capacity to make: KF760.C3
Wills, Contested: KF769.C6
Wills, Joint: KF760.J6
Wind power (Public utilities): KF2140.W56+
Winding up of companies (Taxation): KF6499.D5
Window cleaning (Labor hygiene and safety): KFC586.W5
Windstorm insurance: KF1202.W5
Wine
- Labeling: KF1620.A58
- Liquor laws: KF3924.W5, KFC636.W5, KFN5637.W56, KFA-KFZ 375.5.W56
- Taxation: KF6613.W5

Wiretapping: KF9670, KFC1168, KFN6168, KFA-KFZ 580.5.W5
Wisconsin
- Laws: KFW2401+

Witchcraft trials: KFA-KFZ 78.8.W5
Withholding tax
- Income tax
  - Federal: KF6436+
  - State: KFC870.3

Withholding tax (Income tax)
- State: KF6753, KFN5873, KFA-KFZ 475.5.W5

Witness index to hearings: KF49.W5
Witnesses
- Civil procedure: KF8950+, KFC1040+, KFN6040, KFA-KFZ 541+
- Criminal procedure: KF9672+, KFC1169, KFN6169, KFA-KFZ 580.5.W54

Witnesses, Medical: KF8964
Woman labor: KF3555, KFC581, KFN5581, KFA-KFZ 335.3
Women
- Capacity and disability: KF477+, KFC111.W6, KFN5111.W6, KFA-KFZ 91.W6
- Citizenship: KF4720.W6
- Discrimination against
  - Labor law: KFC573.W65, KFN5573.W64
- Hours of labor: KF3555
- Jury duty: KF8977
- Labor hygiene and safety: KF3555, KFC581, KFN5581, KFA-KFZ 335.3
- Legal handbooks: KF390.W6, KFN5084.W6
- Nationality: KF4720.W6
- Public welfare: KFC602, KFN5602
- Suffrage: KF4895

Women jurors: KF8977
Women lawyers: KF299.W6
Women, Married: KF521+, KFA-KFZ 96+
Women's Bureau (U.S.): KF3555.5
Women's prisons: KF9741+
Women's services
- Air Force: KF7429
- Armed Forces: KF7289
- Army: KF7329
- Coast Guard: KF7469
- Navy: KF7369

Wood-using industries
- Labor hygiene and safety: KF3574.W6, KFC586.W6

Woodworking industries (Labor hygiene and safety): KFA-KFZ 336.S38
Wool
- Import trade: KF1996.W6
- Trade agreements: KF6669.W66

Wool exchanges: KF1086.W6
Wool fabrics
- Labeling: KF1620.T38

Word processing
- Law office management: KF322+

WordPerfect (Computer program)
- Law office management: KF322.5.W66

Words and phrases: KF156, KFA-KFZ 66
WordStar 2000
- Law office management: KF322.5.W67

INDEX

Work and labor, Contract for: KF898+, KFC228+, KFN5228+, KFA-KFZ 155+
Work release of prisoners: KF9750.7
Work rules: KF3542
Workers' compensation: KF3611+, KFC592+, KFN5592+, KFA-KFZ 342+
- Atomic workers: KF3632.A7
- Brewery workers: KF3632.B6
- Coal miners: KF3632.C6
- Construction industry: KFN5594.C6
- Federal employees: KF3626
- Harbor workers: KF3628
- Longshoremen: KF3628
- Merchant mariners: KF1132
- Mining industry: KFC594.M5
- Occupational diseases: KFN5593, KFA-KFZ 342.5
- Public works: KF3632.P8
- Railroads: KF3629

Workers' compensation claims: KFA-KFZ 539.W6
Workload
- Judges: KFA-KFZ 525.5.W67

Workmen's Compensation Appeals Board (California): KFC592.2
Works councils: KF3542
Worthier title: KF615, KFC151
Writ of error: KFN6084
Writs of assistance
- Colonial U.S. law: KF364.W73

Written contract: KF810, KFN5218
Wrongful life: KF1259
Wyoming
- Laws: KFW4201+

Y

Yachts
- Safety regulations: KF2558.P5, KFC524.P5, KFN5524.P5

Yazoo Fraud: KF369.Y3
Yearbooks (General): KF178, KFC70, KFN5070, KFA-KFZ 70
Yellow dog contracts: KF3397
Youth
- Wages: KF3505.Y68

Youth Conservation Corps: KF6075.5

Youth services: KF3731+, KFC603+, KFN5603+

Z

Zero-base budgeting (Public finance): KF6227
Zero budgeting: KF6227
Zoning: KF5697+, KFC811+, KFN5811, KFX2079, KFA-KFZ 458+
- General: KF10D .x2Z62+
- Government liability: KF1325.L36

Zoning, Emission density: KF3812.5.E55